Circuits and Systems: Design and Applications

Volume VI

Circuits and Systems: Design and Applications Volume VI

Edited by **Helena Walker**

New Jersey

Published by Clanrye International,
55 Van Reypen Street,
Jersey City, NJ 07306, USA
www.clanryeinternational.com

Circuits and Systems: Design and Applications
Volume VI
Edited by Helena Walker

International Standard Book Number: 978-1-63240-102-1 (Hardback)

Printed in the United States of America.

Contents

Preface

At a very fundamental level, a circuit refers to an overall, complex arrangement of components such as resistors, conductors etc. which are connected in order to ensure a steady flow of current. It is only through circuits that signals or information is conveyed to the destination. Without a proper circuit system, the functional ability of any device becomes more or less redundant. The complexity and design of electronic circuits is ever increasing. Circuits are classified into analog circuits, digital circuits and mixed-signal circuits.

Circuits and systems in this book explain the handling of theory and applications of circuits and systems, signal processing, and system design methodology. The practical implementation of circuits, and application of circuit theoretic techniques to systems and to signal processing are the topics covered under this discipline. From radio astronomy to wireless communications and biomedical applications, the application of circuits and systems can be found across a varying range of subjects.

Circuits and Systems is an interesting discipline and is emerging as a coveted career option for many students. A lot of research, to develop more efficient systems is also being conducted.

I'd like to thank all the contributors for sharing their studies with us and make this book an enlightening read. I would also like to thank them for submitting their work within the set time parameters. Lastly, I wish to thank my family, whose support has been crucial for the completion of this book.

Editor

1

Fast Signed-Digit Multi-operand Decimal Adders

Jeff Rebacz, Erdal Oruklu, Jafar Saniie
Department of Electrical and Computer Engineering, Illinois Institute of Technology, Chicago, USA

Abstract

Decimal arithmetic is desirable for high precision requirements of many financial, industrial and scientific applications. Furthermore, hardware support for decimal arithmetic has gained momentum with IEEE 754-2008, which standardized decimal floating-point. This paper presents a new architecture for two operand and multi-operand signed-digit decimal addition. Signed-digit architectures are advantageous because there are no carry-propagate chains. The proposed signed-digit adder reduces the critical path delay by parallelizing the correction stage inherent to decimal addition. For performance evaluation, we synthesize and compare multiple unsigned and signed-digit multi-operand decimal adder architectures on 0.18 μm CMOS VLSI technology. Synthesis results for 2, 4, 8, and 16 operands with 8 decimal digits provide critical data in determining each adder's performance and scalability.

Keywords: Computer Arithmetic, Decimal Arithmetic, Signed-Digit, Multi-operand Adder, BCD

1. Introduction

Translating a decimal fraction into a finite floating-point representation is prone to losing precision as a result of rounding errors. In almost all financial settings, decimal arithmetic is desired to guarantee balances are calculated correctly and lawfully. Some industrial and scientific applications require high-precision decimal arithmetic as well. Software packages have been available for most programming languages so that decimal numbers could be evaluated with decimal arithmetic to avoid error [1,2]. IBM recently departed from this software solution by incorporating a decimal floating-point arithmetic unit in the Power6 [3] and z10 processors [4]. A compelling reason to do such is a report [5] showing that 55% of the numbers stored in the databases of 51 major organizations are decimal. One study shows that for a set of five benchmarks, a 1.3 to 12.8 speedup factor was obtained by simulating a processor using virtual decimal arithmetic hardware against software routines [6]. Applications that spend a large proportion of the time consuming decimal calculation stand to benefit from hardware-based decimal operations. Therefore, research into decimal arithmetic has gained momentum. Decimal renditions of binary carry-save [7,8] and carry-lookahead adders [9-11] have been proposed. Decimal floating-point addition is treated in [12-14]. New decimal multipliers [15-18] and dividers [19-21] have also been proposed. In [17], new decimal encodings improve the latency and area for decimal partial product generation and reduction for multiplication. Similarly, in [22], a new redundant digit set is used with special encodings called two-valued digits (twits), resulting in a faster implementation of both addition and subtraction.

The main motivation behind this paper is to introduce a new signed-digit architecture and objectively compare it with signed and unsigned digit adders. Signed-digit decimal adders have the benefit of carry-free addition although a carry-propagate adder must be used to transform the signed-digit sum into an unsigned sum. In the next two sections, we will present the theory of decimal encodings and signed-digit decimal numbers. In the subsequent sections, brief descriptions of other adders are given: the nonspeculative multi-operand adder [7], mixed binary and BCD adder [23], reduced delay BCD adder [10], dynamic decimal CLA [11], Svoboda adder [24], speculative signed-digit adder [25], decimal carry-free adder [26] and Redundant Binary Coded Decimal (RBCD) adder [27,28]. Then, the proposed method for signed-digit addition is discussed. A constant addition technique will be applied to both the correction step in signed-digit decimal addition and conversion to binary-coded decimal (BCD). Multi-operand decimal addition based on signed-digit addition will follow. Finally, the synthesis results will be discussed.

The notation used throughout this paper is as follows:

Variables are represented with a name and a subscript. Take x_i for example, x is the label and i indicates the digit position. If no subscript is present, x will refer to the word-wide variable across all digit positions. Numbers enclosed in square brackets index the bit position. For example, the second bit of *sum* at the first digit position is sum_0 [1].

2. Decimal Encodings

A discussion of decimal encodings is related to signed digit arithmetic because the primary motivation for both are similar, i.e. they are concerned with achieving better performance by leveraging a more convenient number representation for certain tasks. For example, Binary-Coded Decimal (BCD) is the representation usually used for decimal arithmetic. A BCD digit is the binary representation of a decimal number [0,9] with 4 bits. BCD is convenient for arithmetic, but is not optimal for storage because 4 bits for 10 decimal digits wastes 6 encodings. In IEEE 754-2008, storage of decimal floating-point numbers is specified to be in Densely Packed Decimal (DPD) form. In DPD, 3 decimal digits are encoded with 10 bits, which is much more efficient for storage.

For multiplication, several signed and unsigned representations have been developed to increase performance. In [15], it is shown how a signed-digit representation can reduce the number of partial products in a decimal multiplier. These partial products can be efficiently accumulated with a signed digit adder. In [15], the classic Svoboda adder [24] is used for partial product reduction, yet, it will be shown that the proposed signed digit representation can yield better performance. On the other hand, unsigned representations in multiplications are also gaining track. In [17], traditional BCD or BCD-8421 is recoded to BCD-5421, BCD-4221 and BCD-5211 to efficiently generate partial products and reduce the partial product reduction tree. One of the advantages of this scheme is that multiplying by two from one encoding to another may simply require a left shift. Another advantage of the encoding is that it allows the reuse of a binary radix-4 multiplier, sharing components to save area. These new encodings also have advantages over BCD-8421 in division, as demonstrated in [20].

Unsigned decimal adders usually work with BCD numbers, but that is not required. The partial product adder in [29] uses the Overloaded Decimal Representation (ODR), a redundant unsigned 4-bit encoding to store and add intermediate partial products in a carry-save format. In ODR, a decimal digit may take on values 0 through 15. In iterative operations, the decimal correction vector of +6, which is usually required for unsigned decimal addition, is easier to detect and less costly to add. The correction is only needed when a digit exceeds 16, which is easily detected by inspecting the digit's carry out. When the carry out is detected, adding 6 occurs in the next iteration, which shortens the critical path.

Another adder that leverages encodings other than BCD is the mixed binary and BCD multi-operand adder. The mixed binary and BCD multi-operand adder [23], which will later be described in more detail and implemented, uses both binary and BCD representations and operations. Binary addition occurs for a column of BCD digits. The binary result is then converted back to BCD number. The process will repeat until there are two rows of BCD numbers to be inputted into a 2-operand BCD adder.

In signed-digit adders, there appear to be three popular representations: the Svoboda code [24], the two's complement representation (used in the proposed method), and the positive/negative component representation.

The Svoboda code uses 5-bits to represent numbers in the set [−6,6]. A positive number x_i is represented in Svoboda code as $X_i = 3 * x_i$ while a negative number is represented as $X_i = 31 - 3 * x_i$. For example, positive decimal numbers 1 and 6 are represented in Svoboda code as 1_{10} = 00011 and 6_{10} = 10010 respectively; negative decimal numbers −1 and −6 are represented in Svoboda code as -1_{10} = 11100 and -6_{10} = 01101 respectively. There are two representations for zero (00000 and 11111). The Svoboda code allows for quick addition, but the encoding may be difficult to work with or costly to convert to and from.

The two's complement representation for signed-digit numbers is used in the RBCD adder [27,28] and in this work. In RBCD, the digits are 4-bits wide and represent numbers between 7 and −7 inclusive. RBCD's number range requires BCD numbers to go through a conversion step (since 8 and 9 must be recoded). Our proposed adder does not require a conversion step because we use 5-bits to represent a signed decimal digit in the range of [−9,9]. This convenience is a key feature of our design.

In [25,26], a signed-digit is represented as the sum of one positive 4-bit binary vector x^+ and one negative 4-bit binary vector x^-. This positive/negative component representation may store −2 in various ways: as x^+ = 0001 and x^- = 0011 or as x^+ = 0010 and x^- = 0100. With this representation, numbers can be easily inverted by swapping x^+ and x^-. Additionally, no conversion from BCD is needed. However, there are 8 bits to a digit. Though this fact does not automatically imply more area consumption, the results do suggest it.

3. Decimal Signed-Digit Theory

The decimal signed-digit number system used here has

all the properties and limitations set forth in [30]. A decimal signed-digit set D is a special case of general signed-digit sets when $r = 10$ (r is the radix or base).

$$D = \{-\beta, \cdots, -1, 0, \cdots \alpha\} \quad (1)$$

where α, β and r are related by (2).

$$\alpha + \beta + 1 \geq r \quad (2)$$

Usually, symmetric signed-digit sets are used ($\alpha = \beta$). The signed-digit set is said to be redundant (any number has multiple representations) if (3) holds.

$$\alpha > \frac{r-1}{2} \quad (3)$$

The decimal signed-digit set used in this work is [−9,9] or −9 to 9 inclusive ($r = 10$, $\alpha = 9$). With this decimal signed-digit set, to add two decimal signed-digits x_i and y_i, three quantities must be added together: the intermediate sum u_i (*i.e.*, interim sum), the carry c_i (*i.e.*, transfer) which can take values in {−1,0,1}, and the correction $-10 * c_i$. The intermediate sum u_i is $x_i + y_i$ and ranges from −18 to 18 inclusive with the digit set [−9,9]. The carry c_i is generated using a rule set such that $-8 \leq u_i - 10 * c_i \leq 8$ holds. Determining c_i is done by comparing u_i to comparison constants. For the decimal signed-digit set used, one comparison constant is in [−8,−1], the other in [1,8], and are usually chosen to minimize hardware complexity [31]. If −1 and 1 were the comparison constants, then c_i is −1 when u_i is less than −1; c_i is 1 when u_i is greater than 1; c_i is zero when u_i is −1, 0 or 1. The correction is $-10 * c_i$ and adds to the intermediate sum u_i along with the previous digit's carry to obtain the sum. Note that $u_i - 10 * c_i$ is between −8 and 8 inclusive, so an input carry of −1 or 1 will never cause a carry to propagate to the next decimal digit. The above is expressed in (4)-(6).

$$u_i = x_i + y_i \quad (4)$$

$$s_i = u_i - 10 * c_i + c_{i-1} \quad (5)$$

$$c_i = \begin{cases} -1 & \text{if } u_i < -1 \\ 1 & \text{if } u_i > 1 \\ 0 & \text{otherwise} \end{cases} \quad (6)$$

An example demonstrates that the signed-digit technique still produces carries, but never propagates them. In other words, a digit's carry out is not a function of its carry in. In this example, the operands are absent of negative digits only to facilitate demonstration. The comparison constants are −1 and 1. For the least significant digit column, the intermediate sum is 8 + 8 = 16. Since 16 > 1, $c_0 = 1$ is added to the next column and −10 is the correction for the least significant column.

	3	1	3	5	2	8	
+			3	4	7	8	
	3	1	6	9	9	16	*u* vector
	−10	0	−10	−10	−10	−10	correction vector
1	0	1	1	1	1		*c* vector
1	−7	2	−3	0	0	6	*s* vector

The general algorithm is as follows:

1) For each digit, add the two operands to get the intermediate sum, u_i. The range for u_i is −18 to 18 inclusive.

2) If $u_i > 1$, set $correction_i = -10$ and $c_i = 1$. If $u_i < -1$, *set* $correction_i = 10$ and $c_i = -1$. In the example, the c vector is shifted one digit position to the left so that addition occurs within each column.

3) Find the sum of the three vectors, u, *correction* and c. This operation, as those before, will not propagate carries because the method guarantees: $-9 \leq s_i \leq 9$.

4. Prior Work in Unsigned-Digit Decimal Addition

4.1. Nonspeculative Multi-operand Adder

In [7], a nonspeculative multi-operand adder is presented that can sum up to 16 operands. For each digit column, M operands are added using a linear array of M-2 binary carry-save adders. Carries outside the 4-bit range for each digit are transferred to the next column, and saved for later use. A 4-bit CPA finds a 5-bit uncorrected intermediate sum after the carry-save adders. This uncorrected intermediate sum together with the saved carries are inputted into combinational logic to find the carry out and a 4-bit correction vector. Another 4-bit CPA adds the correction vector to the uncorrected intermediate sum to yield the corrected intermediate sum. Finally, the carry-outs and the corrected intermediate sum must be added with a word-wide carry-propagation adder. In this work, multioperand adders requiring decimal carry-propagation addition use the dynamic decimal CLA [10] because it gives the best delay and area usage.

4.2. Mixed Binary and BCD Multi-operand Adder

This adder, proposed in [23], presents a scalable scheme to realize any N-operand addition. First, for each digit column, the N operands are added with N:2 reduction and a CPA. Each column sum is then converted into a decimal number with a network of binary to decimal converter cells. Depending on the number of decimal digits this conversion process produces, another stage of binary addition and binary to decimal conversion may ensue. When the digits of the converted decimal sum is two, a fast decimal carry-propagation adder (in this work, the dynamic decimal CLA adder [10]) is used to obtain the final decimal sum.

For 3 to 11 operands, only one stage is needed because maximum number of digits for the sum of a digit column with 11 operands is $2:9*11=99$. Thus, 2-operand addition follows to calculate the final sum. For 12 to 111 operands, two stages are needed because the maximum decimal sum for a digit column is 999, which is three digits. Adding three digits across each digit column is 3-operand addition, and necessitates another stage.

4.3. The Reduced Delay BCD Adder

In [10], the 2-operand decimal adder is composed of a 4-bit binary adder, an analyzer circuit, a carry network, and another 4-bit binary adder to add the correction vector. Using the intermediate sum from the first 4-bit binary adder, the analyzer circuit finds the generate and propagate signals for that digit. The signals from all digits are passed to a Kogge-Stone carry network to find the carries. Appropriately wiring the generated carries to the final 4-bit adder will add the correction vector (0, 6, 1 or 7), which depends on the carry in and the carry out for that digit.

4.4. The Dynamic Decimal Adder Using Carry Lookahead

Like the reduced delay BCD adder, the dynamic decimal CLA adder [11] is a 2-operand adder that finds digit propagate and generate signals to be used in a carry lookahead scheme for fast carry propagation. These signals are generated per digit using combinational logic on the bit propagate and generate signals of the two input BCD digits. The sum bits are calculated as a function of the bit generate and propagate signals, the carry in, and the carry out. A speculation technique is used for the upper two bits of each digit to speed up the addition time. With dynamic logic, this technique can yield impressive speed.

5. Prior Work in Signed-Digit Decimal Addition

5.1. Svoboda Adder

The Svoboda adder [24] was an early 2-operand design that added digits from −6 to 6 inclusive. The Svoboda adder uses the Svoboda code described in Section 2. This code helps simplify decimal addition. On the other hand, converting BCD operands into the Svoboda code and back requires overhead.

BCD to Svoboda code conversion begins by transforming each input BCD digit to a 5-bit vector corresponding to the Svoboda code of that digit minus 4. Then, a Svoboda adder adds 4 to the Svoboda code of all digits.

To convert back to BCD, a similar, but reversed process is used. Constants are iteratively added with a Svoboda adder until all the digits are between –4 and 5 inclusive. The worst case (*i.e.*, the number of times the loop is executed) depends on the number of digits. We have implemented the Svoboda adder with the suggested BCD to Svoboda code conversion scheme but without the suggested Svoboda code to BCD conversion scheme. Instead, we have replaced it with a faster carry-lookahead conversion scheme. First, the Svoboda code is transformed into a two's complement number ranging from −6 to 6 inclusive. Second, generate and propagate signals are detected and used in a Kogge-Stone prefix network to generate carries so that the proper corrections can be applied to each digit. Also, the Svoboda adder was originally designed with two stages of chained full adders with end-around-carries. In the experiment, we have replaced the full adder chains with prefix adders in order to improve speed performance.

5.2. Speculative SD Adder

This architecture [25] is rather complex as it implements a clever speculation technique that facilitates the addition of input carries. The input operands are in the positive/negative component representation. For example, −3 would be represented like this (let the two vectors be expressed as (x^+, x^-)):

$$\underbrace{(0010,0101)}_{(2-5=-3)}$$

Internally, the speculative SD adder uses compressors to add the input operands. These compressors resemble carry-save addition, but are modified to handle negative bits. The two comparison constants are 1 and −1. A sign detection unit is necessary to determine the carry out. Once the carry out is found, a correction is added if necessary.

No input conversion is necessary since BCD is within the speculative SD's digit set. The adder is speculative because it prepares two pairs of sums, one which can be easily incremented by one and another that can be easily decremented by one. The last step of this adder involves adding a correction vector according to the digit position's carry out.

For conversion back to BCD, the negative component is subtracted from the positive component to yield a 5-bit, two's-complement number between −9 and 9. This number is inputted into an analyzer circuit to find generate and propagate signals to use in a carry-lookahead scheme. Once the carries are known, the right constants can be added to the SD number to get an unsigned BCD result.

5.3. Decimal Carry-Free Adder

The Decimal Carry-Free Adder (DCFA) from [26] uses a digit set from −9 to 9. DCFA represents numbers in the same way [25] does, with two 4-bit vectors (positive/negative component representation). This design is different than [25] because it speculates the addition of several corrections (not just the addition of the transfer in). Two sign detection circuits determine the transfer out (like in [25]). The positive and negative transfer out and the negative transfer in signals select the sum in three levels of multiplexors. The positive transfer in signal is wired into the first bit of the selected sum to effectively add it.

5.4. RBCD Adder

The 2-operand Redundant Binary Coded Decimal adder (RBCD) [27,28] adds 4-bit wide signed-digits between 7 and −7 inclusive represented in two's complement. The reduced digit set dramatically simplifies carry detection at the expense of some initial overhead required to conform BCD operands to the adder's digit range. The adder is implemented with two 4-bit adders, a carry generation block and a correction vector generation block. It is very similar to the proposed 2-operand adder, but differs in the digit set, the carry detection circuit, and especially correction method. Also, RBCD, as well as the other SD adders, do not discuss multi-operand addition.

Additional circuits are described to perform BCD to RBCD and RBCD to BCD conversion. The former case requires less logic. On detection of a 7, 8 or 9, a carry will be sent to the next digit and 6 will be added to the current digit. In the RBCD to BCD conversion, generate and propagate signals are found and used in a carry-lookahead circuit. Once the carries are known, a 4-bit adder corrects the sum in each digit.

6. Proposed Signed-Digit Decimal Adder

6.1. Methodology

In the proposed signed-digit architecture, the digit set used is −9 to 9 inclusive and is represented using a conventional 5-bit, two's complement vector [32]. For the digit at position i, x_i and y_i are added to yield a 6-bit wide intermediate sum, u_i (the carry-propagate adder (CPA) chosen in these designs uses a prefix tree). Then, two levels of simple logic determine the carry c_i, which uses positive and negative magnitude components to represent $\{-1, 0, 1\}$: c_i^- and c_i^+.

$$c_i = c_i^+ - c_i^- \tag{7}$$

The proposed rule set for c_i selects the two comparison constants to be −8 and 7 for reduced hardware complexity. As opposed to the rule set in (6), this rule set can be implemented as a boolean function of 3 variables with 4 minterms as opposed to a boolean function of 6 variables with 9 minterms. The proposed rule set is defined in (8). After an exhaustive design space exploration, it has been found that this rule set requires the minimum logic use. All other valid pairs of comparison constants will have a higher logic complexity and the evidence of this is visible by looking at the upper 3 bits of the two's complement boolean numbers in the set $[-18, 18]$.

$$c_i = \begin{cases} -1 & \text{if } u_i < -8 \\ 1 & \text{if } u_i > 7 \\ 0 & \text{otherwise} \end{cases} \tag{8}$$

Each digit's positive and negative carry signals are easily calculated with (9)-(10). **Figure 1(a)** expresses these equations.

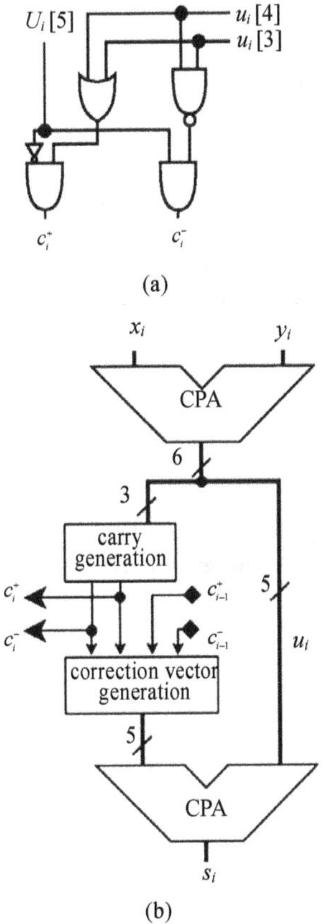

Figure 1. The circuit in (a) elaborates the carry generation block. Once u_i is obtained from the carry propagate adder, c_i^+ and c_i^- are calculated with a few gates. In (b), a high-level diagram depicts the 2-operand SD adder. The upper 3 bits of the intermediate sum are used for carry generation while the lower 5 bits are inputted to the second CPA.

$$c_i^+ = \overline{u_i[5]} \cdot (u_i[4] + u_i[3]) \quad (9)$$

$$c_i^- = u_i[5] \cdot \left(\overline{u_i[4] \cdot u_i[3]}\right) \quad (10)$$

After u_i and c_i are found, the correction vector must be found and added. The correction vector corresponds to $-10 * c_i$ from (5). However, since the incoming carry from the previous digit, c_{i-1}, must eventually be added to u_i as well, it is convenient to think of the correction vector as $-10 * c_i + c_{i-1}$. The correction vector (which is simply the constant term to be added to u_i) is tabulated for every possible input combination in **Table 1**. Addition between u_i and this correction vector will result in a 5-bit sum, s_i. Note that because of the rule set chosen, the final sum for each digit will fall in [−9, 8] meaning that the carry-out of the last CPA will always be 0.

The proposed SD decimal adder is shown in **Figure 1 (b)**. The carry generation block of the proposed adder is shown in **Figure 1(a)**. It is apparent in this figure that carries only propagate to the next digit. There is no ripple effect since carry generation does not depend on the carry in. This design is a necessary precursor to the improved version in the next section.

6.2. Parallel Addition of the Correction Vector

The previously proposed adder's correction generation block and correction vector CPA can be replaced by a parallel speculative structure to reduce delay since the bits of u_i are available before the carries. In these parallel adders, speculative addition of the correction vector and incoming carry take place in one or two stages of logically minimized constant addition. For one stage, the addition of the constants −11, −10, −9, −1, 0, 1, 9, 10, 11 are precomputed and selected with c_i and c_{i-1} in a multiplexor.

Table 1. Correction vector generation.

c_i^+	c_i^-	c_{i-1}^+	c_{i-1}^-	Correction Vector
0	0	0	0	00000_2 (0_{10})
0	0	0	1	11111_2 (-1_{10})
0	0	1	0	00001_2 (1_{10})
0	1	0	0	01010_2 (10_{10})
0	1	0	1	01001_2 (9_{10})
0	1	1	0	01011_2 (11_{10})
1	0	0	0	10110_2 (-10_{10})
1	0	0	1	10101_2 (-11_{10})
1	0	1	0	10111_2 (-9_{10})

For two stages, the addition of −10, 0 and 10 are precomputed and selected by c_i in one stage; −1, 0 and 1 are precomputed and selected by c_{i-1} in the other stage [32]. Depending on the method of constant addition chosen, certain optimizations can be made. For example, the proposed parallel adder uses a method of constant addition such that the addition of $x + c$, where x is the 5-bit input and c is the constant, produces a vector f that indicates which bits in x need to be inverted to obtain the sum. So, five XOR gates are needed to invert r for any constant addition. Hardware can be reduced by placing the XOR gates after the multiplexor instead of having groups of XOR gates for each constant before the multiplexor.

The terminology and concept of the constant addition used were derived from the flag inversion cell (*fic*) sequences in [33]. The method in [33] describes adding two variables and a constant. For this architecture, only one variable and a constant are added. A detailed description of the constant addition mechanism can be found in [33].

In the two-stage parallel adder, the intermediate sum, u_i, is fed to two constant addition blocks for adding and subtracting 10. A 3-to-1 multiplexer will select f for adding −10, 0 or 10 according to the selects: c_i^+ and c_i^-. The multiplexer's output is XORed with u_i to invert the flagged bits. This inversion yields $u_i - 10 * c_i$.

The remaining step is to add the incoming carry. Two more constant addition blocks are used to add or subtract 1 from $u_i - 10 * c_i$. Another 3-to-1 multiplexer is used with XOR gates after it to invert another flagged set of bits and yield the sum. Breaking the addition up into two stages seems to sacrifice speed. However, the two levels involve a very small amount of logic. Both circuits (one-stage and two-stage implementations) have a better area-delay product with parallel constant addition than without.

The one-stage parallel adder is shown in **Figure 2**. This design takes advantage of the fact that u_i is calculated before any of the carries. In fact, the correction vector speculative addition starts as soon as $u_i[0]$ arrives. Therefore, it can be seen that this type of speculation can improve performance. Most other decimal signed-digit adders do not speculate the constant addition.

7. SD and BCD Conversion

Any SD number can be converted to BCD, and vice-versa [30]. The proposed SD adders must extend an unsigned BCD number by one bit for BCD to SD conversion. On the other hand, a carry-propagation operation must be performed for SD to BCD conversion. A Kogge-Stone prefix network is used to accelerate the carry-propagation. The propagate signal p_i is set when the SD

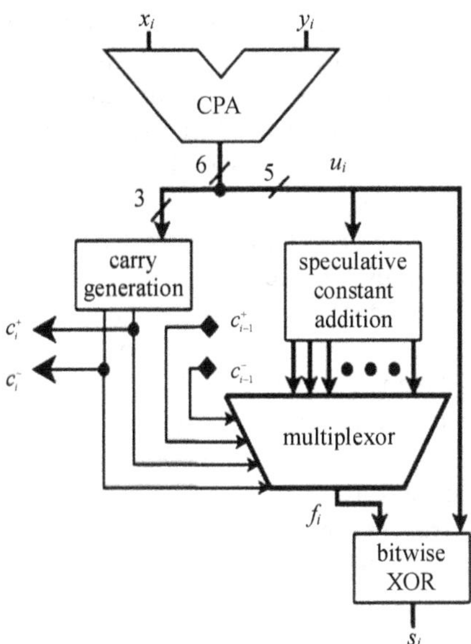

Figure 2. The proposed one-stage signed-digit unit for one digit is shown. This figure shows that the carry generation and constant addition speculation occur in parallel, which is desirable for speed.

digit is 0. The generate signal g_i is set when the SD digit is negative. It should be apparent that −1 and 0 are the two possible values for the carry.

Carries are generated using a Kogge-Stone prefix network, and are used to determine the correction vectors for each sd_i to obtain bcd_i. If there is a carry in to a digit that is greater than 0, −1 is added. If there is a carry in to a negative or 0 digit, 9 is added. If there is no carry in but the digit is negative, 10 is added. Equation (11) expresses these conditions in terms of g_i, p_i, and the carry in c_{in}.

$$bcd_i = \begin{cases} sd_i - 1 & \text{if } c_{in} \cdot \overline{(g_i + p_i \cdot c_{in})} \\ sd_i + 9 & \text{if } c_{in} \cdot (g_i + p_i \cdot c_{in}) \\ sd_i + 10 & \text{if } \overline{c_{in}} \cdot (g_i + p_i \cdot c_{in}) \\ sd_i & \text{if } \overline{c_{in}} \cdot \overline{(g_i + p_i \cdot c_{in})} \end{cases} \quad (11)$$

To perform these corrections, constant addition is used again. The improvement in speed and area-delay inside the conversion circuit is around 20% when using a constant addition correction scheme over conventional addition. **Figure 3(a)** shows the conversion block for 1 digit, **Figure 3(b)** for 8 digits.

In [34], a hybrid SD number system shows that unsigned and signed numbers have a continuum of number representations between them. For example, every third or every fourth digit can be signed. This in turn would limit the carry-propagation chains to those places. However, experiments with hybrid SD representations have shown that the added logic necessary to incorporate the two schemes together costs too much area and delay.

8. Multi-operand Addition

Two-operand signed-digit decimal adders can be used to add multiple numbers if arranged in a tree. In this way, corrections are made after every addition. However, it is apparent that immediate correction is not necessary. The correction step can be postponed in a similar manner as shown in [7] with the addition of new constraints to the problem (see **Table 2**).

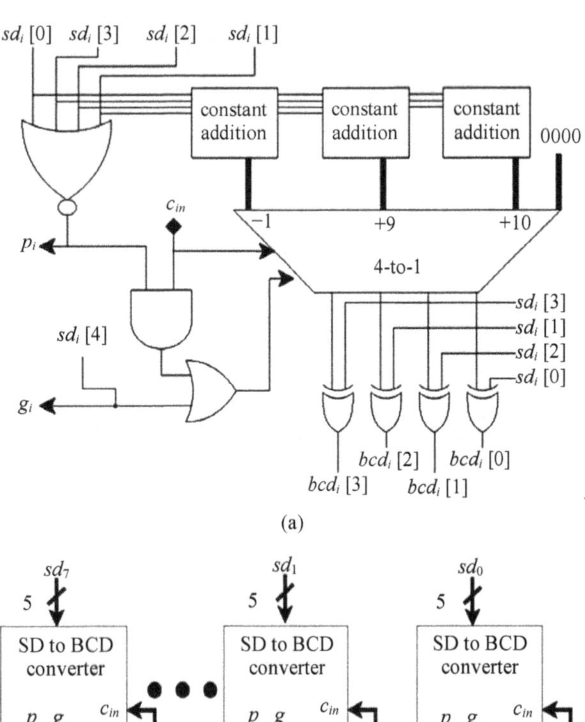

Figure 3. In (a), SD to BCD conversion for one digit is shown. This circuit finds g and p so that a carry-lookahead generator can find c_{in} for all digits. The conversion scheme for 8 decimal digits is shown in (b).

Table 2. Ranges for multi-operand addition.

Number of Operands	Range of u_i	Bounds of $u_i - 10 * c_i$
2 operands	[−18,18]	[−8,8]
3 operands	[−27,27]	[−7,7]
4 operands	[−36,36]	[−6,6]
5 operands	[−45,45]	[−5,5]

The operations for n-operand addition for a digit in the ith position can be summarized in (12)-(14) ($a_{i,n}$ represents the nth input for the ith digit position). These show that an intermediate sum can be calculated from multiple operands and a similar correction procedure can be used to obtain the sum. Equation (14) must be satisfied for a c_i in order for carry-free decimal signed-digit addition to work. For example, for three operand addition, $-7 \geq u_i - 10 * c_i \geq 7$, for all possible u_i in [−27,27], a c_i value can be found that makes $-7 \leq u_i - 10 * c_i \leq 7$ true. Note that (14) finds the maximum bounds, but tighter bounds are possible so long as the bounds can represent all decimal digits.

$$u_i = a_{i,1} + a_{i,2} + \cdots + a_{i,n} \tag{12}$$

$$s_i = u_i - 10 * c_i + c_{i-1} \tag{13}$$

$$\{c_i \in Z : -10 + n < u_i - 10 * c_i \leq 10 - n\} \tag{14}$$

with the maximally redundant digit set of [−9,9], 6 or more operands cannot be added without an intermediate correction since adding 5 carries restricts $u_i - 10 * c_i$ to [−4, 4]. This condition cannot hold for such u_i as −5, 5, 15.

Therefore, only 2, 3, 4 and 5-operand signed-digit adders are possible with the present scheme (see **Figure 4**). Furthermore, only the 2-operand adder can make use of the parallel addition technique; delay cannot be improved since the greater number of parallel additions increases the multiplexer size and the load.

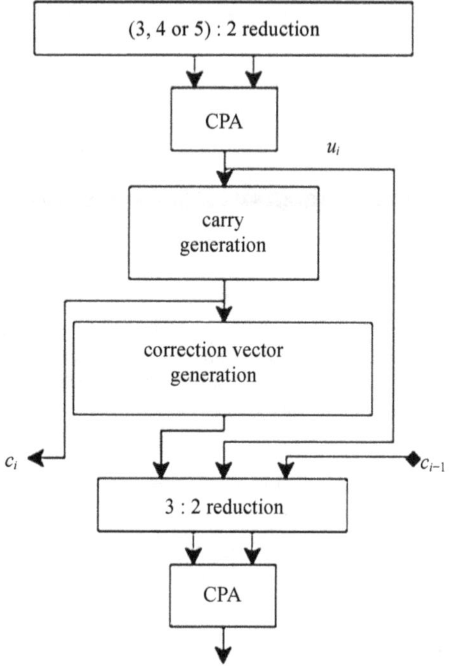

Figure 4. The proposed signed-digit multi-operand addition unit for one digit is shown. This scheme is limited for addition of 3, 4 or 5 operands.

The combinational logic for carry generation becomes more constrained and more complex as n increases. For 2-operand addition, there is a lot of flexibility in choosing the rule set as evidenced by the logic minimization obtained in (8). For 5 operands, fewer rule sets are available to choose from. Since adding 5 SD numbers may result in 45 or −45 (maximum carry in of 4 or −4), the rule set must ensure that $-5 \leq u_i - 10 * c_i \leq 5$. The 2-operand correction logic requires the 3 upper bits from u_i whereas the 5-operand correction logic requires all bits from u_i and many more minterms.

For multi-operand addition requiring multiple modules (*i.e.* $n > 5$), combining reduction where possible can yield better performance [35]. The lower part of the SD adder that reduces and adds u_i, c_{i-1} and $-10 * c_i$ can be combined with the earlier part of the next level's SD adder that reduces and adds n operands. The operation for these parts is addition, so the property of associativity can be exploited.

As an example of multi-operand addition as well as this optimization technique, a 16-operand adder is shown in **Figure 5(a)**. Three 5-operand adders add the first 15 input operands. The 16th input operand is added on the second level with the three sums from the first level using a 4-operand adder. The circuit can be improved by considering the three parallel 5-operand adders together, and summing their internal u_i, c_{i-1}, and $-10 * c_i$ terms together instead of separately. Basically, instead of performing three separate 3:2 reductions followed by a CPA for each 5-operand adder, one large 9:2 reduction followed by a CPA is performed. Adding the 16th input at this stage only involves growing the reduction circuit to 10:2. Furthermore, only one CPA is needed to produce u_i for the 4-operand circuit instead of four (one at the end of each 5-operand adder and one near the beginning of the 4-operand adder). This optimized 16-operand adder is shown in **Figure 5(b)**. The reduction circuit should be organized to reduce the terms that become available first. First, the intermediate sums and leftover operands should be reduced. When the carries become available, their reduction should be merged with the intermediate sums. Likewise, reduction of the correction vector should be merged when it becomes available.

9. Results

All designs were written in Verilog HDL. Synthesis results for area and timing were obtained from Synopsys Design Compiler using MOSIS TSMC 0.18μm standard cell technology. Each design was compiled as an 8-digit (decimal) adder. Several of the designs are 2-operand only, but are arranged in a parallel tree to obtain multi-operand addition.

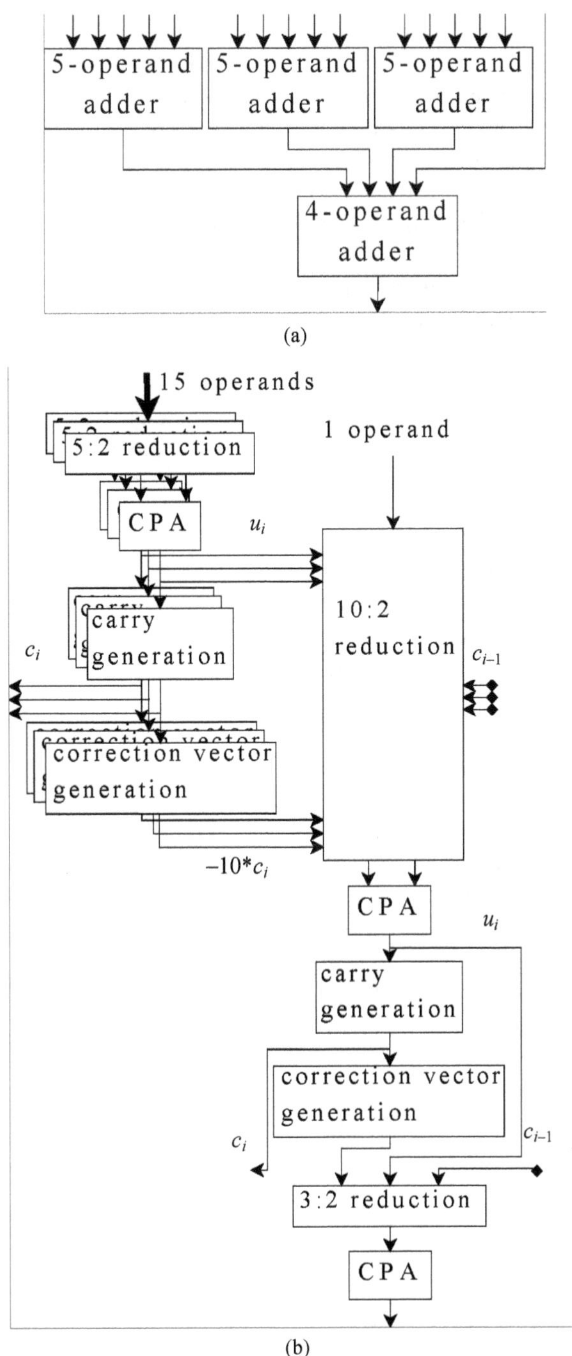

Figure 5. Multi-operand addition. ((a) 16-operand adder is constructed with 4-operand and 5-operand adders from Figure 4; (b) An improved 16-operand adder combines the reduction steps in the last stage of the three 5-operand adders with the first stage of the 4-operand adder.)

The designs in **Table 3** have been synthesized with BCD conversion (if necessary) before the SD operation. Thus, the adders are outputting different number representations, but are adding BCD numbers. The Svoboda adder uses a 5-bit Svoboda code to facilitate addition. We see from **Table 3** that even after accelerating the adders with a prefix tree, the Svoboda adder is still too costly in area. Furthermore, the special Svoboda code requires much more data conversion overhead to and from BCD (compare **Table 3** to the 2-operand rows in **Table 4** which shows 2-operand addition with conversion from and to BCD). The speculative SD adder uses the positive/negative component representation. This representation is advantageous for inverting an operand.

Additionally, there is no overheard required for converting to the adder's representation. However, the area and delay requirements are too much compared to other designs. The DCFA [26] achieves a better area-delay product than the speculative SD while using the same number representation. The RBCD adder is strong in terms of delay and area, but the conversion from BCD puts RBCD behind many of the adders.

The results in **Table 3** for our proposed adders demonstrate two points: i) The adder architecture is efficient in terms of area and delay and ii) The constant addition modification can improve delay or area (see last two rows). The architecture referred to by **Table 3** as the proposed SD is shown in **Figure 1**. The proposed one-stage SD is shown in **Figure 2**. The advantage of the proposed SD's number representation is that it requires no conversion from BCD. Additionally, a digit's sign information is found in the digit's most significant bit. For the representation used in the speculative adder and the DCFA, a sign detector must be used on each digit to determine the digit's sign. Therefore, we believe the proposed designs offer superior performance with the two's complement representation.

For the multi-operand results, every adder inputs decimal digits in the BCD representation and outputs an unsigned BCD sum vector. An additional conversion step is necessary after all SD adders and before the RBCD and Svoboda adders. Since the operand size is 8 digits, the carry-free advantage of the SD adders is not being leveraged.

Table 3. Area and delay comparison for 2-operand SD adders.

Decimal Adder	Delay (ns)	Area (mm^2)	Area-Delay ($ns*mm^2$)	Area-Delay compared to ***Proposed SD***
RBCD [27,28]	1.66	0.0384	0.0637	× 1.26
Svoboda SD [24]	2.18	0.0898	0.1960	× 3.87
Speculative SD [25]	1.40	0.0582	0.0815	× 1.61
DCFA [26]	1.48	0.0498	0.0737	× 1.45
Proposed SD	**1.36**	**0.0373**	**0.0507**	× **1.00**
Proposed 1-stage SD	1.27	0.0385	0.0489	× 0.96
Proposed 2-stage SD	1.36	0.0346	0.0471	× 0.93

Table 4 shows that the multi-operand SD adder proposed in this work outperforms the existing SD designs at every corner (except against the RBCD adder's area for two operands). The RBCD adder occupies the least area for 2 and 4 operands, but falls second to the proposed adder for 8 and 16 operands. For hardware designs that can benefit from the two's complement SD representation, the proposed architecture should be considered. Among the unsigned adders in **Table 5**, the dynamic decimal adder using CLA yields the best delay. It also consumes the least area for 2 and 4 operands. For 8 and 16 operands, the mixed binary and BCD adder architecture yields the best area-delay product. It may be speculated that the mixed binary and BCD approach will scale best, since the main growing component is the fast tree of binary adders.

Table 4. Area and delay comparison for signed multi-operand adders.

Operands	Delay (ns)	Area (mm^2)	Area-Delay ($ns*mm^2$)	Area-Delay compared to ***Proposed SD***
		Svoboda Adder [24]		
2	3.39	0.110	0.373	× 3.42
4	4.93	0.242	1.19	× 5.36
8	6.50	0.477	3.10	× 4.58
16	8.15	0.912	7.43	× 4.17
		Speculative SD Adder [25]		
2	2.51	0.0713	0.179	× 1.64
4	3.89	0.129	0.502	× 2.26
8	5.22	0.288	1.50	× 2.22
16	6.83	0.545	3.72	× 2.09
		DCFA Adder [26]		
2	2.79	0.0675	0.188	× 1.72
4	4.15	0.172	0.714	× 3.22
8	5.90	0.323	1.91	× 2.82
16	7.40	0.649	4.80	× 2.70
		RBCD Adder [27,28]		
2	2.67	0.0486	0.130	× 1.19
4	3.73	0.0794	0.295	× 1.33
8	5.01	0.154	0.772	× 1.14
16	6.21	0.306	1.90	× 1.07
		Proposed SD Adder		
2	2.08	0.0539	0.109	× **1.00**
4	3.18	0.0698	0.222	× **1.00**
8	4.37	0.155	0.677	× **1.00**
16	5.49	0.324	1.78	× **1.00**

Table 5. Area and Delay Comparison for unsigned multi-operand adders.

Operands	Delay (ns)	Area (mm^2)	Area-Delay ($ns*mm^2$)
	Nonspeculative Adder [7]		
2	1.29	.0246	.0317
4	3.15	.0614	.193
8	4.03	.147	.592
16	6.78	.280	1.90
	Mixed Binary and BCD Adder [23]		
2	1.29	.0246	.0317
4	2.71	.0535	.145
8	3.41	.101	.344
16	4.45	.187	.832
	Reduced Delay BCD Adder [10]		
2	1.34	.0284	.0381
4	2.57	.0644	.166
8	3.68	.143	.526
16	4.84	.278	1.34
	Dynamic Decimal using CLA Adder [11]		
2	1.29	.0246	.0317
4	2.38	.0598	.142
8	3.01	.123	.370
16	3.82	.236	.902

Proposed SD multi-operand addition with conversion to BCD does not outperform the best unsigned multi-operand scheme. However, the SD adders' larger functional domain must not be overlooked. That is, the ease at which subtraction can be performed with an SD adder over an unsigned adder strengthens the SD adder's position.

10. Applications

The ideal target applications for the proposed signed-digit schemes would leverage signed-digit advantages. One benefit is the elimination of carry propagation addition with long words (64 or 128 bits) operated on iteratively. If the application does not require iterative computations, then immediate conversion back to an unsigned representation will negate the carry-free addition performance. However, if the application requires knowledge of sign at each iterative step, which signed-digit addition easily provides, then signed-digit addition is promising. Moreover, applications that can conveniently use the signed-digit representation for other operations as well as addition/subtraction stand to benefit. The iterative multiplier in [15] uses a signed-digit adder because an earlier step (partial product generation) found that the signed-digit representation can increase performance. In SRT division, division is executed iteratively and the sign of the dividend is necessary at each iteration. Therefore, the proposed 2-operand adders can potentially serve a core role in division. For the proposed multi-operand scheme, adding multiple partial products to reduce cycles in iterative multiplication appears promising. Finally, advanced financial algorithms may stand to benefit.

11. Conclusions

In this study, new signed-digit two operand and multi-operand decimal adders are proposed. Performance of recent decimal adder architectures have been investigated and compared. The proposed SD adder excels in speed and area usage among previously proposed SD adders. The use of constant addition for speculation and the merging of adjacent modules with sharable operations enable efficient implementation of two operand and multi-operand decimal addition.

12. References

[1] BigDecimal, 2008. http://java.sun.com/products.

[2] DecNumber, AlphaWorks, 2008. http://www.alphaworks.ibm.com/tech/decnumber.

[3] L. Eisen, *et al.*, "IBM POWER6 Accelerators: VMX and DFU," *IBM Journal of Research and Development*, Vol. 51, No. 6, 2007, pp. 663-683.

[4] C. Webb, "IBM z10: The Next-Generation Mainframe Microprocessor," *IEEE Micro*, Vol. 28, No. 2, 2008, pp. 19-29.

[5] A. Tsang and M. Olschanowsky, "A Study of Database 2 Customer Queries," Technical Report TR-03.413, IBM Santa Teresa Laboratory, San Jose, USA, 1991.

[6] L.-K. Wang, C. Tsen, M. Schulte and D. Jhalani, "Benchmarks and Performance Analysis of Decimal Floating-Point Applications," *5th International Conference on Computer Design*, Lake Tahoe, 7-10 October 2007, pp. 164-170.

[7] R. Kenney and M. Schulte, "High-Speed Multioperand Decimal Adders," *IEEE Transactions on Computers*, Vol. 54, No. 8, 2005, pp. 953-963.

[8] I. D. Castellanos and J. E. Stine, "Compressor Trees for Decimal Partial Product Reduction," *GLSVLSI'08: Proceedings of the 18th ACM Great Lakes Symposium on VLSI, ACM*, Orlando, 4-6 May 2008, pp. 107-110.

[9] I. S. Hwang, "High Speed Binary and Decimal Arithmetic Unit," USA Patent No. 4,866,656.

[10] A. Bayrakci and A. Akkas, "Reduced Delay BCD Adder," *IEEE International Conference on Application Specific Systems, Architectures and Processors*, Montreal, 9-11 July 2007, pp. 266-271.

[11] Y. You, Y. D. Kim and J. H. Choi, "Dynamic Decimal Adder Circuit Design by Using the Carry Lookahead,"

IEEE Design and Diagnostics of Electronic Circuits and Systems, Prague, 18-21 April 2006, pp. 242-244.

[12] L.-K. Wang and M. Schulte, "A Decimal Floating-Point Adder with Decoded Operands and a Decimal Leading-Zero Anticipator," *19th IEEE Symposium on Computer Arithmetic*, Portland, 8-10 June 2009, pp. 125-134.

[13] A. Vazquez and E. Antelo, "A High-Performance Significand BCD Adder with IEEE 754-2008 Decimal Rounding," *19th IEEE Symposium on Computer Arithmetic*, Portland, 8-10 June 2009, pp. 135-144.

[14] L.-K. Wang and M. Schulte, "Decimal Floating-Point Adder and Multifunction Unit with Injection-Based Rounding," *18th IEEE Symposium on Computer Arithmetic*, Montpellier, 25-27 June 2007, pp. 56-68.

[15] M. Erle, E. Schwarz and M. Schulte, "Decimal Multiplication with Efficient Partial Product Generation," *17th IEEE Symposium on Computer Arithmetic*, Cape Cod, 27-29 June 2005, pp. 21-28.

[16] M. Erle, M. Schulte and B. Hickmann, "Decimal Floating-Point Multiplication via Carry-Save Addition," *18th IEEE Symposium on Computer Arithmetic*, Montpellier, 25-27 June 2007, pp. 46-55.

[17] A. Vazquez, E. Antelo and P. Montuschi, "A New Family of High-Performance Parallel Decimal Multipliers," *18th IEEE Symposium on Computer Arithmetic*, Montpellier, 25-27 June 2007, pp. 195-204.

[18] G. Jaberipur and A. Kaivani, "Improving the Speed of Parallel Decimal Multipliers," *IEEE Transactions on Computers*, Vol. 58, No. 11, 2009, pp. 1539-1552.

[19] T. Lang and A. Nannarelli, "A Radix-10 Digit-Recurrence Division Unit: Algorithm and Architecture," *IEEE Transactions on Computers*, Vol. 56, No. 6, 2007, pp. 727-739.

[20] A. Vazquez, E. Antelo and P. Montuschi, "A Radix-10 SRT Divider Based on Alternative BCD Codings," *25th International Conference on Computer Design*, Lake Tahoe, 7-10 October 2007, pp. 280-287.

[21] H. Nikmehr, B. Phillips and C. Lim, "Fast Decimal Floating-Point Division," *IEEE Transactions on Very Large Scale Integration (VLSI) Systems*, Vol. 14, No. 9, 2006, pp. 951-961.

[22] A. Kaivani and G. Jaberipur, "Fully Redundant Decimal Addition and Subtraction Using Stored-Unibit Encoding," *Integration, the VLSI journal*, Vol. 43, No. 1, 2010, pp. 34-41.

[23] L. Dadda, "Multioperand Parallel Decimal Adder: A Mixed Binary and BCD Approach," *IEEE Transactions on Computers*, Vol. 56, No. 10, 2007, pp. 1320-1328.

[24] A. Svoboda, "Decimal Adder with Signed Digit Arithmetic," *IEEE Transactions on Computers*, Vol. C-18, No. 3, 1969, pp. 212-215.

[25] J. Moskal, E. Oruklu and J. Saniie, "Design and Synthesis of a Carry-Free Signed-Digit Decimal Adder," *IEEE International Symposium on Circuits and Systems*, New Orleans, 27-30 May 2007, pp. 1089-1092.

[26] H. Nikmehr, B. Phillips and C. Lim, "A Decimal Carry-Free Adder," *Smart Structures, Devices, and Systems-II*, Sydney, 13 December 2005, pp. 786-797.

[27] B. Shirazi, D. Yun and C. Zhang, "RBCD: Redundant Binary Coded Decimal Adder," *IEE Proceedings on Computers and Digital Techniques*, Vol. 136, No. 2, 1989, pp. 156-160.

[28] B. Shirazi, D. Yun and C. Zhang, "VLSI Designs for redundant Binary-Coded Decimal Addition," *7th Annual International Phoenix Conference on Computers and Communications*, Scottsdale, 16-18 March 1988, pp. 52-56.

[29] R. Kenney, M. Schulte and M. Erle, "A High-Frequency Decimal Multiplier," *IEEE International Conference on Computer Design: VLSI in Computers and Processors*, San Jose, 11-13 October 2004, pp. 26-29.

[30] A. Avizienis, "Signed Digit Number Representations for Fast Parallel Arithmetic," *IRE Transactions on Electronic Computers*, Vol. EC-10, No. 3, 1961, pp. 389-400.

[31] B. Parhami, "Generalized Signed-Digit Number Systems: A Unifying Framework for Redundant Number Representations," *IEEE Transactions on Computers*, Vol. 39, No. 1, 1990, pp. 89-98.

[32] J. Rebacz, E. Oruklu and J. Saniie, "High Performance Signed-Digit Decimal Adders," *IEEE International Conference on Electro/Information Technology*, Windsor, 7-9 June 2009, pp. 251-255.

[33] V. Dave, E. Oruklu and J. Saniie, "Design and Synthesis of a Three Input Flagged Prefix Adder," *IEEE International Symposium on Circuits and Systems*, New Orleans, 27-30 May 2007, pp. 1081-1084.

[34] D. Phatak and I. Koren, "Hybrid Signed-Digit Number Systems: A United Framework for Redundant Number Representations with Bounded Carry Propagation Chains," *IEEE Transactions on Computers*, Vol. 43, No. 8, 1994, pp. 880-891.

[35] J. Rebacz, E. Oruklu and J. Saniie, "Performance Evaluation of Multi-Operand Fast Decimal Adders," *52nd IEEE International Midwest Symposium on Circuits and Systems*, Cancun, 2-5 August 2009, pp. 535-538.

An Improved Non-isolated LED Converter with Power Factor Correction and Average Current Mode Control

Renbo Xu[1,2,4], Hongjian Li[1,2], Yongzhi Li[3], Changqian Zhang[1]
[1]*School of Physics Science and Technology, Central South University, Changsha, China*
[2]*School of Materials Science and Engineering, Central South University, Changsha, China*
[3]*College of Physics and Information Science, Hunan Normal University, Changsha, China*
[4]*Hunan Information Science Vocational College, Changsha, China*

Abstract

A new type of high power LED drivers is proposed by adopting an improved two-stages non-isolated configuration. In order to improve power factor and achieve accurate average current control under universal input voltages ranging from 100 Vrms to 240 Vrms, the power factor correction and average current mode control methods operating in continuous current conduction mode are designed and implemented. With the LUMILEDS emitter type LEDs, a laboratory prototype is built and measured. And from the measured results, it could be concluded that the proposed driver has many better performances such as high power factor, low current harmonic, accurate average current control and switch protection.

Keywords: High Power LED, Power Factor Correction, Average Current Mode Control

1. Introduction

In today's world of lighting applications, many electronic engineers are striving to find out a more energy efficient and cost effective way of driving a lighting source. A new type of lighting sources that has a great potential to replace existing lighting sources such as incandescent and fluorescent lamps in the future is the power lighting emitting diode (LED), which is due to its merits: higher efficiency, superior longevity, continuously-improving luminance and environment friendly [1-3]. This interest in LEDs has prompted many power electronic designers to work on driving LED at higher power factor and output current so that it can be applied broader in lighting applications.

In general lighting applications, the line current harmonics should satisfy the limits set by International Electro technical Commission (IEC) 61000-3-2 class *C* regulations [4]. And the input current power factor should be higher than 0.9 required by the Energy-Star [5]. Moreover, with only a small change in the LED current, the corresponding luminous flux and luminous efficiency will change by orders of magnitude. In order to avoid big luminous flux change and meet those regulations, the LED driver should have the power factor correction (PFC) ability and constant average current control.

In view of the development of PFC technology, PFC could be achieved either by passive circuit or by active circuit. With passive PFC, which uses only inductors and capacitors to improve power factor, it is difficult to meet those requirements and become a good candidate because of the disadvantages of high total harmonic distortion (THD) and bulky size [6,7]. In order to overcome these disadvantages, active PFC technology is commonly used in LED drivers due to many advantages such as low THD, fast dynamic response, precise voltage control and universal input voltages. And active PFC method is very suitable for many applications field with high performance requirements, low cost and high control accuracy.

An LED driver with active PFC, which is implemented with two stages, is shown in **Figure 1**. The two-stages structure has many advantages: avoiding the Electro Magnetic Interference (EMI) if only the two stages operate in trailing edge and leading edge respectively; decreasing the capacitance of the output capacitor; reducing the bulk and extending the longevity efficiently [8-12]. The first stage is used to provide a stable voltage for the post stage with AC/DC conversion at the universal input voltage, while the post stage is used for the DC/DC conversion. Unlike conventional LED drivers, it could be applied to both low and high voltage cases, such as it is widely used in car applications because the car power supply voltage is easily changeable [13,14]. With the goal to achieve higher power factor and LED constant average current control, the Boost-Buck converter with higher power rating operating in continuous current conduction mode (CCM) with average current mode control (ACMC) is proposed through adding two control blocks: PFC control and ACMC block.

2. Circuit Description

From the non-isolated LED Boost-Buck converter circuit diagram, it can be seen that the converter consists of rectifier bridge, boost circuit, buck circuit, driving signal and the load. And the Boost-Buck converter uses capacitor as energy transfer component between the first and post stage rather than the inductor mostly used in other conventional converters. It can be known from the analysis that the Boost-Buck converter features fast transient response and excellent frequency response, allowing highly stable feedback regulation to be achieved with simple circuit [15-17]. Two inductors at both input and output side are working in continuous current conduction mode. The inductor ripple current is low and continuous, which can greatly reduce the requirements of input and output filter capacitor. All switch nodes in the circuit are isolated between the two inductors, input and output nodes have no effect on each other, which would make the radiation EMI (Electro Magnetic Interference) from the converter minimized. The operational principles are described and discussed in the next sections.

When the metal oxide semiconductor field effect transistor (MOS-FET) S_1 is turned on, current flows through the rectifier bridge, the input inductor L_1 and the MOS switch S_1. The power supply stores energy in the inductor L_1 and the diode V_{D_1} is off at the moment. When S_1 turns off, current in L_1 flows through the diode V_{D_1}, into the capacitor C_1 and transfer the energy to storage capacitor C_1 as a power supply for the post stage Buck converter. When the MOS switch S_2 is turned on, current flows through the capacitor C_1, the power switch S_2, inductor L_2, capacitor C_2 and LED strings. Transfer the energy to the capacitor C_2 and provide power supply to the load LED strings and the diode V_{D_2} is turned off synchronously. When S_2 turns off, current in inductor L_2 flows through the LED strings and the free-wheeling diode V_{D_2}.

From the analysis it can be known that the average voltage on the inductor L_1 is zero as described in Equation (1).

$$V_{L_1} t_{on_1} = V_{L_1} t_{off_1} \tag{1}$$

where t_{on_1} and t_{off_1} represent the turn-on and the turn-off time of the MOS switch S_1 in a switching period. According to the operational principle described in the former, Equation (1) can be rewritten as

$$V_i D_1 T_S = \left(V_{C_1} - V_i\right)\left(1 - D_1\right) T_S \tag{2}$$

where D_1 is the duty ratio of S_1 and T_S is the switching period. Solving Equation (2) for V_{C_1} as shown in Equation (3), we can see that the output voltage V_{C_1} is increased much.

$$V_{C_1} = \frac{V_i}{\left(1 - D_1\right)} \tag{3}$$

Taking the same switching period T_S and the duty ratio D_2 of S_2, from the similar analysis of the inductor L_2, we have

$$\left(V_{C_1} - V_O\right) D_2 T_S = V_O \left(1 - D_2\right) T_S \tag{4}$$

Substituting (3) into (4), the relation between output voltage and input voltage can be obtained by

$$V_O = \frac{D_2 V_i}{\left(1 - D_1\right)} \tag{5}$$

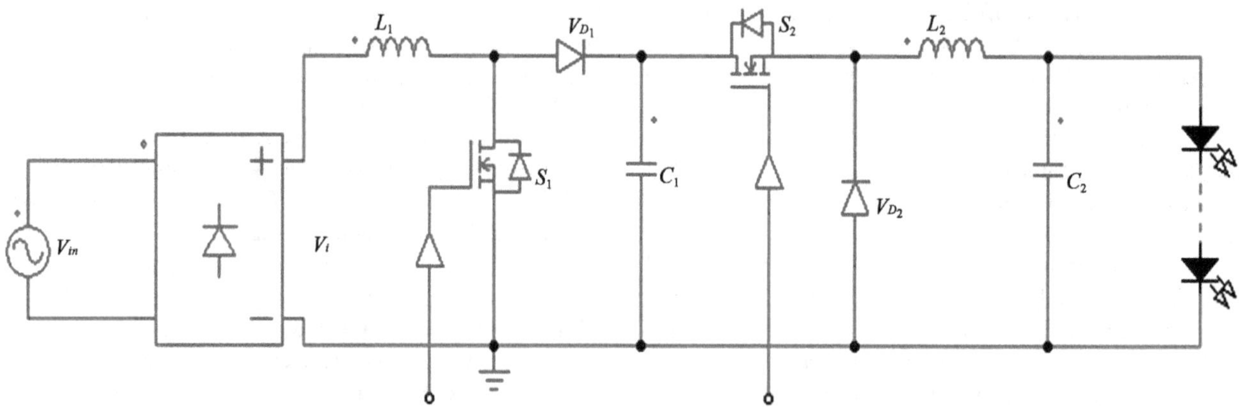

Figure 1. LED Boost-Buck converter diagram.

From the steady-state operational principle [18], it could be known that the average current flowing through the capacitor C_1 must be zero defined as

$$I_{C_1} t_{char} = I_{C_1} t_{unch} \tag{6}$$

where t_{char} and t_{unch} stand for the charging time and uncharging time respectively. (6) could be rewritten as

$$I_{L_1}(1-D_1)T_S = I_{L_2} D_2 T_S \tag{7}$$

Solving (7) for I_{L_1}

$$I_{L_1} = \frac{D_2 I_{L_2}}{(1-D_1)} = \frac{D_2 I_O}{(1-D_1)} \tag{8}$$

3. The Proposed Circuit

From the analysis of the Boost-Buck converter it can be known that the converter has high stability, fast transient response and high efficiency. But the power factor is low because of harmonic distortion and the use of inductors and capacitors, and it can not satisfy the accurate regulation of luminance due to that the light output is proportional to the current delivered to the LEDs string averaged over the utility period. In order to improve the power factor of the input side of the grid and provide a constant average current and lighting output, the technology of active PFC and ACMC is proposed through adding a PFC control loop and an average current control loop as shown in **Figure 2**.

The boost PFC circuit operates in CCM with trailing edge modulator, while the leading edge modulation is adopted in the Buck pulse width modulation (PWM) constant average current control circuit. Although the switches work under turned-on and turned-off state alternately, the proposed converter reduces the harmonic current distortion due to the inductors operated in CCM.

From the system block schematic diagram, it can be known that the error signal between the sampled voltage of the capacitor C_1 and the reference voltage is amplified and sent to the analog multiplier for generating a half-sine reference current signal as same frequency and phase as input voltage V_i. The current regulator is used to compare the sensing current I_i with the half-sine reference current and then generate a current error amplified signal. Compared with the sawtooth wave, the output of the comparator is the control signal of the MOS switch S_1. Thus, through adjusting the duty cycle, the current of inductor L_1 will track the half-sine reference current signal that is to say that the input current I_{in} tracks the sinusoidal input voltage V_{in} well for a high power factor.

To get the working stability of current loop and a good dynamic tracking ability of the average inductor current, the current regulator must be designed to have high low-frequency gain, wide mid-frequency gain, a reasonable margin steady and strong switching ripple suppression ability. A compensation network $G(s)$ with two pole and one zero is taken as a current regulator as shown in Equation (9).

$$G(s) = \frac{\omega_i (1 + s/\omega_Z)}{s(1 + s/\omega_P)} \tag{9}$$

where $\omega_i = \dfrac{1}{R_i(C_1 + C_2)}$, $\omega_P = \dfrac{C_1 + C_2}{R_1 C_1 C_2}$, $\omega_Z = \dfrac{1}{R_1 C_1}$.

Design goal is to adjust the three parameters to meet the system's open loop frequency domain index. And the specific implement circuit of the current regulator is shown in **Figure 3**.

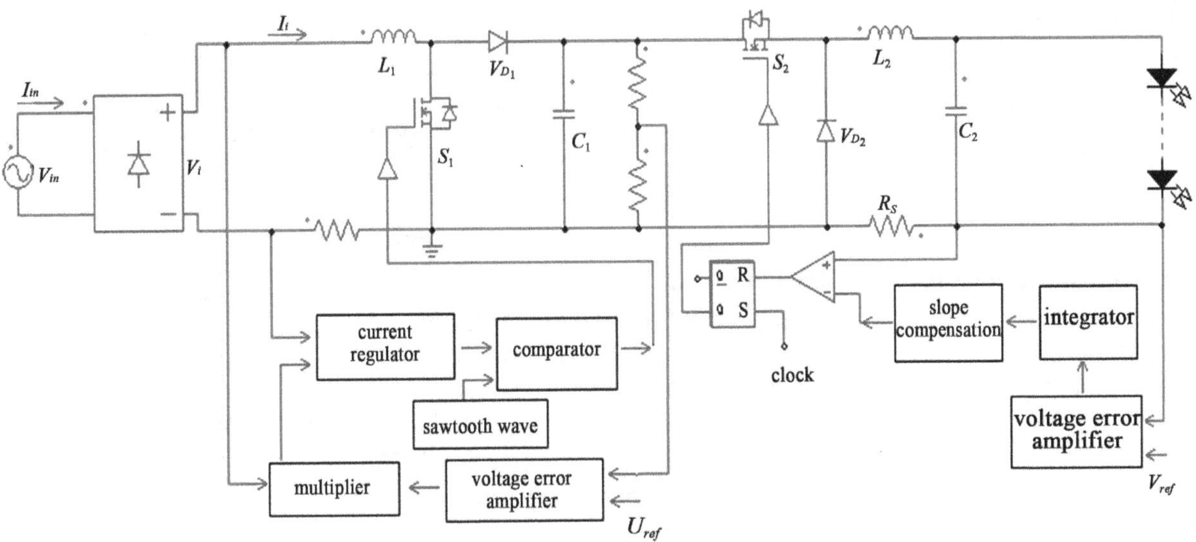

Figure 2. The proposed LED driver with active PFC and ACMC.

To study the discrete control property of the current regulator, a discrete mathematical mode of current sensing is created and then transformed into $He(s)$ at the complex frequency domain.

$$He(s) = 1 + \frac{s}{\omega_n Q_z} + \frac{s^2}{\omega_n^2} \quad (10)$$

where $\omega_n = \frac{\pi}{T_S}$, $Q_z = -\frac{2}{\pi}$.

To avoid aberrance in the inductor current, PFC voltage error amplifier design can't seek rapidity excessively and the output voltage should be relatively constant in a frequency cycle. From the perspective of frequency analysis, the voltage regulation loop bandwidth should be limited. And proportional integral voltage regulator is a good candidate and its implement circuit is shown in **Figure 4**.

The transfer function of the voltage regulator is

$$Gu(s) = \frac{g}{s(1 + s/\omega_z)} \quad (11)$$

where g is the proportional integral coefficient, and $\omega_z = \frac{2}{C_1 R_i}$ according to the stability analysis.

From the system block diagram in **Figure 2**, we can see that there is a sensing resistor R_s to sense the output current. After the output current flowing through the high power LEDs and R_s, the sensing feedback voltage can be acquired. The integral voltage of error value between the feedback voltage and the reference voltage V_{ref} is sent to the slope compensation. Compared with the sensing feedback voltage, the comparator output is obtained to control the RS flip-flop and then the output of RS flip-flop controls the MOS switch S_2 and regulates the output average current precisely.

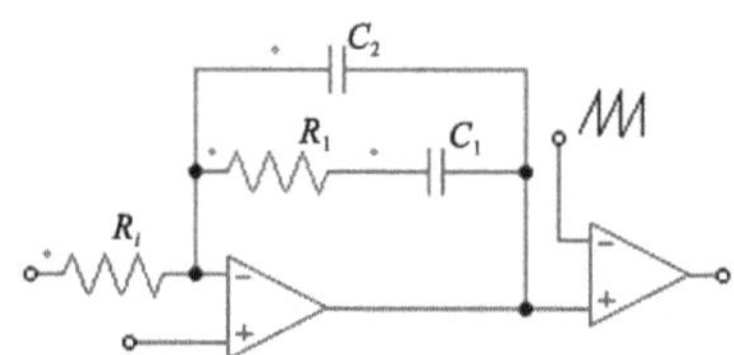

Figure 3. The implement circuit of current regulator.

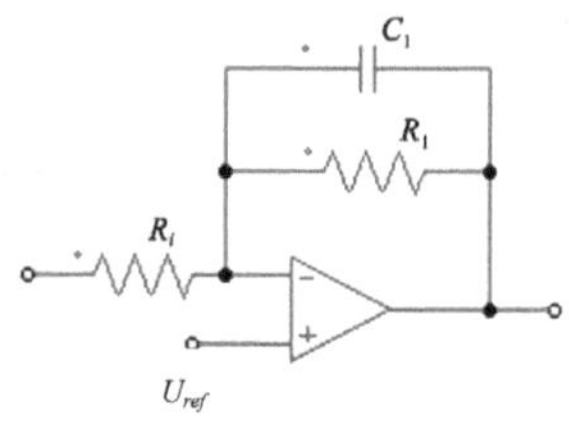

Figure 4. The implement circuit of voltage regulator.

In order to gain the accurate average current, the slope compensation technique is adopted, as shown in **Figure 5**. v_r is the reference voltage, and dotted line v_{avr} is the average voltage of sensing feedback voltage v_s in a switching period. $-m_s$, m_r are the slope of the slope compensation voltage and the sensing voltage v_s respectively. From the steady-state waveforms, it can be seen that the sensing average voltage v_{avr} represents the average current of high power LED.

From the steady-state waveforms, we have

$$\frac{1}{2} m_r d T_S = v_r - v_{avr} - m_s d T_s \quad (12)$$

Take small-signal perturbation of the relevant variables as follows.

$$v_r = V_r + \hat{v}_r \quad v_{avr} = V_{avr} + \hat{v}_{avr}$$
$$m_r = M_r + \hat{m}_r \quad d = D + \hat{d} \quad (13)$$

Among them, the capitalized letters are steady-state values and the variables with "Λ" are small-signal disturbances.

Substituting (12) into (13), we have

$$\frac{T_S}{2}\left(M_r + \hat{m}_r\right)\left(D + \hat{d}\right)$$
$$= V_r + \hat{v}_r - V_{avr} - \hat{v}_{avr} - m_s\left(D + \hat{d}\right)T_s \quad (14)$$

With ignorance of second-order small-signal variables, we can get the characteristics equations of DC steady-state (15) and AC small-signal (16).

$$D = \frac{V_r - V_{avr}}{\frac{1}{2} M_r T_S + m_s T_s} = \frac{2}{n M_r T_S}\left(V_r - V_{avr}\right) \quad (15)$$

Among (15) $-m_s = -M_s$, $n = 1 + \frac{2M_s}{M_r}$.

$$\left(\frac{T_S}{2} M_r + M_s T_s\right)\hat{d} = \hat{v}_r - \hat{v}_{avr} - \frac{D T_s}{2}\hat{m}_r \quad (16)$$

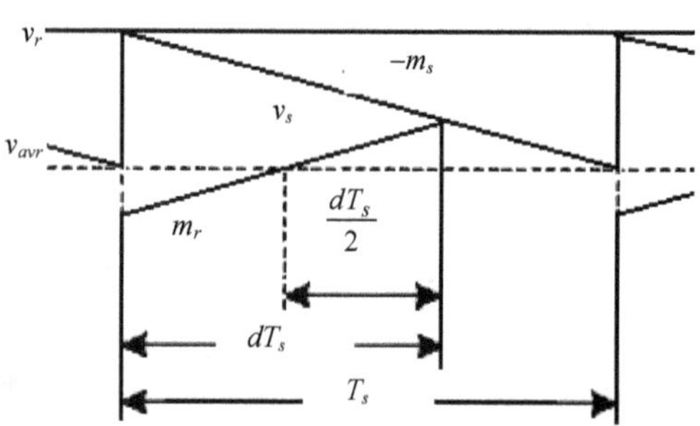

Figure 5. The steady-state waveforms with constant average current control.

As a result of the new control technique, the driver provides a precise constant average output current and high power factor under pieces of LED series connection. Moreover, the proposed converter operating in CCM has many better performances such as variable input source voltages, wide frequency bandwidth, high efficiency and stability.

4. Simulation and Experimental Results

To verify the feasibility of the proposed LED driver, a laboratory prototype with the following specifications were designed and tested.

- Input voltage: 100 - 240 Vrms
- Switching frequency: 200 kHz
- LED current: 350 mA

The circuit parameters for the laboratory prototype are as follows: the rectifier sampling coefficient is 0.0032; the inductor L_1 = 1.47 mH and L_2 = 0.22 mH; the capacitor C_1 = 3500 uF and C_2 = 470 uF, the sensing resistor R_s is 0.1 Ω and the reference voltage V_{ref} = 0.035 V. The series connected LUMILEDS emitter type LEDs is used in this experiment. This LUMILEDS diode is a 1 W high-luminance LED with a nominal forward voltage of 3.42 V. The laboratory prototype is designed to get a high power factor and a constant output average current 350 mA when the input source voltage varies from 100 Vrms to 240 Vrms. **Figure 6** shows the tested waveforms of the input voltage V_{in} and input current I_{in} at the input source voltage of 110 Vrms and 220 Vrms, respectively. It could be seen that I_{in} has a good near-sinusoidal waveform and in phase with the input source voltage V_{in}. Power factor under different input source voltages variations are shown in **Figure 7** and the high power factor is over 0.95.

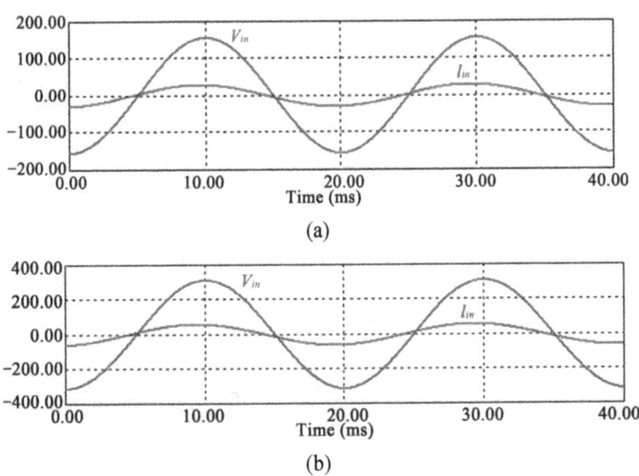

Figure 6. The tested input voltage and current waveforms at V_{in} = 110 Vrms and 220 Vrms. ((a) The tested input voltage and current waveforms at V_{in} = 110 Vrms; (b) The tested input voltage and current waveforms at V_{in} = 220 Vrms).

Figure 8 shows that the line-current harmonics are below the limits set by IEC 61000-3-2 class *C* regulations with enough margin at the input source voltage of 110 Vrms and 220 Vrms, respectively. It can be seen that these high performances such as phase-following, high power factor, low THD are the results of the improved APFC block.

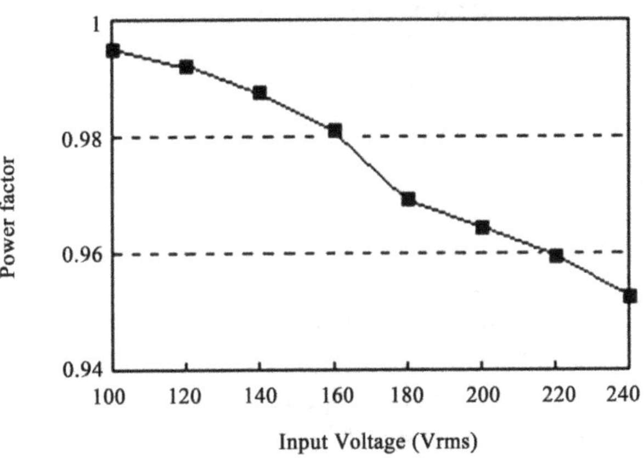

Figure 7. Power factor vs different input voltages.

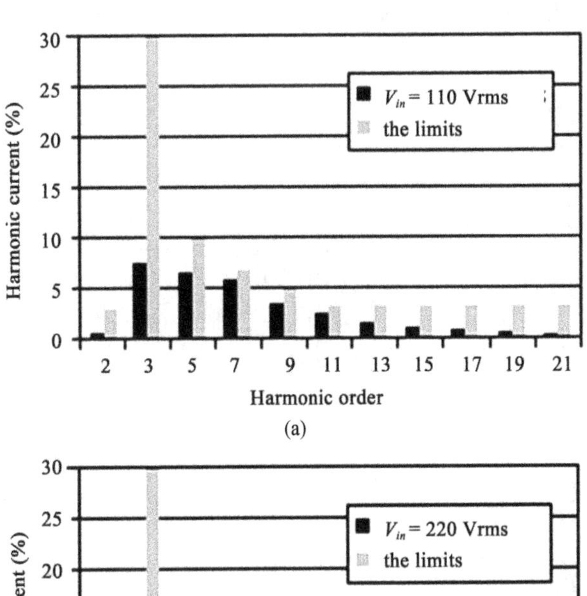

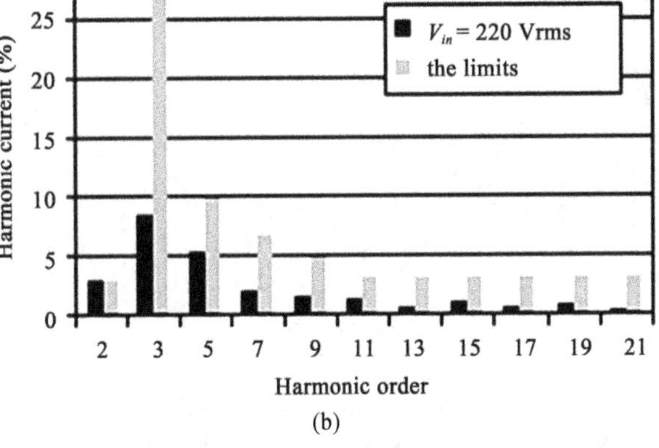

Figure 8. The measured line-current harmonics at V_{in} = 110 Vrms and 220 Vrms. ((a) Line-current harmonics at V_{in} = 110 Vrms; (b) Line-current harmonics at V_{in} = 220 Vrms).

Without the ACMC technique, the LED constant average current is 320 mA below the reference current as shown in **Figure 9(a)**. However, with the proposed method the constant average current of 350 mA can be achieved as shown in **Figure 9(b)**. It is evident that the LED average current and luminous flux can be regulated by adjusting the duty cycle of MOS-FET switch. And the steady and slowly-rising LED current of the new driver can protect the MOS switch due to the improved ACMC block.

All the test results are consistent with expectations well.

5. Conclusions

In this paper, we proposed an improved non-isolated LED converter operating in CCM with PFC and ACMC for driving high power LED lamps. A laboratory prototype with LUMILEDS emitter type LEDs is used to verify the feasibility of the proposed driver. From the measured results, it can be seen that the proposed LED driver achieves a power factor of 0.99 and a THD of 12.2% at input voltage 110 Vrms and a power factor of 0.96 and a THD of 10.4% at input voltage 220 Vrms. Many better performances such as high power factor, accurate average current control, low current harmonic and switch protection are confirmed and the experimental results match well with the analysis results.

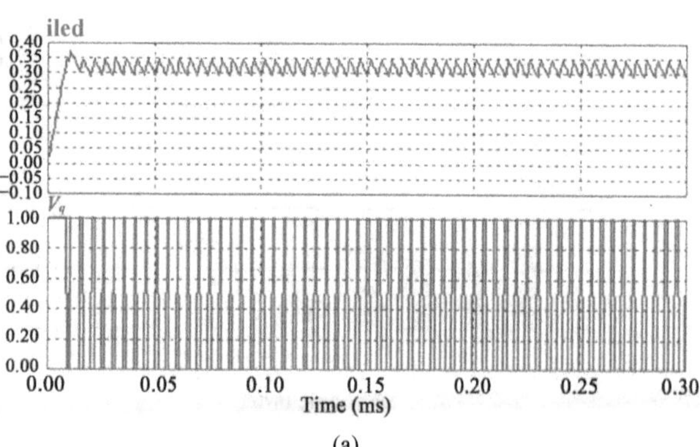

(a)

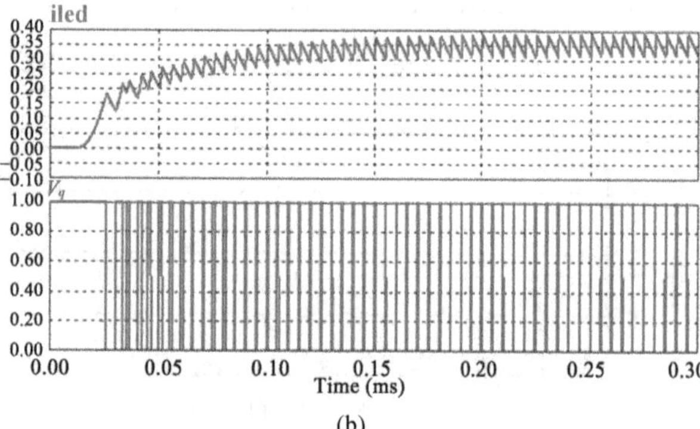

(b)

Figure 9. The LED current simulated waveforms and the switching signal. ((a) The LED current simulated waveforms and the switching signal Without the ACMC; (b) The LED current simulated waveforms and the switching signal With the ACMC).

6. References

[1] J. Y. Tsao, "Solid-State Lighting: Lamps, Chips and Materials for Tomorrow," *IEEE Circuits Devices Magazine*, Vol. 20, No. 3, 2004, pp. 28-37.

[2] T. Komine and M. Nakagawa, "Fundamental Analysis for Visible-Light Communication System Using LED Lights," *IEEE Transactions on Consumer Electronics*, Vol. 50, No. 1, 2004, pp. 100-107.

[3] R. Mehta, D. Deshpande, K. Kulkarni, S. Sharma and D. Divan, "LEDs—A Competitive Solution for General Lighting Applications," *IEEE Energy* 2008, Atlanta, 17-18 November 2008, pp. 1-5.

[4] "Electromagnetic Compatibility (EMC), Part 3-2: Limits—Limits for Harmonic Current Emissions (Equipment Input Current ≤ 16 A per Phase)," International Standard IEC 61000-3-2, 2001.

[5] Energy Star Program Requirements for Solid State Lighting Luminaries. USA, 2007.

[6] J. P. Noon, "Designing High-Power Factor Off-Line Power Supplies," *Proceedings of Unitrode Power Supply Design Seminar Manual SEM*1500, Texas Instruments, August 2003, pp. 2-6.

[7] C. K. Tse, "Circuit Theory of Power Factor Correction in Switching Converters," *International Journal of Circuit Theory and Applications*, Vol. 31, No. 2, 2003, pp. 157-198.

[8] H. van der Broeck, G. Sauerlander and M. Wendt, "Power Driver Topologies and Control Schemes for LEDs," *IEEE Applied Power Electronics Conference*, Anaheim, 25 February-1 March 2007, pp. 1319-1325.

[9] G. Spiazzi and J. P. Pomilio, "Interaction between EMI Filter and Power Factor Pre-regulators with Average Current Control: Analysis and Design Considerations," *IEEE Transactions on Industrial Electronics*, Vol. 46, No. 3, 1999, pp. 577-584.

[10] M. Ogata and T. Nishi, "Gragh-Theoretical Approach to 2-Switch DC-DC Converters," *International Journal of Circuit Theory and Applications*, Vol. 33, No. 2, 2005, pp. 161-173.

[11] A. Lazaro, A. Barrado, M. Sanz, V. Salas and E. Olias, "New Power Correction AC-DC Converter with Reduced Storage Capacitor Voltage," *IEEE Transactions on Industrial Electronics*, Vol. 54, No. 1, 2007, pp. 384-397.

[12] B. Sharifipour, J. S. Hung, P. Liao, L. Huber and M. M. Jovanovic, "Manufacturing and Cost Analysis of Power-Factor-Correction Circuits," *IEEE Applied Power Electronics Conference and Exposition*, Anaheim, 15-19 February 1998, pp.490-494.

[13] M. Rico-Secades, A. J. Calleja, J. Ribas, E. L. Corominas, J. M. Alonso, J. Cardesin and Garcia-Garcia, "Evaluation of a Low-Cost Permanent Emergency Lighting System based on High-Efficiency LEDs," *IEEE Transactions on Industry Applications*, Vol. 41, No. 5, 2005, pp. 1386-1390.

[14] Z. Y. Chen, H. L. Yin and P. Li, "Power Quality Problem and New Technology for Its Improvement," *Power System Technology*, Vol. 26, 2007, pp. 67-70.

[15] M. X. Han, Y. You and H. Liu, "Principle and Realization of Dynamic Voltage Regulator Based on Line Voltage Compensating," *Proceedings of the CSEE*, Vol. 23, 2003, pp. 49-53.

[16] S. Wall and R. Jackson, "Fast Controller Design for Single-Phase Power-Factor Correction Systems," *IEEE Transactions on Industrial Electronics*, Vol. 44, No. 5, 1997, pp. 654-660.

[17] W. Aloisi and G. Palumbo, "Efficiency Model of Boost DC-DC PWM Converters," *International Journal of Circuit Theory and Applications*, Vol. 33, No. 5, 2005, pp. 419-432.

[18] Y. Yueh-Ru and C. Chern-Lin, "Steady-State Analysis and Simulation of a BJT Self-Oscillating ZVS-CV Ballast Driven by a Saturable Transformer," *IEEE Transactions on Industrial Electronics*, Vol. 46, No. 2, 1999, pp. 249-260.

3

Electronically Tunable Minimum Component Biquadratic Filters for Interface Circuits

Mehmet Sağbaş
Department of Electronics Engineering, Maltepe University, Istanbul, Turkey

Abstract

In this paper, two new electronically tunable filter configurations are proposed. The proposed filters operate current-mode (CM), voltage-mode (VM), transimpedance-mode (TIM) and transadmittance-mode (TAM). The first configuration realizes second-order VM band-pass and TAM high-pass filter characteristics from the same configuration. The second one realizes second-order TIM band-pass and CM low-pass filter characteristics from the same configuration. They also use minimum number of electronic components (two capacitors and one active component namely; current controlled current difference transconductance amplifier). The workability of the proposed structures has been demonstrated by simulation results.

Keywords: Second-Order Filters, CC-CDBA, Electronic Tunability, Current-Mode Circuits, Interface Circuits

1. Introduction

It is well known that current-mode and voltage-mode are still important integrated circuit (IC) operations [1-3]. Recently, there is a growing interest in transimpedance-mode and transadmittance-mode operations. A current-input voltage-output filter or voltage-input current-output filter is described as an interface circuit connecting a current-mode circuit to a voltage-mode circuit or a voltage-mode circuit to a current-mode circuit, respectively. These interface circuits are needed in many applications where VM and CM circuits are used together. In addition, the other important application area of transadmittance-mode filters are the receiver baseband blocks of modern radio systems [4,5]. Also the outputs of the many digital/analog converters (DACs) are available as current signals. Then the transimpedance-mode filters can be used for conversion of the signals at the outputs of these DACs, simultaneously. Therefore, several TAM- and TIM-type filters are proposed using different-type active components [6-12].

Simplicity, cost reduction, power consumption and versatility are all important for the integrated circuit manufacturers. Therefore, number of the components is an important parameter. Therefore, numerous circuits are proposed in literature that employing minimum number of component [13-17]. However, these filters use at least four electronic components. The proposed filter is compared to the other filters reported in the literature by the use of **Table 1**. According to **Table 1**, the proposed filter has advantages over the proposed filters in Ref [13-14], since it has electronically tunability property and no external resistors.

In this paper, two new second order filter configurations using only single active component and two capacitors are presented. They realize CM, VM, TIM and TAM second order filter characteristics from the same configuration. Similar kinds of circuits in the literature use more than three elements [13-16] (see **Table 1**).

The paper is organized as in the following sections: In the next section, after a short introduction of CC-CDBA,

Table 1. Comparison of the cited references and the proposed filter.

Ref.	Active Element	External Capacitor	External Resistor	Electronic Tunability
[13]	1 CDBA	2	2	No
[14]	1 CDBA	2	2	No
[15]	1 CCII+	2	2	No
[16]	1 CCCII	2	1	Yes
Proposed Filter	1 CC-CDBA	2	0	Yes

two new filter configurations using CC-CDBA with two capacitors are introduced. Sensitivities and simulation results are discussed in Section 3.

2. Proposed Resistorless Circuit Configurations and Their analysis

In order to accomplish electronic adjustability in CDBA, Maheshwari and Khan have introduced current controlled current controlled differencing buffered amplifier (CC-CDBA) [17]. It has proven to be useful in many voltage-mode and current-mode analog signal-processing applications [17-21]. The circuit symbol of CC-CDBA is shown in **Figure 1** and its terminal equation can be written as follow

$$V_p = R_p i_p, V_n = R_n i_n, i_z = i_p - i_n, v_w = v_z \tag{1}$$

Current controlled CDBA can easily be implemented using bipolar junction transistor (BJT) technologies shown in **Figure 2** [17]. The parasitic input resistances R_p and R_n using BJT implementation for $I_{p,n}(t) \ll 2I_o$ can be obtained as

$$R_p = R_n = \frac{kT/q}{2I_O} = \frac{V_T}{2I_O} \tag{2}$$

where, k is the Boltzman's constant, T is the temperature in Calvin and q is the electron charge; $V_T = kT/q$ is the thermal voltage. Hence, R_p and R_n can be controlled by varying the bias current I_o. In addition to this, the quality factor Q and the undamped natural frequency ω_o depend on R_p and R_n, which makes them electronically adjustable.

Taking the non-idealities of CDBA into account, the above terminal equations can be rewritten as

$$V_p = R_p i_p, V_n = R_n i_n, i_z = \alpha_p i_p - \alpha_n i_n, V_w = \beta V_z \tag{3}$$

where α_p, α_n and β are the current and voltage gains, respectively, and can be expressed as $\alpha_p = 1 - \varepsilon_p$, $\alpha_n = 1 - \varepsilon_n$, $\alpha_\beta = 1 - \varepsilon_v$, with $|\varepsilon_p| \ll 1$, $|\varepsilon_n| \ll 1$, $|\varepsilon_v| \ll 1$. ε_p and ε_n denote the current tracking errors and ε_v denotes voltage tracking error.

The proposed voltage-mode second-order band-pass filter circuit is shown in **Figure 3(a)**. Routine analysis yields the voltage transfer function as follows:

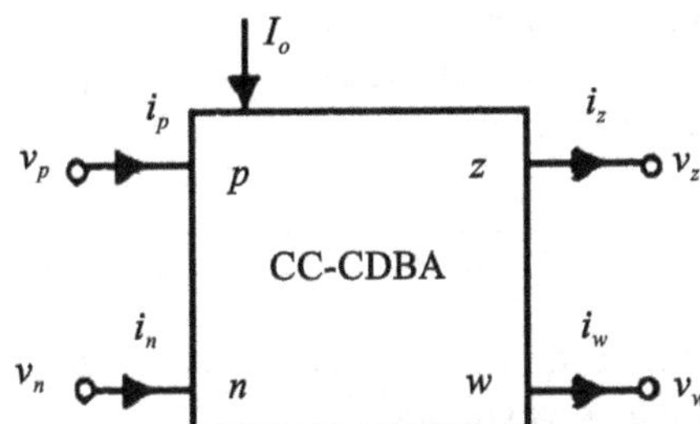

Figure 1. Block diagram of CC-CDBA.

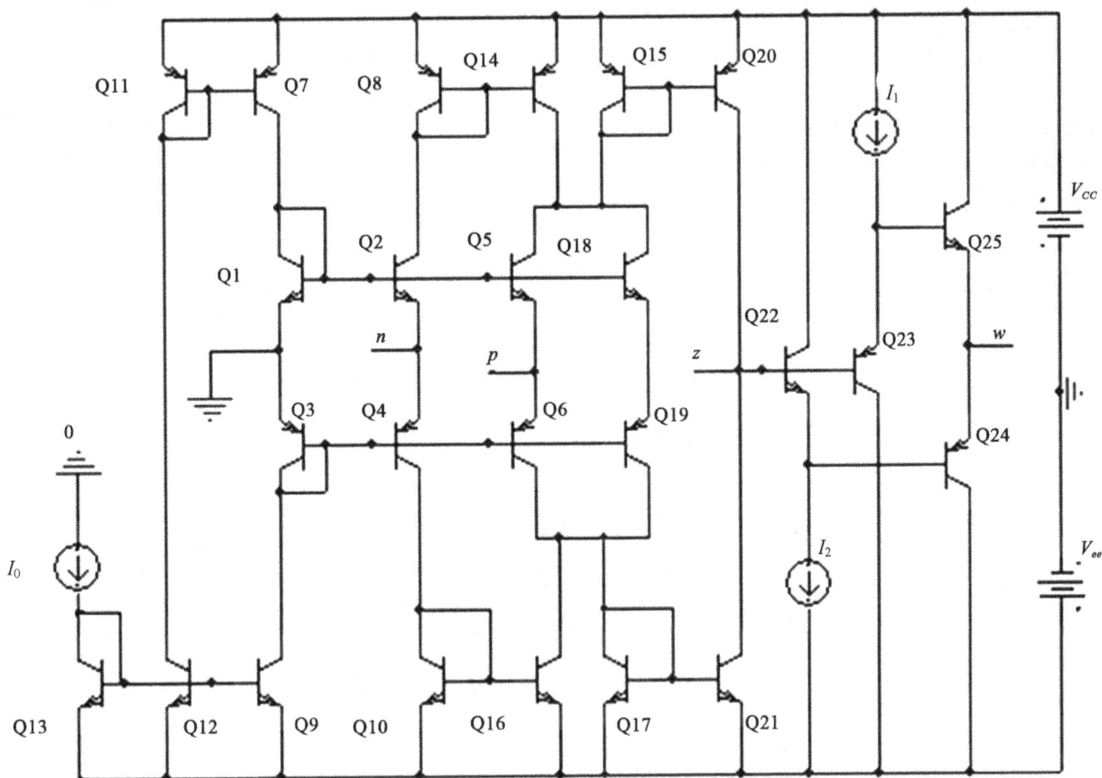

Figure 2. Schematic implementation for CC-CDBA using BJT technology.

$$\frac{V_{out}}{V_{in}} = \frac{sC_1R_n}{s^2C_1C_2R_pR_n + s\left(C_1R_p + C_2R_n\right) + 1} \tag{4}$$

The proposed filter in shown **Figure 3(a)** also gives minimum component transimpedance-mode high-pass filter response. Therefore, the current output response of the proposed circuit is

$$\frac{I_{out}}{V_{in}} = \frac{s^2C_1C_2R_n}{s^2C_1C_2R_pR_n + s\left(C_1R_p + C_2R_n\right) + 1} \tag{5}$$

The proposed current-mode second-order band-pass filter circuit is shown in **Figure 3(b)**. Routine analysis yields the voltage transfer function as follows:

$$\frac{I_{out}}{I_{in}} = \frac{sC_2R_n}{s^2C_1C_2R_pR_n + s\left(C_1R_p + C_2R_n\right) + 1} \tag{6}$$

It also gives minimum component TIM low-pass filter response. Therefore, the voltage output response of the proposed circuit is

$$\frac{V_{out}}{I_{in}} = \frac{R_n}{s^2C_1C_2R_pR_n + s\left(C_1R_p + C_2R_n\right) + 1} \tag{7}$$

The undamped natural frequency and the quality factor of the proposed circuit are obtained from the denominator of the transfer function as follows:

$$\omega_o = \frac{1}{\sqrt{C_1C_2R_pR_n}}, \quad Q = \frac{\sqrt{C_1C_2R_pR_n}}{C_1R_p + C_2R_n} \tag{8}$$

Taking the non-idealities of CC-CDBA given in Equation (3) into account, the denominator polynomial of the transfer function for the proposed filters becomes

$$D(s) = s^2C_1C_2R_pR_n + s\left(\beta\alpha_nC_1R_p + C_2R_n\right) + \beta\alpha_n \tag{9}$$

Using Equation (9), non-ideal the undamped natural frequency and the quality factor becomes

$$\omega_o = \sqrt{\frac{\beta\alpha_n}{C_lC_2R_pR_n}}, \quad Q = \frac{\sqrt{\beta\alpha_nC_lC_2R_pR_n}}{\beta\alpha_nC_lR_p + C_2R_n} \tag{10}$$

From Equation (10), the quality factor Q and the undamped natural frequency ω_o depend on R_p and R_n which can be controlled by varying the bias current I_o. Therefore, they can be adjusted electronically.

3. Sensitivity Consideration and Simulation Results

The ideal sensitivities of the natural frequency and the quality factor with respect to passive components are calculated as follows

$$S_{R_p}^{\omega_o} = S_{R_n}^{\omega_o} = S_{C_l}^{\omega_o} = S_{C_2}^{\omega_o} = -0.5, \tag{11}$$

$$S_{R_p}^{Q} = S_{C_1}^{Q} = 0.5 - C_1R_pk \tag{12}$$

$$S_{R_n}^{Q} = S_{C_2}^{Q} = 0.5 - C_2R_nk \tag{13}$$

where, $k = 1/\left(C_1R_p + C_2R_n\right)$.

If the passive component values are chosen appropriately, the ideal sensitivities will be smaller than 1.

Using Equation (10), the non-ideal sensitivities can be found as

$$S_{\alpha_n}^{\omega_o} = S_{\beta}^{\omega_o} = 0.5, \; S_{\alpha_p}^{\omega_o} = 0 \tag{14}$$

$$S_{\alpha_n}^{Q} = S_{\beta}^{Q} = 0.5 - \beta\alpha_nC_lR_pk \tag{15}$$

where, $k = 1/\left(\beta\alpha_nC_1R_p + C_2R_n\right)$.

Again, if passive component values are chosen appropriately, the sensitivities due to non-ideal effects will also be small than 1.

The performance of the filter topology given in **Figure 3(a)** is verified using PSpice. Each CC-CDBA is realized by its BJT implementation shown in **Figure 2** with the transistor model of PR100N (PNP) and NR100N (NPN) of the bipolar arrays ALA400 from AT & T [22]. In all of the simulations, the voltage supplies of CC-CDBA are taken as $V_{CC} = 2.5$ V and $V_{ee} = -2.5$ V.

To confirm the obtained results with the theoretical results and demonstrate tunability property of the proposed configuration, the gain characteristics obtained by PSPICE for two cases are plotted in **Figure 4** together. In these simulations, bias currents of CC-CDBA are $I_o = 10$ μA and $I_o = 20$ μA, for simulation 1 and 2, respectively.

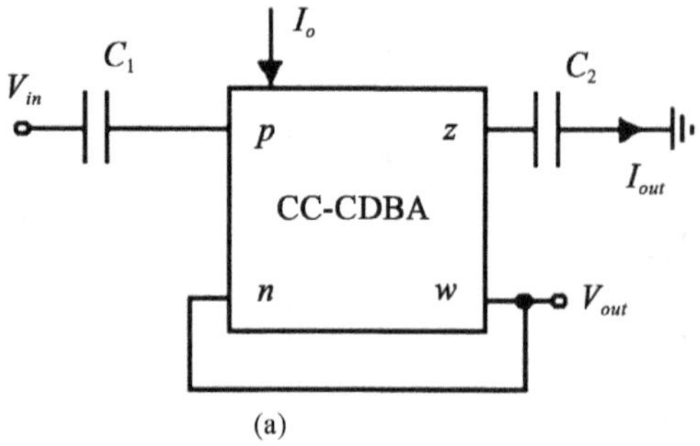

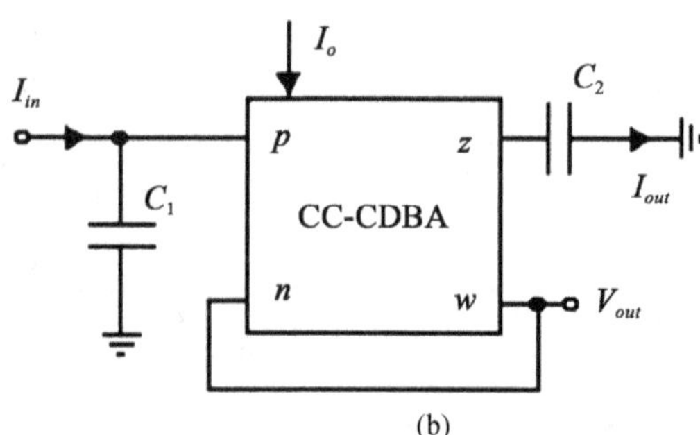

Figure 3. Circuit diagram of the proposed filters. (a) VM and TAM filter; (b) CM and TIM filter.

For these simulations, the passive components are taken as $C_1 = C_2 = 1$ nF. These parameters correspond to a BP filter with the with the center frequency $f_o = 124.34$ kHz and $f_o = 248.68$ kHz, quality factor $Q = 0.5$, which are found by using Equation (2) (with $V_T = 25.5$ mV thermal voltage at 25˚C) to find R_p and R_n, and then Equation (8). The simulation results for the voltage-mode band-pass filter shown in **Figure 4**.

From the results predicted by this figure, it is concluded that the simulation results are in good agreement with the theoretical ones over a wide range of frequencies. Although, the two characteristics well coincide over a wide range of frequency, the numerical data reveal the following differences; The maximum peak attenuations for simulation I are −6.41 dB and −6.02 dB, the maximum peak attenuations for simulation II are 6.76 dB and −6.02 dB, the center frequencies for simulation I are 117.34 kHz and 124.34 kHz, the center frequencies for simulation II are 224.78 kHz and 248.68 kHz for simulation and theoretical results, respectively.

Figure 4 also shows that the dependence of the center frequency on the bias current of CC-CDBA is as predicted theoretically; namely when the bias current increases two times its tuning effect appears increasing the center frequency two times.

In order to demonstrate workability of the other output responses, the simulations are also done. For these simulation, the bias currents of CC-CDBA are taken as I_o = 10 μA ($R_p = R_n = 1.3$ kΩ) and the passive components are taken as $C_1 = C_2 = 1$ nF. The magnitude characteristics of the filters which are shown in **Figures 3(a)** and **3(b)** are given in **Figure 5**.

4. Conclusions

In this paper, an electronically tunable VM band-pass, CM band-pass, TAM high-pass and TIM low-pass filters using current controlled CDBA are proposed. The proposed circuit offers the following advantageous features: 1) use of minimum number of electronic active and passive ele-

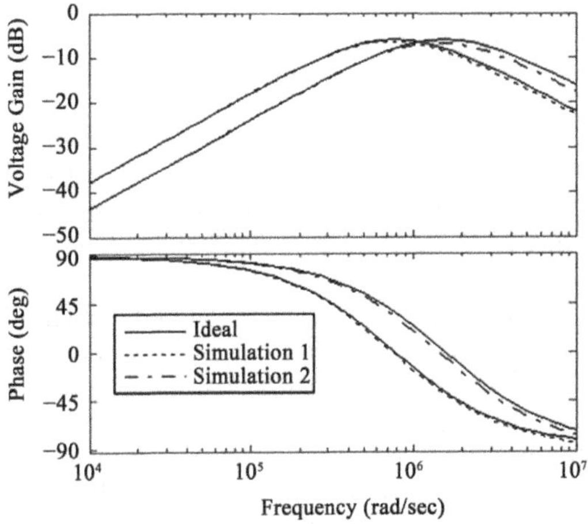

Figure 4. Simulation results for the proposed filter.

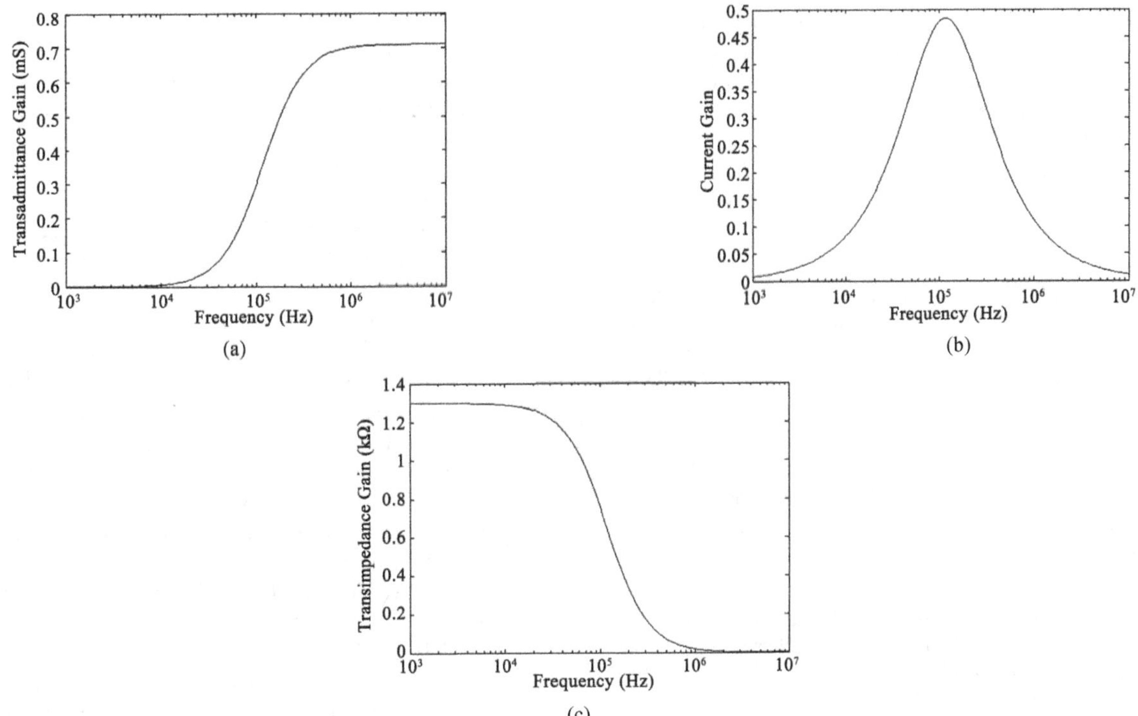

Figure 5. (a) The transadmittance grain for the proposed circuit in Figure 3(a); (b) The current gain for the proposed circuit in Figure 3(b); (c) The transimpedance gain for the proposed circuit in Figure 3(b).

ments, namely; two grounded capacitors and one CC-CDBA; 2) the quality factor and natural frequencies can be adjusted electronically without changing the values of the passive components; 3) single active component, which means less power consumption; 4) having one or more advantages over the proposed configurations in the literature [13-16]; 5) low sensitivities; 6) TIM and TAM outputs, this eliminates the need for current to voltage or voltage to current conversions in DAC and ADC applications; The above properties most of which are well verified by the PSpice simulation make the proposed filter attractive for circuit designers and engineers.

5. References

[1] B. Wilson, "Recent Developments in Current Conveyors and Current-Mode Circuits," *IEE Proceedings of Circuits, Devices and Systems*, Vol. 137, No. 2, 1990, pp. 63-77.

[2] D. C. Wandsworth, "Accurate Current Conveyor Integrated Circuits," *Electronics Letters*, Vol. 25, No. 18, 1989, p. 1251.

[3] G. Gilbert, "Current Mode, Voltage Mode, or Free Mode? A Few Sage Suggestions," *Analog Integrated Circuits and Signal Processing*, Vol. 38, No. 2-3, 2004, pp. 83-101.

[4] G. W. Rundell, J. J. Ou, T. B. Cho, G. Chien, F. Brianti, J. A. Weldon and P. Grey, "A 1.9-Ghz Wide-Band IF Double Conversion CMOS Receiver for Cordless Telephone Applications," *IEEE Journal of Solid-State Circuits*, Vol. 32, No. 12, 1997, pp. 2071-2088.

[5] M. S. Steyaert, J. Janssens, B. D. Muer, M. Borremans and N. Itoh, "A 2-V CMOS Cellular Transceiver Front-End," *IEEE Journal of Solid-State Circuits*, Vol. 35, No. 12, 2000, pp. 1895-1907.

[6] S. Minaei, G. Topcu and O. Cicekoglu, "Low Input Impedance Trans-impedance Type Multifunction Filter Using Only Active Elements," *International Journal of Electronics*, Vol. 92, No. 7, 2005, pp. 385-392.

[7] A. Toker, O. Cicekoglu, S. Ozcan and H. Kuntman, "High-Output-Impedance Transadmittance Type Continuous-Time Multifunction Filter with Minimum Active Elements," *International Journal of Electronics*, Vol. 88, No. 10, 2001, pp. 1085-1091.

[8] U. Cam, "A New Transadmittance Type First-Order All-pass Filter Employing Single Third Generation Current Conveyor," *Analog Integrated Circuits and Signal Processing*, Vol. 43, No. 1, 2005, pp. 97-99.

[9] N. A. Shah, S. Z. Iqbal and B. Parveen, "SITO High Output Impedance Transadmittance Filter Using FTFNs," *Analog Integrated Circuits and Signal Processing*, Vol. 40, No. 1, 2004, pp. 87-89.

[10] U. Cam, C. Cakir and O. Cicekoglu, "Novel Transimpedance Type First-Order All-Pass Filter Using Single OTRA," *International Journal of Electronics and Communication*, Vol. 58, No. 4, 2004, pp. 296-298.

[11] M. Sagbas and M. Koksal, "Voltage-Mode Three-Input Single-Output Multifunction Filters Employing Minimum Number of Components," *Frequenz*, Vol. 61, No. 3-4, 2007, pp. 87-93.

[12] M. Sagbas and M. Koksal, "Current-Mode State-Variable Filter," *Frequenz*, Vol. 62, No. 1-2, 2008, pp. 37-42.

[13] A. U. Keskin, "Voltage-Mode High-*Q* Band-Pass Filters and Oscillators Employing Single CDBA and Minimum Number of Components," *International Journal of Electronics*, Vol. 92, No. 8, 2005, pp. 479-487.

[14] U. Cam, "A Novel Current-Mode Second-Order Notch Filter Configuration Employing Single CDBA and Reduced Number of Passive Components," Computers and Electrical Engineering, Vol. 30, No. 2, 2004, pp. 147-151.

[15] S. Özcan, H. Kuntman and O. Cicekoglu, "Multi-input Single-Output Filter with Reduced Number of Passive Elements Using Single Current Conveyor," *Computers and Electrical Engineering*, Vol. 29, No. 1, 2003, pp. 45-53.

[16] S. Minaei, O. Cicekoglu, H. Kuntman and S. Turkoz, "High Output İmpedance Current-Mode Lowpass, Bandpass and Highpass Filters Using Current Controlled Conveyors," *International Journal of Electronics*, Vol. 88, No. 8, 2001, pp. 915-922.

[17] S. Maheshwari and I. A. Khan, "Current Controlled Current Differencing Buffered Amplifier: Implementation and Applications," *Active and Passive Electronics Components*, Vol. 4, No. 4, 2004, pp. 219-227.

[18] M. Koksal and M. Sagbas, "General Synthesis Procedure for n^{th}-Order Current Transfer Function Using CDBA," *Frequenz*, Vol. 61, No. 3-4, 2007, pp. 94-101.

[19] M. Koksal, M. Sagbas and H. Sedef, "An Electronically Tunable Oscillator Using a Single Active Device and Two Capacitors," Vol. 17, No. 5, 2008, pp. 885-891.

[20] P. Silapan, W. Jaikla and M. Siripruchyanun, "High-Performance BiCMOS Current Controlled CDBA and Application," *International Symposium on Communication and Information Technology*, Vol. 1-3, 2007, pp. 40-43.

[21] W. Tangsrirat, D. Prasertsom and W. Surakampontorn, "Low-Voltage Digitally Controlled Current Differencing Buffered Amplifier and Its Application," *AEU-International Journal of Electronics and Communications*, Vol. 63, No. 4, 2009, pp. 249-258.

[22] D. R. Frey, "Log-Domain Filtering: An Approach to Current-Mode Filtering," *IEE Proceedings-G: Circuits, Devices and Systems*, Vol. 140, No. 6, 1993, 406-416.

4

Analysis and Design Aspects of a Series Power Semiconductor Array with Digital Waveform Control Capability for Single Phase AC Voltage Regulators and Other Applications

Nihal Kularatna, Chandani Jindasa
The University of Waikato, Hamilton, New Zealand

Abstract

A series connected power semiconductor array, with digital control capability could be used for developing single phase AC regulators or other applications such as AC electronic loads. This technique together with an ordinary gapless transformer could be used to develop a low cost AC voltage regulator (AVR) to provide better or comparable specifications with bulky ferro-resonant AVR types. One primary advantage of the technique is that digital control can be used to minimize harmonics. Commencing with a review of AC voltage regulator techniques for single phase power conditioning systems, an analysis and design aspects of this technique is presented with experimental results for AVRs. Guidelines on how to utilize the technique in a generalized basis is also summarized together with a summary of a technique for achieving harmonic control.

Keywords: Power Conditioners, AC Voltage Regulators (AVR), Power Semiconductors, Digital Control, Electronic AC Loads

1. Introduction

With the proliferation of electronic systems based on submicron feature transistors, power quality (PQ) has become a major concern for end users as well as distribution authorities around the world [1-6]. Voltage sags and surges are a very common phenomenon in many distribution circuits, and it is particularly so in overloaded distribution systems. Voltage sags and surges seem to be distributed and tend to follow the daily loading patterns of the utility [2]. Extreme voltage fluctuations in many developing countries [7] and the need for lower cost products with easy manufacturability motivated the preliminary R & D work related to this specific technique. **Figure 1** indicates a typical pattern of voltage fluctuations in an urban location sub-circuit in Sri Lanka [7].

To improve the quality of power at the end user premises, three major considerations are voltage sags and surges, transient surges such as lightning or inductive energy dumps, and harmonics and flicker etc. An AC Voltage Regulator (AVR) is a particularly useful power conditioning equipment. The common AVR techniques used are: 1) motor driven variacs; 2) transformer tap changers; 3) ferro resonant regulators; 4) thyristor based

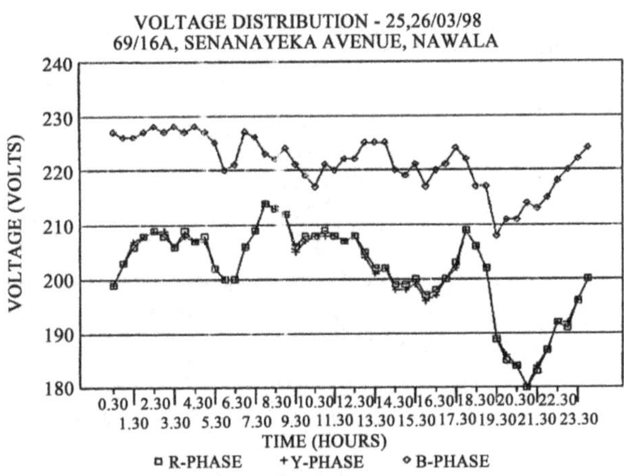

Figure 1. An example of a voltage variation in an overloaded distribution line (Source: Lanka Electricity Company).

systems (v) solid state AC regulators. **Table 1** summarizes the performance of these commercial families in a practical stand point in order to compare with the new technique we introduce in the paper. The information is particularly applicable to the single phase systems used by the end users and with output ratings from few 100Watts to few kilowatts. Magnetic amplifier techniques [8] usable in large capacity single or 3 phase systems etc are not discussed here.

Given the above variety of techniques used in commercial circumstances [9], a consistently popular technique has been the ferro-resonant type. Invented by Joseph Sola in the 1930s, this technique is popular due to its operational reliability, simple construction, and the ability to ride through a couple of AC cycles. However, this line frequency tuned LC resonant circuit based technique has the following disadvantages: 1) dissipates approximately 150 - 250 watts per each KVA of its output, due to the gapped transformer operating near saturation; 2) output regulation is dependant on the power factor of the connected load [10]; 3) various malfunctions when powered by a standby generator where the output frequency fluctuates with the load (due to LC circuit operating beyond resonance). Item 3) was a common occurrence in Sri Lanka during the drought periods with long power outages, where the first part of the work presented in the paper was carried out. In these cases frequent malfunctions of some commercial line interactive type UPS systems with ferro based AVRs were a common occurrence.

Apart from the above approaches used in commercial AVR techniques, there are few other published approaches to achieve AC voltage regulation in single phase power conditioners. Many of these are based on a series AC voltage component generated by a switching PWM scheme [11,12], or electronic transformers, which are also based on a PWM switching technique [13,14]. Another variation of a PWM based series connected AC regulator technique is described in [15,16]. The common problem in these are RFI/EMI due to PWM switching schemes, and the complex cost and manufacturing issues of adapting them to output power levels from few 100W to few kilowatts in single phase environments.

Given the above summary, key requirements in developing AVR techniques suitable for modern power conditioning requirements could be summarized as:

a) Reliability of operation in surge-prone PQ environments;

b) Efficiency under all load levels and load power factor situations;

c) RFI/EMI minimization;

d) Output harmonic minimization;

e) Speed of the control loops within the regulator;

f) Operability within the extremes of input line voltage limits;

g) Energy storage for short duration ride through requirements.

Table 1. Comparison of AC voltage regulators.

Family	Basic Technique used	Advantages	Disadvantages
Motor driven variacs	A servo motor based auto transformer with a voltage feedback loop	▪ Simple construction ▪ High capacity ▪ Simple electronics ▪ High efficiency	▪ Bulky ▪ Slow response ▪ Can get stuck at the lowest input voltage and create an over-voltage when the line voltage returns to normal
Transformer tap changers	A transformer with multiple taps and a feedback loop to automatically change the taps	▪ High efficiency ▪ Easy to design ▪ Simple construction ▪ Low cost	▪ If input voltage fluctuates frequently "tap dancing" could occur ▪ Arcing in taps can create problems, with inductive loads ▪ Voltage transients may appear at the output during tap changes
Thyristor based designs	A series secondary winding or an auto transformer is used with a thyristor phase controlled technique to maintain the RMS voltage constant	▪ Compact ▪ Low cost ▪ Efficient ▪ Fast response	▪ High harmonic content at the output ▪ Could cause problems with inductive loads ▪ Filtering at output may be necessary for reducing RFI/EMI issues
Ferro-resonant regulators	A precisely gapped transformer is used in resonance with a capacitor to create a resonant circuit, while core saturation is used for regulating the output voltage.	▪ Very reliable ▪ Simple design ▪ Can withstand a fractional or few cycle outage at the input side ▪ Differential mode transients can be tolerated	▪ Non sinusoidal output with flattened top ▪ Power factor dependant load regulation ▪ Extremely sensitive to frequency fluctuations on the input side (*i.e.*: when a small standby generator is used as the AC input) ▪ Low efficiency and no load power consumption of 20% - 30% of the VA rating
Solid state types	Either linear amplifier based technique or switching technique based compensation is used	▪ Wide input range is possible ▪ Compact design may be possible (with a switching technique for voltage buck or boost)	▪ Complex circuitry ▪ RFI/EMI problems (in switching technique based ones) ▪ Reliability issues in environments with high common mode transient surges

2. AC Power Control Technique Based on a Series Power Semiconductor Array

Given the above introduction to the commercial design approaches with key design requirements in AVRs, following section introduces the primary design concepts used in this technique. The technique discussed in this paper was developed for single phase end user equipment where the line voltage could fluctuate widely and to achieve a design without any ferro-resonant transformers for easy manufacturability.

This technique based on a series connected power semiconductor array [17-20] is suitable for situations where 230V AC rms voltage fluctuates widely between 160 V to 260 V. The technique has the following advantages and useful features:

1) Fast response and high efficiency at worst case sags
2) Gapless 50/60 Hz transformer;
3) True RMS output control;
4) Electrical isolation between low voltage control circuits and the power stage;
5) Minimum RFI/EMI issues;
6) Lower harmonic distortion at output and less dependence on the load power factor;
7) Equal power dissipation and voltage distribution among transistor elements.

This technique works for both sags and swells without any transformer configuration changes, compared to the technique described in [21]. The technique in [21] with a claim for a high efficiency near 96% is only for a limited range of regulated output which should be lower than the incoming rail with a minimum input voltage of just 4 volts above the regulated output.

The same design approach in [17-22] could also be used in developing an electronic AC load with digital control for harmonic minimization [23,24]. The rest of the paper describes the fundamentals and two applications of the technique, with an in depth discussion on the technique as applied to a single phase, low power AVR with the potential to minimize the harmonics at the output using a digital technique.

3. Concept of Impedance Control and Implementation

3.1. Basic Concept of Series Power Semiconductor Array

A conceptual approach for changing the effective overall AC resistance of a power BJT array over a wide range is shown in **Figure 2**. **Figure 2(a)** shows the simplified concept of control of the transistor. **Figure 2(b)** indicates how an opto isolator can be used to control current diversion in the power semiconductor. **Figure 2(c)** indicates how series connected infrared emitter diodes in an opto isolator can be used to control a series connected bipolar power transistor array with AC operational capability. When the transistor array is used in 230 V AC applications such as in an AC voltage regulator, the instantaneous values could often vary up to a maximum of approximately $330\sqrt{2}$ V for a range of input AC RMS voltages from 160V to 260V [25]. This high voltage requirement at high power loads suggests the use of multiple power semiconductors to share the loading.

For an n-element BJT array similar to the case of **Figure 2(c)**, it can be shown that,

$$R_{Array} \approx \frac{nR_B}{\beta}\left(1+\frac{i_x}{i_b}\right) \tag{1}$$

when

$$R_{B1} = \frac{R_B}{n}; R_{B2} = \frac{R_B}{(n-1)}; R_{B3} = \frac{R_B}{(n-2)}; \cdots R_{Bn} = R_B \tag{2}$$

where R_{Array} is the approximate effective instantaneous resistance at the AC input of the circuit in **Figure 2(c)**, i_b is the instantaneous base current, i_x is the amount of base current diverted by the opto transistors and R_B is the resistance between collector and base of the nth transistor [22]. For the case of the 4 element array in **Figure 2(c)**,

$$R_{Array} \approx \frac{4R_B}{\beta}\left(1+\frac{i_x}{i_b}\right) \tag{3}$$

and,

$$R_1 = \frac{R_B}{4}; R_2 = \frac{R_B}{3}; R_3 = \frac{R_B}{2}; R_4 = R_B \tag{4}$$

Note that the base emitter voltage drops are neglected in these approximations.

Based on the simplified relationship in Equation (3), the resistance between the collector and the emitter can be easily controlled either by varying R_B or suitably changing i_x. This in effect indicates that we need to control the ratio i_x/i_b, which is defined as the base current diversion ratio (BCDR). This technique in addition provides the necessary electrical isolation between the low voltage control circuits and the power stage. In a practical application with Darlington pairs, the compound base emitter voltage will be between 1 to 2 Volts. This practically permits the concept of controlling the BCDR using opto isolators and similar low voltage control circuits. For details [23] is suggested. A similar design approach could be used with other power semiconductors such as MOSFETs and IGBTs, by modifying the above technique, a discussion of which is beyond the scope of the paper.

3.2. Limits and Boundaries of the Achievable AC Resistance

Due to Darlington pairs in **Figure 2(c)** a cutoff condition is reached when the compound V_{BE} value for the Darlington pair is approximately less than about 1.0 Volt. This occurs at a higher value of the opto transistor current and at that point the controllability of the array impedance diminishes. This is the case beyond the maximum BCDR, where the base current of each of the transistors is totally removed by the action of the optoisolators. Under this condition, the effective resistance of the array is not controlled by the transistors, except for the leakage effects. If the transistor leakage effects are neglected and the conditions in Equation (2) are maintained, the effective maximum resistance of the array reaches the value given by the series combination of the resistors R_{B1} to R_{Bn},

$$R_{CE\max} = R_B + \frac{R_B}{2} + \frac{R_B}{3} + \frac{R_B}{4} + \cdots \frac{R_B}{n} \tag{5}$$

At the other extreme, when the current through the input diodes of the optoisolators is zero (the case of minimum BCDR), the effective resistance of the array reduces to nR_B/β. In between these two limits the overall resistance of the array, R_{CE}, can be controlled by varying the current through the series connected diodes.

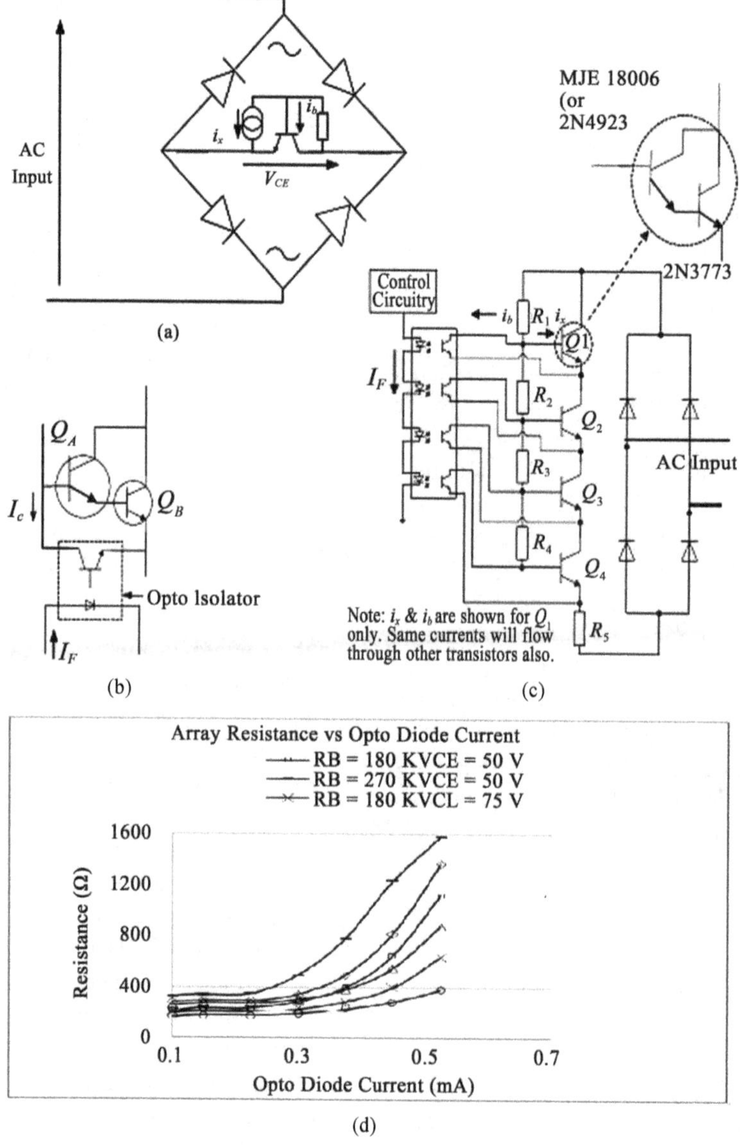

Figure 2. Concept of AC impedance control with a BJT array. (a) Simplified concept; (b) Control of the base current using opto transistor; (c) Implementation of a 4 element system; (d) Effective impedance (R_{array}) of a 4 element array versus opto diode current for R_B values of 180 kΩ and 270 kΩ.

From Equation (5) the maximum value of effective resistance for an array of 4 elements is approximately 2.1 R_B, neglecting the effects of leakage currents in transistors. Equation (3) indicates that the minimum resistance for the array is approximately $4R_B/\beta$. This clearly indicates a wide range of ideal performance possible within the boundaries. If the array is to work as a high voltage capable switching element, the value of R_B can be set to a suitable value for the designer to get the overall result of $4R_B/\beta$ to reach the lowest necessary, based on the circuit components. For a 4-element array the ratio of off-impedance/on-impedance is around $\beta/1.9$ and for a well configured Darlington pair this can be in the range of 3 orders.

Figure 2(d) depicts a typical example of the variation of the effective resistance versus control input I_F (opto-diode current) for R_B values of 270 kΩ and 180 kΩ for a four element array (as in **Figure 2(c)**) capable of 100W dissipation. It is clear that the lowest value reaches the theoretical value expected from $4R_B/\beta$. As indicated in **Figure 2(d)** for the case of 50 V AC input with $R_B = 270$ kΩ, the array reaches a maximum at higher values of I_F as per theoretical predictions and SPICE simulations. However the maximum value is significantly lower than the expected due to leakage effects.

Also the graphs indicate the dependence of the effective resistance on the AC line voltage, due to device nonlinearities and the dependence of β on the instantaneous collector current over the AC cycle. Another practical situation is that the transistors could have non identical β values. However it is easy to compensate for this variation by slightly adjusting the R_B values deviating from the relationship in Equation (2).

4. Application Examples

4.1. Design of an AC Regulator Based on the Technique

Figure 3(a) indicates the basic approach where the transformer T_1 allows the boost or buck operation. If you consider that the transformer is an ideal one, where the series winding has N times the turns as in the primary winding which is in series with the power semiconductor array placed across the bridge points of the full wave rectifier.

Under this arrangement, the following approximate relationship holds true, for any general load connected at the output.

$$\overline{V_{out}} = \overline{V_{in}}(1+N) - R_{array}N^2\overline{I_L} \quad (6)$$

where $\overline{V_{Out}}$ and $\overline{V_{in}}$ are the output and input voltages and $\overline{I_L}$ is the load current in vectors respectively.

Figure 3(b) indicates the phasor diagrams for the case where the input voltage ($|V_{in}|$) is less than the required regulated output ($|V_{out}|$). In this example we consider the load current is lagging the input voltage by an angle Φ. Based on the relationship in Equation (6), and assuming that the impedance of the transistor array is purely resistive, and the transformer is ideal with no leakage inductances or resistances, the control circuits could regulate the output voltage, by maintaining the regulated V_{out} within the arc of the circle with a radius of $|V_{out}|$ in the region where the tangential points of the worst case phase angles of the load falls within $\pm\Phi_{max}$. Beyond these limits of the tangential points T and T' of the phasor diagram, regulation is not possible, for a given turns ratio N.

Few interesting and practically useful observation are that,

1) If the load is purely resistive, the regulated output voltage will be in phase with the input voltage;

2) For a given input voltage if the transformer is configured to have the case of $\overline{V_{out}} = \overline{V_{in}}(1+N)$, dissipation in the array is minimum;

3) Condition 2) above suggests having multiple taps in the transformer, to have the best efficiency under wide range of input voltage fluctuations;

4) When the transformer turns ratio increases, the allowable phase angle of the load decreases.

Figure 3(c) indicates the case of phasor diagram, where the input voltage is higher than the required regulated output voltage. In this situation, by creating a higher voltage across the array, and practically reversing the voltage at the primary winding, the regulation is achieved. In case the load is purely resistive, as expected the regulated output will be in phase with the input voltage. Also in this situation, when the input voltage rises above the required regulated output value, it is possible to reverse the connections of the primary winding, so that the dissipation across the array is reduced. In **Figures 3(b)** and **3(c)** the arc included within T and T' indicates the limits of the reactive component of the load to achieve regulation, assuming that the transformer is considered ideal.

As shown in the phasor diagrams the technique is useful in situations with non resistive loads as well, while regulating the output for both voltage sags and surges with out any transformer configuration changes.

Figure 4(a) indicates the implementation block diagram of a 230 V/50 Hz capable 1 KVA regulator based on the technique[17,18] developed to overcome the frequency sensitivity, waveform distortion and the lower overall efficiency of the commonly used ferro-resonant regulators and the slow response of motor driven variacs [26,27]. To cater for the worst case line voltage situations such as in [8], this AVR prototype was developed to operate within a wide range such as from 160 V to 260 V.

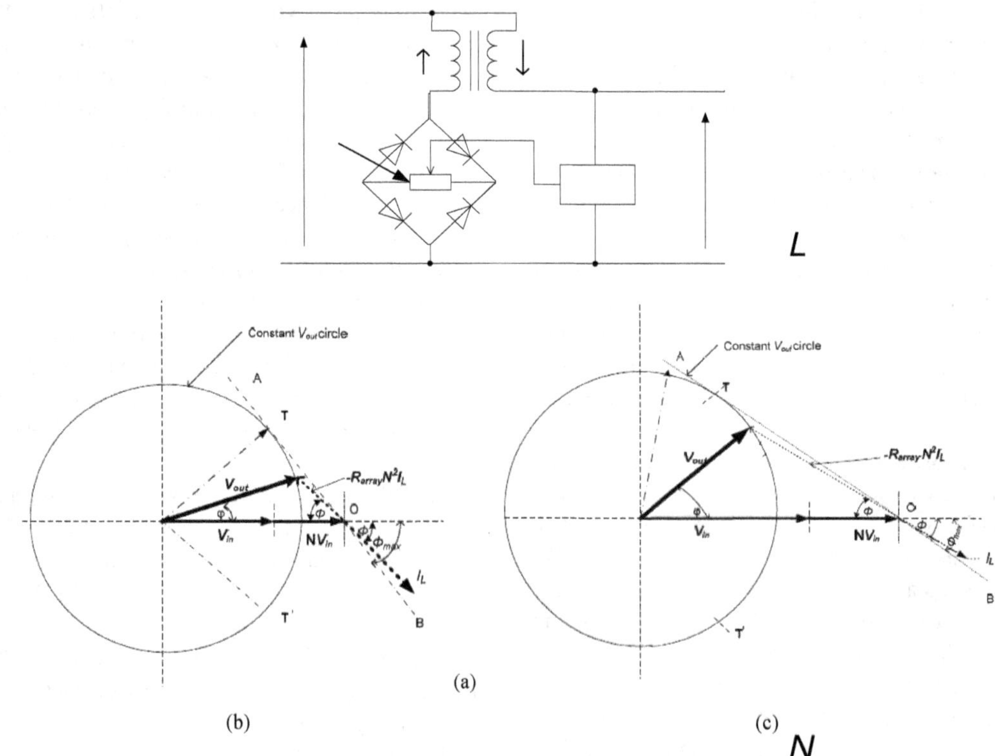

Figure 3. BJT array based AC regulator and phasor diagrams. (a) Basic concept; (b)Phasor diagram when input voltage is less than the regulated output; (c) Phasor diagram when input voltage is higher than the regulated output.

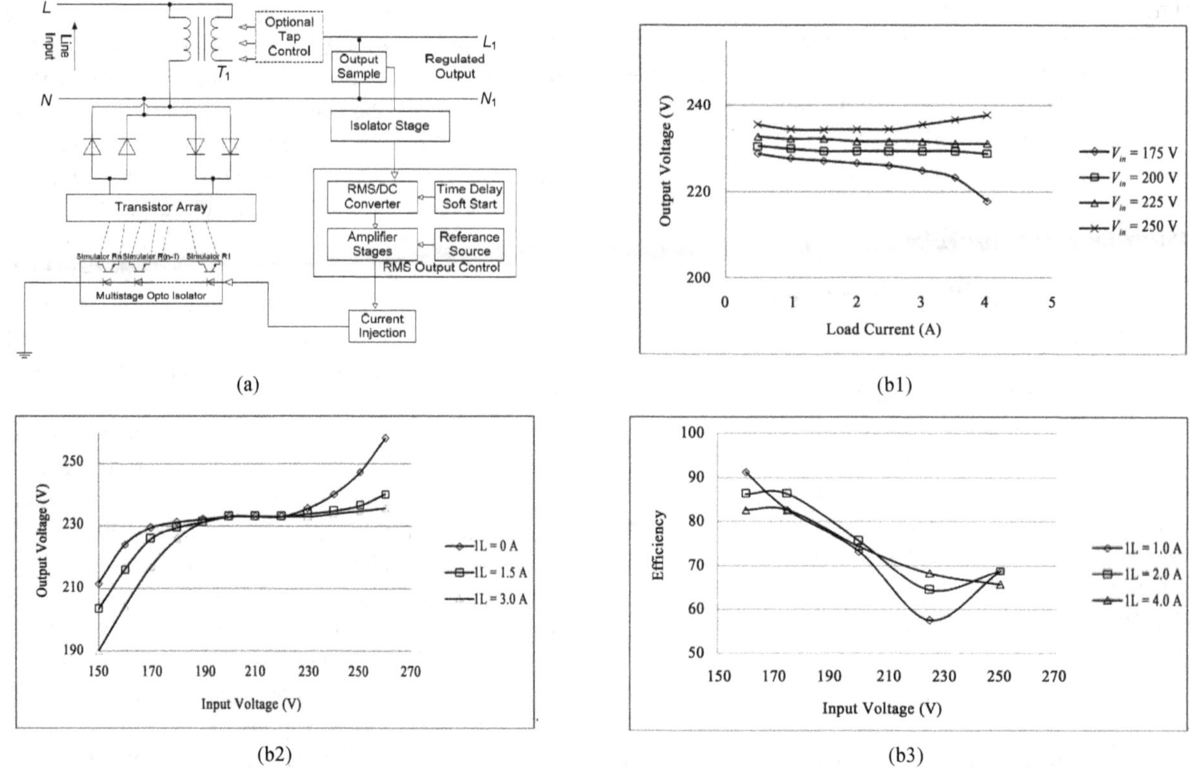

Figure 4. AVR implementation of a 1 kVA prototype and measured performance. (a) Overall block diagram; (b1) Load regulation; (b2) Line regulation; (b3) Efficiency.

For RMS output voltage control, the effective resistance of the array is varied depending on the load and the input voltage. RMS control circuit compares the actual AC output sample, converted to a DC value using an RMS-DC converter IC, with a reference DC voltage. Current injection circuit adjusts the current injected into the series connected input diodes of the opto isolator, based on the output of the RMS control circuits. This effectively controls the value of R_{array} in such a way that the loop keeps the output RMS value regulated at a preset value such as 230 V, for a wide range of input voltages.

Figures 4(b1) to **4(b3)** indicate the measured performance of an AVR prototype of output capacity of 1kVA based on Darlington pairs of 2N3773 and 2N4923 [17]. Load regulation graph in **Figure 4(b1)** indicates that the prototype regulates around 230 ± 6% V AC within an input voltage range of 170 V to over 250 V. The line regulation graph in **Figure 4(b2)** indicates that the technique is usable almost up to 160 V, however needs adjusting the lowest possible resistance of the array.

As per graph of **Figure 4(b3)** we see that the efficiency keeps dropping as the input voltage keeps increasing towards the nominal regulated value of 230 V. In the particular prototype tested [17], we have used a transformer with a turns ratio (N) of 70/160, where the array is expected to have the lowest resistance, at a worst case of input voltage of 160 V rms. If the input voltage reaches 230 V rms, the primary winding should have zero value so that the correction applied at the secondary side is zero. This indicates that the quantity $N^2 R_{Array} I_L$ should be equal to $230 * (70/160)$ V, for the case of a pure resistive load. Similarly if the input voltage goes towards a surge situation with over 230 V rms value, this quantity should be further increased, to generate a negative correction at the secondary winding.

In this prototype where the efficiency is optimized around 160 V, as the input voltage increases the efficiency drops. However the overall performance is comparable with a similar capacity ferro-resonant version. As discussed in a previous paragraph, by using multiple taps and reversing taps under surge voltage conditions at the input overall efficiency could be improved.

This gapless transformer based technique can be enhanced with a digital control subsystem to minimize the harmonics at the output. By suitable control circuitry, transformer tap changes can also be incorporated to further enhance the overall efficiency, recognizing the fact that the technique has a higher efficiency at the worst case sags, where only a minimum resistance value of the array is required as per Equation (6).

4.2. Electronic AC Load

Another useful application of the technique is in an electronic AC load. The design approach for an AC electronic load with processor control is indicated in [23-25]. A discussion on this is beyond the scope of this paper.

5. Processor Based Approach for Linearizing of the Array Resistance

Given the non-linear behaviour of the transistor array as per **Figure 2(d)**, the instantaneous current in the array will be nonlinear under general conditions, and will depend on the instantaneous AC line voltage as well as the dependency of the gain of transistor on its collector current. In order to control the non linearity of the value of R_{Array} which is equivalent to $\frac{V_{Array(rms)}}{I_{Array(rms)}}$, collector current in the opto transistors based on the following relationship could be controlled [27].

$$I_C = K\left(\frac{I_F}{I_{F'}}\right)^p \quad (7)$$

K, $I_{F'}$ and p are the parameters for opto isolator pairs [27].

From the basic transistor parameter relationships and assuming that all transistors are identical,

$$I_{Array} = I_S e^{qV_{BE}/kT} \quad (8)$$

where q is the electron charge, k is the Boltzmann constant and T is the absolute temperature of the transistor junction. I_s is the saturation current for the identical transistors Q_1 to Q_4 in **Figure 2(c)**.

By substituting the relationships in Equation (7) and (8) in Equation (3),

$$R_{CE} \approx \frac{4R_B}{\beta}\left[1+\beta\frac{K\left(\frac{I_F}{I_{F'}}\right)^p}{I_S e^{\frac{qV_{BE}}{kT}}}\right] \quad (9)$$

With suitable mathematical manipulations [23], we can also arrive at the following relationship for voltage across the array (V_{CE}) and the opto-diode forward current (I_F) for a given R_{CE} value, neglecting the v_{BE} compared to the instantaneous values of v_{CE}.

$$\ln V_{CE} = p \ln I_F + \frac{K\beta n R_B R_{CE}}{(\beta R_{CE} - n R_B) I_{F'}{}^p} \quad (10)$$

Based on the relationship of Equation (10) and using experimental data similar to **Figure 2(d)** for the circuit arrangement in **Figure 2(c)**, curve fitting techniques can be used to obtain the logarithmic relationships for voltage across the array (V_{CE}) and the current fed through the photo diodes (I_F) of the opto isolator for each value of expected array resistance. Implementation of this is shown in **Figure 5** depicting the hardware block diagram and the flow chart applicable. By plotting these curves from the experimental results (which tallies with the SPICE simulation results) together with a straight line fit, it could be easily seen that a reasonably accurate values for m and c values for a straight line approximation can be obtained. Two selected examples from [25] are shown for array resistances of 500 Ω and 50 Ω in **Figure 6.** From these graphs, one can see that the relationship is very close to a straight line fit, with matching R^2 values close to 1.

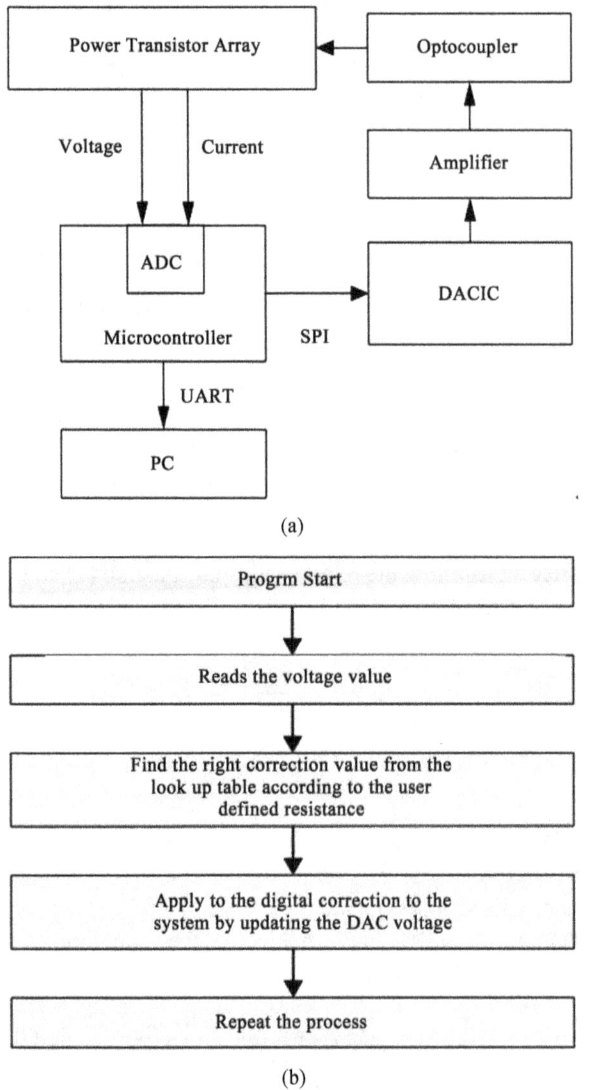

Figure 5. Approach to digital control of the harmonics at the output. (a) Processor and the control; (b) Flow chart.

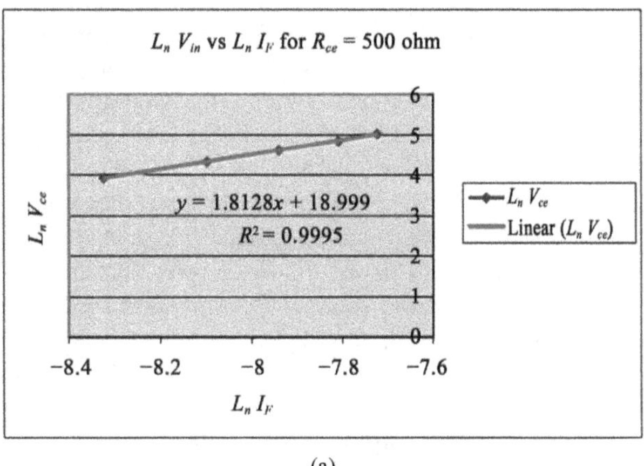

(a)

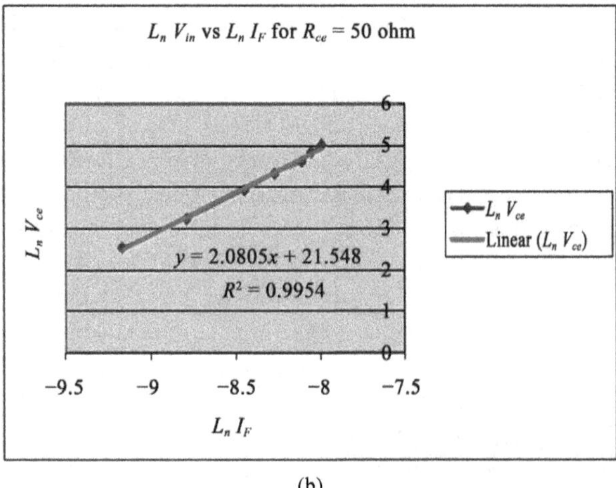

(b)

Figure 6. Graphs of Log$_n$ (V_{CE}) versus Log$_n$ (I_F) for two different R_{CE} values together with straight line fit in each case (a) For R_{CE} = 500 Ω; (b)For R_{CE} = 50 Ω.

Given these relationships for a particular case of a transistor array, the values of m and c can be fed into the digital control algorithm, in an overall arrangement as in **Figure 5(a)**. A look up table can store the experimental values for the particular array, and then derive the approximate values m and c suitable for each case of a straight line fit.

The above discussion leads towards the digital control approach to solve the linearity issue of the array, by controlling the two parameters m and c indicated above. Using a digital control algorithm, injected opto diode current can be controlled to adjust the instantaneous current through the array, by taking relatively larger number of samples of the AC voltage waveform via sampling. Overall effect of the processor based system is to control the opto diode current to achieve the expected impedance, based on the behaviour of the array as per **Figure 2(c)** during each sampling period. 1 kHz sampling rate was used in the proof of concept system. With the sampling of the instantaneous AC line voltage, microprocessor program calculates the required opto diode current (output from the DAC) over each sampling period within the 50 or 60 Hz AC cycle. More details are available in [25] and a related US patent application.

Figure 7 compares the array performance with and without digital control at different resistance settings. It is clear from these oscillographs forms that the digital control technique reduces the harmonics in the waveform. These results were obtained in an electronic AC load capable of 150 VA capacity, based on an 8 bit Zilog Z8 Encore processor [25]. **Figure 8** indicates the fast Fourier transforms (FFT) of the current waveform at 1.3 A with and without the digital controller. This FFT plots indicates that the technique reduces the 3rd, 5th , 7th and 9th harmonic etc by significant amounts, proving that the algorithmic approaches used is clearly suitable. More information is available in [23].

Overall achievements in this work are:

1) A versatile AC impedance control technique which can be used in applications such as AVRs and power conditioners;

2) A new digital control technique where additional digital waveform control can be added to the system to minimize harmonics in the current waveforms.

Array resistance set to 75Ω

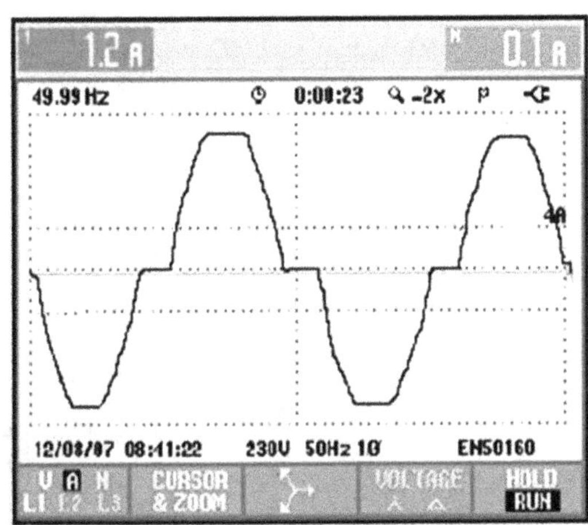

Without digital control

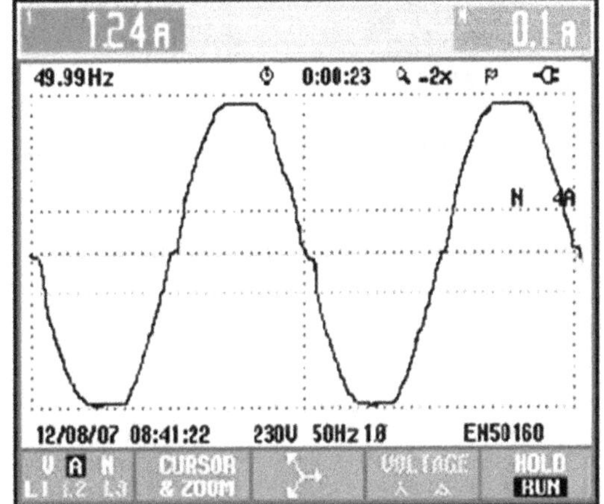

Without digital control

(a)

Array resistance set to 200 Ω

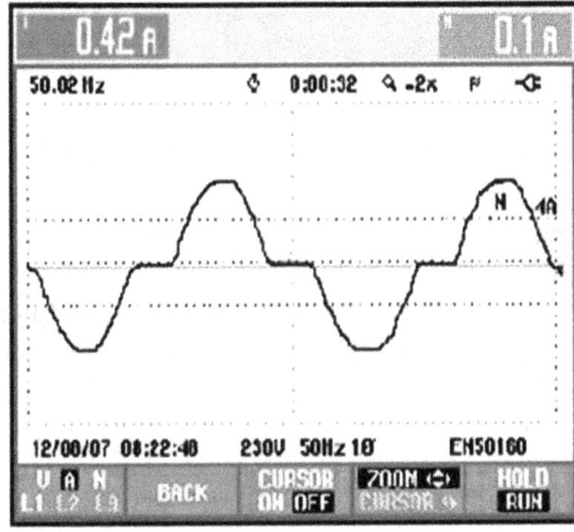

Without digital control

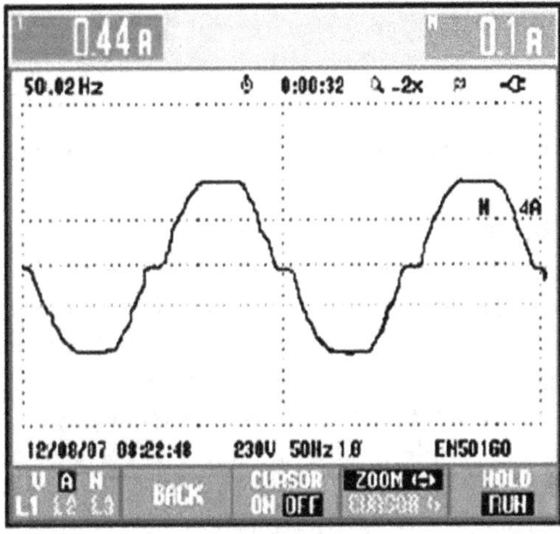

Without digital control

(b)

Figure 7. Current drawn by the array for a different setting of the array resistance with and without digital waveform correction (a)75 Ω setting; (b) 200 Ω setting control.

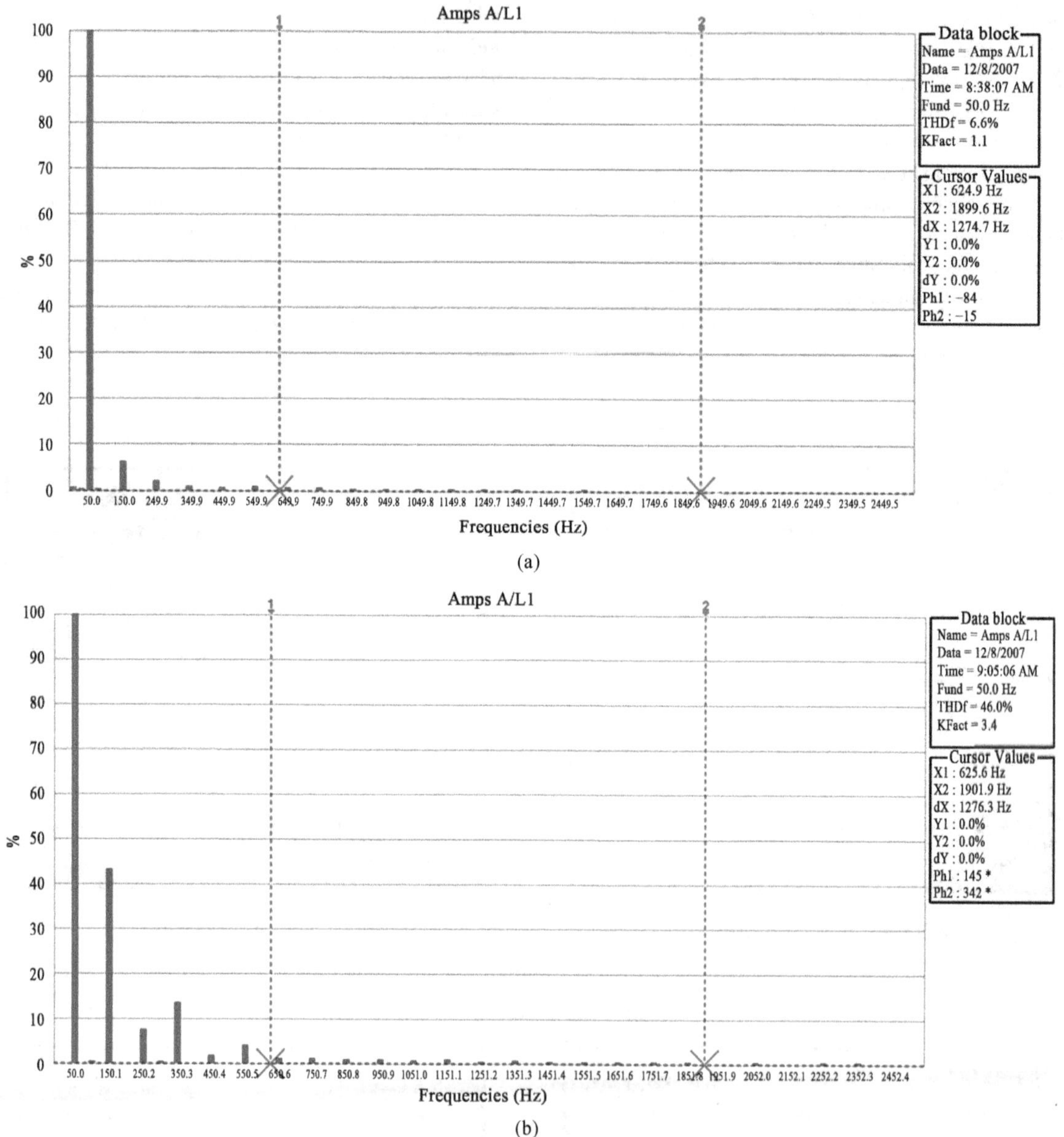

Figure 8. Comparison of the FFT of the current waveform at 1.3 A (a) with digital control; (b) without digital control.

7. Conclusions

The concept of using a series transistor array with opto isolator based isolation can be used in several AC power control applications suitable for low power and single phase requirements. Paper provides a general analysis of the array, and the design details of a 1 KVA capacity AVR prototype, which can be extended into other power levels. One secondary advantage of the technique is its ability to incorporate digital control algorithms to minimize harmonics due to the non linear nature of the power semiconductor array. Given these details, the technique could be used to develop AVRs with performance far superior to ferro-resonant versions and other slow responding transformer tap changers etc.

In addition, this technique has the potential to combine with common AVR techniques such as transformer tap changers etc for higher overall efficiency. Another possible application is in electronic AC loads with harmonic control.

8. References

[1] G. T. Heydt, "Electric Power Quality: A Tutorial Introduction," *IEEE Computer Applications in Power*, Vol. 11, No. 1, 1998, pp. 15-19.

[2] D. O. Koval, R. A. Bocancea, K. Yao and M. B. Hughes, "Canadian National Power Quality Survey: Frequency

and Duration of Voltage Sags and Surges at Industrial Sites," *IEEE Transactions on Industry Applications*, Vol. 34, No. 5, 1998, pp. 904-910.

[3] K. M. Michaels, "Sensible Approaches to Diagnosing Power Quality Problems," *IEEE Transactions on Industry Applications*, Vol. 33, No. 4, 1997, pp. 1124-1130.

[4] A. Domijan, J. T. Heydt, A. P. S. Meliopoulos, M. S. S. Venkata and S. West, "Directions of Research on Electric Power Quality," *IEEE Transactions on Power Delivery*, Vol. 8, No. 1, 1993, pp. 429-436.

[5] R. Ellis and B. Guidry, "Power Quality Concerns and Solutions," *IEEE Industry Applications Magazine*, Vol. 11, No. 6, 2005, pp. 20-24.

[6] W. E. Kazibwe and H. M. Sendaula, "Expert System Targets Power Quality Issues," *IEEE Computer Applications in Power*, Vol. 5, No. 2, 1992, pp. 29-33.

[7] N. Kularatna, "Worst Case Power Quality Environments and Design of Power Electronics Products: Experiences of a Design Team in a Developing Country," *Proceedings of Power Systems World—*2000 *Conference* (*Power Quality*'2000), USA, pp. 109-116.

[8] Magtech Voltage Booster, Magtech.

[9] G. Evans, "Power Quality Source Book," Intertec International, Ventura, 1991.

[10] J. W. Clarke, "AC Power Conditioners," Academic Press, Cambridge, 1990.

[11] C. Chen and D. Divan, "Simple Topologies for Single Phase AC Line Conditioning," *IEEE Transactions on Industry Applications*, Vol. 30, No. 2, 1994, pp. 406-412.

[12] D. Jang and G. Choe, "Step-up/down Ac Voltage Regulator Using Transformer with Tap Changer and PWM AC Chopper," *IEEE Transactions on Industrial Electronics*, Vol. 45, No. 6, 1998, pp. 905-911.

[13] Y. S. Lee, D. K. W. Cheng, and Y. C. Cheng, "Design of a Novel Ac Regulator," *IEEE Transactions on Industrial Electronics*, Vol. 38, No. 2, 1991, pp. 89-94.

[14] J. C. Bowers, S. J. Garret, H. A. NienHaus and J. L. Brooks, "A Solid State Transformer," *IEEE Power Electronics Specialists Conference*, Atlanta, 16-20 June 1980, pp. 253-264.

[15] M. T. Tsai, "Analysis and Design of a Cost-Effective Series Connected AC Voltage Regulator," *IEE Proceedings of Electric Power Applications*, Vol. 151, No. 1, 2004, pp. 107-115.

[16] M. T. Tsai, "Design of a Compact Series-Connected AC Voltage Regulator with an Improved Control Algorithm," *IEEE Transactions on Industrial Electronics*, Vol. 51, No. 4, 2004, pp. 933-936.

[17] A. D. V. N. Kularatna, "Low Cost, Light Weight AC Regulator Employing Bipolar Power Transistors," *Proceedings of the 21st International Power Quality Conference*, Philadelphia, 24 October 1990, pp. 67-76.

[18] A. D. V. N. Kularatna, "Techniques Based on Bipolar Power Transistor Arrays for Regulation of Ac Line Voltage," *Proceedings of the 5th Annual European Conference on Power Electronics and Applications*, Brighton, 13-16 September 1993, pp. 96-100.

[19] A. D. V. N. Kularatna and S. D. Godakumbura, "Use of Spice Simulation for Predicting the Harmonic Capability of an Ac Regulator Technique Based on a Bipolar Power Transistor Array," *Proceedings of the 5th International Conference on Power Electronics and Variable Speed Drives*, London, 26-28 October 1994, pp. 157-162.

[20] A. D. V. N. Kularatna and S. D. Godakumbura, "Use of Voltage Dip and up Simulator for Testing the Transient Behaviour of a Bipolar Power Transistor Array Based Ac Line Voltage Regulator," *Proceedings of European Conference on Power and Applications*, Vol. 3, pp. 3.298-3.303.

[21] C. R. Selvakumar, "Negative Feedback High Efficiency Ac Voltage Regulator," *IEEE Transactions on Industrial Electronics and Control Instrumentation*, Vol. IECI-28, No. 1, 1981, pp. 24-27.

[22] "A Linear technique for Ac Voltage Regulation Using an Ordinary Transformer and Power Semiconductors," Sri Lanka Patent No. 10028, 1990.

[23] N. Kularatna and P. Cho, "A Power Sharing Series Power BJT Array with Isolated Low Voltage Control for AC Power Control Applications," 32*nd Annual Conference on IEEE Industrial Electronics*, Paris, 6-10 November 2006, pp. 1715-1720.

[24] N. Kularatna and P. Cho, "Design Approach to an AC Electronic Load Base Don Generalized Series Power Transistor Array," CD-ROM, Session PQT 17, *Power Quality Conference*, Long beach, October 2006.

[25] C. Jinadasa, "High Power Linear Electronic AC Load for Testing UPS Systems." Master's Thesis, The University of Waikato, Hamilton, 2007.

[26] N. Kularatna, "Power Electronics Design Handbook-Low Voltage Components and Applications, Chapter 6," Butterworth, Oxford, 1998.

[27] K. Goulet, "Automation Equipment of the 90s-Power Conditioning Equipment of the 60s," *Proceedings of the Power Quality*, USA, 1990, pp. 64-77.

[28] "Linear Applications of Optocouplers," Application Note 951-2, Agilent Technologies, 1999.

5

Precision Full-Wave Rectifier Using Two DDCCs

Montree Kumngern
Department of Telecommunications Engineering, Faculty of Engineering, King Mongkut's Institute of Technology Ladkrabang, Bangkok, Thailand

Abstract

A new precision full-wave rectifier employing only two differential difference current conveyors, which is very suitable for CMOS technology implementation, is presented. The proposed rectifier is the voltage-mode circuit, which offers high-input and low-output impedance hence it can be directly connected to load without using any buffer circuits. PSPICE is used to verify the circuit performance. Simulated rectifier results based-on a 0.5 μm CMOS technology with ±2.5 V supply voltage demonstrates high precision rectification and excellent temperature stability. In addition, the application of proposed rectifier to pseudo RMS-to-DC conversion is also introduced.

Keywords: Full-Wave Rectifier, Voltage-Mode Circuit, DDCC, RMS-to-DC Conversion

1. Introduction

Full-wave rectifier is used in RF demodulator, piecewise linear function generator, AC voltmeter, watt meter and various nonlinear analog signal processing circuits. Typically, a conventional rectifier could be realized by using diodes for it rectification. However, this circuit would not be capable of rectifying incoming signals whose amplitudes are less than the threshold voltage (approximately 0.7 V for silicon diode and 0.3 for germanium diode). As a result, diode-only rectifiers are normally used in only those applications in which the precision in the range of threshold voltage is insignificant, such as RF demodulators and DC voltage supply rectifiers. For high precision applications, the diode-only rectifier cannot be used. This can be overcome by using integrated circuit rectifiers instead. The precision rectifiers based on operational amplifier (op-amp), diodes and resistors are presented [1-4]. However, the classical problem with conventional precision rectifiers based on op-amps and diodes is that during the non-conduction/conduction transition of the diodes, the op-amps must recover with a finite small-signal, dv/dt, (slew-rate) resulting in significant distortion during the zero crossing of the input signal. The use of the high slew-rate op-amps does not solve this problem because it is a small signal transient problem. The gain-bandwidth is a parameter of op-amp that limits the high frequency performance of this scheme. Moreover, since these structures use the op-amp and the resistors; therefore these circuits are not suitable for IC fabrication. Second-generation current conveyors (CCIIs) is possessed a very high slew rate and bandwidth if compared to the traditional op-amp. This makes the CCII of primary importance in the design of modern analog integrated circuits.

Several circuits based on CCII for realizing full-wave rectification have been reported in the literature [5-10]. The rectifier circuit in [5-7] employ diodes and resistors in addition to CCIIs. The circuit proposed in [8] employs bipolar current mirrors in addition to a CCII and a number of resistors. The rectifier circuit in [9] employs four CCCIIs and resistors. The circuit proposed in [10] employs two CCII and two MOS transistors. However, the use of resistor makes these circuits not ideal for integration. Recently, Chiu *et al.* [11] proposed a new current conveyor circuit called the differential difference current conveyor (DDCC). The DDCC has the advantages of both the CCII and the differential difference amplifier (DDA) (such as high input impedance and arithmetic operation capability).

In this paper, a new precision full-wave rectifier circuit using only two DDCCs is presented. Compared with previous rectifiers, the proposed structure is more suitable for integrated circuit fabrication. The circuit also offers a low output impedance terminal, which is suitable for low impedance load. Simulation results verifying the theoretical analysis are also included. To demonstrate the advantages of proposed configuration, pseudo RMS-to-DC conversion is also introduced.

2. Circuit Realization

The electrical symbol of DDCC is shown in **Figure 1**. The DDCC has three voltage input terminals: Y_1, Y_2 and Y_3, which have high input impedance. The terminal X is a low impedance input terminal. There is a high impedance current output terminal Z. The CMOS realization for DDCC is shown in **Figure 2** [11]. The input-output characteristics of the ideal DDCC is described as

$$\begin{pmatrix} V_X \\ I_{Y1} \\ I_{Y2} \\ I_{Y3} \\ I_Z \end{pmatrix} = \begin{pmatrix} 1 & -1 & 1 & 0 \\ 0 & 0 & 0 & 0 \\ 0 & 0 & 0 & 0 \\ 0 & 0 & 0 & 0 \\ 0 & 0 & 0 & 1 \end{pmatrix} \begin{pmatrix} V_{Y1} \\ V_{Y2} \\ V_{Y3} \\ I_X \end{pmatrix} \quad (1)$$

The proposed full-wave rectifier circuit is shown in **Figure 3**. The circuit employs only two DDCCs. Compared to previous rectifiers, the proposed rectifier is higher suitable for IC implementation. The DDCC_1 and DDCC_2 are operated as non-inverting and inverting unity-gain voltage buffers. The input voltage V_{in} is connected to Y_1 and Y_2 terminals of DDCC_1 and DDCC_2, respectively, while two outputs (X terminals) are connected. In this case, only positive peak will be appeared at the output voltage V_{out}.

The operation of the proposed full-wave rectifier is as follows: when $V_{in} > 0$, the DDCC_1 is on, the voltage V_{in} is followed by the DDCC_1 to the voltage V_{out} at X terminal. In addition, when $V_{in} < 0$, the voltage $-V_{in}$ is followed by the DDCC_2 to the voltage V_{out} at X terminal ($-V_{Y2} = V_X$). From the operation of the proposed full-wave rectifier explained, the relations between the input voltage, V_{in}, and the output voltage, V_{out}, can be expressed as

$$\left.\begin{matrix} V_{in} > 0 \ ; V_{out} = V_{in} \ : \ \text{DDCC}_1 = \text{on} \\ V_{in} < 0 \ ; V_{out} = -V_{in} \ : \ \text{DDCC}_2 = \text{on} \end{matrix}\right\} \quad (2)$$

The output voltage of the circuit in **Figure 3** can be expressed as

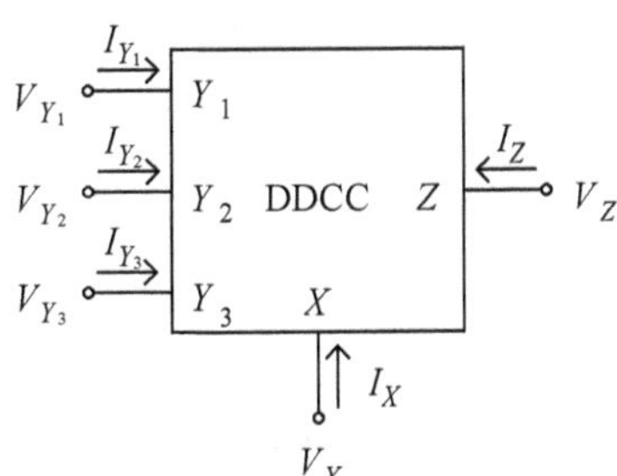

Figure 1. Electrical symbol for DDCC.

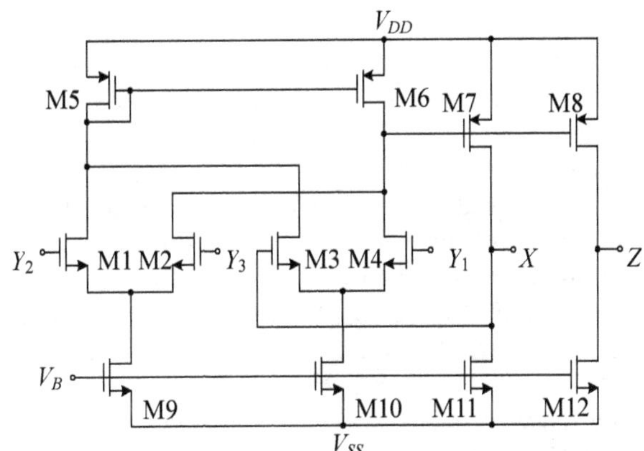

Figure 2. CMOS implementation for DDCC.

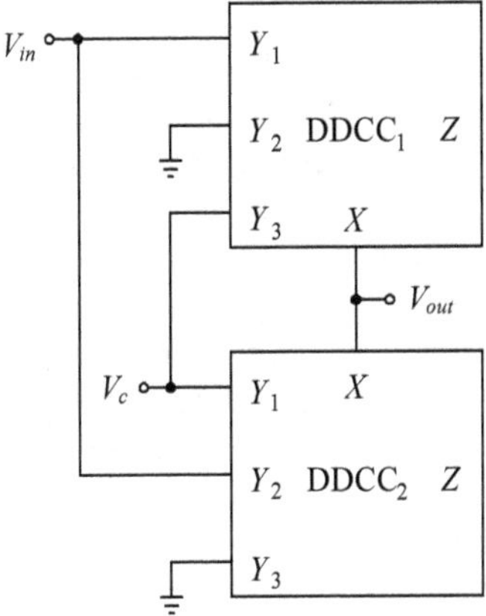

Figure 3. Proposed full-wave rectifier using DDCCs.

$$V_{out} = |V_{in}| \quad (3)$$

Therefore, the proposed circuit provides the full-wave rectification. It can be noted that the proposed circuit has high-input and low-output terminal, hence it is easy to drive loads without using a buffering device. The DC offset output voltage can be controlled by adjusting the voltage V_C.

3. Simulation Results

The proposed full-wave rectifier is simulated using PSPICE program to verify the given theoretical analysis. The DDCCs are simulated using CMOS structure of **Figure 2** that can be implemented using CMOS structures DDCC given in [12]. The aspect ratios of the MOS transistors of the CMOS DDCC are given in **Table 1**.

The device model parameters used for the PSPICE simulation are taken from MIETEC 0.5 μm CMOS process [12]. The supply voltages are selected as $V_{DD} = -V_{SS} = 2.5$ V and the bias voltage is set as $V_B = -1.7$ V. The DC transfer characteristic of the proposed full-wave rectifier is shown in **Figure 4**, which shows the operating voltage ranging from –1 V to 1 V of the input voltage. The magnified zero crossing of **Figure 4** is shown in **Figure 5**. In this figure, the blunting region (b) is found as –2.5 mV < V_{in} < 2.5 mV. Applying the 200 m V_{peak} sine wave at the input of the proposed rectifier, the input and output signals at frequencies of 500 kHz and 1 MHz are shown in **Figures 6** and 7, respectively. This results is confirms the operation that the proposed rectifier can provide the full-wave rectification at the input signal amplitude lower than the threshold voltage of diode (< 0.3 V). It is evident from **Figures 6** and **7** that undistorted full-wave rectified signals are produced at all two frequencies. However, as the input frequency increases to 1MHz and beyond, the output signals have errors at the crossover region, called "corner distortion". This corner distortion results from the non-conduction/conction transition problem of DDCCs. At the frequency of 1 MHz, we simulate the temperature performance of the proposed full-wave rectifier as shown in **Figure 3** by changing temperatures from 50°C to 100°C. **Figure 8** shows the output waveform of the proposed rectifier at temperatures of 50°C, 75°C and 100°C. From simulation results in **Figure 8**, they show that the proposed circuit provides excellence temperature stability. This result is confirmed by Equation (3). The simulated peak outputs V_{out} for the circuit were 199.46 mV and 196.67 mV at 50°C and 100°C, respectively.

Table 1. Transistor aspect ratios of the used DDCC.

Transistor	W (μm)	L (μm)
M1-M4	1.6	1
M5-M6	8	1
M7-M9	20	1
M10-M11	29	1
M12-M14	90	1

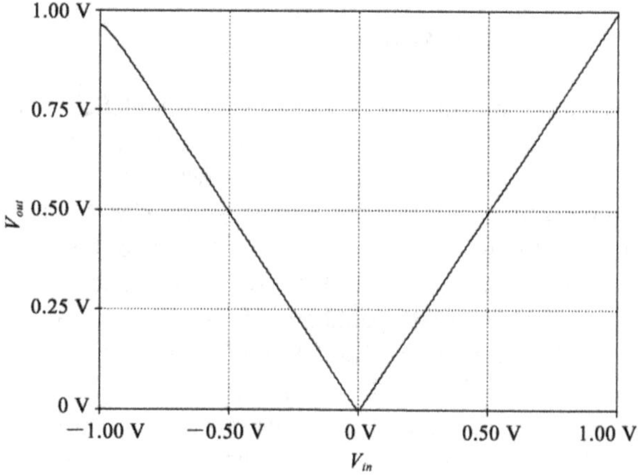

Figure 4. Simulated results for DC transfer characteristic.

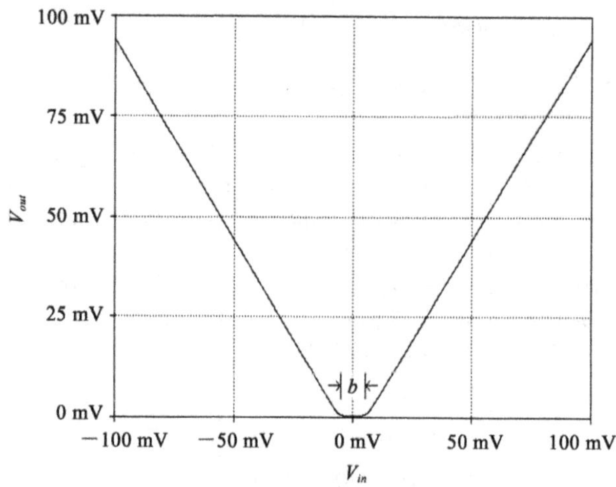

Figure 5. Simulated results for DC transfer characteristic at zero crossing regions.

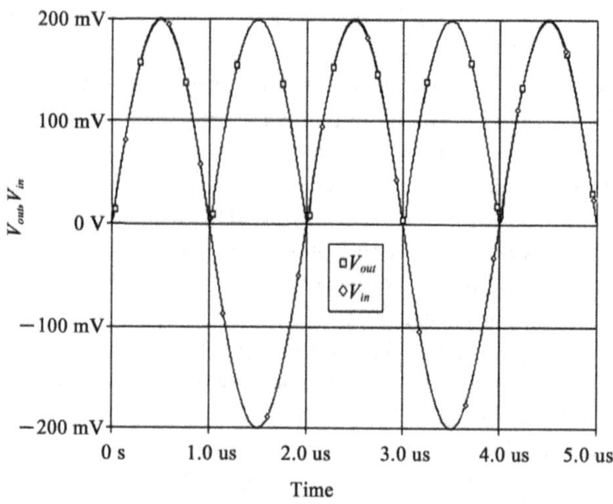

Figure 6. Operation of the proposed full-wave rectifier at 500 kHz frequency for V_{in} = 200 mV peak.

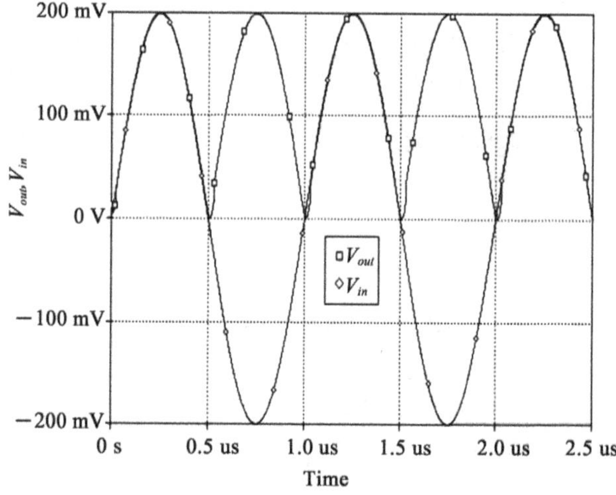

Figure 7. Operation of the proposed full-wave rectifier at 1 MHz frequency for V_{in} = 200 mV peak.

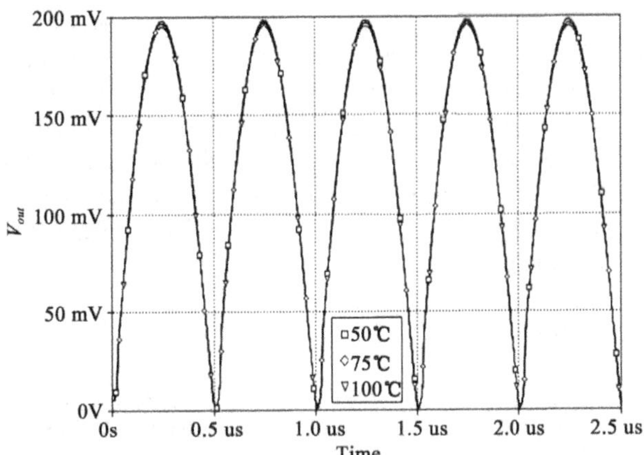

Figure 8. Operation of the proposed full-wave rectifier at different temperatures.

4. Application Examples

To show the advantage of proposed rectifier, author describes a pseudo root-mean-square (RMS)-to-DC conversion as an example. The well-known average value of a signal magnitude is defined by

$$V_{avg} = \frac{1}{T}\int_0^T |v(t)|\,dt \tag{4}$$

where $v(t)$ is the AC signal, T is its period, and V_{avg} is the average value of the rectified signal of $v(t)$. To perform this operation, the AC signal is first full-wave rectified and then low-pass filtered to extract the DC component. For the case of a sinusoidal signal we have $v(t) = V_m \sin(2\pi f t)$, where V_m is the peak amplitude voltage and $f = 1/T$ is the frequency. Substituting $v(t)$ into (4) and integrating yields

$$V_{avg} = \frac{2}{\pi}V_m = 0.637V_m \tag{5}$$

It is customary to calibrate the averaging circuits so that, with a sinusoidal input, the rms value is yield:

$$V_{rms} = \sqrt{\frac{1}{T}\int_0^T v^2(t)\,dt} \tag{6}$$

Substituting $v(t) = V_m \sin(2\pi f t)$ and solving yields

$$V_{rms} = \frac{1}{\sqrt{2}}V_m = 0.707V_m \tag{7}$$

Comparing (5) and (7) we have [13]

$$\frac{V_{rms}}{V_{avg}} = \frac{\pi}{2\sqrt{2}} \approx 1.111 \tag{8}$$

which is the amount of amplification required to obtain V_{rms} from V_{avg}. By using proposed full-wave rectifier, both average value and RMS value of sinusoidal waveform can be readily implemented as shown in **Figure 9**. It should be noted that only grounded components are required. For more suitable IC implementation, all grounded resistors can be replaced by MOS resistor as shown in **Figure 10**. This resistor was presented in 1990 by Wang [14]. Assume MR_1 and MR_2 have the same characteristics and remaining in the saturation region. The resistance value of MOS resistor can be expressed as:

$$R_{eq} = \frac{1}{2K\left(V_{DD} - V_{TH}\right)} \tag{9}$$

where $K = \mu_o C_{ox}(W/L)$, V_{TH} is the threshold voltage and $V_{DD} = |V_{SS}|$ are the supply voltages. It can see that the value of resistor can vary by setting the appropriate aspect ratio.

A first-order low-pass filter is achieved with a properly specified R_L and C. The voltage V_{out} is converted to the input current of the filter in which the AC components are filtered through the capacitor C. The voltage value, V_{avg}, can be obtained by choosing R_{in} and R_{L1} identical. According to (8), V_{rms} can be obtained by setting $R_{L2}/R_{in} = 1.111$. For a symmetrical square input, the ratio of (8) becomes unity thus V_{avg} of **Figure 9** gives the exact RMS value because R_{in} and R_{L1} are identical. If $R_{L1}/R_{in} = 1.155$, the circuit may indicate the RMS value for either sinusoidal or triangular current signals. The criterion for specifying C_L (*i.e.* $C_L = C_{L1} = C_{L2}$) is that it must be large enough to keep the residual output ripple within specified limits, that is [13]

$$C_L \geq \frac{1}{4\pi f_{\min}} \tag{10}$$

where $f_{\min}$ is the low end of the frequency range of interest. C_L should usually exceed the right-hand term by the inverse of the fractional ripple error that can be tolerated at the output [14].

The RMS-to-DC converter in **Figure 9** is simulated using PSPICE program to verify the given theoretical analysis. For this simulation, three resistors (R_{in}, R_{L1} and

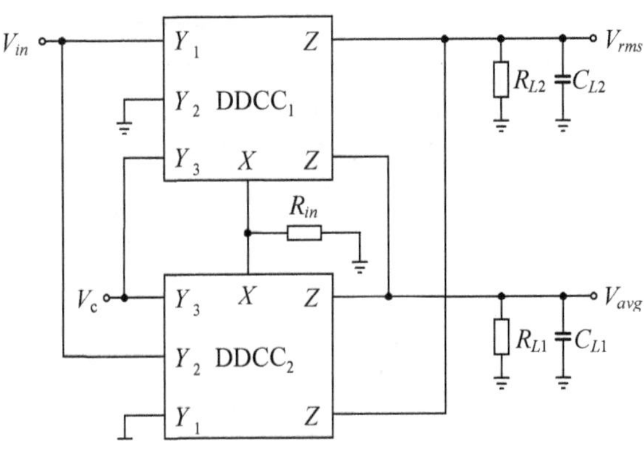

Figure 9. The full-wave rectifier-based RMS-to-DC converter for sinusoidal waveform.

R_{L2}) are replaced by MOS resistor as shown in **Figure 10** According to (8), when R_{in} and R_{L1} are identical to obtain V_{av}, then V_{rms} can be obtained by setting R_{L2}/R_{in} = 1.111. In this case, the aspect ratios (W/L) of MOS transistors, MR_1 and MR_2, for R_{in}, R_{L1} and R_{L2} are 2 μm/2 μm, 2 μm/ 2 μm and 1.8 μm/ 2μm, respectively ($R_{in} = R_{L1}$ = 3.457 kΩ and R_{L2} = 3.844 kΩ). A sinusoidal input with V_{in} = 200 mV and f = 1 MHz was applied to the converter and C = 1 nF. The supply voltages for DDCC are selected as $V_{DD} = -V_{SS}$ = 2.5 V and the bias voltage is set as V_B = −1.7 V. The multiple-output DDCC can be obtained by adding additional current mirrors. **Figure 11** shows the simulation results for V_{avg} = 126.63 mV and V_{rms} = 140.45 mV, with ripple less than 2%. In this case, the RMS voltage converter for both sinusoidal (output V_{rms}) and symmetrical square (output V_{avg}) waveform can be obtained. To achieve this case, the buffer circuits should be used.

5. Conclusions

In this paper, a new DDCC-based full-wave rectifier has been presented. The proposed circuit comprises only two DDCC which is suitable for IC implementation. The proposed circuit has high-input and low-output impedance terminals, hence it easy to drive loads without using a buffering device. It can be applied to various nonlinear analog signal processing circuits. The performance of the proposed circuit is confirmed from PSPICE simulation results. Simulation results show that the proposed rectifier have excellent temperature stability. The application of proposed rectifier to pseudo RMS-to-DC conversion is also included.

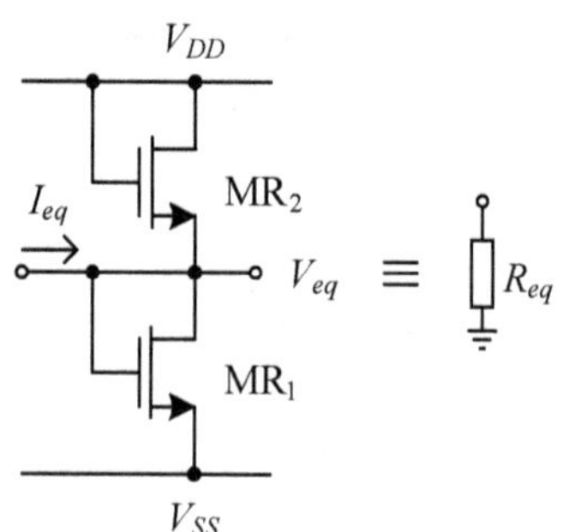

Figure 10. MOS resistor.

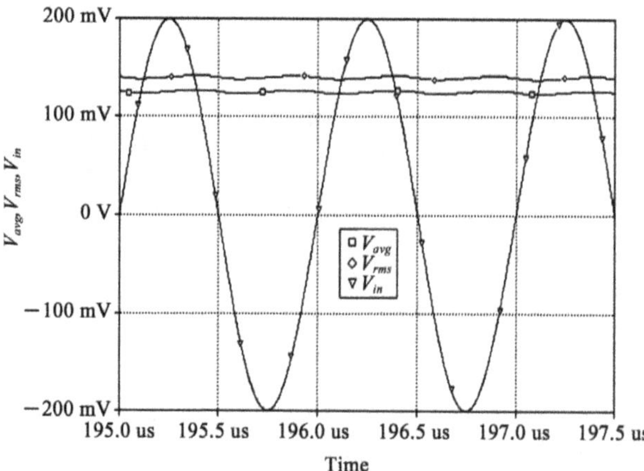

Figure 11. Simulated V_{avg} and V_{rms} for sinusoidal input with amplitude of 200 V_{Peak} and frequency of 1 MHz.

6. References

[1] J. Peyton and V. Walsh, "Analog Electronics with Op Amps: A Source Book of Practical Circuits," Cambridge University Press, New York, 1993.

[2] R. G. Irvine, "Operational Amplifier Characteristics and Applications," Prentice Hall International, Upper Saddle River, 1994.

[3] Z. Wang, "Full-Wave Precision Rectification That is Performed in Current Domain and Very Suitable for CMOS Implementation," *IEEE Transactions on Circuits and Systems-I*, Vol. 39, No. 6, 1992, pp. 456-462.

[4] S. J. G. Gift, "A High-Performance Full-Wave Rectifier Circuit," *International Journal of Electronics*, Vol. 89, No. 8, 2000, pp. 467-476.

[5] C. Toumazou, F. J. Lidgey and S. Chattong, "High Frequency Current Conveyor Precision Full-Wave Rectifier," *Electronics Letters*, Vol. 30, No. 10, 1994, pp. 745-746.

[6] A. Khan, M. A. El-Ela and M. A. Al-Turaigi, "Current-Mode Precision Rectification," *International Journal of Electronics*, Vol. 79, No. 6, 1995, pp. 853-859.

[7] K. Hayatleh, S. Porta and F. J. Lidgey, "Temperature Independent Current Conveyor Precision Rectifier," *Electronics Letters*, Vol. 30, No. 25, 1995, pp. 2091-2093.

[8] A. Monpapassorn, K. Dejhan and F. Cheevasuvit, "A Full-Wave Rectifier Using a Current Conveyor and Current Mirrors," *International Journal of Electronics*, Vol. 88, No. 7, 2001, pp. 751-758.

[9] W. Surakumpontorn, K. Anuntahirunrat and V. Riewruja, "Sinusoidal Frequency Doubler and Full-Wave Rectifier Using Translinear Current Conveyor," *Electronics Letters*, Vol. 34, No. 22, 1998, pp. 2077-2079.

[10] E. Yuce, S. Minaei and O. Cicekoglu, "Full-Wave Rectifier Realization Using Only Two CCII+S and NMOS Transistors," *International Journal of Electronics*, Vol. 93, No. 8, 2006, pp. 533-541.

[11] W. Chiu, S.-I. Liu, H.-W. Tsao and J.-J. Chen, "CMOS Differential Difference Current Conveyors and Their Applications," *IEE Proceeding of Circuits, Devices, System*, Vol. 143, No. 2, 1996, pp. 91-96.

[12] S. Minaei and M. A. Ibrahim, "General Configuration for Realizing Current-Mode First-Order All-Pass Filter Using DDCC," *International Journal of Electronics*, Vol. 92, No. 6, 2005, pp. 347-356.

[13] Z. Wang, "Novel Pseudo RMS Current Converter for Sinusoidal Signals Using a CMOS Precision Current Rectifier," *IEEE Transactions on Instrumentation and Measurement*, Vol. 39, No. 4, 1990, pp. 670-671.

[14] Z. Wang, "2-MOSFET Transistor with Extremely Low Distortion for Output Reaching Supply Voltage," *Electronics Letters*, Vol. 26, No. 13, 1990, pp. 951-952.

Versatile Voltage-Mode Universal Filter Using Differential Difference Current Conveyor

Sudhanshu Maheshwari, Ankita Gangwar
Department of Electronics Engineering, Z. H. College of Engineering and Technology, Aligarh Muslim University, Aligarh, India

Abstract

A novel four-input three-output voltage-mode differential difference current conveyor (DDCC) based universal filter is presented. The circuit uses three DDCCs as active elements, two resistors and two capacitors as passive elements. The circuit along with its versatility enjoys the advantage of minimum number of passive elements employment. SPICE simulation results are given to confirm the theoretical analysis. The proposed circuit is a novel addition to the existing knowledge on the subject.

Keywords: Analog Filters, Current Conveyors, DDCC, Voltage-Mode, Universal Filter

1. Introduction

Current-mode circuits have wider bandwidth, larger linearity, higher slew-rate, and wider dynamic range than voltage-mode circuits, thus they have received considerable attention [1]. A number of applications, such as filters, oscillators, analog-digital converter, and analogue signal processing blocks based on current conveyors have been proposed [2-4]. Recently, current-mode circuits are well used in communication circuits and wireless optical systems due to their larger dynamic range and wider bandwidth [5-6].

In 2004, Jianping Hu [7] proposed a CMOS DDCC along with its filtering applications. In the same year, Horng [8] proposed a similar a voltage mode multifunction filter with a single input and three outputs, which can realize low-pass, band-pass and high-pass filter functions by using two DDCCs, two grounded resistors and two grounded capacitors. But these configurations could not realize all-pass and band-stop functions. In 2004, Temizyurek [9] proposed a three-input single-output voltage mode universal filter. This configuration can realize low-pass, band-pass, band-stop, high-pass and all-pass filter functions using two DDCCs as active device and two resistors and two capacitors as passive devices, but there was no inverted output. In 2007, Chen [10] proposed a universal voltage mode single-input multiple output filter with two DDCCs, two grounded capacitors and three resistors. This configuration can give band-pass, band-stop, high-pass, all-pass and inverting low-pass responses. In 2007 again, Chen [11] proposed two single DDCC based configurations. These were single-input multiple output filters and could provide low-pass, band-pass and high-pass functions. In 2008, a compact voltage-mode multifunction filter employing only one DVCC and four components was reported [12]. Very recently, a single input three output universal filter using three DVCC/DDCC and only four components was also reported [13]. These works [12-13] were based on use of four passive elements and thus lacked non-interactive control of pole-frequency and quality factor. More recently, another biquad filter using DVCC was further proposed [14].

This paper presents a new Biquadratic filter configuration with three DDCCs, two resistors, and two capacitors. This configuration provides low-pass functions, band-pass functions, band-stop functions, high pass functions and all-pass functions, each with inverting and non-inverting transfer functions. The proposed circuit is verified through PSPICE simulations using 0.5 μm CMOS parameters with good results.

2. Differential Difference Current Conveyor

The DDCC, whose symbol is shown in **Figure 1** is a six port building block. The DDCC is characterized by the following equations:

$$I_{Y1} = I_{Y2} = I_{Y3} = 0 \quad (1)$$

$$V_X = V_{Y1} - V_{Y2} + V_{Y3} \quad (2)$$

$$I_{Z+} = I_X \quad (3)$$

$$I_{Z-} = -I_X \quad (4)$$

where, suffixes refer to the respective terminals.

The CMOS Differencial Difference Current Conveyor used in this work was introduced in 2004 [7]. The CMOS implementation of DDCC is shown in **Figure 2**.

The input transconductance elements are realized with two differential stages (M1 and M2, M3 and M4). The high gain stage composed of a current mirror (M7 and M8) which converts the differential current to a single ended output current. Transistors M9-M12 are used to reduce the current error due to different drain voltages of M7 and M8 between currents I7 and I8. The transistors M9 and M13 provide negative feedback to make voltage V_X less dependent of the current drawn from X-terminal. The small resistance R_X [7] can be expressed as

$$R_X = \frac{(g_{d1} + g_{d4} + g_{d8})(g_{d9} + g_{d12})}{g_{m4} g_{m9} g_{m13}} \quad (5)$$

Equation (5) simply gives a measure of intrinsic resistance at X terminal of DDCC. The current through terminal X is conveyed to $Z+$ terminal by the current mirrors formed by transistors M13, M15 and M14, M16. Similarly, M17-M22 performs current inversion so as to provide $Z-$ output [7].

3. Proposed Circuit

3.1. Circuit Description

The proposed circuit configuration is shown in **Figure 3**. The proposed circuit is a multiple input multiple output filter which can give various filter functions at its three outputs based on the combination of input terminals used. The circuit has one high input impedance terminal and three other input terminals and three output terminals. The circuit has three DDCCs, two grounded resistors and two capacitors.

The output transfer functions of **Figure 3** can be expressed as

$$V_{o1} = \frac{sC_2R_2v_{i1} + \left(s^2C_1C_2R_1R_2\right)v_{i2} - \left(sC_2R_2\right)v_{i3} + v_{i4}}{s^2C_1C_2R_1R_2 + sC_2R_2 + 1} \quad (6)$$

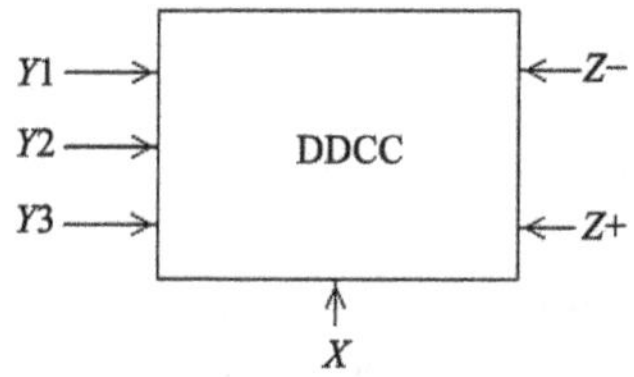

Y1, Y2, Y3, Z−, Z+, X, DDCC

Figure 1. Symbol of DDCC.

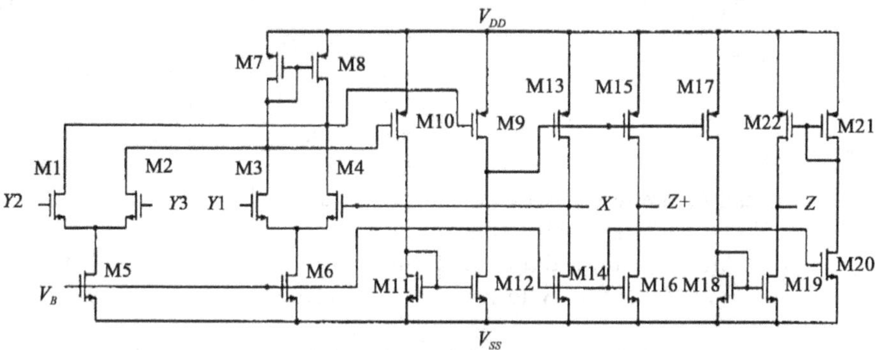

Figure 2. CMOS implementation of DDCC [7].

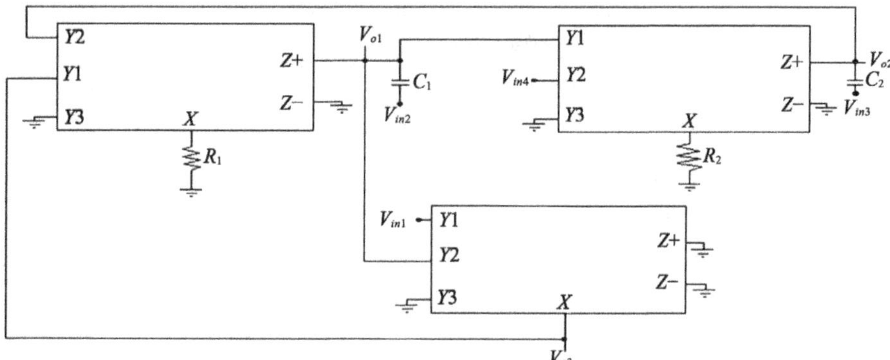

Figure 3. Proposed multi-input multi-output universal filter.

$$V_{o2} = \frac{v_{i1} + sC_1R_1v_{i2} + \left(s^2C_1C_2R_1R_2 + sC_2R_2\right)v_{i3} - \left(sC_1R_1 + 1\right)v_{i4}}{s^2C_1C_2R_1R_2 + sC_2R_2 + 1} \quad (7)$$

$$V_{o3} = \frac{\left(s^2C_1C_2R_1R_2 + 1\right)v_{i1} - s^2C_1C_2R_1R_2v_{i2} + sC_2R_2v_{i3} - v_{i4}}{s^2C_1C_2R_1R_2 + sC_2R_2 + 1} \quad (8)$$

The ω_0 and Q of the filter is given by

$$\omega_0 = \sqrt{\frac{1}{C_1C_2R_1R_2}} \quad Q = \sqrt{\frac{C_1R_1}{C_2R_2}} \quad (9)$$

The proposed configuration is capable of implementing as many as 8 filtering functions with suitable choice of inputs and outputs as depicted in **Table 1**. It may be noted that 'NI' refers to 'non-inverting', whereas 'I' refers to 'inverting'. V_{in} refers to the node's (input) connection to input signal.

3.2. Non-ideal Study

Taking the non-idealities of DDCCs in to account, the relationship of the terminal voltages and currents can be rewritten as

$$\begin{aligned} V_X &= \beta_{1k}V_{Y1} - \beta_{2k}V_{Y2} + \beta_{3k}V_{Y3} \\ I_{Y1} &= I_{Y2} = I_{Y3} = 0 \\ I_{Z+} &= \alpha_{1k}I_X \\ I_{Z-} &= -\alpha_{2k}I_X \end{aligned} \quad (10)$$

In Equation (10), β_{1k}, β_{2k}, and β_{3k} are respectively the voltage transfer gains from Y_1, Y_2 and Y_3 terminals to the X-terminal for the kth DDCC. Moreover, α_{1k} and α_{2k} are the current transfer gains for kth DDCC from X to Z+ and Z– terminals respectively. The non ideal analysis of the proposed circuit gives the characteristic equation as:

$$D(s) = s^2 + \alpha_1\beta_{11}\beta_{32}\left(s/C_1R_1\right) + \alpha_1\alpha_2\beta_{21}\beta_{12}/C_1C_2R_1R_2 \quad (11)$$

Therefore,

$$\omega_0 = \sqrt{\frac{\alpha_1\alpha_2\beta_{21}\beta_{12}}{C_1C_2R_1R_2}} \quad (12)$$

$$Q = \frac{\sqrt{\alpha_2\beta_{21}\beta_{12}/\alpha_1}}{\beta_{11}\beta_{32}}\sqrt{\frac{C_1R_1}{C_2R_2}} \quad (13)$$

Equations (12)-(13) show that the non-ideal transfer gains affect the filter parameters. The sensitivity of parameters to the same is found to be within unity in magnitude, thus showing good sensitivity performance.

4. Simulation Results

To verify the theoretical prediction of the proposed Biquadratic filter, PSPICE simulations were carried out for a designed frequency, f_0 = 1.0065 MHz and gain of all filters as 'unity': C_1 = 10 pF, C_2 = 25 pF, R_1 = 10 K, R_2 = 10 KΩ for few selected combinations. The supply voltages used was ±2.5 V.

Case-1: Low pass, band pass and band stop responses (choice No. 1)

If $V_{i1} = V_{in}$ (the input voltage signal) and $V_{i2} = V_{i3} = V_{i4} = 0$ (namely, the capacitor C_1 and C_2 are grounded), then the non-inverting band-pass (NI-BP), non-inverting low-pass (NI-LP) and non-inverting band-stop (NI-BS) filters are obtained at the node voltages, V_{o1}, V_{o2} and V_{o3}, respectively. Note that the input signal, $V_{i1} = V_{in}$, is connected to the high-input impedance input node of the DDCC (the Y_1 port of the DDCC). So the circuit enjoys the advantage of having high-input impedance, leading to cascadability at the input port.

Table 1. Choice of inputs and outputs to implement different filtering functions.

Choice No.	Input conditions				Outputs		
	V_{i1}	V_{i2}	V_{i3}	V_{i4}	V_{o1}	V_{o2}	V_{o3}
1.	V_{in}	0	0	0	NI-BP	NI-LP	NI-BS
2.	0	V_{in}	0	V_{in}	NI-BS	NI-LP	I-BS
3.	0	V_{in}	0	0	NI-HP	NI-BP	I-HP
4.	V_{in}	0	0	V_{in}	-	I-BP	NI-HP
5.	0	V_{in}	V_{in}	V_{in}	NI-AP	-	I-AP
6.	0	0	0	V_{in}	NI-LP	-	I-LP
7.	V_{in}	V_{in}	0	0	-	-	NI-LP
8.	0	0	V_{in}	0	I-BP	-	NI-BP

Figure 4 shows the filter response for low pass, band pass and band reject functions. The low pass band width found is 0.89615 MHz. Similarly for band pass function the central frequency is 1.042 MHz and the band width is 1.041 MHz. While for the band reject function the central frequency found is 1.0278 MHz. **Figure 5** shows the transient response of band pass filter for a sinusoidal input of 1 MHz.

Case 2 : Inverting, non-inverting HP and BP filter (choice No. 3)

If $V_{i2} = V_{in}$ (the input voltage signal) and $V_{i1} = V_{i3} = V_{i4} = 0$ then non-inverting high-pass (NI-HP) function is implemented at V_{o1} and inverting high pass function is obtained at V_{o3}. It may be noted that band-pass is also obtained at V_{o2}.

Figures 6 and **7** shows the frequency responses of non-inverting and inverting high pass function. The cut off frequency for the high pass function of the proposed filter circuit has been found to be 1.21 MHz. **Figure 8** shows the transient responses of non-inverting and inverting high pass functions respectively for a sinusoidal input of 10 MHz. Also the THD of non-inverting high pass function is found to be 2.3%. It may be noted that the band-pass response is not shown in this case, for brevity reasons, as it was already covered in case 1.

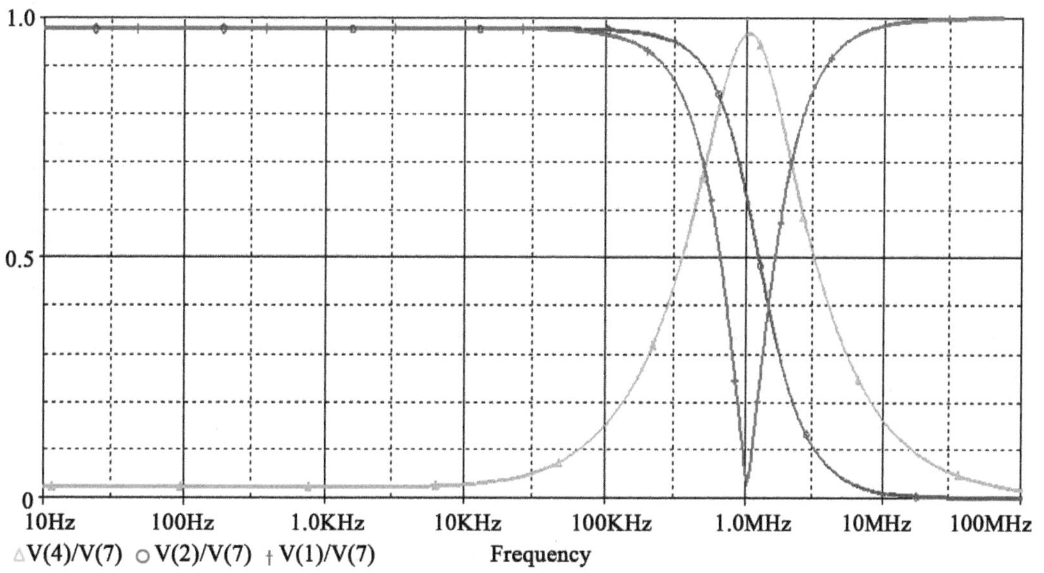

Figure 4. Frequency Response for choice no. 1.

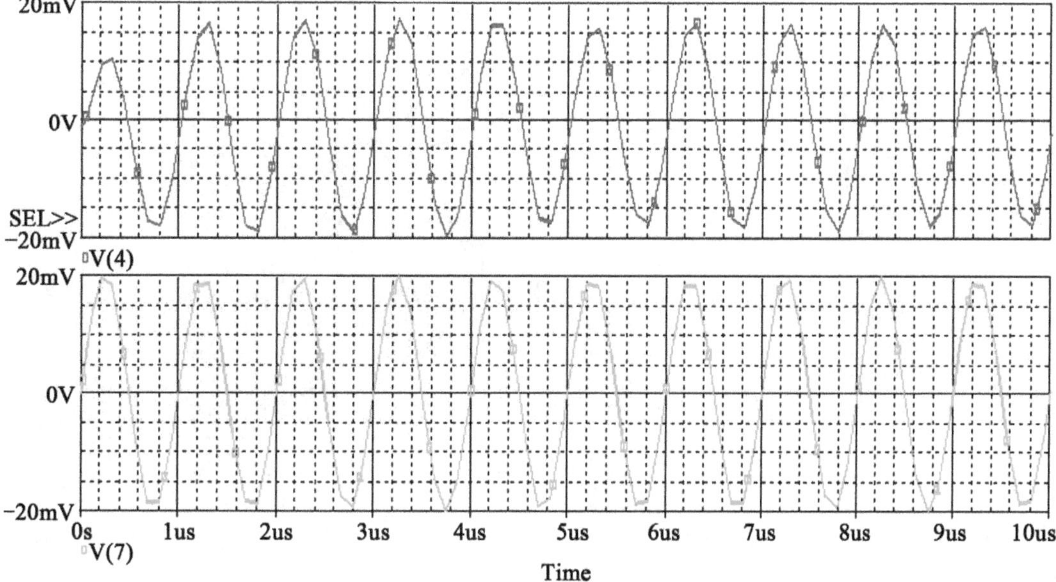

Figure 5. Input and outputs of BP filter at 1 MHz.

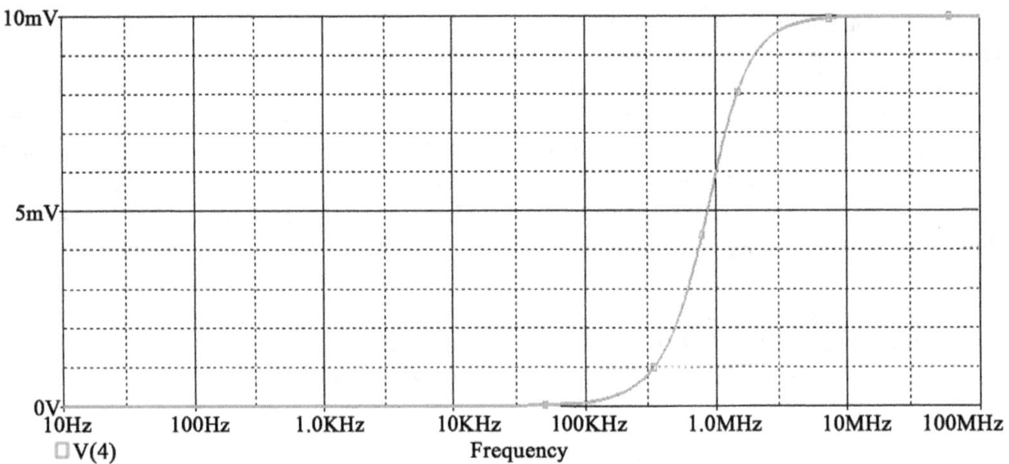

Figure 6. Frequency response of non-inverting high pass function.

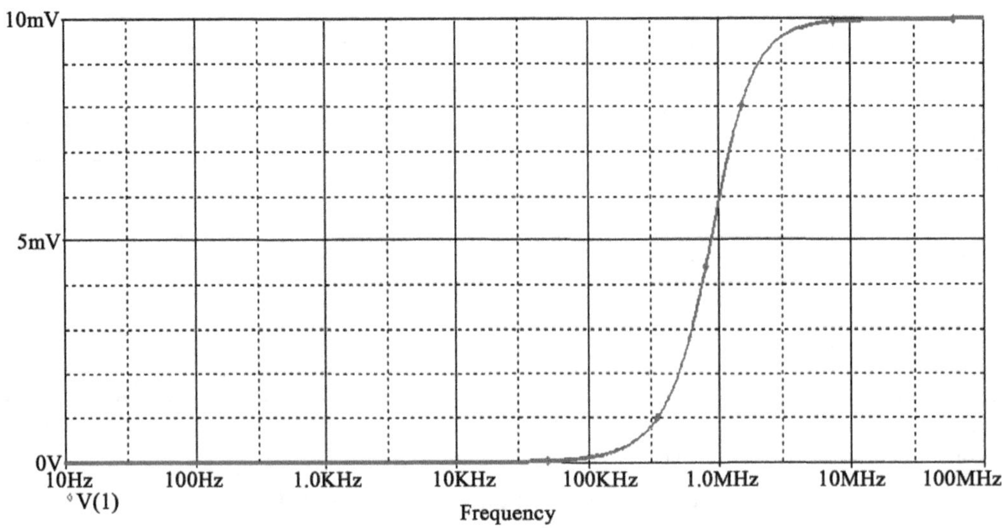

Figure 7. Frequency response of inverting high pass function.

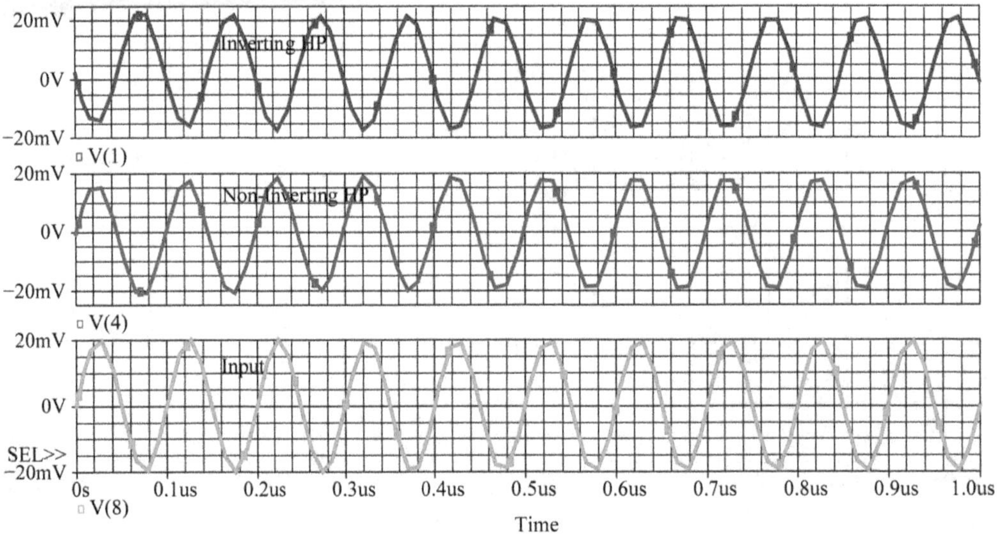

Figure 8. Input and output of HP filters at 10 MHz.

Case 3: Inverting and non-inverting all pass filter (choice No. 5)

If $V_{i1} = 0$ and $V_{i2} = V_{i3} = V_{i4} = V_{in}$ (the input voltage signal) then non- inverting all-pass (NI-AP) function is implemented at V_{o1} and inverting all-pass (I-AP) function is obtained at V_{o3}.

Figures 9 and **10** shows the frequency responses of non-inverting and inverting all pass function. **Figure 11** shows the transient responses of non-inverting and inverting all pass functions respectively for a sinusoidal input of 10 MHz.

5. Conclusions

In this paper, a novel four-input three-output voltage mode universal filter with the use of DDCC has been proposed. The circuit used three DDCCs with only two resistors and two capacitors to realize all the filter functions in inverting as well as in non-inverting form. The proposed configuration employs fewer passive components and can realize low pass, band pass, high pass, all pass and band stop functions, each with inverting and non-inverting transfer functions. Use of all grounded

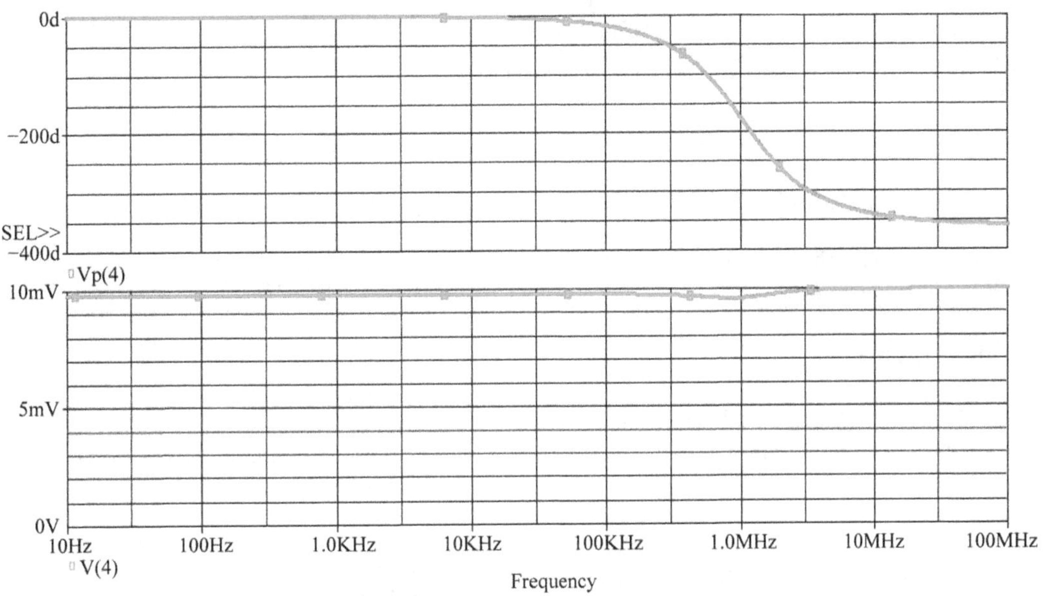

Figure 9. Gain and phase response of inverting all pass.

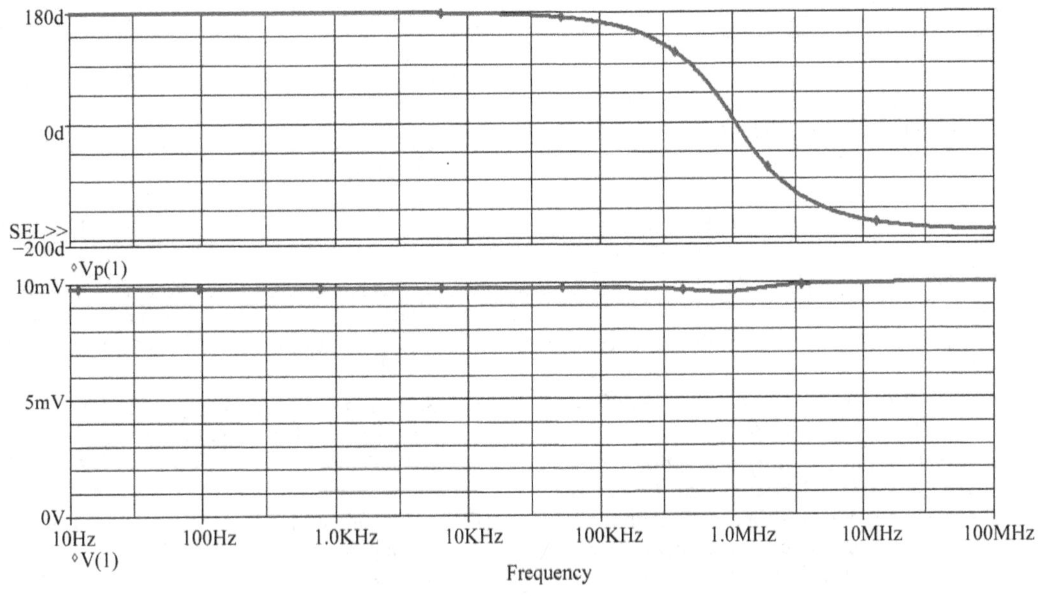

Figure 10. Gain and phase response of non-inverting all pass filter.

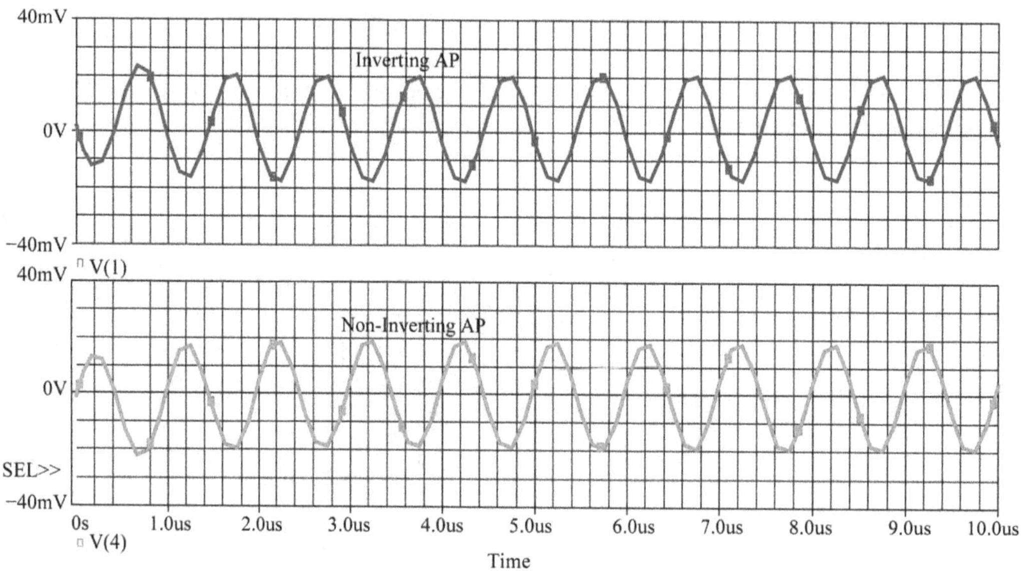

Figure 11. Transient Response of inverting and non-inverting AP functions.

passive components makes the new circuit especially attractive for IC implementation.

6. Acknowledgements

The authors are thankful to the Editorial Board for waiving off the publication fees of this paper.

7. References

[1] C. Toumazou, F. J. Lidgey and D. Haigh, "Analog IC Design: The Current-Mode Approach," PeTer Peregrinus, Exeter, 1990.

[2] A. S. Elwakil and A. M. Soliman, "Current Conveyor Chaos Generators," *IEEE Transactions on Circuits and Systems I: Fundamental Theory and Applications*, Vol. 46, No. 3, 1999, pp. 393-398.

[3] C. C. Chen and C. Y. Wu, "Design Techniques for 1.5-V Low-Power CMOS Current-Mode Cyclic Analog-to-Digital Converters," *IEEE Transactions on Circuits and Systems*, Vol. 45, No. 1, 1998, pp. 319-325.

[4] C. Temizyurek and I. Myderrizi, "Current-Mode Universal Filter Implemented with DVCCs," *International Conference on Electrical and Electronics Engineering*, Bursa, 3-7 December 2003.

[5] L. N. Alves and R. L. Aguiar, "Maximizing Bandwidth in CCll for Wireless Optical Applications," *The* 8*th IEEE International Conference on Electronics, Circuits and System*, Vol. 3, 2001, pp. 1107-1110.

[6] E. Vasconcelos, J. L. Cura, R. L. Aguiar and D. M. Santos, "A Novel High-Gain, High-Bandwidth CMOS Differential Front-End for Wireless Optical Systems," *Proceedings of the* 1999 *IEEE International Symposium on Circuits and Systems*, Vol. 4, 1999, pp. 431-434.

[7] J. Hu, Y. Xia, T. Xu and H. Dong, "A New CMOS Differential Difference Current Conveyor and Its Applications," 2004 *International Conference on Communications, Circuits and Systems*, Vol. 2, 2004, pp. 1156-1160.

[8] J. W. Horng, W. Y. Chiu and H. Y. Wei, "Voltage-Mode Highpass, Bandpass and Lowpass Filters Using Two DDCCs," *International Journal of Electronics*, Vol. 91, No. 8, 2004, pp. 461-464.

[9] C. Temizyurek and I. Myderrizi, "A Novel Three-nput One-Output Voltage-Mode Universal Filter Using Differential Difference Current Conveyor (DDCC)," *Proceedings of the* 12*th IEEE Mediterranean Electrotechnical Conference*, Dubrovnik, 12-15 May 2004, pp. 103-106.

[10] H.-P. Chen, "Universal Voltage-Mode Filter Using Only Plus-Type DDCCs," *Analog Integrated Circuits and Signal Processing*, Vol. 50, No. 2, 2007, pp. 137-139.

[11] H.-P. Chen and K.-H. Wu, "Single DDCC Based Voltage-Mode Multifunction Filter," *IEICE Transactions on Fundamentals of Electronics, Communications and Computer Sciences*, Vol. E90-A, No. 9, 2007, pp. 2029-2031.

[12] S. Maheshwari, "High Performance Voltage-Mode Multifunction Filter with Minimum Component Count," *WSEAS Transactions on Electronics*, Vol. 5, No. 6, 2008, pp. 244-249.

[13] S. Maheshwari, "Analogue Signal Processing Applications Using a New Circuit Topology," *IET: Circuits Devices and Systems*, Vol. 3, No. 3, 2009, pp. 106-115.

[14] S. Minaei and E. Yuce, "All-Grounded Passive Elements Voltage-Mode DVCC-Based Universal Filters," *Circuits Systems and Signal Processing*, Vol. 29, No. 2, 2010, pp. 295-305.

7

Algorithmic Optimization of BDDs and Performance Evaluation for Multi-level Logic Circuits with Area and Power Trade-offs

Saurabh Chaudhury[1], Anirban Dutta[2]
[1]*Department of Electrical Engineering, National Institute of Technology, Silchar, India*
[2]*Department of Electronics & Communication Engineering, National Institute of Technology, Silchar, India*

Abstract

Binary Decision Diagrams (BDDs) can be graphically manipulated to reduce the number of nodes and hence the area. In this context, ordering of BDDs play a major role. Most of the algorithms for input variable ordering of OBDD focus primarily on area minimization. However, suitable input variable ordering helps in minimizing the power consumption also. In this particular work, we have proposed two algorithms namely, a genetic algorithm based technique and a branch and bound algorithm to find an optimal input variable order. Of course, the node reordering is taken care of by the standard BDD package *buddy*-2.4. Moreover, we have evaluated the performances of the proposed algorithms by running an exhaustive search program. Experimental results show a substantial saving in area and power. We have also compared our techniques with other state-of-art techniques of variable ordering for OBDDs and found to give superior results.

Keywords: Algorithmic Optimization, BDDs, Genetic Algorithm, Branch & Bound, Variable Ordering, Area-Power Trade-offs

1. Introduction

Binary decision diagram (BDD) is an important data structure which finds wide applications specially, in the area of Boolean logic manipulation, logic synthesis, formal verification and testing. A Boolean function that describes a digital circuit can be represented as a BDD which is a directed acyclic graph with respect to an order and satisfying a set of properties. The number of its non-terminal nodes gives their size. For multiplexer based design styles such as Pass Transistor Logic (PTL), a smaller number of nodes directly transfers to a smaller chip area. A BDD can be implemented either in canonical form, reduced order (ROBDD) or in any other specific order (OBDD). If all identical nodes are shared and all redundant nodes are eliminated, the OBDD is said to be reduced (an ROBDD). The size of a BDD is strongly dependent on the order of input variables.

In the current problem of variable ordering, a number of algorithms exist in this context. These variable ordering algorithms can be broadly classified as *static variable ordering*, *dynamic variable ordering* and *evolutionary algorithms*. Most of the variable ordering algorithms from circuit topology are based on a depth first traversal through a circuit from the primary outputs to the primary inputs [1,2]. Such an ordering works well if the circuit is tree-structured. Yet another approach to variable ordering is gradual improvement based on variable exchange [3,4]. Though this approach is effective, the results depend on the initial variable orders and hence on circuit topology. R. Rudell [5] describes a dynamic variable ordering technique for an OBDD and propose two algorithms. The technique allows maintaining all advantages provided by the ordered BDD data structure, such as, canonicity and efficient recursive algorithms. A new variable ordering algorithms for multiple output circuits has been presented in [6] use variable *interleaving*, while conventional algorithms use variable *appending*. Christoph Meinel and Fabio Somenzi [7] propose another algorithm called *linear shifting*, which in many cases it leads to substantially more compact diagrams when compared to simple variable reordering. Another heuristic technique for deciding which BDD variables to reorder is simulated annealing (SA) [8]. But this technique is very slow, especially if the cost function is expensive to compute. A first attempt to use evolutionary algorithms for the variable ordering problem for BDDs is presented in [9] where the main genetic operations are partially-mapped crossover and mutation which yield better results (smaller BDDs) than other dynamic reordering techniques, but they are comparably slow. Many such evolutionary algorithms are presented in [10-12]. In [13], a low power optimization technique for BDD mapped circuits using temporal correlation has been presented. Output phase assignment technique for area and power minimization has been proposed in [14], which optimizes the BDD by finding suitable output polarity of a multi-output circuit using genetic algorithm. A new and powerful class of optimization techniques based on scatter search [15] has been proposed, which is very aggressive and attempts to find high quality solutions at a fast rate. Scatter search optimization techniques offers a reasonable compromise between quality (BDD size) and time. In [16] we see a technique to minimize the BDD complexity and the time of evaluation of the function based on *minimum path length* which is decided by initial variable order. A detailed survey of static variable ordering heuristics (such as topological, influential, priority ordering and variable weighing etc.) has been presented in [17] in order to minimize the overall size of resulting decision diagram. Prasad, Assi, Harb and Prasad [18] propose an improved variable ordering method to obtain the minimum number of nodes in ROBDD which uses the graph topology to find the best variable ordering.

Most recently, a double hybridized genetic algorithm has been proposed in [19] for the optimization of variable order in ROBDD. The proposed technique combines a branch & bound technique with the basic genetic algorithm and then uses the linear shifting algorithm as the second hybridization to find ROBDD with reduced complexity.

We can see that variable ordering has been potentially used for reducing the size of OBDDs. In this paper, we propose some efficient variable ordering algorithms, namely, a genetic algorithm based technique and a branch and bound technique. Each of which not only reduces the size of the BDD but at the same time also minimizes power consumption. Section 2 defines the problem with some examples and then Section 3 describes the methodology of adopting the two algorithms with respect to the current problem, followed by results of experimentation. Convergence to global optimum is given in Section 4. Analysis and comparison of results with other techniques are presented in Section 5. Finally, Section 6 draws the conclusion.

2. Defining the Problem of Variable Ordering in BDDs

Digital integrated circuits often represented as Boolean functions can be best-manipulated graphically in the form of Binary Decision Diagrams (BDD). A BDD can be expressed mathematically as follows.

$$f : B \rightarrow B, B = \{0,1\} \quad (1)$$

where f is a switching function and π—a total order on a fixed set of Boolean variables $x_1, x_2, \cdots, x_n$. An OBDD with respect to order π is a single rooted direct acyclic graph that satisfies the properties as described in [20]. It is already mentioned that the size of a BDD is strongly dependent on the ordering of variables and is also explained in **Figure 1**.

Improving the variable ordering of BDDs is NP-Complete and finding the best order is NP-hard. However, the most tedious job in case of OBDDs is to find an optimal variable order. An optimal variable order has a greater impact on power minimization also, as because, node switching and leakage is dependent on the number of BDD nodes and its order. Majority of the heuristic techniques discussed here has stressed only upon the size or complexity of the resulting BDD. However, power is considered to be one of the critical design issues especially when there is drastic device scaling and increasing use of portable, battery-operated digital devices in recent times. In this paper, due weightage is given to both the area (complexity) and power consumption of the resulting BDD after optimization.

The next section proposes two techniques to tackle the problem of finding optimal variable order in order to minimize BDD complexity (area) and power.

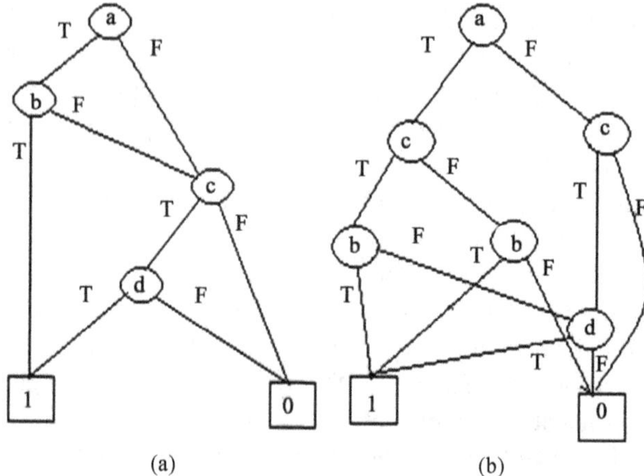

Figure 1. The influence of the variable ordering for $f(a,b,c,d) = ab + cd$ with the order a, b, c, d (a) and order a, c, b, d (b).

3. Proposed Approaches

We have attempted two different algorithmic approaches for efficient ordering of variables in OBDD, namely, the genetic algorithm which is an excellent multi-objective optimization technique and a branch and bound optimization approach, which is an exact method. At first, we will put our variable ordering problem in the framework of GA and constitute a GA-based program to obtain the best possible order decided by the minimal node count and power consumption of the resulting BDD. This will be followed by the experimentation with a number of benchmark circuits. The flowchart of **Figure 2** shows a pictorial representation of the proposed GA based technique.

Next, we will go for the same variable ordering problem by adopting a branch and bound (BB) based greedy algorithmic approach which is also an excellent optimization technique for multi-objective problems and has a finite but usually very large number of feasible solutions. A BB algorithm searches the complete space of solutions (exact method) for a given problem for optimum solution. However, in the current variable ordering problem for optimizing area and power, in combinational logic circuits realized as BDDs, explicit enumeration is normally impossible due to the exponentially increasing number of potential solutions (*factorial n* number of solutions), so a modified BB algorithm is taken up, the details of which we will see in Section 3.2.

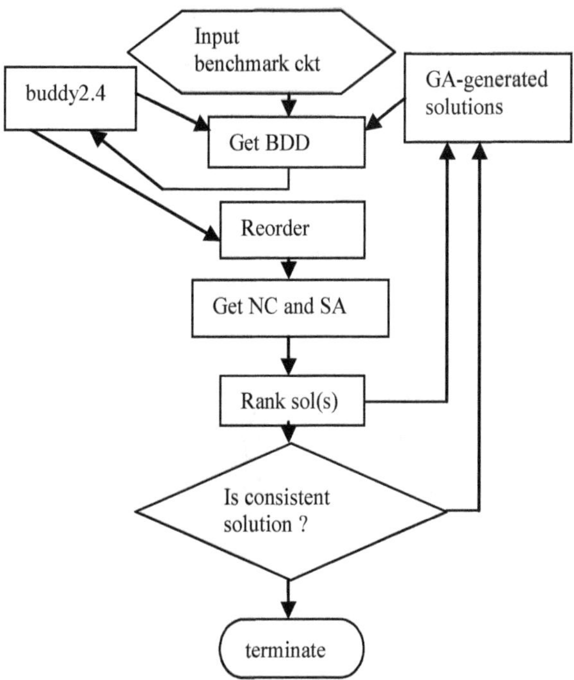

Figure 2. Flow-chart of the proposed GA-based technique.

3.1. Genetic Algorithm Based Approach

Genetic Algorithms (GA) are stochastic optimization based on principle of natural selection and natural genetics. They start with an initial population (solution space) consisting of a set of randomly generated solutions. Based on some reproductive plan especially, the crossover and mutation, they are allowed to evolve over a number of generations. After each generation, the chromosomes are evaluated based on some fitness criteria. Depending upon the selection policy and fitness value, the set of chromosomes for next generation are selected. Finally, the algorithm terminates when there is no improvement in solution over a fixed number of generations. The best solution at that generation is accepted as the solution produced by GA.

The formulation of Genetic Algorithm for any problem involves the careful and efficient encoding of the solutions to form chromosomes, cross-over and mutation operators and a cost function measuring the fitness of the chromosomes in a population. We discuss each of these in subsequent sections.

3.1.1. Solution Representation

Here, given a multilevel, multi-output circuit with n number of input (variables), the problem is to find an optimal order and as such the chromosome is a set of n variables (i_1, i_2, i_3, i_4, i_5, ⋯, i_n) of any order with no repetition of variables. For example, a combinational logic circuit consisting of 7 variables (inputs) then according to above,

2	3	1	4	5	7	6

is a chromosome, where, each decimal number represents an input (variable) taken in some order.

3.1.2. Genetic Operators

Two types of genetic operators namely the crossover and the mutation, are applied to selected parents for generating offspring. Crossover is performed between two selected individuals, called parents, by exchanging parts of their features (*i.e.* encodings) to form two new individual, called offspring. The crossover point is selected randomly, and the substrings of two parent chromosomes are exchanged to form the offspring. Care must be taken to see that neither a variable is repeated in a chromosome nor a duplicate chromosome is generated as offspring. To generate better offspring, whole population is sorted according to fitness value and the best-fit chromosomes take part in crossover.

The mutation operator brings variety into population by selecting a chromosome randomly from the population and modifies the chromosome at a point depending upon the value of a generated random number. To modify a chromosome, a randomly selected bit is complemented if the chromosome is a binary string. Here, as the chromosome is a string of n variables so it can be done by subtracting the randomly selected variable, n_i from n and swapping it with the variable n_i. This becomes the new chromosome. Once again the generated chromosome cannot be a duplicate.

3.1.3. Fitness Measure

The fitness function is used to determine how better a particular solution is. In this problem, initially we take it as a linear combination of area (node count) and switching activity (neglecting leakage) which can be determined by using the following formula.

$$\text{Fitness Value (F1)} = \text{A} \times \text{Number of nodes} + \text{B} \times \text{Switching Activity} \quad (2)$$

Next, we consider the leakage which is no longer a negligible quantity. In fact, it is a dominant contributor to the total power consumption in today's device scaling scenario. So the modified fitness function ($F2$) becomes,

$$\text{Fitness (F2)} = \text{A} \times \text{Number of nodes} + (1 - \text{A}) \times (\text{B} \times \text{Switching Activity} + (1 - \text{B}) \times \text{leakage}) \quad (3)$$

where number of nodes for each BDD representation based on a particular order is given by the standard BDD package (such as, *buddy*-2.4) and switching activity is obtained by traversing through the BDD in a bottom up fashion. Since this fitness value is dominated by area (node count) a modified fitness function is taken where switching activity (for dynamic power) and number of nodes at any generation is divided by the corresponding maximum values of first generation. Lesser the value of fitness function better is the offspring.

For a particular chromosome, the two-level circuit is represented with a BDD. Each BDD-node is essentially a multiplexer and suppose the function to be relaized is $f = a - c + bc$, then $Prob\ (f = 1) = Prob\ (a = 1) \times Prob\ (c = 0) + Prob\ (b = 1) \times Prob\ (c = 1)$ and $Prob\ (f = 0) = 1 - Prob\ (f = 1)$. So the switching activity of a BDD node (f) is then, $= 2 \times Prob\ (f = 1) \times Prob\ (f = 0)$. Thus SA's of all individual nodes are added up to get the overall SA for the BDD.

Leakage is again dependent mainly on sub-threshold and junction leakage at 0.18 um technology level considered here for realizing the BDD nodes with PTL. It however also depends on input patterns, gate fan-outs.

3.1.4. Experimental Results

The GA based program as defined above is implemented with C codes and experimented by running on a Pentium core-2 duo processor having 1Gb of RAM with a number of benchmark combinational logic circuits from *LGSynth* 93 benchmark suite. The GA based program takes a population size of 500 for large circuits (having more than 20 inputs) and 200 for small sized circuits (less than 20 inputs) with 80% crossover rate and 5% mutation rate. The result of experimentation for about 30 benchmark circuits with different area and power weights have been displayed in **Figure 3**. The average power reduction is more than 75% (highest) and average saving in area is about 39.35% as shown in bar diagram of **Figure 3**. When the emphasis is mostly on power the chart shows that although we achieve highest reduction in power, there is absolutely no control on area minimization (NC) and instead it becomes negative for many circuits which mean there is an increase in area. When we give more emphasis on area, it keeps on reducing, which is quite natural. Similarly, when we keep on increasing the emphasis on power, we achieve a gradual improvement in power reduction. However, we can take the best trade-off point to be at around A = 0.4 and 0.6, when both area and power reductions are considerably high and are found to be more than 32% and 71% respectively. **Figure 4** shows the area, dynamic power and leakage trade-offs (for A = 0.4, B = 0.6 and A = 0.4, B = 0.8). Overall improvement in area, dynamic power and leakage is found to be 33.163%, 57.28% and 29.234% respectively.

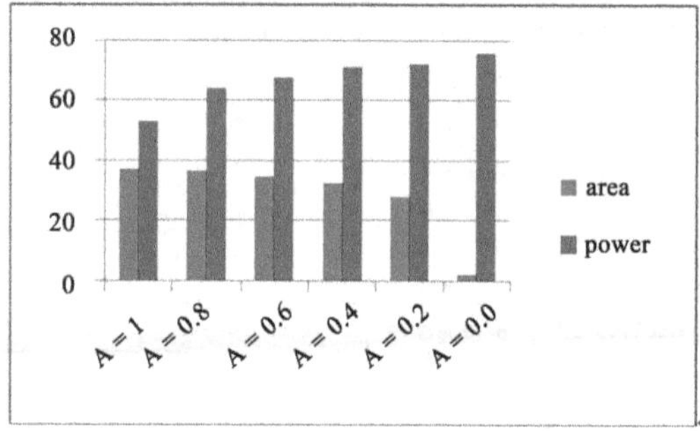

Figure 3. Bar diagram of average area and power reductions for different trade-offs.

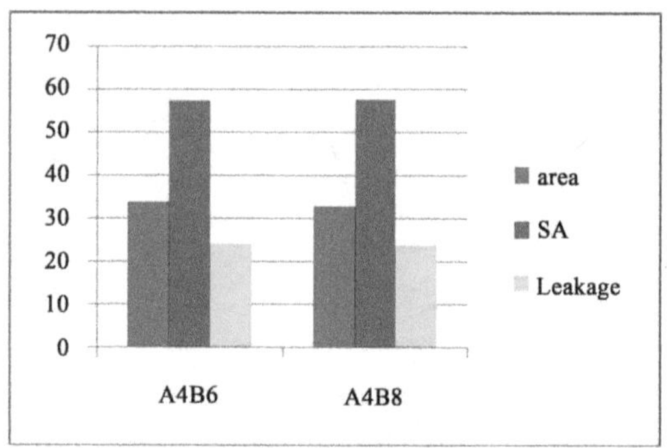

Figure 4. Plot showing area, dynamic power and leakage trade-offs.

It is also observed that the area saving can be as high as 97.33% (with 100% area weight) and power reduction of 97.46% (with 100% power weight) for a large circuit, such as, *seq* which is quite promising. In fact the benefit of area and power reduction is more for large circuits.

3.2. Branch and Bound Algorithm

In this section, we take up the problem of BDD optimization by formulating a branch and bound algorithm (BB). As the target is for an optimal trade-off between area and power, we propose here a greedy search technique using BB for the current variable ordering problem. A BB algorithm searches the whole solution space for the best solution. This is done by an iteration process which has three main components: selection of the *solution set* for *bound* calculation, and *branching*. The sequence of these may vary according to the strategy chosen for selecting the next *solution set* to process. Here the selection of next *solution set* is based on the *bound value* of the *solution sets* obtained after branching from the previous level. For each of these iterations, it is checked whether the subspace consists of a lower bound, in that case, it is compared with the current best solution thereby retaining the better of the two while pruning the other sets.

3.2.1. Branching Scheme

This step is called branching as its recursive application defines a tree structure (the *search tree*) whose *nodes* are obtained from the previous level by a *splitting* procedure *i.e.* subdivision of the solution space of the nodes into two or more subspaces to be investigated in a subsequent iteration. Since the efficiency of the method depends strongly on the node-splitting procedure and on the lower bound estimators, we start the search from a set of sorted, non-duplicate potential solutions and applied variable's sequence *inversion* of a solution and the technique can be categorized as *variable appending*. Accordingly, we have three different types of solutions space, namely *leftside_inverted*, *rightside_inverted* and *bothside_inverted*. This splitting technique provides maximum non-overlapping subsets or no overlapping subsets as shown in **Figure 5**.

3.2.2. Bounding Scheme

The next step of the proposed BB technique is a procedure that computes only the lower bounds of the *solution_set* by calculating the bounds for each of the solutions, within the given *solution_set*. This step is called bounding. The lower bounds are calculated by setting the objective function of the proposed problem based on the fitness as defined in Equations (2) and (3). The key idea of the BB algorithm is: if the *lower* bound for some tree nodes (set of candidates) A is greater than the lower bound for some other node B in the same level, then A may be safely discarded from the search. This step is called *pruning*, and is usually implemented by maintaining a global variable *m* (shared among all nodes of the tree) that records the minimum lower bound seen among all solutions examined so far. Any node whose lower bound is greater than *m* can be discarded. Otherwise, the bounding function for the subspace is calculated and compared with the current best solution.

3.2.3. Termination Criteria

The search terminates when we reach Level-(n-2), where n is the number of variables and the optimal solution is then the one recorded as "current best". Ideally the procedure stops when all nodes of the search tree are either pruned or solved. At that point, all non-pruned sub-regions will have their upper and lower bounds equal to the global minimum of the function. To check whether the solution obtained converges to the local minimum or not, we have repeated the above algorithmic steps by starting the search from a different *solution set* obtained by reversing the set of Level-1.

3.2.4. Experimentation and Result

The proposed BB algorithms is written in C and exhaustive experimentation has been done with the same set up as was done for GA based algorithm, with the same set of benchmarks. An input combinational logic circuit is first converted to BDD, the order of which is decided by the proposed algorithm while trading off area and power. The trade off is done by taking different weights for area (node count) and power (switching activities). Simulation is carried out for *n*-2 levels where *n* is the number of inputs in the circuit. The parameters taken for the experimentation purpose are as follows:

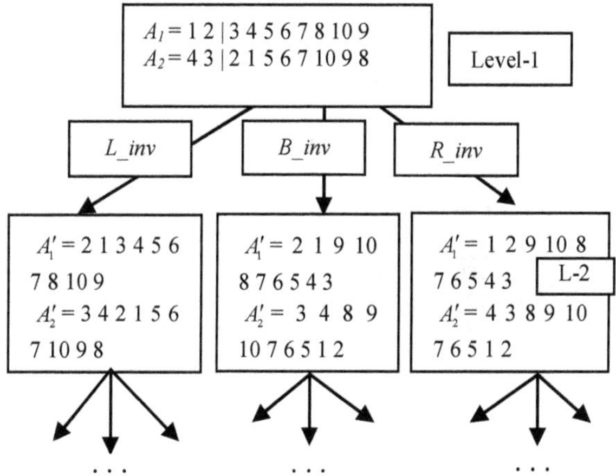

Figure 5. Branching scheme.

Solution Set size-50 for large circuits (inputs > 20) and 100 for small and medium circuits (inputs < 20)

The weights varies from 0 to 1 (0, 0.2, 0.4, 0.6, 0.8 and 1 are taken in present work). The result of experimentation for about 30 benchmark circuits taking different area and power weights has been shown in **Figure 6**. It shows the results in terms of percentage improvement in area and power against different weights. As it is clear from the bar diagram that the average power reduction is more than 78% (highest) and average saving in area is about 38.225%. It is also to be noted that even for the area weights A = 0.8 and A = 1.0, there is no negative values of switching activity, which means in almost all circuits there is a reduction in power consumption or zero reduction but no increase in power consumption. When power weight of B = 0.0, area is optimized maximally. Again, when the emphasis is mostly on power the chart shows that although we achieve highest reduction in power, but there is absolutely no control on area minimization (NC). When we give more emphasis on area, saving in power keeps on reducing, which is quite natural. Similarly, when we keep on increasing the emphasis on power, we achieve a gradual improvement in power reduction. However, we can take the best trade-off point to be at around A = 0.4 and 0.6, when both area and power reductions are considerably high and are found to be more than 30% and 70% respectively.

It is also observed that the area saving can be as high as 95.9% (with 100% area weight) and power reduction of 98.429% (with 100% power weight) for a large circuits, such as, seq and *cps*, which is quite promising. In fact, the benefit of area and power reduction is more for large circuits.

4. Convergence of the Approaches

In this section we will see the convergence of the proposed GA based and BB based approaches towards global optimum by framing an exhaustive search program and running it for a few benchmarks circuits taking all possible input (variable) orders. To minimize CPU time, we have confined our simulations to circuits having variables (inputs) less than 7. When we compare the GA based optimization results with exhaustively searched ones, we find that both GA and BB results in same area reduction for the five benchmarks circuits considered *i.e.* converges to exhaustive search. However, for power, we find that the convergence is about 1.50% to 4.44% (for A = 0.4 and B = 0.6) to optimum value. Whereas, with BB algorithm, we find the convergence of power is about 1.05% to 9.09% (for different area and power trade-offs) to optimum value. This explains that the GA based approach converges more to the optimum value than the BB based approach, thus indicating the effectiveness of the GA based approach.

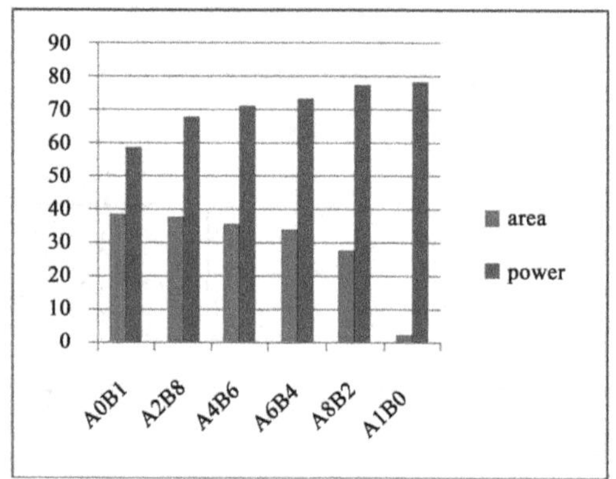

Figure 6. Bar diagram of average area and power reductions (BB based approach) for different trade-offs.

5. Comparison of Different Approaches

If we observe the results of our GA-based approach and BB approach then we find that the overall results are much better compared to the most binate sort of ordering as shown **Table 1**. Output phase assignment technique [14] for area and power minimization on the other hand can produce a maximum of 15.72% and 19.18% saving in area and power respectively. While with dynamic variable ordering as proposed in [5] and the hybrid algorithm in [9], the average area reduction is as high as 45% and 30%, respectively, compared to the initial value. However they do not take power minimization into account. We then compare the results of the proposed two algorithms, with the most recent heuristic search algorithm based on scatter search [15], for some of the benchmark circuits as shown in **Table 1**.

The average results for each of the algorithms in terms of percentage improvement in area are shown in the last row of **Table 1**. We can see that the modified BB algorithm and the GA based algorithm will be a better option when the area reduction is given the highest priority, while the scatter search approach will be preferable from the point of view of minimal computational time complexity (of the order of 0.053 hr) as shown in **Figure 7**.

6. Conclusions

Presented here two techniques for BDD optimization namely, GA based optimization and Branch and Bound based Greedy optimization. Exhaustive experimentation has been done with ISCAS93 benchmark circuits to see the effectiveness of the proposed two techniques for area and power optimization. Finally, the comparison with other established techniques such as, scatter search tech nique and dynamic variable ordering have been done and

Table 1. Percentage Improvement in Area for the Various Heuristic Approaches.

Benchmark circuits/PLA	Complexity	% improvement in Area for BB based optimization	% improvement in Area for GA based optimization	% improvement in Area for scatter search heuristics algorithm [15]	% improvement in Area for Most Binate Ordering algorithm
apex1	45	92.64204645	93.20777	81.6123	94.07568783
clip	9	64.09266409	64.09266	58.323	34.74903475
cm162a	14	58.10810811	56.75676	55.6234	43.24324324
con1	7	25	25	25.5123	0
b12	15	42	36	35.2345	14
cm163a	16	53.96825397	52.38095	52.7123	36.50793651
Cu	14	47.36842105	44.73684	45.734	1.315789474
sao2	10	44.93670886	43.67089	30.7345	37.97468354
AVERAGE		53.51452532	51.98073375	48.1625	32.73329692

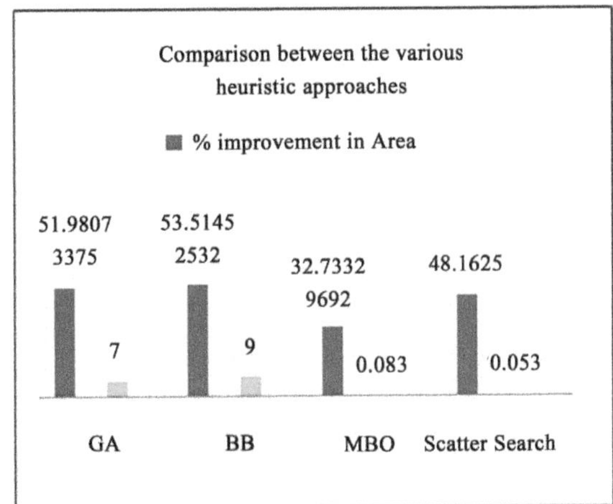

Figure 7. Comparison of various heuristic approaches.

found that the proposed two techniques are superior compared to others in fulfilling the objectives.

7. References

[1] S. Malik, A. R. Wang, R. K. Brayton and A. Sangiovarmi-Vincentelli, "Logic Verification Using Binary Decision Diagrams in a Logic Synthesis Environment," *Proceedings of International Conference on Computer-Aided Design*, Santa Clara, 7-10 November 1988, pp. 6-9.

[2] M. Fujita, H. Fujisawa and Y. Matsnnaga, "Variable Ordering Algorithms for Ordered Binary Decision Diagrams and Their Evaluation," *IEEE Transactions on Computer-Aided Design*, Vol. 12, No. 1, 1993, pp. 6-12.

[3] M. Fujita, Y. Matsmraga and T. Kakuda, "On Variable Ordering of Binary Decision Diagrams for the Application of Multi-level Logic Synthesis," *Proceedings of European Design Automation Conference*, Amsterdam, 25-28 February 1991, pp. 50-54.

[4] N. Ishiura, H. Sawada and S. Yajima, "Minimization of Binary Decision Diagrams Based on Exchange of Variables," 1991 *IEEE International Conference on Computer-Aided Design*, Santa Clara, 11-14 November 1991, pp. 472-475.

[5] R. Rudell, "Dynamic Variable Ordering for Ordered Binary Decision Diagrams," *Proceedings of the* 1993 *IEEE/ACM International Conference on Computer-Aided Design*, Santa Clara, 7-11 November 1993, pp. 42-47.

[6] H. Fujii, G. Ootomo and C. Hori, "Interleaving Based Variable Ordering Methods for Ordered Binary Decision Diagrams," *Proceedings of the* 1993 *IEEE/ACM International Conference on Computer-Aided Design*, Santa Clara, 7-11 November 1993, pp. 38-41.

[7] C. Meinel and F. Somenzi, "Linear Sifting of Decision Diagrams," *Proceedings of the* 34*th Annual Automation Conference*, Anaheim, 9-13 June 1997, pp. 202-207.

[8] B. Beate, L. Martin and W. Ingo, "Simulated Annealing to Improve Variable Orderings for OBDDs," *Proceedings of the International Workshop on Logic Synthesis*, May 1995, pp. (5-1)-(5-10).

[9] R. Drechsler and N. Göckel, "Minimization of BDDs by Evolutionary Algorithms," *International Workshop on Logic Synthesis* (*IWLS*), Lake Tahoe, 1997.

[10] M. A. Thornton, J. P. Williams, R. Drechsler, N. Drechsler and D. M. Wessels, "SBDD Variable Reordering Based on Probabilistic and Evolutionary Algorithms," 1999 *IEEE Pacific Rim Conference on Communications, Computers and Signal Processing*, Victoria, 22-24 August 1999, pp. 381-387.

[11] R. Drechsler, B. Becker, N. Göckel, "Learning Heuristics for OBDD Minimization by Evolutionary Algorithms," *Lecture Notes in Computer Science*, Vol. 1141, 1996, pp.

730-739.

[12] W. Günther and R. Drechsler, "Improving EAs for Sequencing Problems," *Proceedings of the Genetic and Evolutionary Computation Conference*, 2000.

[13] R. Drechsler, M. Kerttu, P. Lindgren and M. Thornton, "Low Power Optimization Techniques for BDD Mapped Circuits Using Temporal Correlation," *Canadian Journal of ECE*, Vol. 27, No. 4, 2002, pp. 159-164.

[14] S. Chaudhury and S. Chattopadhyay, "Output Phase Assignment for Multilevel Multi-output Logic Synthesis with Area and Power Trade-offs," 2006 *Annual IEEE India Conference*, New Delhi, 15-17 September 2006, pp, 1-4.

[15] W. N. N. Hung, X. Song, E. M. Aboulhamid and M. A. Driscoll, "BDD Minimization by Scatter Search," *IEEE transactions on Computer-Aided Design of Integrated Circuits and Systems*, Vol. 21, No. 8, 2006, pp. 974-979.

[16] P. W. C. Prasad, M. Raseen, A. Assi and S. M. N. A. Senanayake, "BDD Path Length Minimization Based on Initial Variable Ordering", *Journal of Computer Science*, Vol. 1, No. 4, 2005, pp. 520-528.

[17] M. Rice and S. Kulhari, "A Survey of Static Variable Ordering Heuristics for Efficient BDD/MDD Construction," Technical Report, 2008.

[18] P. W. C. Prasad, A. Assi, A. Harb and V. C. Prasad, "Binary Decision Diagrams: An Improved Variable Ordering using Graph Representation of Boolean Functions," *International Journal of Computer Science*, Vol. 1, No. 1, 2006, pp. 1-7.

[19] O. Brudaru, R. Ebendt and I. Furdu, "Optimizing Variable Ordering of BDDs with Double Hybridized Embryonic Genetic Algorithm," *Proceedings of 12th IEEE International Symposium on Symbolic and Numeric Algorithms for Scientific Computing*, Timisoara, 23-26 September 2010, pp. 167-173.

[20] R. Ebendt, F. Gorschwin and R. Drechsler, "Advanced BDD Minimization", Springer, New York, 2005.

8

Low Noise Phase CMOS Quadrature VCO with Superharmonic Coupling Using Cross-Couple Pair*

Seyed Reza Hadianamrei, Masoud Sabaghi, Maziyar Niyakan Lahiji, Mehdi Rahnama
Research School of National Science & Technology Research Institute (N.S.T.R.I), Tehran, Iran

Abstract

This paper aims to introduce a quadrature VCO (voltage control oscillator) which applies superharmonic coupling. The presented quadrature VCO is suitable to be used, both with 2 × subharmonic mixers, as well as 4× subharmonic mixers. It would be impossible to avoid the presence of harmonics in CMOS VCO circuits. These harmonics are in general, undesirable signals which tend to accompany the desired fundamental signal. There are common-mode nodes (similar to those in the two source nodes in a cross-coupled VCO) in deferential VCO at which higher-order harmonics are present while the fundamental is absent in essence. We can make use of these second-order harmonics which are present at the common-mode nodes of two VCO in order to implement a quadrature connection between the fundamental outputs. The technique through which this is done is called superharmonic coupling. This CMOS quadrature VCO which applies active superharmonic coupling puts an excellent performance in show, with an output power –0.942 dBm for fundamental and –9.751 dBm for subharmonic, phase noise –107.2 dBc/Hz for fundamental and –114.8 dBc/Hz at a 1MHz offset. All of circuit applied are designed and simulated by ADS, 2008.

Keywords: Quadrature VCO, Cross-Couple, Phase Noise, CMOS

1. Introduction

Oscillators are fundamental components in wireless communications systems that can be used for several applications. Communication systems that use phase shift keying modulation frequently require a pair of LO signals that are in quadrature, or 90° out-of-phase.

Quadrature VCO (voltage control oscillator) is one of the most important components in direct conversion transceivers. These VCOs are of a basic role in image-rejection techniques which are based on the appropriate phasing of the signals. Furthermore, they eliminate the immense and non-planar high-frequency filters. it also should be added that, some digital radio communication systems (e.g. GSM and DECT) in which complex digital modulation schemes are applied in order to reduce the signal bandwidth to the possible minimum level, need quadrature VCO [1]. In all the applications mentioned above, departures from the quadrature phase or the existence of an amplitude imbalance between the two signals leads to a damaging effect on the performance of the whole system. There are a number of techniques which can be applied to produce quadrature signals.

1) The first technique is a standard VCO which a RC-CR phase-shift network follows. If the real values of R and C are not accurate, it may result in errors in the quadrature which, in turn, necessitate compensation of some form [2].

The complete LO input circuit with balun and phase shifters is shown in **Figure 1** with relative phase shifts indicated at the output for clarity. Using a reference 0°

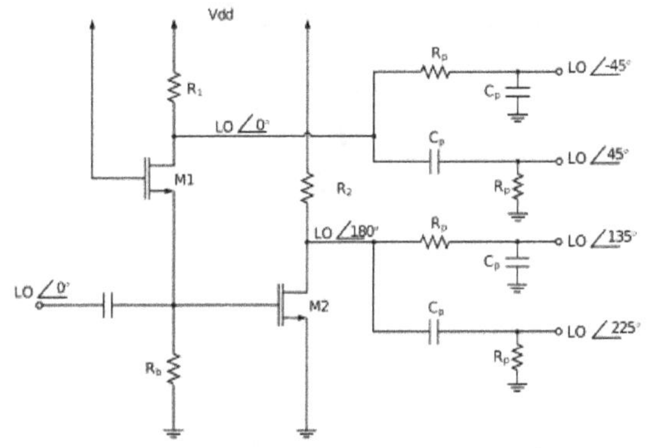

Figure 1. RC-CR phase-shift network.

*This work was supported in part by N.S.T.R.I Tehran, Iran.

phase of an LO input signal, the phase shift at the outputs in **Figure 1** would be –45°, 45°, 135°, 225° from top output to bottom relative to the input phase.

2) The second technique which can be applied is a VCO which runs at double frequency and a digital frequency divider based on flip-flops follows it. Here, the sections of the circuit which work at the double frequency may turn into a speed or power bottleneck.

3) Another technique is employing two cross-coupled VCO's [3].

4) Using active polyphase filters such as ring oscillator designs is another technique in this list. In four-delay stage ring oscillators, for example, taps at diametrically opposite points yield quadrature phases [4].

An alternative method for obtaining quadrature VCO based on the differential coupling at the second harmonics of two differential VCOs is introduced in this paper. As a matter of fact, if s 180-degrees phase shift occurs between the second harmonics of two VCOs, their basic frequency components will be in quadrature states.

2. Design of a 4.8 GHz VCO

The cross-coupled VCO is the most frequently used microwave VCO topology in CMOS technology. We can prepare a model of a LC VCO with the capacitor and inductor, parallel with a resistor to simulate the losses in the tank, and also a negative resistance to simulate the active device. In order to produce the negative resistance to compensate for the losses in the LC tank, employing a cross-coupled differential pair, as shown in **Figure 2**, would be a choice. The resistance, R_{in} looking into the cross-coupled pair is obtained by:

$$R_{in} = -\frac{2}{g_m} \tag{1}$$

g_m is the transconductance of each of the BJTs in the cross-coupled pair.

Therefore, by choosing a proper device size and biasing, the value of negative resistance necessary to counteract, we are able to find the losses in the tank.

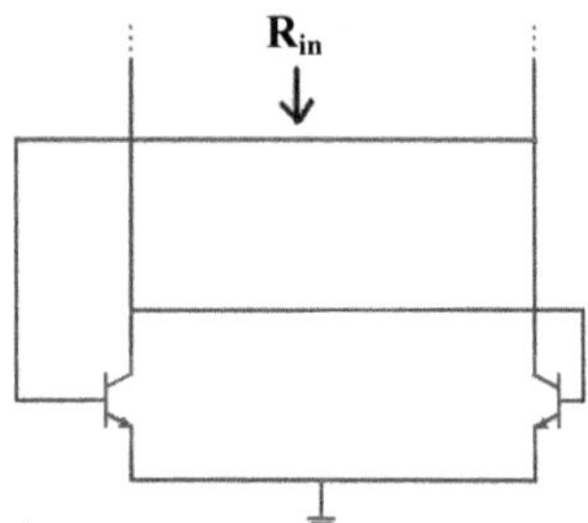

Figure 2. Negative resistance generated from cross-coupled BJT.

Figure 3 illustrates a frequently employed LC VCO circuit using the cross coupled differential pair. A moderately low supply voltage is possible to be used for this implementation because there are only two levels of transistors. However, it calls for two inductors, which require considerable chip area.

The VCO topology illustrated in **Figure 3** was applied (with BJT transistor) in [5].

CMOS technology was applied to design fundamental C band VCO for the present experiment. The Diode varactor illustrated in **Figure 2** allows the tuning of frequency.

Simulation Results for Cross-Coupled VCO

The signal output power was about 0.942 dBm and the phase noise at a 1 MHz offset was –107.2 dBc/Hz.

Figure 4 illustrates the phase noise graph. **Figure 5** illustrates the output power spectrum and **Figure 6** illustrates Time-domain VCO outputs.

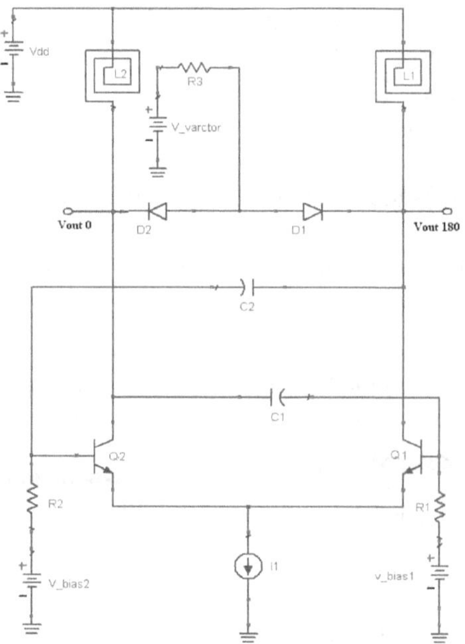

Figure 3. Cross-coupled BJT VCO.

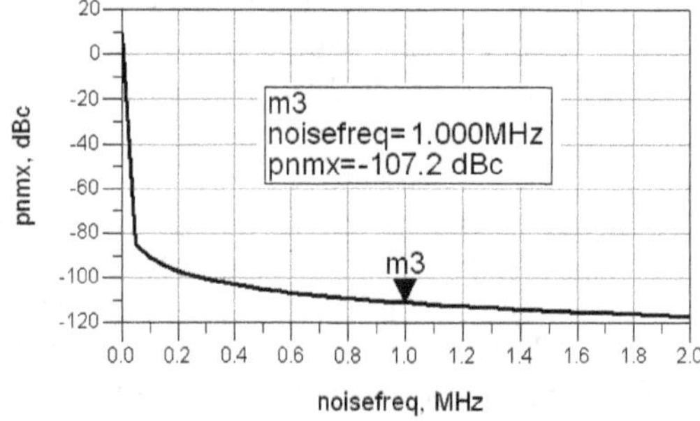

Figure 4. Phase noise 4.8 GHz VCO.

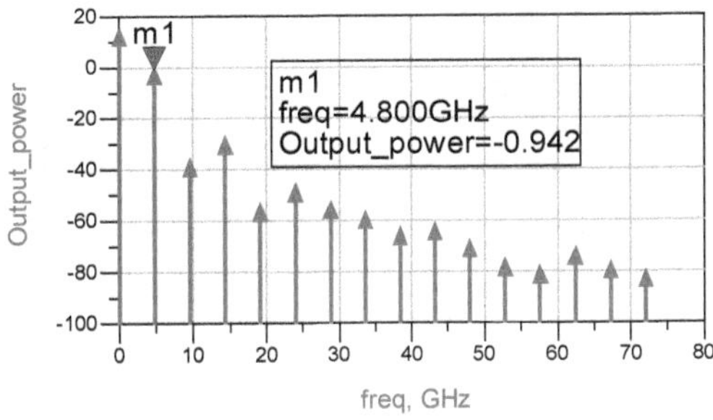

Figure 5. Output power VCO.

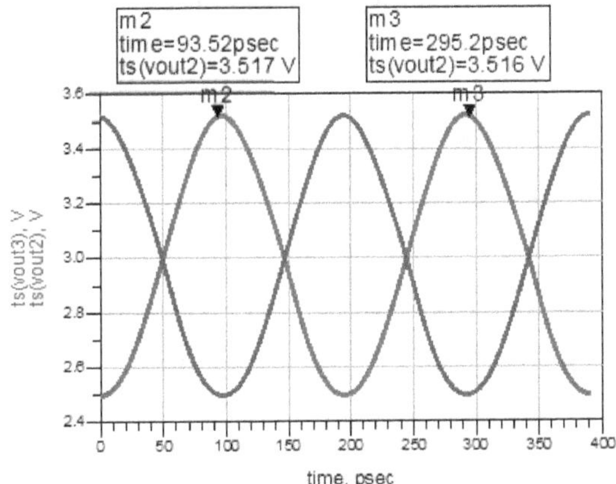

Figure 6. Time-domain VCO outputs.

3. Concept of the Quadrature VCO

In most CMOS processes, resistors are particularly of large tolerances. Hence, this method may result in a low degree of accuracy in the quadrature signals that generated. In order to generate quadrature signals, another method is to employ a digital frequency divider which follows a VCO running at the frequency two times larger than the fundamental frequency [6]. There are some essential restrictions against using this technique at high frequencies for it calls for a VCO operating at double the desired frequency. A third frequent technique is to force two VCOs to run in quadrature through applying coupling transistors running at the fundamental frequency [7]. The problem with this technique is a trade-off between quadrature accuracy and phase noise which is due to the effects the coupling circuit imposes on the oscillation frequency. In order to overcome this problem, we may take advantage of realizing a quadrature VCO through superharmonic coupling. As shown in **Figure 7(a)**, quadrature signals are produced at the fundamental frequency by using differential coupling at the common-mode nodes where the second harmonic is predominant. In order to implement the coupling of the second harmonic with a 180° phase shift, the on-chip transformer has been inverted [8-10] (**Figure 7(b)**).

The method of superharmonic coupling implements a 180° connection between the even-ordered harmonics of the two VCO circuits, and this happens while both passive and active superharmonic coupling circuits are achievable. The performance of the two individual deferential VCOs, as alongside with the coupling network will determine the performance of a quadrature VCO which applies the superharmonic coupling topology. This results in an anti-phase relationship between the second-order harmonics at the common-mode nodes.

4. Proposed Quadrature VCO

A frequently method used for implementing a CMOS differential LC VCO is applying a cross-coupled pair for generating the negative resistance needed for compensating for the losses in the tank. Hence, by choosing the proper device size and biasing, we are able to realize the negative resistance needed to counteract the losses in the tank. The core quadrature VCO circuit investigated in this work is shown in **Figure 8**. It is made of two cross-coupled VCOs connected through a cross coupled pair. It has been shown that the phase noise of the VCO can be enhanced notably by including cross-coupled inductor above the cross-coupled NPN transistors, due to the higher transconductance and faster switching speed of the corresponding structure [10]. We can find the oscillation frequency for each VCO via the common formula for finding the resonant frequency of an LC tank, in which L is the value of the on-chip spiral inductor and C is the total capacitance at the tank nodes. The inductors employed in this circuit of the capacitance less than 1.1 nH. The overall capacitance, including the lumped capacitor, and adding the parasitic capacitance was 0.925 pF which provided oscillation at 4.8 GHz.

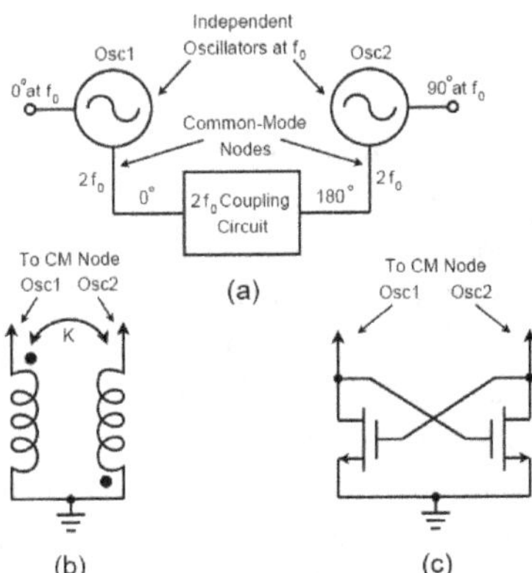

Figure 7. (a) Superharmonic coupling of the second harmonic to enforce quadrature at the fundamental; (b) Coupling using an inverting transformer; (c) Coupling using a cross-coupled pair.

The network which is employed to implement the 180° phase difference in the second-order harmonics is a vital component of the quadrature VCO. This anti-phase association is the factor which generates the quadrature phase relationship at the fundamental frequency. Convenient common-mode nodes which are used for coupling the second harmonic are the common source nodes in each of the cross-coupled differential pairs, which are signified by CM1 and CM2 in the comprehensive VCO circuit schematic illustrated in **Figure 8**. DC blocking capacitors were used so that transistors N5-N6 could be biased for optimal coupling. Owing to the fact that any practical use of a VCO requires connecting its output to other circuitry, buffers are required to be employed in order to guarantee that loading does not disrupt the oscillations. For each of the four outputs we have used source follower buffers that we were able to measure the VCO using equipment with 50 Ω input impedances. The 180° and 270° outputs were terminated on-chip with 50 Ω loads and the 0° and 90° were linked to CPW pads for on-chip inquiring.

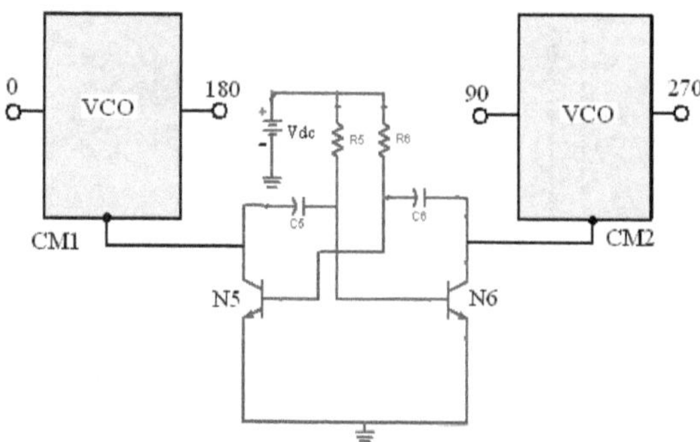

Figure 8. Schematic quadrature VCO.

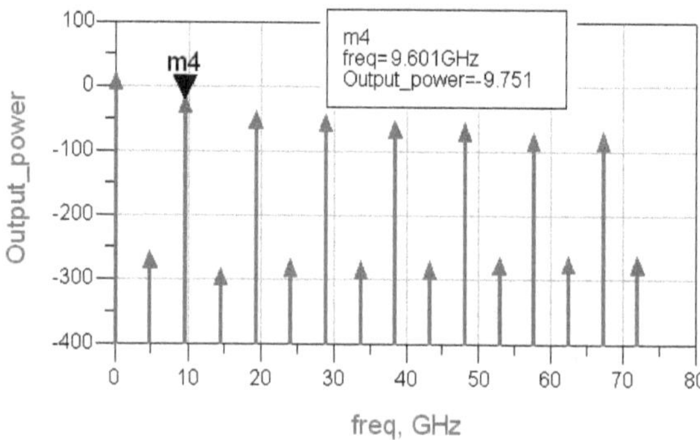

Figure 9. Output power quadrature VCO.

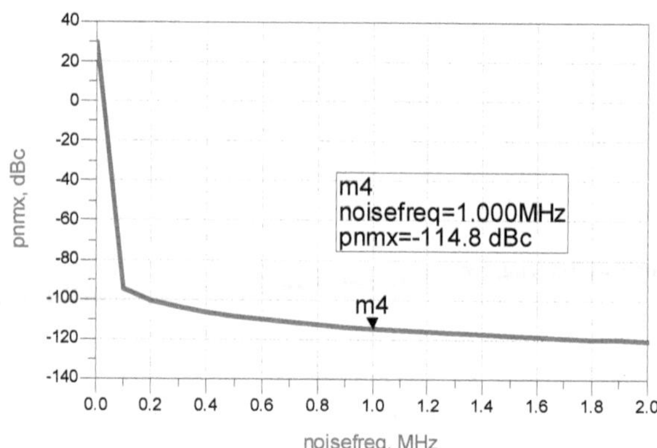

Figure 10. Phase noise quadrature VCO.

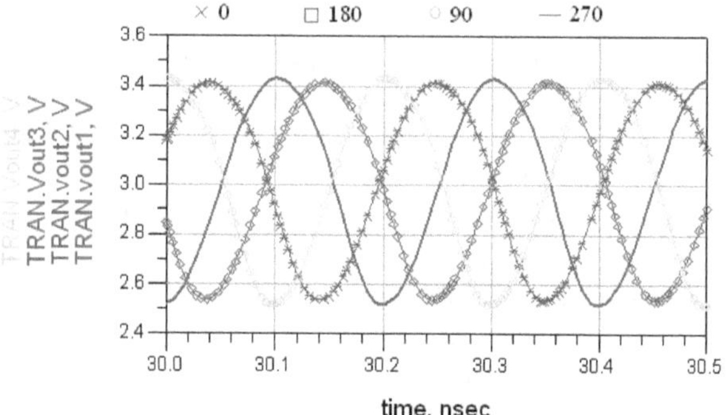

Figure 11. Time-domain Quadrature VCO.

Simulation Results for Quadrature Cross-Coupled VCO

In Quadrature VCO at subharmonic frequency (9.6 GHz) the signal output power was approximately –9.751 dBm and the phase noise at a 1 MHz offset was –114.8 dBc/Hz.

Figure 9 shows spectrum of output power **Figure 10** shows Graph of phase noise. And **Figure 11** shows Time-domain VCO outputs. **Table 1** shows result of fundamental and subharmonic VCO. **Table 2** shows result of compare with other VCO designs.

5. Conclusions

This paper represents a CMOS quadrature VCO which was designed at 4.8 GHz by applying superharmonic coupling. This technique focuses on coupling the second-order harmonics between two VCO and obliges an anti-phase connection, which, in turn, compels a quadrature relationship at the fundamental. In order for this coupling with a 180° phase shift to be implemented, a cross-coupled differential NPN pair was employed at the common-mode nodes. This CMOS quadrature VCO which employs an active superharmonic coupling demonstrates a very fine performance with an output power of –0.942 dBm for fundamental and –9.751 dBm for subharmonic, phase noise of –107.2 dBc/Hz for fundamental and –114.8 dBc/Hz at a 1 MHz offset. it creates the 180° phase shift in the second-order harmonics by using a cross-coupled differential pair.

Table 1. Compare fundamental and subharmonic VCO.

	Fundamental	Subharmonic
Freq	4.8 GHz	9.6 GHz
Output Power	–0.942 dBm	–9.751 dBm
Phase Noise	–107.2 dBc/Hz	–114.8 dBc/Hz

Table 2. Compare with other VCO designs.

Reference	f_c(GHz)	Phase noise(dBc/Hz)	Device
[11]	8.7	–110	SiGe BiCMOS
[12]	2.2	–111	CMOS0.35 μm
[13]	11.02	–86.83	CMOS RF
[14]	1.6	–114.7	CMOS 0.18° μm
This Work	9.6	–114.8	CMOS 0.18° μm

6. References

[1] A. A. Abidi, "Direct-Conversion Radio Transceivers for Digital Wmmunications," *IEEE Journal of Solid-State Circuits*, Vol. 30, No. 12, 1995, pp. 1399-1410.

[2] J. Craninckx and M. S. J. Steyaert, "A Fully Integrated GaAs DCS-1800 Frequency Synthesizer," *IEEE Journal of Solid-State Circuits*, Vol. 33, No. 12, 1998, pp. 2054-2065.

[3] A. Rofougaran, J. Rael, M. Rofougaran and A. Abidi, "A 900 MHz CMOS LC-Oscillator with Quadrature Outputs," *IEEE International Solid-State Circuits Conference*, San Francisco, February 1996, pp. 392-393.

[4] P. Vancorenland and M. Steyaert, "A 1.57 GHz Fully Integated Very Low Phase Noise Quadrature VCO," *VLSI* 2001 *Symposium on Circuits, Digest of Technical Papers*, Kyoto, 14-16 June 2011, pp. 111-114.

[5] Z. Liu, E. Skadas and R. Evans, "A 60 GHz VCO with 6 GHz Tuning Range in 130 nm Bulk CMOS," *IEEE Journal of Solid-State Circuits*, Vol. 1, 2008, pp. 209-211.

[6] J. P. Maligeorgos and J. R. Long, "A Low-Voltage 5.1 - 5.8 GHz Imagereject Receiver with Wide Dynamic Range," *IEEE Journal of Solid-State Circuits*, Vol. 35, No. 12, 2000, pp. 1917-1926.

[7] A. Rofougaran, *et al.*, "A Single-Chip "A-Voltage 5.1-5.8 GHz Imagereject 900-MHz spread-Spectrum Wireless Transceiver in 1-μmm CMOS-Part I: Architecture and Transmitted Design," *IEEE Journal of Solid-State Circuits*, Vol. 33, 1998, pp. 515-534.

[8] C. Meng, Y. W. Chang and S. C. Tseng, "4.9-GHz Low-Phase-Noise Transformer-Based Superharmonic-Coupled GaInP/GaAs HBT QVCO," *IEEE Microwave and Wireless Component Letters*, Vol. 16, No. 6, 2006, pp. 339-341.

[9] J. Cabanillas, L. Dussopt, J. Lopez-Villegas and G. Rebeiz, "A 900 MHz Low Phase Noise CMOS Quadrature Oscillator," 2002 *IEEE Radio Frequency Integrated Circuits Symposium*, Seattle, 2-4 June 2002, pp. 63-66.

[10] S. Gierkink, S. Levantino and R. Frye, C. Samori and V. Boccuzzi, "A Low-Phase-Noise 5-GHz GaAs Quadrature VCO Using Superharmonic Coupling," *IEEE Journal of Solid-State Circuits*, Vol. 38, No. 7, 2003, pp. 1148-1154.

[11] X. Y. Geng and F. F. Dai,, "An x-Band Transformer-Coupled Varactor-Less Quadrature Current-Controlled Oscillator in 0.18 μm SIGE BICMOS," *IEEE Journal of Solid-State Circuits*, Vol. 45, No. 9, 2010, pp. 1669-1677.

[12] A. Thanachayanont and M. krairiksh, "Implementation of an rf CMOS Quadrature lc Voltage-Controlled Oscillator Based on the Switched Tail Transistor Topology," *World SciNet, Journal of Circuit System And Computer*, Vol. 20, No. 7, 2010, pp. 1280-1285.

[13] Y. Wu, M. Ismail and H. Olsson, "An 8.7 - 13.8 GHz Transformer-Coupled Varactor-Less Quadrature VCO," *Proceeding of IEEE International Symposium Circuit and System*, Geneva, May 2000, pp. 149-152.

[14] A. Tang, F. Yuan and E. Lawkrairiksh "CMOS Active Transformers and Their Applications in Voltage-Controlled Quadrature Oscillators," *Analog Integrated Circuits and Signal Processing,* Vol. 62, No. 1, 2009, pp. 83-90.

9

A State Variable Method for the Realization of Universal Current-Mode Biquads

Raj Senani[1], Kasim Karam Abdalla[2], Data Ram Bhaskar[2]
[1]*Division of Electronics and Communication Engineering, Netaji Subhas Institute of Technology, Delhi, India*
[2]*Department of Electronics and Communication Engineering, Faculty of Engineering and Technology, Jamia Millia Islamia, New Delhi, India*

Abstract

A state variable method of converting single-resistance-controlled-oscillators (SRCO), into universal current-mode biquad (offering realizations of all the five standard filter functions namely, low pass, band pass, high pass, notch and all pass) has been highlighted. The workability of the exemplary implementation of the derived current-mode universal biquad has been demonstrated by PSPICE simulation results based upon 0.35 μm technology. It is expected that the proposed method can be applied to other SRCOs to generate other multifunction filter structures.

Keywords: Analog Electronics, Circuit Theory and Design, Current Mode Circuits, Universal Biquads, Current Conveyors

1. Introduction

Current-mode universal filters employing current conveyors (CC) and their many variants have been extensively investigated during the past two decades for instance, see [1-19] and those cited therein. Current-mode universal filters can be broadly classified in two categories namely the single input multi-output (SIMO)-type ([11-18]) and the multiple-input-single-output (MISO)-type ([5,10,14,19]). It may be mentioned that while most of the proposers of current-mode (CM) universal filters have come up with a specific topology rather than disclosing any general method of systematic derivation of such filters. It may also be noted that while a general method for realizing SIMO-type CM universal filters has been known earlier [20], to the best knowledge of the authors, any systematic method of synthesizing MISO-type CM universal biquads has not been reported explicitly in the open literature yet. The purpose of this paper is to fill this void.

The main object of this paper is to present a state variable method by which a given single resistance controlled oscillator (SRCO) can be re-configured as a multiple-input-single-output (MISO)-type current-mode (CM) universal biquad. Although the method to convert a SRCO into universal current-mode biquad proposed here might appear simple but it has not been explicitly published in the open literature earlier.

2. The Proposed Method

Although the proposed method is quite general and can be applied to any given SRCO using any kind of active element, we illustrate the method by choosing an earlier proposed SRCO as an example using fully differential second generation current conveyor (FDCCII) as an active element.

It may be recalled that a FDCCII and its applications for analog VLSI were introduced by El-Adawy, Soliman and Elwan in [1]. FDCCII has since then been used in realizing various signal processing and signal generation circuits for instance, see [1-6]. Simultaneously, improved implementations of FDCCII have also been advanced; see [7] and [8].

Some time back, Chang, Al-Hashimi, Chen, Tu and Wan [2] presented two novel single-resistance-controlled-oscillators (SRCO) using a single FDCCII and all grounded passive elements, which is advantageous for integrated circuit implementation.

Consider now one of the CM SRCOs from [2] (Figure 1 therein). The condition of oscillation (CO) for this circuit is given by $R_1 = R_3$ and frequency of oscillation

(FO) is given by $\omega_0 = 1/\sqrt{R_2 R_3 C_1 C_2}$.

With all its y-input terminals unconnected, the circuit can be redrawn as shown in **Figure 1(a)**.

Note that with Y_1 connected to $Z+$ and Y_3 connected to $Z-$ with Y_2 and Y_4 connected to ground, one obtains the SRCO of **Figure 1** of [2].

To synthesize a filter providing independent control of ω_0 (say, by the resistor R_2) and independent control of bandwidth (ω_0 / Q_0) (say, by the resistor R_1), one must have a transfer function $\frac{I_{out}}{I_{in}} = \frac{N(s)}{D(s)}$ with its characteristic polynomial $D(s)$ given by

$$D(s) = s^2 + \left(\frac{\omega_0}{Q_0}\right) s + \omega_0^2 = s^2 + \frac{s}{R_1 C_2} + \frac{1}{C_1 C_2 R_2 R_3} \quad (1)$$

From the above, the characteristic equation of the circuit (assuming zero input) is given by

$$s^2 + \frac{s}{R_1 C_2} + \frac{1}{C_1 C_2 R_2 R_3} = 0 \quad (2)$$

It can be easily worked out that assuming that the circuit to be synthesized has to have two capacitors and three resistors only, if the voltages across the assumed capacitors C_1 and C_2 are taken as x_1 and x_2 respectively

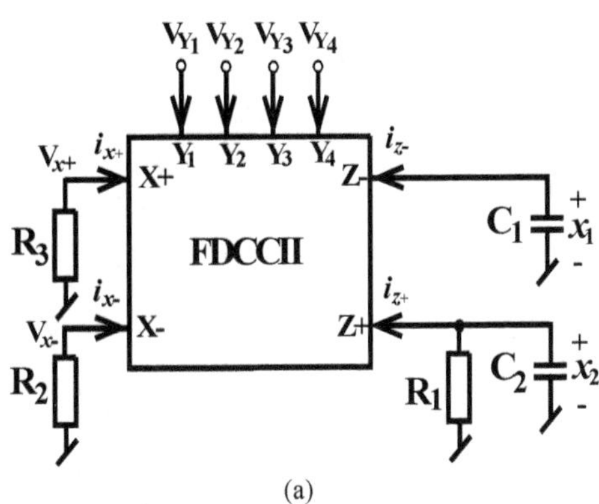

(a)

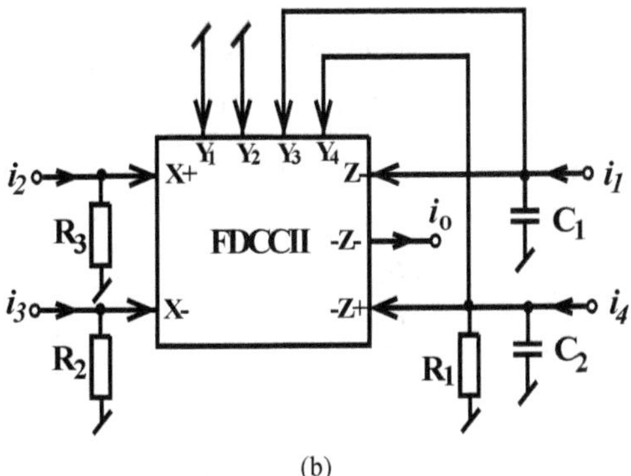

(b)

Figure 1. (a) Circuit arrangement with un-committed *y*-inputs of FDCCII, derived from SRCO of [2]; (b) An exemplary MISO-type universal CM biquad.

such a circuit should be characterized by the following matrix state equation

$$\begin{bmatrix} \frac{dx_1}{dt} \\ \frac{dx_2}{dt} \end{bmatrix} = \begin{bmatrix} 0 & \frac{1}{C_1 R_2} \\ -\frac{1}{C_2 R_3} & -\frac{1}{C_2 R_1} \end{bmatrix} \begin{bmatrix} x_1 \\ x_2 \end{bmatrix} = [A] \begin{bmatrix} x_1 \\ x_2 \end{bmatrix} \quad (3)$$

so that the consequent characteristic equation

$$det\{s[I] - [A]\} = 0 \quad (4)$$

would, indeed, result in the characteristic Equation (2).

Equation (3) can now be re-arranged as follows:

$$C_1 \frac{dx_1}{dt} = \frac{x_2}{R_2} \quad (5)$$

$$C_2 \frac{dx_2}{dt} = -\frac{x_1}{R_3} - \frac{x_2}{R_1} \quad (6)$$

The above equations can be considered to be the node equations (NE) of the circuit to be synthesized. In view of the FDCCII characterization, which is given by the equations: $i_{Yk} = 0,\ k = 1 - 4$; $v_{X+} = (v_{Y1} - v_{Y2} + v_{Y3})$, $v_{X-} = (-v_{Y1} + v_{Y2} + v_{Y4})$, $i_{-Z+} = -i_{X+}$, $i_{Z-} = i_{X-}$, the circuit shown in **Figure 1(a)** (where terminal Z+ is replaced by –Z+) is characterized by the following equation

$$\begin{bmatrix} \frac{dx_1}{dt} \\ \frac{dx_2}{dt} \end{bmatrix} = \begin{bmatrix} 0 & 0 \\ 0 & -\frac{1}{C_2 R_1} \end{bmatrix} \begin{bmatrix} x_1 \\ x_2 \end{bmatrix} + \begin{bmatrix} -\frac{1}{C_1 R_2} & \frac{1}{C_1 R_2} & 0 & \frac{1}{C_1 R_2} \\ -\frac{1}{C_2 R_3} & \frac{1}{C_2 R_3} & -\frac{1}{C_2 R_3} & 0 \end{bmatrix} \begin{bmatrix} v_{Y1} \\ v_{Y2} \\ v_{Y3} \\ v_{Y4} \end{bmatrix} \quad (7)$$

where voltages across capacitors C_1 and C_2 are chosen as state variables x_1 and x_2 respectively. If the various Y-terminal voltages of FDCCII are chosen as:

$$v_{Y1} = 0,\ v_{Y2} = 0,\ v_{Y3} = x_1,\ v_{Y4} = x_2 \quad (8)$$

then it can be verified that resulting state equations will be same as in Equations (5) and (6).

After having made the above *state variable assignment* and by appropriately connecting the required external terminals of the FDCCII in accordance with the requirements in Equation (8), a non-autonomous circuit with multiple-inputs and single-output (MISO) is subsequently created by augmenting the circuit with four external current input signals i_1, i_2, i_3 and i_4 and extending the FDCCII to have one additional Z+ output terminal (henceforth to be referred as multiple output FDCCII (MO-FDCCII)). The output current of the resulting circuit (shown in **Figure 1(b)**) is found to be:

$$i_0 = \frac{-i_3\left(s^2 + \frac{s}{C_2R_1}\right) + (i_2 + i_4)\frac{s}{C_2R_2} - i_1\frac{1}{C_1C_2R_2R_3}}{s^2 + \frac{s}{C_2R_1} + \frac{1}{C_1C_2R_2R_3}} \quad (9)$$

Note that the D(s) of (9) is exactly same as (1).

The five filter responses can be realized from the circuit of **Figure 1(b)** as follows: Low pass (LP): making $i_2 = i_3 = i_4 = 0$ and taking $i_1 = i_{in}$. Band pass (BP): making $i_1 = i_3 = 0$ and taking one of i_2 or i_4 as i_{in}. High pass (HP): making $i_1 = 0$ and taking i_2 or $i_4 = i_3 = i_{in}$[1] along with $R_2 = R_1$. Notch: making i_2 or $i_4 = i_1 = i_3 = i_{in}$ along with $R_2 = R_1$. All pass (AP): making $i_1 = i_2 = i_3 = i_4 = i_{in}$ along with $R_2 = R_1$.

The various parameters of the realized filters are given by

$$\omega_0 = \sqrt{\frac{1}{C_1C_2R_2R_3}}; \ \text{BW} = \frac{1}{C_2R_1}; \ Q_o = R_1\sqrt{\frac{C_2}{C_1R_2R_3}} \quad (10)$$

$$H_0 = \begin{cases} \frac{R_1}{R_2} \text{ for BP} \\ -1, \text{ for LP / HP / AP / Notch} \end{cases} \quad (11)$$

where ω_0 = cut-off frequency in radian/sec, BW = bandwidth, Q_o = quality factor and H_0 = gain. In the last three cases, having fixed the bandwidth (BW) by R_1, ω_0 can be independently controlled by R_3 while in the first two cases ω_0 (with R_2 and/or R_3) and BW (by R_1) are independently adjustable.

3. Analysis Incorporating Nonideal Parameters

Considering the non-ideal MO-FDCCIIs sources, two parameters, α and β (where $\alpha = (1-\varepsilon_i)$ and $\beta = (1-\varepsilon_v)$, with $\varepsilon_i(\varepsilon_i \langle\langle 1)$ and $\varepsilon_v(\varepsilon_v \langle\langle 1)$ denote the current and voltage tracking errors respectively) need to be considered. Incorporating these sources of error, we have the following non-ideal characterization of the MO-FDCCII:

$$\begin{bmatrix} V_{X+} \\ V_{X-} \\ I_{-Z+} \\ I_{Z-} \end{bmatrix} = \begin{bmatrix} 0 & 0 & \beta_{11} & -\beta_{12} & \beta_{13} \\ 0 & 0 & -\beta_{21} & \beta_{22} & \beta_{24} \\ -\alpha_{01} & 0 & 0 & 0 & 0 \\ 0 & \alpha_{02} & 0 & 0 & 0 \end{bmatrix} \begin{bmatrix} I_{X+} \\ I_{X-} \\ V_{Y1} \\ V_{Y2} \\ V_{Y3} \\ V_{Y4} \end{bmatrix} \quad (12)$$

Taking Equation (12) into consideration, the non-ideal expression for the output current is given by (13)

Considering above, the non-ideal expressions for ω_o, Q_o and H_0 are found to be:

$$\omega_o = \sqrt{\frac{\alpha_{01}\alpha_{02}\beta_{13}\beta_{24}}{C_1C_2R_2R_3}}; \ Q_o = R_1\sqrt{\frac{C_2\alpha_{01}\alpha_{02}\beta_{13}\beta_{24}}{C_1R_2R_3}} \quad (14)$$

The non-ideal gains and realization conditions (wherever applicable) are modified as follows:

$H_{0LP} = -1$ (remains unaffected by non-ideal voltage/current gains)

$$H_{0BP} = \alpha_{01}\alpha_{02}\beta_{24}\frac{R_1}{R_2}.$$

$H_{0HP} = -\alpha_{02}$; where the condition of realization modifies to $\alpha_{01}\beta_{24}R_1 = R_2$.

$H_{0Notch} = -1$, if $\alpha_{02} = 1$; realization condition being same as in *HP*.

$H_{0AP} = -1$, if $\alpha_{01} = \alpha_{02} = \beta_{24} = 1$ and $R_2 = R_1$.

From the above, the active and passive sensitivities of the non-ideal ω_0 and Q_o are given by

$$S_{C_1}^{\omega_o} = S_{C_2}^{\omega_o} = S_{R_2}^{\omega_o} = S_{R_3}^{\omega_o} = -\frac{1}{2},$$

$$S_{\alpha_{01}}^{\omega_o} = S_{\alpha_{02}}^{\omega_o} = S_{\beta_{13}}^{\omega_o} = S_{\beta_{24}}^{\omega_o} = \frac{1}{2}, \ S_{R_1}^{\omega_o} = 0,$$

$$S_{C_2}^{Q_o} = S_{\alpha_{01}}^{Q_o} = S_{\alpha_{02}}^{Q_o} = S_{\beta_{13}}^{Q_o} = S_{\beta_{24}}^{Q_o} = \frac{1}{2},$$

$$S_{C_1}^{Q_o} = S_{R_2}^{Q_o} = S_{R_3}^{Q_o} = -\frac{1}{2}, \ S_{R_1}^{Q_o} = 1 \quad (15)$$

From Equation (15) the active and passive sensitivities of ω_o and Q_o are found to be in the range $-\frac{1}{2} \le S_x^F \le 1$, and the circuit, thus, enjoys low sensitivities.

$$i_0 = \frac{-\alpha_{02}i_3\left(s^2 + \frac{s}{C_2R_1}\right) + \alpha_{02}\beta_{24}(\alpha_{01}i_2 + i_4)\frac{s}{C_2R_2} - i_1\frac{\alpha_{01}\alpha_{02}\beta_{13}\beta_{24}}{C_1C_2R_2R_3}}{s^2 + \frac{s}{C_2R_1} + \frac{\alpha_{01}\alpha_{02}\beta_{13}\beta_{24}}{C_1C_2R_2R_3}} \quad (13)$$

[1]Although additional circuitry e.g. a multiple-output current follower will be needed at the front end of the proposed universal CM filter circuits to realize the conditions of the kind $i_4 = i_3 = i_{in}$, the total amount of the hardware required, even after including such additional circuitry, will be lesser than the three-FDCCII-based universal filter structures of [1].

4. Simulation Results

To verify the validity of the proposed configuration, current mode filters have been simulated in SPICE by making a CMOS MO-FDCCII based upon the FDCCII from [3] (Figure 3 therein) which is shown here in **Figure 2**.

PSPICE simulation implementation was based upon a CMOS MO-FDCCII in 0.35 μm technology where the aspect ratios of the MOSFETs are shown in **Table 1**.

The CMOS MO-FDCCII was biased with DC power supply voltages V_{DD} = +1.5 V, V_{SS} = −1.5V, I_B = 35 μA, I_{SB} = 100 μA, V_{bp} = 0.2 V, and V_{bn} = −0.66 V. To achieve the filters with f_o = 1 MHz, the component values chosen were $R_1 = R_2 = 0.71\ \text{k}\Omega$, R_3 = $1.39\ \text{k}\Omega$, and $C_1 = C_2 = 0.16\ nF$. The frequency responses of LPF, BPF, HPF, Notch and APF are shown in **Figure 3**. Thus, a very good correspondence between theoretical values and PSPICE simulations is observed.

To test the input dynamic range of the proposed filters, the simulation of the band-pass filter as an example has been done for a sinusoidal input signal of f_o = 1 MHz. **Figure 4** shows that the input dynamic range of the filter extends up to amplitude of 300 μA without significant distortion. The dependence of the output harmonic distortion on the input signal amplitude is illustrated in **Figure 5**.

Although FDCCII-based filters have been proposed by many authors as [1,3-6], with the exception of [1] (Figure 11 therein), [6] (Figure 2 therein), all others deal with voltage-mode filters.

In view of this, a comparison with MISO-type CM universal biquads using FDCCIIs presented recently in [1] (Figure 11 there in) and [6] (Figure 2 therein) is now in order. When compared with the circuit of [1], the circuit of **Figure 2** has the advantage of using only one active building block (one FDCCII) as against three FDCCII's in biquads proposed in [1] and use of all grounded passive elements (AGPE) which is an attractive feature for IC implementation. On the other hand, when compared with the circuit of [6] (Figure 2 there in) our circuit has

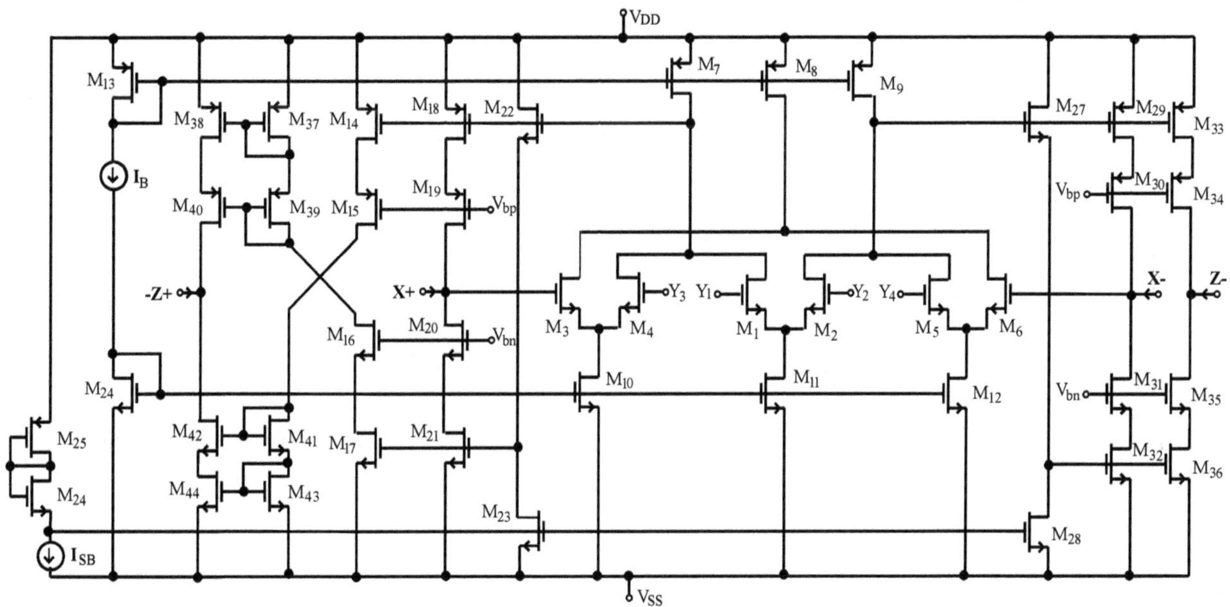

Figure 2. CMOS realization of the FDCCII.

Table 1. Aspect ratios of MOSFETs.

MOS transistors	W/L
M_1 - M_6	0.7/0.35
M_7, M_8, M_9, M_{13}	15/1.2
M_{10}, M_{11}, M_{12}, M_{24}	0.7/0.35
M_{14}, M_{15}, M_{18}, M_{19}, M_{25}, M_{29}, M_{30}, M_{33}, M_{34}, M_{37}, M_{38}, M_{39}, M_{40}	20/0.35
M_{16}, M_{17}, M_{20}, M_{21}, M_{26}, M_{31}, M_{32}, M_{35}, M_{36}, M_{41}, M_{42}, M_{43}, M_{44}	25/0.35
M_{22}, M_{23}, M_{27}, M_{28}	0.35/0.35

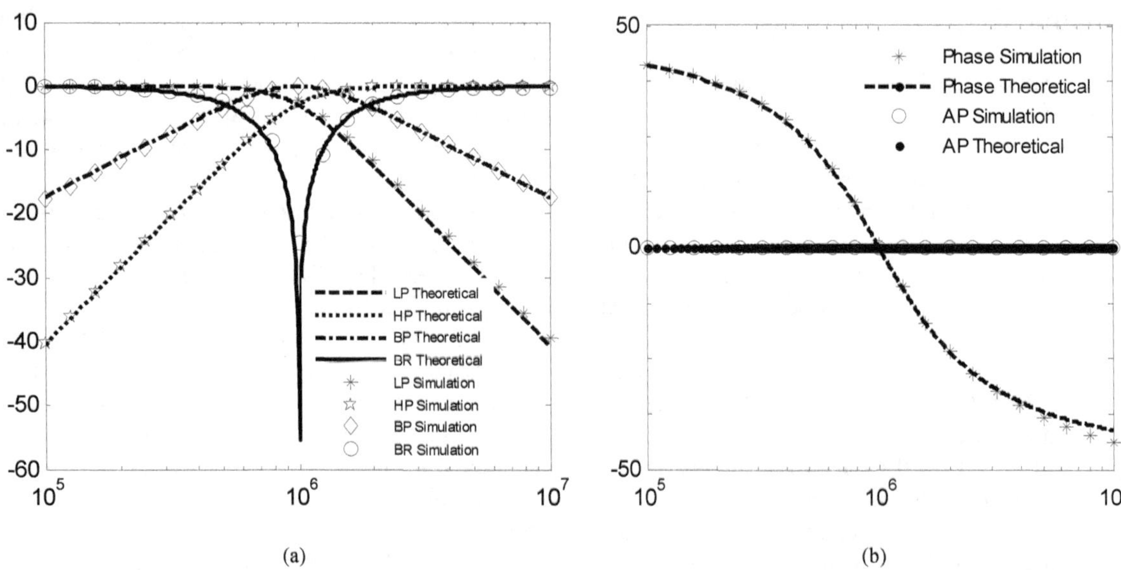

(a) (b)

Figure 3. PSPICE simulation results. (a) Gain response of LPF, BPF, HPF and Notch. (b) Gain and phase response of APF.

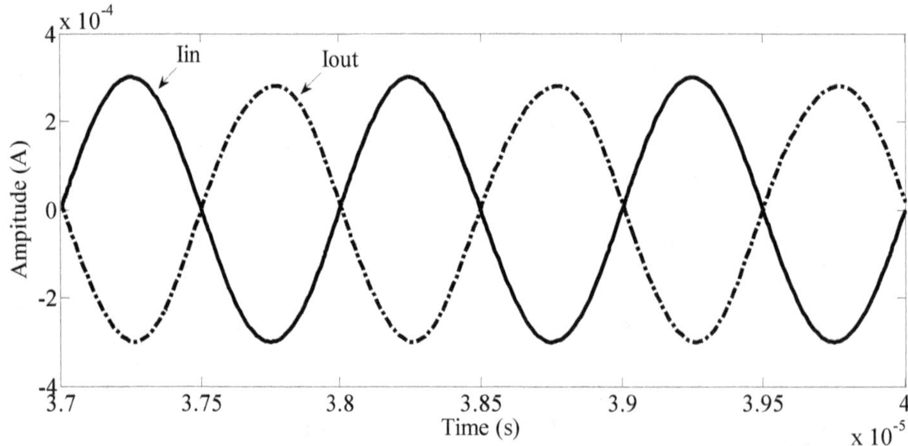

Figure 4. Input and output waveforms of the band-pass filter of the proposed circuit for 1 MHz sinusoidal input current of 300 μA.

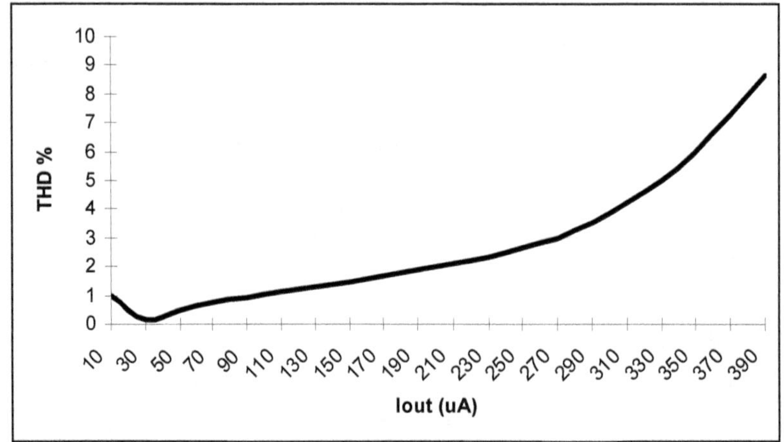

Figure 5. Dependence of output current total harmonic distortion on input current amplitude for the band-pass filter realized from the proposed configuration.

the advantages of independent tunability of BW or Q_o which is not feasible in the quoted circuit of [6] which also needs two outputs to implement APF. Our FDCCII has nine terminals in contrast to the FDCCII in [6] which has eleven terminals to implement the biquad filter.

The comparison with [9] and [10] is now in order, The circuit of [9] (Figure 8 there in) is also current-mode MISO type and uses five grounded passive elements but used two FDCCIIs (the first has ten terminals and the other has nine terminals to implement the biquad filter) and not independent tunability of BW or Q_o.

The circuit of [10] although uses one FDCCII (eleven terminals to implement the biquad filter in current –mode and voltage mode) but has one floating resistance and needs two outputs to implement LPF and APF.

5. Concluding Remarks

A method has been presented by which the FDCCII-based CM SRCOs of [2] can be reconfigured as MISO-type universal biquads offering realizations of all the five standard filter functions also, thereby enhancing their capabilities. One exemplary biquad resulting from the application of the proposed method was presented and its workability was demonstrated by SPICE simulation using an FDCCII implementation in 0.35 μm CMOS technology.

The methodology presented here could also be applied to all other SRCOs published earlier using other kinds of active building blocks thereby giving rise to a large number of new MISO-type CM universal biquads, some of which may possess some interesting features. This, however, is left for further investigations.

6. Acknowledgements

The authors wish to thank an anonymous reviewer for his constructive feedback, which has been helpful in improving the presentation. The material presented here has its origin in an earlier unpublished report[2] of Analog Signal Processing Research Lab of NSIT, where part of this work was performed.

7. References

[1] A. A. El-Adawy, A. M. Soliman and H. O. Elwan, "A Novel Fully Differential Current Conveyor and Its Applications for Analog VLSI," *IEEE Transactions on Circuits and Systems II: Analog and Digital Signal Processing*, Vol. 47, No. 4, April 2000, pp. 306-313.

[2] C. M. Chang, B. M. Al-Hashimi, H. P. Chen, S. H. Tu and J. A. Wan, "Current Mode Single Resistance Controlled Oscillators Using Only Grounded Passive Elements," *Electronics Letters*, Vol. 38, No. 39, 2002, pp. 1071-1072.

[3] H. P. Chen, "Single FDCCII-Based Universal Voltage-Mode Filter," *International Journal of Electronics and Commun* (AEU), Vol. 63, No. 9, 2009, pp. 713-719.

[4] F. Gür and F. Anday, "First-Order Allpass Sections-Based High-Input Low-Output Impedance Voltage-Mode Universal Filter Using FDCCIIs," *Proceeding of 18th European Conference on Circuit Theory and Design*, Seville, 27-30 August 2007, pp. 428-431.

[5] C. M. Chang and H. P. Chen, "Single FDCCII-Based Tunable Universal Voltage-Mode Filter," *Circuits Systems Signal Processing*, Vol. 24, No. 2, 2005, pp. 221-227.

[6] C. M. Chang, B. M. Al-Hashimi, C. L. Wang and C. W. Hung, "Single Fully Differential Current Conveyor Biquad Filters," *IEE Proceeding of Circuits Devices System*, Vol. 150, No. 5, 2003, pp. 394-398.

[7] S. A. Mahmoud, M. A. Hashiesh and A. M. Soliman, "Low-Voltage Digitally Controlled Fully Differential Current Conveyor," *IEEE Transactions on Circuits and Systems I*, Vol. 52, No. 10, 2005, pp. 2055-2064.

[8] H. A. Alzaher, "CMOS Highly Linear Fully Differential Current Conveyor," *Electronics Letters*, Vol. 40, No. 4, 2004, pp. 214-216.

[9] F. Gür and F. Anday, "Simulation a Novel Current-Mode Universal Filter Using FDCCIIs," *Analog Integrated Circuits and Signal Processing*, Vol. 60, 2009, pp. 231-236.

[10] C. N. Lee and C. M. Chang, "Single FDCCII-Based Mixed-Mode Biquad Filter with Eight Outputs," *International Journal of Electronics and Communication* (AEU), Vol. 63, No. 9, 2009, pp. 736-742.

[11] R. Senani and A. K. Singh, "A New Universal Current-Mode Biquad Filter," *Frequenz*, Vol. 56, 2002, pp. 55-59.

[12] R. Senani, A. K. Singh and V. K. Singh, "New Tunable SIMO-Type Current-Mode Universal Biquad Using Only Three MOCCs and All Grounded Passive Elements," *Frequenz*, Vol. 57, 2003, pp. 160-161.

[13] J. W. Horng, "Current Conveyor Based Current-Mode Universal Biquadratic Filter," *Journal of the Chinese Institute of Electrical Engineering*, Vol. 9, 2002, pp. 147-150.

[14] H. Y. Wang and C. T. Lee, "Versatile Insensitive Current Mode Universal Biquad Implementation Using Current Conveyors," *IEEE Transactions CAS-II. Analog and Digital Signal Processing*, Vol. 48, 2001, pp. 409-413.

[15] M. Siripruchyanun and W. Jaikla, "Cascadable Current-Mode Biquad Filter and Quadrature Oscillator Using

[2]R. Senani, "Re-Configuring FDCCII-Based SRCOs into Universal Current mode Biquads", TCASII ID-2267, November 14, 2003 (Unpublished).

DO-CCCIIs and OTA," *Circuits Systems and Signal Processing*, Vol. 28, No. 1, 2009, pp. 99-110.

[16] E. Yuce and S. Minaei, "Universal Current-Mode Filters and Parasitic Impedance Effects on the Filter Performances," *International Journal of Circuit Theory and Applications*, Vol. 36, No. 2, 2008, pp. 161-171.

[17] S. Minaei, "Electronically Tunable Current-Mode Universal Biquad Filter Using Dual-X Current Conveyors," *Journal of Circuits, Systems, and Computers*, Vol. 18, No. 4, 2009, pp. 665-680.

[18] C.-M. Chang, B. M. Al-Hashimi and J. N. Ross, "Unified Active Filter. Biquad Structures," *IEE Proceeding of Circuits Devices System*, Vol. 151, No. 4, 2004, pp. 273-277.

[19] R. Senani, "New Universal Current Mode Biquad Employing All Grounded Passive Components But Only Two DOCCs," *Journal of Active and Passive Electronic Devices*, Vol. 1, 2006, pp. 281-288.

[20] R. Senani, "A Simple Approach of Deriving Single-Input-Multiple-Output Current Mode Biquad Filters," *Frequenz*, Vol. 50, No. 5-6, 1996, pp. 124-127.

10

Study and Enhanced Design of RF Dual Band Bandpass Filter Validation and Confirmation of Experimental Measurements

Mohamed Mabrouk, Leila Bousbia

CIRTACOM and ISETCOM of Tunis, University of Carthage, Tunis, Tunisia

Abstract

Dual band bandpass filter is designed and optimized for RF wireless applications. The performances of that RF dual band filter are improved especially parameters describing the insertion loss, return losses and rejection. Dual band bandpass filter using stub loaded resonators is designed and characterized. Theoretical results are compared with experimental data. This comparison shows that the magnitude of reflection coefficient S_{11} from ADS^{TM} simulation is better than 28.0 dB, and the insertion loss S_{21} is less than 0.5 dB. The two rejections are also better than 32.0 dB. The simulated results also show that two central frequencies are located at desired 1.82 and 2.95 GHz. Comparison of measured and simulated results shows frequency drift. The main reason for this frequency shifting is due to some uncertainties. These are obviously due to geometrical and physical parameters H and εr respectively of Duroid substrate used during design and measurements.

Keywords: RF Filters, Dual Bandpass, Effective Permittivity, Physical and Geometrical Parameters

1. Introduction

RF circuits with a dual pass band operation are required by modern wireless communication systems [1]. For example, the RF transceiver length (TX/RX) for second generation GSM and third-generation WCDMA mobile communications must be able to receive and transmit 900 MHz and 1900 MHz signals. Also 2.4 GHz and 5.2 GHz bands are two bands operated by high-speed wireless LANs [1,2]. The band pass filter is necessary to generate two or more transmission frequency bands, in particular dual-band filters, as they have an essential role in transmit-receive systems [2]. RF filters have particularly an important role for signals filtering, rejection and isolation between parts in transceivers systems (TX/RX). Filters have the characteristic to be frequency selective devices for transmitting and attenuating signal in desired frequency ranges [3]

Many different ways are considered to design dual-band bandpass filters such combination of two filters operating on two different bandwidths [4] and using dual band stepped impedances resonator [5] or dual band stubs resonators [6]. Quasi lumped with open loop band pass filters operating at different frequency bands [7] and using square loop dual mode resonators [8] are also used for designing this type of filters. Small insertion loss, low return loss and high rejection band are the desired characteristics of a good filter. The design of this kind of filter is considered using electromagnetic (EM) simulators. The studied filter was simulated using IE3D^{TM} [6], and in this paper we report our ADS^{TM} simulation optimized results which are very close to the experimental measurements. ADS^{TM} software has been used successfully many times for simulation design filter so that the resulting performances meet the microwave filter specifications. Simulated results confirm that two central frequencies are located at desired values 1.82 GHz and 2.95 GHz.

2. Design Description of Band Pass Filter

The studied filter is composed of two ring-resonators loaded with two open stubs. **Figure 1** shows the physical layout of the dual band pass filter using uniform microstrip lines. This filter consists of two microstrip open loops. Two open circuited stubs are attached [6] at the center of the respective microstrip lines. The total length of each resonator is around half wave length ($\lambda_g/2$).

The design parameters dimensions are chosen [6] as following: W = 1.2 mm; W_1 = 1.5 mm; W_2 = 0.9 mm; L=11.2 mm; L_1 = 6.7 mm; g_1 = g_2 = 0.3 mm. The structure of open-loop resonators filter with center frequency of 1.82 GHz and 2.94 GHz is designed on an RT Duroid 6006 substrate with a thickness H = 0.635 mm ± 0.0254 and a relative dielectric constant ε_r = 6.15 ± 0.15 [9].

3. Analysis and Comparison of Simulation with Measurement Results

Figures 2 and **3** illustrate simulated and measured S_{21} and S_{11} parameters respectively of our studied dual band filter.

Simulated results show that two central frequencies are located at the desired values 1.82 GHz and 2.95 GHz, and a small frequency shifting is observed. Thus, the ADS^{TM} simulation results are shifted of –5.0 MHz, (1.825 GHz instead 1.830 GHz), and of +13.0 MHz (2.953 GHz instead 2.940 GHz). To understand the main reason for this frequency shifted aberration which is certainly due to the uncertainties on the guided wave length λ_g, we have highlighted the following relationships:

$$\lambda_g = \frac{c}{F\sqrt{\varepsilon_{eff}}} \quad (1)$$

where F is the center frequency of the filter and c is the light velocity. The effective dielectric constant is depending on relative permittivity ε_r and ratio W/H between the width W of the transmission line and the thickness H of the substrate which is given in the following forms. The RT Duroid 6006 laminate substrate is available with relative permittivity ε_r value ε_r = 6.15 ± 0.15.

It's known that the Equation (2) shows below the effective permittivity ε_{eff} of the microstrip structure, used

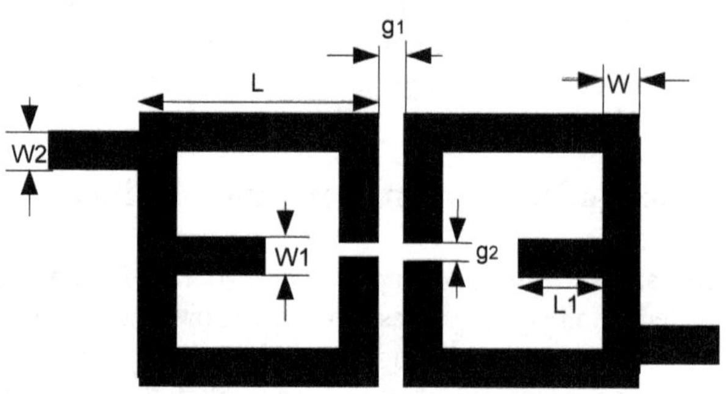

Figure 1. Layout of dual band filter.

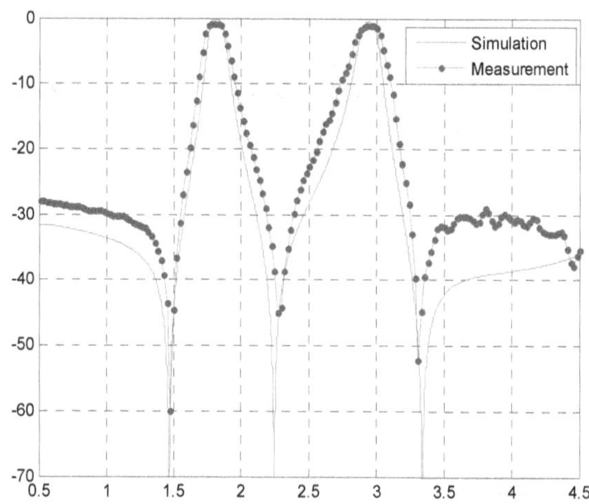

Figure 2. Simulated and measured S_{21} parameters of dual band filter.

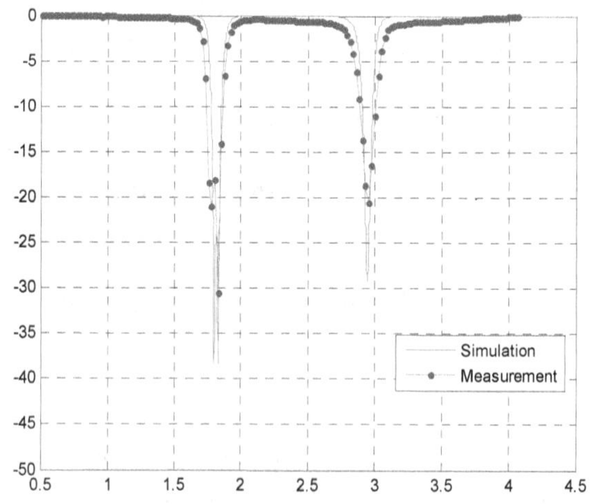

Figure 3. Simulated and measured S_{11} parameters of dual band filter.

in our design, depends on the relative dielectric constant ε_r, which is one of physical parameters of Duroid substrate, and the guided wave length λ_g also depends on ε_{eff}, so the resonant frequencies of our filter are closely depending on λ_g according to the Equation (1).

For W/H ≥ 1, the empirical relationship of the effective permittivity is summarized below [10-12]:

$$\varepsilon_{eff} = \frac{\varepsilon_r + 1}{2} + \frac{\varepsilon_r - 1}{2}\left[1 + 12\frac{H}{W}\right]^{-\frac{1}{2}} \quad (2)$$

Because of the uncertainty on the dielectric relative permittivity ε_r of Duroid substrate recalled previously (in §2), we can evaluate ε_{eff} as following:

$$4.476 \leq \varepsilon_{eff} \leq 4.553 \quad (3)$$

$$76 \text{ mm} \leq \lambda_g \leq 78 \text{ mm} \quad (4)$$

Thus, we can deduce that the first resonant frequency F_{C1} is the following:

$$1.79 \text{ GHz} \leq F_{C1} \leq 1.84 \text{ GHz} \quad (5)$$

For the second frequency F_{C2}, we can also do the same line of argument as following:

$$47 \text{ mm} \leq \lambda_g \leq 48 \text{ mm} \quad (6)$$

That means F_{C2} is:

$$2.94 \text{ GHz} \leq F_{C2} \leq 3.06 \text{ GHz} \quad (7)$$

These equations confirm the first explicit reason for this frequency shifting is due to the uncertainty on the first physical parameter, *i.e.* the dielectric relative permittivity ε_r of Duroid substrate.

In the same line of argument, we can see that the uncertainty on the substrate thickness H can lead the following limits for the first frequency F_{C1}:

$$4.47 \leq \varepsilon_{eff} \leq 4.507 \quad (8)$$

$$77 \text{ mm} \leq \lambda_g \leq 78 \text{ mm} \quad (9)$$

$$1.810 \text{ GHz} \leq F_{C1} \leq 1.850 \text{ GHz} \quad (10)$$

For the second frequency F_{C2}:

$$4.47 \leq \varepsilon_{eff} \leq 4.507 \quad (11)$$

$$47 \text{ mm} \leq \lambda_g \leq 48 \text{ mm} \quad (12)$$

$$2.910 \text{ GHz} \leq F_{C2} \leq 3.0 \text{ GHz} \quad (13)$$

Here again, it's confirmed that the uncertainty on thickness H can obviously contribute to the frequency shifting that we observed, and the differences between center frequencies are surely due to the cumulative effects of both uncertainties on ε_r and H. We have made a comparative study of our simulation results and experimental measurements obtained and provided by our partner Zhang. Nevertheless, these differences that we observed on the frequency values, between our simulations and the measurements of our partner Zhang, are remaining very small. Thus, the difference of 5.0 MHz on the first resonance frequency (1.830 GHz) between our simulation results and the measurements of Zhang is about 0.27%, while the difference of 150.0 MHz observed (1.680 GHz instead 1.830 GHz) between the first simulation results of Zhang and the experimental measurements is about 8.0%. The difference of 13.0 MHz on the second resonance frequency (2.94 GHz) between our simulation results and the measurements of Zhang is about 0.44%, and the difference of 130.0 MHz observed by Zhang (2.81 GHz instead 2.94 GHz) is about 4.4%. The little disagreement we have obtained with the experimental measurements confirms our predictions, and our indepth analysis shows that we can notably improve some characteristics of the studied filter with going in detail and making further development, consequently of the global performances become enhanced.

Regarding the insertion and return losses, **Figure 4** shows simulated and measured insertion loss S_{21} and return loss S_{11} parameters respectively of our dual band filter. We obtained S_{21} significantly lower than 0.28 dB instead of 0.9 dB measured at F_{C1}, and 0.4 dB instead of 1.1 dB measured at F_{C2} respectively. Our simulated S_{21} results depicted on **Figure 2** are up to 10.0 dB better at 4.0 GHz than the measurements. **Figure 3** also shows that our simulated results of return loss S_{11} are up to 8.0 dB better at 4.0 GHz than the measurements, and the obtained return loss S_{11} is better than 28.0 dB.

Moreover, the simulated filter using two open loop ring resonators shows better rejections than the measured ones, 31.0 dB instead of 28.0 dB measured at 0.5 GHz and 37.0 dB instead of 31.0 dB measured at 4.5 GHz. **Table 1** shows comparative results.

4. Conclusions

We have studied and enhanced the design of dual band bandpass filter for RF and wireless applications. The performances of RF dual-band filter are improved especially parameters describing the insertion loss, return losses and rejections. We have obtained a good agreement between our simulations and experimental results. Insertion loss S_{21} lower than 0.5 dB and return loss S_{11} better than 28.0 dB were obtained from ADS simulations. The rejections are also better than 32.0 dB. Simulated results show that two central frequencies are located at desired 1.820 and 2.950 GHz. Comparison of measured and simulated results shows frequency shift. This is obviously due to the uncertainties on the geometrical and

Table 1. Comparison of Zhang measurements [5] and our simulations.

	Measurement Results of Zhang [5]	Our results
Resonance Frequency F_{C1}	1. 830 GHz	1.825 GHz
Resonance frequency F_{C2}	2.940 GHz	2.953 GHz
Band Pass 1	9.4%	6.7%
Band Pass 2	7.5%	4.37%
Insertion losses at F_{C1}	0.9 dB	0.28 dB
Insertion losses2 at F_{C2}	1.1 dB	0.4 dB
Return loss at F_{C1}	24.0 dB	29.25 dB
Return loss at F_{C2}	20.0 dB	28.81 dB
Rejection at 0.5 GHz	28.0 dB	31.64 dB
Rejection at 4.0 GHz	31.0 dB	38.64 dB

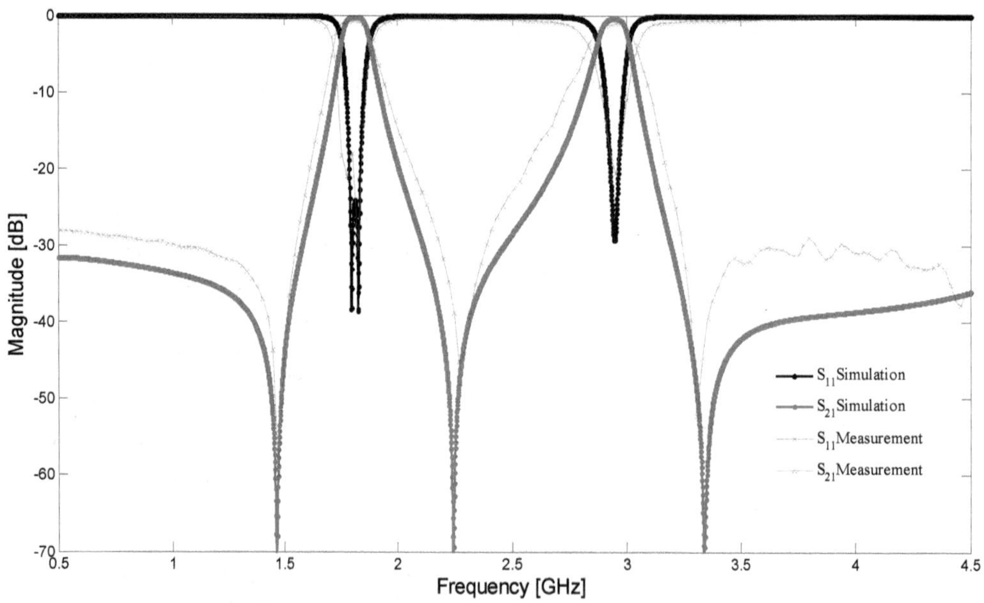

Figure 4. Simulated and measured S_{11}, S_{21} parameters of dual-band filter.

physical parameters H and ε_r respectively of Duroid substrate used during design and measurements.

5. Acknowledgements

The authors would like to acknowledge and extend their gratitude to our partner Xiu Yin Zhang, Associate Professor with the School of Electronic and Information Engineering (South China University of Technology, Guangzhou, 510641, China) who has carried out and provided the experimental measurements of studied prototype of filter.

6. References

[1] C. Y. Chen, C. Y. Hsu and H. R. Chuong, "Design of Miniature Planar Dual Band Filter Using Dual-Feeding Structures and Embedded Resonators," *IEEE Microwave and Wireless Components Letters*, Vol. 16, No. 12, 2006, pp. 669-671.

[2] S. F. Chang, Y. H. Jeng and J. L. Chen, "Dual-Band Step Impedance Band Pass Filter for Multimode Wireless LANs," *Electronic Letters*, Vol. 40, No. 1, 2004, pp. 38-39.

[3] I. C. Hunter, L. Billonet, B. Jarry and P. Guillon, "Microwave Filters—Applications and Technology," *IEEE Microwave Theory and Techniques Transactions*, Vol. 50, No. 3, March 2002, pp. 794-805.

[4] H. Miyake, S. Kitazawa, T. Ishizaki, T. Ymanda and Y. Nagatomi, "A Miniaturized Monolithic Dual-band Filter Using Ceramic Lamination Technique for Dual Mode Portable Telephones," *IEEE MTT-S International Microwave Symposium Digest*, 8-13 June 1997, Vol. 2, pp. 789-792.

[5] J. T. Kuo, T. H. Yeh and C. Yeh, "Design of Microstrip Bandpass Filters with a Dual Pass Band Response," *IEEE Microwave Theory and Techniques Transactions*, Vol. 53, No. 4, April 2005, pp. 1331-1337.

[6] X. Y. Zhang, J. X. Chen and Q. Xue, "Dual-band Band Pass Filters Using Stub-Loaded Resonators," *IEEE Microwave and Wireless Components Letters*, Vol. 17, No. 8, 2007, pp. 583-585.

[7] A. Balalem, W. Menzel and A. Omar, "Quasi Lumped Open Loop Suspended Stripline Bandpass Filters," 36th *European Microwave Conference*, Manchester, 10-15 September 2006, pp. 568-571.

[8] A. Balalem, J. Machac and A. Omar, "Dual-band Bandpass Filter by Using Square Loop Dual Mode Resonator," *International Journal of Microwave and Optical Technology*, Vol. 50, No. 6, June 2008, pp. 1567-1570.

[9] "RT/duroid® 6006/6010LM High Frequency Laminates," 1998. http://www.rogerscorp.com/documents/612/acm/RT-duroid-6006-6010-laminate-data-sheet

[10] M. V. Schneider, "Microstrip Lines for Microwave Integrated Circuits," *The Bell System Technical Journal*, Vol. 48, No. 5, 1969, pp. 1421-1444.

[11] H. A. Wheeler, "Transmission Line Properties of a Strip on a Dielectric Sheet on a Plane," *IEEE Microwave Theory and Techniques Transactions*, Vol. 25, No. 8, 1977, pp. 631-647.

[12] K. C. Gupta, *et al*., "Computer-Aided Design of Microwave Circuits," Artech House, Dedham, 1981, pp. 131-134.

11

Polymorphic Computing: Definition, Trends, and a New Agent-Based Architecture

David Hentrich, Erdal Oruklu, Jafar Saniie

Department of Electrical and Computer Engineering, Illinois Institute of Technology Chicago, Illinois, USA

Abstract

Polymorphic computing is widely seen as next evolutionary step in designing advanced computing architectures. This paper presents a brief history of reconfigurable and polymorphic computing, and highlights the recent trends and challenges. A novel polymorphic architecture featuring programmable memory event triggers and a new concept of control agents is proposed. This architecture can provide dynamic load balancing, distributed control, separated memory and processing fabrics, configurable memory blocks, and task-optimized computation.

Keywords: Polymorphic Computing, Reconfigurable Computing, Agents, Processing Fabric

1. Introduction

Microprocessor performance has advanced at a staggering pace during the past two decades. This can be attributed to:

1) Circuit architectural improvements,
2) Scaling of transistor sizes down, and
3) Scaling of clock frequency up.

Historically, each of the categories has contributed equally to the general performance increase [1]. Unfortunately, the rate of improvement in all of these areas is slowing or showing signs of slowing. Continual innovations in these areas are required to maintain the pace of improvement.

Polymorphic computing is a circuit architectural improvement technique that promises to improve overall computing performance. This work presents a definition of polymorphic computing, a brief history of the field of polymorphic computing, a summary of the current trends, a set of views on the current state of the field, and a novel polymorphic architecture.

2. Definition and History of Polymorphic Computing

The definition of a polymorphic computer is a computing machine that can dynamically arrange the underlying hardware computing architecture model in both time and space to match the computational demands of the moment. **Figure 1** shows how polymorphic computing sits in the set of all types of computation.

General computing is the set of all possible types of computation (*i.e.* any physical system that has a set of inputs and outputs). *Static computing* is the subset of general computing where the program (transfer function) is fixed in a device. Examples of static computing are simple NAND circuits, ASICs, and computers where the program is ROM'ed. On the other hand, *programmable computing* is composed of the set of computing devices where the program (transfer function) is intentionally changeable after manufacturing time. The programs may be hardware-based and/or software-based. *Reconfigurable computing* is the proper subset of general computing where the hardware configuration can be changed after manufacturing time. PLDs and FPGAs are the best examples of reconfigurable computing. *Polymorphic computing* is the proper subset of reconfigurable computing that includes devices that can reconfigure their hardware in time and space during runtime. FPGAs that can be configured only at startup time are reconfigurable computing devices, but not polymorphic computing devices. However, FPGAs that can be partially configured during runtime are both reconfigurable and polymorphic computing devices.

The history of polymorphic computing begins with the history of reconfigurable computing. The earliest thoughts for the creation of a reconfigurable computer were from Gerald Estrin of UCLA in 1960 [2]. His idea was to create a computer where the hardware could be

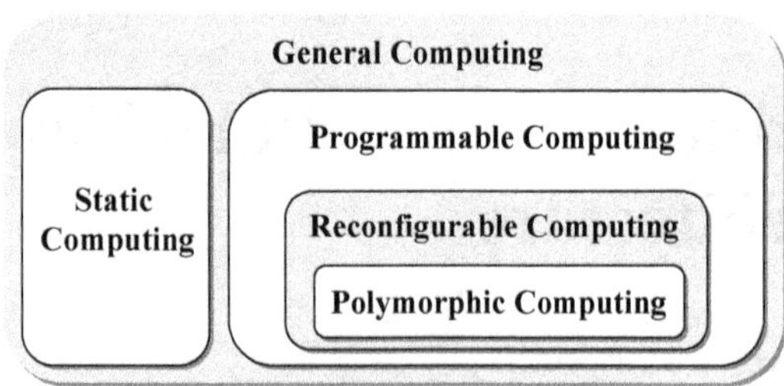

Figure 1. Categories of computing.

reconfigured to match the computational demands of the program. (In those days, a single computer filled an entire room and a single processor inhabited one or more equipment racks.) Research work on reconfigurable computing continued at UCLA under Estrin's leadership through the 1960s and 1970s [3]. Estrin's idea was about 40 years before its time and pre-dates the invention of the microprocessor.

The industrial origins of reconfigurable computing lie in the creation of programmable logic devices (PLDs) in the 1970s. These early devices were simply fixed arrays of AND and OR gates where the connections could be configured (usually just once) after manufacturing time. The key ideas that emerged from PLDs were that hardware could be configured by the users rather than the manufacturer and that the configuration of the circuits could be generated using software. PALASM and ABEL are early examples of the languages and tools for generating custom circuits in PLDs [4].

The next big advance in reconfigurable computing was the invention of the field programmable logic array (FPGA) in 1984 by Ross Freeman (one of the founders of Xilinx, Inc.) [5]. The important innovations were:

1) a programmable signal routing fabric,

2) a flexible logic cell that could perform any logic function,

3) arranging the logic cells in a tiled manner, and

4) configuration of the configurable logic at device start-up time.

Freeman's seminal observation was that the transistor density penalties of configurable logic devices would be more than offset by the transistor manufacturing density increases described by Moore's law and the efficiencies realized in circuit design effort. FPGAs are the general template for reconfigurable computing and polymorphic computing devices.

Polymorphic computing is the next logical step in the advancement of reconfigurable computing. Essentially, the hardware architecture can be deliberately modified during runtime to improve performance. The performance improvements all come from exploitations of parallelization (coarse-grained and/or fine-grained parallelism). A general trend (but not a rule) is that polymorphic computers are similar to FPGAs with small microprocessors in the place of configurable logic blocks.

In the late 1990's and early 2000's, DARPA funded several promising polymorphic computing architectures: Raw, Smart Memories, TRIPS, and MONARCH. Of these, Raw and MONARCH have transitioned to commercial products.

The Raw architecture was developed at MIT and is a replicated series of identical tiles arranged in a grid [6] [7]. Each tile contains a programmable compute processor and programmable network interfaces. Of the four DARPA sponsored projects, Raw most resembles an FPGA with full processors in the place of logic blocks. A primary contribution of the architecture was to keep critical wire lengths small since the length of wires is not scaling down as quickly as transistor geometries and wire resistance increases as the wires get smaller [8]. This was accomplished by keeping the individual processors small and strictly limiting the network interfaces to only point-to-point connections between adjacent tiles. A company called Tilera now offers Raw architecture chips commercially. Thus far, the Tilera chips have seen success in network switches.

Smart Memories is a polymorphic computing architecture from Stanford University [9,10]. Each tile contains four processors. Each individual processor is paired with a private memory fabric that can be configured as standard addressable memory, cache, streaming memory, and (in a later version of the design) transactional memory [11]. Different combinations of these configurations are available simultaneously. The primary contribution of this project was the notion that memories, as well as processing units, can be configured to exploit parallelism to improve performance.

TRIPS is a polymorphic computing architecture from the University of Texas at Austin [12-14]. Its primary contributions were showing that a dataflow architecture [15] can be used as the basis of a polymorphic computer, showing how to implement a single processor in a fundamentally parallel fashion, and demonstrating that a von Neumann instruction set can co-exist with a dataflow instruction set. Dataflow instruction set architectures are an idea from the mid-1970's that allows data to be executed upon as soon as it is available. It inherently supports parallel execution. Dataflow is a concept that is still ahead of its time. It promises vast parallelization of programs, but no practical implementation of a dataflow machine has yet fully emerged.

MONARCH is a combination of the University of Southern California's Data IntensiVe Architecture (DIVA) RISC processor system [16-18] and Raytheon's Field Programmable Compute Array (FPCA) [19-21]. The FPCA is essentially a systolic array of arithmetic and memory units, and is the portion of the architecture that makes MONARCH a polymorphic computer. MONARCH's primary contribution was the demonstration that a polymorphic computing fabric can be based on a simpler execution unit than a full microprocessor (like the other three DARPA funded architectures). MONARCH is currently in production and is used primarily for military signal processing applications. For a list of other polymorphic architectures, see also Hartenstein [22].

3. Current Trends in Polymorphic Computing

A study of the existing architectures reveals the following observations and trends in current polymorphic computer design:

1) Polymorphic hardware architectures strongly tend to be tile based. This allows designs to be scaled up by simply adding more tiles.

2) No clear "best processing cell" type has yet emerged.

3) Critical circuit path lengths are intentionally limited to roughly the diameter of a tile. Smaller critical path lengths allow higher clock frequencies to be utilized.

4) Network links tend to be point-to-point connections between only directly adjacent tiles. This is an easily scalable network strategy for tile based arrays. It also supports the trend of limiting the length of critical paths in the system.

5) Processing elements are trending toward simpler designs compared to today's single-core and multi-core processors.

6) Configurable memories are an emerging trend.

7) Algorithms tend to be statically scheduled and placed in the computing fabric. Programs tend to be compiled and mapped to array elements at compile time, not runtime.

8) Polymorphic architectures require extensive compiler and software support.

9) Polymorphic computers support multiple different programming models. Their fabrics tend be configurable into SIMD units, pipelines, and systolic architectures.

10) There is a clear trend towards hybrid computer architectures. For example, Raw tiles are a combination of a compute processor and a network processor. MONARCH is a collection of RISC processors combined with a configurable systolic array.

11) Polymorphic architectures tend to have both current and future scaling strategies. Most designs have currently available options to connect multiple chips together. Additionally, tiled designs scale up easily by adding more tiles.

4. Issues and Views

With regards to current polymorphic architectures, the authors perceive that:

1) Dynamic processing balancing is not addressed by current architectures. Process mapping is currently handled as a design-time and compile-time problem.

2) Performance monitoring capabilities in current architectures are lacking. Monitoring is necessary in order to perform dynamic load balancing.

3) Processing control is either centralized or determined pre-runtime. These are generally non-scalable techniques. As systems get larger, centralized control will become a bottleneck. Distributed control will become necessary. Additionally, dynamic control will require runtime decisions.

4) The rule, "direct communication links are strictly limited to only between directly adjacent tiles" is too restrictive. This rule is in place in tiled architectures because it fits nicely with the tiling scalability strategy and it helps limit the length of critical path wire lengths. However, this can route some communication through disinterested tiles and increase communication latencies. This rule could be relaxed to allow direct communication between neighboring, non-adjacent tiles.

5) The single processors at the heart of the tiles may be too complicated. Most processing elements are pipelined. This could prove to be too complicated for processing elements.

6) Pure meshes of processor may not necessarily scale with mesh size. The current square array tiling strategy cannot be efficiently scaled indefinitely. All inputs and outputs must enter and exit, respectively, through the edges of the array. It is conceivable that arrays could be scaled so large that it would be rare for execution graphs to penetrate very far into the array before completing and being routed back out. Interior array elements may be underutilized. Other array geometries should be considered, such as rectangular arrays.

7) Debugging strategies must be built into polymorphic systems. Polymorphic computing systems are unavoidably complex. The ability to view machine state and capture problems as they occur is vital.

5. A New Polymorphic Architecture

Given the trends and views in the current state of polymorphic computing, a new polymorphic computing architecture is proposed (shown in **Figure 2**) in this work. At a high level, the architecture is partitioned into a configurable processing fabric and a configurable memory fabric connected via a crossbar bus. The crossbar contains a large number of channels and provides connectivity for the entire system, including external processors and the interrupt/event controller. In addition, the crossbar arbiter provides the ability to "park" channels on particular connections between the processing fabric and

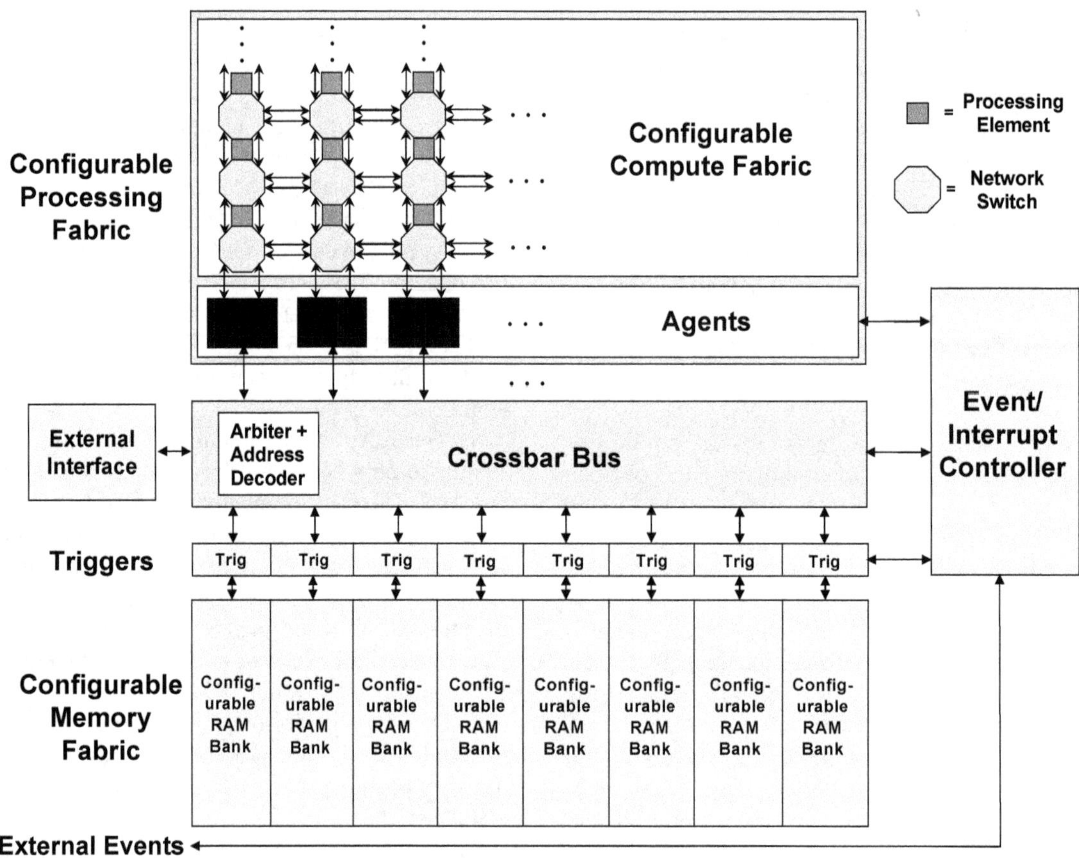

Figure 2. Proposed polymorphic architecture.

the memory fabric to support consistent and deterministic memory access times.

5.1. Memory Fabric

The memory fabric is composed of two types of components: independent, configurable memory banks and event triggers. Each memory bank has its own independent connection to the crossbar. In addition, each memory bank is associated with its own set of event triggers. From a configuration perspective, each memory bank can be selected as a traditional addressable memory, a streaming memory (FIFO and burst modes), a transactional memory [11], or a combination of the different modes. Caching has intentionally been omitted as an operational mode for deterministic memory access performance reasons. It is also expected that if a "wider" data path is needed, that the memory banks could be ganged together into a single "wider" memory bank.

The event triggers are mechanisms that associate arbitrary addresses within a memory bank with system events. They are akin to trace points and data breakpoints in modern embedded microprocessors. These enable writes to a particular memory location to be detected and communicated to interested entities throughout the system. The event triggers are a unique contribution of this work.

5.2. Processing Fabric

The processing fabric is abstracted into two partitions: a compute fabric and a layer of agents between the compute fabric and the rest of the system (*i.e.* the bus and the memories). The compute fabric is composed of a regular array of processing elements. These can be arithmetic logic units or simple microprocessors. The role of an element in the compute fabric is to receive operands, perform arithmetic operations upon them, and output the results. Memory accesses are not an intended role for compute fabric elements. The processing elements are intended to be workers with only a very local view of the system. They should only know how to do their assigned jobs, know on which of their ports to receive inputs, and know upon which of their ports to place their outputs.

The agents have a more global view of the system. They are the "department managers" in the overall computational enterprise. Their duties are to monitor for events that are relevant to their assignments, perform relevant memory accesses (both input and output), deliver/sequence inputs into the compute fabric, receive outputs from the compute fabric, perform their own transform functions to the data, and route the results to the appropriate system location (which could be the memory fabric, another agent, or an external location accessible via the crossbar). The agents are expected to be full microprocessors with their own local memories.

One of the reasons for distinguishing between agents and processing elements is to recognize the distinction between I/O bound algorithms and compute-bound algorithms. The act of memory accesses (I/O) and the act of computation are fundamentally different operations. Load/store computing architectures (RISC) have long recognized this distinction by providing completely separate instructions for memory accesses and arithmetic operations. For example, search algorithms are typically memory-bound operations and matrix operations are typically compute-bound algorithms. Concurrent execution opportunities in both algorithm types can usually be exploited to realize performance gains. In the case of a search algorithm, most of the effort is in the memory accesses. The search can typically be partitioned into smaller concurrently executing jobs with an agent assigned to each independent search effort. In this case, there is typically little reason to involve the processing elements. The search may be executed with only a collection of agents. On the other hand, matrix operations require more arithmetic operations than memory accesses and are easily parallelized. In this example, it is expected that there would be one or more agents assigned to the memory accesses and quite a few processing elements assigned to exploit concurrency in the arithmetic.

Another reason for distinguishing between agents and processing elements is geometric. Most processing elements are typically buried in the interior of a compute fabric. They tend to be relatively distant from the memories and memory access mechanisms (buses). The elements that are in the most convenient place to access memory are the elements on the edge of a compute fabric. Consequently, the edge elements need to be burdened with memory access circuitry. However, interior elements don't necessarily need to be burdened with memory access circuitry if they are directly given their inputs by neighboring elements. In this case, interior elements can be made smaller and simpler than the fabric periphery elements.

Yet another reason for distinguishing between agents and processing elements is managerial. A polymorphic system is expected to dynamically monitor loading and algorithmic demands, and continually adjust its architecture appropriately. Agents participate in this activity in a distributed manner. However, not every element in the fabric needs to participate in this activity and be burdened with this capability (*i.e.* extra circuitry).

The compute fabric itself (not including the agents) is composed of two types of elements: processing elements and network switches. Within the compute array itself, the roles of processing and routing are logically separated. Consequently, there are two types of elements within the array: processing elements and network elements. (Note, the agents are considered part of the overall processing fabric, but they are not included in the compute fabric subset.)

5.3. Data and Control Networks

There are two classes of networks within the compute fabric: a data network and a control network. All processing data are intended to be transmitted on the data network and all configuration, management, monitoring, and debug information are intended to be transmitted on the control network.

The data network is a configurable routing fabric composed of one or more channels that may be either circuit-switched or packet-switched depending on the implementation. All data network routing is performed by the network switches. The data network connectivity strategy is shown in **Figure 3**. The network switches are connected with their neighboring network switches and neighboring processing elements. However, processing elements are only connected with the neighboring network switches in the north and south directions. Processing elements are not directly connected together because they do not participate in data network routing.

The control network is a static network composed of individual buses terminated on the system crossbar (see **Figure 4**). Collectively, the buses map all agents, network switches, and processing elements into a global address space. Each "column" in the processing fabric will get its own control bus with the agent acting as the bus arbiter.

5.4. Polymorphism

The proposed system is polymorphic because the agents and processing elements can be reconfigured into different models. For instance, a pipelined processor might be created with an agent and a single column of processing elements; a SIMD unit could be created by arranging several agents and processing units together in a parallel fashion; and a systolic array could easily be configured from the processing fabric. Collectively, the array could be configured to cooperatively work on a single problem, or partitioned into independent subunits to work on different problems utilizing different processing models.

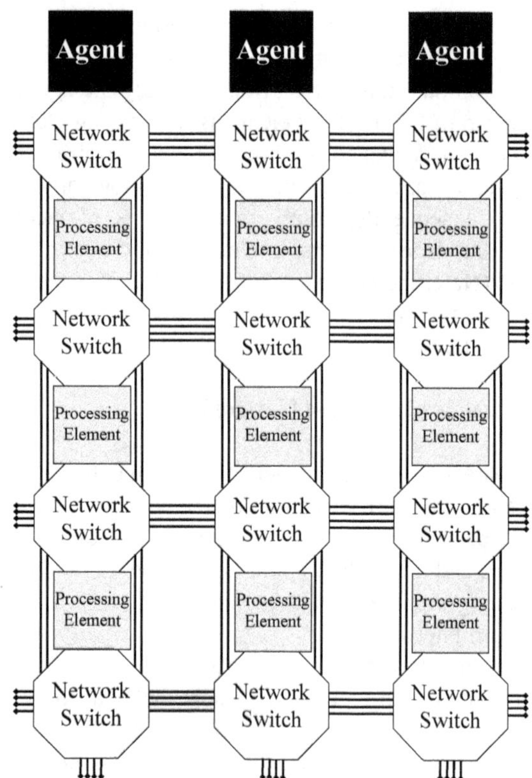

Figure 3. Data network.

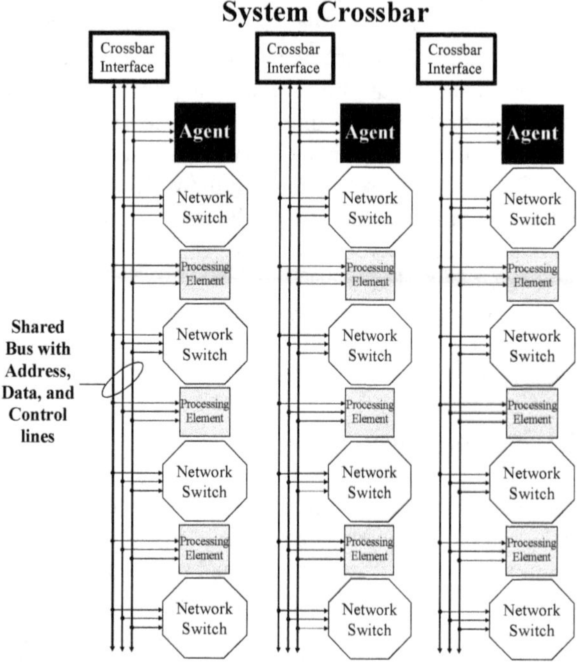

Figure 4. Control Network.

The monitoring and load balancing capabilities of the system are largely software-based. However, a series of programmable counters are also built into the agents and processing elements to facilitate system monitoring.

6. Conclusions

Overall, this work presents a definition of polymorphic computers, briefly sketches the history and development of the field, presents a list of trends occurring in the field, lists a series of views on the current state of field, and presents a novel polymorphic architecture. The significant contributions of the architecture are a clean partitioning between memory and computation, a method for globally detecting system events (the triggers), the concept of an agent, and a clear division of roles between agents and processing elements.

7. References

[1] D. Harris, "Skew-Tolerant Circuit Design," Morgan Kaufmann Publishers, Waltham, 2001.

[2] G. Estrin, "Organization of Computer Systems—The Fixed Plus Variable Structure Computer," *Proceedings of the Western Joint Computer Conference*, New York, 3-5 May 1960, pp. 33-40.

[3] G. Estrin, "Reconfigurable Computer Origins: The UCLA Fixed-Plus Variable (F+V) Structure Computer," *IEEE Annals of the History of Computing*, Vol. 24, No. 4, 2002, pp. 3-9.

[4] M. A. Baker and V. J. Coli, "The PAL20RA10 Story—The Customization of a Standard Product," *IEEE Micro*, Vol. 6, No. 5, 1986, pp. 45-60.

[5] R. Freeman, Configurable Electrical Circuit Having Configurable Logic Elements and Configurable Interconnects, US Patent No. 4,870,302, 26 September 1989.

[6] A. Agarwal, "Raw Computation," *Scientific American*, Vol. 281, No. 2, pp. 60-63.

[7] M. B. Taylor, *et al.*, "The Raw Microprocessor: A Computational Fabric for Software Circuits and General-Purpose Programs," *IEEE Micro*, Vol. 22, No. 2, 2002, pp. 25-35.

[8] R. Ho, K. W. Mai and M. A. Horowitz, "The Future of Wires," *Proceedings of the IEEE*, Vol. 89, No. 4, 2001, pp. 490-504.

[9] K. Mai, T. Paaske, N. Jayasena, R. Ho, W. J. Dally and M. Horowitz, "Smart Memories: A Modular Reconfigurable Architecture," *Proceedings of the 27th International Symposium on Computer Architecture*, Vancouver, 14 June 2000, pp. 161-171.

[10] A. Firoozshahian, A. Solomatnikov, O. Shacham, Z. Asgar, S. Richardson, C. Kozyrakis and M. Horowitz, "A Memory System Design Framework: Creating Smart Memories," *Proceedings of the 36th Annual International Symposium on Computer Architecture*, New York, 2009, pp. 406-417.

[11] M. Herlihy and J. E. B. Moss, "Transactional Memory: Architectural Support for Lock-Free Data Structures," *Proceedings of the 20th Annual Symposium on Computer Architecture*, San Diego, 16-19 May 1993, pp. 289-300.

[12] D. Burger, S. W. Keckler, K. S. McKinley, M. Dahlin, L. K. John, C. Lin, C. R. Moore, J. Burrill, R. G. McDonald and W. Yoder, "Scaling to the End of Silicon with EDGE Architectures," *IEEE Computer*, Vol. 37, No. 7, 2004, pp. 44-55.

[13] R. McDonald, D. Burger, S.W. Keckler, K. Sankaralingam and R. Nagarajan, "TRIPS Processor Reference Manual," Technical Report, Department of Computer Sciences, The University of Texas at Austin, Austin, 2005.

[14] M. Gebhart, B. A. Maher, K. E. Coons, J. Diamond, P. Gratz, M. Marino, N. Ranganathan, B. Robatmili, A. Smith, J. Burrill, S. W. Keckler, D. Burger and K. S. McKinley, "An Evaluation of the TRIPS Computer System (Extended Technical Report)," Technical Report TR-08-31, Department of Computer Sciences, The University of Texas at Austin, Austin, 2008.

[15] J. B. Dennis and D. P. Misunas, "A Preliminary Architecture for a Basic Dataflow Processor," *Proceedings of the 2nd Annual Symposium on Computer Architecture* New York, 1975, pp. 126-132.

[16] J. Draper, J. Sondeen, S. Mediratta and I. Kim, "Implementation of a 32-Bit RISC Processor for the Data-Intensive Architecture Processing-in Memory Chip," *Proceedings of the IEEE International Conference on Application-Specific Systems, Architectures, and Processors*, San Jose, 17-19 July 2002, pp. 163-172.

[17] J. Draper, J. Sondeen and C. W. Kang, "Implementation of a 256-Bit Wide-Word PROCESSOr for the Data-Intensive Architecture (DIVA) Processing in Memory (PIM) Chip," *Proceedings of the 28th European Solid-State Circuits Conference, Florence*, 2002, pp. 77-80.

[18] J. Draper, J. Chame, M. Hall, C. Steele, T. Barrett, J. LaCoss, J. Granacki, J. Shin, C. Chen, C. W. Kang, I. Kim and G. Daglikoca, "The Architecture of the DIVA Processing-in-Memory Chip," *Proceedings of the 16th International Conference on Supercomputing* 2002, New York, 2002, pp. 14-25.

[19] J. Granacki, and M. Vahey," MONARCH: A Morphable Networked Micro-ARCHitecture," Technical Report, USC/Information Sciences Institute and Raytheon, Marina del Rey, May 2003.

[20] J. J. Granacki, "MONARCH: Next Generation SoC (Supercomputer on a Chip)," Technical Report, USC/Information Sciences Institute, Marina del Rey, February 2005.

[21] K. Prager, L. Lewins, M. Vahey and G. Groves, "World's First Polymorphic Computer—MONARCH," *11th Annual High Performance Embedded Computing Workshop* 2007, 2007. http://www.ll.mit.edu/HPEC/agendas/proc07/agenda.html

[22] R. Hartenstein, "A Decade of Reconfigurable Computing: A Visionary Retrospective," *Proceedings of the Conference on Design, Automation and Test in Europe* 2001, Munich, 13-16 March 2001, pp. 642-649.

12

New Stability Tests of Positive Standard and Fractional Linear Systems*

Tadeusz Kaczorek
Faculty of Electrical Engineering, Bialystok University of Technology, Bialystok, Poland

Abstract

New tests for checking asymptotic stability of positive 1D continuous-time and discrete-time linear systems without and with delays and of positive 2D linear systems described by the general and the Roesser models are proposed. Checking of the asymptotic stability of positive 2D linear systems is reduced to checking of suitable corresponding 1D positive linear systems. It is shown that the stability tests can be also applied to checking the asymptotic stability of fractional discrete-time linear systems with delays. Effectiveness of the tests is shown on numerical examples.

Keywords: Fractional, Positive, Linear, System, Asymptotic Stability, Test

1. Introduction

A dynamical system is called positive if its trajectory starting from any nonnegative initial state remains forever in the positive orthant for all nonnegative inputs. An overview of state of the art in positive theory is given in the monographs [1,2]. Variety of models having positive behavior can be found in engineering, economics, social sciences, biology and medicine, etc.

New stability conditions for discrete-time linear systems have been proposed by M. Busłowicz in [3] and next have been extended to robust stability of fractional discrete-time linear systems in [4]. The stability of positive continuous-time linear systems with delays has been addressed in [5]. The independence of the asymptotic stability of positive 2D linear systems with delays of the number and values of the delays has been shown in [6]. The asymptotic stability of positive 2D linear systems without and with delays has been considered in [7,8]. The stability and stabilization of positive fractional linear systems by state-feedbacks have been analyzed in [9,10]. The Hurwitz stability of Metzler matrices has been investigated in [11] and some new tests for checking the asymptotic stability of positive 1D and 2D linear systems have been proposed in [12].

In this paper new tests for checking asymptotic stability of positive 1D continuous-time and discrete-time linear systems without and with delays and of positive 2D linear systems described by the general and the Roesser models will be proposed. It will be shown that the checking of the asymptotic stability of positive 2D linear systems can be reduced to checking of suitable corresponding 1D positive linear systems.

The paper is organized as follows. In Section 2 new stability tests for positive continuous-time linear systems are proposed. An extension of these tests for positive discrete-time linear systems is given in Section 3. Application of these tests to checking the asymptotic stability of positive 1D linear systems with delays is given in Section 4. In Section 5 the tests are applied to positive 2D linear systems described by the general and Roesser models and in Section 6 the fractional discrete-time linear systems with delays. Concluding remarks are given in Section 7.

The following notation will be used: $\Re$ —the set of real numbers, $\Re^{n\times m}$ —the set of $n\times m$ real matrices, $\Re_+^{n\times m}$ —the set of $n\times m$ matrices with nonnegative entries and $\Re_+^n = \Re_+^{n\times 1}$, M_n —the set of $n\times n$ Metzler matrices (real matrices with nonnegative off-diagonal entries), I_n —the $n\times n$ identity matrix.

2. Continuous-Time Linear Systems

Consider the continuous-time linear system

$$\dot{x}(t) = Ax(t) \tag{2.1}$$

where $x(t)\in\Re^n$ is the state vector and $A\in\Re^{n\times n}$.

The system (2.1) is called (internally) positive if

*This work was supported by Ministry of Science and Higher Education in Poland under work No. N N514 6389 40.

$x(t) \in \Re_+^n$, $t \geq 0$ for any initial conditions $x(0) = x_0 \in \Re_+^n$ [1, 2].

Theorem 2.1. [1,2] The system (2.1) is positive if and only if A is a Metzler matrix.

The positive system is called asymptotically stable if

$$\lim_{t\to\infty} x(t) = \lim_{t\to\infty} e^{At}x_0 = 0 \quad \text{for all} \quad x_0 \in \Re_+^n$$

Theorem 2.2. [1,2] The positive system (2.1) is asymptotically stable if and only if all principal minors Δ_i, $i = 1, \cdots, n$ of the matrix $-A$ are positive, *i.e.*

$$\begin{aligned} &\Delta_1 = -a_{11} > 0, \\ &\Delta_2 = \begin{vmatrix} -a_{11} & -a_{12} \\ -a_{21} & -a_{22} \end{vmatrix} > 0, \\ &\vdots \\ &\Delta_n = \det[-A] > 0 \end{aligned} \tag{2.2}$$

Theorem 2.3. [1,2] The positive system (2.1) is asymptotically stable only if all diagonal entries of the matrix A are negative.

Let $A = [a_{ij}] \in \Re^{n\times n}$ be a Metzler matrix with negative diagonal entries ($a_{ii} < 0$, $i = 1, \cdots, n$). Let define

$$A_n^{(0)} = A = \begin{bmatrix} a_{11}^{(0)} & \dots & a_{1,n}^{(0)} \\ \vdots & \dots & \vdots \\ a_{n,1}^{(0)} & \dots & a_{n,n}^{(0)} \end{bmatrix} = \begin{bmatrix} a_{11}^{(0)} & b_{n-1}^{(0)} \\ c_{n-1}^{(0)} & A_{n-1}^{(0)} \end{bmatrix},$$

$$A_{n-1}^{(0)} = \begin{bmatrix} a_{22}^{(0)} & \dots & a_{2,n}^{(0)} \\ \vdots & \dots & \vdots \\ a_{n,2}^{(0)} & \dots & a_{n,n}^{(0)} \end{bmatrix}, \tag{2.3a}$$

$$b_{n-1}^{(0)} = [a_{12}^{(0)} \ \dots \ a_{1,n}^{(0)}], \quad c_{n-1}^{(0)} = \begin{bmatrix} a_{21}^{(0)} \\ \vdots \\ a_{n,1}^{(0)} \end{bmatrix}$$

and

$$A_{n-k}^{(k)} = A_{n-k}^{(k-1)} - \frac{c_{n-k}^{(k-1)} b_{n-k}^{(k-1)}}{a_{k+1,k+1}^{(k-1)}} = \begin{bmatrix} a_{k+1,k+1}^{(k)} & \dots & a_{k+1,n}^{(k)} \\ \vdots & \dots & \vdots \\ a_{n,k+1}^{(k)} & \dots & a_{n,n}^{(k)} \end{bmatrix}$$

$$= \begin{bmatrix} a_{k+1,k+1}^{(k)} & b_{n-k-1}^{(k)} \\ c_{n-k-1}^{(k)} & A_{n-k-1}^{(k)} \end{bmatrix},$$

$$A_{n-k-1}^{(k)} = \begin{bmatrix} a_{k+2,k+2}^{(k)} & \dots & a_{k+2,n}^{(k)} \\ \vdots & \dots & \vdots \\ a_{n,k+2}^{(k)} & \dots & a_{n,n}^{(k)} \end{bmatrix}, \tag{2.3b}$$

$$b_{n-k-1}^{(k)} = [a_{k+1,k+2}^{(k)} \ \dots \ a_{k+1,n}^{(k)}], \quad c_{n-k-1}^{(k)} = \begin{bmatrix} a_{k+2,k+1}^{(k)} \\ \vdots \\ a_{n,k+1}^{(k)} \end{bmatrix}$$

for $k = 1, \cdots, n-1$.

Let us denote by $R[i + j \times c]$ the following elementary column operation on the matrix A: addition to the i-th column the j-th column multiplied by a scalar c. It is well-known that using these elementary operations we may reduce the matrix

$$A = \begin{bmatrix} a_{11} & a_{12} & \dots & a_{1,n} \\ a_{21} & a_{22} & \dots & a_{2,n} \\ \vdots & \vdots & \dots & \vdots \\ a_{n,1} & a_{n,2} & \dots & a_{n,n} \end{bmatrix} \tag{2.4}$$

to the lower triangular form

$$\tilde{A} = \begin{bmatrix} \tilde{a}_{11} & 0 & \dots & 0 \\ \tilde{a}_{21} & \tilde{a}_{22} & \dots & 0 \\ \vdots & \vdots & \ddots & \vdots \\ \tilde{a}_{n,1} & \tilde{a}_{n,2} & \dots & \tilde{a}_{n,n} \end{bmatrix}. \tag{2.5}$$

The reduction of the matrix (2.4) to the form (2.5) is equivalent to postmultiplication of the matrix (2.4) by the upper triangular matrix of the elementary column operations of the form

$$R = \begin{bmatrix} 1 & r_{12} & \dots & r_{1,n} \\ 0 & 1 & \dots & r_{2,n} \\ \vdots & \vdots & \ddots & \vdots \\ 0 & 0 & \dots & 1 \end{bmatrix} \tag{2.6}$$

i.e.

$$\tilde{A} = AR \tag{2.7}$$

Note that to reduce to zero the entries $a_{12}, \cdots, a_{1n}$ of the matrix (2.4) we postmultiply it by the matrix

$$R_1 = \begin{bmatrix} 1 & -\dfrac{a_{12}}{a_{11}} & \dots & -\dfrac{a_{1,n}}{a_{11}} \\ 0 & 1 & \dots & 0 \\ \vdots & \vdots & \ddots & \vdots \\ 0 & 0 & \dots & 1 \end{bmatrix} \tag{2.8}$$

and we obtain

$$\bar{A} = AR_1 = \begin{bmatrix} a_{11} & 0 & \dots & 0 \\ a_{21} & \bar{a}_{22} & \dots & \bar{a}_{2,n} \\ \vdots & \vdots & \dots & \vdots \\ a_{n,1} & \bar{a}_{n,2} & \dots & \bar{a}_{n,n} \end{bmatrix} \tag{2.9}$$

where

$$\bar{a}_{22} = a_{22} - \frac{a_{12}\cdot a_{21}}{a_{11}}, \cdots, \bar{a}_{2,n} = a_{2,n} - \frac{a_{21}\cdot a_{1,n}}{a_{11}},$$

$$\bar{a}_{n,2} = a_{n,2} - \frac{a_{n,1}\cdot a_{12}}{a_{11}}, \cdots, \bar{a}_{n,n} = a_{n,n} - \frac{a_{n,1}\cdot a_{1,n}}{a_{11}}.$$

Next we postmultiply the matrix (2.9) by the matrix

$$R_2 = \begin{bmatrix} 1 & 0 & 0 & \dots & 0 \\ 0 & 1 & -\dfrac{\bar{a}_{23}}{\bar{a}_{22}} & \dots & -\dfrac{\bar{a}_{2,n}}{\bar{a}_{22}} \\ 0 & 0 & 1 & \dots & 0 \\ \vdots & \vdots & \vdots & \ddots & \vdots \\ 0 & 0 & 0 & \dots & 1 \end{bmatrix}. \tag{2.10}$$

In a similar way we define matrices $R_3,\cdots,R_n$. The matrix (2.6) is the product of the elementary column operations matrices $R_1,R_2,\cdots,R_n$, *i.e.* $R = R_1,R_2,\cdots,R_n$.

It is easy to show that if the matrix (2.4) is Metzler matrix with negative diagonal entries then the matrix (2.5) is also a Metzler matrix.

Theorem 2.4. The positive systems with the matrix (2.5) is asymptotically stable if and only if all diagonal entries of the matrix are negative.

Proof. The eigenvalues of the matrix (2.5) are equal to its diagonal entries $\tilde{a}_{11},\cdots,\tilde{a}_{nn}$ and the positive system is asymptotically stable if and only if all the diagonal entries are negative.

Theorem 2.5. The positive continuous-time linear system (2.1) is asymptotically stable if and only if one of the equivalent conditions is satisfied:

1) the diagonal entries of the matrices defined by (2.3)

$$A_{n-k}^{(k)} \text{ for } k = 1,\cdots,n-1 \tag{2.11}$$

are negative,

2) the diagonal entries of the lower triangular matrix (2.5) are negative, *i.e.*

$$\tilde{a}_{kk} < 0 \text{ for } k = 1,\cdots,n \tag{2.12}$$

Proof. Let $A_{j_1,\cdots,j_q}^{i_1,\cdots,i_q}$ be the $q\times q$ ($q \le n$) minor of the matrix A obtained by the deleting all rows except the rows $i_1,\cdots,i_q$ and all columns except the columns $j_1,\cdots,j_q$. In a similar way we define the minors of the matrices $\tilde{A}$ and R. Applying the Cauchy-Binet theorem to (2.7) we obtain

$$\tilde{A}_{i_1,\cdots,i_q}^{i_1,\cdots,i_q} = \sum_{1\le k_1<\cdots<k_q\le n} A_{k_1,\cdots,k_q}^{i_1,\cdots,i_q} R_{i_1,\cdots,i_q}^{k_1,\cdots,k_q} \tag{2.13}$$

From the structure of the matrix (2.6) it follows that

$$R_{i_1,\cdots,i_q}^{k_1,\cdots,k_q} = \begin{cases} 1 \text{ for } k_1 = i_1,\cdots,k_q = i_q \\ 0 \text{ for } k_1 \ne i_1,\cdots,k_q \ne i_q \end{cases} \tag{2.14}$$

Taking into account (2.14) from (2.13) we obtain

$$\tilde{A}_{i_1,\cdots,i_q}^{i_1,\cdots,i_q} = A_{i_1,\cdots,i_q}^{i_1,\cdots,i_q} \text{ for } q = 1,\cdots,n \tag{2.15}$$

From (2.15) follows the equivalence of the conditions (2.2) and (2.11). To show the equivalence of the conditions (2.11) and (2.12) note that the computation of the matrix $A_{n-1}^{(1)}$ by the use of (2.3b) for $k = 1$ is equivalent to the reduction to zero of the entries $a_{i,j}$, $j = 2,\cdots,n$ of the matrix (2.4) by elementary column operations since

$$A_{n-1}^{(1)} = \begin{bmatrix} a_{22} & \cdots & a_{2,n} \\ \vdots & \cdots & \vdots \\ a_{n,2} & \cdots & a_{n,n} \end{bmatrix} - \frac{1}{a_{11}} \begin{bmatrix} a_{21} \\ \vdots \\ a_{n,1} \end{bmatrix} \begin{bmatrix} a_{12} & \cdots & a_{1,n} \end{bmatrix}. \tag{2.16}$$

Note that $-\frac{a_{1,i}}{a_{11}} > 0$ for $i = 2,\cdots,n$ and $-\frac{a_{1,i}a_{i,1}}{a_{11}} > 0$ for $i = 2,\cdots,n$ since $a_{11} < 0$ and $a_{i,j} \ge 0$ for $i \ne j$.

Thus, the matrix $A_{n-1}^{(1)}$ is a Metzler matrix. Continuing this procedure after n steps we obtain the Metzler lower triangular matrix (2.5). Therefore, the conditions (2.11) and (2.12) are equivalent.

Example 2.1. Consider the positive system (2.1) with the matrix

$$A = \begin{bmatrix} -2 & 1 & 0 \\ 0 & -1 & 1 \\ 1 & 1 & -2 \end{bmatrix}. \tag{2.17}$$

Check the asymptotic stability using the conditions (2.11) and (2.12).

Using (2.3) for (2.17) we obtain

$$\begin{aligned} A_2^{(1)} &= A_2^{(0)} - \frac{b_2^{(0)}c_2^{(0)}}{a_{33}^{(0)}} \\ &= \begin{bmatrix} -1 & 1 \\ 1 & -2 \end{bmatrix} + \frac{1}{2}\begin{bmatrix} 0 \\ 1 \end{bmatrix}[1 \quad 0] = \begin{bmatrix} -1 & 1 \\ 1.5 & -2 \end{bmatrix} \\ A_1^{(2)} &= A_1^{(1)} - \frac{b_1^{(1)}c_1^{(1)}}{a_{22}^{(1)}} = -2 + \frac{1.5}{1} = -0.5. \end{aligned} \tag{2.18}$$

The conditions (2.11) of Theorem 2.5 are satisfied and the positive system is asymptotically stable.

Using the elementary column operations to the matrix (2.17) we obtain

$$\begin{aligned} A = \begin{bmatrix} -2 & 1 & 0 \\ 0 & -1 & 1 \\ 1 & 1 & -2 \end{bmatrix} &\xrightarrow{R[2+1\times 0.5]} \begin{bmatrix} -2 & 0 & 0 \\ 0 & -1 & 1 \\ 1 & 1.5 & -2 \end{bmatrix} \\ &\xrightarrow{R[3+2\times 1]} \begin{bmatrix} -2 & 0 & 0 \\ 0 & -1 & 0 \\ 1 & 1.5 & -0.5 \end{bmatrix} \end{aligned} \tag{2.19}$$

The conditions (2.12) of Theorem 2.5 are also satisfied and the positive system is asymptotically stable.

3. Discrete-Time Linear Systems

Consider the discrete-time linear system

$$x_{i+1} = \bar{A}x_i, \quad i \in Z_+ = \{0,1,\cdots\} \tag{3.1}$$

where $x_i \in \Re^n$ is the state vector and $\bar{A} \in \Re^{n\times n}$.

The system (3.1) is called (internally) positive if $x_i \in \Re_+^n$, $i \in Z_+$ for any initial conditions $x_0 \in \Re_+^n$.

Theorem 3.1. [1,2] The system (3.1) is positive if and only if $A \in \Re_+^{n\times n}$.

The positive system is called asymptotically stable if

$$\lim_{i\to\infty} x_i = \lim_{i\to\infty} A^i x_0 = 0 \text{ for all } x_0 \in \Re_+^n.$$

From Theorem 2.2 and 3.1 it follows that the nonnegative matrix $\bar{A}$ is asymptotically stable if and only if the Metzler matrix $\bar{A} - I_n$ is asymptotically stable.

Theorem 3.2. [1,2] The positive system (3.1) is asymptotically stable if and only if all principal minors $\hat{\Delta}_i$, $i=1,\cdots,n$ of the matrix $\hat{A}=I_n-\overline{A}=[\hat{a}_{ij}]\in\Re^{n\times n}$ are positive, *i.e.*

$$\hat{\Delta}_1=\hat{a}_{11}>0,\ \hat{\Delta}_2=\begin{vmatrix}\hat{a}_{11} & \hat{a}_{12}\\ \hat{a}_{21} & \hat{a}_{22}\end{vmatrix}>0,\cdots,\ \hat{\Delta}_n=\det[\hat{A}]>0 .$$

Theorem 3.3. [1,2] The positive system (3.1) is asymptotically stable only if all diagonal entries of the matrix $\overline{A}$ are less than 1.

It is assumed that $\overline{a}_{ii}<1$, $i=1,\cdots,n$ of the matrix $\overline{A}=[\overline{a}_{ij}]\in\Re_+^{n\times n}$ since otherwise by Theorem 3.3 the system is unstable. Using (2.3) in a similar way as for the matrix A we define for the matrix $\hat{A}=\overline{A}-I_n=[\hat{a}_{ij}]$ the matrices $\hat{A}_{n-k}^{(k)}$ for $k=0,1,\cdots,n-1$. Using the elementary column operations we reduce the matrix $\hat{A}$ to the lower triangular form

$$\tilde{A}'=\begin{bmatrix}\tilde{a}'_{11} & 0 & \dots & 0\\ \tilde{a}'_{21} & \tilde{a}'_{22} & \dots & 0\\ \vdots & \vdots & \ddots & \vdots\\ \tilde{a}'_{n,1} & \tilde{a}'_{n,2} & \dots & \tilde{a}'_{n,n}\end{bmatrix}. \tag{3.4}$$

Theorem 3.4. The positive discrete-time system with the matrix (3.4) is asymptotically stable if and only if all diagonal entries of the matrix $\hat{A}'$ are less than 1.

Proof is similar to the proof of Theorem 2.4.

Theorem 3.5. The positive discrete-time linear system (3.1) is asymptotically stable if and only if one of the equivalent conditions is satisfied:

1) the diagonal entries of the matrices

$$\hat{A}_{n-k}^{(k)} \text{ for } k=1,\cdots,n-1 \tag{3.5}$$

are negative,

2) the diagonal entries of the lower triangular matrix (3.4) are negative, *i.e.*

$$\tilde{a}'_{kk}<0 \text{ for } k=1,\cdots,n. \tag{3.6}$$

Proof. The positive discrete-time system (3.1) is asymptotically stable if and only if the corresponding continuous-time system with the Metzler matrix $\hat{A}=\overline{A}-I_n$ is asymptotically stable. By Theorem 2.5 the positive discrete-time system (3.1) is asymptotically stable if one of its conditions is satisfied. □

Example 3.1. Check the asymptotic stability of the positive system (3.1) with the matrix

$$\overline{A}=\begin{bmatrix}0.5 & 0.1\\ 0.2 & 0.4\end{bmatrix}. \tag{3.7}$$

In this case

$$\hat{A}=\overline{A}-I_n=\begin{bmatrix}-0.5 & 0.1\\ 0.2 & -0.6\end{bmatrix}. \tag{3.8}$$

Using (3.5) for $n=2$ we obtain

$$\hat{A}_1^{(1)}=\hat{a}_{22}-\frac{\hat{a}_{12}\hat{a}_{21}}{\hat{a}_{11}}=-0.6+\frac{0.1\cdot 0.2}{0.5}=-0.56<0 .$$

Condition i) of Theorem 3.5 is satisfied and the positive system (3.1) with (3.7) is asymptotically stable.

Similarly, using the elementary column operations to the matrix (3.8) we obtain

$$\hat{A}=\begin{bmatrix}-0.5 & 0.1\\ 0.2 & -0.6\end{bmatrix}\xrightarrow{R[2+1\times 0.2]}\begin{bmatrix}-0.5 & 0\\ 0.2 & -0.56\end{bmatrix}.$$

The condition ii) of Theorem 3.5 is also satisfied and the positive system is asymptotically stable.

4. Linear Systems with Delays

Consider the continuous-time linear system with q delays [5]

$$\dot{x}(t)=A_0x(t)+\sum_{k=1}^{q}A_kx(t-d_k) \tag{4.1}$$

where $x(t)\in\Re^n$ is the state vector, $A_k\in\Re^{n\times n}$, $k=0,1,\cdots,q$ and $d_k>0$, $k=1,\cdots,q$ are delays.

The initial conditions for (4.1) have the form

$$x(t)=x_0(t) \text{ for } t\in[-d,0],\ d=\max_k d_k . \tag{4.2}$$

The system (4.1) is called (internally) positive if $x(t)\in\Re_+^n$, $t\geq 0$ for any initial conditions $x_0(t)\in\Re_+^n$.

Theorem 4.1. The system (4.1) is positive if and only if

$$A_0\in M_n \text{ and } A_k\in\Re_+^{n\times n},\ k=1,\cdots,q \tag{4.3}$$

where M_n is the set of $n\times n$ Metzler matrices.

Proof is given in [5].

Theorem 4.2. The positive system with delays (4.1) is asymptotically stable if and only if the positive system without delays

$$\dot{x}=Ax,\ A=\sum_{k=0}^{q}A_k\in M_n \tag{4.4}$$

is asymptotically stable.

Proof is given in [5].

To check the asymptotic stability of the system (4.1) Theorem 2.5 is recommended. The application of Theorem 2.5 to checking the asymptotic stability of the system (4.1) will be demonstrated on the following example.

Example 4.1. Consider the system (4.1) with $q=1$ and the matrices

$$A_0=\begin{bmatrix}-1 & 0.2\\ 0.2 & -1.4\end{bmatrix},\ A_1=\begin{bmatrix}0.5 & 0.1\\ 0.2 & 0.8\end{bmatrix}. \tag{4.5}$$

The matrix of the positive system (4.4) without delays has the form

$$A = A_0 + A_1 = \begin{bmatrix} -0.5 & 0.3 \\ 0.4 & -0.6 \end{bmatrix} \in M_2 . \quad (4.6)$$

Using (2.3) for the matrix (4.6) we obtain

$$\hat{A}_1^{(1)} = -0.6 + \frac{0.4 \cdot 0.3}{0.5} = -0.36 < 0 . \quad (4.7)$$

Condition i) of Theorem 2.5 is satisfied and the positive system (4.1) with (4.5) is asymptotically stable.

Using the elementary column operations to the matrix (4.6) we obtain

$$A = \begin{bmatrix} -0.5 & 0.3 \\ 0.4 & -0.6 \end{bmatrix} \xrightarrow{R\left[2+1\times\frac{3}{5}\right]} \begin{bmatrix} -0.5 & 0 \\ 0.4 & -0.36 \end{bmatrix}$$

The condition ii) of Theorem 2.5 is also satisfied and the positive system is asymptotically stable.

Now let us consider the discrete-time linear system with q delays [3]

$$x_{i+1} = \sum_{k=0}^{q} A_k x_{i-k}, \quad i \in Z_+ \quad (4.8)$$

where $x_i \in \Re^n$ is the state vector and $A_k \in \Re^{n\times n}$, $k = 0,1,\cdots,q$.

The initial conditions for (4.8) have the form

$$x_{-k} \in \Re^n \ \text{ for } k = 0,1,\cdots,q. \quad (4.9)$$

The system (4.8) is called (internally) positive if $x_i \in \Re_+^n$, $i \in Z_+$ for any initial conditions $x_{-k} \in \Re_+^n$ for $k = 0,1,\cdots,q$.

Theorem 4.3. [2] The system (4.8) is positive if and only if $A_k \in \Re_+^{n\times n}$, $k = 0,1,\cdots,q$.

Theorem 4.4. The positive discrete-time system with delays (4.8) is asymptotically stable if and only if the positive system without delays

$$x_{i+1} = \bar{A}x_i , \quad \bar{A} = \sum_{k=0}^{q} A_k , \ i \in Z_+ \quad (4.10)$$

is asymptotically stable.

Proof is given in [3].

To check the asymptotic stability of the system (4.8) Theorem 3.5 is recommended. The application of Theorem 3.5 to checking the asymptotic stability of the system (4.8) will be demonstrated on the following example.

Example 4.2. Consider the positive system (4.8) with $q = 1$ and the matrices

$$A_0 = \begin{bmatrix} 0.2 & 0.2 \\ 0.1 & 0.2 \end{bmatrix}, \quad A_1 = \begin{bmatrix} 0.2 & 0.1 \\ 0.1 & 0.3 \end{bmatrix}. \quad (4.11)$$

The matrix of the positive system (4.10) without delays has the form

$$\bar{A} = A_0 + A_1 = \begin{bmatrix} 0.4 & 0.3 \\ 0.2 & 0.5 \end{bmatrix}. \quad (4.12)$$

In this case

$$\hat{A} = \bar{A} - I_n = \begin{bmatrix} -0.6 & 0.3 \\ 0.2 & -0.5 \end{bmatrix} \quad (4.13)$$

and using the elementary column operation to (4.13) we obtain

$$\begin{bmatrix} -0.6 & 0.3 \\ 0.2 & -0.5 \end{bmatrix} \xrightarrow{R[2+1\times 0.5]} \begin{bmatrix} -0.6 & 0 \\ 0.2 & -0.4 \end{bmatrix}.$$

The condition ii) of Theorem 3.5 is satisfied and the positive system is asymptotically stable.

5. 2D Linear Systems

Consider the general autonomous model of 2D linear systems

$$x_{i+1,j+1} = A_0 x_{i,j} + A_1 x_{i+1,j} + A_2 x_{i,j+1}, \quad i,j \in Z_+ \quad (5.1)$$

where $x_{i,j} \in \Re^n$ is the state vector and $A_k \in \Re^{n\times n}$, $k = 0,1,2$.

Boundary conditions for (5.1) have the form

$$x_{i,0} \in \Re^n , \ i \in Z_+ \text{ and } x_{0,j} \in \Re^n , \ j \in Z_+ . \quad (5.2)$$

The model (5.1) is called (internally) positive if $x_{i,j} \in \Re_+^n$, $i,j \in Z_+$ for any initial conditions $x_{i,0} \in \Re_+^n$, $i \in Z_+$, $x_{0,j} \in \Re_+^n$, $j \in Z_+$.

Theorem 5.1. [2] The system (5.1) is positive if and only if

$$A_k \in \Re_+^{n\times n} , k = 0,1,2. \quad (5.3)$$

The Roesser autonomous model of 2D linear systems has the form [2]

$$\begin{bmatrix} x_{i+1,j}^h \\ x_{i,j+1}^v \end{bmatrix} = \begin{bmatrix} A_{11} & A_{12} \\ A_{21} & A_{22} \end{bmatrix} \begin{bmatrix} x_{i,j}^h \\ x_{i,j}^v \end{bmatrix}, \quad i,j \in Z_+ \quad (5.4)$$

where $x_{i,j}^h \in \Re^{n_1}$ and $x_{i,j}^v \in \Re^{n_2}$ are the horizontal and vertical state vectors at the point (i, j) and $A_{k,l} \in \Re^{n_k \times n_l}$, $k, l = 1,2$.

Boundary conditions for (5.4) have the form

$$x_{0,j}^h \in \Re^{n_1} , \ j \in Z_+ \text{ and } x_{i,0}^v \in \Re^{n_2} , \ i \in Z_+ . \quad (5.5)$$

The model (5.4) is called (internally) positive if $x_{i,j}^h \in \Re_+^{n_1}$ and $x_{i,j}^v \in \Re_+^{n_2}$ for any initial conditions $x_{0,j}^h \in \Re_+^{n_1}$, $j \in Z_+$ and $x_{i,0}^v \in \Re_+^{n_2}$, $i \in Z_+$.

Theorem 5.2. [2] The Roesser model (5.4) is positive if and only if

$$\begin{bmatrix} A_{11} & A_{12} \\ A_{21} & A_{22} \end{bmatrix} \in \Re_+^{n\times n}, \quad n = n_1 + n_2 . \quad (5.6)$$

The positive general model (5.1) is called asymptotically stable if

$$\lim_{i,j\to\infty} x_{i,j} = 0 \ \text{ for all } x_{i,0} \in \Re_+^n , \ i \in Z_+$$

and $$x_{0,j} \in \Re_+^n, \quad j \in Z_+. \tag{5.7}$$

Similarly, the positive Roesser model (5.4) is called asymptotically stable if

$$\lim_{i,j\to\infty} \begin{bmatrix} x_{i,j}^h \\ x_{i,j}^v \end{bmatrix} = 0 \ \text{ for all } x_{0,j}^h \in \Re_+^{n_1}, \ j \in Z_+$$
$$\text{and } x_{i,0}^v \in \Re_+^{n_2}, \ i \in Z_+. \tag{5.8}$$

Theorem 5.3. The positive general model (5.1) is asymptotically stable if and only if the positive 1D system

$$x_{i+1} = Ax_i, \ A = A_0 + A_1 + A_2, \ i \in Z_+ \tag{5.9}$$

is asymptotically stable.

Proof is given in [8, 6].

Theorem 5.4. The positive Roesser model (5.4) is asymptotically stable if and only if the positive 1D system

$$x_{i+1} = \begin{bmatrix} A_{11} & A_{12} \\ A_{21} & A_{22} \end{bmatrix} x_i, \ i \in Z_+ \tag{5.10}$$

is asymptotically stable.

Proof is given in [8, 6].

To check the asymptotic stability of the positive general model (5.1) and the positive Roesser model (5.4) the Theorem 3.5 is recommended. The application of Theorem 3.5 to checking the asymptotic stability of the models (5.1) and (5.4) will be demonstrated on the following examples.

Example 5.1. Consider the positive general model (5.1) with the matrix

$$A_0 = \begin{bmatrix} 0.1 & 0.2 \\ 0.1 & 0.1 \end{bmatrix}, \ A_1 = \begin{bmatrix} 0 & 0.1 \\ 0 & 0.1 \end{bmatrix}, \ A_1 = \begin{bmatrix} 0.2 & 0.3 \\ 0.1 & 0.2 \end{bmatrix}. \tag{5.11}$$

In this case

$$\bar{A} = A_0 + A_1 + A_2 = \begin{bmatrix} 0.3 & 0.6 \\ 0.2 & 0.4 \end{bmatrix} \tag{5.12}$$

and

$$\hat{A} = \bar{A} - I_n = \begin{bmatrix} -0.7 & 0.6 \\ 0.2 & -0.6 \end{bmatrix}. \tag{5.13}$$

Using the elementary column operation to (5.13) we obtain

$$\hat{A} = \begin{bmatrix} -0.7 & 0.6 \\ 0.2 & -0.6 \end{bmatrix} \xrightarrow{R\left[2+1\times\frac{6}{7}\right]} \begin{bmatrix} -0.7 & 0 \\ 0.2 & -\frac{3}{7} \end{bmatrix}.$$

The condition ii) of Theorem 3.5 is satisfied and the positive general model with (5.11) is asymptotically stable.

Example 5.2. Consider the positive Roesser model (5.4) with the matrices

$$A = \begin{bmatrix} A_{11} & A_{12} \\ A_{21} & A_{22} \end{bmatrix} \tag{5.14a}$$

and

$$A_{11} = \begin{bmatrix} 0.6 & 0.2 \\ 0.1 & 0.4 \end{bmatrix}, \ A_{12} = \begin{bmatrix} 0.1 \\ 0.2 \end{bmatrix},$$
$$A_{21} = [0.2 \ \ 0.1], \ A_{22} = [0.8]. \tag{5.14b}$$

In this case

$$\hat{A} = A - I_n = \begin{bmatrix} -0.4 & 0.2 & 0.1 \\ 0.1 & -0.6 & 0.2 \\ 0.2 & 0.1 & -0.2 \end{bmatrix}. \tag{5.15}$$

Using the elementary column operation to (5.15) we obtain

$$\begin{bmatrix} -0.4 & 0.2 & 0.1 \\ 0.1 & -0.6 & 0.2 \\ 0.2 & 0.1 & -0.2 \end{bmatrix} \xrightarrow[R[3+1\times 0.25]]{R[2+1\times 0.5]} \begin{bmatrix} -0.4 & 0 & 0 \\ 0.1 & -0.55 & 0.225 \\ 0.2 & 0.2 & -0.15 \end{bmatrix}$$
$$\xrightarrow{R\left[3+2\times\frac{22.5}{55}\right]} \begin{bmatrix} -0.4 & 0 & 0 \\ 0.1 & -0.55 & 0 \\ 0.2 & 0.2 & -0.0682 \end{bmatrix}$$

The condition ii) of Theorem 3.5 is satisfied and the positive Roesser model with (5.14) is asymptotically stable.

In a similar way as for 1D linear systems using the approach given in [7] the considerations can be easily extended to 2D linear systems with delays and to fractional 1D and 2D linear systems.

6. Fractional Positive Discrete-Time Linear Systems

Consider the autonomous fractional discrete-time linear systems with q delays [10]

$$x_{i+1} = \sum_{j=1}^{i+1} (-1)^{j+1} \binom{\alpha}{j} x_{i-j+1} + \sum_{k=0}^{q} A_k x_{i-k}, \ 0 < \alpha < 1 \tag{6.1}$$

where α is the fractional order, $x_i \in \Re^n$ is the state vector, $A_k \in \Re^{n\times n}$, $k = 0,1,\cdots,q$ and

$$\binom{\alpha}{j} = \begin{cases} 1 & \text{for } \ j = 0 \\ \dfrac{\alpha(\alpha-1)\ldots(\alpha-j+1)}{j!} & \text{for } \ j = 1,2,\cdots \end{cases} \tag{6.2}$$

The fractional system (6.1) is called (internally) positive if $x_i \in \Re_+^n$, for any initial conditions $x_{-k} \in \Re_+^n$, $k = 0,1,\cdots,q$.

Theorem 6.1. [10] The fractional system (6.1) is positive if and only if $A_k + c_{k+1} I_n \in \Re_+^{n\times n}$ for $k = 0,1,\cdots,q$

where $c_k = (-1)^k \binom{\alpha}{k}$.

The fractional positive system (6.1) is called asymptotically stable if

$$\lim_{i\to\infty} x_i = 0 \quad \text{for all } x_{-k} \in \Re_+^n, \; k = 0,1,\cdots,q. \qquad (6.3)$$

Theorem 6.2. [10] The fractional positive system (6.1) is asymptotically stable if and only if the positive discrete-time system without delays

$$x_{i+1} = \bar{A}x_i, \quad \bar{A} = -I_n + \sum_{k=0}^{q} A_k \qquad (6.4)$$

is asymptotically stable.

Proof is given in [10].

To check the asymptotic stability of the fractional positive system (6.1) Theorem 3.5 is recommended. The application of Theorem 3.5 to checking the asymptotic stability of the system (6.1) will be demonstrated on the following example.

Example 6.1. Consider the fractional system (6.1) for $\alpha = 0.5$ with $q = 1$ and the matrices

$$A_0 = \begin{bmatrix} 0.55 & 0.1 \\ 0.05 & 0.5 \end{bmatrix}, \quad A_1 = \begin{bmatrix} 0.2 & 0.1 \\ 0.05 & 0.2 \end{bmatrix}. \qquad (6.5)$$

The fractional system is positive since

$$A_0 + c_1 I_2 = A_0 - \alpha I_2 = \begin{bmatrix} 0.05 & 0.1 \\ 0.05 & 0 \end{bmatrix} \in \Re_+^{2\times 2} \qquad (6.6a)$$

and

$$A_1 + c_2 I_2 = A_2 + \frac{\alpha(\alpha-1)}{2} I_2 = \begin{bmatrix} 0.075 & 0.1 \\ 0.05 & 0.075 \end{bmatrix} \in \Re_+^{2\times 2} \qquad (6.6b)$$

Therefore, to check the asymptotic stability of the positive system we may use Theorem 3.5.

Using (3.5) for $n = 2$ and (6.4) we obtain

$$\hat{A} = \bar{A} - I_2 = A_0 + A_1 - 2I_2 = \begin{bmatrix} -1.25 & 0.2 \\ 0.1 & -1.3 \end{bmatrix} \qquad (6.7)$$

and

$$\hat{A}_1^{(1)} = \hat{a}_{22} + \frac{\hat{a}_{12}\hat{a}_{21}}{\hat{a}_{11}} = -1.3 + \frac{0.2\cdot 0.1}{1.25} = -1.284 < 0\,. \qquad (6.8)$$

The condition i) of Theorem 3.5 is also satisfied and the positive system is asymptotically stable.

Using the elementary column operations to the matrix (6.7) we obtain

$$\begin{bmatrix} -1.25 & 0.2 \\ 0.1 & -1.3 \end{bmatrix} \xrightarrow{R[2+1\times 0.16]} \begin{bmatrix} -1.25 & 0 \\ 0.1 & -1.284 \end{bmatrix}.$$

The condition ii) of Theorem 3.5 is satisfied and the positive system is asymptotically stable.

This approach can be also applied to checking the asymptotic stability of the positive 2D linear systems with delays.

7. Concluding Remarks

New tests for checking asymptotic stability of positive 1D continuous-time and discrete-time linear systems without and with delays and of positive 2D linear systems described by the general and the Roesser models have been proposed. The tests are based on the Theorem 2.5 and Theorem 3.5. Checking of the asymptotic stability of positive 2D linear systems has been reduced to checking of suitable corresponding 1D positive linear systems. It has been shown that the stability tests can be also applied to checking the asymptotic stability of fractional discrete-time linear systems with delay. The tests can be also extended to 2D continuous-discrete linear systems and to 1D and 2D fractional linear systems. An open problem is extension of these considerations to 2D positive switched linear systems.

8. References

[1] L. Farina and S. Rinaldi, "Positive Linear Systems; Theory and Applications," John Wiley & Sons, Hoboken, 2000.

[2] T. Kaczorek, "Positive 1D and 2D Systems," Springer Verlag, London, 2002.

[3] M. Busłowicz, "Simple Stability Conditions for Linear Systems with Delays," *Bulletin of the Polish Academy of Sciences*, Vol. 56, No. 4, 2008, 319-324.

[4] M. Busłowicz, "Robust Stability of Positive Discrete-Time Linear Systems of Fractional Order," *Bulletin of the Polish Academy of Sciences*, Vol. 58, No. 4, 2010, 567-572.

[5] T. Kaczorek, "Stability of Positive Continuous-Time Linear Systems with Delays," *Bulletin of the Polish Academy of Sciences*, Vol. 57, No. 4, 2009, 395-398.

[6] T. Kaczorek, "Independence of Asymptotic Stability of Positive 2D Linear Systems with Delays of Their Delays," *International Journal of Applied Mathematics and Computer Science*, Vol. 19, No. 2, 2009, 255-261.

[7] T. Kaczorek, "Asymptotic Stability of Positive 2D Linear Systems with Delays," *Bulletin of the Polish Academy of Sciences*, Vol. 57, No. 2, 2009, 133-138.

[8] T. Kaczorek, "Asymptotic Stability of Positive 2D Linear Systems," Computer Applications in Electrical Engineering, Poznan University of Technology, Electrical Engineering Committee of Polish Academy of Sciences, IEEE Poland Section, Poznan.

[9] T. Kaczorek, "Stability and Stabilization of Positive Fractional Linear Systems by State-Feedbacks," *Bulletin of the Polish Academy of Sciences*, Vol. 58, No. 4, 2010, 517-554.

[10] T. Kaczorek, "Selected Problems of Fractional System Theory," Springer Verlag, London, 2011.

[11] K. S. Narendra and R. Shorten, "Hurwitz Stability of Metzler Matrices," *IEEE Transactions on Automatic Control*, Vol. 55, no. 6 June 2010, pp. 1484-1487.

[12] T. Kaczorek, "New Stability Tests of Positive 1D and 2D Linear Systems," *Proceeding of 25th European Conference Modelling and Simulation*, Krakow, 7-10 June 2011.

13

Stability and Leakage Analysis of a Novel PP Based 9T SRAM Cell Using N Curve at Deep Submicron Technology for Multimedia Applications

Shilpi Birla[1*], Rakesh Kumar Singh[2], Manisha Pattanaik[3]

[1]*Department of Electronics and Communication (ECE), Sir Padampat Singhania University (SPSU), Udaipur, India*
[2]*Department of Electronics and Communication (ECE), Bipin Tripathi Kumaon Institute of Technology (BTKIT), Dwarahat Almora, India*
[3]*VLSI Group, Atal Bihari Vajpayee Indian Institute of Information Technology & Management (ABV-IIITM), Gwalior, India*

Abstract

Due to continuous scaling of CMOS, stability is a prime concerned for CMOS SRAM memory cells. As scaling will increase the packing density but at the same time it is affecting the stability which leads to write failures and read disturbs of the conventional 6T SRAM cell. To increase the stability of the cell various SRAM cell topologies has been introduced, 8T SRAM is one of them but it has its limitation like read disturbance. In this paper we have analyzed a novel PP based 9T SRAM at 45 nm technology. Cell which has 33% increased SVNM (Static Voltage Noise Margin) from 6T and also 22% reduced leakage power. N curve analysis has been done to find the various stability factors. As compared to the 10T SRAM cell it is more area efficient.

Keywords: N Curve, Scaling, SVNM (Static Voltage Noise Margin), Leakage Power, 9T SRAM Cell

1. Introduction

The high demand of increasing packaging density and low power SRAMs for multimedia applications leads to the problem of data stability. As ultra low power supply voltages suppresses power consumption, gate leakage and stand by current which results in increase of life time of battery. Various Read & Write assist methods were introduced to enhance the write margin and read stability of 6T Cells. Some of the techniques are CVDD (Cell Vdd) adjustment, CVSS (Cell virtual ground), dual rail power supply, negative bitline etc. But still the voltage of the conventional 6T SRAM cannot be reduced beyond 0.6 V for successful operation. Various topologies of SRAM cell has been introduced, 7T SRAM cell in which a read static noise margin is achieved by cutting off a pull down path during read operation but has limited write capability due to single end write operations [1]. 8T SRAM cell which is one of the popular topology which increases the stability but has its own limitation. In this paper the limitation of 8T has been removed and alternative topologies have been discussed to increase the stability [2]. Although other 9T SRAM cell as in [3] is also been discussed but it suffers from read disturbance. As far as best of my knowledge this cell has not been reported yet.

In section II various factors of SRAM functional Margins has been reported. In section III the novel PP based 9T SRAM cell has been explained in detail. In section IV N curve has been discussed. In section V the analysis of various stability parameters with respect to Vdd and temperature has been discussed. In section VI the leakage power of the proposed cell has been discussed and in the end conclusion.

2. SRAM Functional Margins

SRAM functional margins are determined by three SRAM design Parameters: static noise margin (SNM), write margin (WRM), and cell current (Icell). Since all of them strongly depend on operating voltage (*V*DD), transistor channel length (Lg), and width (Wg). So the cell stability depends on the amount of V_T mismatch caused by the random variation (σV_T) of threshold voltage V_T

and operation voltage VDD as well as cell ratios: γ-ratio for write and β-ratio for read [4].

2.1. Static Noise Margin

The static noise margin (SNM) is the maximum amount of noise voltage VN that can be tolerated at the both inputs of the cross-coupled inverters in different directions while inverters still maintain bi-stable operating points and cell retains its data [5]. In other words, the static noise margin (SNM) quantifies the amount of noise voltage VN required at the storage nodes of SRAM to flip the cell data. The cell becomes more vulnerable to noise during a read access since the "0" storage node rises to a voltage higher than ground (GND) due to a voltage division along the Pass gate transistors and inverter Pull-down devices between the pre-charged BL and the GND terminal of the cell. The ratio of the transistor width of Pull-down to Passgate, commonly referred to as the β-ratio determines how high the "0" storage node rises during a read access [4] as shown in **Figure 1** for conventional 6T SRAM cell. Due to the scaling of the device to nanometer regime, the variation of β-ratio is significantly increased. This is the primary reason for increasing SNM challenge in nanometer-scale SRAM. The ratio of inverter pull-down transistors (M1 or M2) and pull-up transistors (M3 or M4) also directly impacts the cell immunity to noise. Weaker pull-up due to the variations makes the cell easier to flip as lowering its trip point of inverter, making the cell more vulnerable to noise.

When the WL is off, the SNM becomes larger than that for read access because of no rising of "0" storage node from GND level [4]. The two kinds of SNMs for data retention and read access are referred to as "hold SNM margin" and "read SNM margin" [6].

2.2. Write Margin

The cell data is written by forcing the BL pair to the differential levels of "1" and "0" while WL is asserted to allow pass gate transistors (M5 or M6) connected to the BL. The potential of the corresponding storage node is pulled down to the critical level that is dependent on the ratio of transistor strengths between M5 and M3 (or M6 and M4). This ratio is referred to as γ -ratio. In order to ensure robust write operation, the critical level has to be lowered than the trip point of connected inverter before the level of "0" written BL is reached to the end-point (e.g., GND). The write margin (WRM) is defined as the rest of potential difference between the BL level at which the data is flipped and the end-point (e.g., GND) as shown in **Figure 1**. If the cell data is flipped when the BL comes at X mV, where X mV is allowed to reach to the GND level, WRM is defined as X mV. As the device sizes of Pass gate and Pull-up are scaled down to nanometer regime, the variation of γ-ratio is significantly increased. That is the reason why WRM has become just as difficult as read in nanometer-scale SRAM [7].

2.3. Cell Current (Icell)

The BL discharging time takes a large percentage of the total access time. The discharging time (TBL) depends on the BL capacitance, the cell current, and the required BL discharging level (VSEN). The amount of cell current (Icell) is determined by the strength of passgate and pull-down connected in series between the BL and GND as shown in **Figure 1**. The higher VT settings for pass gate, pull-down, and pull-up transistors in SRAM can suppress the sub-threshold leakage but it causes not only the reduction of Icell but also increases its variation [5].

3. Proposed Novel PP Based 9T Cell

In this paper we have proposed a novel PP based 9T SRAM Cell **Figure 2**. In this cell one extra signal RWL is used during read operation, during read operation we keep it at gnd voltage otherwise the value remains high. The true storage nodes are separated from the two virtual storage nodes connected between the stacked PMOS. If we look at the figure we will find that there is one extra NMOS transistor is used which creates a discharging path. It is connected to the RWL. The discharging path is used such that to discharge a precharged high bitline during the read operation.

This circuit has certain advantages like it does not have read problem as the discharging path is isolated from the true storage nodes. The write ability is also not disturbed in this structure. We have used a single wordline for both the operations read and write .This cell has better stability and it is power efficient.

3.1. Detailed Structure of the Cell

In this section, we describe our cell design in **Figure 2**. As mentioned previously, it is composed of two cross coupled P-P-N inverters, and data is stored in node Q and

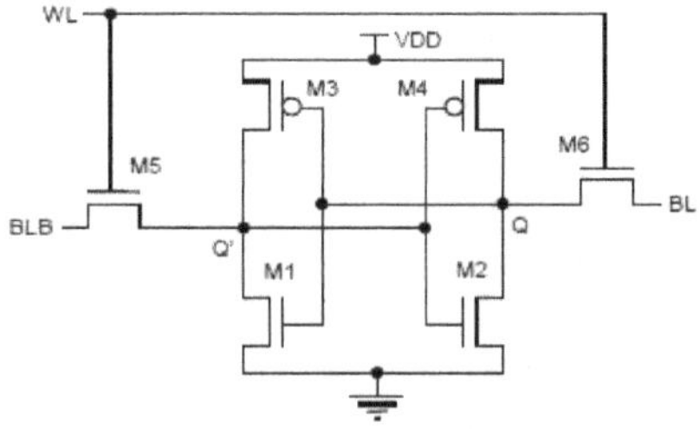

Figure 1. Conventional 6T SRAM cell.

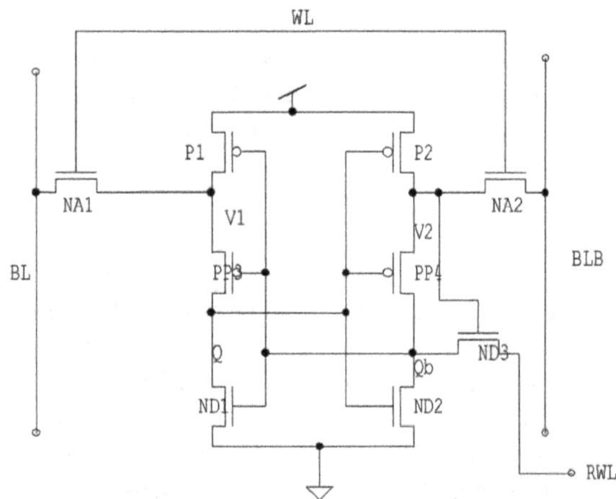

Figure 2. Proposed PP based 9T SRAM cell.

node Qb in a complementary manner. Transistors P1, PP3, and ND1 form a P-P-N inverter and P1, PP4, ND2 form another.

ND1 provides the read current path for discharging a bitline (BL) or its complementary (BLB), depending on the stored values of Q and Qb, respectively. The source terminal of this transistor is connected to the VGND pin, which connects to the ground voltage only during the read operation. Anytime else, it stays high to curb unnecessary leakage current.V1 and V2 are located between the two cascaded P-MOS transistors forming the P-P-N inverter. Q and Qb are the storage nodes .BL and BLB are bitlines while Wl is the word line as in conventional 6T SRAM cell.

3.2. Working of the Novel 9T Cell

3.2.1. Write Operation

During a write operation .initially in this PP based 9T SRAM **Figure 2**, storage node Q stores "0" while Qb stores "1". To perform a write operation, the wordline WL is enabled and one bitline, e.g., BLB, is pulled down to ground in advance. When the supply voltage is relatively high (e.g., 1 V), node Qb (storing "1") here in this case will be pulled down directly through the discharging path formed by. In turn, node Q will be charged up to complete the data-flipping process.

In general, the lower portion of our P-P-N inverter pair can be viewed as a latch consisting of PP3-ND1and PP4-ND2. In some sense, this latch takes node V1and node V2 as the pseudo supply terminals. In step 1, Qb is pulled down quickly to nearly the ground voltage at the beginning of the write operation since it is driven by BLB tied to strong "0". Qb via the PMOS between them (PP3), reducing the voltage of Qb to a lower middle voltage. During this time period, PP3 and PP4 controlled by Qb still conducts weakly to pull up voltage at node Q, Due to the coupling effect of parasitic capacitances the voltage of Qb, which is in the floating state, rises with node Q but only slightly. In step 2, the data flipping finally takes place when Q is strong enough to conduct the PDR transistor to discharge Qb down to the ground voltage.

It is worth mentioning that even though such a write mechanism takes relatively longer time to accomplish the data flipping, it is still shorter than the read access time, and therefore, overall it does not introduce any operating frequency penalty. We can also further improve the cell's write-ability by strengthening the access transistors (NA1 and NA2). It does not affect the read performance.

3.2.2. Read Operation

To perform a read operation, the wordline WL is enabled and RWL is pulled down to ground to allow bitline discharging. Assuming that the data stored at Q is now "0". Since data node Q and Qb are isolated from bitline BL by PP2 and PP3 (which is between the true storage node Q) and thus the so-called *read current* (which is the current used to discharge a bitline) does not flow through the storage node Qb but through the *bypassing ND*3 as indicated in **Figure 2**. This is the main reason why the read stability does not degrade at all in our cell. As for a 6T cell, the read current flows through the storage node directly, thereby causing *read disturbance*, *i.e.*, the voltage at data node Q will rise temporarily. This will degrade the read stability because the cell flipping will be more likely to take place.

The pull-up transistors P1 and P2 are usually made weaker for easy write operation just like in a conventional 6T cell. While the pull-down transistors ND1 and ND2, forming the cell discharging paths, need to be stronger to facilitate a larger read current and thereby a quicker access. The pass gate transistors NA1 and NA2 need to be strong enough to serve as high-conduction paths between the accessed cell and the bitlines during both the read and write operations. The two pull-up transistors, PP2 and PP3, need to be slightly stronger, to compensate for the conductivity degradation of the cascaded PMOS structure linking the storage nodes (*i.e.*, Q and Qb) and Vdd, which help contribute to a good hold SNM. Unlike a 6T cell, the pull-down transistors do not have to be strong, since they do not involve in the cell discharging paths. However, their strengths are made comparable to the cascaded PMOS structure mentioned above to achieve a more balanced cell structure which could lead to a larger hold SNM.

In our cell we have seen that the SVNM has been 1.53times greater than that of conventional 6T cell. In our cell we achieved 460mv while for 6T it is 300 mv. The leakage power has also been reduced by 3.3 times than that of conventional 6T.

4. Stability Measurement: N Curve Analysis

Numerous analytical models of the static noise margin (SNM) have been developed to optimize the cell design, to predict the effect of parameter changes on the SNM and to assess the impact of intrinsic parameter variations on the cell stability. Furthermore, new SRAM cell circuit designs have been developed to maximize the cell stability for future technology nodes [8]. The set up for N curve is as shown in **Figure 3**. In an ideal case, each of the two cross-coupled inverters in the SRAM cell has an infinite gain. As a result, the butterfly curves delimit a maximal square side of maximum, being an asymptotical limit for the SNM. Therefore, scaling limits the stability of the cell. An additional drawback of the SNM is the inability to measure the SNM with automatic inline testers [4], due to the fact that after measuring the butterfly curves of the cell the static current noise margin (SINM) still has to be derived by mathematical manipulation of the measured data. An alternative definition for the SRAM read stability is based on the N-curve of the [5]. N-curve contains information both on the read stability and on the write-ability, thus allowing a complete functional analysis of the SRAM cell with only one N-curve [8].

Parameters which are find by using N curve these 4 parameters are useful for measuring the write ability and read ability of the cell.

- *The static voltage noise margin* (*SVNM*)

The static voltage noise margin is the voltage difference between points A and B in **Figure 4** and it indicates the maximum tolerable DC noise voltage at the input of the inverter of the cell before its content changes [4].

- *The static current noise margin* (*SINM*)

The static current noise margin is defined as the maximum value of DC current that can be injected in the SRAM cell before its content changes [4]. It is given by the peak value of Iin during read operation that is between points A and B in the **Figure 4**.

- *The Write Trip Voltage* (*WTV*)

The SRAM N-curve also provides information regarding the write ability of the cell. WTV is the voltage drop needed to flip the internal node "1" of the cell with both the bit lines clamped at Vdd [4]. It is given by the voltage difference between the second (B) and the last zero crossing point (C) in **Figure 4**.

- *The Write Trip Current* (*WTI*)

It is the amount of current needed to write the cell when both bit lines are clamped at supply voltage equal to Vdd [5]. The peak value of Iin after the second zero crossing of N-curve gives WTI.

For better read stability, the values of SVNM, and the magnitude of SINM and hence the value of static power noise margin SPNM (product of mean of SVNM and mean of SINM) should be larger. For better write ability the value of WTV, the absolute value of WTI and hence the value of WTP (product of mean of WTV and mean of WTI) must be smaller.

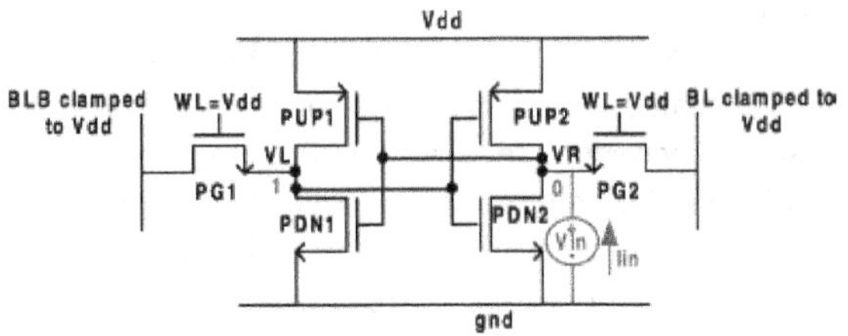

Figure 3. Set up for N curve analysis.

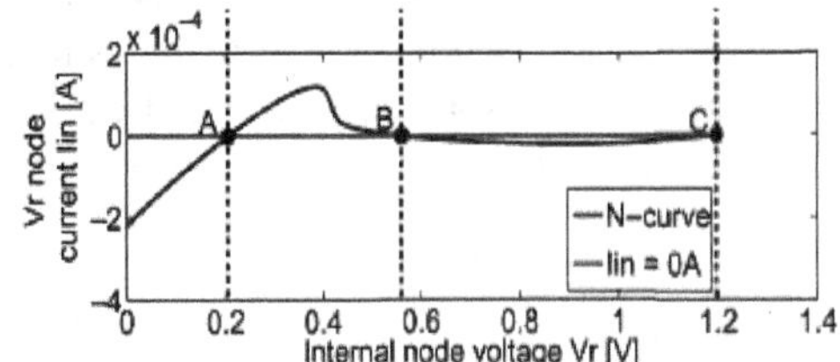

Figure 4. Ncurve for 6 T SRAM cell [2].

5. Analysis of N Curve Metrics

N-curve analysis has been done at 45nm technology in order for low voltage operation. Various factors of stability has been analyses with the affect of temperature and voltage on them. **Figure 5** shows one N curve analysis at Vdd = 1 V at temperature varies from –25°C to 125°C [2].

5.1. Effect of Power Supply (Vdd)

We have seen that there is significant affect of power supply on the 4 parameters which we have obtained from the Ncurve.As Vdd increases the stability also increases [9]. This is also been observed here that as the Vdd increased the SINM, WTV, SVNM and WTI the four parameters has been increased as shown in the given graphs.

5.1.1. Effect on SVNM

As shown in the graph **Figure 6**, we see that at Vdd = 1 V it is maximum 460 mv and reduces when we go to Vdd = 0.6 V. As we know that SVNM it is the maximum DC tolerable voltage before the cell changes it contents so it means that as Vdd reduces the cell tolerance is also reduces.

5.1.2. Effect on WTI

As discussed above the write-trip current (WTI) is the

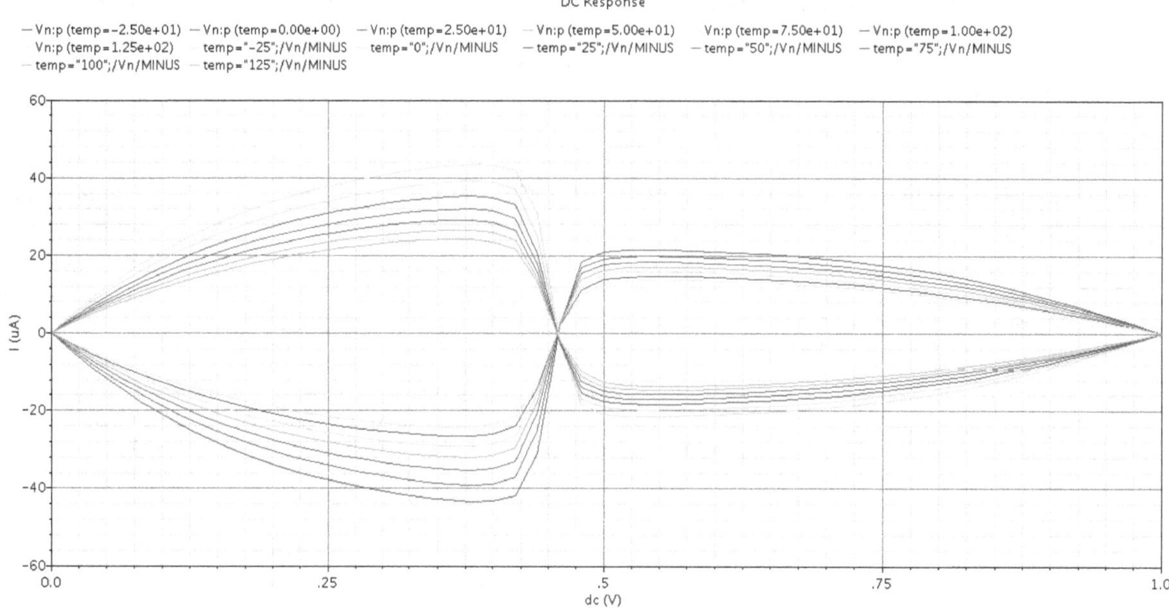

Figure 5. N curve of 9T SRAM cell.

amount of current needed to write the cell when both bit-lines are kept at Vdd . This is the current margin of the cell for which its content changes as in (**Figure 7**). The ability to write a cell with both bit-lines clamped at results actually in a destructive read operation; therefore, the absolute value of WTI should be large enough to cope with the read stability requirement. On the other hand, the lower the absolute WTI is, the higher the write-trip point of the cell. It shows an exponential relation with Vdd. WTI is measure at various temperatures.

5.1.3. Effect on WTV

Write-trip voltage (WTV) is the voltage drop needed to flip the internal node "1" of the cell with both the bit-lines clamped at Vdd. Write ability requires both WTI and WTV.WTV increases with Vdd. At 1 V the cell has maximum stability and it decreases drastically when the Vdd reaches to 0.6 V. As shown in **Figure 8**.

5.1.4. Effect on SINM

By using the combined SVNM and SINM, the read stability criteria for the cell are defined properly. For example, a small SVNM combined with a large SINM will still result in a stable cell since the amount of required noise charged disturb the cell is large. At Vdd 1V we have good SINM but it reduces exponentially at Vdd = 0.6 V, as shown in **Figure 9**.

5.2. Effect of Temperature

As we have varied the temperature from 0˚C to 125˚C we have seen that the SVNM and WTV is unaffected by the temperature variation but the currents *i.e.* the write trip current and static noise margin current has been affected by temperature variation. As temperature increases both the SINM and WTI reduces. As shown in **Figures 10** and **11** respectively. The variation has been observed at varying Vdd from 1 V to 0.6 V.

6. Analysis of Leakage Current for Proposed Cell

In this cell we have achieved 33% less leakage power with respect to 6T SRAM cell, as in this cell we have used the PMOS cell and also we used ND3 which is used to reduced the leakage power. We have seen the affect of Vdd and temperature on leakage power. As we know it depends exponential to Temperature and increases with temperature the same affect is seen here **Figure 12**. It also shows the effect of Vdd which shows that there is 7X increases in Leakage current when we increase the Vdd from 0.6 V to Vdd 1 V.

We have also analyzed the Leakage power with SINM as shown in **Figure 13** and found that as SINM increases the Leakage power also increases which shows that with increasing Vdd the SINM increases and at the same time increasing Vdd results in increasing the leakage power [10].

7. Conclusions

We have proposed a novel 9T SRAM cell which has

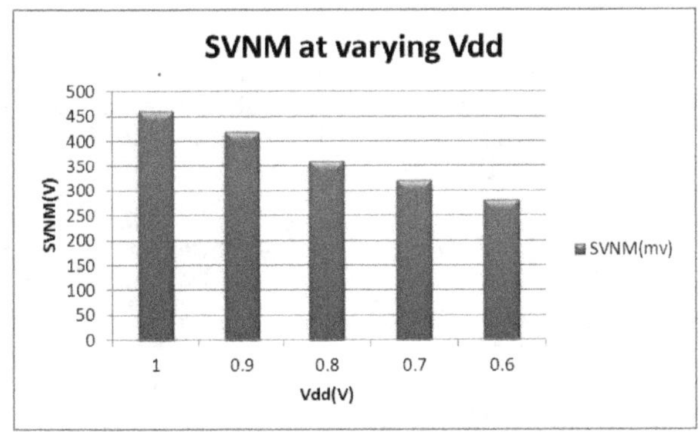

Figure 6. Vdd vs. SVNM.

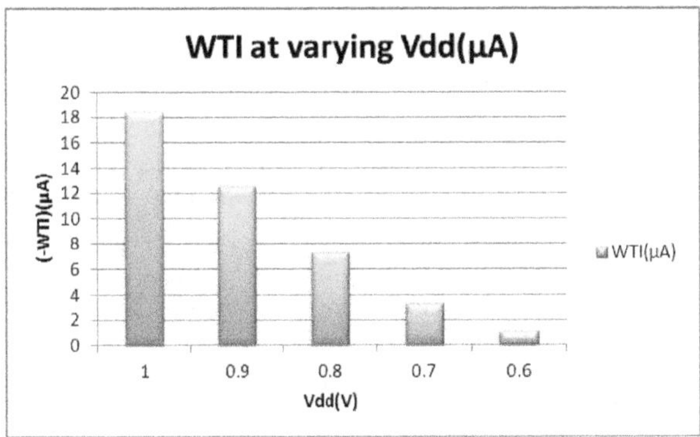

Figure 7. Vdd vs. WTI.

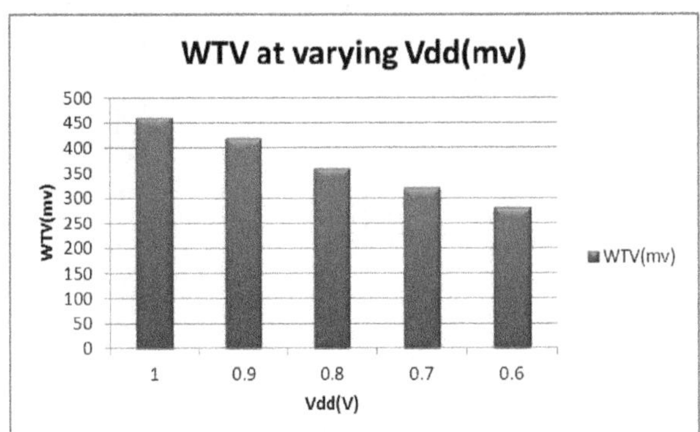

Figure 8. Vdd vs. WTV.

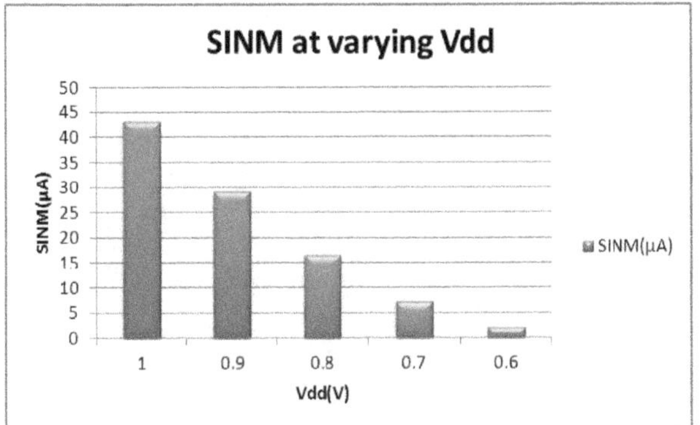

Figure 9. Vdd vs. SINM.

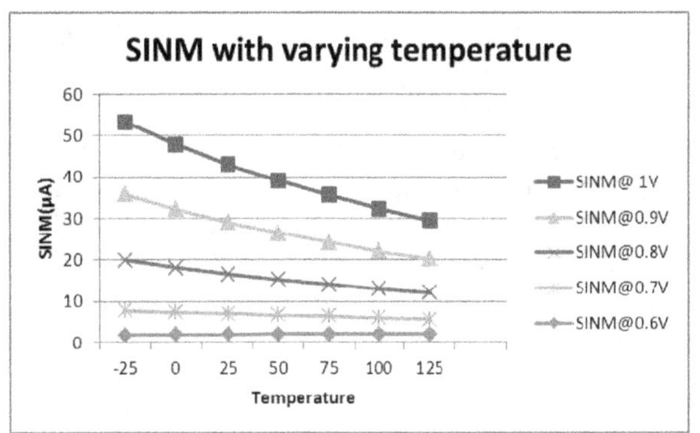

Figure 10. Temperature vs. SINM.

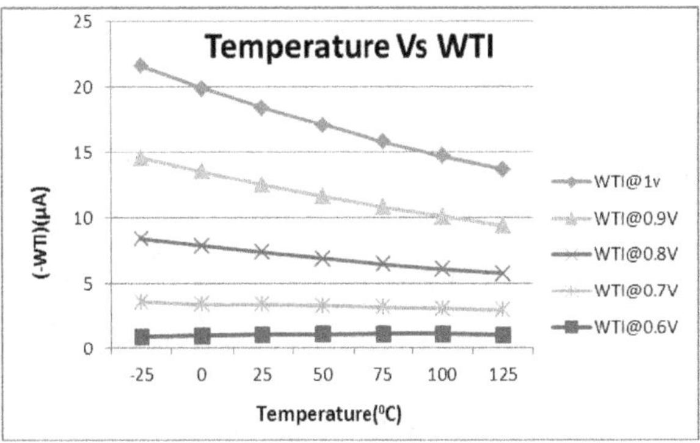

Figure 11. Temperature vs. WTI.

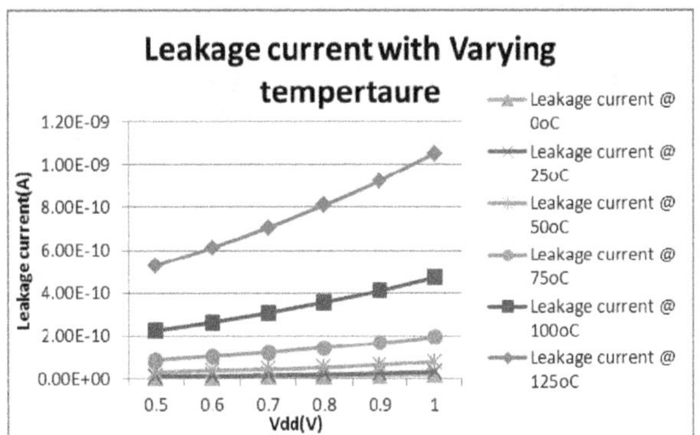

Figure 12. Temperature vs. leakage current.

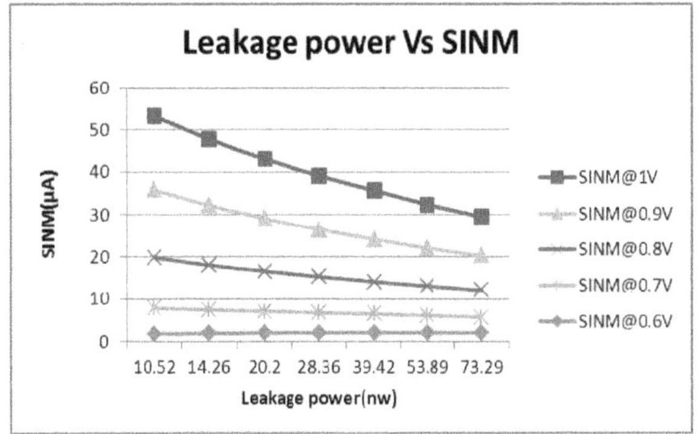

Figure 13. Leakage power vs. SINM.

been simulated at 45 nm 65% increase in SVNM compared to 6T SRAM cell. The cell has 33% leakage power reduction also with respect to 6T SRAM cell and in this we have not used any leakage reduction techniques. So the future expansion can be done by sizing the cell to increase the stability *i.e.* the write ability and read ability of the cell. Also power can be reduced by using various leakage reduction methods. Although the area with respect to 6T has been increased but at lower technology it is comparable to 6T. The SNM measured is 380mv which can be improved by sizing the transistor widths.

8. Acknowledgements

The authors are very grateful to the respective organization for their support and encouragement.

9. References

[1] M. Sinangil, V. Naveen and A. P. Chandrakasan, "A Reconfigurable 8T Ultra–Dynamic Voltage Scalable (U-DVS) SRAM in 65 nm CMOS," *IEEE Journal Solid-State of Circuits*, Vol. 44, No. 11, 2009, pp. 3163-3173.

[2] R. E. Aly and M. A. Bayoumi, "Low-Power Cache Design Using 7T SRAM Cell," *IEEE Transactions on Circuits and Systems II: Express Briefs*, Vol. 54, No. 4, 2007, pp. 318-322.

[3] Z. Liu and V. Kursun, "Characterization of a Novel Nine-Transistor SRAM Cell," *IEEE Transaction of Very large Scale Integration Systems*, Vol. 16, No. 4, 2008, pp. 488-492.

[4] B. H. Calhoun and A. P. Chandrakasan "Static Noise Margin Variation for Sub-threshold SRAM in 65 nm CMOS," *IEEE Journal of Solid-State Circuits*, Vol. 41, No. 7, 2006, pp. 1673-1679.

[5] Y. Chung and S.-H. Song, "Implementation of Low-Voltage Static RAM with Enhanced Data Stability and Circuit Speed," *Microelectronics Journal*, Vol. 40, No. 6, 2009, pp. 944-951.

[6] E. Seevinck, *et al.*, "Static-Noise Margin Analysis of MOS SRAM Cells," *IEEE Journal of Solid-State Circuits*, Vol. 22, No. 5, 1987, pp. 748-754.

[7] C. Wann, *et al.*, "SRAM Cell Design for Stability Methodology," 2005 *IEEE VLSI-TSA International Symposium on VLSI Technology*, 25-27 April 2005, pp. 21-22.

[8] E. Grossar, M. Stucchi and K. Maex, "Read Stability and Write-Ability Analysis of SRAM Cells for Nanometer Technologies," *IEEE Journal of Solid-State Circuits*,Vol. 41, No. 11, 2006, pp. 2577-2588.

[9] S. Birla, M. Pattanaik and R. K. Singh, "Static Noise Margin Analysis of Various SRAM Topologies," IACSIT *International Journal of Engineering and Technology*, Vol. 3, No. 3, 2011, pp. 304-309.

[10] S. Birla, N. Kr. Shukla, M. Pattanaik and R. K. Singh, "Device and Circuit Design Challenges for Low Leakage SRAM for Ultra Low Power Applications," *Canadian Journal on Electrical & Electronics Engineering*, Vol. 1, No. 7, 2010, pp. 157-167.

14

Distortionless Lossy Transmission Lines Terminated by in Series Connected *RCL*-Loads

Vasil G. Angelov[1], **Marin Hristov**[2]
[1]*Department of Mathematics, University of Mining and Geology, Sofia, Bulgaria*
[2]*Department of Microelectronics, Technical University of Sofia, Sofia, Bulgaria*

Abstract

The paper deals with a lossy transmission line terminated at both ends by non-linear *RCL* elements. The mixed problem for the hyperbolic system, describing the transmission line, to an initial value problem for a neutral equation is reduced. Sufficient conditions for the existence and uniqueness of periodic regimes are formulated. The proof is based on the finding out of suitable operator whose fixed point is a periodic solution of the neutral equation. The method has a good rate of convergence of the successive approximations even for high frequencies.

Keywords: Lossy Transmission Line, *RCL*-Nonlinear Loads, Fixed Point, Periodic Solution

1. Introduction

The principal importance of transmission lines investigations has been discussed in many papers (cf. for instance [1-8]). In a previous paper [9] we have investigated lossless transmission lines terminated by in series connected *RCL*-loads. In [10] we have considered a lossy transmission line terminated by a resistive load with exponential *V-I* characteristic. In [11] we have considered periodic regimes for lossy transmission lines terminated by parallel connected *RCL*-loads. Here we investigate lossy transmission lines terminated at both ends by in series connected *RCL*-loads but in contrast of [11] the capacitive element has a nonlinear *V-C* characteristic. Unlike of the usually accepted approach (cf. for instance [12,13]) we consider first order hyperbolic system instead of the Telegrapher's equation derived from it. First we reduce the mixed problem for the hyperbolic system to an initial value problem for neutral system of equations on the boundary [14]. Extending ideas from [15-17] we introduce operators whose fixed points are periodic solutions of the neutral system. Our treatment is based on the fixed point method (cf. [18]). All derivation are performed under assumption

$$R/L = G/C \quad (R \neq 0, G \neq 0).$$

The last condition is known as Heaviside one and it implies that the waves propagate without distortion.

We would like to mention the advantages of our method in comparison of the other used ones: lumped element method, finite element method and finite-difference time-domain method (cf. for instance [19-21]). If we use numerical methods we have to keep one and same accuracy. But here we consider nonlinearities of polynomial and transcendental type (for exponential ones cf. [10]). For such "bad" nonlinearities (cf. [2]) there are examples showing that if we want to keep the same accuracy it should be reduced step thousands of times. Here we obtain (even though approximate) an analytical solution for voltage and current beginning with simple initial approximations.

We proceed from the system:

$$C\frac{\partial u(x,t)}{\partial t} + \frac{\partial i(x,t)}{\partial x} + Gu(x,t) = 0, \tag{1}$$

$$L\frac{\partial i(x,t)}{\partial t} + \frac{\partial u(x,t)}{\partial x} + Ri(x,t) = 0,$$

$$(x,t) \in \Pi = \{(x,t) \in R^2 : (x,t) \in [0,\Lambda] \times [0,\infty)\},$$

$$u(x,0) = u_0(x),\ i(x,0) = i_0(x),\ x \in [0,\Lambda] \tag{2}$$

where L, C, R and G are prescribed specific parameters of the line and $\Lambda > 0$ is its length. Here the current $i(x,t)$ and voltage $u(x,t)$ are unknown functions. The initial conditions for the foregoing system (1) are prescribed functions $u_0(x)$, $i_0(x)$. The boundary conditions can be derived from the loads and sources at the ends of the line (cf. **Figure 1**).

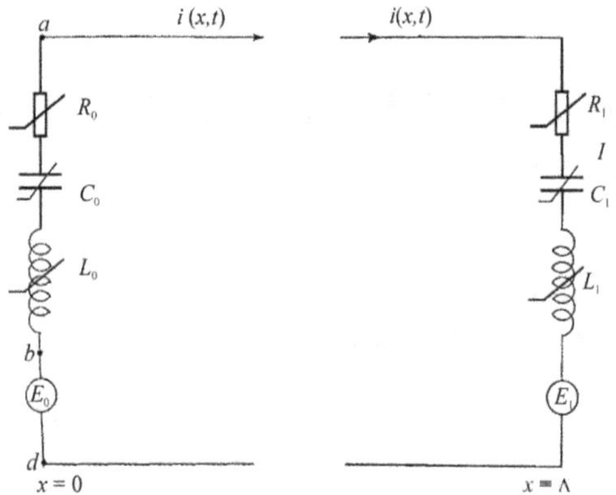

Figure 1. Lossy transmission line terminated by nonlinear *RCL*-loads.

In view of the Kirchoff's voltage law for the voltages between the nodes *a*, *b* and *d* for $x = 0$ we obtain:

$$-u(0,t) = -u_{ad} = u_{ba} - u_{bd} = u_{ba} - E_0(t), \tag{3}$$

where $E_0(t)$ is the source voltage. The voltage u_{ba} is:

$$u_{ba} = u_{R_0} + u_{C_0} + u_{\Psi_0} = R_0(i(0,t)) + u_{C_0} + \frac{\mathrm{d}\Psi_0}{\mathrm{d}t}.$$

To calculate the voltage of the condenser C_0 we proceed from the relation (assuming

$$u_{C_0}(T) \equiv u(T) = 0),$$

$$i = \frac{\mathrm{d}q}{\mathrm{d}t} = \frac{\mathrm{d}(C_0(u).u)}{\mathrm{d}t} \Rightarrow \int_T^t i(x,\tau)\mathrm{d}\tau = C_0(u)\cdot u \equiv \bar{C}_0(u)$$

or

$$u_{C_0} = u(0,t) = \bar{C}_0^{-1}\left(\int_T^t i(0,\tau)\mathrm{d}\tau\right).$$

To calculate the voltage of the inductor L_0 we proceed from

$$u_{\Psi_0} = \frac{\mathrm{d}\Psi_0}{\mathrm{d}t} = (L_0(i)\cdot i) = \left(i\frac{\mathrm{d}L_0(i)}{\mathrm{d}i} + L_0(i)\right)\frac{\mathrm{d}i}{\mathrm{d}t}.$$

Therefore the first boundary condition is:

$$u_{ba} = R_0(i(0,t)) + \bar{C}_0^{-1}\left(\int_T^t i(0,\tau)\mathrm{d}\tau\right) + \left[i(0,t)\frac{\mathrm{d}L_0(i(0,t))}{\mathrm{d}i} + L_0(i(0,t))\right]\frac{\mathrm{d}i(0,t)}{\mathrm{d}t}$$

or

$$u(0,t) = E_0(t) - R_0(i(0,t)) - \bar{C}_0^{-1}\left(\int_T^t i(0,\tau)\mathrm{d}\tau\right) - \left[i(0,t)\frac{\mathrm{d}L_0(i(0,t))}{\mathrm{d}i} + L_0(i(0,t))\right]\frac{\mathrm{d}i(0,t)}{\mathrm{d}t}. \tag{4}$$

Analogously for $x = \Lambda$ (cf. **Figure 1**) we obtain

$$u(\Lambda,t) = E_1(t) + R_1(i(\Lambda,t)) + \bar{C}_1^{-1}\left(\int_T^t i(\Lambda,t)\mathrm{d}\tau\right) + \left[i(\Lambda,t)\frac{\mathrm{d}L_1(i(\Lambda,t))}{\mathrm{d}i} + L_1(i(\Lambda,t))\right]\frac{\mathrm{d}i(\Lambda,t)}{\mathrm{d}t}. \tag{5}$$

Here $R_1(.), C_1(.)$ and $L_1(.)$ are characteristics (in general, nonlinear functions) of *RCL*-loads at right end.

Now we are able to formulate the initial-boundary (mixed) value problem for the hyperbolic transmission line system of equations: to find a solution $(u(x,t), i(x,t))$ of the hyperbolic system (1) for

$$(x,t) \in \Pi = \{(x,t) \in R^2 : 0 \le x \le \Lambda,\ t \ge 0\},$$

satisfying the initial conditions

$$u(x,0) = u_0(x),\ i(x,0) = i_0(x) \text{ for } x \in [0,\Lambda] \tag{6}$$

and the boundary conditions

$$u(0,t) = E_0(t) - R_0(i(0,t)) - \bar{C}_0^{-1}\left(\int_T^t i(0,\tau)\mathrm{d}\tau\right) - \left[i(0,t)\frac{\mathrm{d}L_0(i(0,t))}{\mathrm{d}i} + L_0(i(0,t))\right]\frac{\mathrm{d}i(0,t)}{\mathrm{d}t}, \tag{7}$$

$$u(\Lambda,t) = E_1(t) + R_1(i(\Lambda,t)) + \bar{C}_1^{-1}\left(\int_T^t i(\Lambda,t)\mathrm{d}\tau\right) + \left[i(\Lambda,t)\frac{\mathrm{d}L_1(i(\Lambda,t))}{\mathrm{d}i} + L_1(i(\Lambda,t))\right]\frac{\mathrm{d}i(\Lambda,t)}{\mathrm{d}t} \tag{8}$$

where $u_0(x), i_0(x), E_k(t), R_k(.), C_k(.)$ and $L_k(.)$ $(k = 0, 1)$ are prescribed functions.

So the system (1) and conditions (6) - (8) form a mixed problem for a lossy transmission line equations.

2. Reducing the Mixed Problem for the Transmission Line System to an Initial Value Problem for a Nonlinear Neutral System

First we present system (1) in matrix form:

$$A_1U_t + A_2U_x + A_3U = 0 \left(U_t \equiv \frac{\partial U}{\partial t}, U_x \equiv \frac{\partial U}{\partial x}\right) \tag{9}$$

where $A_1 = \begin{bmatrix} C & 0 \\ 0 & L \end{bmatrix}$, $A_2 = \begin{bmatrix} 0 & 1 \\ 1 & 0 \end{bmatrix}$, $A_3 = \begin{bmatrix} G & 0 \\ 0 & R \end{bmatrix}$,

$$U = \begin{bmatrix} u \\ i \end{bmatrix}, U_t = \begin{bmatrix} u_t \\ i_t \end{bmatrix}, U_x = \begin{bmatrix} u_x \\ i_x \end{bmatrix}.$$

Since $|A_1| = LC \ne 0$, then multiplying Equation (9) by A_1^{-1} we obtain

$$U_t + AU_x + BU = 0 \quad (10)$$

where $A = \begin{bmatrix} 0 & 1/C \\ 1/L & 0 \end{bmatrix}$, $B = \begin{bmatrix} G/C & 0 \\ 0 & R/L \end{bmatrix}$. In order to transform the matrix $A = A_1^{-1}A_2 = \begin{bmatrix} 0 & 1/C \\ 1/L & 0 \end{bmatrix}$ in a diagonal form we solve the characteristic equation:

$$\begin{vmatrix} -\lambda & 1/C \\ 1/L & -\lambda \end{vmatrix} = 0$$

whose roots are $\lambda_1 = 1/\sqrt{LC}$ and $\lambda_2 = -1/\sqrt{LC}$. Denote the matrix formed by eigenvectors by

$$H = \begin{bmatrix} \sqrt{C} & \sqrt{L} \\ -\sqrt{C} & \sqrt{L} \end{bmatrix}$$

and its inverse one—by

$$H^{-1} = \frac{1}{2}\begin{bmatrix} 1/\sqrt{C} & -1/\sqrt{C} \\ 1/\sqrt{L} & 1/\sqrt{L} \end{bmatrix}.$$

If we denote by

$$A^{can} = \begin{bmatrix} 1/\sqrt{LC} & 0 \\ 0 & -1/\sqrt{LC} \end{bmatrix},$$

then $A^{can} = HAH^{-1}$.

Introduce new variables $Z = HU$ (or $U = H^{-1}Z$):

$$Z = \begin{bmatrix} V(x,t) \\ I(x,t) \end{bmatrix}, U = \begin{bmatrix} u(x,t) \\ i(x,t) \end{bmatrix}.$$

Then

$$\begin{vmatrix} V(x,t) = \sqrt{C}u(x,t) + \sqrt{L}i(x,t) \\ I(x,t) = -\sqrt{C}u(x,t) + \sqrt{L}i(x,t), \end{vmatrix} \quad (11)$$

$$\begin{vmatrix} u(x,t) = V(x,t)/2\sqrt{C} - I(x,t)/2\sqrt{C} \\ i(x,t) = V(x,t)/2\sqrt{L} + I(x,t)/2\sqrt{L}. \end{vmatrix} \quad (12)$$

Replacing $U = H^{-1}Z$ in Equation (10) we obtain

$$\frac{\partial(H^{-1}Z)}{\partial t} + A\frac{\partial(H^{-1}Z)}{\partial x} + B(H^{-1}Z) = 0.$$

Since H^{-1} is a constant matrix we have:

$$H^{-1}Z_t + (AH^{-1})Z_x + (BH^{-1})Z = 0.$$

After multiplication from the left by H we obtain

$$Z_t + H(AH^{-1})Z_x + H(BH^{-1})Z = 0, \text{ i.e.}$$

$$Z_t + A^{can}Z_x + (HBH^{-1})Z = 0. \quad (13)$$

But

$$HBH^{-1} = \frac{1}{2}\begin{bmatrix} (G/C)+(R/L) & (-G/C)+(R/L) \\ (-G/C)+(R/L) & (G/C)+(R/L) \end{bmatrix}$$

and then

$$\begin{bmatrix} V_t \\ I_t \end{bmatrix} + \begin{bmatrix} 1/\sqrt{LC} & 0 \\ 0 & -1/\sqrt{LC} \end{bmatrix}\begin{bmatrix} V_x \\ I_x \end{bmatrix} + \frac{1}{2}\begin{bmatrix} (G/C)+(R/L) & (-G/C)+(R/L) \\ (-G/C)+(R/L) & (G/C)+(R/L) \end{bmatrix}\begin{bmatrix} V \\ I \end{bmatrix} = \begin{bmatrix} 0 \\ 0 \end{bmatrix}.$$

We consider distortionless lossy transmission lines that means the following Heaviside condition is fulfilled:

$$R/L = G/C.$$

Then HBH^{-1} can be simplified and the last system becomes:

$$\begin{bmatrix} V_t \\ I_t \end{bmatrix} + \begin{bmatrix} 1/\sqrt{LC} & 0 \\ 0 & -1/\sqrt{LC} \end{bmatrix}\begin{bmatrix} V_x \\ I_x \end{bmatrix} + \begin{bmatrix} R/L & 0 \\ 0 & R/L \end{bmatrix}\begin{bmatrix} V \\ I \end{bmatrix} = \begin{bmatrix} 0 \\ 0 \end{bmatrix}$$

or

$$\begin{gathered} V_t + (1/\sqrt{LC})V_x + (R/L)V = 0 \\ I_t - (1/\sqrt{LC})I_x + (R/L)I = 0. \end{gathered} \quad (14)$$

The new initial conditions we obtain from conditions (6) and system (12):

$$\begin{aligned} V(x,0) &= \sqrt{C}\,u(x,0) + \sqrt{L}\,i(x,0) \\ &= \sqrt{C}\,u_0(x) + \sqrt{L}\,i_0(x) \equiv V_0(x),\ x \in [0,\Lambda], \end{aligned} \quad (15)$$

$$\begin{aligned} I(x,0) &= -\sqrt{C}\,u(x,0) + \sqrt{L}\,i(x,0) \\ &= -\sqrt{C}\,u_0(x) + \sqrt{L}\,i_0(x) \equiv I_0(x),\ x \in [0,\Lambda]. \end{aligned} \quad (16)$$

Further on we set

$$\begin{gathered} W(x,t) = e^{(R/L)t}V(x,t),\ J(x,t) = e^{(R/L)t}I(x,t) \\ \Leftrightarrow V(x,t) = e^{-(R/L)t}W(x,t),\ I(x,t) = e^{-(R/L)t}J(x,t). \end{gathered} \quad (17)$$

Then system (14) can be written in the form:

$$W_t + vW_x = 0,\quad J_t - vJ_x = 0\ \left(v = 1/\sqrt{LC}\right). \quad (18)$$

The initial conditions (15), (16) remain the same ones:

$$W(0,t) = V(0,t) = V_0(x),\ J(0,t) = I(0,t) = I_0(x).$$

From system (12) and denotation (17) we obtain

$$\begin{aligned} u(x,t) &= [W(x,t) - J(x,t)]e^{-(R/L)t}/(2\sqrt{C}), \\ i(x,t) &= [W(x,t) + J(x,t)]e^{-(R/L)t}/(2\sqrt{L}) \end{aligned} \quad (19)$$

and then

$$W(x,t) = e^{(R/L)t}\sqrt{C}\,u(x,t) + e^{(R/L)t}\sqrt{L}\,i(x,t),$$

$$J(x,t) = -e^{(R/L)t}\sqrt{C}\,u(x,t) + e^{(R/L)t}\sqrt{L}\,i(x,t).$$

Replacing in system (19) $x=0$ we have

$$u(0,t)=\left[W(0,t)-J(0,t)\right]e^{-(R/L)t}\Big/\left(2\sqrt{C}\right),$$
$$i(0,t)=\left[W(0,t)+J(0,t)\right]e^{-(R/L)t}\Big/\left(2\sqrt{L}\right) \tag{20}$$

and replacing $x=\Lambda$ —

$$u(\Lambda,t)=\left[W(\Lambda,t)-J(\Lambda,t)\right]e^{-(R/L)t}\Big/\left(2\sqrt{C}\right),$$
$$i(\Lambda,t)=\left[W(\Lambda,t)+J(\Lambda,t)\right]e^{-(R/L)t}\Big/\left(2\sqrt{L}\right). \tag{21}$$

Now replace expressions (20) into the first boundary condition and obtain:

$$\begin{aligned}
&\left[W(0,t)-J(0,t)\right]e^{-(R/L)t}\Big/\left(2\sqrt{C}\right)\\
&=E_0(t)-R_0\left(\left(W(0,t)+J(0,t)\right)e^{-(R/L)t}\Big/\left(2\sqrt{L}\right)\right)\\
&-\bar{C}_0^{-1}\left(\int_T^t\left[W(0,\tau)+J(0,\tau)\right]e^{-(R/L)t}\Big/\left(2\sqrt{L}\right)\mathrm{d}\tau\right)\\
&-\left[\left(i(0,t)\right)\frac{\mathrm{d}L_0\left(i(0,t)\right)}{\mathrm{d}i}+L_0\left(i(0,t)\right)\right]\\
&\times\frac{\mathrm{d}}{\mathrm{d}t}\left(\left(W(0,t)+J(0,t)\right)e^{-(R/L)t}\Big/\left(2\sqrt{L}\right)\right).
\end{aligned} \tag{22}$$

Replacing expressions (21) into the second boundary condition we obtain the following equation

$$\begin{aligned}
&\left[W(\Lambda,t)-J(\Lambda,t)\right]e^{-(R/L)t}\Big/\left(2\sqrt{C}\right)\\
&=E_1(t)+R_1\left(\left(W(\Lambda,t)+J(\Lambda,t)\right)e^{-(R/L)t}\Big/\left(2\sqrt{L}\right)\right)\\
&+\bar{C}_1^{-1}\left(\int_T^t\left[W(\Lambda,s)+J(\Lambda,s)\right]e^{-(R/L)s}\Big/\left(2\sqrt{L}\right)\mathrm{d}s\right)\\
&+\left[i(\Lambda,t)\frac{\mathrm{d}L_1\left(i(\Lambda,t)\right)}{\mathrm{d}i}+L_1\left(i(\Lambda,t)\right)\right]\\
&\times\frac{\mathrm{d}}{\mathrm{d}t}\left(\left(W(\Lambda,t)+J(\Lambda,t)\right)e^{-(R/L)t}\Big/\left(2\sqrt{L}\right)\right).
\end{aligned} \tag{23}$$

Introduce denotations

$$\begin{aligned}
\tilde{L}_0(t)&=i(0,t)\frac{\mathrm{d}L_0\left(i(0,t)\right)}{\mathrm{d}i}+L_0\left(i(0,t)\right)\\
&=\left(\left(W(0,t)+J(0,t)\right)e^{-(R/L)t}\Big/\left(2\sqrt{L}\right)\right)\frac{\mathrm{d}L_0\left(i(0,t)\right)}{\mathrm{d}i}\\
&+L_0\left(\left(W(0,t)+J(0,t)\right)e^{-(R/L)t}\Big/\left(2\sqrt{L}\right)\right),
\end{aligned}$$

$$\begin{aligned}
\tilde{L}_1(t)&=i(\Lambda,t)\frac{\mathrm{d}L_1\left(i(\Lambda,t)\right)}{\mathrm{d}i}+L_1\left(i(\Lambda,t)\right)\\
&=\left(\left(W(\Lambda,t)+J(\Lambda,t)\right)e^{-(R/L)t}\Big/\left(2\sqrt{L}\right)\right)\frac{\mathrm{d}L_1\left(i(\Lambda,t)\right)}{\mathrm{d}i}\\
&+L_1\left(\left(W(\Lambda,t)+J(\Lambda,t)\right)e^{-(R/L)t}\Big/\left(2\sqrt{L}\right)\right).
\end{aligned}$$

We assume that the unknown functions are $W(\Lambda,t)=W(t)$, $J(0,t)=J(t)$. An integration along the charateristics yields $W(\Lambda,t+T)=W(0,t)$, $J(\Lambda,t)=J(0,t+T)$ and then Equations (22) and (23) become

$$\begin{aligned}
&\left(W(0,t+T)-J(0,t)\right)e^{-(R/L)t}\Big/\left(2\sqrt{C}\right)\\
&=E_0(t)-R_0\left(\left(W(0,t+T)-J(0,t)\right)e^{-(R/L)t}\Big/\left(2\sqrt{C}\right)\right)\\
&-\bar{C}_0^{-1}\left(\int_T^t\left(\left(W(0,t+T)+J(0,\tau)\right)e^{-(R/L)\tau}\Big/\left(2\sqrt{L}\right)\right)\mathrm{d}\tau\right)\\
&-\tilde{L}_0(t)\frac{\mathrm{d}}{\mathrm{d}t}\left(\left(W(0,t+T)+J(0,\tau)\right)e^{-(R/L)\tau}\Big/\left(2\sqrt{L}\right)\right)
\end{aligned}$$

and

$$\begin{aligned}
&\left(W(\Lambda,t)-J(0,t+T)\right)e^{-(R/L)t}\Big/\left(2\sqrt{C}\right)\\
&=E_1(t)+R_1\left(\left(W(\Lambda,t)+J(0,t+T)\right)e^{-(R/L)t}\Big/\left(2\sqrt{L}\right)\right)\\
&+\bar{C}_1^{-1}\left(\int_T^t\left(\left[W(\Lambda,\tau)+J(0,\tau+T)\right]e^{-(R/L)\tau}\Big/\left(2\sqrt{L}\right)\right)\mathrm{d}\tau\right.\\
&\left.+\tilde{L}_1(t)\frac{\mathrm{d}}{\mathrm{d}t}\left(\left(W(\Lambda,t)+J(0,t+T)\right)e^{-(R/L)t}\Big/\left(2\sqrt{L}\right)\right)\right).
\end{aligned}$$

Then we put $t+T\equiv t$ and change the variables in the integrals:

$$\begin{aligned}
&\left(W(t)-J(t-T)\right)e^{-(R/L)(t-T)}\Big/\left(2\sqrt{C}\right)\\
&=E_0(t-T)-R_0\left(\left(W(t)+J(t-T)\right)e^{-(R/L)(t-T)}\Big/\left(2\sqrt{L}\right)\right)\\
&-\bar{C}_0^{-1}\int_T^t\left(\left(W(\theta)+J(\theta-T)\right)e^{-(R/L)(\theta-T)}\Big/\left(2\sqrt{L}\right)\right)\mathrm{d}\theta\\
&-\tilde{L}_0(t-T)\frac{\mathrm{d}}{\mathrm{d}t}\left(\left(W(t)+J(t-T)\right)e^{-(R/L)(t-T)}\Big/\left(2\sqrt{L}\right)\right),
\end{aligned}$$

$$\begin{aligned}
&\left(W(t-T)-J(t)\right)e^{-(R/L)(t-T)}\Big/\left(2\sqrt{C}\right)\\
&=E_1(t-T)+R_1\left(\left(W(t-T)+J(t)\right)e^{-(R/L)(t-T)}\Big/\left(2\sqrt{C}\right)\right)\\
&+\bar{C}_1^{-1}\int_T^t\left(\left(W(\theta-T)+J(\theta)\right)e^{-(R/L)(\theta-T)}\Big/\left(2\sqrt{L}\right)\right)\mathrm{d}\theta\\
&+\tilde{L}_1(t-T)\frac{\mathrm{d}}{\mathrm{d}t}\left(\left(W(t-T)+J(t)\right)e^{-(R/L)(t-T)}\Big/\left(2\sqrt{L}\right)\right).
\end{aligned}$$

To solve the above equations with respect to the derivatives $\mathrm{d}W(t)/\mathrm{d}t$ and $\mathrm{d}J(t)/\mathrm{d}t$ we have to divide the above equations into $\tilde{L}_0(t-T)$ and $\tilde{L}_1(t-T)$, respectively.

But

$$u_{\Psi_k}=\frac{\mathrm{d}\Psi_k}{\mathrm{d}t}=\frac{\mathrm{d}\tilde{L}_k(i)}{\mathrm{d}t}\equiv\frac{\mathrm{d}L_k(i).i}{\mathrm{d}t}=\left(i\frac{\mathrm{d}L_k(i)}{\mathrm{d}i}+L_k(i)\right)\frac{\mathrm{d}i}{\mathrm{d}t}$$

$(k=0,1)$ where $L_k(i)=\sum_{n=0}^{m}a_n^{(k)}i^n$. Then since

$$\Psi_k(i)=i.L_k(i)=i.\sum_{n=0}^{m}a_n^{(k)}i^n=\sum_{n=0}^{m}a_n^{(k)}i^{n+1}.$$

we get

$$\begin{aligned}\frac{\mathrm{d}\tilde{L}_k(i)}{\mathrm{d}i}&=i\frac{\mathrm{d}L_k(i)}{\mathrm{d}i}+L_k(i)\\&=i\sum_{n=0}^{m}na_n^{(k)}i^{n-1}+\sum_{n=0}^{m}a_n^{(k)}i^n\\&=\sum_{n=0}^{m}(n+1)a_n^{(k)}i^n,\ (k=0,1).\end{aligned}$$

Introduce denotations

$$\Pi_0(W,J)(t)=e^{-(R/L)(t-T)}\left(W(t)+J(t-T)\right)/\left(2\sqrt{L}\right),$$

$$\Pi_1(W,J)(t)=e^{-(R/L)(t-T)}\left(W(t-T)+J(t)\right)/\left(2\sqrt{L}\right).$$

Therefore

$$\begin{aligned}\tilde{L}_0(t-T)&=\Pi_0(W,J)(t)\frac{\mathrm{d}L_0(\Pi_0(W,J)(t))}{\mathrm{d}i}\\&\quad+L_0(\Pi_0(W,J)(t))\\&=\sum_{n=0}^{m}(n+1)a_n^{(0)}(\Pi_0(W,J)(t))^n,\end{aligned}$$

$$\begin{aligned}\tilde{L}_1(t-T)&=\Pi_1(W,J)(t)\frac{\mathrm{d}L_1(\Pi_1(W,J)(t))}{\mathrm{d}i}\\&\quad+L_1(\Pi_1(W,J)(t))\\&=\sum_{n=0}^{m}(n+1)a_n^{(1)}(\Pi_1(W,J)(t))^n.\end{aligned}$$

We have to ensure a strict positive lower bound for $\tilde{L}_k(t-T),\ (k=0,1)$. We can find an interval $|i|\le i_0$ such that the inequalities

$$\begin{aligned}&\left|\Pi_0(W,J)(t)\right|\le e^{(\mu-(R/L))T_0}\left(W_0+J_0e^{-\mu T}\right)/\left(2\sqrt{L}\right)\le i_0,\\&\left|\Pi_1(W,J)(t)\right|\le e^{(\mu-(R/L))T_0}\left(W_0e^{-\mu T}+J_0\right)/\left(2\sqrt{L}\right)\le i_0\end{aligned}\tag{24}$$

imply

$$\tilde{L}_k(t-T)=\sum_{n=0}^{m}(n+1)a_n^{(k)}(\Pi_k(W,J)(t))^n\ge\overline{L}_k>0$$

$$\Rightarrow 1/\tilde{L}_k(t-T)\le 1/\overline{L}_k\le 1/\overline{L}\ (k=0,1)$$

where $1/\overline{L}=\max\{1/\overline{L}_k:k=0,1\}$.

This can be done if the polynomials have suitable properties (cf. 4. Numerical example).

We also briefly recall:

$$i=\frac{\mathrm{d}q}{\mathrm{d}t}=\frac{\mathrm{d}(C_0(u).u)}{\mathrm{d}t}\Rightarrow\int_T^t i(x,\tau)\mathrm{d}\tau=C_0(u).u\equiv\overline{C}_0(u)$$

and

$$u_{C_0}=u(0,t)=\overline{C}_0^{-1}\left(\int_T^t i(0,\tau)\mathrm{d}\tau\right)$$

where $c_k,\Phi_k,\ h\in[2,3]$,

$$C_k(u)=\frac{c_k}{\sqrt[h]{1-(u/\Phi_k)}}=\frac{c_k\sqrt[h]{\Phi_k}}{\sqrt[h]{\Phi_k-u}}\ (k=0,1)$$

are constants and

$$|u|\le W_0<\Phi=\min\{\Phi_0,\Phi_1\}\le(h/(h-1))\Phi.$$

The derivatives of the functions $\overline{C}_k(u)=uC_k(u)$ are

$$\begin{aligned}\frac{\mathrm{d}\overline{C}_k(u)}{\mathrm{d}u}&=C_k(u)+u\frac{\mathrm{d}C_k(u)}{\mathrm{d}u}\\&=\frac{c_k\sqrt[h]{\Phi_k}(h\Phi_k-hu+u)}{h(\Phi_k-u)^{\frac{1}{h}+1}},u\in[-W_0,W_0].\end{aligned}$$

Since $\frac{\mathrm{d}\overline{C}_k(u)}{\mathrm{d}u}>0$ the inverse function exists for $|u|<\frac{h\Phi_k}{h-1}$.

Since

$$\overline{C}_k(u)=uC_k(u)=\frac{c_ku\sqrt[h]{\Phi_k}}{\sqrt[h]{\Phi_k-u}}:[-W_0,W_0]$$

$$\to\left[\frac{-c_k\sqrt[h]{\Phi_k}\,W_0}{\sqrt[h]{\Phi_k+W_0}},\frac{c_k\sqrt[h]{\Phi_k}\,W_0}{\sqrt[h]{\Phi_k-W_0}}\right]$$

then

$$\overline{C}_k^{-1}(I):\left[\frac{-c_k\sqrt[h]{\Phi_k}\,W_0}{\sqrt[h]{\Phi_k+W_0}},\frac{c_k\sqrt[h]{\Phi_k}\,W_0}{\sqrt[h]{\Phi_k-W_0}}\right]\to[-W_0,W_0],$$

or $\left|\overline{C}_k^{-1}(I)\right|\le W_0$.

The explicit form of the inverse function for $h=2$ is:

$$\begin{aligned}&c_k\sqrt{\Phi_k}\,u/\sqrt{\Phi_k-u}=I\\&\Rightarrow c_k^2\Phi_ku^2=\Phi_kI^2-I^2u\\&\Rightarrow c_k^2\Phi_ku^2+I^2u-\Phi_kI^2=0,\\&\overline{C}_k^{-1}(I)\\&\quad=\frac{-I^2+\sqrt{I^4+4c_k^2\Phi_k^2I^2}}{2c_k^2\Phi_k}\ (k=0,1).\end{aligned}$$

We need the derivative given below (see Equation (26))

and the following estimates:

$$|I| \le \frac{c_k \sqrt{\Phi_k}\ W_0}{\sqrt{\Phi_k + W_0}} = \min\left\{ \left| \frac{-c_k \sqrt[h]{\Phi_k}\ W_0}{\sqrt[h]{\Phi_k + W_0}} \right|,\ \left| \frac{c_k \sqrt[h]{\Phi_k}\ W_0}{\sqrt[h]{\Phi_k - W_0}} \right| \right\}$$

and

$$\begin{aligned}\left|\frac{\mathrm{d}\bar{C}_k^{-1}(I)}{\mathrm{d}I}\right| &\le \frac{1}{c_k^2\Phi_k}\left(|I| + \frac{I^2 + 4c_k^2\Phi_k^2}{\sqrt{I^2 + 4c_k^2\Phi_k^2}}\right) \\ &\le \frac{1}{c_k^2\Phi_k}\left(|I| + \sqrt{I^2 + 4c_k^2\Phi_k^2}\right) \\ &\le \frac{1}{c_k^2\Phi_k}\left(\frac{c_k\sqrt{\Phi_k}\,W_0}{\sqrt{\Phi_k + W_0}} + \sqrt{\left(\frac{c_k\sqrt{\Phi_k}\,W_0}{\sqrt{\Phi_k + W_0}}\right)^2 + 4c_k^2\Phi_k^2}\right) \\ &\le \frac{2}{c_k}\sqrt{1 + \frac{W_0}{\Phi_k}}\,(k = 0,1).\end{aligned} \tag{25}$$

Therefore the arguments

$$\int_T^t \left(\left[W(\theta) + J(\theta - T)\right]e^{-(R/L)(\theta - T)} \big/ \left(2\sqrt{L}\right)\right)\mathrm{d}\theta,.$$

$$\int_T^t \left(\left[W(\theta - T) + J(\theta)\right]e^{-(R/L)(\theta - T)} \big/ \left(2\sqrt{L}\right)\right)\mathrm{d}\theta$$

of $\bar{C}_0^{-1}(.), \bar{C}_1^{-1}(.)$ should satisfy the inequalities

$$\left|\int_T^t \left(\left[W(\theta) + J(\theta - T)\right]e^{-(R/L)(\theta - T)} \big/ \left(2\sqrt{L}\right)\right)\mathrm{d}\theta\right| \le \frac{c_k\sqrt{\Phi_k}\ W_0}{\sqrt{\Phi_k + W_0}},$$

$$\left|\int_T^t \left(\left[W(\theta - T) + J(\theta)\right]e^{-(R/L)(\theta - T)} \big/ \left(2\sqrt{L}\right)\right)\mathrm{d}\theta\right| \le \frac{c_k\sqrt{\Phi_k}\ W_0}{\sqrt{\Phi_k + W_0}}$$

or in view of the inequality

$$\left|\int_T^t \left(\left[W(\theta - T) + J(\theta)\right]e^{-(R/L)(\theta - T)} \big/ \left(2\sqrt{L}\right)\right)\mathrm{d}\theta\right|$$

$$\le \left(\left(W_0 + J_0 e^{-\mu T}\right) \big/ \left(2\sqrt{L}\right)\right)\left(\left(e^{(\mu - (R/L))T_0} - 1\right) \big/ \left(\mu - (R/L)\right)\right)$$

we obtain

$$\frac{W_0 + J_0 e^{-\mu T}}{2\sqrt{L}} \frac{e^{(\mu - (R/L))T_0} - 1}{\mu - (R/L)} \le \frac{c_k\sqrt{\Phi_k}\ W_0}{\sqrt{\Phi_k + W_0}}$$

and

$$\frac{W_0 e^{-\mu T} + J_0}{2\sqrt{L}} \frac{e^{(\mu - (R/L))T_0} - 1}{\mu - (R/L)} \le \frac{c_k\sqrt{\Phi_k}\ W_0}{\sqrt{\Phi_k + W_0}}.$$

For the *I-V* characteristics we assume that they are polynomial functions

$$R_k(i) = \sum_{n=1}^{m} r_n^{(k)} i^n, (k = 0,1).$$

Now we are able to formulate a periodic problem for the obtained neutral system:

$$\frac{\mathrm{d}\bar{C}_k^{-1}(I)}{\mathrm{d}I} = \begin{cases} \dfrac{1}{c_k^2\Phi_k}\left(-I - \dfrac{I^2 + 2c_k^2\Phi_k^2}{\sqrt{I^2 + 4c_k^2\Phi_k^2}}\right), I \in \left[\dfrac{-c_k\sqrt{\Phi_k}\ W_0}{\sqrt{\Phi_k + W_0}}, 0\right) \\ \dfrac{1}{c_k^2\Phi_k}\left(-I + \dfrac{I^2 + 2c_k^2\Phi_k^2}{\sqrt{I^2 + 4c_k^2\Phi_k^2}}\right), I \in \left(0, \dfrac{c_k\sqrt{\Phi_k}\ W_0}{\sqrt{\Phi_k - W_0}}\right] \end{cases}, \tag{26}$$

$$\begin{aligned}\frac{\mathrm{d}W(t)}{\mathrm{d}t} = &-\frac{\mathrm{d}J(t - T)}{\mathrm{d}t} + \frac{R}{L}W(t) + \frac{R}{L}J(t - T) + \left(2e^{(R/L)(t - T)}\sqrt{L}E_0(t - T) - \left(W(t) - J(t - T)\right)Z_0\right) \big/ \tilde{L}_0 \\ &- \frac{2e^{(R/L)(t - T)}\sqrt{L}}{\tilde{L}_0} R_0\left(\frac{e^{-(R/L)(t - T)}}{2\sqrt{L}}\left(W(t) + J(t - T)\right)\right) \\ &- \frac{2e^{(R/L)(t - T)}\sqrt{L}}{\tilde{L}_0}\bar{C}_0^{-1}\left(\int_T^t \frac{e^{-(R/L)(t - T)}}{2\sqrt{L}}\left(W(\theta) + J(\theta - T)\right)\mathrm{d}\theta\right) \equiv U(W, J)(t).\end{aligned} \tag{27}$$

$$\begin{aligned}\frac{\mathrm{d}J(t)}{\mathrm{d}t} = &-\frac{\mathrm{d}W(t - T)}{\mathrm{d}t} + \frac{R}{L}W(t - T) + \frac{R}{L}J(t) - 2e^{(R/L)(t - T)}\sqrt{L}E_1(t - T) \big/ \tilde{L}_1 \\ &+ \left(\left(W(t - T) - J(t)\right)Z_0\right) \big/ \tilde{L}_1 - \frac{2e^{(R/L)(t - T)}\sqrt{L}}{\tilde{L}_1} R_1 \frac{e^{-(R/L)(t - T)}}{2\sqrt{L}}\left(W(t - T) + J(t)\right) \\ &- \frac{2e^{-(R/L)(t - T)}\sqrt{L}}{\tilde{L}_1}\bar{C}_1^{-1}\left(\int_T^t \frac{e^{-(R/L)(t - T)}}{2\sqrt{L}}\left(W(\theta - T) + J(\theta)\right)\mathrm{d}\theta\right) \equiv I(W, J)(s),\ t \in [T, T + T_0],\end{aligned} \tag{28}$$

$$W(t) = \upsilon_0(t),\ \dot{W}(t) = \dot{\upsilon}_0(t),$$
$$J(t) = \iota_0(t),\ \dot{J}(t) = \dot{\iota}_0(t),\ \ t \in [0,T].$$

The initial functions $\upsilon_0(t)$, $\iota_0(t)$ can be obtained from the initial conditions (7) by shifting along the characteristics of the initial functions $u_0(x)$, $i_0(x)$ (cf. [9-11]).

3. Main Results

Here we formulate conditions for the existence-uniqueness of a periodic solution of neutral functional differential system (27), (28) (for definition of neutral equation see [15]). First we define a suitable operator generating by the right-hand sides of the Equations (27), (28). We find a T_0 – periodic solution of Equations (27), (28) on the interval $[T, T+T_0)$ coinciding with prescribed T_0 – periodic function on $[0,T]$ and then one can continue it periodically because our system is autonomous one.

By $L_{T_0}^{1,\infty}[T,\infty)$ we mean the space consisting of all measurable essentially bounded T_0 – periodic functions whose derivatives are also essentially bounded and T_0 – periodic.

Introduce the sets:

$$M_u = \left\{ f \in L_{T_0}^{1,\infty}[T,\infty) : \int_{T_0}^{T+T_0} f(t)\mathrm{d}t = 0 \wedge f(t) = \upsilon_0(t),\ t \in [-T,T] \right\},$$

$$M_i = \left\{ f \in L_{T_0}^{1,\infty}[T,\infty) : \int_{T}^{T+T_0} f(t)\mathrm{d}t = 0 \wedge f(t) = \iota_0(t),\ t \in [-T,T] \right\}.$$

Lemma 1. If $f(.) \in M_u$ (respectively $f(.) \in M_i$) then $F(t) = \int_T^t f(\tau)\mathrm{d}\tau$ is T_0 – periodic function.

Assumption (E) $E_k(.) \in L_{T_0}^{1,\infty}[-T,\infty)$, $\int_T^{T+T_0} E_k(t)\mathrm{d}t = 0$, $|E_k(t)| \le W_0 e^{\mu(t-T)}, t \in [T, T+T_0]$, $E_k(-T) = 0\ (k = 0,1)$.

Assumption (IN) $\upsilon_0(t), \iota_0(t)$ are essentially bounded T_0 – periodic functions where $T = mT_0, m \in \{2,3,4,5,\cdots\}$, $\upsilon_0(0) = \iota_0(0) = 0$, $|\upsilon_0 t| \le W_0$, $|\iota_0(t)| \le J_0$. Here W_0, J_0 are prescribed positive constants.

Lemma 2. If the assumptions **(IN)** and **(E)** are fulfilled and $(W,J) \in M_u \times M_i$ then $R_0(\Pi_0(W,J)(t))$, $R_1(\Pi_1(W,J)(t))$, $\Psi_0(t) = \int_T^t (\Pi_0(W,J)(\tau))\mathrm{d}\tau$ and $\Psi_1(t) = \int_T^t (\Pi_1(W,J)(\tau))\mathrm{d}\tau$ are T_0 – periodic functions.

Define the operator $B = (B_u, B_i)$ on the set $M_u \times M_i$ by the formulas:

$$B_u(W,J)(t) := \upsilon_0(t), t \in [0,T],$$
$$B_i(W,J)(t) := \iota_0(t), t \in [0,T],$$

$$B_u(W,J)(t) := \int_T^t U(W,J)(s)\mathrm{d}s - \left(\frac{t-T}{T_0} - \frac{1}{2}\right)\int_T^{T+T_0} U(W,J)(s)\mathrm{d}s - \frac{1}{T_0}\int_T^{T+T_0}\int_T^t U(W,J)(s)\mathrm{d}s\mathrm{d}t,\ t \in [T, T+T_0]$$

$$B_i(W,J)(t) := \int_T^t I(W,J)(s)\mathrm{d}s - \left(\frac{t-T}{T_0} - \frac{1}{2}\right)\int_T^{T+T_0} I(W,J)(s)\mathrm{d}s - \frac{1}{T_0}\int_T^{T+T_0}\int_T^t I(W,J)(s)\mathrm{d}s\mathrm{d}t,\ t \in [T, T+T_0].$$

Remark 1. It is easy to see that changing the integration order one obtains

$$\int_T^{T+T_0}\int_T^t U(W,J)(s)\mathrm{d}s\mathrm{d}t = (T+T_0)\int_T^{T+T_0} U(W,J)(s)\mathrm{d}s - \int_T^{T+T_0} sU(W,J)(s)\mathrm{d}s$$

and

$$\int_T^{T+T_0}\int_T^t I(W,J)(s)\mathrm{d}s\mathrm{d}t = (T+T_0)\int_T^{T+T_0} I(W,J)(s)\mathrm{d}s - \int_T^{T+T_0} sI(W,J)(s)\mathrm{d}s.$$

Lemma 3. The periodic problem (27), (28) has a solution $(W(.), J(.)) \in M_u \times M_i$ iff the operator B has a fixed point $(W,J) \in M_u \times M_i$, that is, $W = B_u(W,J)$, $J = B_i(W,J)$.

Introduce the sets

$$X_u = \left\{ f \in M_u : |f(t)| \le W_0 e^{\mu(t-T)}, t \in [T, T+T_0] \right\},$$

$$X_i = \left\{ f \in M_i : |f(t)| \le J_0 e^{\mu(t-T)}, t \in [T, T+T_0] \right\}.$$

Here the constant $\mu > 0$ will be prescribed below.

The sets X_u and X_i turn out into metric spaces with metrics

$$\rho(W,\bar{W}) = \operatorname{ess\,sup}\left\{ e^{-\mu(t-T)} \left|W(t) - \bar{W}(t)\right| : t \in [T, T+T_0] \right\},$$

$$\rho(\dot{W},\dot{\bar{W}}) = \operatorname{ess\,sup}\left\{ e^{-\mu(t-T)} \left|\dot{W}(t) - \dot{\bar{W}}(t)\right| : t \in [T, T+T_0] \right\},$$

$$\rho(J,\bar{J}) = \operatorname{ess\,sup}\left\{ e^{-\mu(t-T)} \left|J(t) - \bar{J}(t)\right| : t \in [T, T+T_0] \right\},$$

$$\rho(\dot{J},\dot{\bar{J}}) = \text{ess sup}\left\{e^{-\mu(t-T)}\left|\dot{J}(t)-\dot{\bar{J}}(t)\right|: t\in[T,T+T_0]\right\}.$$

Define a metric on $X_u \times X_i$ in the following way:

$$\rho\left((W,J),(\bar{W},\bar{J})\right) = \max\left\{\rho\left(W,\bar{W}\right),\rho\left(J,\bar{J}\right),\rho\left(\dot{W},\dot{\bar{W}}\right),\rho\left(\dot{J},\dot{\bar{J}}\right)\right\}.$$

Assumption (LC): $\dfrac{e^{(\mu-(R/L))T_0}\left(W_0+J_0e^{-\mu T}\right)}{2\sqrt{L}} \le i_0$,

$$\frac{e^{(\mu-(R/L))T_0}\left(W_0e^{-\mu T}+J_0\right)}{2\sqrt{L}} \le i_0,$$

$$\frac{W_0+J_0e^{-\mu T}}{2\sqrt{L}}\,\frac{e^{(\mu-R/L)T_0}-1}{\mu-(R/L)} \le \frac{c_k\sqrt{\Phi_k}\,W_0}{\sqrt{\Phi_k+W_0}},$$

$$\frac{W_0e^{-\mu T}+J_0}{2\sqrt{L}}\,\frac{e^{(\mu-(R/L))T_0}-1}{\mu-(R/L)} \le \frac{c_k\sqrt{\Phi_k}\,W_0}{\sqrt{\Phi_k+W_0}},\quad \mu>\frac{R}{L}.$$

Theorem 1. Let the assumptions **(LC)**, **(E)** and **(IN)** be fulfilled. Then there exists a unique T_0 – periodic solution $(W,J)\in X_u\times X_i$ of the problem (27), (28).

Proof: Define the operator $B\equiv(B_u,B_i):X_u\times X_i\to X_u\times X_i$ by the above formulas. In what follows we show

$$|W(t)|\le W_0e^{\mu(t-T)}\wedge|J(t)|\le J_0e^{\mu(t-T)}$$

$$\Rightarrow|B_u|\le W_0e^{\mu(t-T)}\wedge|B_i|\le J_0e^{\mu(t-T)}.$$

Using inequality (24) and proceeding as in [11] we obtain (for sufficiently large $\mu>(R/L)$):

$$\begin{aligned}|B_u(W,J)(t)\le&\left|\int_T^t U(W,J)(s)ds\right|+\frac{1}{2}\left|\int_T^{T+T_0}U(W,J)(s)ds\right|\\&+\frac{1}{T_0}\int_T^{T+T_0}\left|\int_T^t U(W,J)(s)ds\right|dt\le e^{\mu(t-T)}\Bigg[\frac{e^{\mu_0}+\mu_0-1}{\mu_0}e^{-\mu T}J_0\\&+\frac{(\mu_0+2)e^{\mu_0}+\mu_0-2}{2\mu_0}\left(\frac{R}{L}+\frac{Z_0}{\bar{L}_0}\right)\frac{\left(W_0+J_0e^{-\mu T}\right)}{\mu}+\frac{2\sqrt{L}\,W_0(e^{-\mu T}+1)}{\bar{L}_0(\mu+R/L)}e^{(R/L)T_0}\frac{(\mu_0+2)e^{\mu_0}+2\mu_0-2}{\mu_0}\\&+\frac{1}{\bar{L}_0}\sum_{n=1}^m\frac{\left|r_n^{(0)}\right|\left(W_0+J_0e^{-\mu T}\right)^n}{n\left(2\sqrt{L}\right)^{n-1}\left(\mu-(((n-1)R)/(nR))\right)}\times\left(e^{(n-1)(\mu-(R/L))T_0}\frac{2e^{\mu_0}+3\mu_0-2}{2\mu_0}-\frac{1}{2}\right)\Bigg]\le e^{\mu(t-T)}W_0.\end{aligned}$$

For the second component of the operator we obtain

$$\begin{aligned}|B_i(W,J)(t)\le&\left|\int_T^t I(W,J)(s)ds\right|+\frac{1}{2}\left|\int_T^{T+T_0}I(W,J)(s)ds\right|+\frac{1}{T_0}\int_T^{T+T_0}\left|\int_T^t I(W,J)(s)ds\right|dt\\\le&\, e^{\mu(t-T)}\Big[W_0e^{-\mu T}\left(e^{\mu_0}+\mu_0-1\right)/\mu_0+\left(W_0\left(e^{-\mu T}+1\right)/\mu\right)\\&\times\left((R/L)+\left(Z_0/\bar{L}_1\right)\right)\left((\mu_0+2)e^{\mu_0}+\mu_0-2\right)/(2\mu_0)+\left(4e^{(R/L)T_0}+e^{(\mu+(R/L))T_0}-1\right)\frac{\sqrt{L}\,W_0\left(e^{-\mu T}+1\right)}{\bar{L}_1\left((R/L)+\mu\right)}\\&+\left(2e^{\mu_0}+3\mu_0-2\right)/\left(2\mu_0\bar{L}_1\right)\times\sum_{n=1}^m\frac{\left|r_n^{(1)}\right|\left(W_0e^{-\mu T}+J_0\right)^n}{\left(2\sqrt{L}\right)^{n-1}n}\,\frac{e^{(n\mu-(n-1)(R/L))T_0}-1}{\mu-(((n-1)R)/(nR))}\Big]\le J_0e^{\mu(t-T)}.\end{aligned}$$

Therefore the operator B maps the set $X_u\times X_i$ into itself. In what follows we show that B is contractive operator. We need the following preliminary inequalities

$$\left|\Pi_0(W,J)(t)-\Pi_0\left(\bar{W},\bar{J}\right)(t)\right|\le\frac{e^{(\mu-(R/L))(t-T)}}{2\mu\sqrt{L}}\left(\rho\left(\dot{W},\dot{\bar{W}}\right)+\rho\left(\dot{J},\dot{\bar{J}}\right)e^{-\mu T}\right),$$

$$\left|\Pi_1(W,J)(t)-\Pi_1\left(\bar{W},\bar{J}\right)(t)\right|\le\frac{e^{(\mu-(R/L))(t-T)}}{2\mu\sqrt{L}}\left(\rho\left(\dot{W},\dot{\bar{W}}\right)e^{-\mu T}+\rho\left(\dot{J},\dot{\bar{J}}\right)\right),$$

$$\left|[\Pi_0(W,J)(t)]^n - \left[\Pi_0\left(\bar{W},\bar{J}\right)(t)\right]^n\right|$$
$$\le n\left[e^{(\mu-(R/L))T_0}\left(W_0+J_0e^{-\mu T}\right)/\left(2\sqrt{L}\right)\right]^{n-1}\times e^{(\mu-(R/L))(t-T)}\left(\rho\left(\dot{W},\dot{\bar{W}}\right)+\rho\left(\dot{J},\dot{\bar{J}}\right)e^{-\mu T}\right)/\left(2\mu\sqrt{L}\right).$$

$$\left|[\Pi_1(W,J)(t)]^n - \left[\Pi_1\left(\bar{W},\bar{J}\right)(t)\right]^n\right|$$
$$\le n\left[e^{(\mu-(R/L))T_0}\left(W_0e^{-\mu T}+J_0\right)/\left(2\sqrt{L}\right)\right]^{n-1}\times e^{(\mu-(R/L))(t-T)}\left(\rho\left(\dot{W},\dot{\bar{W}}\right)e^{-\mu T}+\rho\left(\dot{J},\dot{\bar{J}}\right)\right)/\left(2\mu\sqrt{L}\right).$$

Then for the first operator component we obtain:

$$\left|B_u(W,J)(t)-B_u\left(\bar{W},\bar{J}\right)(t)\right|$$
$$\le \int_T^t\left|U(W,J)(s)-U\left(\bar{W},\bar{J}\right)(s)\right|\mathrm{d}s+\left(\frac{t-T}{T_0}-\frac{1}{2}\right)\left|\int_T^{T+T_0}U(W,J)(s)\mathrm{d}s-\int_T^{T+T_0}U\left(\bar{W},\bar{J}\right)(s)\mathrm{d}s\right|$$
$$+\frac{1}{T_0}\int_T^{T+T_0}\left|\int_T^t U(W,J)(s)\mathrm{d}s-\int_T^t U\left(\bar{W},\bar{J}\right)(s)\mathrm{d}s\right|\mathrm{d}t$$
$$\le e^{\mu(t-T)}\left[\rho\left(W,J),\left(\bar{W},\bar{J}\right)\right)\frac{e^{\mu_0}+\mu_0-1}{\mu_0}\frac{e^{-\mu T}}{\mu}+\frac{(\mu_0+2)e^{\mu_0}+\mu_0-2}{2\mu_0}\frac{1+e^{-\mu T}}{\mu^2}\right.$$
$$\left.\cdot\left((R/L)+\left(Z_0/\bar{L}_0\right)+\frac{1}{\bar{L}_0}\sum_{n=1}^m\left|r_n^{(0)}\right|\frac{ne^{(n-1)(\mu-(R/L))T_0}(W_0+J_0e^{-\mu T})^{n-1}}{\left(2\sqrt{L}\right)^{n-1}}+2\sqrt{1+(W_0/\Phi_0)}\Big/\left(c_0\bar{L}_0\left(\mu-(R/L)\right)\right)\right)\right]$$
$$\equiv e^{\mu(t-T)}K_u\,\rho\left((W,J),\left(\bar{W},\bar{J}\right)\right).$$

Further on we have

$$\left|B_i(W,J)(t)-B_i(\bar{W},\bar{J})(t)\right|$$
$$\le \int_T^t\left|I(W,J)(s)-I(\bar{W},\bar{J})(s)\right|\mathrm{d}s+\left(\frac{t-T}{T_0}-\frac{1}{2}\right)\left|\int_T^{T+T_0}I(W,J)(s)\mathrm{d}s-\int_T^{T+T_0}I(\bar{W},\bar{J})(s)\mathrm{d}s\right|$$
$$+\frac{1}{T_0}\int_T^{T+T_0}\left|\int_T^t I(W,J)(s)\mathrm{d}s-\int_T^t I(W,\bar{J})(s)\mathrm{d}s\right|\mathrm{d}t$$
$$\le e^{\mu(t-T)}\rho((W,J),(\bar{J},\bar{W}))\left[\frac{e^{\mu_0}+\mu_0-1}{\mu_0}\frac{e^{-\mu T}}{\mu}+\frac{(\mu_0+2)e^{\mu_0}+\mu_0-2}{2\mu_0}\frac{(e^{-\mu T}+1)}{\mu^2}\right.$$
$$\left.\cdot\left(\left((R/L)+\left(Z_0/\bar{L}_0\right)+\frac{2}{\bar{L}_1}\sum_{n=1}^m\left|r_n^{(1)}\right|\frac{ne^{(n-1)(\mu-(R/L))T_0}(W_0e^{-\mu T}+J_0)^{n-1}}{\left(2\sqrt{L}\right)^{n-1}}+\frac{2}{c_1\bar{L}_1\left(\mu-(R/L)\right)}\sqrt{1+(W_0/\Phi_1)}\right)\right]$$
$$\equiv e^{\mu(t-T)}K_i\,\rho\left((W,J),\left(\bar{J},\bar{W}\right)\right).$$

Finally we have to obtain an estimate for $t\in[T,T+T_0]$. It is easy to prove the following inequalities:

$$\left|\dot{B}_u(W,J)(t)-\dot{B}_u(\bar{W},\bar{J})(t)\right|$$

$$\leq \left|U(W,J)(t)-U(\bar{W},\bar{J})(t)\right|+\frac{1}{T_0}\left|\int_T^{T+T_0} U(W,J)(s)\mathrm{d}s-\int_T^{T+T_0} U(\bar{W},\bar{J})(s)\mathrm{d}s\right|$$

$$\leq e^{\mu(t-T)}\rho((W,J),(\bar{W},\bar{J}))\left[e^{-\mu T}+\frac{e^{\mu_0}+\mu_0-1}{\mu_0}\frac{\left(1+e^{-\mu T}\right)}{\mu}\times\left(\frac{R}{L}+\frac{Z_0}{\bar{L}_0}+\frac{1}{\bar{L}_0}\sum_{n=1}^{m}\left|r_n^{(0)}\right|\frac{ne^{(n-1)(\mu-(R/L))T_0}\left(W_0+J_0e^{-\mu T}\right)^{n-1}}{\left(2\sqrt{L}\right)^{n-1}}\right.\right.$$

$$\left.\left.+\frac{2\sqrt{1+W_0/\Phi_0}}{\bar{L}_0c_0\left(\mu-(R/L)\right)}\right)\right]$$

$$\equiv e^{\mu(t-T)}\dot{K}_u\rho\left((W,J),(\bar{J},\bar{W})\right).$$

For the derivative of the second component of B we obtain

$$\left|\dot{B}_i(W,J)(t)-\dot{B}_i(\bar{W},\bar{J})(t)\right|$$

$$\leq \left|I(W,J)(t)-I(\bar{W},\bar{J})(t)\right|+\frac{1}{T_0}\left|\int_T^{T+T_0} I(W,J)(s)\mathrm{d}s-\int_T^{T+T_0} I(\bar{W},\bar{J})(s)\mathrm{d}s\right|$$

$$\leq e^{\mu(t-T)}\rho((W,J),(\bar{W},\bar{J}))\left[e^{-\mu T}+\frac{e^{\mu_0}+\mu_0-1}{\mu_0}\frac{(e^{-\mu T}+1)}{\mu}\right.$$

$$\left.\times\left(\frac{R}{L}+\frac{Z_0}{\bar{L}_1}+\frac{1}{\bar{L}_1}\sum_{n=1}^{m}n\left|r_n^{(1)}\right|\frac{e^{(n-1)\left(\mu-\frac{R}{L}\right)T_0}(W_0e^{-\mu T}+J_0)^{n-1}}{(2\sqrt{L})^{n-1}}+\frac{2\sqrt{1+W_0/\Phi_1}}{c_1\bar{L}_1\left(\mu-(R/L)\right)}\right)\right]$$

$$\equiv e^{\mu(t-T)}\dot{K}_i\,\rho\left((W,J),(\bar{J},\bar{W})\right).$$

The above inequalities imply

$$\rho(B(W,J),B(\bar{W},\bar{J}))\leq K\,\rho((W,J),(\bar{W},\bar{J}))$$

where $K=\max\left\{K_u,K_i,\dot{K}_u,\dot{K}_i\right\}$ should be chosen smaller than 1.

Therefore B is contractive operator and has a unique fixed point in M (cf. [18]). It is a unique periodic solution of system (26), (27).

Theorem 1 is thus proved.

4. Numerical Example

For a transmission line with length $\Lambda=1\,\mathrm{m}$,

$L=0.45\,\mu H/\mathrm{m}$, $C=80\,pF/\mathrm{m}$, cross-section area

$S=6\ \mathrm{mm}^2$, specific resistance for the cuprum

$\rho_c=0.0175$, that is, $R=(\rho_c\Lambda)/S\approx 3.10^{-3}\,\Omega$,

$v=1/\sqrt{LC}=1/(6\cdot 10^{-9})=1.66\cdot 10^{8}$,

$Z_0=\sqrt{L/C}=75\Omega$. Then $T=\Lambda\sqrt{LC}=6\cdot 10^{-9}\,\sec$.

Let us check the propagation of millimeter waves $\lambda_0=(1/6)\cdot 10^{-3}\,\mathrm{m}$. We have

$$f_0=1/\left(\lambda_0\sqrt{LC}\right)=10^{12}\,Hz\Rightarrow T_0=1/f_0=10^{-12}.$$

We choose $\mu=2\cdot 10^{12}$. Then $\mu T_0=\mu_0=2$ and $T=6\cdot 10^{-9}\cdot 2\cdot 10^{12}T_0=12000\,T_0$. Consequently

$\mu T=2\cdot 10^{12}\cdot 6\cdot 10^{-9}\approx 12\cdot 10^{3}\Rightarrow e^{-\mu T}\approx 0,\ RT/L\approx 0,$

$R/L=0.0029/(0.45\cdot 10^{-6})\approx 0.6\cdot 10^{4},\ e^{\pm(RT/L)}\approx e^{0}\approx 1$

$\mu\pm(R/L)=2\cdot 10^{12}\pm 10^{4}=10^{12}(2\pm 10^{-8})\approx 2\cdot 10^{12},$

$(R/L)T_0\approx 0\Rightarrow e^{(R/L)T_0}-1\approx 6.6\cdot 10^{-6},$

$\mu-(R/L)\approx 10^{12},\ e^{(\mu-(R/L))T_0}=e^{\mu_0}e^{-(R/L)T_0}\approx e^{2}.$

We choose resistive elements with the following *V-I* characteristics $R_0(u)=R_1(u)=0.028u-0.125u^3$ *i.e.* $r_1=0.028,\ r_2=0,\ r_3=0.125$, and inductive element with $L_0(i)=L_1(i)=3i-(1/12)i^3$. Then

$$\tilde{L}_0(i)=i\left(\mathrm{d}L_0(i)/\mathrm{d}i\right)+L_0(i)=6i-(1/3)i^3.$$

If we choose $i_0=1$ one obtains

$$6i-(1/3)i^3>6-(1/3)=17/3$$

and consequently $1/\bar{L}=3/17$.

Let us take

$$C_0(u)=C_1(u)=c/\sqrt{1-(u/\Phi)}=c\sqrt{\Phi}/\sqrt{\Phi-u},$$

where $h=2,\ c=50\,pF=5\cdot 10^{-11}F$ and $\Phi=0.4\ V\Rightarrow$

$W_0 < 0.4$. Then the inequalities of Theorem 1 become

$$e^{(\mu-(R/L))T_0}\left(W_0+J_0e^{-\mu T}\right)/\left(2\sqrt{\bar{L}}\right)\le 1$$

$$\Rightarrow e^2W_0/\left(2\sqrt{\bar{L}}\right)\le 1 \Rightarrow W_0\le 2\sqrt{\bar{L}}/e^2\approx 0.18\cdot 10^{-3},$$

$$e^{(\mu-R/L)T_0}\left(W_0e^{-\mu T}+J_0\right)/\left(2\sqrt{\bar{L}}\right)\le 1$$

$$\Rightarrow e^2J_0/\left(2\sqrt{\bar{L}}\right)\le 1 \Rightarrow J_0\le 2\sqrt{\bar{L}}/e^2\approx 0.18\cdot 10^{-3}$$

$$\frac{W_0}{2\sqrt{L}}\frac{e^2-1}{\mu}\le\frac{cW_0\sqrt{\Phi}}{\sqrt{\Phi+W_0}}\Leftrightarrow\sqrt{\Phi+W_0}\le\frac{2c\mu\sqrt{L\Phi}}{e^2-1}$$

$$\Rightarrow W_0\le\min\left\{13.25^2-0.4;\ 0.18\cdot 10^{-3}\right\}=0.18\cdot 10^{-3},$$

$$\frac{J_0}{2\sqrt{L}}\frac{e^2-1}{\mu}\le\frac{cW_0\sqrt{\Phi}}{\sqrt{\Phi+W_0}}$$

$$\Rightarrow J_0\le\frac{2\cdot c\sqrt{L}\sqrt{\Phi}\cdot W_0\mu}{(e^2-1)\sqrt{\Phi+W_0}}\approx 6\cdot 10^{-6};$$

and

$$\frac{1}{\mu}\left[e^2\left(\frac{R}{L}+\frac{Z_0}{\bar{L}}\right)+\frac{(4e^2+2)\sqrt{L}}{\bar{L}}+\frac{1}{\bar{L}}\left(0,028\frac{e^2+1}{2}+\frac{0,125W_0^2}{L}\frac{e^6+2e^4-1}{24}\right)\right]\le 1,$$

$$\frac{1}{\mu}\left[\left(\frac{R}{L}+\frac{Z_0}{\bar{L}}\right)e^2W_0+\frac{(e^2+3)\sqrt{L}\,W_0}{\bar{L}}+\frac{e^2+2}{2\bar{L}}\left(0.028J_0(e^2-1)+\frac{0,125J_0^3}{12L}(e^6-1)\right)\right]\le J_0,$$

$$\dot{K}_u=\frac{e^2+1}{2\mu}\left[\frac{R}{L}+\frac{Z_0}{\bar{L}}+\frac{1}{\bar{L}}\left(0.028+0.125\frac{3e^4W_0^2}{4L}\right)+2\sqrt{1+(W_0/\Phi)}/(\mu\bar{L}c)\right]<1,$$

$$\dot{K}_i=\frac{e^2+1}{2\mu}\left[\frac{R}{L}+\frac{Z_0}{\bar{L}}+\frac{1}{\bar{L}}\left(0.028+0.125\frac{3e^4J_0^2}{4L}\right)+2\sqrt{1+(W_0/\Phi)}/(\mu\bar{L}c)\right]<1.$$

Taking into account $R/L+Z_0/\bar{L}=10^4(0.6+13.24\cdot 10^{-4})\approx 0.6\cdot 10^4$, $W_0<0.18\cdot 10^{-3}$ and $J_0\le 3\cdot 10^{-6}$ we see that

$$1/(2\cdot 10^{12})\left[4.44\cdot 10^4+5.58\sqrt{0.45\cdot 10^{-6}}+(13/17)(0.118+3.4)\right]\le 1,$$

$$10^{-6}\left[8+0.83\left(0.54\cdot 10^{-6}+(3.375\cdot 10^{-12})404/5.4\right)\right]\le 6,$$

$$K_u,K_i<\dot{K}_i\le\dot{K}_u\approx\approx(2,1/10^{12})(0.6\cdot 10^4+0.072+0.0036)13\cdot 10^{-7}<1.$$

Most often the initial approximation is chosen to be simple functions, namely:

$$W^{(0)}(t)=\begin{cases}W_0\sin\omega_0t,\ t\in[0,T]\\ 0,\ t\in[T,T+T_0]\end{cases};$$

$$J^{(0)}(t)=\begin{cases}J_0\sin\omega_0t, t\in[0,T]\\ 0,\ t\in[T,T+T_0]\end{cases}$$

($\omega_0=2\pi/T_0$) and $E_0(t)=E_1(t)=E_0\sin\omega_0t$.

Then we have $W^{(n+1)}(t)=B_u(W^{(n)},J^{(n)})$,

$$J^{(n+1)}(t)=B_i(W^{(n)},J^{(n)})$$

$(n=0,1,2,\cdots)$ and

$$\rho((W^{(n+1)},J^{(n+1)}),(W^{(n)},J^{(n)}))$$

$$\le\left(1.13\cdot 10^{-7}\right)^n/\left(1-1.13\cdot 10^{-7}\right)\rho\left(\left(W^{(1)},J^{(1)}\right),\left(W^{(0)},J^{(0)}\right)\right),$$

$(n=1,2\cdots)$

We notice that $\tilde{L}_0(i)=\tilde{L}_1(i)=6i-(1/3)i^3$ imply

$$\tilde{L}_0(t-T)$$

$$=6\left(e^{-(R/L)(t-T)}\left(W(t)+J(t-T)\right)/\left(2\sqrt{\bar{L}}\right)\right)$$

$$-(1/3)\left(e^{-(R/L)(t-T)}\left(W(t)+J(t-T)\right)/\left(2\sqrt{\bar{L}}\right)\right)^3,$$

$$\tilde{L}_1(t-T)$$

$$=6\left(e^{-(R/L)(t-T)}\left(W(t-T)+J(t)\right)/\left(2\sqrt{\bar{L}}\right)\right)$$

$$-(1/3)\left(e^{-(R/L)(t-T)}\left(W(t-T)+J(t)\right)/\left(2\sqrt{\bar{L}}\right)\right)^3$$

and therefore (recall $|\Pi_0|\le i_0=1, |\Pi_1|\le i_0=1$):

$$\left|2\sqrt{\bar{L}}\int_T^t e^{(R/L)(s-T)}R_0\left(\Pi_0(W^{(0)},J^{(0)})(s)\right)/\left(\tilde{L}_0(s-T)\right)ds\right|$$

$$\le 2\sqrt{\bar{L}}\int_T^t e^{(R/L)(s-T)}\left|R_0(i_0)\right|/\left(\tilde{L}_0(s-T)\right)ds$$

$$\le 2\sqrt{\bar{L}}\int_T^t e^{(R/L)(s-T)}\left(0,028+0,125\right)/(\bar{L})ds$$

$$\le 0.31L\sqrt{\bar{L}}\left(e^{(R/L)T_0}-1\right)/\left(\bar{L}R\right)\le 0.074\cdot 10^{-12}\approx 0.$$

Analogously

$$\left|2\sqrt{\bar{L}}\int_T^t e^{(R/L)(s-T)}R_1\left(\Pi_1(W^{(0)},J^{(0)})(s)\right)/\tilde{L}_1(s-T)\mathrm{d}s\right| \le \left(6\sqrt{\bar{L}}/17\right)(0.028+0.125)\left(e^{(R/L)T_0}-1\right)L/R\approx 0.$$

We find the first approximation

$$W^{(1)}(t)=B_u(W^{(0)},J^{(0)})(t)=\int_T^t U(W^{(0)},J^{(0)})(s)\mathrm{d}s-\left(\frac{t-T}{T_0}-\frac{1}{2}\right)\int_T^{T+T_0}U(W^{(0)},J^{(0)})(s)\mathrm{d}s$$

$$-\frac{1}{T_0}\int_T^{T+T_0}\int_T^t U(W^{(0)},J^{(0)})(s)\mathrm{d}s\mathrm{d}t$$

$$=-J_0\sin\omega_0 t+(R/L)\int_T^t J_0\sin\omega_0 s\,\mathrm{d}s+2E_0\sqrt{\bar{L}}\int_T^t e^{(R/L)(s-T)}\sin\omega_0 s/\left(\tilde{L}_0(s-T)\right)\mathrm{d}s$$

$$+Z_0J_0\int_T^t\sin\omega_0 s/\left(\tilde{L}_0(s-T)\right)\mathrm{d}s-2\sqrt{\bar{L}}\int_T^t\frac{e^{(R/L)(s-T)}}{\tilde{L}_0(s-T)}\frac{\bar{C}_0^{-1}}{2\sqrt{\bar{L}}}\left(\int_T^s e^{-(R/L)(\theta-T)}J_0\sin\omega_0\theta\mathrm{d}\theta\right)\mathrm{d}s$$

$$-\left(\frac{t-T}{T_0}-\frac{1}{2}\right)\left[2E_0\sqrt{\bar{L}}\int_T^{T+T_0}e^{(R/L)(s-T)}\sin\omega_0 s/\left(\tilde{L}_0(s-T)\right)\mathrm{d}s+Z_0J_0\int_T^{T+T_0}\sin\omega_0 s/\left(\tilde{L}_0(s-T)\right)\mathrm{d}s\right.$$

$$\left.-2\sqrt{\bar{L}}\int_T^{T+T_0}\frac{e^{(R/L)(s-T)}}{\tilde{L}_0(s-T)}\bar{C}_0^{-1}\left(\frac{J_0}{2\sqrt{\bar{L}}}\int_T^s e^{-(R/L)(\theta-T)}\sin\omega_0\theta\mathrm{d}\theta\right)\mathrm{d}s\right]$$

$$-\frac{1}{T_0}\int_T^{T+T_0}\left[-J_0\sin\omega_0 t+(R/L)\int_T^t J_0\sin\omega_0 s\mathrm{d}s+2E_0\sqrt{\bar{L}}\int_T^t e^{(R/L)(s-T)}\sin\omega_0 s\tilde{L}_0(s-T)\mathrm{d}s\right.$$

$$\left.+Z_0J_0\int_T^t\sin\omega_0 s/\left(\tilde{L}_0(s-T)\right)\mathrm{d}s-2\sqrt{\bar{L}}\int_T^t\frac{e^{(R/L)(s-T)}}{\tilde{L}_0(s-T)}\bar{C}_0^{-1}\left(\frac{J_0}{2\sqrt{\bar{L}}}\int_T^s e^{-(R/L)(\theta-T)}\sin\omega_0\theta\,\mathrm{d}\theta\right)\mathrm{d}s\right]\mathrm{d}t.$$

Since $\left|(R/L)\int_T^t J_0\sin\omega_0 s\,\mathrm{d}s\right|\approx J_0\cdot 10^{-9}$ and

$$2\sqrt{\bar{L}}\left|\int_T^t\frac{e^{(R/L)(s-T)}}{\tilde{L}_0(s-T)}\bar{C}_0^{-1}\left(\frac{J_0}{2\sqrt{\bar{L}}}\int_T^s e^{-(R/L)(\theta-T)}\sin\omega_0\theta\mathrm{d}\theta\right)\mathrm{d}s\right|\le W_0\frac{2\sqrt{\bar{L}}}{\bar{L}}\frac{L}{R}\left(e^{(R/L)T_0}-1\right)\approx W_0 3.6\cdot 10^{-8}\approx 0$$

we can disregard this terms and obtain

$$W^{(1)}(t)=-J_0\sin\omega_0 t+2E_0\sqrt{\bar{L}}\int_T^t\frac{e^{(R/L)(s-T)}\sin\omega_0 s}{\tilde{L}_0(s-T)}\mathrm{d}s+Z_0J_0\int_T^t\sin\omega_0 s/\left(\tilde{L}_0(s-T)\right)\mathrm{d}s$$

$$-\left(\frac{t-T}{T_0}-\frac{1}{2}\right)\left(2E_0\sqrt{\bar{L}}\int_T^{T+T_0}e^{(R/L)(s-T)}\sin\omega_0 s/\left(\tilde{L}_0(s-T)\right)\mathrm{d}s+Z_0J_0\int_T^{T+T_0}\sin\omega_0 s/\left(\tilde{L}_0(s-T)\right)\mathrm{d}s\right)$$

$$-\frac{1}{T_0}\int_T^{T+T_0}\left(2E_0\sqrt{\bar{L}}\int_T^t e^{(R/L)(s-T)}\sin\omega_0 s/\left(\tilde{L}_0(s-T)\right)\mathrm{d}s+Z_0J_0\int_T^t\sin\omega_0 s/\left(\tilde{L}_0(s-T)\right)\mathrm{d}s\right)\mathrm{d}t,$$

and then

$$\left|W^{(1)}(t)-W^{(0)}(t)\right|$$

$$\le J_0+\left(2E_0L\sqrt{\bar{L}}/R\bar{L}\right)\left(e^{(R/L)T_0}-1\right)+\left(Z_0J_0/\bar{L}\right)\left|\int_T^t e^{\mu(s-T)}\mathrm{d}s\right|+\left(E_0L\sqrt{\bar{L}}/R\bar{L}\right)\left(e^{(R/L)T_0}-1\right)$$

$$+\left(Z_0J_0/2\bar{L}\right)\left|\int_T^{T+T_0}e^{\mu(s-T)}\mathrm{d}s\right|+\frac{1}{T_0}\int_T^{T+T_0}\left(\left(2E_0L\sqrt{\bar{L}}/R\bar{L}\right)\left(e^{(R/L)T_0}-1\right)+\left(Z_0J_0/\bar{L}\right)\left|\int_T^t e^{\mu(s-T)}\mathrm{d}s\right|\right)\mathrm{d}t\le J_0$$

$$+\left(5L^{3/2}/\bar{L}R\right)\left(e^{(R/L)T_0}-1\right)E_0+5Z_0J_0\left(e^{\mu_0}-1\right)/\left(2\bar{L}\mu\right)$$

$$\le e^{\mu_0}J_0=e^2J_0.$$

For the derivative we have

$$\dot{W}^{(1)}(t) = U(W^{(0)},J^{(0)})(t) - \frac{1}{T_0}\int_T^{T+T_0} U(W^{(0)},J^{(0)})(s)\mathrm{d}s$$

$$= -\omega_0 J_0 \cos\omega_0 t + \frac{R}{L}J_0 \sin\omega_0 t + \frac{2e^{(R/L)(t-T)}E_0\sqrt{L}}{\tilde{L}_0(t-T)}$$

$$+\frac{Z_0}{\tilde{L}_0}\ J_0\sin\omega_0 t - \frac{2e^{(R/L)(t-T)}\sqrt{L}\ R\left(\Pi_0(W^{(0)},J^{(0)})(t)\right)}{\tilde{L}_0(t-T)}$$

$$-\frac{2e^{(R/L)(t-T)}\sqrt{L}}{\tilde{L}_0(t-T)}\tilde{C}_0^{-1}\left(\int_T^t \Pi_0(W^{(0)},J^{(0)})(\theta)\mathrm{d}\theta\right) - \frac{1}{T_0}\left(2E\sqrt{L}\int_T^{T+T_0} e^{(R/L)(s-T)/\tilde{L}_0(s-T)}\mathrm{d}s\right)$$

$$+\frac{1}{T_0}\left(Z_0\int_T^{T+T_0} J_0\sin\omega_0\big/\left(\tilde{L}_0(s-T)\right)\mathrm{d}s - 2\sqrt{L}\int_T^{T+T_0} e^{(R/L)(s-T)}R_0\left(\Pi_0(W^{(0)},J^{(0)})(s)\right)\big/\left(\tilde{L}_0(s-T)\right)\mathrm{d}s\right)$$

$$+\frac{1}{T_0}\left(2\sqrt{L}\int_T^{T+T_0}\frac{e^{(R/L)(s-T)}}{\tilde{L}_0(s-T)}\tilde{C}_0^{-1}\left(\int_T^s \Pi_0(W^{(0)},J^{(0)})(\theta)\mathrm{d}\theta\right)\mathrm{d}s\right).$$

Then we obtain

$$\left|\dot{W}^{(1)}(t) - \dot{W}^{(0)}(t)\right|$$

$$\le \left(\omega_0 + \frac{R}{L} + \frac{Z_0}{\overline{L}} + \frac{Z_0}{\overline{L}}(e^{\mu_0}-1)/\mu_0\right)J_0 + \left(2\sqrt{L}/\overline{L}\right)\left(e^{RT_0/L} + \left(e^{RT_0/L}-1\right)/\left(RT_0/L\right)\right)\left(E_0+W_0\right)$$

$$+\left(2\sqrt{L}/\overline{L}\right)(0.028+0.125)\left(e^{RT_0/L} + (e^{RT_0/L}-1)/\left(RT_0/L\right)\right) + \left(2\sqrt{L}/\overline{L}\right)\left(e^{RT_0/L}-1\right)/\left(RT_0/L\right)W_0.$$

Since $\left(e^{RT_0/L}-1\right)/\left(RT_0/L\right)\approx 1,\ E_0 = 0.5\ V$ we have

$$\left|\dot{W}^{(1)}(t) - \dot{W}^{(0)}(t)\right| \le \left(2\pi\cdot 10^{12} + 0,6.10^4 + \frac{225(e^2-1)}{34}\right)J_0 + \frac{3\sqrt{0.45\cdot 10^{-6}}}{17}(2+6W_0+0,612)\approx 3.768\cdot 10^7.$$

It follows $\rho\left(\dot{W}^{(1)},\dot{W}^{(0)}\right)\le 18.84\cdot 10^6$. Consequently

$$\rho((W^{(n+1)},J^{(n+1)}),(W^{(n)},J^{(n)}))\le \frac{\left(1.13\cdot 10^{-7}\right)^n}{1-1.13\cdot 10^{-7}}3.8\cdot 10^7\quad (n=0,1,\cdots)$$

or

$$\left|\dot{W}^{(n+1)}(t) - \dot{W}^{(n)}(t)\right| \le 7.4(1.13\cdot 10^{-7})^n 3.8\cdot 10^7 \le (1.13\cdot 10^{-7})^n\cdot(2.82)\cdot 10^8.$$

In the same way we can obtain an estimate for the second component of the operator B:

$$J^{(1)}(t) = B_i(W^{(0)},J^{(0)})(t) = \int_T^t I(W^{(0)},J^{(0)})(s)\mathrm{d}s - \left(\frac{t-T}{T_0}-\frac{1}{2}\right)\int_T^{T+T_0} I(W^{(0)},J^{(0)})(s)\mathrm{d}s - \frac{1}{T_0}\int_T^{T+T_0}\int_T^t I(W^{(0)},J^{(0)})(s)\mathrm{d}s\mathrm{d}t$$

$$= -W_0\sin\omega_0 t + \frac{RW_0}{L}\int_T^t \sin\omega_0 s\,\mathrm{d}s + 2E_0\sqrt{L}\int_T^t \frac{e^{R/L(s-T)}}{\tilde{L}_1(s-T)}\mathrm{d}s$$

$$+Z_0\int_T^t \frac{W_0\sin\omega_0 s}{\tilde{L}_1(s-T)}\mathrm{d}s - \left(\frac{t-T}{T_0}-\frac{1}{2}\right)\left(2E_0\sqrt{L}\int_T^{T+T_0}\frac{e^{(R/L)(s-T)}}{\tilde{L}_1(s-T)}\mathrm{d}s + Z_0\int_T^{T+T_0}\frac{W_0\sin\omega_0 s}{\tilde{L}_1(s-T)}\mathrm{d}s\right)$$

$$-\frac{1}{T_0}\int_T^{T+T_0}\left(2E_0\sqrt{L}\int_T^t \frac{e^{(R/L)(s-T)}}{\tilde{L}_1(s-T)}\mathrm{d}s + Z_0\int_T^t \frac{W_0\sin\omega_0 s}{\tilde{L}_1(s-T)}\mathrm{d}s\right)\mathrm{d}t.$$

5. Acknowledgements

The research described in this paper was carried out within the frame work of Contract No. DUNK-01/03 -12.2009 (UNIK).

6. References

[1] M. Shimura, "Analysis of Some Nonlinear Phenomena in a Transmission Line," *IEEE Transactions on Circuit Theory*, Vol. 14, No. 1, 1967, pp. 60-68.

[2] L. O. Chua and P.-M. Lin, "Machine Analysis of Electronic Circuits," in Russian, Energy, Moscow, 1980.

[3] D. M. Pozar, "Microwave Engineering," 2nd Edition, New York, Wiley, 1998.

[4] P. Chirlian, "Analysis and Design of Integrated Electronic Circuits," Harper & Row, Publishers, Inc., New York, 1987.

[5] C. R. Paul, "Analysis of Multiconductor Transmission Lines," Wiley-Interscience Publications, John Wiley & Sons, Hoboken, 1994.

[6] L. O. Chua, C. A. Desoer and E. S. Kuh, "Linear and Nonlinear Circuits," McGraw-Hill Book Company, New York, 1987.

[7] A. H. Zemanian, "Hyperreal Waves on Transfinite, Terminated Distortionless and Lossless Transmission Lines," *International Journal of Circuit Theory and Applications*, Vol. 33, No. 3, 2005, pp.183-193.

[8] S. Rosenstark, "Transmission Lines in Computer Engineering," McGraw-Hill, Inc., New York, 1994.

[9] V. G. Angelov, "Transmission Lines Terminated by Series Nonlinear RLC-Loads," *Annual of the University of Architecture, Civil Engineering and Geodesy*, Vol. 41, Sofia, 2000-2001, pp. 9-29.

[10] V. G. Angelov, "Lossy Transmission Lines Terminated by Nonlinear R-Loads with Exponential V-I Chara- cteristics," *Journal Nonlinear Analysis*, Vol. 8, No. 2, 2007, pp. 579-589.

[11] V. G. Angelov, "Periodic Regimes for Distortionless Lossy Transmission Lines Terminated by Parallel Connected RCL-Loads," In: Transmission Lines: Theory, Types and Applications. Ser. Electrical Engineering Developments, Nova Science Publishers, New York, 2011.

[12] S. Grivet-Talocia, H. M. Huang, A. E. Rudehli, F. Canavero and I. M. Elfadel, "Transient Analysis of Lossy Transmission Lines: An Efficient Approach Based on the Method of Characteristics," *IEEE Transactions on Advanced Packaging*, Vol. 27, No. 1, 2004, pp. 45-56.

[13] V. Rasvan, "Functional Differential Equations and One-Dimensional Distortionless Propagation," *Tatra Mountains Mathematical Publications*, Vol. 43, 2009, pp. 215-228.

[14] K. L. Cooke and D. W. Krumme, "Differential-Difference Equations and Nonlinear Initial Boundary Value Problems for Linear Hyperbolic Partial Differential Equations," *Journal of Mathematical Analysis and Applications*, Vol. 24, No. 2, 1968, pp. 372-387.

[15] A. D. Myshkis, "Linear Differential Equations with Retarded Arguments," in Russian, Nauka, Moscow, 1972.

[16] M. A. Krasnoselskii, "The Shift Operator along the Trajectories," in Russian, Moscow, 1970.

[17] Y. G. Borisovich, "Nonlinear Fredholm Mappings and Periodic Solutions of Functional Differential Equations," in Russian, *Proceedings of Mathematical Faculty*, Vol. 10, 1973, pp. 12-25.

[18] V. G. Angelov, "Fixed Points in Uniform Spaces and Applications," Cluj University Press, Cluj-Napoca, 2009.

[19] T. Dhaene and D. D. Zutter, "Selection of Lumped Models for Coupled Lossy Transmission Lines," *IEEE Transaction on Computer-Aided Design*, Vol. 11, No. 7, 1992, pp. 805-815.

[20] S. Y. Lee, A. Konrad and R. Saldanha, "Lossy Transmission Line Transient Analysis by the Finite Element Method," *IEEE Transactions on Magnetics*, Vol. 29, No. 2, 1993, pp. 1730-1732.

[21] Taflove and S. C. Hagness, "Computational Electromagnetics: The Finite-Difference Time-Domain Method," 2nd Edition, Artech House, Boston, 2000.

15

Derivation of Floquet Eigenvectors Displacement for Optimal Design of LC Tank Pulsed Bias Oscillators

Stefano Perticaroli, Nikend Luli, Fabrizio Palma
Department of Information Engineering, Electronics and Telecommunications, Sapienza Università di Roma, Rome, Italy

Abstract

The paper presents an approximated and compact derivation of the mutual displacement of Floquet eigenvectors in a class of LC tank oscillators with time varying bias. In particular it refers to parallel tank oscillators of which the energy restoring can be modeled through a train of current pulses. Since Floquet eigenvectors are acknowledged to give a correct decomposition of noise perturbations along the stable orbit in oscillator's space state, an analytical and compact model of their displacement can provide useful criteria for designers. The goal is to show, in a simplified case, the achievement of oscillators design oriented by eigenvectors. To this aim, minimization conditions of the effect of stationary and time varying noise as well as the contribution of jitter noise introduced by driving electronics are deduced from analytical expression of eigenvectors displacement.

Keywords: Floquet Eigenvectors Noise Decomposition, Pulsed Bias Oscillator, Oscillator Phase Noise

1. Introduction

Noise decomposition through Floquet eigenvectors is widely acknowledged to be a correct methodology for the analytical treatment of phase noise in electronic oscillators [1]. For this reason, numerical algorithms which rely also on the Floquet eigenvectors have been developed in order to obtain accurate prediction of power density spectrum (PDS) around the fundamental oscillation frequency. A well known example is found in the commercial simulator SpectreRF that computes Floquet eigenvectors from the shooting matrix and use them as a theoretical based correction for the PNoise analysis [2]. Although electronic simulators offer results in good agreement with effective measurements, they cannot be used to infer general properties of the underlying system. Despite the great amount of work presented even recently in literature [3, 4], since the pioneeristic work of Kaertner [5] and the latter efforts accomplished by Hajimiri-Lee [6], Demir [7, 8] and Buonomo [9] not many significant theoretical contributions have really extended the capability to develop innovative techniques in the design of oscillators systems.

In authors opinion the innovation should be founded on derivation of architecture-related expressions of Floquet eigenvectors [10], leading to a proper design methodology. This approach has been limited in the past by the fact that, also in relatively simple cases, Floquet eigenvectors cannot be obtained in analytical closed form.

Mutual displacement among eigenvectors along the period of oscillation regulates indeed how noise perturbations affect the spectral purity of oscillator system. In particular projections of noise on the eigenvectors determine the PDS of the oscillator [11]. We notice that mutual displacement depends in general on the quality factor of tank and on the way the lost energy is restored, i.e. on the chosen architecture. Even if in recent years several new architectural solutions were proposed for the reduction of phase noise in CMOS technologies [12-15], none of them was justified on eigenvectors based considerations. In particular, to knowledge of the authors, in literature there is no attempt to establish a direct relationship between Floquet eigenvectors and circuit parameters for a certain class of oscillators.

In this paper we present an analytical derivation of mutual displacement of Floquet eigenvectors and of their relationship with design parameters in the class of the LC tank oscillators with pulsed bias. First, we propose to introduce a parametrical model for the pulsed bias concept. Then we extend Floquet theory for the class in study in order to analyze noise dynamics and thus to optimize oscillators implemented through architectures with time varying bias. Finally we validate the proposed analysis and optimization criteria through the comparison with numerical results from a dedicated Matlab simulator of introduced model.

2. Simplified Model of LC Tank Pulsed Bias Oscillator

In order to characterize the class of LC tank oscillators with pulsed current bias we adopt the simplified parallel RLC model in **Figure 1**: it presents only two state variables, corresponding to the capacitor voltage V_C and the inductor current I_L of tank. This assumption can be seen as a rather drastic simplification for a model of a real oscillator, nevertheless, if pulsed bias circuitry does not introduce parasitic comparable to those in tank, the additional state variables can be neglected.

In this model the energy refilling is demanded to pulsed current generator $i(t)$ which is controlled, in particular, by the capacitor voltage V_C. Crossing of a threshold $|V_{th}|$ by the capacitor voltage, occurring at time defined as T_{th}, triggers the accumulation of a fixed delay T_1. After this delay the current generator is turned on for a time T_2 at fixed amplitude I_{max}. The turning on and off are assumed to be instantaneous, thus application of the ideal pulses gives rise to non derivable points of the capacitor voltage. In order to clarify the aforementioned timings and parameters of the model, a sketch of the generator current and of the resulting capacitor voltage waveform is reported in **Figure 2**.

The differential algebraic equations (DAE) describing dynamic of the proposed model is reported in Equation (1).

$$\begin{bmatrix} \dot{V}_C(t) \\ \dot{I}_L(t) \end{bmatrix} = \begin{bmatrix} -\frac{1}{RC} & -\frac{1}{C} \\ \frac{1}{L} & 0 \end{bmatrix} \cdot \begin{bmatrix} V_C(t) \\ I_L(t) \end{bmatrix} + \begin{bmatrix} \frac{1}{C} \\ 0 \end{bmatrix} \cdot i(t) \quad (1)$$

We choose to not explicitly express the large signal dependence of $i(t)$ as a function of V_C, since in this paper we are interested in a variational analysis for the study of noise only. However the existence of a stable orbit can be easily proved by means of mathematical approach for the analysis of nonlinear systems (e.g. the describing function technique) and will be not reported here.

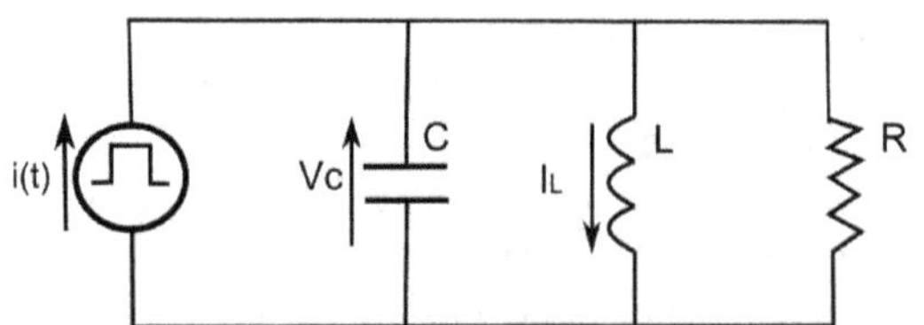

Figure 1. Model of the simplified LC tank pulsed bias oscillator.

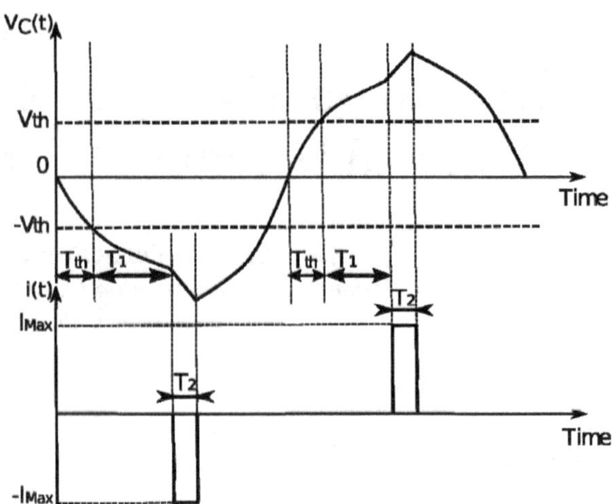

Figure 2. Sketch of capacitor voltage and current pulse of the generator in time.

In **Figure 3(a)** sketch of the stable orbit and the projections onto eigenvectors of superimposed noise perturbation $\underline{b}$ at certain time instant are reported. Due to the adopted symmetrical model, every half of the orbit can be subdivided into two different portion delimited by dashed lines in **Figure 3**. A first one corresponds to the RLC dumped evolution only and the second one corresponds to the evolution when the refilling current pulse is also active.

3. Floquet Theory for the Study of Noise

Floquet theory describes the periodical linear time varying (LPTV) response of oscillators systems to small perturbations superimposed on the stable oscillation orbit. Floquet eigenvectors are usually extracted from Mono-

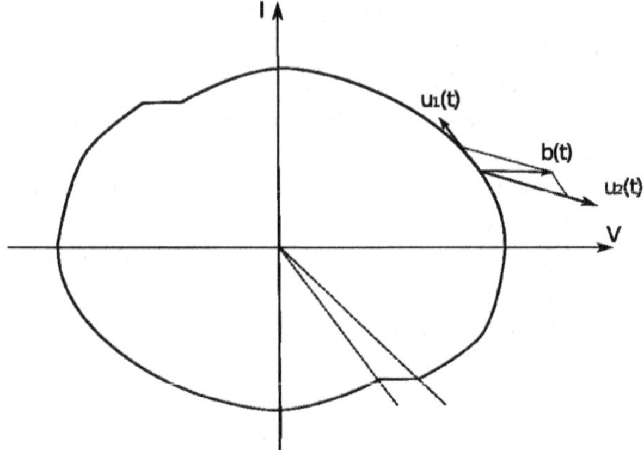

Figure 3. Sketch of the stable orbit and of the projections onto eigenvectors of superimposed noise perturbation $\underline{b}$ at certain time instant. Dashed lines indicate phase portion when pulsed bias current is active in a half of period.

dromy matrix. In general Monodromy matrix is obtained as the product of sequence of eventually different transition matrices along one oscillation period. In our treatment Monodromy matrix is calculated by following the evolution of the state variation vector $[v_C\ i_L]^T$ in the system along the orbit, apart from non derivable points. Evolution is derived from (1) imposing $i(t) = 0$ and is given by

$$\begin{bmatrix} \dot{v}_C(t) \\ \dot{i}_L(t) \end{bmatrix} = \begin{bmatrix} -\frac{1}{RC} & -\frac{1}{C} \\ \frac{1}{L} & 0 \end{bmatrix} \cdot \begin{bmatrix} v_C(t) \\ i_L(t) \end{bmatrix}, \quad (2)$$

The state transition matrix $\Phi(t)$ of dumped RLC system (2) results in

$$\Phi(t) = \begin{bmatrix} \Phi_{11}(t) & \Phi_{12}(t) \\ \Phi_{21}(t) & \Phi_{22}(t) \end{bmatrix} \quad (3)$$

Every component of (3) can be obtained by direct integration of (2) and hence assumes the form of dumped sinusoidal evolution as expressed in Equation (4)

$$\begin{cases} \Phi_{11}(t) = \frac{e^{-\mu t}}{\omega}\sqrt{\mu^2+\omega_n^2}\cos(\omega_n t - \varphi) \\ \Phi_{12}(t) = \frac{-Le^{-\mu t}}{\cos(-\varphi)}\sqrt{\mu^2+\omega_n^2}\sin(\omega_n t) \\ \Phi_{21}(t) = \frac{e^{-\mu t}}{L\omega}\sin(\omega_n t) \\ \Phi_{22}(t) = \frac{e^{-\mu t}}{\cos(-\varphi)}\cos(\omega_n t - \varphi) \end{cases} \quad (4)$$

where

$$\omega_0 = \sqrt{\frac{1}{LC}}, \quad \omega_n = \frac{2\pi}{T_n} = \omega_0\sqrt{1-\left(\frac{\mu}{\omega_0}\right)^2}$$

$$Q = \frac{R}{\omega_0 L} = \frac{\omega_0}{2\mu}, \quad \mu = \frac{1}{2RC} = \frac{\omega_0}{2Q} \quad (5)$$

$$\varphi = arctg\left(-\frac{\mu}{\omega_n}\right) \approx arctg\left(-\frac{\mu}{\omega_0}\right) = arctg\left(-\frac{1}{2Q}\right)$$

It has to be noticed that real period T differs in general from the nominal period T_n as a main effect of the pulsed bias.

The above described model holds until current pulse edges are reached. Since at this time instants the capacitor voltage is not derivable, we will need to introduce Interface matrices [16,17] to properly describe state evolution.

In the simplified adopted model only two Floquet eigenvectors exist, with two corresponding eigenvalues. We call "first eigenvector", $\underline{u}_1(t)$, the one which is tangent to the orbit with unitary eigenvalue and the "second eigenvector", $\underline{u}_2(t)$, the one with corresponding eigenvalue lower than 1. Once the evolution of the eigenvectors is available, we may project the perturbation $\underline{b}(t)$ multiplying it by inverse eigenvectors. The effect of noise projection is a state deviation which evolves as the eigenvector itself and sum in square to further noise projections along the orbit. Projections depend on the instant when $\underline{b}(t)$ is applied, so that the system appears as periodic time variant. In **Figure 4(a)** sketch of power density spectrum of the eigenvectors is reported [11]. Contribution to the PDS of noise projected on the first eigenvector, can be described by a transfer function with square modulus $1/\omega^2$, where is the offset with respect to the fundamental. We notice that at very low offset a cut-off must be assumed, not reported in the figure, due to nonlinear behaviour of the system for large values of phase deviation [7]. Noise projected on the second eigenvector can be instead described by a transfer function with square modulus $1/(\gamma_2^2+\omega^2)$, where γ_2 is the pole pulsation related to the second Floquet multiplier.

As a result the main contribution to the overall power density spectrum at frequencies close to the fundamental arises from projection on the first eigenvector. On the contrary contribution arising from the second eigenvector becomes relevant only at high frequency offsets ($\omega >> \gamma_2$) due to its low-pass shape with respect to the fundamental.

Only noise contributions parallel to $\underline{u}_2$ produce null contributions on $\underline{u}_1$ and thus do not increase the phase noise [1]. Floquet decomposition points out that eigenvectors, in general, are not orthogonal. As a result, assuming a white noise current generator in parallel to the RLC resonator, as it will be discussed in next section, a noise contribution in the direction $[1\ 0]^T$ (the voltage

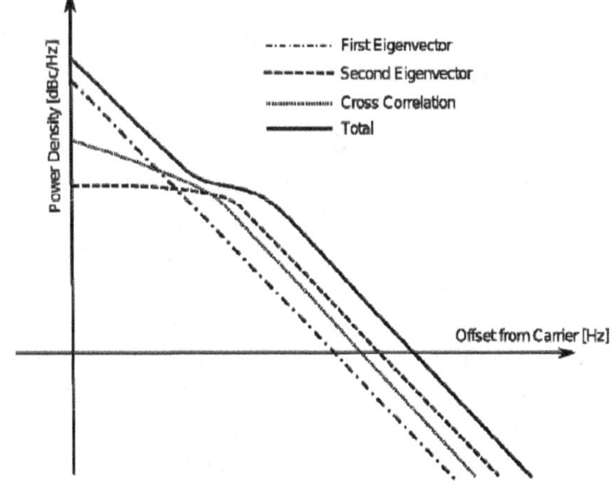

Figure 4. Sketch of power density spectrum contributions due to the eigenvectors.

variation axis) applied in correspondence of the voltage maximum may not yield to a null projection on $\underline{u}_1$.

These considerations lead to investigate a pulsed bias strategy, designed to activate the bias only when the projection of noise related to the biasing electronics on the first eigenvector is at least around a minimum. Nevertheless a complete evaluation of the proposed architectcture must take into account also the effect of eigenvectors displacement due to the pulsed bias on all the other noise sources present in the circuit.

As formerly stated, the eigenvectors evolutions are almost everywhere derived from state transition matrix of the dumped RLC system except for time instants when the generator switches on/off. Since an oscillator has no time reference, in the adopted model we may assume that at $t = 0$ the first eigenvector must be equal to $\underline{u}_1(0) = [V_{u1}(0)\ I_{u1}(0)] = k[1\ 0]^T,\ k \in \mathbb{R}$ with null current component (an eigenvector can always be defined by means of a proportionality constant). Until the first discontinuity, occurring at $t = T_{th} + T_1$, eigenvectors evolutions can then be described by the following equations normalized to amplitude of superimposed perturbation

$$\underline{u}_1(t) = \begin{bmatrix} V_{u1}(t) \\ I_{u1}(t) \end{bmatrix} = \begin{bmatrix} e^{-\mu t}\cos(\omega_n t - \varphi) \\ \dfrac{e^{-\mu t}}{F}\sin(\omega_n t) \end{bmatrix}$$
$$\underline{u}_2(t) = \begin{bmatrix} V_{u2}(t) \\ I_{u2}(t) \end{bmatrix} = \begin{bmatrix} e^{-\mu t}\cos(\omega_n t - \varphi + \beta) \\ \dfrac{e^{-\mu t}}{F}\sin(\omega_n t + \beta) \end{bmatrix} \quad (60)$$

where coefficient F depends on the quality of the tank and on resonating elements as in (7) and β represents the *phase displacement* between eigenvectors.

$$F = \sqrt{\frac{L}{C}} \cdot \sqrt{1 + \frac{1}{(2Q)^2}} \quad (7)$$

4. Phase Displacement between Eigenvectors as a Function of Pulse Paramaters

Figures 5 and **6** show a sketch of the evolutions respectively of first and second eigenvector. The effect of turning on and off of the bias current, taking place at $t = T_{th} + T_1$ and $t = T_{th} + T_1 + T_2$ respectively, corresponds to discontinuities of eigenvectors states, in direction $[1\ 0]^T$ (the V voltage variation axis). Due to the introduction of the Interface matrix theory [16], and as shown in **Figure 7**, we have to consider that any state variation along each eigenvector, evolved from $t = 0$ until T_{th}, produces a delay t with respect to the crossing of the threshold $|V_{th}|$.

The same delay is reported at the time of the turning on and off of the current generator. The delay is calculated as

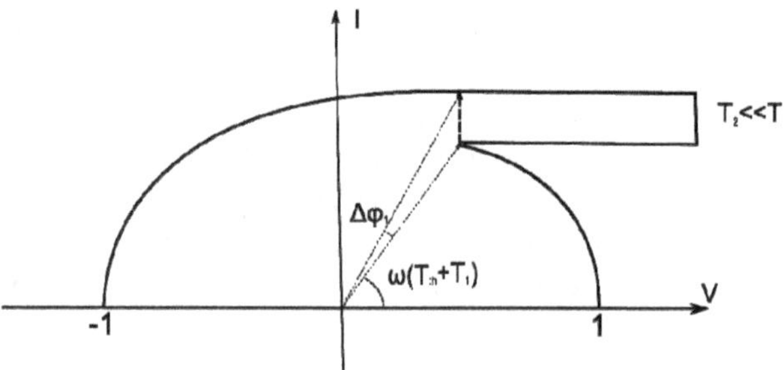

Figures 5. Sketch of evolution of the first eigenvector for a half of the period.

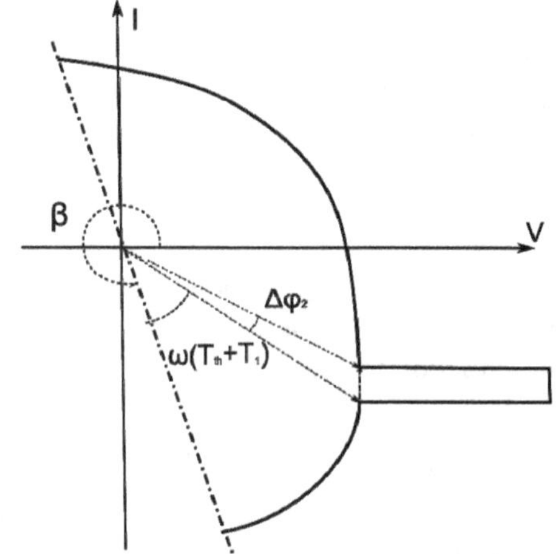

Figures 6. Sketch of evolution of the second eigenvector for a half of the period.

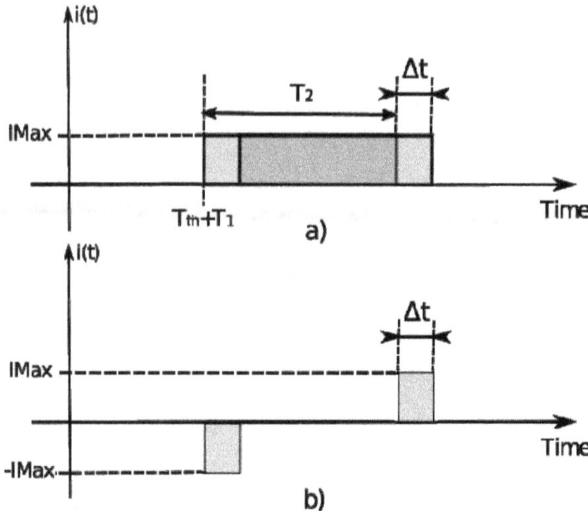

Figure 7. Current of the generator in time with delay due to the variation (a) and additional contributions at the pulse edges (b).

the ratio of voltage variation to the time derivative of the capacitor voltage at threshold crossing. Using a smart notation with subscript $J = 1,2$ where $X_{J=1} = 0$ and $X_{J=2} = \beta$, delay for both eigenvectors results in

$$\Delta t_J = \frac{e^{-\mu T_{th}}}{\dot{V}_C\big|_{t=T_{th}}}\cos\left(\omega_n T_{th} - \varphi + X_J\right) \tag{8}$$

Implicit voltage variation at numerator ensures dimensional balance in Equation (8). As a result of the delay, at the pulse edges two additional contributions opposite in sign sum to the former state variation. Since we are dealing with a pulsed bias for hypothesis, we now assume $T_2 << T$ and then we neglect the relative phase rotation between the pulse edges in both eigenvectors evolutions. As depicted in **Figure 5**, this allows us to approximate the effect of the bias current pulse as a unique discontinuity of the state in direction $[0\ 1]^T$ (the I current variation axis). We hence calculate discontinuity amplitude for both eigenvectors using (6) and (8) as the sum of opposite contributions approximating sinusoidal function for small T_2 in

$$\Delta I_J = \frac{\mathrm{I}_{\max}}{C\dot{V}_C\big|_{t=T_{th}}F} e^{-\mu T_{th}}\omega_n T_2 \cos\left(\omega_n T_{th} - \varphi + X_J\right) \tag{9}$$

The overall state variation, including the effect due to discontinuities, evolves along a new orbit. The second part of the evolution can be obtained for both the eigenvectors as

$$\underline{u}_J(t) = \begin{bmatrix} V_J(t) \\ I_J(t) \end{bmatrix} = \begin{bmatrix} \mathrm{A}^{-\mu t}\cos\left(\omega_n t - \varphi + X_J + \Delta\varphi_J\right) \\ \dfrac{\mathrm{A}}{F}e^{-\mu t}\sin\left(\omega_n t + X_J + \Delta\varphi_J\right) \end{bmatrix} \tag{10}$$

where A and $\Delta\varphi_J$ are unknown general solution parameters.

We notice that at $t = T_{th} + T_1$ the voltage components remain unaltered due to the assumption $T_2 << T$, whereas the current components of state variations are affected by the ΔI_J drops. This observation leads to define a system of two non-linear equations in the two unknown A and $\Delta\varphi_J$:

$$\begin{cases} \mathrm{A}e^{-\mu(T_{th}+T_1)}\cos\left(\omega_n T_{th} + \omega_n T_1 - \varphi + X_J + \Delta\varphi_J\right) \\ = e^{-\mu(T_{th}+T_1)}\cos\left(\omega_n T_{th} + \omega_n T_1 - \varphi + X_J\right) \\ \dfrac{\mathrm{A}}{F}e^{-\mu(T_{th}+T_1)}\sin\left(\omega_n T_{th} + \omega_n T_1 + X_J + \Delta\varphi_J\right) \\ = \dfrac{1}{F}e^{-\mu(T_{th}+T_1)}\sin\left(\omega_n T_{th} + \omega_n T_1 + X_J\right) + \Delta I_J. \end{cases} \tag{11}$$

In order to achieve an approximate solution of system (11) we expand the trigonometric function containing $\Delta\varphi_J$ in Mac Laurin series, limited to the first order and obtain:

$$\Delta\varphi_J = \frac{\Delta I_J F\cos\left(\omega_n T_{th} + \omega_n T_1 - \varphi + X_J\right)}{\cos(-\varphi) + \Delta I_J F\sin\left(\omega_n T_{th} + \omega_n T_1 - \varphi + X_J\right)}. \tag{12}$$

Since in most of practical cases tank quality factor Q is at least greater than 5 we further observe that

$$\cos(-\varphi) \approx \cos\left(arctg\left(\frac{1}{2Q}\right)\right) \approx \cos\left(\frac{1}{2Q}\right) \approx 1 \qquad \Delta I_J F << 1 \tag{13}$$

thus we may reformulate (12) neglecting terms due to pulse in the sum at denominator to solve the general parameter $\Delta\varphi_J$ for both the eigenvector as

$$\begin{aligned} \Delta\varphi_1 &\cong \frac{\Delta I_1 F\cos\left(\omega_n T_{th} + \omega_n T_1 - \varphi\right)}{\cos(-\varphi)} \\ \Delta\varphi_2 &\cong \frac{\Delta I_2 F\cos\left(\omega_n T_{th} + \omega_n T_1 - \varphi + \beta\right)}{\cos(-\varphi)} \end{aligned} \tag{14}$$

where $\Delta\varphi_1$ and $\Delta\varphi_2$ account the phase discontinuities due to the bias current pulse, respectively, for the first and the second eigenvector.

Since, by the definition, eigenvectors are periodic, and, due to the symmetry of the adopted model in the two halves of period they cover the same phase angle, we may infer that phase discontinuities caused by the bias current pulse must be equal, *i.e.*

$$\Delta\varphi_1 = \Delta\varphi_2 \tag{15}$$

From these observations, substituting the condition (15) in Equation (14) and expanding ΔI_J drops, it is straightforward to obtain the value of the phase displacement between the eigenvectors $\underline{u}_1$ and $\underline{u}_2$, at least out of the orbit portion when pulsed current is active as

$$\beta = -\left(2\omega_n T_{th} + \omega_n T_1 - 2\varphi\right). \tag{16}$$

We want to remark that in Equation (16) β is only a function of the threshold crossing time, of the delay of current pulse application, and of the tank quality factor (related to parameter φ).

5. Optimal Phase Displacement between Eigenvectors

Phase displacement between eigenvectors becomes here the main tool toward the paper goal to offer design insights for the reduction of phase noise which, in our treatment, means to minimize projection of noise on the first eigenvector. To this aim we are now going to demonstrate optimum conditions on phase displacement between eigenvectors, in order to reduce noise due to bias, parasitic resistance and jitter on accumulation of delay time T_1.

We assume perturbations to be realizations of white Gaussian noise processes with zero time average. This is not a restrictive assumption. In fact, also noise sources with non-delta autocorrelations, *i.e.* $1/f^{\alpha}$ with $\alpha \in \mathbb{R}^{+}$, may be taken into account through the projections on the eigenvectors. Referring to [5], in particular Sections 6 and 7, the power density of a flicker noise source is obtained as an infinite sum of autocorrelation spectra of statistically independent Ornstein-Uhlenbeck processes (that are also Gaussian processes). Since we are dealing with a parallel RLC tank, perturbations are introduced as parallel noise current sources. Such noise current sources cause a variation of the capacitor voltage, hence we model the normalized noise perturbation through a constant vector

$$\underline{b} = \begin{bmatrix} V_b \\ I_b \end{bmatrix} = \begin{bmatrix} 1 \\ 0 \end{bmatrix}. \quad (17)$$

In order to determine the PDS we need to calculate the projection of vector $\underline{b}$ on the base formed by the two eigenvectors. Integration along the orbit of the square value of the projection on $\underline{u}_1$ leads to the c_1 coefficient of Demir [7], while projection on $\underline{u}_2$ must be multiplied before integration by a properly evaluated exponential factor [11].

We first search for the condition which zeroes the projection on $\underline{u}_1$ of noise due to the bias current, usually the largest source of noise in integrated technologies. Bias current noise is cyclostationary because it arises only during the bias pulse. Assuming again $T_2 << T$ we may consider constant the projection angle during the pulse, then integration reduces to the multiplication of the projection by time T_2. We notice that noise projection has to be performed after the turning on of the bias current, after the eigenvector discontinuity in $T_{th} + T_1$ has occurred. As depicted in **Figures 5** and **6**, the additional component is in the direction $[1\ 0]^T$, thus the necessary and sufficient condition which ensures that once added the Interface matrix component the eigenvector has null current component is

$$\underline{u}_2\left(T_{th}+T_1\right)\cdot \underline{b} = 0 \rightarrow \underline{u}_2\left(T_{th}+T_1\right)\cdot \begin{bmatrix} 1 \\ 0 \end{bmatrix} = 0. \quad (18)$$

Following the definition of $\underline{u}_2$ in Equation (6) and substituting in its expression the phase displacement of Equation (16), condition (18) is equivalent to:

$$\begin{gathered} \omega_n(T_{th}+T_1)+\beta \\ = \omega_n(T_{th}+T_1) - \left(2\omega_n T_{th} + \omega_n T_1 - 2\varphi\right) = 0 \\ \downarrow \\ \omega_n T_{th} = 2\varphi. \end{gathered} \quad (19)$$

Equation (19) states that, in possible implementations of pulsed bias oscillators, the $|V_{th}|$ threshold should be chosen around the zero crossing of the oscillation voltage.

We may further search for the minimization of the contribution arising from parasitic resistance, which remains active all along the orbit. We recall that, from Equation (16) and following condition $T_2 << T$ which led to (15) phase displacement between eigenvectors remains constant along the entire evolution except for region where the pulsed current bias is active.

However, since we assumed bias active for a short time compared to period, the projections of noise on the two eigenvectors, respectively u_{1p} and u_{2p}, are given by

$$\begin{cases} u_{1p}(t) = \dfrac{\sin(\beta+\omega_n t)}{\sin(\beta)} \\ u_{2p}(t) = \dfrac{\sin(\omega_n t)}{\sin(\beta)} \end{cases} \quad (20)$$

then we obtain the integral of the square of the projections

$$\begin{cases} \int_0^T u_{1p}(t)^2\, dt = \dfrac{1}{\sin^2(\beta)} \int_0^T \sin^2(\beta+\omega_n t) dt = \dfrac{1}{\sin^2(\beta)} \dfrac{T}{2} \\ \int_0^T u_{2p}(t)^2\, dt = \dfrac{1}{\sin^2(\beta)} \int_0^T \sin^2(\omega_n t) dt = \dfrac{1}{\sin^2(\beta)} \dfrac{T}{2} \end{cases} \quad (21)$$

As expected the two terms in Equation (21) are equal. The first one is the Demir c_1 coefficient [7], while the second is only a majorant term in the expression of phase noise due to $\underline{u}_2$.

The actual period T depends on the angle β between the eigenvectors, however in hypothesis $Q > 5$ it results very close to T_n (the nominal period). This leads to state that factor $\sin^2(\beta)$ predominates the result of integration and allows us to infer that minimization of phase noise distribution due to a stationary noise source occurs if the condition $\beta = \pm\pi/2$ holds.

Further considerations can be derived from this result and from condition expressed in (19). For example, we notice that a jitter noise contribution arises from the electronic circuit when we introduce the delay T_1. This jitter is proportional to the delay itself and inversely proportional to the power used to accumulate the delay [18]. The choice to avoid any delay may be of interest in order to save an additional source of noise and to reduce energy dissipation [19]. Imposing $T_1 = 0$ in combination with condition (21) we obtain that the optimum choice is to set

$$\begin{cases} T_1 = 0 \\ \beta = -2\left(\omega_n T_{th} - \varphi\right) = -\dfrac{\pi}{2} \Rightarrow \omega_n T_{th} - \varphi = \dfrac{\pi}{4} \end{cases} \quad (22)$$

It results that condition on minimization of stationary noise (21) together with condition on minimization of accumulated jitter can be simultaneously satisfied only for a very low quality factor ($Q = 0.5$). Then in any practical case a suboptimal condition must be searched, e.g. accepting a non zero delay time T_1.

Hence the last optimum condition we can search for is derived from minimization of both resistance noise and bias current noise for a given quality factor Q and in presence of a delay time of the current pulse T_1. Using results from Equations (19) and (21) in Equation (16) we obtain

$$\omega_n T_1 = \frac{\pi}{2} + 2\varphi = \frac{\pi}{2} - 2\text{arctg}\left(\frac{1}{2Q}\right) \quad (23)$$

6. Numerical Comparison and Discussion

In order to evaluate the accuracy of the proposed analytical expressions we need to compare them with numerical simulations. In fact, at the knowledge of the authors, there is no measurement setup and/or post-processing that can extract eigenvectors from measure of physical quantities in a real circuital implementation.

Moreover there are no commercial circuit simulator which can compute Floquet eigenvectors in presence of discontinuities in space state. Then we developed a dedicated Matlab simulator for the model defined in Section III. The simulator derives the Monodromy matrix through a shooting algorithm which use Interface matrices for the treatment of discontinuities.

Even if the proposed analysis is not dependent on the oscillation period, in the following simulations we fixed frequency at $f_n = \omega_n/(2\pi) = 5$ GHz. Along with frequency, we choose to keep constant quality factor $Q = 7.5$, pulse duration $T_2 = T/15$ and amplitude $I_{\max} = 60$ mA ensuring the oscillator to be refilled by a fixed amount of energy and to be perturbed by the same amount of noise power. Moreover in case $V_{th} \neq 0$ V we keep constant also the sum $T_{th}+T_1$, allowing to reach the same limit cycle of $V_{th} = 0$ V simulations set. The two case of study, respectively $V_{th} \neq 0$ V and $V_{th} \neq 0$ V, differ only in the starting point with respect to period of T_1 delay accumulation and in the weight of jitter contribution which is proportional to T_1. All kind of noise sources are modeled as parallel current generators that adds to the model in **Figure 1**. Stationary noise is introduced as thermal noise of the parasitic resistance depending on quality factor Q through $4k_BT_{amb}/R$ [A^2/Hz] relation (k_B is Boltzmann constant T_{amb} is ambient temperature in Kelvin) whereas the cyclostationary noise is introduced as shot noise (modeling eventual devices) related to current $I_{\max}$ through $2qI_{\max}$ [A^2/Hz] relation (q is electron charge). Jitter noise source is instead considered as an additional time shift due to the accumulation of both T_1 and T_2 delay and it is added to the one due to evolution of the initial variation until time of threshold crossing T_{th} (8). Jitter source is the result of the charging of a capacitor through a dissipative media (again assume a MOS device) so it has been modeled through $8k_BT_{amb}\gamma\, T_1(K_{MOS}/I_D^3)^{0.5}$ [s] relation where is γ transistor noise constant, K_{MOS} and I_D are respectively the large signal current gain and drain current of MOS device. We choose to fix drain current to $I_D = I_{\max}/10 = 6$ mA. In fact the eventual auxiliary circuit suited for the introduction of desired delay must necessarily have a lower power consumption with respect the refilling process of the tank in a real design.

In **Figure 8** the phase displacement β is reported in function of T_1 normalized to period T in two cases $V_{th} = 0$ V and $V_{th} = 0.75$ V.

Amplitude and period of oscillation, as stated before, vary in function of pulse position between [2.45 V, 3.11 V] and [4.8 GHz, 5.2 GHz] respectively.

It can be observed a good match between simulated and calculated (16) trend with a maximum absolute error of about 13 in the evaluated range for case $V_{th} = 0.75$ V.

Former considerations on factor $\sin^2(\beta)$ in case $V_{th} = 0$ V suggest that in correspondence of $T_1/T \approx 0.223$ when $\beta \approx \pi/2$ a minimization of noise projection on the first eigenvector should occur. Moreover for $T_1/T \approx 0.223$ the maximum of amplitude and the nominal frequency are obtained. In case $V_{th} = 0.75$ V the enhancement of time shift (8) due to late starting point T_{th} of delay accumulation overwhelm any reduction of jitter weight due to shorter T_1.

In **Figure 9** the simulated PDS of the oscillator is reported for three typical frequency offsets (100 KHz, 1 MHz and 10 MHz) from the fundamental in function of

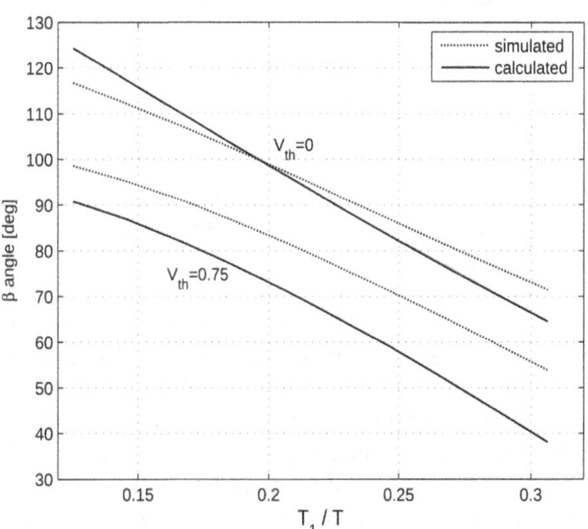

Figure 8. Eigenvectors phase displacement out of the fast region simulated (dotted trace) and calculated (continue trace) in function of normalized pulse position T_1 for $T_2 = T/15$, $Q = 7.5$ in cases $V_{th} = 0$ V and $|V_{th}| = 0.75$ V.

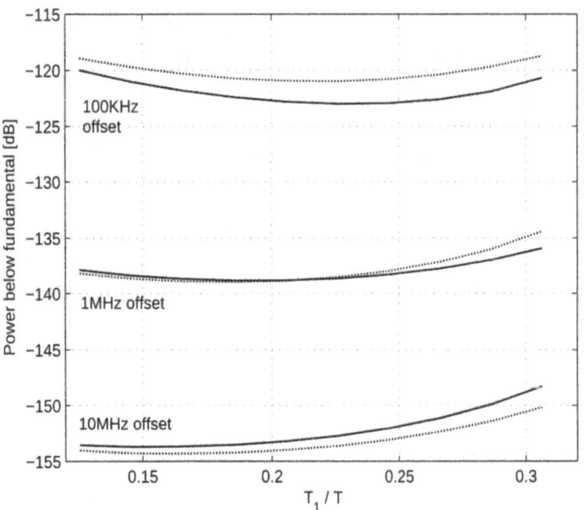

Figure 9. Simulated PDS evaluated at three different offset from fundamental frequency in function of normalized pulse position T_1 for $T_2 = T/15$, $Q = 7.5$ in cases $V_{th} = 0$ V (continue trace) and $|V_{th}| = 0.75$ V (dotted trace).

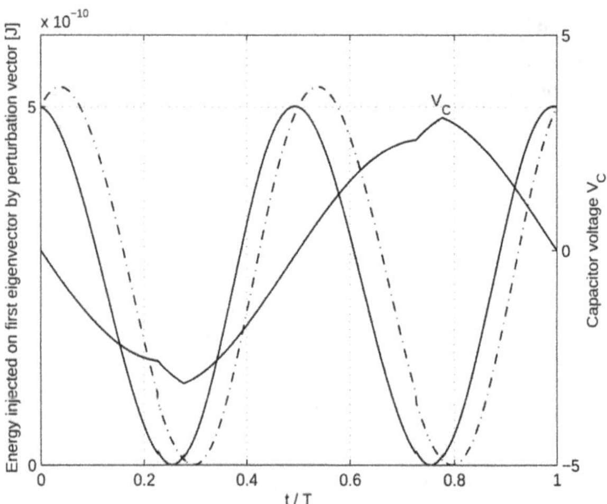

Figure 10. Simulated energy injected on first eigenvector by perturbation vector $\underline{b}$ in cases $V_{th} = 0$ V (continue trace) and $|V_{th}| = 0.75$ V (dotted trace) on left y-axis and capacitor voltage V_C right y-axis along oscillation period for $T_1/T = 0.24$, $T_2 = T/15$, $Q = 7.5$.

T_1 in case of $V_{th} = 0$ V and $V_{th} = 0.75$V.

PDS has been computed following [11]. It can be observed that the continue trace related to the lowest offset, where the major contribution to PDS arises from projection on first eigenvector, exhibits the minimum exactly in correspondence of the prediction made by means of $\beta \approx \pi/2$ criterion for $V_{th} = 0$ V. At higher offsets contributions arising from projections on cross-correlations between eigenvectors and on second eigenvector become preponderant and the minima shift toward earlier T_1/T ratio for both V_{th} cases. However it can be noticed that the $V_{th} = 0$ V case achieves the better performance at the lowest offset whereas the $V_{th} = 0.75$ V case reaches the best results at large offsets for quite all T_1/T ratio.

In order to justify this observed trend we propose to monitor noise introduced through first eigenvector (referring to $u_{1p}(t)$ noise projection) in term of injected level of energy from all noise sources on first eigenvector.

In **Figure 10** the energy injected along the normalized period on first eigenvector by perturbation vector $\underline{b}$ is reported in cases $V_{th} = 0$ V and $V_{th} = 0.75$ V for $T_1/T = 0.24$, $T_2 = T/15$, $Q = 7.5$. It can be noticed that the zero of injected energy occurs during the current bias pulse only in case $V_{th} = 0$ V. For any $V_{th} \neq 0$ V the zero shifts toward later time instant. Moreover, as a result of non orthogonal phase displacement between eigenvectors in case $V_{th} \neq 0$ V the maxima of injected energy on first eigenvector (when only stationary and jitter noise sources are present) can be greatly increased, thus degrading phase noise especially at low offsets. This observation is congruent with former defined design criterion (19) and validates the proposed analysis.

7. Concluding Remarks

The paper presented an approximated and compact derivation of the mutual displacement of Floquet eigenvectors in the class of parallel RLC tank oscillators with pulsed current bias. Mutual displacement was proved to be strongly connected with the chosen architecture and consequently to determine phase noise distribution. As appreciable result, the derived expression of displacement is compact and straightforward, thus it can suggest primary guide lines for designers in the field of oscillators architectures with time varying bias.

In particular we demonstrated conditions for minimization of stationary as well as cyclostationary noise. Also the jitter noise introduced in the positioning of the pulsed bias is taken into account and its relation with noise projections on the eigenvectors is determined. Minimization conditions were formulated using parameters of the proposed model for the pulsed bias class, allowing to directly infer the circuit design. Finally the analytical results are compared with a dedicated simulator, showing that proposed criteria for noise reduction are congruent with observed trend in the simulated PDS.

Future works will provide developments and extensions of the proposed analytical noise treatment to VCOs and PLLs systems.

8. References

[1] G. J. Coram, "A Simple 2-D Oscillator to Determine the Correct Decomposition of Perturbations into Amplitude and Phase Noise," *IEEE Transactions on Circuits and*

Systems-I: Fundamental Theory and Applications, Vol. 48, No. 7, July 2001, pp. 896-898.

[2] Affirma™ RF Simulator (SpectreRF™) User Guide, Product Version 4.4.6, June 2000, pp. 696-699.

[3] F. O'Doherty and J. P. Gleeson, "Phase Diffusion Coefficient for Oscillators Perturbed by Colored Noise," *IEEE Transactions on Circuits and Systems-II: Express Briefs*, Vol. 54, No. 5, May 2007, pp. 435-439.

[4] T. Djurhuus, V. Krozer, J. Vidkjaer and T. K. Johansen, "Oscillator Phase Noise: A Geometrical Approach," *IEEE Transactions on Circuits and Systems-I: Regular Papers*, Vol. 56, No. 7, July 2009, pp. 1373-1382.

[5] F. X. Kaertner, "Analysis of White And f-α Noise in Oscillators," *International Journal of Circuit and Theory Applications*, Vol. 18, No. 5, March 1990, pp. 485-519.

[6] T. H. Lee and A. Hajimiri, "Oscillator Phase Noise: A Tutorial," *IEEE Journal of Solid-State Circuits*, Vol. 35, No. 6, March 2000, pp. 326-336.

[7] A. Demir, "Floquet Theory and Non-Linear Perturbation Analysis Foroscillators with Differential-Algebraic Equations," *International Journal of Circuit and Theory Applications*, Vol. 28, No. 2, March 2000, pp. 163-185.

[8] A. Demir, A. Mehrotra and J. S. Roychowdhury, "Phase Noise in Oscillators: A Unifying Theory and Numerical Methods for Characterization," *IEEE Transactions on Circuits and Systems-I: Fundamental Theory and Applications*, Vol. 47, No. 5, May 2000, pp. 655-674.

[9] A. Buonomo, "Nonlinear Analysis of Voltage-Controlled Oscillators: A Systematic Approach," *IEEE Transaction on Circuit and Systems-I: Regular Papers*, Vol. 55, No. 6, June 2008, pp. 1659-1670.

[10] A. Carbone, A. Brambilla and F. Palma, "Using Floquet Eigenvectors in the Design of Electronic Oscillators," 2005 *IEEE 7th CAS Symposium on Emerging Technologies: Circuits and Systems for* 4G *Mobile Wireless Communications*, St. Petersburg, 23-24 June 2005, pp. 100-103.

[11] A. Carbone and F. Palma, "Considering Orbital Deviations on the Evaluation of Power Density Spectrum of Oscillators," *IEEE Transactions on Circuits and Systems-II: Express Briefs*, Vol. 53, No. 6, June 2006, pp. 438-442.

[12] B. Razavi, "A Study of Phase Noise in CMOS Oscillators," *IEEE Journal of Solid-State Circuits*, Vol. 31, No. 3, March 1996, pp. 331-343.

[13] R. Aparicio and A. Hajimiri, "A Noise-Shifting Differential Colpitts VCO," *IEEE Journal of Solid-State Circuits*, Vol. 37, No. 12, December 2002, pp. 1728-1736.

[14] S. K. Magierowski and S. Zukotynski, "CMOS LC-Oscillator Phase Noise Analysis Using Nonlinear Models," *IEEE Transactions on Circuits and Systems-I: Regular Papers*, Vol. 51, No. 4, April 2004, pp. 664-677.

[15] T. H. Lee, "Design of CMOS Radio-Frequency Integrated Circuits," Cambridge Press, Cambridge, 1998, pp. 669-677.

[16] A. Carbone and F. Palma, "Discontinuity Correction in Piecewise-Linear Models of Oscillators for Phase Noise Characterization," *International Journal of Circuit Theory and Applications*, Vol. 35, No. 1, 2007, pp. 93-104.

[17] R. I. Leine, D. H. Van Campen and B. L. Van der Vrande, "Bifurcations in Nonlinear Discontinuous Systems," *Nonlinear Dynamics*, Vol. 23, No. 2, October 2000, pp. 105-164.

[18] M. Aleksic, N. Nedovic K. W. Current and V. G. Oklobdzija, "Jitter Analysis of Nonautonomous MOS Current-Mode Logic Circuits," *IEEE Transaction on Circuit and Systems-I: Regular Papers*, Vol. 55, No. 10, November 2008, pp. 3038-3049.

[19] S. Perticaroli and F. Palma, "Phase and Quadrature Pulsed Bias LC-CMOS VCO," *SCIRP Circuit and Systems*, Vol. 2, No. 1, January 2011, pp. 18-24.

An Efficient Method for Vehicle License Plate Detection in Complex Scenes

Mahmood Ashoori-Lalimi, Sedigheh Ghofrani*
Electrical Engineering Department, Islamic Azad University, South Tehran Branch, Tehran, Iran

Abstract

In this paper, we propose an efficient method for license plate localization in the images with various situations and complex background. At the first, in order to reduce problems such as low quality and low contrast in the vehicle images, image contrast is enhanced by the two different methods and the best for following is selected. At the second part, vertical edges of the enhanced image are extracted by sobel mask. Then the most of the noise and background edges are removed by an effective algorithm. The output of this stage is given to a morphological filtering to extract the candidate regions and finally we use several geometrical features such as area of the regions, aspect ratio and edge density to eliminate the non-plate regions and segment the plate from the input car image. This method is performed on some real images that have been captured at the different imaging conditions. The appropriate experimental results show that our proposed method is nearly independent to environmental conditions such as lightening, camera angles and camera distance from the automobile, and license plate rotation.

Keywords: License Plate Detection, Image Enhancement, Background and Noise Removing, Morphological Operations

1. Introduction

With the rapid development of highway and the wide use of vehicle, researchers start to pay more attention on efficient and accurate intelligent transportation systems (ITS). It is widely used for detecting car's speed, security control in restricted areas, highway surveillance and electric toll collection [1]. Vehicle license plate (VLP) recognition is one of the most important requirements of an ITS. Although any ITS and specifically any VLP recognition contains two part in general, license plate detection and recognition, detecting and segmenting VLP correctly is most important because of existing conditions such as poor illumination, vehicle motion, viewpoint and distance changes. The problem of automatic VLP recognition has been studied since 1990s. The first approach was based on characteristics of boundaries [2,3]. In this method, an image was binarized and then processed by certain algorithms, such as Hough transform, to detect lines. In general, the most common approaches for VLP detection include texture [1,4], color feature [5], edge extraction [6], combining edge and color [7], morphological operation [5,8] and learning-based method [9]. Using color feature is benefit when lightening is unchanged and stable. However methods based on edge and texture are nearly invariant to different illumination and so they are widely used for VLP detection. These methods use the fact that there are many characters in the license plate, so the area contains rich edge and texture information. Zhang *et al.* [9] proposed learning-based method using AdaBoost for VLP detection. They used both global (statistical) and local (Haar-like) features to detect the license plate.

In this paper, we do pre processing for image enhancement at first. The some regions are candidate as a license plate during three procedures. Finally considering geometrical features, the license plate is segmented nearly independent of image capturing conditions.

This paper is organized as follows: in Section 2, different styles of Iranian license plates are illustrated in Section 3. We express how our image bank is provided. In Section 4, the proposed algorithm is described and in Section 5 the experimental results are reported. Finally, in Section 6 we have conclusion.

2. Iranian Vehicle License Plate

We have considered 3 classes for Iranian VLP, they are private, public (such as taxi, truck and bus) and governmental vehicles. Each class has own plate and character color. In addition, though Farsi characters are 32, only some characters are used for VLP. Color arrangement, characters and outline of the Iranian VLP are shown in **Table 1**.

3. Provided Image Bank

As respects, the aim of this paper is detecting the Iranian license plates in images with complex scenes. Due to the unavailability of required images, in several stages by using 2 digital cameras and mobile cameras, we have provided 350 images under various illumination (lightening), different distances and angles of stationary and moving vehicles. After providing images, in order to increase the processing speed and facilitate the license plate detection, input color image is converted to grayscale image. The size of images is 640 × 480 pixels.

4. Efficient License Plate Detection

Our proposed method is composed of several parts, **Figure 1** shows the flowchart.

4.1. Pre Processing

Low contrast may have the most important effect on failing a license plate detection algorithm. Severe lightening conditions, changing plate orientation and various distances are main reasons for having low contrast and quality in the car images. Therefore, contrast enhancement seems to be necessary, specially at locations where might be a license plate. So, in following we improve different images using two methods, they are intensity variance [6] and edge density [7], and choose the best for pre processing images.

4.1.1. Intensity Variance

Zheng *et al.* [6] used the local variance of pixel intensities to improve image contrast at regions that may be plate. They proposed an enhancement function which increases image contrast at regions that local variance of intensity is around 20. The enhancement function was suggested as follows:

$$I'_{ij} = f\left(\sigma_{w_{ij}}\right)\left(I_{ij} - \bar{I}_{w_{ij}}\right) + \bar{I}_{w_{ij}} \quad (1)$$

where I_{ij}, and I'_{ij} denote the intensities of the pixel in the input grayscale image and enhanced image, and w_{ij} is a window centered on pixels of grayscale image. $\bar{I}_{w_{ij}}$, and $\sigma_{w_{ij}}$ are average luminance and standard deviation respectively. The enhanced coefficient is defined as follows:

$$f(\sigma_{w_{ij}}) = \begin{cases} \dfrac{3}{\dfrac{2}{400}\left(\sigma_{w_{ij}} - 20\right)^2 + 1} & \text{if} \quad 0 \le \sigma_{w_{ij}} < 20 \\ \dfrac{3}{\dfrac{2}{1600}\left(\sigma_{w_{ij}} - 20\right)^2 + 1} & \text{if} \quad 20 \le \sigma_{w_{ij}} < 60 \\ 1 & \text{if} \quad \sigma_{w_{ij}} \ge 60 \end{cases} \quad (2)$$

With respect to **Figure 2**, the intensities of pixels in the input grayscale images with local variance between 0 and 60 are enhanced.

Figure 3 shows the result of image enhancement using the zheng's method.

4.1.2. Edge Density

Abolghasemi *et al.* [7] used the density of vertical edges (instead of the variance of intensity) as criterion for local enhancement of car image. License plate of the car consist of several characters (8 characters for Iranian VLP), so the license plate area contains rich edge information. We can employ the edge information to find the location of plate in an image. At first, they [7] used the vertical sobel mask and obtained the gradient image:

Table 1. Different styles of Iranian VLP.

Vehicle Type	Plate Color	Character Color	Outline of VLP
Private (automobile)	white	black	
Public (taxi, truck and bus)	yellow	black	
Governmental	red	white	

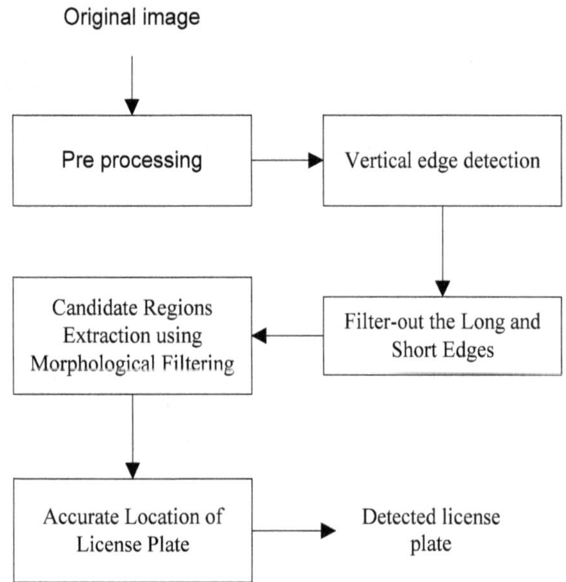

Figure 1. Flowchart of our proposed system for VLP detection.

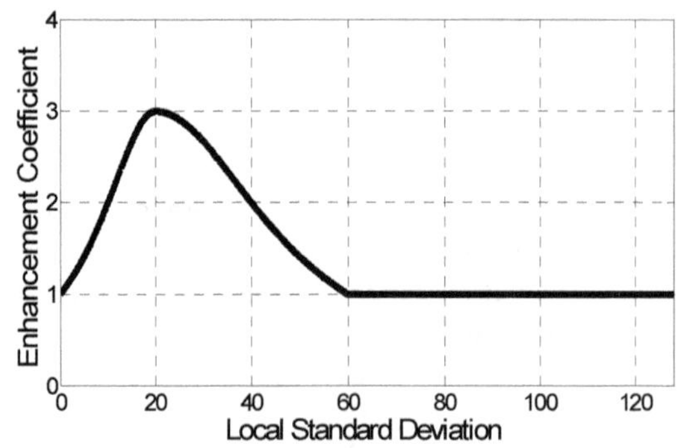

Figure 2. The graph of enhancement coefficient, $f(\sigma_{w_{ij}})$, based on the local standard deviation, $\sigma_{w_{ij}}$.

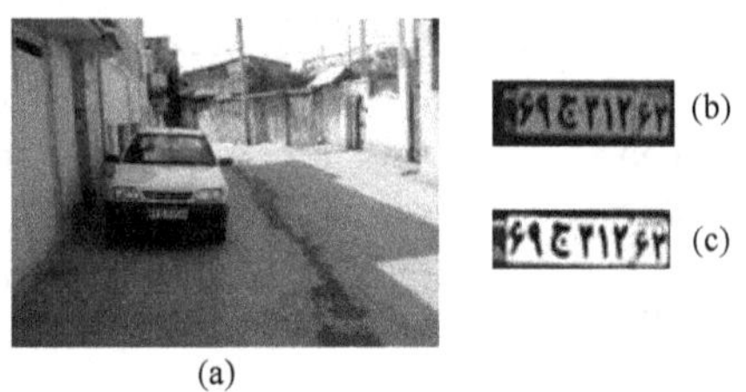

Figure 3. (a) input grayscale image. Iranian license plate before (b) and after (c) enhancement using intensity variance method.

$$h = \begin{bmatrix} -1 & 0 & 1 \\ -2 & 0 & 2 \\ -1 & 0 & 1 \end{bmatrix} \tag{3}$$

Then, they compared pixel values with a predefined threshold and the vertical edge image has been achieved.

In the next step, the vertical edge image is convolved with the 2-D Gaussian kernel and estimation of the edge density is yielded. The results on a sample image are shown in **Figure 4**.

In order to enhance the input image with respect to the estimations of edge density, an enhancement coefficient is suggested as follows:

$$I'_{ij} = f\left(\rho_{w_{ij}}\right)\left(I_{ij} - \overline{I}_{w_{ij}}\right) + \overline{I}_{w_{ij}} \tag{4}$$

where I_{ij}, I'_{ij} and $\overline{I}_{w_{ij}}$ are explained in the previous step. $f\left(\rho_{w_{ij}}\right)$ is the weighting function, regarding the estimation of edge density. This function is sketched in **Figure 5**.

As can be seen in **Figure 5**, the intensity of pixels with the edge density among 0.15 to 0.45 is to be enhanced. The enhancement coefficient $f\left(\rho_{w_{ij}}\right)$ is defined as follows:

$$f\left(\rho_{w_{ij}}\right) = \begin{cases} \dfrac{3}{\dfrac{2}{0.15^2}\left(\rho_{w_{ij}} - 0.15\right)^2 + 1}, & \text{if } 0 \le \rho_{w_{ij}} < 0.15 \\ \dfrac{3}{\dfrac{2}{(0.5-0.15)^2}\left(\rho_{w_{ij}} - 0.15\right)^2 + 1}, & \text{if } 0.15 \le \sigma_{w_{ij}} < 0.5 \\ 1, \quad \text{if } \rho_{w_{ij}} \ge 0.5 \end{cases} \tag{5}$$

Figure 6 shows the result of enhancement by this method.

Even though for normal images, as it can be seen in **Figure 7(a)**, both intensity variance [6] and edge density [7] can improve the VLP, when the distance and angle

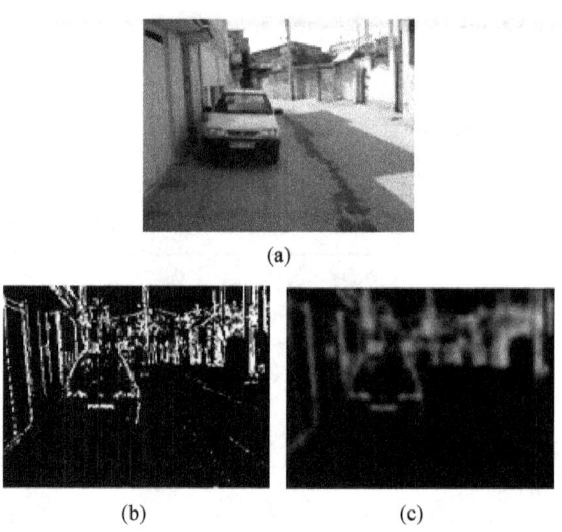

Figure 4. (a) Input grayscale image, (b) vertical edge image and (c) the edge-density estimation image.

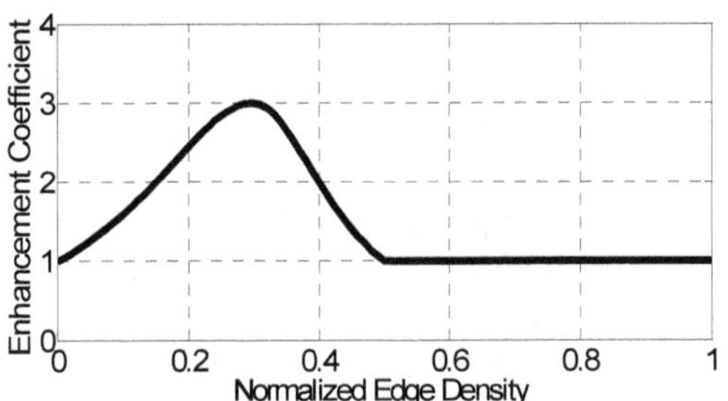

Figure 5. The graph of enhancement coefficient, $f\left(\rho_{w_{ij}}\right)$, based on normalized edge density, $\rho_{w_{ij}}$.

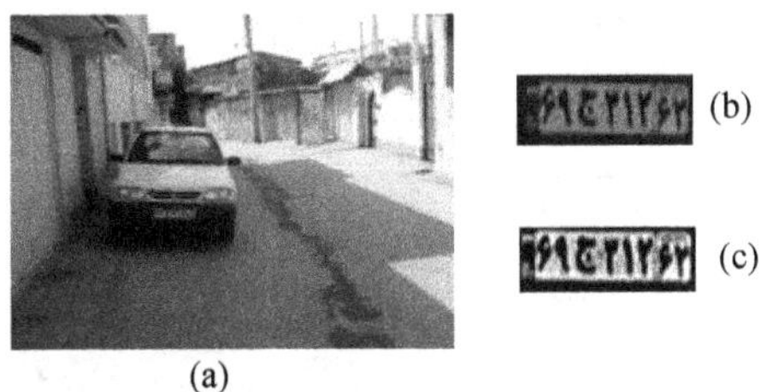

(a)

Figure 6. (a) input grayscale image. Iranian license plate before (b) and after (c) enhancement using edge density method.

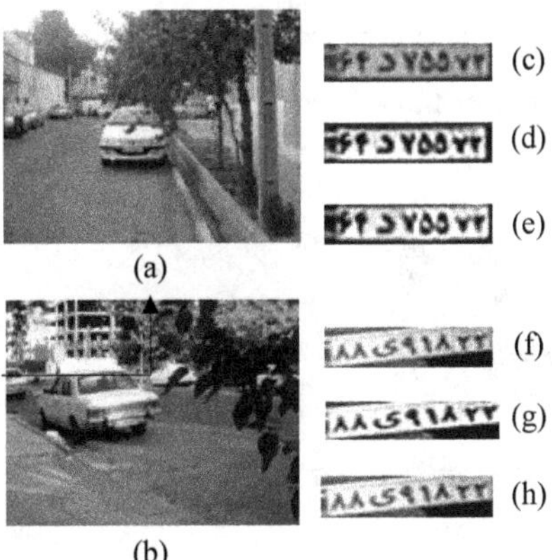

Figure 7. (a),(b) input grayscale image. Iranian license plate (c),(f) without enhancement (d),(g) improved using edge density method (e), (h) improved using intensity variance method.

between camera and vehicle are increased, zheng's method fails while abolghasemi's method already improves the quality of VLP considerably, **Figure 7(b)**. so, in this work we employ edge density method for pre processing.

4.2. Detecting the VLP

After enhancing an input image by using suitable method (edge density), we should detect any existed license plate in the improved image. We do the following stages for this purpose.

4.2.1. Vertical Edge Detection

Edge detection is one of the most important processes in image analysis. An edge represents the boundary of an object which can be used to identify the shapes and area of the particular object. When there is contrast difference between the object and the background, after applying edge detection, the object edges will be illustrated. We select the vertical sobel operator, Equation (3), to detect the vertical edges.

After convolving the enhanced car image with the vertical sobel operator, an estimation of vertical gradient image is yielded. Finally, we get a binary image, as shown in **Figure 8(a)**, by using a threshold value.

4.2.2. Filter-Out the Long and Short Edges

After extracting vertical edges from the enhanced image, using morphological filtering obtains candidate regions those may be a license plate. But, as it can be seen in **Figure 8(a)**, there are many long background and short noise edges that may interference in the morphological filtering process. In order to resolve this problem, an effective algorithm is used to remove the background and noise edges [6]. The filter-out image after removing unwanted edges is shown in the **Figure 8(b)**.

4.2.3. Candidate Regions Extraction Using Morphological Filtering

Morphological filtering is used as a tool for extracting image components and so representing and describing region shapes such as boundaries. In this part, we use a morphological operation for extracting candidate regions. Hence, we implement the morphological closing and opening that defined as follows:

Closing operation $I \bullet S_{m\times n} = (I \oplus S_{m\times n})\Theta S_{m\times n}$

Opening operation $I \circ S_{m\times n} = (I\Theta S_{m\times n}) \oplus S_{m\times n}$

where $\oplus$, and Θ denote dilation and erosion operations, respectively. $S_{m\times n}$ denote a structuring element with size $m\times n$, all entries in $S_{m\times n}$ are one. The output of this stage is shown in **Figure 9(a)**.

4.2.4. Accurate Location of License Plate

After using morphological filtering, still many regions

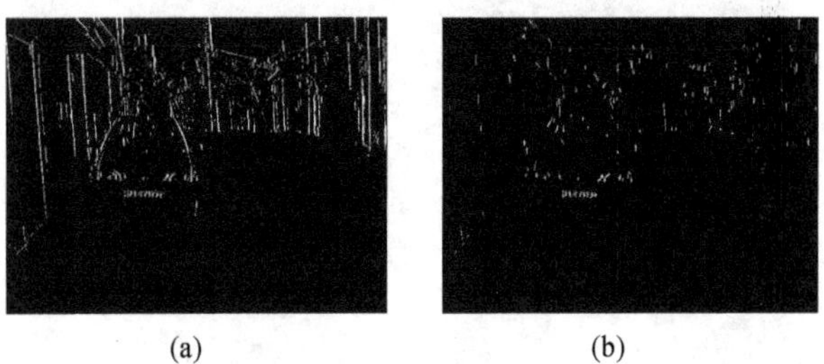

(a) (b)

Figure 8. (a) vertical edge image, (b) removing background and noise edges (filter-out the long and short edges).

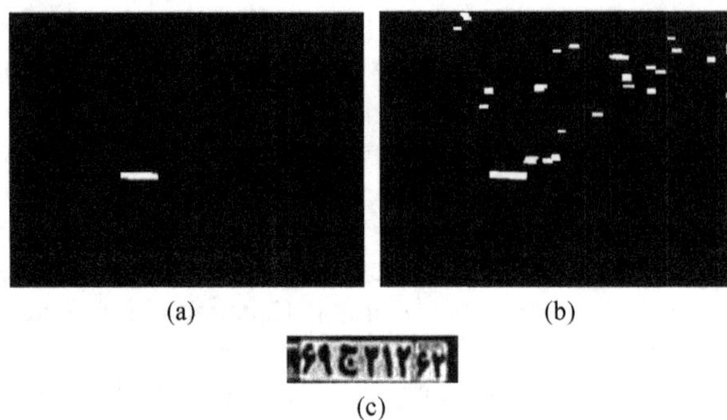

Figure 9. (a) Connected regions obtained from morphological process, (b) after applying features (c) cropped image.

are candidating as a license plate. So we consider some features such as area, aspect ratio (height per width) and edge density in order to discard wrong candidate regions. Values for these features are set experimentally based on our test images. These features are scale-, luminance- and rotation-variant. Progressive of using these features to remove non-plate candidate regions can be seen in **Figure 9(b)**.

5. Experimental Results

We have run our proposed algorithm on laptop Core 2 Due CPU 2.26 MHz with 2 GB of RAM under MATLAB R2008b environment. In Section 3, we described how the vehicle images are provided. Some sample images of our database are shown in **Figure 10**.

Now, in order to evaluate the accuracy of our proposed method, we categorize the provided database into three categories including: Angle (high angle (>30 degree & <60 degree) and low angle (<30 degree)), Distance (short distance (<4 m) and normal distance (>4 m & <12 m) and low quality or contrast (evening, sunlight, and rainy or cloudy weather).

Figure 10. Some sample images of our database.

Table 2 shows the accuracy of the proposed algorithm under mentioned conditions.

As it is written in **Table 2**, the average accuracy achieved by our proposed method for license plate detection is 95.2%. It means that we could detect 333 Iranian license plate correctly. Although our achieved accuracy is less than what zheng [6] got but we believe our provided image bank is more complex. Because of showing in **Figure 7**, the zheng's method is sensitive to real situations such as existing long distance and high angle. **Table 3** shows the result of license plate detection for several vehicle images in our categories.

Table 2. Accuracy achieved by our proposed method.

Images in Different Situations		Number of Images	Accuracy (%)
Distance	short	100	97
	normal	100	95
Angle	low	50	98
	high	50	94
Low Quality		50	92
Average (350 Images)			95.2

Table 3. Detected license plate by our proposed algorithm.

Input Gray Scale Image	Detected License Plate	Different Situations
		short distance
		normal distance
		low angle
		high angle
		low quality (sunlight)

6. Conclusions

In this paper, an efficient license plate detection method is proposed which performed on images with complex scenes. We used edge density as pre processing for image enhancement. Then by using vertical sobel mask, removing background and noise edges, and employing morphological filter, some regions are candidate as license plate. Finally considering geometrical features (such as area of the regions, aspect ratio and edge density), the license plate from the input car image is extracted. Although the proposed algorithm performs on the Iranian vehicle license plates under various situations such as different lightening conditions, varied distances and existence angle between the camera and the vehicle and varied weather conditions, we believe its performance is yet appropriate if we try to detect the foreign license plate.

7. References

[1] V. Shapiro, G. Gluhchev and D. Dimov, "Toward a Multinational Car License Plate Recognition System," *Machine Vision Application*, Vol. 17, No. 3, July 2006, pp. 173-183.

[2] V. Kamat and S. Ganesan, "An Efficient Implementation of the Hough Transform for Detecting Vehicle License Plates Using DSP's," *Proceedings of Real Time Technology and Applications*, Chicago, 15-17 May 1995, pp. 58-59.

[3] Y. Yanamura, M. Goto and D. Nishiyama, "Extraction and Tracking of the License Plate Using Hough Transform and Voted Block Matching," *IEEE proceedings of Intelligent Vehicles Symposium*, Columbus, 9-11 June 2003, pp. 243-246.

[4] C. N. E. Anagnostopoulos and I. E. Anagnostopoulos, "A License Plate Recognition Algorithm for Intelligent Transportation System Applications," *IEEE Transaction on Intelligent Transportation System*, Vol. 7, No. 3, 2006, pp. 377-392.

[5] W. G. Zhu, G. J. Huo and X. Jia, "A Study of Locating Vehicle License Plate Based on Color Feature and Mathematical Morphology," *6th International Conference on Signal Processing*, Vol. 1, 2002, pp. 748-751.

[6] D. Zheng, Y. Zhao and J. Wang, "An Efficient Method of License Plate Location," *Pattern Recognition Letters*, Vol. 25, No. 6, 2005, pp. 2431-2438.

[7] V. Abolghasemi and A. R. Ahmadyfard, "An Edge-Based Color-Aided Method for License Plate Detection," *Elsevier Journal of Image and Vision Computing*, Vol. 27 No. 8, 2009, pp. 1134-1142.

[8] J. W. Hsieh, S. H. Yu and Y. S. Chen, "Morphology-Based License Plate Detection from Complex Scenes," 16 *th International Conference on Pattern Recognition*, Vol. 3, 2002, pp. 176-179.

[9] H. Zhang, W. Jia, X. He and Q. Wu, "Learning-Based License Plate Detection Using Global and Local Features," *ICPR*, Vol. 2, 2006, pp. 1102-1105.

17

Analysis of 8T SRAM Cell at Various Process Corners at 65 nm Process Technology

Shilpi Birla[1*], Neeraj Kumar Shukla[2], Kapil Rathi[3], Rakesh Kumar Singh[4], Manisha Pattanaik[5]
[1]*Department of Electronics & Communications, Sir Padampat Singhania University, Udaipur, India*
[2]*Department of ECE, ITM University, Gurgaon, India*
[3]*Texas Instruments, Bangalore, India*
[4]*Department of Electronics & Communications, Bipin Chandra Tripathi kumaon Engineering College, Almora, India*
[5]*VLSI Group, Atal Bihari Vajpayee Indian Institute of Information Technology and Management, Gwalior, India*

Abstract

In Present scenario battery-powered hand-held multimedia systems become popular. The power consumption in these devices is a major concern these days for its long operational life. Although various techniques to reduce the power dissipation has been developed. The most adopted method is to lower the supply voltage. But lowering the V_{dd} reduces the gate current much more rapidly than the sub-threshold current and degrades the SNM. This degraded SNM further limits the voltage scaling. To improve the stability of the SRAM cell topology of the conventional 6T Static Random Access Memory (SRAM) cell has been changed and revised to 8T and 10T cell, the topologies. This work has analyzed the SRAM's Static Noise Margin (SNM) at 8T for various process corners at 65 nm technology. It evaluates the SNM along with the write margins of the cell along with the cell size of 8T SRAM bit-cell operating in sub-threshold voltage at various process corners. It is observed that an 8T cell has 13% better write margin than conventional 6T SRAM cell. This paper analyses the dependence of SNM of SRAM memory cell on supply voltage, temperature, transistor sizing in 65 nm technology at various process corners (TT, SS, FF, FS, and SF).

Keywords: SNM, Sub-Threshold Current, Gate Current, Process Corners

1. Introduction

Due to increase in demand of wireless sensor nodes and mobile multimedia applications, the demand of small size SRAM memory on chips increases. However, as the voltage is scaled down to combat the rise in power and other issues, e.g., the lower noise margins (responsible for cell stability) arise in conventional 6T SRAM cells. Solutions involving additional transistors, *i.e.*, 7T, and 8T have been explored to lower power consumption while reducing these adverse effects in the cell performance. We will therefore look into one of these SRAM Cells topologies, the 8T SRAM cell which operates at sub-threshold voltages, successfully. The ultra-low leakage regime for static random-access memories (SRAM) designs imposes unique constraints on the cell design in many ways different from those imposed by performance-driven scaling concerns. The bit-cell size is of paramount importance regardless of the device threshold voltage but beyond that the similarity ends. The high threshold voltage associated with the ultra-low leakage design point provides substantial relief to the static noise margin (SNM) for a given design, but the intrinsic threshold variation limits the performance available from the cell [1]. The intrinsic threshold variation affects the leakage as well, but in a less significant manner. In this paper we have analyzed the Static Noise Margin (SNM) of 8T SRAM cell at various process corners of the design environment at 65 nm.

This paper is organized as follows; SNM is described in section II. Section III deals with the working of 8T SRAM cell. Section IV shows the analysis of SNM, Write margin, Read Margin with respect to various process corners. Finally, conclusion is drawn in section V.

2. Static Noise Margin

The best measure of the ability of these inverters to

maintain their states is the bit-cell's SNM. The SNM is the maximum amount of noise voltage that can be introduced at the output of the two inverters, such that the cell retains its data. SNM quantifies the amount of noise voltage required at the internal nodes of a bit-cell to flip the cell's contents [2]. The static noise margin is a measure of the cell's ability to retain its data state. The worst-case situation is usually under "read-disturb" condition [3]. When the word-line device is turned on and connects the pre-charged bit-line to the low side of the cell. The state of the cell may flip if the internal node voltage rises to a high enough level. The problem is exacerbated if the ratio of the conductance of the pull-down and the word-line devices (often called beta) is too small.

3. Analysis of 8T SRAM Cell

This topology was originally proposed for a sub-threshold SRAM design. It is optimized for functionality and performance over a large voltage range in this design. Two NMOS devices (N3 and N2), **Figure 1**, constitute the read-buffer. A write operation is performed through WWL, WBL and WBLX ports, whereas single-ended read operation is exercised through RWL and RBL ports. RBL is pre-charged at the end of each read cycle and kept pre-charged during a write cycle [4]. In this bit-cell, read and write ports are decoupled in contrast to the traditional 6T cell so that the,

1) read-SNM (RSNM) problem is eliminated;

2) 6T SRAM part can be sized for better write-ability without trading-off RSNM and;

3) 2T read-buffer can be sized for larger read-current independently.

This makes the voltage drop across unaccessed read-buffers zero and hence leakage on read-bit-lines is highly reduced. V_{dd} is the virtual supply nodes for the cross-coupled inverters and its voltage can be brought down during a write access to weaken PMOS load devices (P1 and P2), **Figure 1**, and ease write-ability problem at low voltages. Since all the bit-cells on a row are written and read at the same time, V_{dd} is shared across one row of memory cells [5].

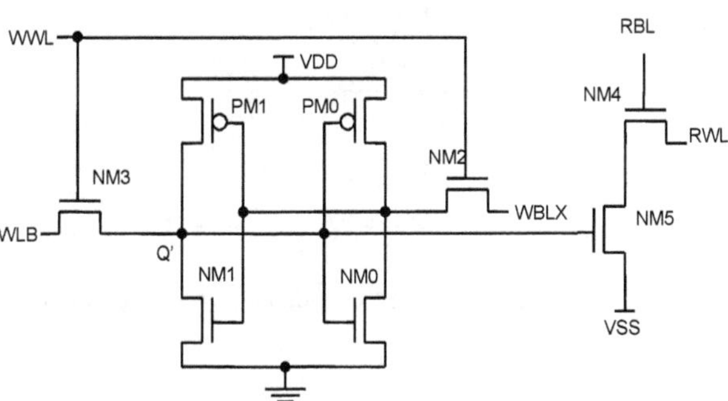

Figure 1. 8T SRAM Cell.

4. Analysis at Different Process Corners

Process Corners (PCs) represent the extremes of these parameter variations within which a circuit that has been etched onto the wafer must function correctly. A circuit running on devices fabricated at these process corners may run slower or faster than specified and at lower or higher temperatures and voltages, but if the circuit does not function at all at any of these process extremes the design is considered to have inadequate design margin.

There are therefore five possible process corners: typical-typical (TT), fast-fast (FF), slow-slow (SS), fast-slow (FS), and slow-fast (SF). The first three corners (TT, FF, SS) are called even corners, because both types of devices are affected evenly, and generally do not adversely affect the logical correctness of the circuit. The resulting devices can function at slower or faster clock frequencies, and are often binned as such. The last two corners (FS, SF) are called "skewed" corners, and are cause for concern. This is because one type of FET will switch much faster than the other, and this form of imbalanced switching can cause one edge of the output to have much less slew than the other edge.

4.1. Analysis of Static Noise Margin at Various Process Corners

A simulation and analysis has been performed on the static noise margin at 65 nm at various process corners. The results shows that at SF corner the SNM is the maximum and at FS corner the SNM is minimum, **Table 1**. TT corner shows moderate value. As we measure the SNM at varying temperature at 40˚C and 100˚C, we found that as the temperature increases and the SNM decreases. As the V_{dd} increases the SNM has also increased but this increase in V_{dd} leads to increase in leakage current.

4.2. Analysis of Write Margin at Various Process Corners

Write SNM (WSNM) is measured using butterfly (or VTC) curves. For a successful write, only one cross point should be found on the butterfly curves, indicating that the cell is monostable. WSNM for writing "1" is the width of the smallest square that can be embedded between the lower-right half of the curves. WSNM for writing "0" can be obtained from a similar simulation. The final WSNM for the cell is the minimum of the margin for writing "0" and writing "1". A cell with lower

Table 1. SNM at various V_{dd} and PCs for 8T SRAM Bit-Cell at 65 nm.

V_{dd} (V)	SNM (V) (TT Corner)		SNM (V) (SS Corner)		SNM (V) (FF Corner)		SNM (V) (FS Corner)	
	100°C	40°C	100°C	40°C	100°C	40°C	100°C	40°C
1.2	0.207	0.192	0.232	0.242	0.142	0.157	0.117	0.137
1.1	0.187	0.202	0.217	0.227	0.137	0.152	0.112	0.132
1	0.177	0.187	0.202	0.207	0.132	0.147	0.107	0.122
0.9	0.162	0.172	0.182	0.187	0.127	0.137	0.096	0.107
0.8	0.147	0.152	0.162	0.167	0.117	0.127	0.081	0.086
0.7	0.127	0.132	0.137	0.142	0.107	0.117	0.061	0.066
0.6	0.107	0.112	0.117	0.117	0.091	0.096	0.041	0.046
0.5	0.086	0.067	0.091	0.096	0.076	0.081	0.021	0.026
0.4	0.066	0.066	0.071	0.071	0.057	0.061	0.004	0.009
0.3	0.041	0.041	0.046	0.046	0.041	0.011	failed	failed

WSNM has poorer write-ability. The BL voltage can also be used as a measure of write margin [6]. The 6T cell is configured for a write "1" case. The voltage of BLB the bit-line connected to the node holding "1" initially is swept downward during simulation. The write margin is defined as the BLB value at the point when Q and QB flip, which we will call VBL. The lower that value is, the harder it is to write the cell, implying a smaller write margin. From **Figures 2** and **3**, it can seen that as the V_{dd} increases the write margin increases, this trend of increasing write margin can be seen in each process corner. As the temperature increases the write margin increases too, as we can see that at 40°C (**Figure 2**), the write margin at TT is 0.148 V and at 100°C it is 0.167 V, (**Figure 3**), an increase in 0.19 V.

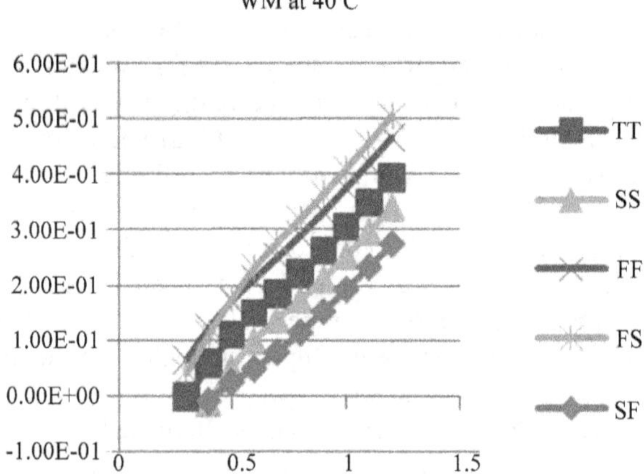

Figure 2. Write margin at 40°C measured at various process corners.

4.3. Analysis of Read Current at Various Process Corners

In some sense, stability can be viewed from write ability and read access time. The more stable the cell, the more difficult it will be to write the cell into a different state. A cell design with a narrower word-line device is more stable, but as the current through such a device is smaller, it will require more time to develop a signal of a given magnitude on the bit-line. The rate at which the cell can pull down the bit-line is limited by the series combination of the pull down device and the word-line device, and is increased by increasing the conductance of either or both devices [7]. The relative importance of the two devices to the read current is a consequence of the details of the device design and the operating conditions, and may not be precisely equal. For minimum read delay the widths of both devices should therefore be as wide as possible. While SNM evaluate cell functionality, the cell read current, "I_{read}" is a major component in designing array access time.

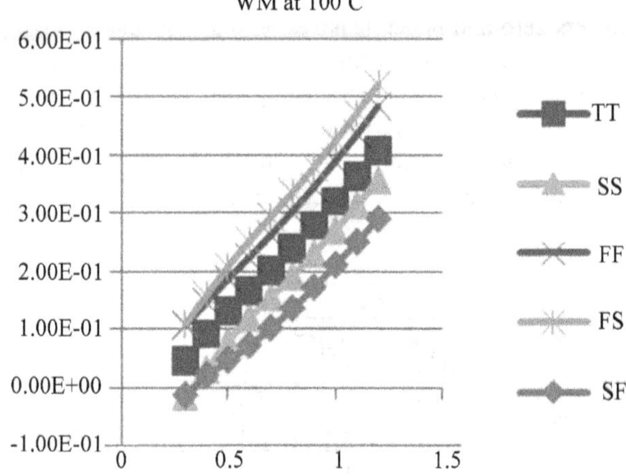

Figure 3. Write margin at 100°C measured at various process corners.

The correct write operation requires that stored data be overwritten by the access devices; however, the relative device strengths necessary to ensure this cannot practically be guaranteed. Further, the increased sensitivity to variation also results in extremely low worst case read-current. The resulting effect on performance is drastic, but, even more importantly; the effect on functionality can be fatal, where the read-current can be exceeded by the aggregate bit-line leakage-current. As shown in **Figures 4** and **5**, we can analyze, as the temperature increases the read current decreases and it is the highest for FF corner. So, increase in temperature degrades the read current which degrades the stability.

5. Conclusions

Voltage scaling enables energy minimization and leakage power reduction in micro-power systems. However, the design techniques and circuit peripherals are necessary to overcome the process variations in the ultra-low voltage regime. This work analyzed the SRAM Bit-cell's stability of the 8T cell at the 65 nm technology. The cell size of the 8T cell is 0.525 μm^2 and it is seen that as the voltage decreases, the SNM decreases. The temperature also affects the stability when it is at the higher side. On the other side, if the supply voltage V_{dd} increased, it increases the leakage and may lead in exceed in the read current. To minimize the V_{dd}, other low-voltage techniques may be used, so that the leakage can be minimized with maximized stability. It is also observed that the stability is the best with FF process corner and it has intermediate stability at the TT process corner.

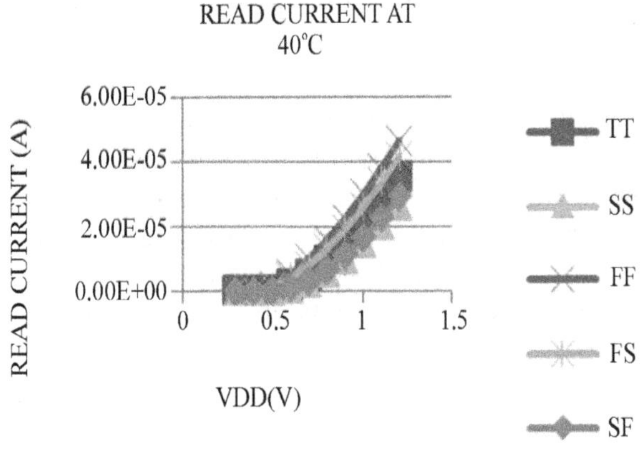

Figure 4. Read current at 40°C measured at various process corners.

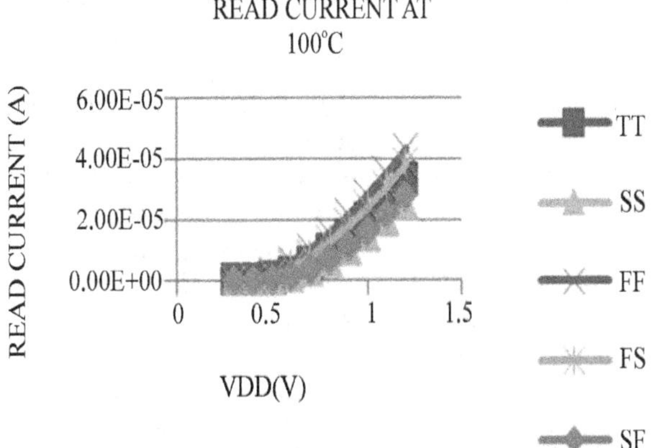

Figure 5. Read current at 100°C measured at various process corners.

6. Acknowledgements

All the authors are grateful to their respective organizations.

7. References

[1] S. Birla, N. Kr. Shukla, M. Pattanaik and R. K. Singh, "Device and Circuit Design Challenges for Low Leakage SRAM for Ultra Low Power Applications," *Canadian Journal on Electrical & Electronics Engineering*, Vol. 1, No. 7, 2010, pp. 156-167.

[2] B. H. Calhoun and A. P. Chandrakasan "Static Noise Margin Variation for Sub-Threshold SRAM in 65 nm CMOS," *IEEE Journal of Solid-State Circuits*, Vol. 41, No. 7, 2006, pp. 1673-1679.

[3] Y. Chung and S.-H. Song, "Implementation of Low-Voltage Static RAM with Enhanced Data Stability and Circuit Speed," *Microelectronics Journal*, Vol. 40, No. 6, 2009, pp. 944-951.

[4] N. Hiroki, S. Okumura, Y. Iguchi, *et al.*, "Which Is the Best Dual Port SRAM in 45 nm Process Technology? 8T, 10T Single End and 10T Differential," *IEEE International Conference on Integrated Circuit Design and Technology and Tutorial*, Austin, 2-4 June 2008, pp. 55-58.

[5] B. H. Calhoun and A. P. Chandrakasan "A 256-kb 65-nm Sub-Threshold SRAM Design for Ultra-Low-Voltage Operation," *IEEE Journal of Solid-State Circuits*, Vol. 42, No. 3, 2007, pp. 680-688.

[6] Koichi Takeda, *et al.*, "A Read Static Noise Margin Free SRAM Cell for Low V_{dd} and High Speed Applications," *IEEE Journal of Solid-State Circuits*, Vol. 41, No. 1, 2006, pp. 113-121.

[7] R. Keerthi and H. Chen, "Stability and Static Noise Margin Analysis of Low Power SRAM," *IEEE International Instrumentation & Measurement Technology Conference*, Victoria, May 2008, pp. 1541-1544.

18

Artificial Intelligence in the Estimation of Patch Dimensions of Rectangular Microstrip Antennas

Vandana Vikas Thakare[1], **Pramod Singhal**[2]
[1]*Department of Electronics and Instrumentation Engineering, Anand Engineering College, Keetham, Agra, India*
[2]*Department of Electronics Engineering, Madhav Institute of Technology & Science, Gwalior, India*

Abstract

Artificial Neural Network (ANNs) techniques are recently indicating a lot of promises in the application of various micro-engineering fields. Such a use of ANNs for estimating the patch dimensions of a microstrip line feed rectangular microstrip patch antennas has been presented in this paper. An ANN model has been developed and tested for rectangular patch antenna design. The performance of the neural network has been compared with the simulated values obtained from IE3D EM Simulator. It transforms the data containing the dielectric constant (ε_r), thickness of the substrate (h), and antenna's dominant-mode resonant frequency (f_r) to the patch dimensions *i.e.* length (L) and width (W) of the patch. The different variants of back propagation training algorithm of MLFFBP-ANN (Multilayer feed forward back propagation Artificial Neural Network) and RBF-ANN (Radial basis function Artificial Neural Network) has been used to implement the network model. The results obtained from artificial neural network when compared with simulation results, found satisfactory and also it is concluded that RBF network is more accurate and fast as compared to different variants of back propagation training algorithms of MLPFFBP. The ANNs results are more in agreement with the simulation findings. Neural network based estimation has the usual advantage of very fast and simultaneous response of all the outputs.

Keywords: Microstrip Antenna, Bandwidth, Simulation, Modelling, Neural Networks, CAD

1. Introduction

Microstrip antennas are used in a wide range of mobile communication applications which demands multi band and/or wideband frequency operations, high power gain omni directional radiations patterns etc. Therefore design of printed antennas to meet the requirements of multiple operational services becomes a difficult task. This warrants in the very high accuracy of the calculation of various design parameters of microstrip patch antennas. Patch dimensions of a rectangular microstrip antenna is a vital parameter in deciding the performance and the utility of an antenna. In the present work, microstrip line feeding is taken as a preferred method of feeding the input power to the antenna. The calculation of exact patch dimensions of rectangular microstrip patch antenna becomes extremely important where the antenna size is drastically small. A number of papers have been appeared on the calculation of patch dimension of microstrip antennas [1-3]. However, these papers suffer considerable deviation in the calculated value of patch dimensions compared to theoretical and simulation findings. In this paper, an attempt has been made to exploit the capability of artificial neural networks to calculate the length (L) and width (W) of microstrip patch antenna over a ground plane with a substrate thickness h and dielectric constants ε_r. The results are in good agreement with the simulation findings.

Neural networks have recently gained attention as a fast and flexible vehicle to EM /Microwave modeling, simulations and optimization. Recently CAD approach based on neural networks has been introduced in the microwave community for modeling of passive and active microwave component. Number of research papers [4-14] indicates how ANN can be used efficiently to calculate different design and performance parameters of microstrip antennas. However the literature shows that only three layer MLPFFBP has been preferred to prove the utility of ANN in the area of microstrip antenna design. In this work, the authors extend the work on the use of the artificial neural network (ANN) technique taking into account different variants of back propagation training algorithm with MLPFFBP and RBF ANN model is stressed upon in place of conventional numerical techniques for the microstrip antenna design.

2. Design and Data Generation

The rectangular microstrip antennas are made up of a rectangular patch with dimensions width (W) and length (L) over a ground plane with a substrate thickness h having dielectric constant ε_r. There are numerous substrates that can be used for the design of microstrip antennas, and their dielectric constants are usually in the range of $2.2 < \varepsilon_r < 12$. Thin substrates with higher dielectric constants are desirable for microwave circuitry because they require tightly bound fields to minimize undesired radiation and coupling, and lead to smaller element.

The software used to model and simulate the proposed microstrip patch antenna is Zeland Inc's IE3D software. IE3D is a full-wave electromagnetic simulator based on the method of moments. It analyses 3D and multilayer structures of general shapes. It has been widely used in the design of MICs, RFICs, patch antennas, wire antennas, and other RF/wireless antennas. It can be used to calculate and plot the S11 parameters, VSWR, current distributions as well as the radiation patterns.

As an example microstrip line feed rectangular patch microstrip antenna is designed to resonate at 8 Ghz frequency with dielectric constant (ε_r) = 2, substrate thickness h = 1 mm, L = 12.6 mm, W = 15.3 mm. The length and the width of the patch are calculated by the given relationships. (1), (2), (3) and (4) mentioned in [15,16].

$$W = \frac{v_o}{2f_r}\sqrt{\frac{2}{\varepsilon_r + 1}} \quad (1)$$

$$L = \frac{v_o}{2f_r\sqrt{\varepsilon_{reff}}} - 2\Delta L \quad (2)$$

where v_o is the free space velocity of the light.

$$\frac{\Delta L}{h} = 0.412\frac{(\varepsilon_{reff}+0.3)\left(\frac{W}{h}+0.264\right)}{(\varepsilon_{reff}-0.258)\left(\frac{W}{h}+0.8\right)} \quad (3)$$

where ΔL is extension in length due to fringing effects and effective dielectric constant is given by

$$\varepsilon_{reff} = \frac{\varepsilon_r+1}{2} + \frac{\varepsilon_r-1}{2}\left[1+12\frac{h}{W}\right]^{-1/2} \quad (4)$$

The transmission line model is applicable to infinite ground planes only. However, for practical considerations, it is essential to have a finite ground plane. It is known that similar results for finite and infinite ground plane can be obtained if the size of the ground plane is greater than the patch dimensions by approximately six times the substrate thickness all around the periphery. Hence, for this design, the ground plane dimensions would be given as:

$$Lg = 6\,(h) + L = 6(1) + 12.6 = 17.6 \text{ mm} \quad (5)$$

$$Wg = 6\,(h) + W = 6(1) + 15.3 = 21.3 \text{ mm} \quad (6)$$

With the calculated values of various design parameters the patch antenna is designed for 8 GHz resonating frequency. The exact position of feed point can be determined by using IE3D Electromagnetic Simulator. The width W_o of microstrip line taken as 0.5 mm and the feed length is 2 mm. The patch is energized electromagnetically using 50 ohm microstrip feed line. The geometry of the example antenna is as shown in the **Figure 1**.

IE3D software has been used to calculate the return loss (S11) & hence the dominant resonating frequency of the antenna and the data is generated in the form of f_r (resonating frequency) for different specified range *i.e.* 1.5_ ε_r _ 3.5, 1 mm _h _5 mm, 11 mm _ L _ 16.5 mm and 13 mm _W _19 mm and has been used to train the various ANN model. The generated data were then arranged in five matrices. The feed coordinates and dimensions of microstrip line are kept constant and corresponding resonating frequencies are recorded and this data has been used as a training data and test data for MLFFBP and RBF ANN. The three matrices containing the values of ε_r, h and f_r are used as the input to the network. The other two matrices containing the corresponding values of L and W *i.e.* length and width of the patch are the outputs of the neural network.

Figure 2 shows the return loss (S11) vs. frequency curve for the given physical dimension for the example antenna indicating that antenna is resonating at 8 GHz.

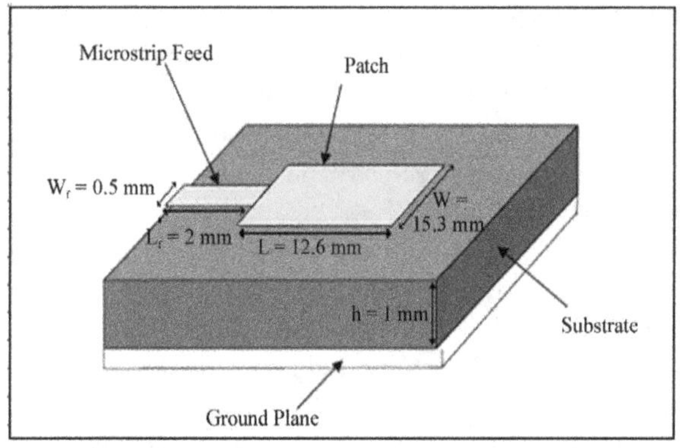

Figure 1. Microstrip line feed rectangular patch antenna.

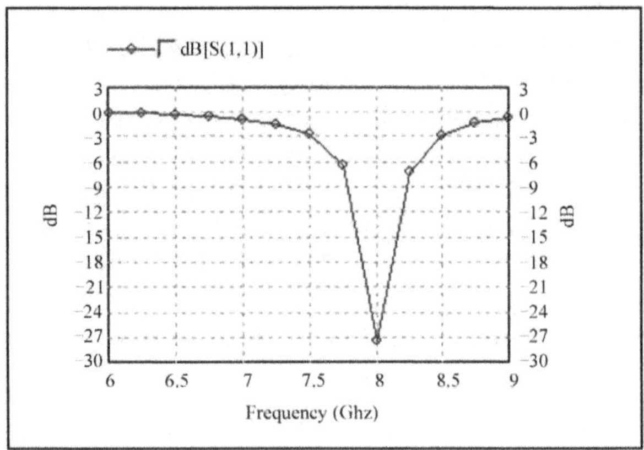

Figure 2. The return loss (S11) in dB vs. resonating frequency of microstrip antenna.

The length, width, substrate thickness h and dielectric constant (ε_r), were varied for the specified range to see the effect on the microstrip antenna bandwidth. It was observed that antenna performance could be controlled by varying these parameters to a large extent.

3. Network Architecture and Training

For the present work three layer network MLFFBP [17,18] with 6 different training algorithms and RBF network is preferred to model the microstrip line feed patch antenna.

3.1. Multi Layer Feed Forward Back Propagation (MLFFBP)

MLP networks are feed forward networks trained with the standard back propagation algorithm as shown in **Figure 3**. They are supervised networks and also they required a desired response to be trained. With one or two hidden layers they can approximate virtually any input output map. The weights of the network are usually computed by training the network using the back propagation algorithm.

In the present work three layers multilayer perceptron feed-forward back propagation artificial neural network with one hidden layer and trained by six different variants of back propagation training algorithms is used and compared to design microstrip patch antenna.

Back propagation [17] was created by generalizing the Window-Hoff learning rule to multiple-layer networks and nonlinear differentiable transfer functions. Standard back propagation is a gradient descent algorithm, in which the network weights are moved along the negative of the gradient of the performance function.

There are many variations of the back propagation algorithm. The simplest implementation of back propagation learning updates the network weights and biases in the direction in which the performance function decreases most rapidly—the negative of the gradient. Six different variants of back propagation algorithm have been used to train the MLPFFBP network model developed for the proposed design.

Scaled Conjugate Gradient (SCG) This belongs to the class of conjugate gradient methods which show super linear convergence on the most problems. This was designed to avoid the time consuming line approach. The algorithm is an implementation of avoiding the complicated line search procedure of conventional conjugate gradient algorithm

Bayesian Regularization algorithm (BR) This algorithm updates the weight and bias values according to the Levenberg-Marquardt optimization and minimizes a linear combination of squared errors and weight. It also modifies the linear combination so that at the end of training the resulting network has good generalization quality.

Levenberg-Marquardt optimization algorithm (LM) This is a least square estimation method based on the minimum neighborhood idea and does not suffer from the problem of slow convergence. The LM method combines the best feature of the Gauss Newton technique and the steepest decent method but avoid many of their limitations.

Quasi Newton algorithm (QN) This is based on Newton's method but doesn't require calculation of second derivatives; an approximate Hessian Matrix is updated. At each iteration of the algorithm the update is computed as a function of gradient Conjugate.

Gradient of Fletcher Reeves algorithm (CGF) In this algorithm a search is performed along the conjugate directions which produces generally faster convergence than steepest descends direction. The algorithm updates weight and biases values according to the formulas proposed by Fletcher and Reeves.

Adaptive Gradient Decent algorithm (AGD) It trains any network as long as its weight, net input, and transfer functions have derivative functions. Back propagation is used to calculate derivatives of performance with respect to the weight and bias variables. Each variable is adjusted according to gradient descent.

ANN structure *i.e.* number of layers, number of neurons in each layer, neurons activation function, learning algorithm and training parameters is not known in advance. Hence the network model is analysed with different number of hidden layers in the structure and also the numbers of processing elements are also varied to acquire the accuracy. Hence it is concluded that three layer MLP with one hidden layer and 20 processing elements in the hidden layer is the optimum network structure for the

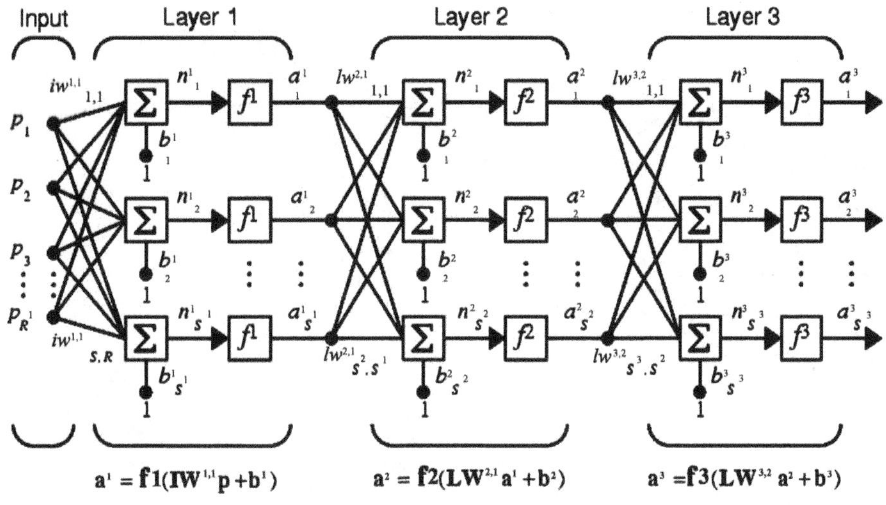

Figure 3. Three layer feed forward artificial neural network.

proposed problem. The network is trained with six different training algorithms to achieve the required degree of accuracy and hence compared for network performance.

In the network there are three input neurons in the input layer, 20 hidden neurons in the hidden layer and two output neurons in the output layer. The various inputs to the network are ε_r, h and fr and the outputs of the neural network are L and W *i.e.* length and width of the patch. The training time is 35 seconds and training performs in 361 epochs. In this work, different algorithms are used for training the proposed neural model and a comparative evaluation of relative performance is carried out for estimating patch dimensions L and W of microstrip antenna. In order to evaluate the performance of proposed MLFFBP-ANN based model for the design of microstrip antenna, simulation results are obtained using IE3D Simulator and generated 120 input-output training patterns and 30 inputs-output test patterns to validate the model. The network has been trained for different ε_r, h and f_r values of the proposed example but in a specified range. During the training process the neural network automatically adjusts its weights and threshold values such that the error between predicted and sampled outputs is minimized. The adjustments are computed by the back propagation algorithm. The training algorithm most suitable is trainlm .The error goal is 0.001 and learning rate is 0.1. The other network parameters used were noise factor of 0.004 and momentum factor of 0.075. The transfer function preferred is tansig in the architecture.

3.2. RBF Networks

Radial basis function network [17,18] is a feed forward neural network with a single hidden layer that use radial basis activation functions for hidden neurons. RBF networks are applied for various microwave modeling purposes. The RBF neural network has both a supervised and unsupervised component to its learning. It consists of three layers of neurons—input, hidden and output. The hidden layer neurons represent a series of centers in the input data space. Each of these centers has an activation function, typically Gaussian. The activation depends on the distance between the presented input vector and the centre. The further the vector is from the centre, the lower is the activation and vice versa. The generation of the centers and their widths is done using an unsupervised k-means clustering algorithm. The centers and widths created by this algorithm then form the weights and biases of the hidden layer, which remain unchanged once the clustering has been done. A typical RBF network structure is given in **Figure 4**.

The parameters c_{ij} and λ_{ij} are centers and standard deviations of radial basis activation functions. Commonly used radial basis activation functions are Gaussian and Multiquadratic. Given the inputs x, the total input to the ith hidden neuron γ_i is given by Equation (7).

$$\gamma_i = \sqrt{\sum_{j=1}^{n}\left(\frac{x_j - c_{ij}}{\lambda_{ij}}\right)^2}, i = 1,2,3,\cdots,N \qquad (7)$$

where N is the number of hidden neurons. The output value of the ith hidden neuron is $z_{ij} = \sigma(\gamma_i)$ where $\sigma(\gamma_i)$ is a radial basis function. Finally, the outputs of the RBF network are computed from hidden neurons as shown in Equation (8)

$$y_k = \sum_{i=0}^{N} w_{ki} z_{ki} \qquad (8)$$

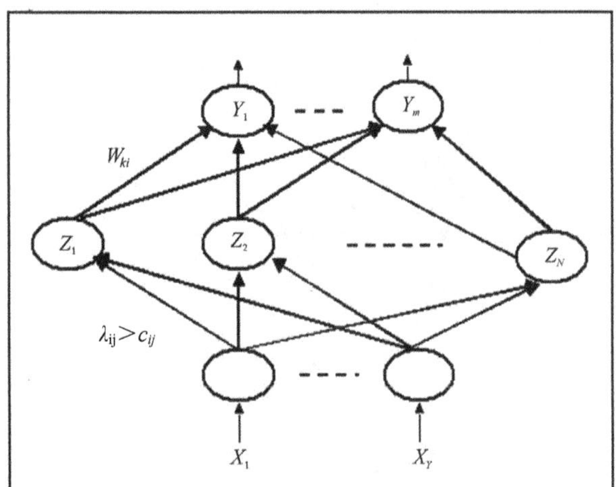

Figure 4. Radial basis function (RBF) artificial neural network.

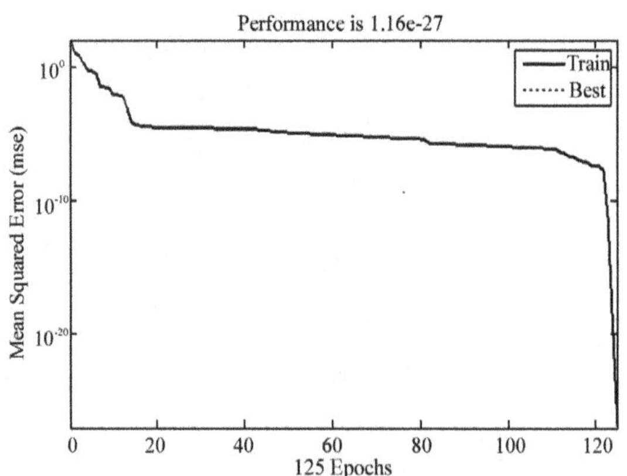

Figure 5. Number of epochs to achieve minimum mean square error level with Levenberg-Marquardt (LM) as a training algorithm in case of MLPFFBP.

where w_{ki} is the weight of the link between the *i*th neuron of the hidden layer and the *k*th neuron of the output layer. Training parameters w of the RBF network include w_{k0}, w_{ki}, c_{ij}, λ_{ij}, $k = 1,2, \cdots, m$, $I = 1,2, \cdots, N$, $j = 1,2, \cdots, n$.

In the RBF network, the spread value was chosen as 0.01, which gives the best accuracy. The network was trained with 120 samples and tested with 30 samples. In the structure there are 3 inputs and 2 outputs are chosen for the present synthesis ANN Model. RBF networks are more fast and effective as compared to MLPFFBP for this antenna design example. The RBF network automatically adjusts the number of processing elements in the hidden layer till the defined accuracy is reached. In the present work the RBF ANN model the network is choosing 26 processing elements in the hidden layer. The training time is 25 seconds and training performs in 212 epochs and the training algorithm is unsupervised k-means clustering algorithm.

4. Results and Conclusions

4.1. Results

It has been established from **Table 1** that the Levenberg-Marquardt algorithm with structure (3-20-2) is the suitable model to achieve optimal values of speed of convergence and accuracy in case of MLPFFBP. It has been observed that total number of 125 epochs as shown in **Figure 5** is needed to reduce MSE level to a low value 1.6e - 027 for three layers MLPFFBP. With Levenberg-Marquardt (LM) training algorithm and tansig as a transfer function achievement of such a low value of performance goal (MSE) indicates that trained ANN model with trainlm as a training algorithm is an accurate model for designing the Microstrip patch antenna. The maximum absolute error at each value of L and W (patch dimensions) antenna is estimated for the random values of input parameters but in specified range *i.e.* the range for which network is trained. Various transfer functions are used for training the network and average minimum MSE on training and CV data is measured. It is observed that tansig as shown in **Figure 6** is most suitable transfer function for the present work. The MLP neural network is trained using learning rules namely Levenberg-Marquardt (LM), Scale Conjugate Gradient Back propagation (SC-GBP), Gradient of Fletcher Reeves algorithm (GFR), Quasi Newton algorithm (QN), Bayesian Regularization Algorithm (BR) and Adaptive Gradient Decent (AGD). Minimum MSE and maximum absolute error is measured on training and test data and is indicated in **Table 1** and **Figure 7**. It is concluded that Levenberg- Marquaradt is most suitable learning rule for our neural network with 3-20-2 structure. For generalization the randomized data is fed to the network and is trained for different hidden layers. It is observed that MLP with single hidden layer gives better performance as shown in **Figure 8**. The number of Processing Elements (PEs) in the hidden layer is also varied. The network is trained and minimum MSE is obtained when 20 PEs are used in hidden layer as shown in **Figure 9**.

As the work signifies RBF ANN is also used to model the microstrip line feed patch antenna. It is established from **Table 1** and **Figure 7** that RBF is giving results not only more accurate but fast also. The presented RBF network has performed training in only 74 epochs to the MSE value of 6.79e-28 as shown in **Figure 10**. So it is concluded that RBF architecture is better from MLPFFBP to the accuracy of 99.69% and quite faster comparatively.

4.2. Conclusions

In this paper, an attempt has been made to indicate to the

Table 1. Comparison of different variants of back propagation training algorithm for the design of microstrip line feed rectangular patch Antenna using artificial neural network.

Training algorithms	Number of epochs	Mean square error	Estimation of length (L) Maximum Absolute Error Training data	Test data	Estimation of (W) Maximum Absolute Error Training data	Test data
Levenberg-Marquardt (LM)	125	1.6e - 027	0.0141	0.1813	0.0227	0.1765
Scale Conjugate Gradient Back propagation (SCGBP)	450	9.20e - 25	0.0784	0.6221	0.1334	0.4190
Gradient of Fletcher Reeves algorithm (CGF)	640	2.65e - 13	0.1519	1.6140	0.1724	1.9992
Quasi Newton algorithm (QN)	800	8.03e - 19	0.1290	1.7645	0.1645	1.3004
Bayesian Regularization Algorithm (BR)	590	3.67e - 20	0.1721	1.8999	0.1205	1.4143
Adaptive Gradient Decent(AGD)	485	1.77e - 026	0.0667	0.3215	0.0814	0.5216
RBF	74	6.79e - 28	0.0008	0.0748	0.0016	0.1027

Table 2. Comparisons of results of IE3D EM simulator and RBF ANN for the calculation of patch dimensions of microstrip antenna.

S. No.	ε_r	h mm	f_r GHz	W (IE3D) mm	W (RBF ANN) mm	L (IE3D) mm	L (RBF ANN) mm
1	2	1	8.0	15.3	15.23	12.6	12.54
2	2.2	1.4	7.51	15.6	15.56	12.8	12.72
3	2.5	1.7	6.82	15.9	16.0	13.1	12.99
4	2.7	1.9	6.45	13.9	14.01	13.3	13.31
5	2.9	1	7.12	13.7	13.72	13.5	13.48
6	2.6	1.8	6.73	13.2	12.99	12.2	12.30
7	3	1.2	6.84	14.4	14.38	12.4	12.43
8	2.4	1.7	8.83	15.4	15.50	13.4	13.21
9	2.1	1.5	8.79	13	13.10	11.0	11.10
10	2.8	1.6	6.39	15.2	15.13	13.2	13.10
11	2.9	1.7	7.34	15.4	15.51	13.4	13.31

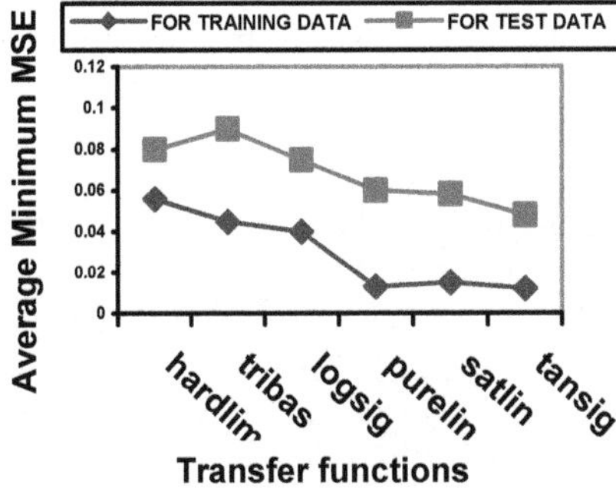

Figure 6. Graph showing variation of average minimum MSE on Training and Test data set for different transfer functions in the neural network.

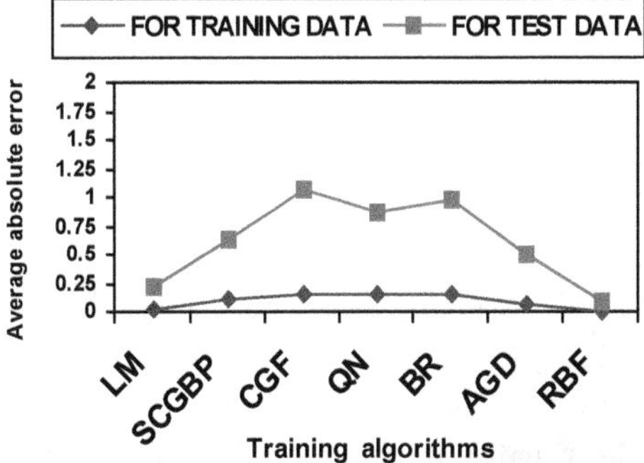

Figure 7. Graph showing variation of average absolute error on training and test data for different training algorithms

reader's one of the approach to model the patch antenna using MLFFBP and RBF-ANN. The results obtained with the present technique were closer to the simulation results generated by simulating the example antenna in IE3D Simulator. **Table 1** shows the comparison of results of different variant of back propagation algorithm of MLPFFBP ANN and RBF ANN. The paper concludes that results obtained using present ANN techniques are quite satisfactory and also that RBF ANN is giving the best approximation to the design as compared to MLPFFBP ANN. **Table 2** respectively depicts the comparison of results between RBF ANN and simulated values

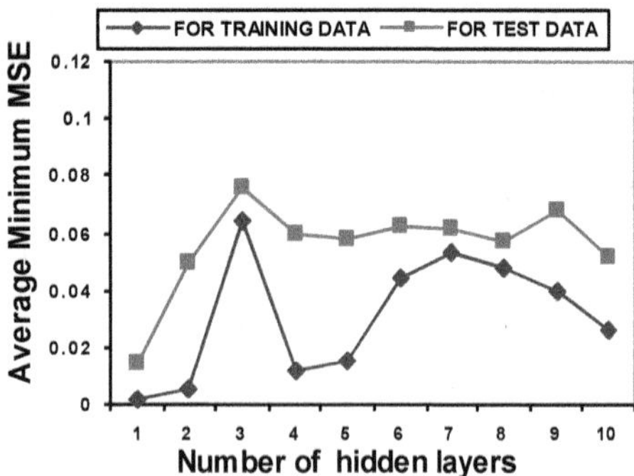

Figure 8. Graph showing variation of average minimum MSE on Training and Test data set for different no. of the hidden layers in the neural network.

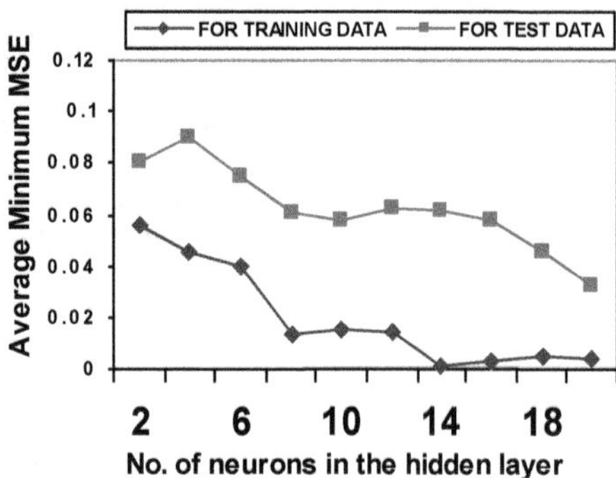

Figure 9. Graph showing variation of average minimum MSE on Training and Test data set for different no. of hidden layers in the network.

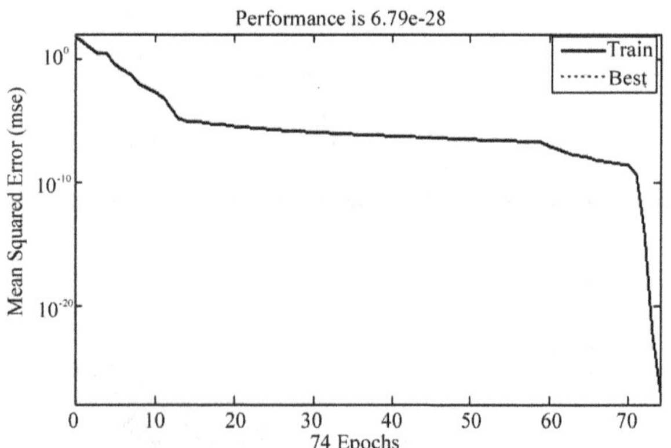

Figure 10. Number of epochs to achieve minimum mean square error level with RBF ANN.

for those 11 input combinations which are not included in the set of training data and found satisfactory.

A neural network-based CAD model is developed for the design of a rectangular patch antenna, which is robust both from the angle of time of computation and accuracy. A distinct advantage of neuro computing is that, after proper training, a neural network completely bypasses the repeated use of complex iterative processes for new cases presented to it. The developed network structure can predict the results for patch dimensions provided that the values of ε_r, f_r and h are in the domain of training values.

5. References

[1] R. K. Mishra and A. Patnaik, "Neural Network-Based CAD Model for the Design of Square-Patch Antennas," *IEEE Transactions on Antennas and Propagation*, Vol. 46, No. 12, 1998, pp. 1890-1891.

[2] J. L. Narayan, K. Sri R. Krishna and L. P. Reddy, "Design of Microstrip Antenna Using Artificial Neural Networks," *International Conference on Computational Intelligence and Multimedia Applications*, Vol. 1, 2007, pp. 332-334.

[3] N. Turker, F. Gunes and T. Yildirim, "Artificial Neural Design of Microstrip Antennas," *Turkish Journal of Electrical Engineering*, Vol. 14, No. 3, 2006, pp. 445-453.

[4] A. Patnaik, R. K. Mishra, G. K. Patra and S. K. Dash, "An Artificial Neural Network Model for Effective Dielectric Constant of Microstripline," *IEEE Transactions on Antennas Propagation*, Vol. 45, No. 11, 1997, p. 1697.

[5] D. Karaboga, K. Giiney, S. Sagıroglu and M. Erler, "Neural Computation of Resonant Frequency of Electrically Thin and Thick Rectangular Microstrip Antennas," *IEEE Proceedings of Microwaves, Antennas and Propagation*, Vol. 146, No. 2, 1999, pp. 155-159.

[6] S. Sagiroglu, K. Guney and M. Erler, "Computation of Radiation Efficiency for a Resonant Rectangular Microstrip Patch Antenna using Back Propagation Multilayered Perceptrons," *Journal of Electrical and Electronics*, Vol. 3, 2003, pp. 663-671.

[7] Q. J. Zhang and K. C. Gupta, "Neural Networks for RF and Microwave Design," Artech House Publishers, London, 2000.

[8] F. Peik, G. Coutts and R. R. Mansour, "Application of Neural Networks in Microwave Circuit Modelling," 1998 *IEEE Canadian Conference of Electrical and Computer Engineering*, Waterloo, 24-28 May 1998, pp. 928-931.

[9] S. Devi, D. C. Panda and S. S. Pattnaik, "A Novel Method of Using Artificial Neural Networks to Calculate Input Impedance of Circular Microstrip Antenna," *Antennas and Propagation Society International Symposium*, Vol. 3, 2000, pp. 462-465.

[10] R. K. Mishra and A. Patnaik, "Design of Circular Microstrip Antenna Using Neural Networks," *IETE Journal of Research*, Vol. 44, No. 122, 1998, pp. 35-39.

[11] S. Sagiroglu and K. Guney and M. Erler, "Calculation of Resonant Frequency for an Equilateral Triangular Microstrip Antenna Use with the of Artificial Neural Networks," *Microwave and Optical Technology Letters*, Vol. 14, No. 3, 2003, pp. 89-93.

[12] R. K. Mishra and A. Patnaik, "ANN Techniques in Mi-

crowave Engineering," *IEEE Microwave Magazine*, Vol. 1, 2000, pp. 55-60.

[13] M. Naser-Moghaddasi, P. D. Barjoei and A. Naghsh, "Heuristic Artificial Neural Network for Analysing and Synthesizing Rectangular Microstrip Antenna," *International Journal of Computer Science and Network Security*, Vol. 7, No. 12, 2007, pp. 278-281.

[14] V. V. Thakare and P. K. Singhal, "Bandwidth Analysis by Introducing Slots in Microstrip Antenna Design Using ANN," *Progress in Electromagnetic Research M*, Vol. 9, 2009, pp. 107-122.

[15] D. M. Pozar, "Microstrip Antennas," John Wiley and Sons, Hoboken, 1995, pp. 79-81.

[16] C. A. Balanis, "Antenna Theory," John Wiley & Sons, Hoboken, 1997.

[17] S. Haykin, "Neural Networks," 2nd Edition, Prentice-Hall of India, Delhi, 2000.

[18] M. H. Hassoun," Fundamentals of Artificial Neural Networks," Prentice Hall of India, New Delhi, 1999.

Integrated Off-Line Ballast for High Brightness LEDs with Dimming Capability

Jorge Garcia, Antonio J. Calleja, Emilio L. Corominas, David Gacio, Lidia Campa, Ramón E. Díaz
Department of Electrical Engineering, EEC-IEL Research Group, University of Oviedo, Asturias, Spain

Abstract

This paper presents an off-line integrated full ballast to supply a 35 W assembly of Power LEDs. The proposed solution integrates an input PFC stage (a flyback converter operating in DCM) and a DC-DC output converter (a buck converter) into a single switch power stage, operating with peak current control. As it will be shown, this control scheme maintains the current through the load constant, regardless of the instantaneous value of the DC link voltage. This issue allows the use of a small capacitor for the DC link, which enhances the overall system reliability. The complete ballast has full dimming capability, and all the analysis and design steps are presented, thus ensuring the fulfilling of the existing regulations. The novelty of the final solution comes from the simplicity and robustness of the control scheme in an integrated compact single-switch power stage. A final prototype of the ballast has been built and tested, and experimental results are shown in the last part of the paper. Finally, conclusions and future developments are shown.

Keywords: High Brightness LEDs, Light Dimming, Electrolytic Capacitor Avoidance, Integration of Stages

1. Introduction

At present, significant efforts are being performed in the development of lighting electronic systems, as one of the major research fields related to energy savings and sustainable development. Among other causes, this is due to the continuous improvement of High Brightness (HB) and Power LEDs as outstanding light sources [1-8]. In fact, these devices exhibit a continuous increase in its luminous efficiency and a high operating life and reliability. These features turn them the preferred device for an increasing number of applications [5-8].

Both the thermal and electrical behaviors of such devices make necessary the use of drivers with current limiting capability, in order to achieve stable operation The most efficient approach for this driver is the use of multi-stage Switch-Mode Power Supplies (SMPS) [9-19]. **Figure 1** shows a typical block diagram of such a driver supplied from AC mains.

The overall components count of such drivers is relatively high, due the number of stages. Moreover, this scheme implies the use of a low ripple voltage DC link after the input Power Factor Correction (PFC) stage, commonly provided by an electrolytic capacitor. As these devices have a relatively small operating life, it penalizes the overall life span of the system [2,20-22].

In this paper, a novel complete integrated electronic dimmer for Power LEDs is presented to overcome these drawbacks. The input stage of the proposed design operates from AC mains and delivers energy to a DC bus. The output stage with the proposed peak current control provides a DC current to the assembly of LEDs, regardless of the DC bus voltage. Thus, the DC bus voltage ripple can be significantly high, so the electrolytic capacitor can be removed and substituted by a small capacitance device. Provided that both power stages are single-switch topologies, the integration of the circuitry can be explored as an optimization strategy. As it will be shown in the present work, this integration is feasible, yielding to a final electronic driver with a single con

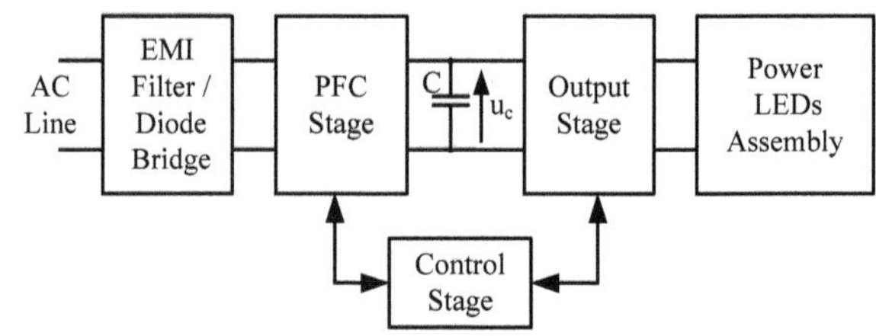

Figure 1. Block diagram of an offline electronic driver for Power LEDs.

trolled switch, presenting a block diagram as the one shown in **Figure 2**. The proposed solution allows the use of a simple and reliable control method, particularly effective in a circuit that avoids the use of electrolytic capacitors [21,22]. This simplicity and robustness, along with the compact scheme inherent to integrated power stages, provides a new feasible solution for power LEDs drivers.

In addition, light dimming can also be studied as a key issue of the full ballast. The most used diming schemes, AM and PWM dimming, will be investigated applied to the resulting integrated topology. As it will be shown, AM dimming can be attained by simply changing the peak control reference, while PWM dimming can be carried out by modulating the HF switching scheme of the integrated switch.

This paper analyzes more deeply the basic scheme presented in [22]. The effects of the integration in both the waveforms and the size of the power switches is considered. A revised design procedure is presented, and the design implications considering universal input line voltage condition are also presented. Both PWM and AM dimming schemes are also discussed in this paper.

The paper is organized as follows. Section 2 takes care of the power stage and the control strategy of the output converter. Later, Section 3 deals with the input PFC stage. Section 4 covers the topics related with the integration of stages and the design constraints, as well as with the effects on the input Power Factor (PF) and current harmonics. After that, Section 5 summarizes a design procedure for the full power operation of the driver. Section 6 deals with the experimental setup for the full power nominal operation of a built prototype, while section 7 takes care of both AM and PWM dimming procedures for the proposed topology. A final discussion on the extension of the design for universal AC input voltage is carried out in Section 8, while Section 9 comments on the conclusions and future developments of this work.

2. The Output Stage

Figure 3 shows the output stage, used in the full ballast

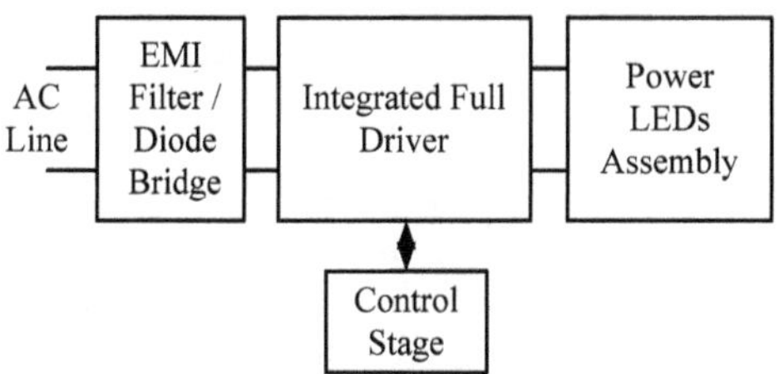

Figure 2. Block diagram of an integrated electronic driver for Power LEDs.

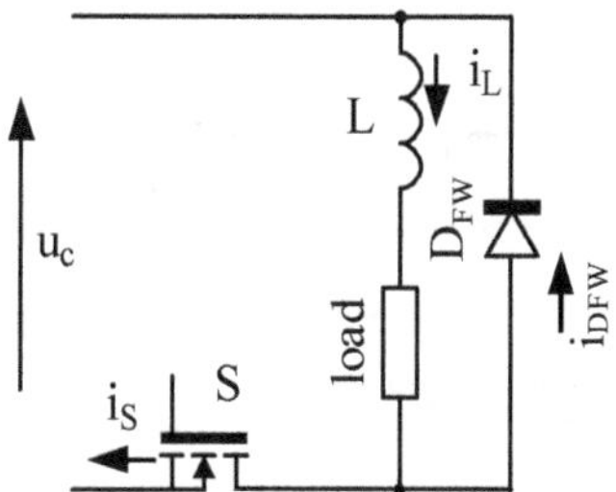

Figure 3. Scheme of the output stage

presented in [21]. It is a reverse buck converter stage, but removing the output filter capacitor. The final circuit is formed by the inductor L, the freewheeling diode D_{FW} and the controlled switch S. As it is shown, the current through the LEDs (modeled by the block called 'load') is the inductor current. Thus, ensuring a low AC ripple at the inductor current guarantees a proper current waveform to supply the LEDs.

2.1. The Power Stage

The operation of the converter is the same than in the usual buck converter. Although the output capacitor has been removed, the equivalent output characteristic of the LEDs assembly [23], resembles a voltage source, and thus the charging and discharging subintervals of the inductor can be considered at constant voltage [21,22]. This issue allows the usual analysis of the operation of the buck converter.

Thus, the expression of the inductor current, considering Continuous Conduction Mode (CCM), can be calculated as:

$$i_L(t) = \begin{cases} i_0 + \dfrac{u_C - u_{LEDs}}{L} \cdot t & 0 \le t < T_{ON} \\ i_{MAX} - \dfrac{u_{LEDs}}{L} \cdot (t - T_{ON}) & T_{ON} \le t < T \end{cases} \quad (1)$$

where i_0 and i_{MAX} are the initial and peak value of the inductor current, respectively, u_C is the input voltage, u_{LEDs} is the output voltage, L is the inductance, and T_{ON} and T are the turn-on time and the switching period of the switch S, respectively.

Obviously, the static gain expression of this converter can be defined as:

$$\frac{V_{out}}{V_{in}} = \frac{u_{LEDs}}{u_C} = \frac{T_{ON}}{T} = d \quad (2)$$

where d is the duty ratio of the converter.

Figure 4 shows the main theoretical waveforms of this converter.

Also, the current through the switch S, i_S, can be easily calculated:

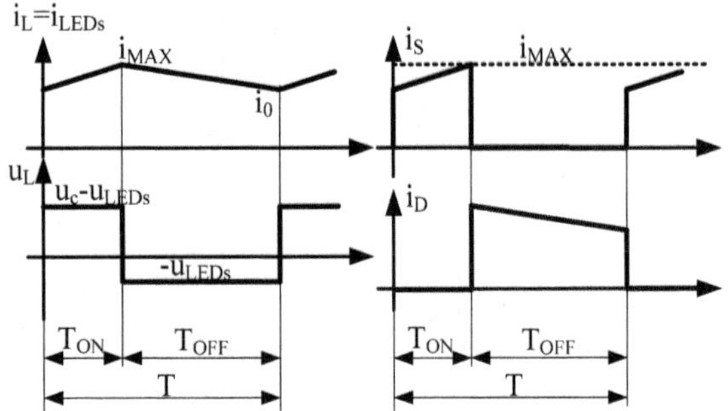

Figure 4. Main waveforms at the buck converter.

$$i_S(t)=\begin{cases} i_0+\dfrac{u_C-u_{LEDs}}{L}\cdot t & 0\le t<T_{ON} \\ 0 & T_{ON}\le t<T \end{cases} \tag{3}$$

The average value of this input current in one high frequency switching period, i_{SAVG}, can be obtained from (3):

$$i_{SAVG}=\frac{i_0+i_{MAX}}{2}\cdot d \tag{4}$$

2.2. The Control Stage

Different control strategies can be implemented to drive this stage. In order to supply properly the LEDs, an output current control mode must be considered. The proposed control method fixes the maximum current through the switch and the turn-off time of the switch, T_{OFF}. Obviously,

$$T=T_{ON}+T_{OFF} \tag{5}$$

Considering (1) and (5), if T_{OFF} and I_{MAX} are fixed, the value of the current i_0, and hence that of the current ripple through the LEDs, Δi_{LEDs}, is also fixed:

$$i_{MAX}-i_0=\Delta i_{LEDs}=\frac{u_{LEDs}}{L}\cdot T_{OFF} \tag{6}$$

Thus, the i_{MAX} - T_{OFF} control ensures a maximum peak current value through the LEDs as well as a fixed current ripple through the LEDs. Notice how this assertion is true whatever the voltage u_C is present (provided that u_C is greater than u_{LEDs}, and hence the inductor can be charged during T_{ON}). That is to say, for every value of u_C greater than u_{LEDs}, the control ensures a current waveform of a fixed maximum value and ripple.

Another consequence of this control is that the turn-on time of the switch, T_{ON}, is not an independent variable of the system for the selected control scheme. From (2) and (5), T_{ON} can be expressed as:

$$T_{ON}=\frac{u_{LEDs}}{u_C-u_{LEDs}}\cdot T_{OFF} \tag{7}$$

Thus, T_{ON} depends on the input voltage, u_C, and hence the switching frequency of the converter also depends on u_C:

$$f=\frac{1}{T}=\frac{1}{T_{ON}+T_{OFF}}=\frac{u_C-u_{LEDs}}{u_C\cdot T_{OFF}} \tag{8}$$

In order to define the operation of the complete system it is interesting to express the average input current as a function of the input and output voltages as well as of the control parameters. From (4), (6) and (7), the expression of the average input current, i_{SAVG}, can be rewritten as a function of i_{MAX}, T_{OFF} and u_C, yielding to:

$$i_{SAVG}=\frac{2\cdot i_{MAX}-\dfrac{u_{LEDs}}{L}\cdot T_{OFF}}{2}\cdot\frac{u_{LEDs}}{u_C} \tag{9}$$

So finally, it can be seen how the average input current is also a function of u_C.

3. The Input Stage

The input PFC stage is a flyback converter, operating in Discontinuous Conduction Mode (DCM). The schematic diagram of this stage is shown in **Figure 5**. Prior to the integration of both stages, an analysis of the main waveforms must be carried out. The current flowing through the magnetizing inductor at the primary side of the flyback transformer, i_{LF}, can be expressed as:

$$i_{LF}(t)=\begin{cases} \dfrac{V_{INPK}\cdot|\sin(\theta)|}{L_F}\cdot t & 0\le t<T_{ONF} \\ i_{LFPK}-\dfrac{N_P}{N_S}\dfrac{u_C}{L_F}\cdot(t-T_{ONF}) & T_{ONF}\le t<T_{ONF}+T_d \\ 0 & T_{ONF}+T_d\le t<T_F \end{cases} \tag{10}$$

where $V_{INPK}\cdot\sin(\theta)$ is the line input voltage, considered constant during the switching period of the flyback stage, T_F; L_F is the magnetizing inductance at the primary side of the transformer; N_P and N_S are the turns ratio at the primary and secondary side of the transformer, respectively;

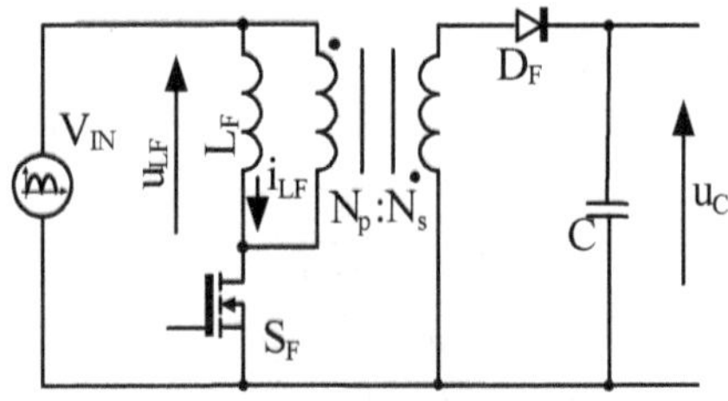

Figure 5. Schematics of the flyback input stage.

T_{ONF} is the interval during which the switch S_F is turned on, T_d is the demagnetizing time of L_F, u_C is the output voltage of this stage, and i_{LFPK} is the peak value of the current through the magnetizing inductor. This value can be described as:

$$i_{LFPK} = \frac{V_{INPK} \cdot |\sin(\theta)|}{L_F} \cdot T_{ONF} \qquad (11)$$

Figure 6 depicts the voltage and current waveforms in the magnetizing inductor at the primary side of the transformer.

On the other hand, the instant current waveform, i_{IN}, at the input (line input current) can be easily obtained considering (10):

$$i_{IN}(t,\theta) = \begin{cases} \frac{V_{INPK} \cdot |\sin(\theta)|}{L_F} \cdot t & 0 \le t < T_{ONF} \\ 0 & T_{ONF} \le t < T_F \end{cases} \qquad (12).$$

The average value of this input current in a switching period, i_{INAVG}, can be calculated as:

$$i_{INAVG}(\theta) = \frac{V_{INPK} \cdot |\sin(\theta)| \cdot T_{ONF}^2}{L_F \cdot T_F \cdot 2} \qquad (13)$$

The current in the secondary side of the transformer, that is to say, the forward current of the diode D_F, can be expressed by (14):

The demagnetizing time, T_d, can be expressed from (14):

$$T_d = \frac{V_{INPK} \cdot |\sin(\theta)|}{u_C} \cdot T_{ONF} \cdot \frac{N_S}{N_P} \qquad (15)$$

Thus, the average value of the output current in a switching period, i_{DFAVG}, can be calculated as:

$$i_{DFAVG} = \frac{V_{INPK} \cdot |\sin(\theta)|}{2 \cdot L_F} \cdot \frac{N_P}{N_S} \cdot T_{ONF} \cdot \frac{T_d}{T_F} \qquad (16)$$

From (15) and (16), this expression can be calculated as:

$$i_{DFAVG} = \frac{V_{INPK}^2 \cdot \sin^2(\theta)}{2 \cdot L_F \cdot u_C} \cdot \frac{T_{ONF}^2}{T_F} \qquad (17)$$

4. Dealing with the Integration

Figure 7 depicts the resulting full ballast, with the proposed stages connected in series. Each stage has a controlled switch, represented by a MOSFET, with its source terminal connected to ground. The integration can be carried out by equaling the switching periods of both stages and their turn-on times:

$$T_{ONF} = T_{ON};\ T_F = T \qquad (18)$$

A scheme of the final ballast can be seen in **Figure 8**, while **Figure 9** depicts the switching intervals of the integrated ballast operation. When the integrated switch, S_{INT}, is turned on (T_{ON}), the input current charges the magnetizing inductance of the primary side of the transformer (**Figure 9(a)**). At the same time, the capacitor C provides the current that flows through the inductor L and through the load in the output converter. This interval corresponds to the turn-on intervals of the input and output stages.

After the current through inductor reaches i_{MAX}, S_{INT} is turned off. The magnetizing inductance at the primary side of the flyback transformer discharges through D_F towards the capacitor (**Figure 9(b)**). Also, the freewheeling diode D_{FW} turns on, thus discharging L through the load. At a certain time after being started, the demagnetizing of the flyback transformer ends up, and the diode D_F turns off again (**Figure 9(c)**). Nevertheless, the output stage remains unchanged.

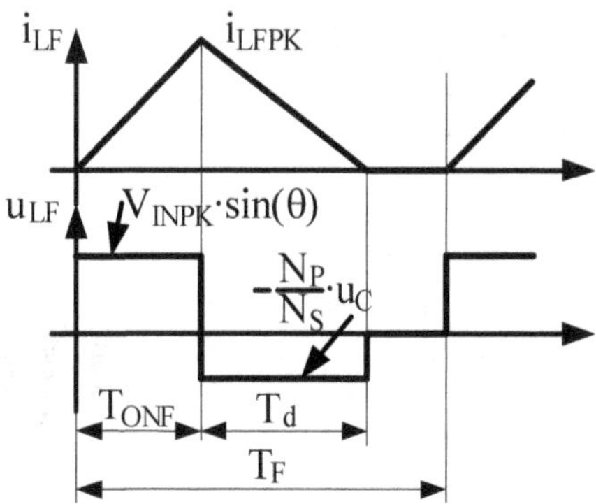

Figure 6. Main waveforms in the magnetizing inductor at the primary side of the transformer of the input stage.

$$i_{DF}(t) = \begin{cases} 0 & 0 \le t < T_{ONF} \\ i_{LFPK} \cdot \frac{N_P}{N_S} - \frac{N_P^2}{N_S^2} \cdot \frac{u_C}{L_F} \cdot (t - T_{ONF}) & T_{ONF} \le t < T_{ONF} + T_d \\ 0 & T_{ONF} + T_d \le t < T_F \end{cases} \qquad (14)$$

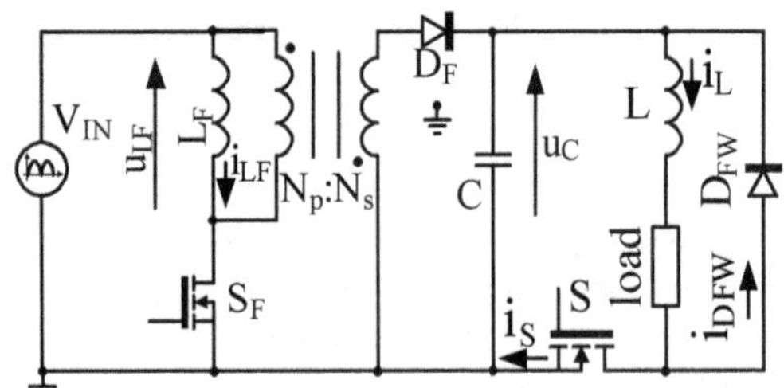
Figure 7. Full ballast with the proposed stages.

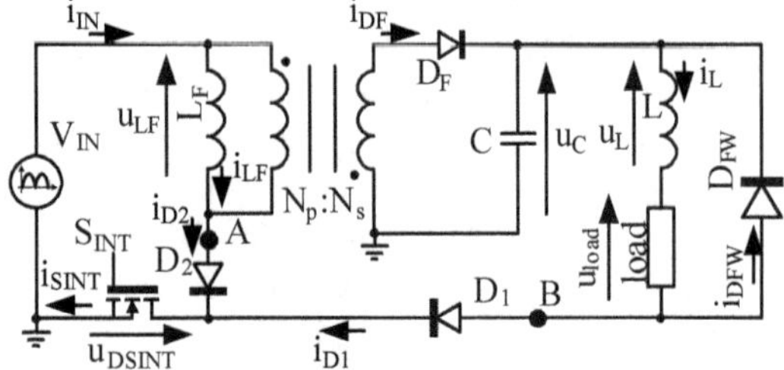
Figure 8. Full ballast with the integration of the stages.

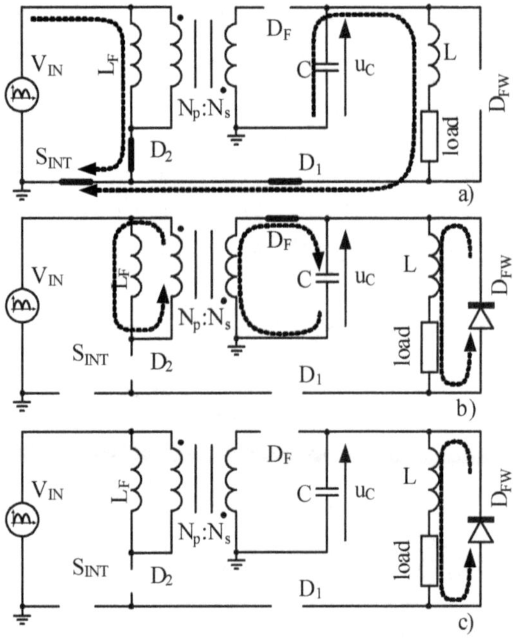
Figure 9. Switching modes of the integrated proposed driver.

In order to dimension the switches of the proposed topology, a study of the obtained waveforms has been carried out, taking into account the requirements for the new semiconductors after the integration, S_{INT}, D_1 and D_2.

From the point of view of the current stresses, **Figure 9(a)** shows how the current flowing through S_{INT} is the sum of the input switch (S in **Figure** 7) and output switch (S_F in **Figure** 7) currents. Provided that the operation of the independent stages is the one previously discussed (**Figures 3** and **6**), the main current waveforms of the proposed topology are depicted in **Figure 10**. In fact, as it can be seen, the peak current trough S_{INT}, i_{SINTPK}, is the sum of both peak currents:

$$i_{SINTPK} = i_{MAX} + i_{LFPK} \tag{19}$$

The current waveform through diode D_1 is the same current waveform obtained for the input switch (S in **Figure** 7), whereas the current through D_2 is the one obtained for the output switch (S_F in **Figure** 7). The currents through the rest of devices are the same that were obtained at the analysis of the input and output independent stages.

The analysis of the voltage waveforms is not so easy, as the voltage waveforms in D_1 and D_2 change depending on the relative value of the line instant voltage and the capacitor voltage, which in turn depends on the turns ratio, N_P/N_S. In order to simplify the study, it is assumed that:

$$N_P > N_S \tag{20}$$

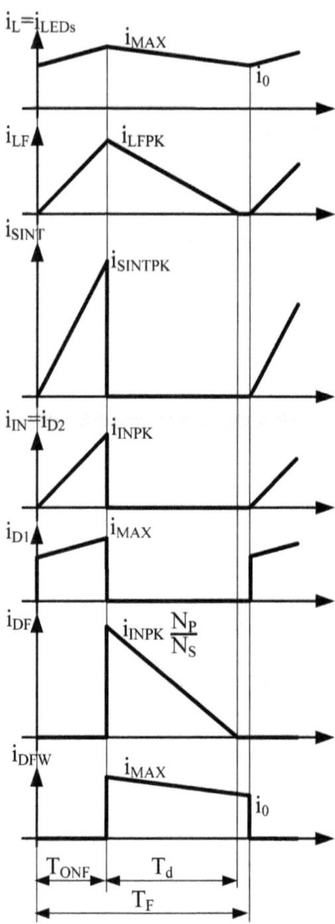
Figure 10. Main current waveforms at the proposed topology.

This assumption will be justified later, in the design section. Depending on these relative values, two different conditions of the input line voltage are present.

4.1. Relative Values of V_A and V_B during the Demagnetization Interval

When S_{INT} is turned on, D_1 and D_2 are forward biased, and no voltage requirement is obtained. However, once the main switch is turned off, the resulting waveforms depend on the line instant angle, θ.

While the flyback rectifying diode, D_F, is directly biased, the voltage at the anode of D_2 (point A in **Figure 8**) is defined by:

$$V_A = V_{INPK} \cdot |\sin(\theta)| + \frac{N_P}{N_S} \cdot u_C \tag{21}$$

On the other hand, the voltage at the anode of D_1 (point B in **Figure 8**), can be expressed by:

$$V_B = u_C \tag{22}$$

as the diode D_{FW} is directly biased, and thus withstands no voltage. Considering (20), (21) and (22), the relative values of V_A and V_B yield to:

$$V_A = V_{INPK} \cdot |\sin(\theta)| + \frac{N_P}{N_S} u_C > u_C = V_B \Rightarrow V_A > V_B \tag{23}$$

This condition reversely biases the diode D_1, which withstands the following voltage:

$$V_{D1AK} = V_{INPK} \cdot |\sin(\theta)| + \left(\frac{N_P}{N_S} - 1\right) u_C \tag{24}$$

On the other hand, diode D_2 is directly biased, but with no current passing through. Provided that (20) is fulfilled, this condition is satisfied for every line instant.

4.2. Relative Values of V_A and V_B after the Demagnetization Interval

Once the demagnetization of the magnetizing inductance L_F ends up, the value of V_B is still represented by (22), but diode D_F turns off, and the voltage at node A changes yielding to:

$$V_A = V_{INPK} \cdot |\sin(\theta)| \tag{25}$$

Now, the relative values of V_A and V_B depend on the line input voltage instant. In fact, at high instant input voltage values, the following equation if fulfilled:

$$V_{INPK} \cdot |\sin(\theta)| > u_C \tag{26}$$

what yields again to the condition

$$V_A > V_B \tag{27}$$

and diodes D_1 and D_2 remain as in the previous stage.

However, for low instant input voltage (near the zero crossing of the line voltage), the following equation is eventually satisfied:

$$V_{INPK} \cdot |\sin(\theta)| < u_C \tag{28}$$

what yields to the opposite condition:

$$V_A < V_B \tag{29}$$

In this case, this condition reversely biases D_2, that withstands a voltage given by:

$$V_{D1AK} = u_C - V_{INPK} \cdot \sin(\theta) \tag{30}$$

In this case, D_1 remains directly biased but without driving forward current.

Thus, depending of the relative values of the instant line rectified input voltage and the capacitor voltage, the state of the diodes D_1 and D_2 change. **Figure 11(a)** depicts the voltage waveforms for high instant line voltage, given by (26), while **Figure 11(b)** shows the voltage waveforms for the alternate low instant line voltage condition, defined by (28).

The value of this capacitor, C, is the key parameter of the operation of the converter. This capacitance fixes the DC link voltage instant waveform. As the flyback input current is a function of this DC link voltage, the line input current depends also on the capacitance C. Thus, to properly design the ballast, the waveform of the capacitor voltage, as a function of the capacitance C, must be calculated. The average current in a switching period flowing into the capacitor C can be calculated. As can be seen, the input current of the capacitor is the output current of the input stage, and the output current of the capacitor is the input current through the output stage.

$$i_{CAVG} = i_{DFAVG} - i_{SAVG} \tag{31}$$

Thus, from (9), (17) and (31): (32)

Considering (5) and (18), this current can be expressed as a function of the control parameters, i_{MAX} and T_{OFF} (33)

$$i_{CAVG} = \frac{{V_{INPK}}^2 \cdot \sin^2(\theta)}{2 \cdot L_F \cdot u_C} \cdot \frac{{T_{ONF}}^2}{T_F} - \frac{2 \cdot i_{MAX} - \frac{u_{LEDs}}{L} \cdot T_{OFF}}{2} \cdot \frac{u_{LEDs}}{u_C} \tag{32}$$

$$i_{CAVG} = \frac{{V_{INPK}}^2 \cdot \sin^2(\theta) \cdot {u_{LEDs}}^2}{2 \cdot L_F \cdot {u_C}^2 \cdot (u_C - u_{LEDs})} T_{OFF} - \frac{u_{LEDs}}{u_C}\left(i_{MAX} - \frac{u_{LEDs}}{2 \cdot L} \cdot T_{OFF}\right) \tag{33}$$

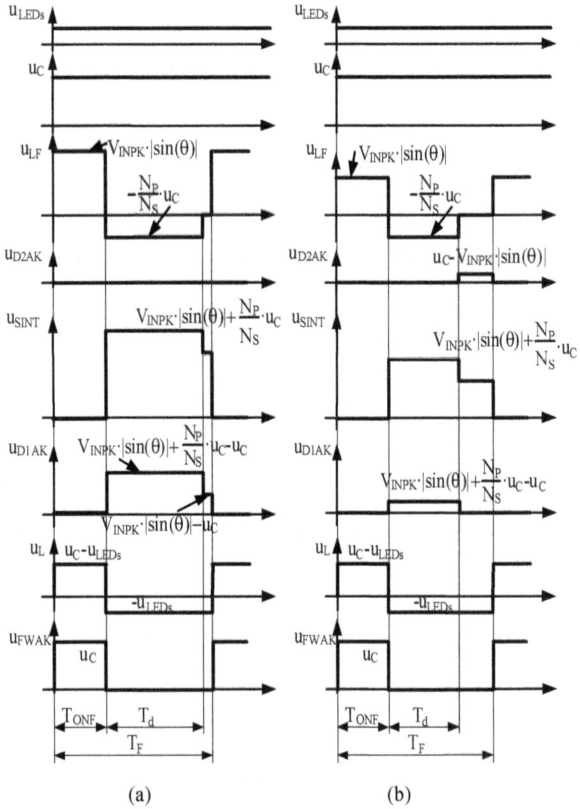

Figure 11. Main voltage waveforms at the proposed topology. (a) High line instant input voltage condition. (b) Low line instant voltage condition.

The fundamental equation of a capacitor, combined with (33), yield to: (34)

This differential equation must be solved numerically. The time expression of the capacitor voltage can be solved as a function of the control parameters, i_{MAX} and T_{OFF}, and the capacitance C:

$$u_C(\theta) = f(\theta, i_{MAX}, T_{OFF}, C) \tag{35}$$

After the integration, the expression of the input line current as a function of the line angle can be expressed from (2), (8) and (13) as: (36)

Finally, substituting (35) in (36), the final expression of the input current value is found, what yields to the calculation of both the power factor and the input current harmonics.

5. Design Procedure for 115 V_{RMS}-60 Hz Line Voltage

This section proposes the design procedure for a LED driver, calculating the input current harmonics to verify if they fulfill the corresponding regulations. In a first approach ideal components will be considered.

The selected input is the American input mains voltage range, 115 V_{RMS}-60 Hz, and an allowed variation of ±20% in the amplitude will be considered. At the final part of this section, once the rest of the components are designed, the rated voltage and current values of the main switches will be selected for this input condition. This will yield to a proper sizing of these devices. An additional discussion at the final part of the paper will consider the Universal input mains voltage range, and its effects on the design procedure.

5.1. Desired Operation Parameters

The first thing to settle is the target load and its nominal operation point. In this case, a 32 W assembly of Power LEDs will be the target load. The selected device is the Luxeon LXK2-PW14-U00, from Lumileds Lighting [23]. To obtain such a power load, the selected assembly is formed by the series connection of 10 LEDs. In previous works, it has been demonstrated how the proposed control scheme allows a proper operation of the system, regardless the evolution of the electric and thermal parameters of the LEDs [21].

Thus, the rated electrical parameters of this load are:

$$P_{LEDs} = 32\text{ W} \quad u_{LEDs} = 32\text{ V} \quad i_{LEDs} = 1\text{ A} \tag{37}$$

where u_{LEDs} is the total voltage drop of the assembly of LEDs.

The design current ripple has been selected as:

$$\Delta i_{LEDs} = i_{MAX} - i_0 = 0.1\text{ A} = 10\% \tag{38}$$

and, in order to keep the average forward value selected in (37), the values of i_{MAX} and i_0 are:

$$i_{MAX} = i_{LEDs} + \frac{\Delta i_{LEDs}}{2} = 1.05\text{ A} \tag{39}$$

$$i_0 = i_{LEDs} - \frac{\Delta i_{LEDs}}{2} = 0.95\text{ A} \tag{40}$$

$$2\pi f_L C \cdot \frac{du_C}{d\theta} = \frac{V_{INPK}^2 \cdot \sin^2(\theta) \cdot u_{LEDs}^2}{2 \cdot L_F \cdot u_C^2 (u_C - u_{LEDs})} T_{OFF} - \frac{u_{LEDs}\left(i_{MAX} - \dfrac{u_{LEDs} \cdot T_{OFF}}{2 \cdot L}\right)}{u_C} \tag{34}$$

$$i_{INAVG}(\theta) = \frac{V_{INPK} \cdot |\sin(\theta)| \cdot T_{ON}^2}{L_F \cdot T_F \cdot 2} = \frac{V_{INPK} \cdot |\sin(\theta)| \cdot u_{LEDs}^2 \cdot T_{OFF}}{2 \cdot L_F \cdot u_C(\theta) \cdot (u_C(\theta) - u_{LEDs})} \tag{36}$$

As described in previous sections, the values of T_{ON}, and hence of T and d, are a function of θ. Nevertheless, the averaged values of these parameters must be settled in order to start the design. Thus, the selected average switching frequency will be 100 kHz, whereas the target duty ratio will be 50%:

$$f = 100 \text{ kHz} \quad T = 10 \text{ μs} \quad T_{OFF} = 5 \text{ μs} \tag{41}$$

With these initial design parameters, the values of the rest of the circuit parameters can be calculated.

5.2. Calculation of the Magnetic Components

The value of the inductor at the output stage can be obtained from (6):

$$L = \frac{u_{LEDs}}{\Delta i_{LEDs}} \cdot T_{OFF} = 1.67 \text{ mH} \tag{42}$$

Although this inductance is high, it must be noticed that the current ripple through the inductor will be very low. This condition makes possible the design optimization of the magnetic device, thus maintaining low enough the power losses in this component.

The flyback transformer must now be calculated. To ensure the DCM, the demagnetizing time of the transformer, T_d, must fulfill:

$$T_d \le T_{OFF} \tag{43}$$

From (15) and (43), the limit value of the turns ratio, N_P/N_S, that keeps DCM condition can be obtained:

$$\frac{N_P}{N_S} \ge \frac{T_{ON}(\theta)}{T_{OFF}} \cdot \frac{V_{INPK} \cdot |\sin(\theta)|}{u_C(\theta)} \tag{44}$$

Taking into account (7),

$$\frac{N_P}{N_S} \ge \frac{u_{LEDs}}{u_C(\theta) - u_{LEDs}} \cdot \frac{V_{INPK} \cdot \sin(\theta)}{u_C(\theta)} \tag{45}$$

Notice how in (44) and (45) the V_{INPK} value is the highest possible. For instance, considering the ±20% input line variation, in this case a 120% of V_{INPK} should be selected.

It can also be seen how prior to settle the turns ratio of the transformer, the limit values of u_C must be calculated. Nevertheless, the magnetizing inductance at the primary side of the transformer can be calculated considering the equation that expresses the average input power in a switching period. Considering (36), the instant input power as a function of the line angle, θ, can be calculated as:

$$P_{IN}(\theta) = \frac{V_{INPK}^2 \cdot \sin^2(\theta) \cdot T_{ON}^2}{2 \cdot L_F \cdot T} \tag{46}$$

And finally, the average input power in a line period can be obtained:

$$P_{IN-AVG} = \frac{V_{INPK}^2 \cdot T_{ON}^2}{4 \cdot L_F \cdot T} \tag{47}$$

If an efficiency of η is considered, the maximum allowable value of the input inductor can be solved:

$$P_{IN-AVG} = P_{LEDs} \cdot \eta \quad \Rightarrow \quad L_F \le \frac{V_{INPK}^2 \cdot T_{ON}^2}{4 \cdot P_{LEDs} \cdot \eta \cdot T} \tag{48}$$

In this case V_{INPK} value must be the smallest possible. For the aforementioned specification of ±20% input voltage variation, now a 80% of V_{INPK} should be selected.

From (41) and (48), and considering η = 0.85, the magnetizing inductor L_F is: (43)

$$L_F \le 425 \text{ μH} \Rightarrow L_F = 420 \text{ μH} \tag{49}$$

5.3. Solution of the Equation of the Capacitor Voltage

Equation (34) has been solved numerically for different capacitor values. The obtained voltage waveforms at the capacitor, u_C, have been plotted in **Figure 12**.

After analyzing the value of $u_C(\theta)$, it has been verified that the minimum value of C that allows a correct operation of the system is:

$$C_{MIN} = 18 \text{ μF} \tag{50}$$

For lower values, $u_C(\theta)$ reaches voltage values smaller than u_{LEDs}, which would imply negative currents through the LEDs (obviously an impossible condition). For greater capacitance values, the system operates properly, and the larger the C value, the smaller the DC link voltage ripple, as shown in **Figure 12**.

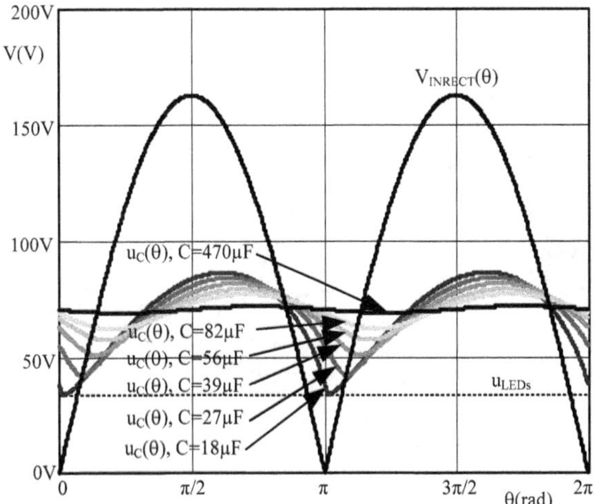

Figure 12. Theoretical waveforms of the capacitor voltage, u_C, as a function of different capacitance values.

Although the output stage will operate properly for capacitance values greater than C_{MIN}, the input current will present different shapes depending on C. **Figure 13** plots this input current for different values of C. As can be seen, the current trends to be sinusoidal for high values of C, while high distortion is present for low C values. To quantify this distortion, the values of PF and THD, as a function of C, have been calculated. **Figure 14** plots both parameters as a function of C. The amplitudes of the line current harmonics, as a function of C, have been obtained, and they are shown in **Figure 15**.

In order to choose an appropriate value of C, the fulfilling of the corresponding standards must be verified. For this driver, both the limits provided by the IEC61000-3-2 and the Energy Star Program Requirements for Solid-State Lighting Products are applicable. The latter sets the minimum PF as 0.7 for residential and as 0.9 for commercial applications. The values corresponding to the IEC61000-3-2 are given in **Table 1**. This table also shows the values of the theoretical current harmonics calculated for different C values. In bold letters are those values that fulfill the mentioned standard. As can be seen, the minimum capacitance value to verify the standards is $C = 47$ μF. Moreover, this capacitance value also fulfills the Energy Star standards for residential and commercial applications, as the PF raises above 0.9. The theoretical current harmonics for this capacitor value, as well as the limits provided by the standard are depicted in **Figure 16**.

Solving (34) also provides a relationship between the maximum voltage values and C. This relationship, depicted in **Figure 17**, can be used to size the capacitor. As it can be seen, in this case the maximum voltage value for the selected capacitor, u_{CMAX}, is given by:

$$u_{CMAX} = 81\text{ V} \tag{51}$$

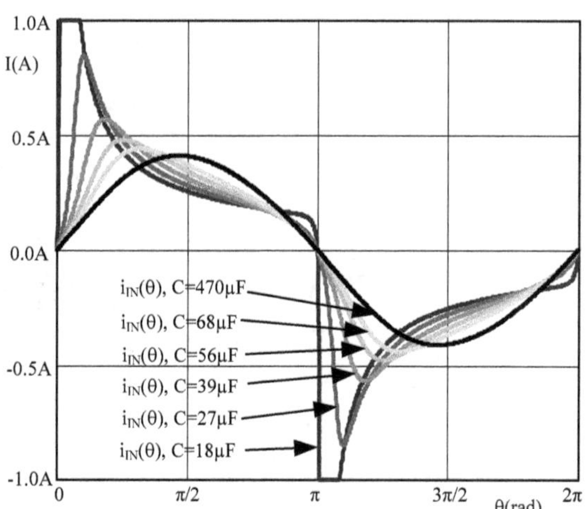

Figure 13. Theoretical waveforms of the AC line input current, i_{IN}, as a function of different capacitance values.

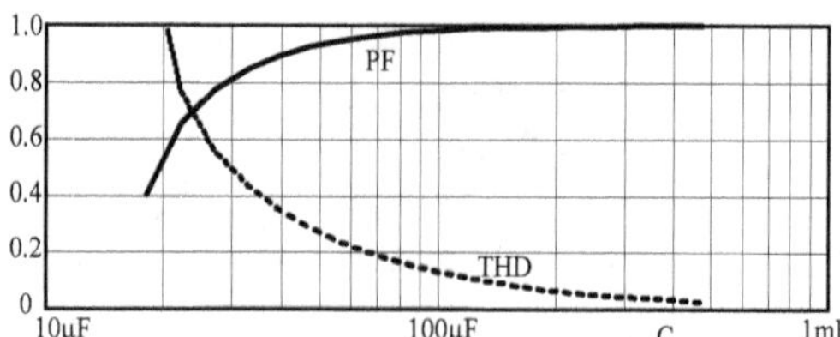

Figure 14. Theoretical values of *PF* (filled line) and THD (dotted line) of the input current, for different *C* values.

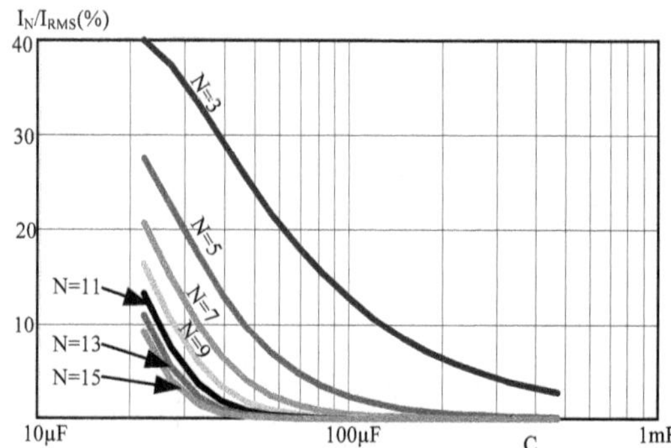

Figure 15. Theoretical values of the amplitudes of the line current harmonics for different capacitance values.

Table 1. Current harmonics of the input current limited by IEC-61000-3-2, and theoretical values for different *C* values.

Current Harmonics	*PF*	1st	3rd	5th	7th	9th	11th to 39th
Standard (%)		-	30·PF	10	7	5	3
Theor. (%) $C = 18$ μF	0.407	60.1	36.8 (12.2)	28.8	24.2	21.1	≤19
Theor. (%) $C = 27$ μF	0.774	87.5	37.3 (23.2)	22.4	14.9	10.4	≤8.0
Theor. (%) $C = 33$ μF	0.850	91.9	33.2 (25.5)	17.2	9.80	5.88	≤4.0
Theor. (%) $C = 39$ μF	0.892	94.3	29.5 (26.8)	13.2	6.57	3.43	≤1.9
Theor. (%) $C = 47$ μF	0.926	96.1	25.4 (27.7)	9.65	4.06	1.79	≤0.8

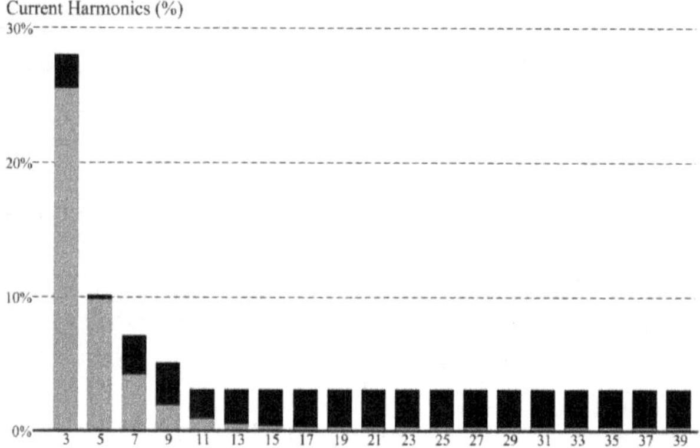

Figure 16. Theoretical harmonics of the input current of the integrated ballast for the selected value of 47 μF (grey), and current harmonic limits given by IEC 61000-3-2 (black).

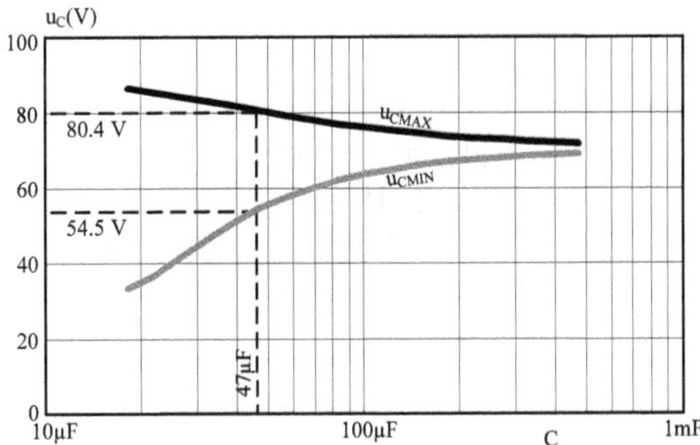

Figure 17. Theoretical value of the peak (maximum) and valley (minimum) voltage values in a line period at capacitor *C* for different capacitance values.

Also, the final turns ratio of the transformer can be designed. Considering (45), for the selected value of *C*, the value of the turns ratio is:

$$\frac{N_P}{N_S} \geq 3.1 = 4 \quad (52)$$

5.4. Dimension of the Power Switches

From the above discussion, the values of the absolute maximum voltage and current values for the switches of the converter can be selected considering **Figure 11**. Considering (51) and (52), the maximum voltage at the drain of the integrated switch is given by:

$$u_{SINT\_MAX} = V_{INPK} + \frac{N_P}{N_S} \cdot u_{CMAX} = 520 \text{ V} \quad (53)$$

The maximum reverse voltages in diodes D_1 and D_2 can also be calculated from **Figure 11**:

$$u_{D1AK\_MAX} = V_{INPK} + \left(\frac{N_P}{N_S} - 1\right) \cdot u_{CMAX} = 438 \text{ V} \quad (54)$$

$$u_{D2AK\_MAX} = u_{CMAX} = 81 \text{ V} \quad (55)$$

Equations (53) and (54) have been calculated considering the aforementioned ±20% input line variation. It must also be noticed that these calculations do not consider an input clamp voltage snubber to store the energy handled by the leakage inductance of the primary side of the transformer. This snubber rises up significantly the maximum drain voltage, usually around 20% - 25%, what must be considered in the final implementation.

6. Built Prototype and Experimental Results

A built prototype of the integrated driver has been built and tested, for the stated load of 10 power LEDs connected in series.

Figure 18 shows experimental waveforms measured in the built prototype in steady state. **Figure 18(a)** depicts the capacitor voltage, the voltage and current through the LEDs, and the drain to source voltage at the switch S_{INT}, for an input voltage of 100 V ($\theta \approx 50°$). **Figure 18(b)** shows these waveforms for an input voltage of 162 V ($\theta = 90°$)

The line frequency waveforms of the prototype are shown in **Figure 19(a)**. As can be seen, the current through the LEDs is kept constant through all the line cycle, although the capacitor voltage, u_C, presents a significant voltage ripple. **Figure 19(b)** plots the experimental and theoretical waveforms of the capacitor voltage, u_C, and the line input current, i_{IN}. As can be seen, the experimental waveforms are in good agreement with the expected values.

Table 2 shows the PF and the amplitude of the input current harmonics for both the theoretical and the experimental waveforms. The experimental input current harmonics are depicted in **Figure 20**, along with the limits given by the IEC 61000-3-2 standard. As can be seen, the waveform fulfills these standards, although the experimental values of the current harmonics are slightly greater than the theoretical ones. In fact, the experimental THD is 36%, while the theoretical THD is 25%. The

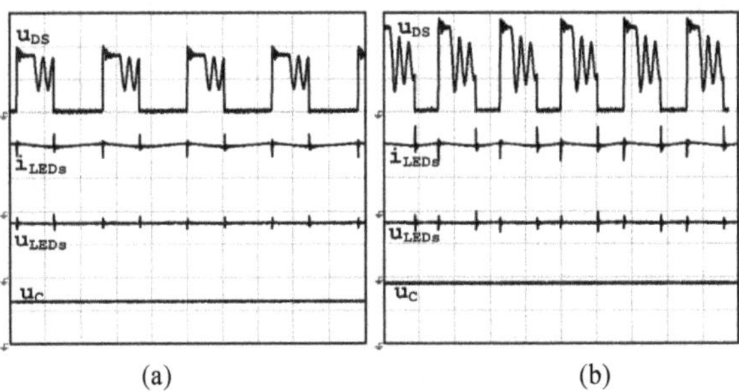

Figure 18. Main experimental high frequency waveforms in the built prototype, at different line angles. (a) V_{IN}= 100 V ($\theta \approx 50°$). (b) V_{IN}= 162 V ($\theta \approx 90°$). (all traces: u_C 50 V/div; u_{LEDs}: 20 V/div; u_{DS}: 200 V/div, i_{LEDs}: 500 mA/div; time: 5 μs/div).

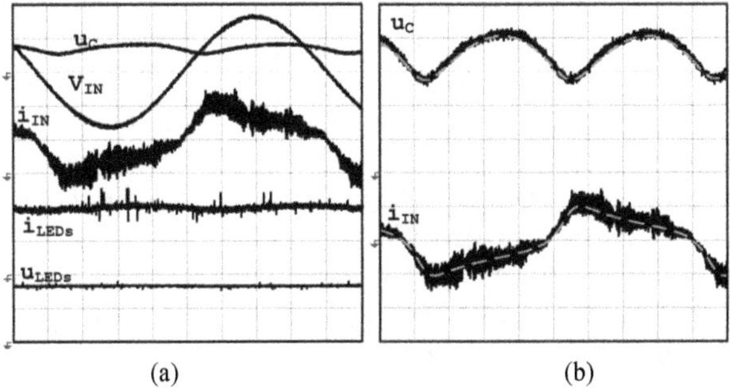

Figure 19. (a) Main experimental line frequency waveforms (u_C and u_{LEDs}: 50 V/div; u_{RECT}: 100 V/div; i_{LEDs}: 1 A/div; i_{IN}: 500 mA/div; time: 2 ms/div); (b) Comparison between theoretical and experimental waveforms of u_C and i_{IN} (u_C 20 V/div; i_{IN}: 500 mA/div; time: 2 ms/div).

Table 2. Theoretical vs. experimental values of the input current harmonics.

Current Harm.	*PF*	1st	3rd	5th	7th	9th	11th to 39th
Standard (%)		-	30·PF	10	7	5	3
Theor.(%) $C = 47\ \mu F$	0.926	96.1	25.4 (27.7)	9.65	4.06	1.79	≤0.8
Exp. (%) $C = 47\ \mu F$	0.911	95.2	26.3 (27.7)	9.01	2.67	2.28	≤2.47

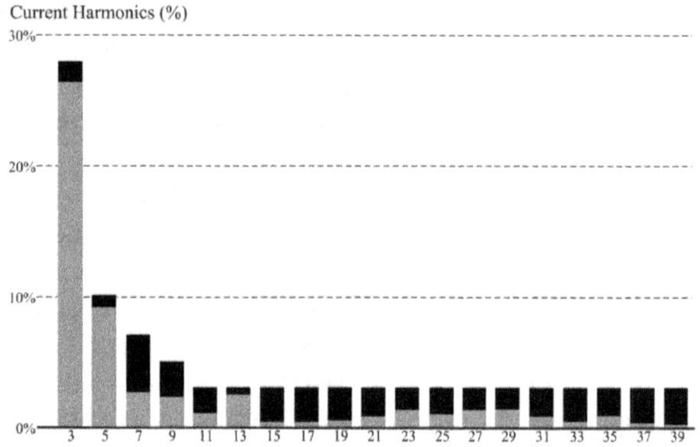

Current Harmonics (%)
30%
20%
10%
0%
3 5 7 9 11 13 15 17 19 21 23 25 27 29 31 33 35 37 39

Figure 20. Experimental harmonics of the input current of the integrated ballast for the selected value of 47 μF (grey), and current harmonic limits given by IEC 61000-3-2 (black)

overall system efficiency is 85.8%, while the output power is 31.2 W.

7. The Dimming Procedure

As it has been mentioned before, both AM and PWM dimming schemes can be carried out in the proposed integrated ballast. This section explains the main advantages and drawbacks of both strategies in the proposed ballast, and finally selects the best dimming option.

7.1. PWM Dimming

For the PWM dimming scheme, the basic idea is to modulate the operation of switch S_{INT} at a low fixed frequency, with a duty ratio d_{DIM} proportional to the output light level required. Thus, a PWM dimming scheme will be obtained at the output current waveform. As the proposed topology is an integrated circuit, with only one controlled switch, the PWM diming scheme can only be implemented by completely turning on and off the full converter. Thus, the dimming frequency is limited by the dynamic behavior of the whole ballast. The theoretical current through the LEDs and the line input current, both in a line period, have been depicted in **Figure 21**. **Figure 21(a)** shows the theoretical line and LEDs currents at full power operation, that is to say without dimming, while **Figure 21(b)** shows the same waveforms if operated under PWM dimming scheme (modulated with a low frequency). In fact, **Figure 21(b)** shows the typical PWM dimming current waveform. Notice how if this scheme is carried out, the input current would be pulsated at the dimming frequency (**Figure 21(b)**). Thus, the input EMI filter must guarantee a correct filtering of the input current, at the dimming frequency rather than at the switching frequency. In order to achieve a feasible driver, this dimming frequency should be high enough as to allow reasonable values for the EMI filter values. **Figure 22** shows the LEDs current for a PWM scheme, by turning on and off the complete driver at a frequency of 500 Hz. As can be seen, the turn on and turn off transients seen in the current waveform prevent the use of higher frequencies for the dimming scheme, which yields to non-practical too bulky EMI filters. **Figure 23** shows the main waveforms of the converter for different PWM dimming ratios. Particularly, **Figure 23(a)** shows the input current waveforms for those dimming ratios (100%, 50% and 10%). As can be seen, the pulsating input current waveforms increase significantly the THD and decrease the PF to non-admissible values. Thus, this dimming scheme is not feasible for this topology.

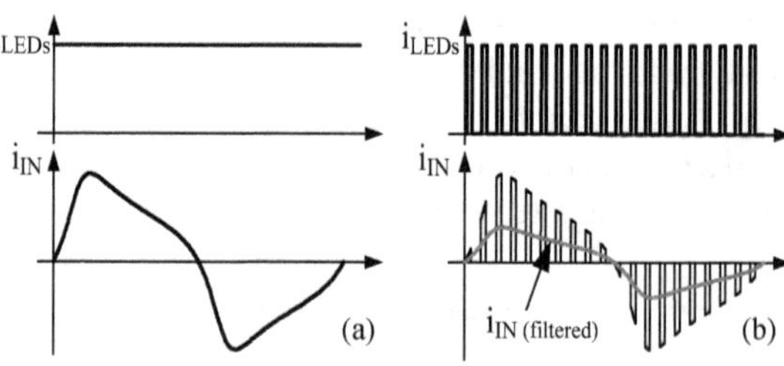

Figure 21. Current through the LEDs, i_{LEDs}, and line input current, i_{IN}, for a line period. (a) without PWM dimming; (b) with PWM dimming.

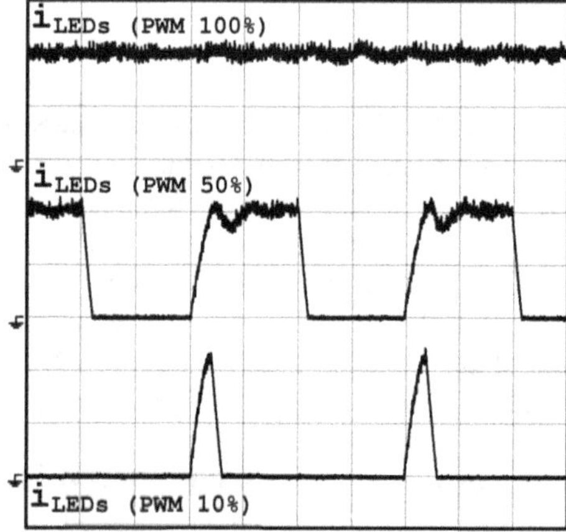

Figure 22. Experimental waveforms of the current through the LEDs for PWM dimmed operation of converter (PWM dimming 100%, 50% and 10%). All traces 500 mA/div, 500 μs/div.

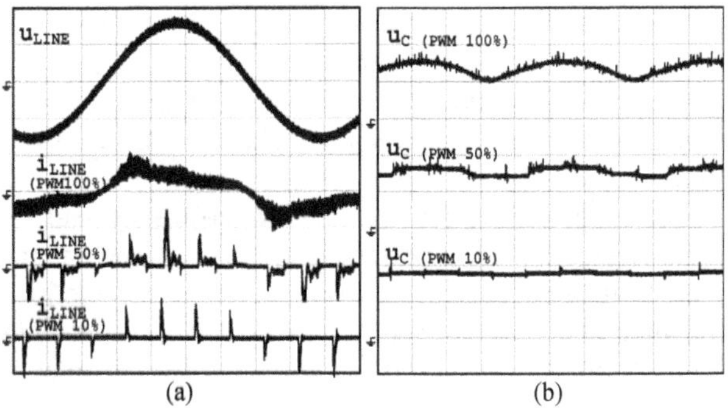

Figure 23. (a) Input AC line voltage, u_{LINE} (50 V/div), input AC line current, i_{LINE} (1 A/div), for different PWM dimming ratios (100%, 50% and 10%); time 2 ms/div. (b) DC link capacitor voltage, u_C (50 V/div), for different PWM dimming ratios (100%, 50% and 10%); time 2 ms/div.

7.2. AM Dimming

AM dimming scheme consists in changing the DC current level flowing through the LEDs. For this topology, it can be easily done by changing the peak current reference of the control stage, in the high frequency switching scheme. As the output current level decreases, the output power level also decreases. As the power flows through the output through the DC link capacitor, that is loaded from the input stage at twice the line frequency, a smaller power output yields to a smaller voltage ripple in the DC link capacitor voltage. This yields to an input current waveform with smaller harmonics, and hence the THD and the PF increase for higher AM dimming ratios. This can be observed in **Figures 24-26**, where the main waveforms of the proposed converter for AM diming ratios of 100%, 50% and 10%, respectively, are shown. It can be seen how the line input current is more sinusoidal as the diming ratio increases. It can also be seen how the voltage ripple in the DC link capacitor is also smaller for higher dimming ratios. Hence, this dimming scheme is selected for this application as the best option.

8. Design Considerations for Universal Input Voltage

This section deals with an analysis of the effect in the design parameters when considering Universal input voltage range in the proposed ballast. To carry out an effective comparison, it is necessary to explore which are the design parameters affected by this input margin increase. In fact, the lower limit remains constant at 115 V_{RMS} (–20%), while the higher voltage limit considered will be 230 V_{RMS} (+20%). The frequency range considered will be 50 - 60 Hz.

The main design parameters for American and Universal input voltage ranges are presented in **Table 3**.

The values of the magnetizing inductance of the primary side of the transformer, L_F, and the bulk DC capacitor, C, were calculated in (49) and (51) respectively for the minimum input voltage range, thus their design values are not affected by the input range increase. Analogously, the turns ratio can be calculated from (45) for the new input margin, but as the most restrictive condition comes from the smaller input voltage, this parameter also remains constant.

However, the maximum capacitor voltage depends on the maximum input voltage range, and thus this value increases significantly for the one calculated for American input range. A similar capacitor voltage plot (like the one depicted in **Figure 17**) can be calculated but for universal input voltage, yielding to an increase in the capacitor maximum voltage from 81 V to 130 V.

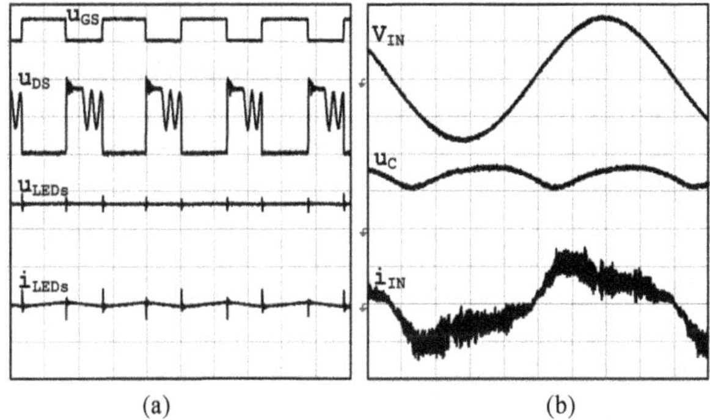

Figures 24. Experimental waveforms for full power operation of converter (AM dimming 100%). (a) Gate to source voltage, U_{GS} (20 V/div); drain to source voltage, U_{DS} (200 V/div); LEDs forward current, i_{LEDs} (500 mA/div) and LEDs voltage, u_{LEDs} (20 V/div); time 5 μs/div; (b) Input AC line voltage, u_{LINE} (100 V/div), input AC line current, i_{LINE} (500 mA/div), DC link capacitor voltage, u_C (50 V/div); time 2 ms/div.

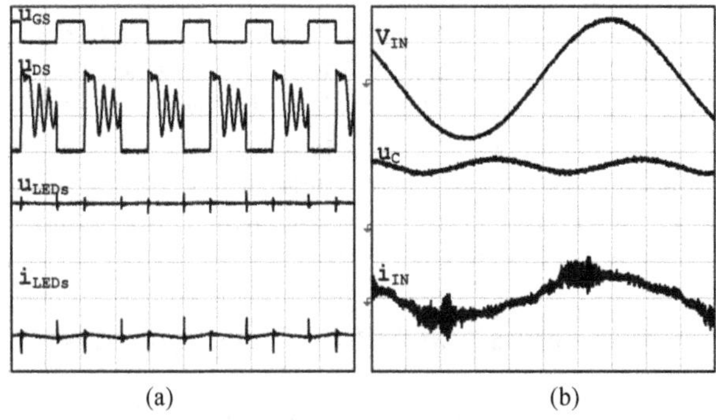

Figures 25. Experimental waveforms for 50% AM dimmed operation of converter (AM dimming 50%). (a) Gate to source voltage, U_{GS} (20 V/div); drain to source voltage, U_{DS} (200 V/div); LEDs forward current, i_{LEDs} (500 mA/div) and LEDs voltage, u_{LEDs} (20 V/div); time 5 μs/div; (b) Input AC line voltage, u_{LINE} (50 V/div), input AC line current, i_{LINE} (500 mA/div), DC link capacitor voltage, u_C (50 V/div); time 2 ms/div.

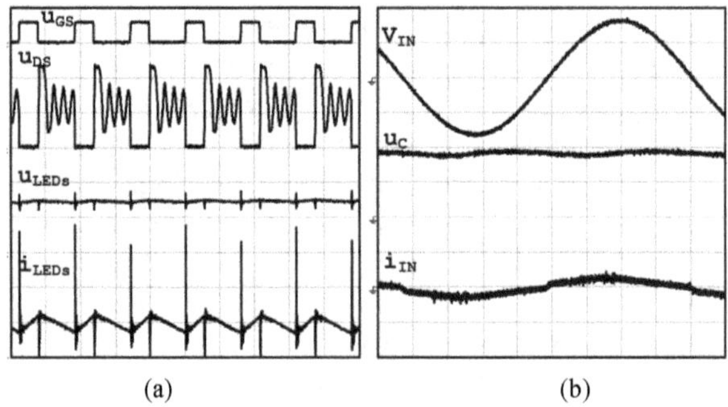

(a) (b)

Figures 26. Experimental waveforms for 10% AM dimmed operation of converter (AM dimming 10%). (a) Gate to source voltage, U_{GS} (20 V/div); drain to source voltage, U_{DS} (200 V/div); LEDs forward current, i_{LEDs} (200 mA/div) and LEDs voltage, u_{LEDs} (20 V/div); time 5 µs/div; (b) Input AC line voltage, u_{LINE} (50 V/div), input AC line current, i_{LINE} (500 mA/div), DC link capacitor voltage, u_C (50 V/div); time 2 ms/div.

Table 3. Design values for American and Universal input voltage range.

Input voltage range.	L_F	C	N_P/N_S	u_{C_MAX}	u_{SINT_MAX}	u_{D1AK_MAX}	u_{D2AK_MAX}
115 V_{RMS}(±20%), 60 Hz	420 µH	47 µF	4	81 V	520 V	438 V	81 V
115 V_{RMS} (−20%) - 230 V_{RMS}(+20%), 50 - 60 Hz.	420 µH	47 µF	4	130 V	898 V	767 V	130 V

Also, the peak limit voltage values of the switches depend on this input voltage, and thus the values of u_{SINT_MAX}, u_{D1AK_MAX} and u_{D2AK_MAX} can be recalculated from (53), (54) and (55) for this new voltage condition. The results of this calculations are presented in **Table 3**.

As can be seen, the obtained voltage ratings for the universal input voltage range, up to 900 V in the case of the integrated switch, are too high, even without considering the increase in these values that will provide the clamp voltage snubber at the primary side of the transformer. Thus, this Universal input range design is beyond the scope of this paper, and will be addressed in future developments.

9. Conclusions and Future Developments

A novel integrated ballast for driving power LEDs from AC mains has been presented, deeply analyzed, designed, built and tested. The proposed driver has only one controlled switch, thus obtaining a simpler and more cost-effective system. Also, the obtained value of capacitance and voltage rating of the DC capacitor, 47 µF/81 V, allows the use of a non-electrolytic device, which also increases the reliability of the whole ballast. The proposed driver also allows AM dimming very easily, which is enough for a number of applications with no special constraints in color rendering, which are the target uses for this converter (e.g. emergency lighting systems, street lighting, etc.).

The main drawbacks are the low efficiency and the high stresses of the electronic devices. Also, and although the input current fulfills the harmonic regulations, the harmonic distortion of this waveform is relatively high. Another drawback is the lack of galvanic isolation due the integration process, although this drawback is not as critical as it could be in other kind of lamps (for instance HID lamps, where very high input voltage pulses must be provided to the lamp).

Future developments include a deep study of the design for Universal input voltage range, as well as the circuit optimization to increase efficiency. There are significant losses due to the high current values at turn-off of the semiconductors. Operating the input stage in CCM would decrease those current stresses. In fact, this optimization of the efficiency has both design aspects and constructive aspects, which must be discussed in future works.

10. Acknowledgements

This work was supported by the Spanish Government, Innovation and Science Office (MCINN), under research grant no. DPI-2007-61522, project "BENAPI", and by the European Union through the ERFD Structural Funds (FEDER).

11. References

[1] M. Dyble, N. Narendran, A. Bierman and T. Klein, "Impact of Dimming White LEDs: Chromaticity Shifts Due to Different Dimming Methods," *5th International Conference on Solid State Lighting*, Bellingham, 1 August 2005.

[2] N. Narendran and Y. Gu, "Life of LED-Based White Light Sources," *IEEE Journal of Display Technology*, Vol. 1, No 1, 2005, pp. 167-171.

[3] J. Garcia, M. A. Dalla-Costa, J. Cardesin, J. M. Alonso and M. Rico-Secades, "Dimming of High-Brightness LEDs by Means of Luminous Flux Thermal Estimation," *IEEE Transactions on Power Electronics*, Vol. 24, No. 2, 2009, pp. 1107-1114.

[4] J. Bielecki, A. S. Jwania; F. El Khatib and T. Poorman, "Thermal Considerations for LED Components in an Automotive Lamp," *23rd Annual IEEE Semiconductor Thermal Measurement and Management Symposium*, San Jose, 18-22 March 2007, pp. 37-43.

[5] C. C. Chen, C. Y. Wu, Y. M. Chen and T. F. Wu, "Se-

quential Color LED Backlight Driving System for LCD Panels," *IEEE Transactions on Power Electronics*, Vol. 22, No. 3, 2007, pp. 919-925.

[6] M. Rico-Secades, A. J. Calleja, J. Ribas, E. L. Corominas, J. M. Alonso, J. Cardesín and J. García, "Evaluation of a Low-Cost Permanent Emergency Lighting System Based on High Efficiency LEDs," *IEEE Transactions on Industry Applications*, Vol. 41, No. 5, 2005, pp. 1386-1390.

[7] Y.-K. Lo, K.-H. Wu, K.-J. Pai and H.-J. Chiu, "Design and Implementation of RGB LED Drivers for LCD Backlight Modules," *IEEE Transactions on Industrial Electronics*, Vol. 56, No. 12, 2009, pp. 4862-4871.

[8] H.-J. Chiu, Y.-K. Lo, J.-T. Chen, S.-J. Cheng, C.-Y. Lin, and S.-C. Mou, "A High-Efficiency Dimmable LED Driver for Low-Power Lighting Applications," *IEEE Tran-sactions on Industrial Electronics*, Vol. 57, No. 2, 2010, pp. 735-743.

[9] K. Zhou, J. G. Zhang, S. Yuvarajan and D. F. Weng, "Quasi-Active Power Factor Correction Circuit for HB LED Driver," *IEEE Transactions on Power Electronics*, Vol. 23, No. 3, 2008, pp. 1410-1415.

[10] M. Rico-Secades, J. Garcia, J. Cardesin and A. J. Calleja, "Using Tapped Inductor Converters as LED Drivers," *Conference Record of the* 2006 *IEEE Industry Applications Conference* 41*st IAS Annual Meeting*, Tampa, 8-12 October 2006, pp. 1794-1800.

[11] X. Qu, S. Ch. Wong and Ch. K. Tse, "Isolated PFC Pre-Regulator for LED Lamps," *Proceedings of* 34*th Industrial Electronics Annual Conference*, Orlando, 10-13 November 2008, pp. 1980-1987.

[12] Y. X. Qin, H. S. H. Chung, D. Y. Lin and S. Y. R. Hui, "Current Source Ballast for high Power Lighting Emitting Diodes without Electrolytic Capacitor," *Proceedings of* 34*th Industrial Electronics Annual Conference*, Orlando, 10-13 November 2008, pp. 1968-1973,

[13] Y. Hu and M. M. Jovanovic, "LED Driver with Self-Adaptive Drive Voltage," *IEEE Transaction on Power Electronics*, Vol. 23, No. 6, 2008, pp. 3116-3125.

[14] Y. Fang; S.-H. Wong and L. L. Hok-Sun, "A Power Converter with Pulse-Level-Modulation Control for Driving High Brightness LEDs," *Proceedings of the Twenty-Fourth Annual IEEE Applied Power Electronics and Exposition Conference*, Washington DC, 15-19 February 2009, pp. 577-581.

[15] D. Rand, B. Lehman and A. Shteynberg, "Issues, Models and Solutions for Triac Modulated Phase Dimming of LED Lamps," *Proceedings of the IEEE Power Electronics Specialists Conference* 2007, Orlando, 17-21 June 2007, pp. 1398-1404.

[16] X. R. Xu and X. B. Wu, "High Dimming Ratio LED Driver with Fast Transient Boost Converter," *Proceedings of the IEEE Power Electronics Specialists Conference* 2008, Rhodes, 15-19 June 2008, pp. 4192-4195.

[17] N. Prathyusha and D. S. Zinger, "An Effective LED Dimming Approach," 2004 *IEEE Industry Applications Conference*, 39*th IAS Annual Meeting*, Seattle, 3-7 October 2004, pp. 1671-1676.

[18] D. Gacio, J. M. Alonso, J. Garcia, L. Campa, M. Crespo and M. Rico-Secades, "High Frequency PWM Dimming Technique for High Power Factor Converters in LED Lighting," *Proceedings of the Twenty-Fifth Annual IEEE Applied Power Electronics and Exposition Conference* 2010, Palm Springs, 21-25 February 2010, pp. 743-749.

[19] D. Gacio, J. Alonso, J. Garcia, L. Campa, M. Crespo Ramos and M. Rico-Secades, "PWM Series Dimming for Slow-Dynamics HPF LED Drivers: The High Frequency Approach," *IEEE Transactions on Industrial Electronics*, No. 99, p. 1.

[20] L. Gu, X. Ruan, M. Xu and K. Yao, "Means of Eliminating Electrolytic Capacitor in AC/DC Power Supplies for LED Lightings," *IEEE Transactions on Power Electronics*, Vol. 24, No. 5, 2009, pp. 1399-1408.

[21] J. Garcia, A. J. Calleja, E. L. Corominas, D. Gacio and J. Ribas, "Electronic Driver without Electrolytic Capacitor for Dimming High Brightness LEDs," 35*th Annual Conference of the IEEE Industrial Electronics Society*, Porto, 2-5 November 2009, pp. 3518-3513.

[22] J. Garcia, A. J. Calleja, E. L. Corominas, J. Ribas, L. Campa and R. E. Díaz, "Integrated Driver for Power LEDs," 36*th Annual Conference of the IEEE Industrial Electronics Society*, Glendale, 2-5 November 2010, pp. 2578-2583.

[23] Luxeon LXK2 white LED datasheet, DS51, 2006. http://www.lumileds.com.

Research on a High-Efficiency LED Driving Circuit Based on Buck Topology

Renbo Xu[1,2,3*], Hongjian Li[1,2], Yongzhi Li[4], Xiaomao Hou[3]
[1]*School of Materials Science and Engineering, Central South University, Changsha, China*
[2]*School of Physics Science and Technology, Central South University, Changsha, China*
[3]*Hunan Information Science Vocational College, Changsha, China*
[4]*College of Physics and Information Science, Hunan Normal University, Changsha, China*

Abstract

A high efficiency LED (Light Emitting Diode) driver based on Buck converter, which could operate under a wide AC input voltage range (85 V - 265 V) and drive a series of high power LEDs, is presented in this paper. The operation principles, power loss factors of the LED driver in this study are analyzed and discussed in detail and some effective ways to improve efficiency are proposed through system design considerations. To verify the feasibility, a laboratory prototype is also designed and tested for an LED lamp which consists of 16 LUMILEDS LEDs in series. Experimental results show that a high efficiency of 92% at I_o = 350 mA can be achieved and the studied driver might be practical for driving high power LEDs. In the last, the overall efficiency over 90% is gained through some experiments under variable input and output voltages and verifies the validity of the designed driver.

Keywords: LED Driver, Buck Type, High Efficiency, Universal Input Voltage

1. Introduction

Among the many artificial lighting sources, high power LED characterized by high luminous intensity, superior longevity, cost-effective and less environment impact, is one of the most competitive to replace the conventional incandescent lamp and fluorescent lamp and gradually becomes a commonly used solid-state lighting source in many lighting applications [1-3]. It has been extensively used in the offline lighting field, such as automotive illuminations, liquid crystal display (LCD) backlights and street lighting, where multiple strings of LED driving techniques are often needed. The increased popularity of high power LED has given a requirement for electronic engineers to propose a series of driving circuits with high efficiency and low-cost.

LED dimming control methods could be simply divided into two categories: analog dimming and pulse width modulation (PWM) dimming regulators [4-7]. Analog dimming method is not a good candidate due to colour variation, even though it is simple and cost effective. To avoid colour variation and get accurate current control over full range, PWM dimming regulators in which the pulse current is kept constant.

To research the overall efficiency of LED lighting, a PWM dimming method, Buck converter is chosen in this paper as shown in **Figure 1**, and the power dissipation factors are analyzed with all the particulars, then a detailed LED driver example with high power efficiency is designed and implemented. In addition to the integrated circuit(IC), the main components mainly includes a power MOS switch S, a Schottky diode D, an inductor L directly connected with the load LEDs and the current sampling resistor Rs. In fact, the major power dissipation of Buck converter is on these components. Next to make a detail analysis of them.

2. Operation Principle and Power Loss Analysis

During the time interval of state 1, the metal oxide semiconductor field effect transistor (MOS-FET) S is turned on, current flows through MOS switch S, input inductor L, storage capacitor C, the load LED strings and sampling resistor Rs. The power supply stores energy in the inductor L, the storage capacitor C and the free-wheeling diode

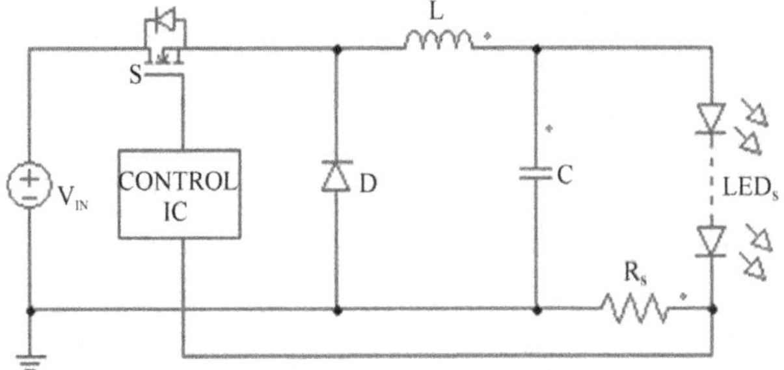

Figure 1. Circuit diagram of Buck converter.

D is off at the moment. During the time interval of state 2, the MOS switch S turns off. The LED strings power is provided by the storage capacitor C, and the energy stored in inductor L flows through the free-wheeling diode D simultaneously. Then the circuit proceeds back to stage 1 when the MOS switch *S* turns on again.

From the analysis it can be known that the power dissipation on the power switch *S* is described in following Equation (1):

$$P_{S(on)} = I_O^2 \times R_{S(on)} \times D \tag{1}$$

where $R_{S(on)}$ is conduction resistor of MOS switch, I_O is the LED strings current and D is the duty cycle of the power switch.

In fact, there is still some power dissipation in the MOS switch when it operates in high frequency. Especially when LED constant-current driving circuit is working in frequency more than 100 kHz, this power dissipation is quite substantial which can be expressed as follows [8]:

$$P_{S(high-freq)} = Q_{gs} \times V_{GS} \times f_s + \frac{1}{2} \times V_{IN} \times I_O \times (t_r + t_d) \times f_s \tag{2}$$

where Q_{gs} is the MOS gate-source charge and V_{GS} is the MOSFET gate drive voltage, V_{IN} is the input voltage, t_r, t_d are the needed time of MOS turn-on and turn-off respectively, f_s is the switching frequency. From the Equation (2), it is clear that the power dissipation is proportional to the switching frequency. Combining Equation (1) together with Equation (2), we can get the total power dissipation as described in Equation (3):

$$\begin{aligned} P_S &= P_{S(on)} + P_{S(high-freq)} \\ &= I_O^2 \times R_{S(on)} \times D + Q_{gs} \times V_{GS} \times f_s \\ &\quad + \frac{1}{2} \times V_{IN} \times I_O \times (t_r + t_d) \times f_s \end{aligned} \tag{3}$$

in order to decrease the total power dissipation, on one hand we should choose a MOS switch with a small conduction resistance, on the other hand the high-frequency characteristic of MOS switch should be taken into consideration if the driving circuit operates in a high frequency.

Inductor L in the Buck converter which is connected directly to the load LED strings plays an important role of energy storage and transformation. As an LED constant current driver, the Buck converter usually operates in continuous current conduction mode (CCM) so that most of the system power dissipation is consumed on the inductor L. Similar to other switched-mode power supplies, the inductor power dissipation can be divided into two parts: iron loss and copper loss [9,10]. Copper loss is determined by the output current and inductor DC resistance, and iron loss caused by eddy current is determined by the switching frequency. The total power consumption of the inductor can be expressed as follows:

$$P_L = I_O^2 \times R_{L(DC)} + P_c \tag{4}$$

where $R_{L(DC)}$ is inductor DC resistance, P_c is iron loss of the inductor.

In the LED constant current driver circuit, using a large inductor can effectively reduce the ripple current flowing through the LED strings [11]. However, a problem arises that it would bring greater power loss due to a greater inductor DC resistance. Another method to decrease the ripple current is to parallel a large capacitor with the output LED strings [12,13]. But large capacitance means slow frequency response which is not suitable in high precision control requirement occasion.

In the Buck converter, the function of the diode *D* is to provide a free-wheeling path for the inductor current when MOS switch turns off. Because of high working frequency, a reverse fast recovery Schottky diode has been chosen. When MOS switch is turned-on, the Schottky diode is reverse biased and there is no power dissipation. When the MOS switch is turned-off, the power consumption of free-wheeling diode can be derived by:

$$P_D = I_O \times V_{D(on)} \times (1 - D) \tag{5}$$

where $V_{D(on)}$ is the corresponding forward voltage drop when following through the LED current I_O.

It could be seen from the Equation (5) that the diode power dissipation is proportional to the forward voltage drop and decreases with the duty cycle increasing. As a matter of fact, the control chip has a limited output duty cycle which makes the diode a minimum power loss. Another way to reduce the power consumption is synchronous rectifier technique [14,15]. The diode is replaced by a MOS switch with a low resistance, and the power loss is significantly decreased even if the LED output current is high. However, the synchronous rectification is bound to bring a complicated driving circuit, which needs a balance between performance and cost.

The last system efficiency factor is the driving chip and the sampling resistor Rs. With the development of LED driving IC, the chip commonly adopts a low comparison voltage about 200 mV, so the power consumption of the sampling resistor is not great.

3. System Design Considerations

In order to design an efficient LED constant-current driver, a certain process is given as follows about how to select components.

According to the LED constant driving current requirements, a suitable driving chip and a sampling resistor should be selected. Referring to the relevant LED materials of manufacturers, we can get the output voltage under rated current. As mentioned in Equation (6), the corresponding minimum input voltage can be chosen when the chip operating in the allowed maximum duty cycle.

$$D = \frac{V_O}{V_{IN}} \tag{6}$$

If the chip has no built-in MOS switch, a external MOS switch is needed to choose. Generally speaking, the higher voltage endurance is, the worse the other corresponding characteristics is. Therefore, according to the working environment we should choose a suitable MOS switch with an appropriate voltage endurance and with the conduction resistance and the gate-source charge as an important choice standard. Next to find out the required inductance value calculated by the Equation (7) [16]:

$$L = V_O \times T \times (1 - D)/\Delta i \tag{7}$$

where T is a cycle time of Buck converter, and Δi is the allowed maximum ripple current. The inductor should have small DC induction resistance and meet with the frequency requirement. Then, decide whether to use an output capacitor according to the requirements of PWM dimming system and circuit volume. In the case of meeting the ripple current requirements, we should choose a small inductance due to small power consumption.

A suitable diode should be selected according to the reverse bias voltage endurance and its frequency response should be fast enough. Generally speaking, a Schottky diode with low forward voltage drop can be used in most situations blew 100 V. Otherwise, we should choose a fast diode with a high forward voltage drop and a high reverse bias voltage endurance.

4. Example Design and Experimental Results

In this section, an LED constant current driver with high power efficiency is designed and implemented according to the following configuration:

- Input voltage: AC 85 - 265 V (nominal 220 V)
- LED string voltage: DC 30 - 60 V
- LED current: 350 mA
- Expected efficiency: 90%

An LED constant current Buck topology driving IC SL221 from SYNCOAM with a input DC supply voltage range from 9 V to 550 V is chosen as a controller and the schematic diagram shown in **Figure 2**. And it is used to drive an LED string with 16 LUMILEDS LED with a 3.3 V working voltage.

The AC 220 V input voltage is converted to $V_{IN} = 310\text{ V}$ after following through the rectifier bridge and the filtering capacitors. The system output voltage is $V_O = n \times V_{LED} = 52.8\text{ V}$ and the duty cycle is 0.17 calculated by Equation (6). High switching frequency will reduce the size of the inductor L, but it will increase the circuit's switch dissipation. The oscillator frequency of SL221 is from 20 kHz to 150 kHz and we choice a typical constant switching frequency 40 kHz. The timing resistor should be 620 kΩ and connect to the ground referring to SL221 manual. During the MOSFET switch is on, the gate is charged by high-frequency current pulse. And in order to maintain stability of the internal power supply voltage, C3 a typical capacitance value 2.2 uF,16 V is recommended.

Next to choose the capacitance values of C1 and C2. In order to satisfy the stability requirements at constant switching frequency, the maximum LED string voltage must be less than the half of the minimum input voltage. The minimum input voltage is shown in Equation (8):

$$V_{IN(\min)} = 2 \times V_{O(\max)} = 120\text{ V} \tag{8}$$

The capacitance value C1 should be calculated at the minimum AC input voltage, and the nominal voltage should be larger than the input peak voltage as shown in the following Equations (9) and (10):

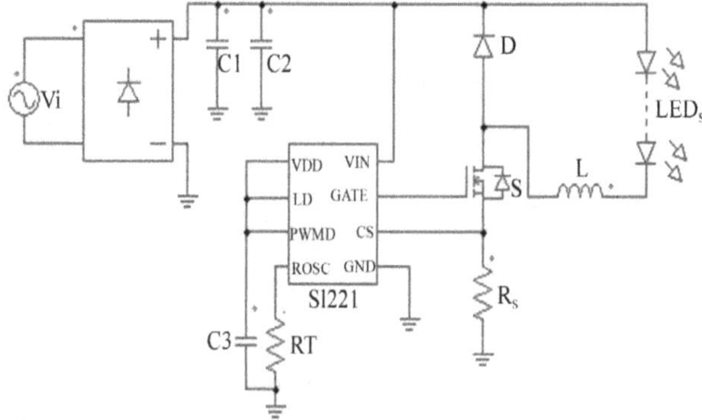

Figure 2. Schematic diagram of the studied LED driver.

$$C_1 \geq \frac{I_{O(\max)} \times V_{O(\max)}}{\left(2\times V_{i(\min)}^2 - V_{IN(\min)}^2\right)\times f_s \times \eta} \Rightarrow C_1 \geq 11.67\ \mu\text{F} \quad (9)$$

$$V_{C_1(\max)} \geq \sqrt{2}\times V_{i(\max)} \Rightarrow V_{C_1(\max)} \geq 375\ \text{V} \quad (10)$$

From the mentioned above, we choose a electrolytic capacitor with 33 uF, 450 V. The stability of the electrolytic capacitor is good. However, it is not suitable for high frequency ripple current absorption which is generated by the Buck converter due to large ESR (Equivalent Series Resistance). So a metalized polypropylene capacitor in parallel with the electrolytic capacitor is used to absorb the high frequency ripple current. The high frequency capacitance 0.47 uF and withstanding voltage 400 V is determined by the following equation:

$$C_2 \geq \frac{0.25\times I_{O(\max)}}{\left(0.05\times V_{IN(\min)}\right)\times f_s} \Rightarrow C_2 \geq 0.365\ \mu\text{F} \quad (11)$$

Next to calculate the inductance value which is determined by the permissible ripple current and we assume that the existence of LED ripple current is allowed ±15% (total ripple is 30%). During the MOSFET is off, the inductor supplies energy to the LED string as shown in Equation (12):

$$E_L = V_{\text{LED}} = V_{O(\max)} = L\frac{\text{d}i}{\text{d}t} \Rightarrow L = V_{O(\max)}\frac{\text{d}t}{\text{d}i} \quad (12)$$

where $di = 0.3\times I_{o,\max}$ is the ripple current, $\text{d}t$ is the off time described as follows:

$$dt = \frac{1-\dfrac{V_{O(\max)}}{\sqrt{2}\times V_{i(rated)}}}{f_s} \quad (13)$$

From Equations (12) and (13), the inductance value L can be represented as the following equation:

$$L = \frac{V_{O(\max)}\times\left(1-\dfrac{V_{O(\max)}}{\sqrt{2}\times V_{i(rated)}}\right)}{0.3\times I_{O(\max)}\times f_s} \quad (14)$$

The standard inductance value 4.7 mH is selected which is larger than the calculated value, so the ripple current would be less than 30%. The DC resistance is 3.2 Ω and the inductor dissipation can be derived by the Equation (4).

MOSFET peak voltage is equal to the maximum input voltage and the safety margin is 50% described as follows:

$$V_{\text{MOSFET}} = 1.5\times\left(\sqrt{2}\times V_{i(\max)}\right) = 562\ \text{V} \quad (15)$$

The maximum RMS of MOSFET current depends on the maximum duty cycle, so the nominal current can be expressed as:

$$I_{\text{MOSFET}} \approx I_{o(\max)}\times\sqrt{0.17} = 0.144\ \text{A} \quad (16)$$

In order to get the minimum switching power dissipation, STD2NM60 with rated voltage 600 V and rated current 2 A is selected. Refer to its manual, the conduction resistance is 2.8 Ω, $t_r = 8\ \text{ns}$, $t_d = 25\ \text{ns}$ and $Q_{gs} = 1.8\ \text{n}C$, $V_{GS} = 7.5\ \text{V}$.

Next to select the diode. Its nominal peak voltage should be equal to MOSFET switch peak voltage and diode average current described as follows:

$$V_D = V_{\text{MOSFET}} = 562\ \text{V} \quad (17)$$

$$I_D = 0.83\times I_{O(\max)} = 0.291\ \text{A} \quad (18)$$

So we can choose the fast diode STTH1R06 with a forward voltage drop 1 V, rated voltage 600 V and rated current 1 A, and the switching power dissipation would be low due to the short reverse recovery time 25 ns.

The relationship between the output current and the sensing resistor can be expressed as:

$$R_s = \frac{0.25}{1.15\times I_{O(\max)}} \Rightarrow R_s = 0.621\ \Omega \quad (19)$$

If the internal threshold voltage is 0.25 V, the result of the above equation is correct. Otherwise, LD pin voltage should be used to replace the internal threshold voltage. In this case, an appropriate standard resistance 0.62 Ω is selected.

From all the above equations, the theory calculated results are: $P_S = 0.130\ \text{W}$, $P_L = 0.412\ \text{W}$, $P_D = 0.291\ \text{W}$, $P_{IC} = 0.477\ \text{W}$, $P_{Rs} = 0.076\ \text{W}$. Combining all the power loss, the theory total power loss is described as:

$$\begin{aligned} P_{loss(\text{theory})} &= P_S + P_L + P_D + P_{IC} + P_{Rs} \\ &= 1.386\ \text{W} \end{aligned} \quad (20)$$

In order to verify the feasibility, a laboratory prototype is designed and tested as shown in **Figure 3**. The experimental results are expressed as follows:

$$P_{in} = 17.38\ \text{W},\ P_{\text{LEDs}} = 15.97\ \text{W},$$
$$P_{loss(real)} = 1.41\ \text{W},\ \eta = 92\% \quad (21)$$

From the theory and experimental results, it can be seen that the theory power loss is almost equal with the measured power loss and the main power dissipation is on diode *D*, inductor *L* and IC due to high input voltage and the voltage error value between output and input. However, the power dissipation on the MOS switch is not large because of small duty cycle.

In order to confirm the LED driver's universal validity, a series of experiments under variable input and output voltages are tested, and the efficiencies are shown in **Figure 4**. It is clear that the system efficiency is over the expected value 90%.

Figure 3. Photograph of the tested prototype driving system.

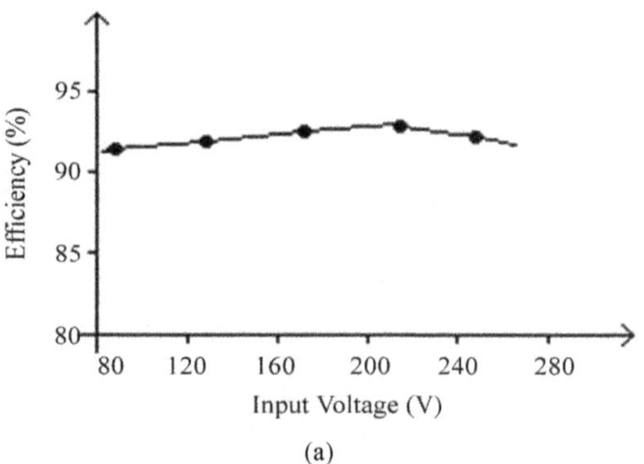

(a)

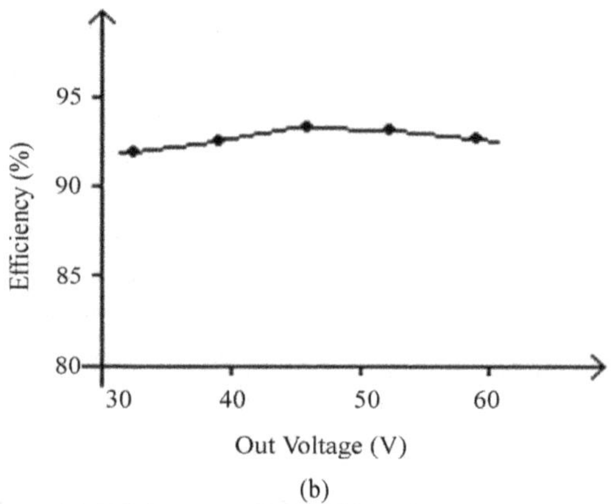

(b)

Figure 4. Measured efficiency vs. input and output voltages. (a) Measured efficiency vs. input voltage; (b) Measured efficiency vs. output voltage.

5. Conclusions

LED constant current drive circuit efficiency is determined by several factors, and these factors are interrelated and influenced. To optimize and improve the efficiency of the driving system, the circuit performance and the appropriate components selections must be taken into consideration. In this paper, a high efficiency Buck LED driver with AC input voltage range from 85 V to 265 V, which could drive an LED lamp consists of 16 LUMILEDS LEDs, is designed and tested. The measured results on a laboratory prototype show a high efficiency of 92% at $I_o = 350$ mA. Next, a series of experiments results under variable input and output voltages show that the efficiency is over 90% and reach the design requirements.

6. References

[1] Y. K. Cheng and K. W. E. Cheng, "General Study for Using LED to replace Traditional Lighting Devices," *2nd International Conference on Power Electronics Systems and Applications*, Hong Kong, 12-14 November 2006, pp. 173-177.

[2] E.-W. Wu, T.-Fu. Wu, J.-R. Tsai, Y.-M. Chen and C.-C. Chen, "Multistring LED Backlight Driving System for LCD Panels with Color Sequential Display and Area Control," *IEEE Transactions on Industrial Electronics*, Vol. 54, No. 10, 2008, pp. 3791-3800.

[3] M. Rico-Secades, A. J. Calleja, J. Ribas, E. L. Corominas, J. M. Alonso, J. Cardesin and J. Garcia-Garcia, "Evaluation of a Low-Cost Permanent Emergency Lighting System Based on High-Efficiency LEDs," *IEEE Transactions on Industry Applications*, Vol. 41, No. 5, 2005, pp. 1386-1390.

[4] K. H. Loo, W.-K. Lun, S.-C. Tan, Y. M. Lai and C. K. Tse, "On Driving Techniques for LEDs: Toward a Generalized Methodology," *IEEE Transactions on Power Electronics*, Vol. 24, No. 12, 2009, pp. 2967-2976.

[5] M. Nishika, Y. Ishizuka, H. Matsuo, *et al.*, "An LED Drive Circuit with Constant Output Current Control and Constant Luminance Control," *28th Telecommunications Energy Conference*, Providence, September 2006, pp. 1-6.

[6] H. V. D. Broeck, G. Sauerlander and M. Wendt, "Power Driver Topologies and Control Schemes for LEDs," *Twenty Second Annual IEEE of Applied Power Electronics Conference*, Anaheim, 25 February-1 March 2007, pp. 1319-1325.

[7] F.-F. Ma, W.-Z. Chen and J.-C. Wu, "A Monolithic Current-Mode Buck Converter with Advanced Control and Protection Circuits," *IEEE Transactions on Power Electronics*, Vol. 22, No. 5, 2007, pp. 1836-1846.

[8] H.-J. Chiu, Y.-K. Lo, J.-T. Chen, S.-J. Cheng, C.-Y. Lin and S.-C. Mou, "A high-Efficiency Dimmable LED Driver for Low-Power Lighting Applications," *IEEE Transactions on Industrial Electronics*, Vol. 57, No. 2, 2010, pp. 735-743.

[9] D. Gacio, J. M. Alonso, A. J. Calleja, J. Garcia and M. Rico-Secades, "A Universal-Input Single-Stage High-Power-Factor Power Supply for HB-LEDs Based on Integrated Buck-Flyback Converter," *Twenty-Fourth Annual IEEE of Applied Power Electronics Conference and Exposition*, Washington, DC, 15-19 February 2009 pp. 570-576.

[10] J. M. Alonso and M. A. Dalla Costa, "Integrated Buck-Flyback Converter as a High-Power-Factor Off-Line Power Supply," *IEEE Transactions on Industrial Elec-*

tronics, Vol. 55, 2009, pp. 1090-1100.

[11] J. A. Villarejo, J. Sebastian, F. Soto and E. de Jodar, "Optimizing the Design of Single-Stage Power-Factor Correctors," *IEEE Transactions on Industrial Electronics*, Vol. 54, No. 3, 2007, pp. 1472-1482.

[12] B. Wang, X. Ruan, K. Yao and M. Xu, "A Method of Reducing the Peak-to-Average Ratio of LED Current for Electrolytic Capacitor-Less AC-DC Drivers," *IEEE Transactions on Power Electronics*, Vol. 25, No. 3, 2010, pp. 592-601.

[13] L. Zhao and A. Q. Zhu, "Design of Energy-Saving Intelligent LED Illumination System," *Semiconductor Technology*, Vol. 33, No. 2, 2008, pp. 137-140.

[14] W. Lin, H. Song, Z. Y. Lu and G. Hua, "A High Efficiency Gate-Driving Scheme of Synchronous Rectifiers in Wide-Input-Voltage-Range CCM Flyback Converter," 37*th IEEE Power Electronics Specialists Conference*, Jeju, 18-22 June 2006, pp. 1-6.

[15] M. Schmid, D. Kuebrich, M. Weiland, and T. Duerbaum, "Evaluation on the Efficiency of Power LEDs Driven with Currents Typical to Switch Mode Power Supplies," *Conference Record of the* 2007 *IEEE Industry Applications Conference*, New Orleans, 23-27 September 2007, pp. 1135-1140.

[16] Y. Hu and M. M. Jovanovic, "LED Driver with Self-Adaptive Drive Voltage," *IEEE Transactions on Power Electronics*, Vol. 23, No. 6, 2008, pp. 3116-3125.

21

Single-Stage Vernier Time-to-Digital Converter with Sub-Gate Delay Time Resolution

Chin-Hsin Lin, Marek Syrzycki
School of Engineering Science Simon Fraser University, Burnaby, Canada

Abstract

This paper presents a single-stage Vernier Time-to-Digital Converter (VTDC) that utilizes the dynamic-logic phase detector. The zero dead-zone characteristic of this phase detector allows for the single-stage VTDC to deliver sub-gate delay time resolution. The single-stage VTDC has been designed in 0.13 μm CMOS technology. The simulation results demonstrate a linear input-output characteristic for input dynamic range from 0 to 1.6 ns with a time resolution of 25 ps.

Keywords: Vernier Time-to-Digital Converter, Dynamic-Logic Phase Frequency Detector

1. Introduction

The Vernier Time-to-Digital Converter (VTDC) is a circuit that has been commonly used to provide on-chip timing measurement with fine resolution. These circuits are being implemented in PLL-based frequency synthesis systems [1,2], for on-chip PLL jitter measurement [3,4], and for time-of-flight measurement units in particle physics and medical imaging, such as Positron-Emission Tomography (PET) imaging [5]. In all these applications the adaptation of the Vernier method allows to achieve sub-gate delay time resolution. Despite this fine time resolution characteristic, the conventional VTDC still has some disadvantages due to the linear structure of the Vernier Delay Line (VDL), since the length of the VDL determines the measurement range of the VTDC. Hence, increasing the measurement range will increase the chip area and the power consumption of the circuit. Moreover, since the measurement accuracy of VTDC depends on the matching of the delay cells, the mismatches in the VDL delay cells lead to differential non-linearity (DNL) and integral non-linearity (INL) errors. Although careful layout techniques can help to minimize these mismatches, these problems cannot be completely eliminated in the design of VTDC. In order to improve the time resolution, the TDC architecture has evolved from multistage VDL [3,6] to 2-dimensional [7] and 3-dimensional [8] delay-space scheme, and to the Δ-Σ architecture [9], leading to a dramatic increase in circuit complexity. However, the increased complexity makes the circuits more susceptible to process variation. In order to eliminate the problems caused by the large structures of VDL, single-stage VTDC designs have been proposed [4]. In a single-stage VTDC circuit, the linear VDL has been replaced by a single Vernier stage that consists of two triggerable oscillators featuring different oscillation periods, T_s and T_f (**Figure 1**).

The input signals of the single-stage VTDC, START and STOP, are used to trigger oscillators. When the START signal arrives at the single-stage VTDC, the slow oscillator is triggered and starts to oscillate with a period of T_s. On the arrival of the STOP signal, the fast oscillator is activated to oscillate with a period of T_f, and the counter starts to count the number of its oscillations. After both oscillators have been triggered, the phase difference between signals ST_s and ST_f is initially equal T_{in}. Since T_f is smaller than T_s, the phase difference between ST_f and ST_s gets reduced each cycle by an oscillation period difference of $(T_s - T_f)$, and the signal edge of ST_f gradually catches up with ST_s. When these two signal edges are coincident, the phase detector signal will disable the counter. The input phase difference, T_{in}, can be determined using the following equation:

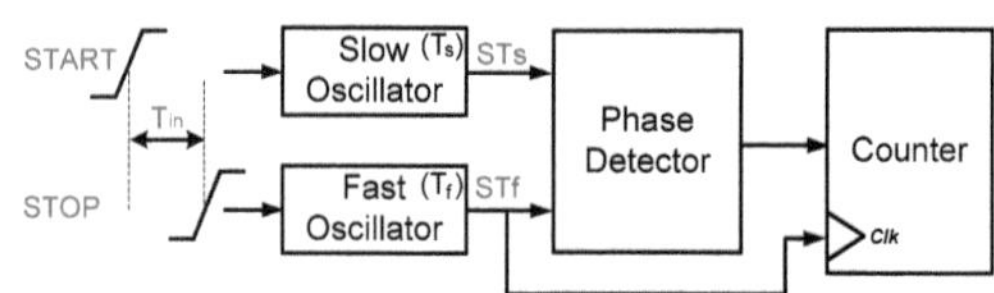

Figure 1. Concept of a single-stage Vernier Time-to-Digital Converter [4].

$$T_{in} = \left(T_s - T_f\right) \times \text{CNT} \quad (1)$$

where CNT is the number of oscillation cycles counted by the counter. The performance of the single-stage VTDC surpasses the conventional VTDC in measurement accuracy, chip size, and power consumption. However, the measurement resolution of a single-stage VTDC is limited by the phase detectors' performance. The resolution of a single-stage VTDC cannot be smaller than the minimum detectable phase error of its phase detector. The measurement range of the single-stage VTDC is also limited by the detection range of the phase detector. Although the use of single-stage VTDC alleviates the component mismatch problems in the conventional VTDC, the single-stage VTDC can be still unable to achieve sub-gate delay time resolution due to the limitations of the adopted phase detector [4]. This paper presents a single-stage VTDC with a dynamic-logic phase detector that has an extended phase detection range and zero dead-zone characteristics, allowing for reliable sub-gate delay time resolution.

This paper is organized as follows. Section II describes the single-stage VTDC with classic register type phase detectors. The design details of the single-stage VTDC with a dynamic-logic phase detector proposed in this work are presented in Section III. The simulation results are in Section IV and Section V provides conclusions and a summary.

2. Single-Stage Vernier Time-to-Digital Converter with Classic Register Type Phase Detector

A single-stage VTDC is the VTDC that utilizes two triggerable oscillators with a precise oscillation frequency difference to replace the VDL in the conventional VTDC. In the previously reported implementation of the single-stage VTDC [4], the classic phase detector with two D-type registers and an AND gate has been utilized in to control the timing measurement process (**Figure 2**). The phase detector keeps track of the history of the phase difference between two oscillators and stops the measurement process once ST_f begins to lead ST_s. On the first rising ST_f edge after the rising edge of ST_s, the output of the first register Q1 goes high. On the following rising edge of ST_f, the second register keeps the value of Q1 and switches Q2 to high. When the signal edge of ST_f catches up with ST_s, the output QB1 rises and switches the output of the AND gate to generate the Phase Detected signal, as shown in **Figure 3**. The Phase Detected signal is fed to the counter where it stops the time measurement process.

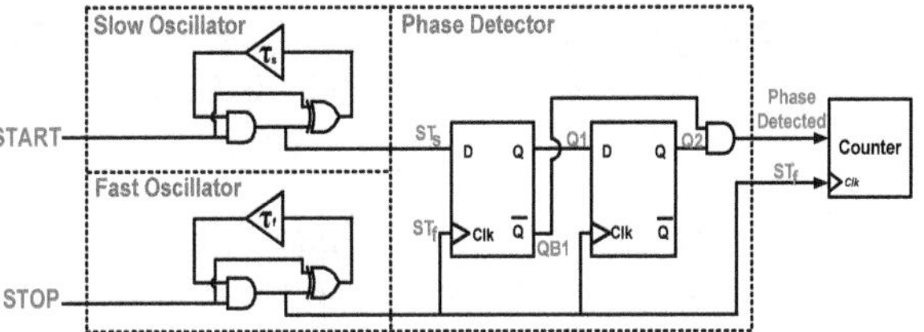

Figure 2. Single-stage VTDC with a classic two-register phase detector [4].

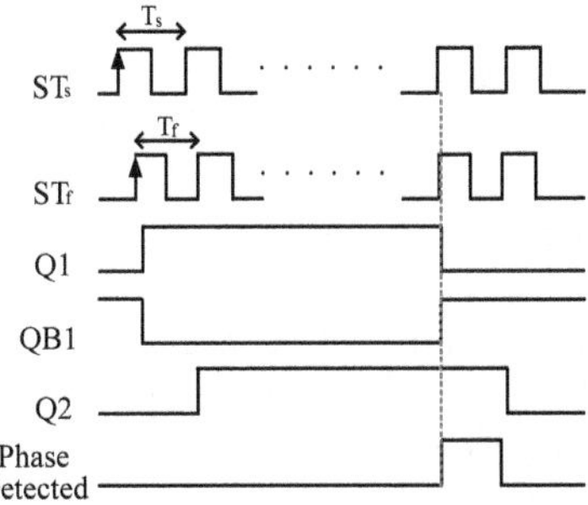

Figure 3. Timing diagram of the correct phase detection [4].

The classic two-register phase detection mechanism relies on the proper operation of D-type register. However, if the time difference between the rising edges of Clock and Data signals violates the setup time constraint of the registers, the outputs of the registers will not be correct. This problem is generally referred as meta-stability [10]. In order to prevent the meta-stability, the Data signal should be held steady for certain amount of time before the Clock event, and the minimum value of this time constraint is called a setup time. The meta-stability is likely to happen in the classic two-register phase detector, when the ST_f signal catches up with ST_s signal and the phase difference between these two signals is smaller than the required setup time. The unpredictable outputs of the registers will further cause the phase detector unable to stop the measurement process accurately. Therefore, the requirement for the non-zero setup time in the classic two-register phase detector is equivalent to the dead-zone characteristic of the phase detector. Due to the dead-zone characteristic, the single-stage VTDC designed with a classic two-register phase detector will feature a serious limitation on the time measurement resolution. The single-stage VTDC with the two-register phase detector built in 0.18 μm CMOS technology has been reported to achieve only a 54.5 ps measurement resolution [4].

Hence, it becomes evident that any further improvements in the time resolution of the single-stage VTDC would require the using of the phase detector that is not limited by the meta-stability error and thus eliminates the dead-zone in the phase detector.

3. The Single-Stage Vernier Time-to-Digital Converter with Dynamic-Logic Phase Detector

3.1. The Architecture of the Single-Stage VTDC with the Dynamic-Logic Phase Detector

The new single-stage VTDC (**Figure 4**) exploits the concept of the single-stage Vernier circuit, similar to the circuit proposed by [4]. In order to further improve the measurement resolution of the single-stage VTDC, a dynamic-logic phase detector with zero dead-zone is proposed in this work. The dynamic-logic Delayed-Input-Pulse Phase Frequency Detector (DIP-PFD) is known to have zero dead-zone and an extended detection range [11]. Therefore it is a promising candidate to improve the time measurement resolution of the VTDC. The proposed single-stage VTDC (**Figure 4**) is composed of two triggerable ring oscillators, the dynamic-logic phase detector, and the counter. The functional blocks of the single-stage VTDC are described below.

3.2. Triggerable Voltage-Controlled Ring Oscillators

The triggerable voltage-controlled ring oscillators are built similarly to the circuit proposed by [6]. However, for the simplicity, we do not use Phase-Locked Loops (PLL) to stabilize the oscillator frequencies. The triggerable ring oscillators have been designed using voltage controlled delay cells and NAND gates, as shown in **Figure 5**. Instead of generating different oscillation frequencies by using PLLs [6], the different oscillation frequencies are generated by using voltage-controlled delay cells. This solution is sufficient for the proof of the concept and also provides a degree of controllability to the time measurement resolution.

The NAND gate is used to accommodate the triggering signal, START or STOP. When the triggering signal is high, the NAND gate operates as an inverter closing the feedback loop, and creating the conditions for oscillations to take place. When the triggering signal is low, the NAND gate deactivates the feedback loop and stops the circuit from oscillating. The schematic of the triggerable voltage-controlled oscillator is shown in **Figure 6**.

The slow and fast triggerable voltage-controlled oscillators have the same architecture. The different oscillation frequencies are achieved by applying different control voltages. The control voltage of the fast oscillator is connected to the V_{DD} allowing a fast oscillation frequency. Meanwhile, the control voltage of the slow oscillator is connected to a lower externally controlled voltage, producing a slower but tunable oscillation frequency (**Figure 7**). The slow oscillator features a tunable oscillation period of 4.47 ns down to 2.61 ns that depends on the control voltage within the 0.5 V to 1.2 V range, while the fast oscillator has a steady oscillation period of 2.61 ns. In order to achieve a measurement resolution of 25 ps, the oscillation period of the slow oscillator is kept at 2.635 ns by applying the control voltage around 1.1 V.

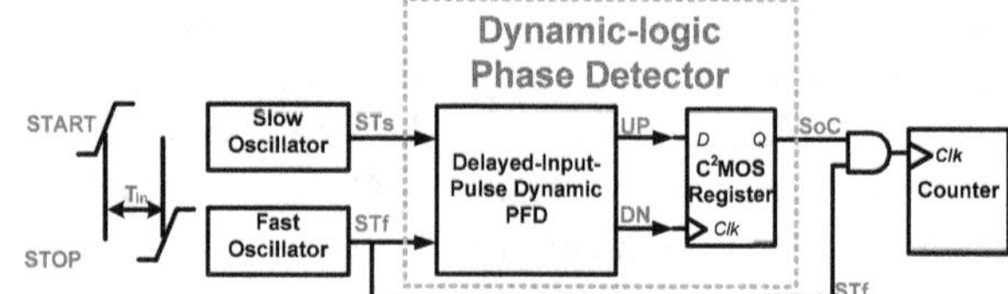

Figure 4. Single-stage VTDC with dynamic-logic phase detector.

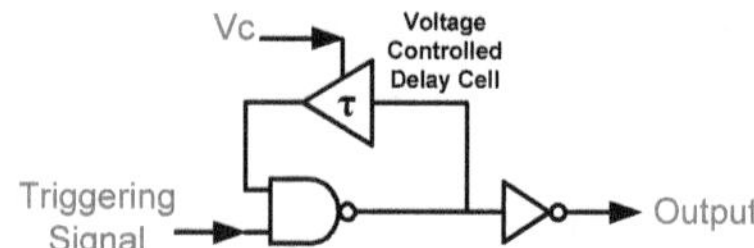

Figure 5. Concept of the triggerable voltage-controlled oscillator.

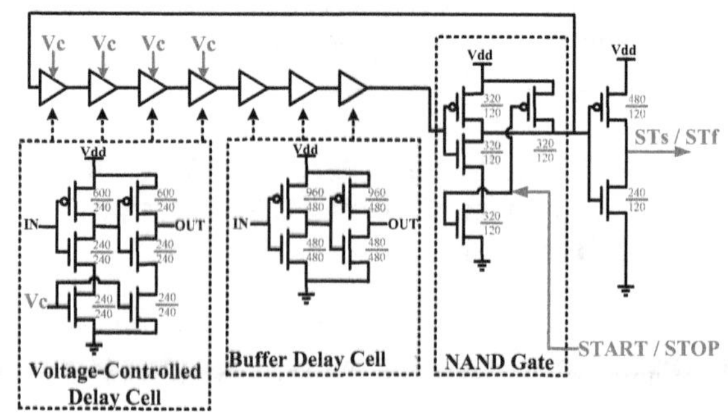

Figure 6. Schematic of the triggerable voltage-controlled oscillator.

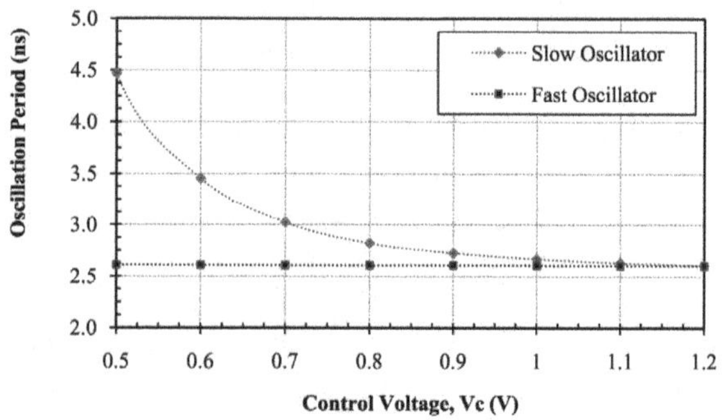

Figure 7. Oscillation periods of the voltage-controlled oscillators versus control voltage.

3.3. Dynamic-Logic Phase Detector

The dynamic-logic phase detector is a two stage phase detector constructed with a Delayed-Input-Pulse Dynamic Phase Frequency Detector (DIP-PFD) [11] followed by a C^2MOS register (**Figure 8**). The dynamic-logic phase detector compares the phase difference between the ST_s and the ST_f signals and generates the Start-of-Conversion signal (SoC) to control the measurement process.

The first stage of the dynamic-logic phase detector is the Delayed-Input Pulse Phase-Frequency Detector (DIP-PFD) proposed in [11]. It has been chosen because of its zero dead-zone and extended detection range characteristics. The PFD (**Figure 9**) compares the phases and frequencies of the input signals, andgenerates the UP and DN error pulses based on the phase and frequency difference between the input signals.

In this DIP-PFD, when the ST_s and ST_f signals are low, the U1 and D1 nodes are precharged high. When ST_s rises, the UPb node is discharged, producing the UP pulse. On the arrival of the rising edge of ST_f, the DNb node is pulled low, generating the DN pulse. When both outputs UP and DN are high, the U1 and D1 node will be pulled low, causing the UPb and DNb nodes to go high. This condition will deactivate the UP and DN pulses and reset the PFD. The difference in the pulse width between the UP and DN signals is therefore equal to the phase difference between ST_s and ST_f. Since the dynamic-logic PFD uses its own output signals directly to reset itself, there is virtually no dead-zone in this design. The DIP-PFD was simulated with the ring oscillators presented in the previous section. The outputs of the ring oscillators have been connected to the DIP-PFD to verify the dead-zone characteristic. The triggerable ring oscillators were triggered by two rising signal edges with a phase difference of 500 ps. The phase difference between ST_s and ST_f was gradually decreasing (by 25 ps in each oscillation cycle), finally reaching zero in the 21st cycle. The simulation result (**Figure 10**) shows that the DIP-PFD is capable of detecting phase error in a single picosecond range. This makes the DIP-PFD a good solution to eliminate the dead-zone of the phase detector in single-stage VTDCs.

The second stage of the dynamic-logic phase detector (**Figure 8**) is a C^2MOS register. The error signals, UP and DN, generated by the DIP-PFD are connected to a C^2MOS register (**Figure 11**). The register is used to sample the UP signal by the DN signal as the clock. In the case when the UP signal leads the DN signal, the C^2MOS register will generate SoC signal to enable the counter clock. When ST_f catches up to ST_s, the UP and DN signals will overlap each other. The Data input signal of the C^2MOS register will change at the same time as the Clock signal so that the output signal, SoC, will fall to deactivate the counter clock (**Figure 12**).

However, since the required setup time of the C^2MOS register is sensitive to process variation, the SoC signal may remain high for additional oscillation cycles. This will result a minor time offset to the time measurement. This time offset can be easily determined and removed

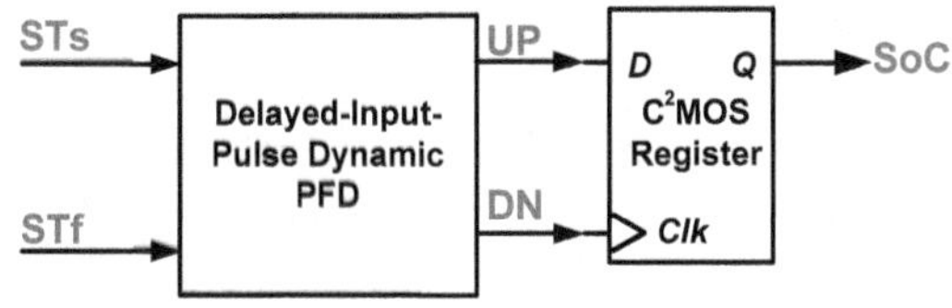

Figure 8. Dynamic-logic phase detector.

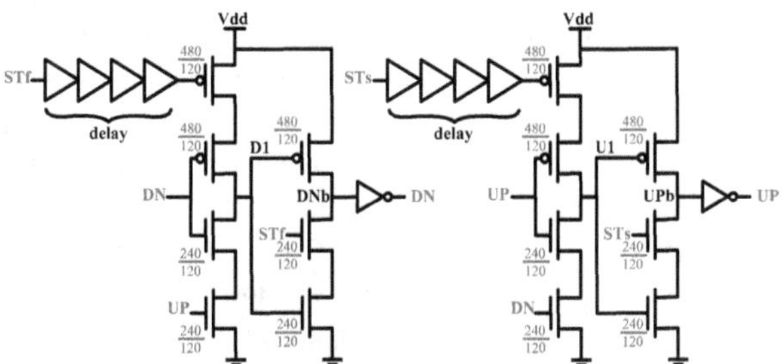

Figure 9. Delay-input-pulse phase frequency detector [11].

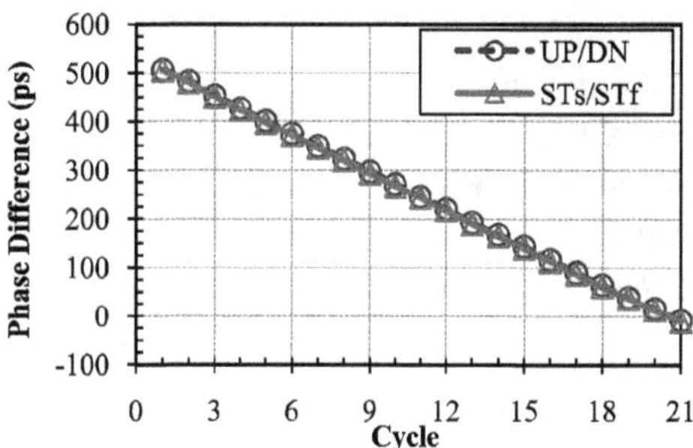

Figure 10. Zero dead-zone characteristic of the Delayed-Input-Pulse Phase Frequency Detector.

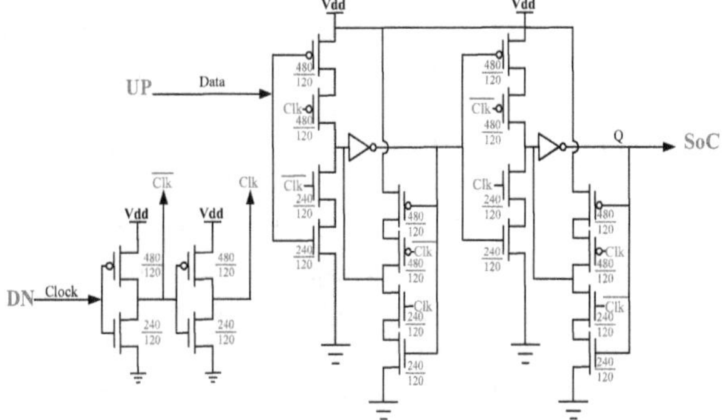

Figure 11. C^2 MOS register.

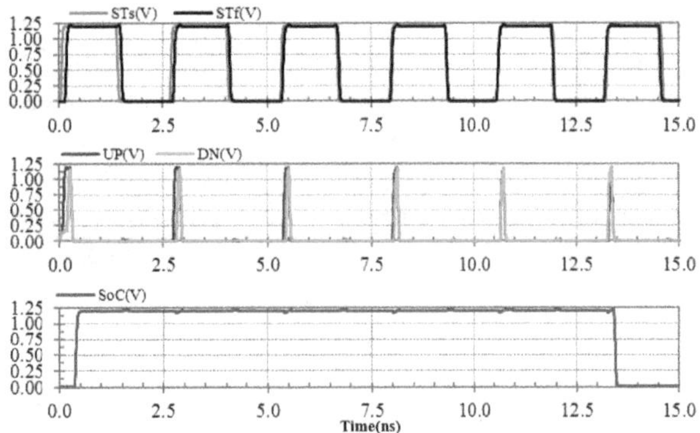

Figure 12. Timing diagram of dynamic-logic phase detector.

by measuring zero input phase difference [4]. Due to the offset, the input phase different T_{in} calculation must be modified. Taking offset into account, the measured input phase difference T_{in} is equal:

$$T_{in} = \left(T_s - T_f\right) \times \left(\text{CNT} - \text{offset}\right) \quad (2)$$

3.4. Counter

The SoC signal generated by the dynamic-logic phase detector controls the operation of a counter, which counts the number of cycles the measurement takes (CNT). A 6-bit counter has been designed with C^2MOS registers, as shown **Figure 13**. The counter is enabled by the SoC signal and clocked by the ST_f signal. Each stage of the counter divides the clock frequency signal by half. Therefore, the output signal of each register oscillates two times slower than its input clock signal. The final output signal levels [Q0:Q5] can be interpreted as the binary value of the CNT. The input phase difference, T_{in}, can be calculated with the CNT by using Equation (2).

4. Simulation Result

The single-stage VTDC with the dynamic-logic phase detector has been designed using the 0.13 μm IBM CMOS technology using the 1.2 V power supply. The **Figure 14** shows the schematic diagram of the single-stage VTDC with dynamic-logic phase detector.

The **Figure 15** shows digital output as a function of the input phase difference, simulated in the typical-typical (TT) technology corner. The control voltage has been set to 1.10V to achieve the resolution approximately 25 ps. The output characteristics of the single-stage VTDC with dynamic-logic phase detector are linear within the time range from 0 to 1600 ps. These results demonstrate that the circuit can correctly detect the phase difference and control the measurement process even at an oscillation period difference of 25 ps.

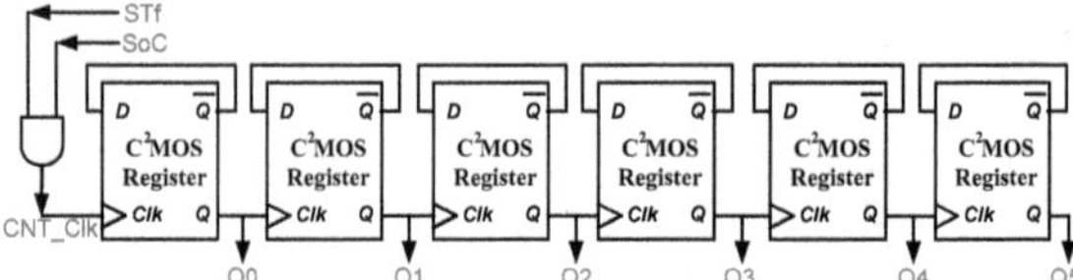

Figure 13. Block diagram of the 6-bit counter.

Next we compared the characteristics of the single-stage VTDC with the dynamic-logic phase detector with those of the single-stage VTDC with a classic register-type phase detector (**Figure 16**) implemented in the TSMC 0.35 μm CMOS as reported in [6]. The corresponding time resolution of this design was 37.5ps, and the characteristics offset estimated as 125 ps. [6]. The single-stage VTDC with the dynamic-logic phase detector has much smaller offset, in the order of 25 ps. We attribute the large offset of this VTDC [6] to the classic register-type phase detector. The offset results from a substantial dead-zone of the classic register-type phase detector, when for small phase differences (smaller than the width of the detector's dead-zone) the VTDC is unable to produce a digital output. Using the dynamic-logic phase detector clearly decreases the characteristics offset and makes measurements of small phase differences possible.

The ability to vary the VCO's oscillation frequency can be used to control the resolution of the single-stage VTDC with the dynamic-logic phase detector. Example results (**Figure 17**) show that varying the control voltage, one can achieve better resolution of the time measurements and further minimization of the offset. The increased resolution leads to a smaller input time range. Hence, the control voltage adjustment can be used for applications that require different time resolutions and input time ranges.

We also observed that without the PLL-type stabilization of the VCO, the single-stage VTDC characteristics will vary with process variations. The results presented in **Figure 18** show significant variations in time measurement resolution, and in the circuit gain and offset. To diminish this effect while keeping the circuit architecture simple, we postulate to compensate the process variations through appropriate adjustment of the control voltage, which varies the VCO oscillation frequency. The compensated results are shown in **Figure 19**, demonstrating that it is possible to obtain nearly identical output characteristics in different process corners by adjusting the control voltage. The characteristics in the TT corner (V_c = 1.10 V, **Figure 19(a)**, are almost the same as in the FF corner (but for V_c = 1.06 V, **Figure 19(b)**, and as in the SS corner (but for V_c = 1.13 V, **Figure 19(c)**. Hence, the control voltage can be used not only for setting up the parameters of the single-stage VTDC, but also for calibration if necessary.

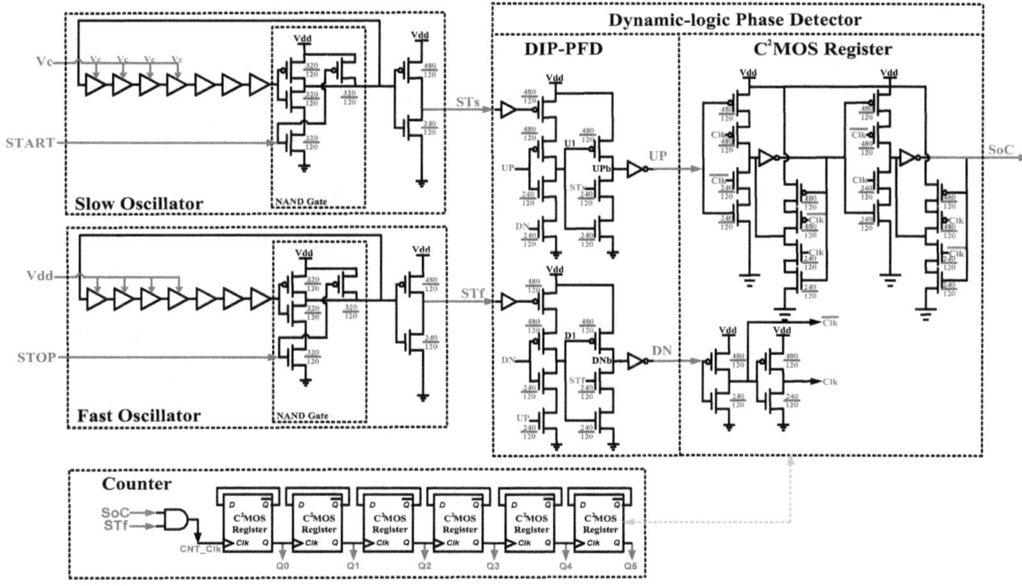

Figure 14. Schematic diagram of the single-stage VTDC.

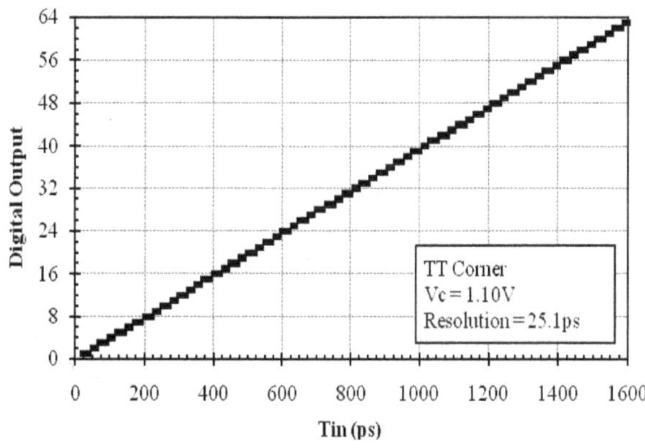

Figure 15. Digital output characteristic of the single-stage VTDC with the dynamic-logic phase detector (TT corner).

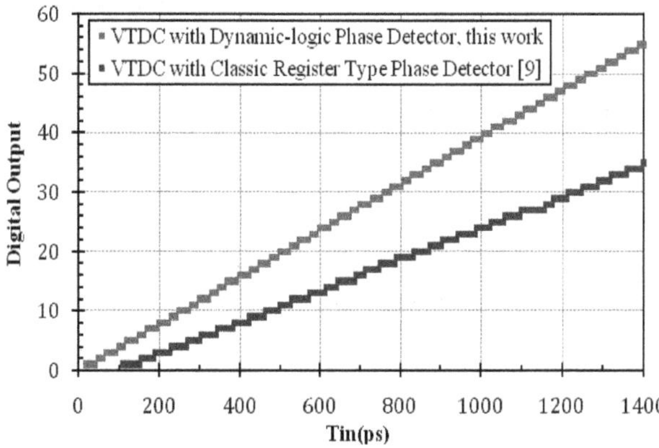

Figure 16. Comparison of the digital output characteristics of the single-stage VTDC with the dynamic-logic phase detector with the characteristics of the single-stage VTDC with the classic register-type phase detector from [6].

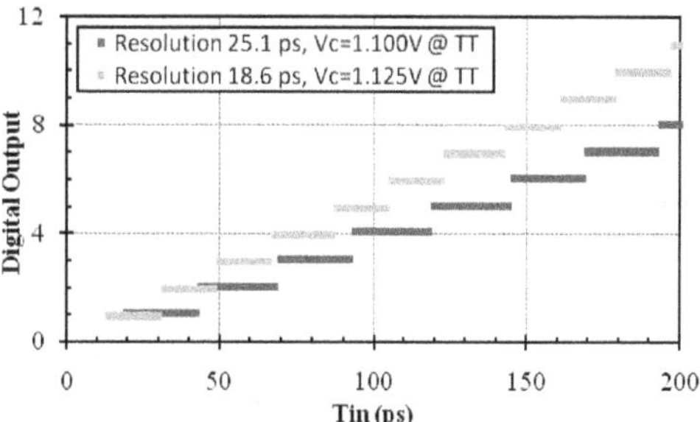

Figure 17. Digital output characteristics of the single-stage VTDC with the dynamic-logic phase detector in which the control voltage has been used to set up different time measurement resolution. Only the 0 - 200 ps fraction of the entire time scale has been shown for simplicity. (A small vertical offset in the digital output has been introduced for better readability).

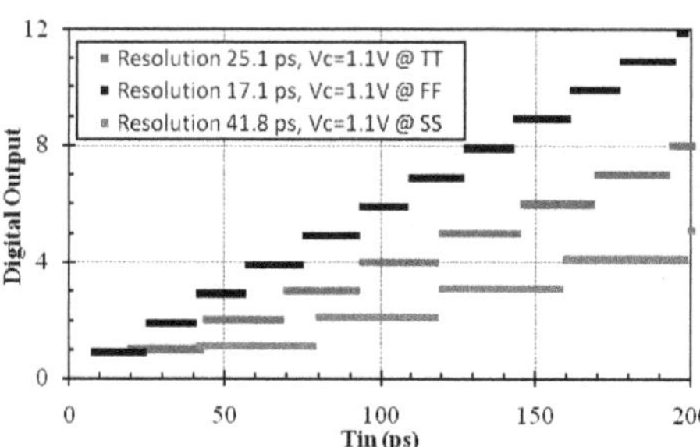

Figure 18. Variability of the digital output characteristics of the single-stage VTDC with the dynamic-logic phase detector as a function of process variations (in the TT, FF, and SS process corners), for a constant control voltage, V_c = 1.10 V. Only the 0 - 200 ps fraction of the time scale has been shown for simplicity. (A small vertical offset in the digital output has been introduced for better readability).

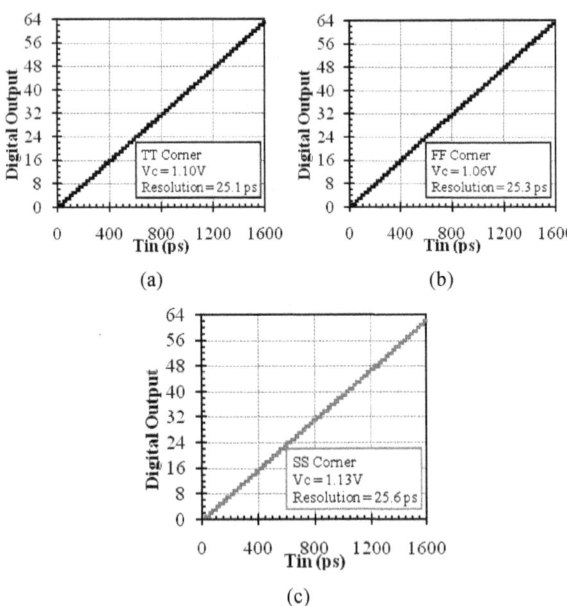

Figure 19. Digital output characteristics of the single-stage VTDC with the dynamic-logic phase detector in the different process corners compensated using different values of the control voltage (a) TT corner V_c = 1.10 V; (b) FF corner, V_c = 1.06V; (c) SS corner, V_c = 1.13 V.

5. Conclusions

This paper presents a single-stage Vernier Time-to-Digital Converter with sub-gate delay time resolution. By utilizing the dynamic-logic phase detector that eliminates the dead-zone problem, the single-stage Vernier Time-to-Digital Converter in this work has demonstrated a linear digital output characteristic with a 25 ps time resolution. The presented simulation results have confirmed the very important role of the phase detector quality for the performance of single-stage Vernier Time-to-Digital Converters with sub-gate delay resolutions.

6. References

[1] R. B. Staszewski, S. Vernulapalli, P. Vallur, *et al.*, "1.3V 20ps Time-to-Digital Converter for Frequency Synthesis in 90-nm CMOS," *IEEE Transactions on Circuits and Systems II*, Vol. 53, No. 3, 2006, pp. 220-224.

[2] R. B. Staszewski, C.-M. Hung, K. Maggio, *et al.*, "All-Digital Phase-Domain TX Frequency Synthesizer for Bluetooth Radios in 0.13μm CMOS," *IEEE International Solid-State Circuit Conference* (*ISSCC*), Vol. 1, 15-19 Feburary 2004, pp. 272-527.

[3] C.-C. Chung and W.-J. Chu, "An All-Digital On-Chip Jitter Measurement Circuit in 65 nm CMOS Technology," *International Symposium on VLSI Design, Automation and Test*, Hsinchu, 25-28 April 2011, pp. 1-4.

[4] A. H. Chan and G. W. Roberts, "A Jitter Characterization System Using a Component-Invariant Vernier Delay Line," *IEEE Transactions on Very Large Scale Integration* (*VLSI*) *Systems*, Vol. 12, No. 1, 2004, pp. 79-95.

[5] B. K. Swann, B. J. Blalock, L. G. Clonts, *et al.*, "A 100-ps Time-Resolution CMOS Time-to-Digital Converter for Positron Emission Tomography Imaging Applications," *IEEE Journal of Solid-State Circuits*, Vol. 39, No. 11, 2004, pp. 1830-1845.

[6] P. Chen, C.-C. Chen, J.-C. Zheng and Y.-S. Shen, "A PVT Insensitive Vernier-Based Time-to-Digital Converter with Extended Input Range and High Accuracy," *IEEE Transactions on Nuclear Science*, Vol. 54, No. 2, 2007, pp. 294-302.

[7] A. Liscidini, L. Vercesi and R. Castello, "Time to Digital Converter Based on a 2-Dimensions Vernier Architecture," 2009 *IEEE Custom Integrated Circuits Conference*, San Jose, 13-16 September 2009, pp. 45-48,

[8] J. J. Yu and F. F. Dai, "A 3-Dimensional Vernier Ring Time-to-Digital Converter in 0.13μm CMOS", *IEEE Custom Integrated Circuit Conference* (*CICC*), San Jose, 19-22 September 2010, pp. 1-4.

[9] Y. Cao, P. Leroux, W. De Cock and M. Steyaert, "A 1.7 mW 11b 1-1-1-MASH Δ-Σ Time-to-Digital Converter," 2011 *IEEE International Solid State Circuits Conference*, San Francisco, 20-24 February 2011, pp. 480-482.

[10] T. A. Jackson and A. Albicki, "Analysis of Metastable Operation in D Latches," *IEEE Transactions on Circuits and Systems*, Vol. 36, No. 11, 1989, pp. 1392-1404.

[11] Z. Cheng and M. Syrzycki, "Modifications of a Dynamic-Logic Phase Frequency Detector for Extended Detection Range," 2010 53*rd IEEE International Midwest Symposium on Circuits and Systems*, Seattle, 1-4 August 2010, pp. 105-108.

A New CMOS Current Controlled Quadrature Oscillator Based on a MCCII

Ashwek Ben Saied[1,2], Samir Ben Salem[2,3], Dorra Sellami Masmoudi[1,2]
[1]*Computor Imaging and Electronic Systems Group (CIEL), Research Unit on Intelligent Design and Control of complex Systems (ICOS), Sfax, Tunisia*
[2]*University of Sfax, National Engineering School of Sfax (ENIS), Sfax, Tunisia*
[3]*Development Group in Electronics and Communications (EleCom) Laboratory of Electronics and Information Technology (LETI), Sfax, Tunisia*

Abstract

In this paper, we propose a design of a current controlled Quadrature Sinusoidal Oscillator. The proposed circuit employs three optimized Multi-output translinear second generation current conveyer (MCCII). The oscillation condition and the oscillation frequency are independently controllable. The proposed Quadrature Oscillator frequency can be tuned in the range of [198 - 261 MHz] by a simple variation of a DC current. PSpice simulation results are performed using CMOS 0.35 μm process of AMS.

Keywords: Quadrature Sinusoidal Oscillator, Optimized MCCII

1. Introduction

Controlled Quadrature Sinusoidal Oscillator is a basic signal-generating block frequently needed in communication systems, instrumentation and control systems. In communication it is require for Quadrature mixer and single side band generators.

MCCII based Quadrature oscillator presents a good solution to avoid limitations of Surface Acoustic Wave, such as problems of integration, impedance matching, tuning, linearity, etc.

In order to get controllable characteristics for the proposed Quadrature Qscillator, translinear Multi-output second generation current controlled conveyer based structure seems to be the most attractive [1-3]. In fact, being able to control the output resistance at port X by means of a current source [4-6], one may exploit this in the synthesis of electronically adjustable functions [5-8].

Translinear MCCII family is wathly extended to MOS submicron technologies going towards VLSI design. Indeed, reaching sub-micron technologies, the MOS transistor becomes able to achieve high transit frequencies [1,7,9,11]. These Multi-output conveyors are employed in different RF controllable applications such as oscillators, quadrature oscillator and filters [1,2,7,11].

In this paper, we are interested in the design of MCCII based Quadrature Oscillator. This paper is organized as follows: in section II, we present the MCCII based Quadrature oscillator architecture [1]. Then After presenting the inconvenient of this oscillator, we present the general characteristics of Multi-output second generation translinear current conveyor in section III. In section IV, we give the proposed Controlled Quadrature Oscillator. Finally, the proposed structure is designed and simulated using PSPICE.

2. The Controlled Quadrature Oscillator

Parven Beg [1] presents a novel single resistance controlled sinusoidal quadrature oscillator shown in **Figure 1**. This architecture uses only two CMOS multioutput CCIIs along with the grounded resistors and capacitors.

The corresponding oscillation condition is given by:

$$s^2 + s\left[\frac{1}{R_1} - \frac{1}{R_2}\right]\frac{1}{C_2} + \frac{1}{C_1C_2R_2R_3} = 0 \qquad (1)$$

It leads to the following condition

$$R_1 = R_2 \qquad (2)$$

and following oscillation frequency:

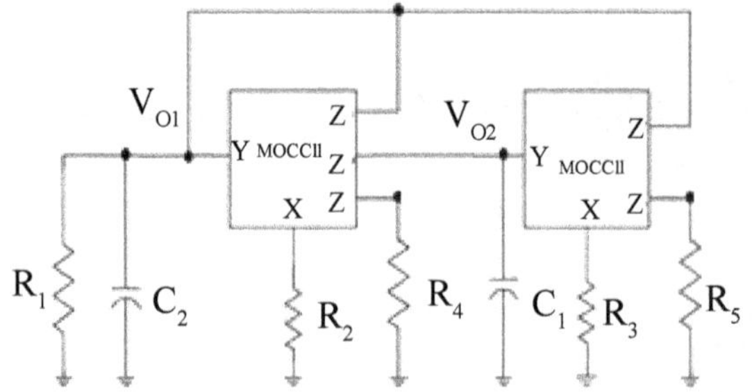

Figure 1. Quadrature oscillator implementation proposed by Parven Beg.

$$f_0 = \frac{1}{2\Pi\sqrt{C_1 C_2 R_3 R_2}} \quad (3)$$

From Equation (3), we get a variable frequency oscillator. The oscillation frequency can be adjusted independently without modification of the oscillation condition by varying R_3 [1]. However, to avoid tuning R_3 after integration, one can change this external resistance by an internal active controllable one corresponding to the X port parasitic resistance of the MCCII.

CMOS Implementation of the MCCII

The MCCII can be represented by the symbol of **Figure 2**. The port relations of the MCCII can be characterized by the following expression:

$$I_Y = 0,\ V_X = V_Y + I_X R_X,\ I_{Zi+} = I_X \text{ and } I_{Zi-} = -I_X$$

where, R_X denote the parasitic resistance at the X input terminal of the MCCII and i = 1, 2, 3. The plus and minus sign of the current transfer ratio represent the positive and negative types of the MCCII outputs

The terminal characteristic of the MCCII can be described by the following matrix equation:

$$\begin{bmatrix} I_Y \\ V_X \\ I_{Z1+} \\ I_{Z2+} \\ I_{Z3+} \\ I_{Z1-} \\ I_{Z2-} \\ I_{Z3-} \end{bmatrix} = \begin{bmatrix} 0 & 0 & 0 \\ 1 & 0 & 0 \\ 0 & 1 & 0 \\ 0 & 1 & 0 \\ 0 & 1 & 0 \\ 0 & -1 & 0 \\ 0 & -1 & 0 \\ 0 & -1 & 0 \end{bmatrix} \begin{bmatrix} V_Y \\ I_X \\ V_Z \end{bmatrix} \quad (4)$$

The MCCII implementation is given in **Figure 3**. Assuming the same gain factors for both NMOS and PMOS transistors, the parasitic impedances are described by the following expressions (5)

$$Ry = \frac{1}{I_o * (\lambda_N + \lambda_P)} \quad (6)$$

$$Rzi = \frac{1}{I_o * (\lambda_N + \lambda_P)} \quad (i = 1+, \cdots, 3+ \text{ or } 1-, \cdots, 3-) \quad (7)$$

We notice that the optimization process can be done in the same way for other simulation conditions [7,9,10]. **Table 1** shows the optimal device scaling that we get after applying the optimization approach.

Figure 4 shows the simulated parasitic resistance at port X (R_X) in the optimized configuration. It can be tuned on more than a decade over [427 Ω, 7.1 kΩ] by varying Io in the range [1 μA - 400 μA]. Such control is very important, since it will be used to replace the resistance R$_3$ in the Quadrature Oscillator giving in **Figure 3**. **Figure 4** depicts results obtained from both PSPICE software simulations (R_X) and MAPLE theoretical calculus of (R_{Xthe}). We Notice a global agreement between both characteristics.

3. Proposed Oscillator

The basic idea in the improved structure consists on replacing the resistance R_3 by the parasitic resistance on port X. We then use this implementation of MCCII, presenting a variable resistance on port X. The Quadrature oscillator, will be in that case controlled by means of the bias current I_o in the MCCII3.

The proposed Quadrature Sinusoidal Oscillator is presented in **Figure 5**. The modified oscillation condition and oscillation frequency are respectively given by the following expressions:

$$R_1 = R_2 \quad (8)$$

$$f_0 = \frac{1}{2\Pi\sqrt{C_1 C_2 R_{X3} R_2}} \quad (9)$$

From Equation (9), we get a variable frequency oscillator. In fact, the oscillation frequency can be adjusted independently without modification of the oscillation condition by varying R_{X3} (by varying I_{o3} current of the MCCII3). The proposed Quadrature oscillator is simulated for different MCCII3 bias currents. Simulation results are shown in **Figure 6**. When varying the control current between 10 μA and 400 μA, the oscillation frequency is tuned in the range [198 MHz - 261MHz].

$$Rx = \frac{1}{\sqrt{I_o} * \left[\sqrt{2K_N \left(\frac{W}{L}\right)_{NXX}} (1 + \lambda_N V_{DS}) + \sqrt{2K_P \left(\frac{W}{L}\right)_{PXX}} (1 + \lambda_P V_{DS}) \right]} \quad (5)$$

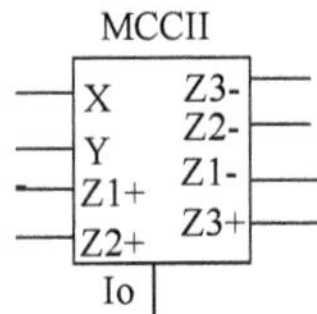

Figure 2. MCCII block.

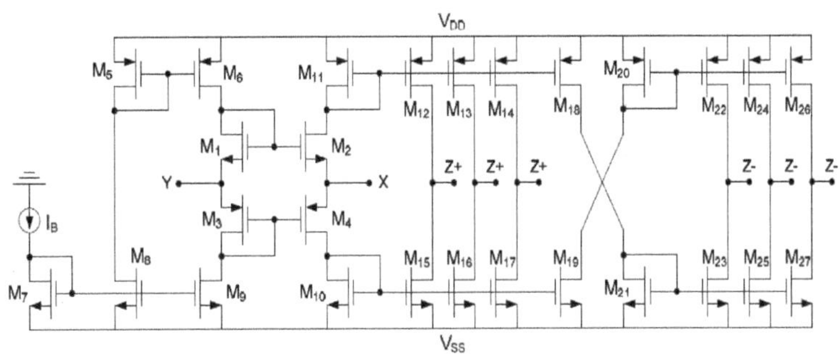

Figure 3. MCCII implementation using translinear loop I_o.

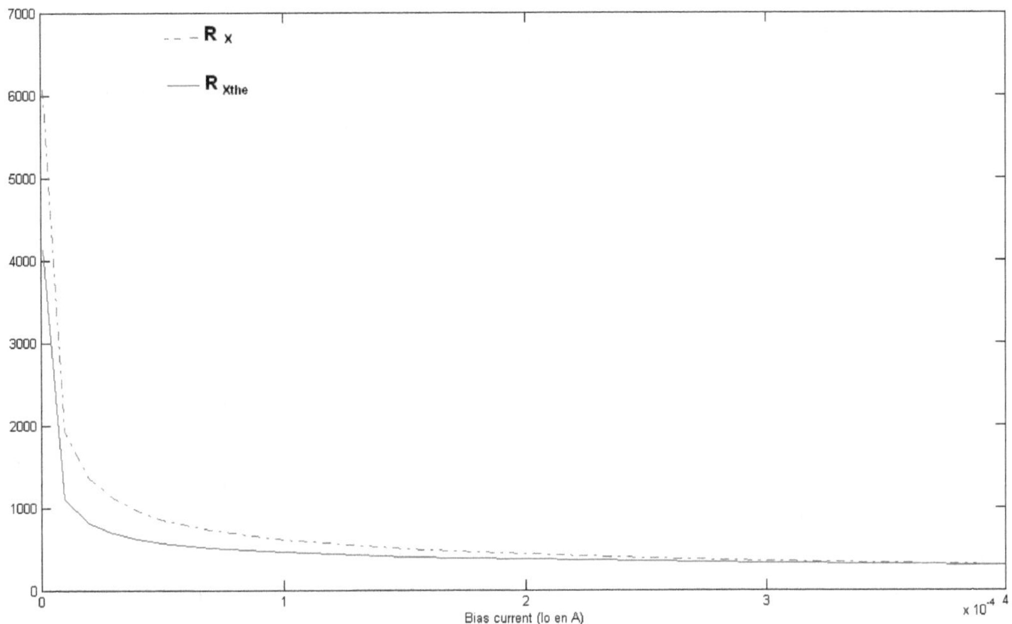

Figure 4. Parasitic resistance at port X versus the control current I_o (___R_{xthe}, ---R_X).

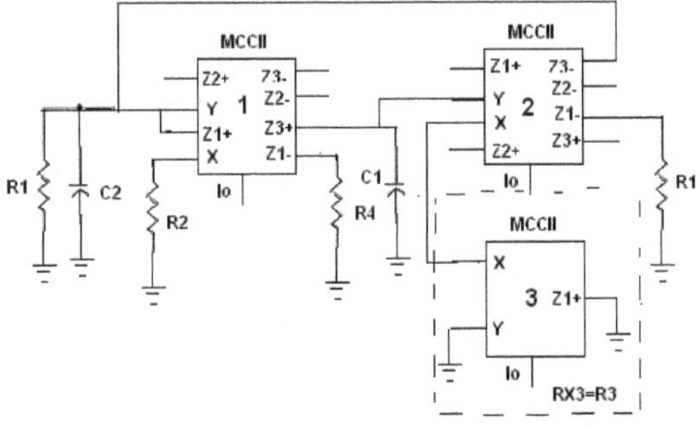

Figure 5. The proposed quadrature oscillator implementation.

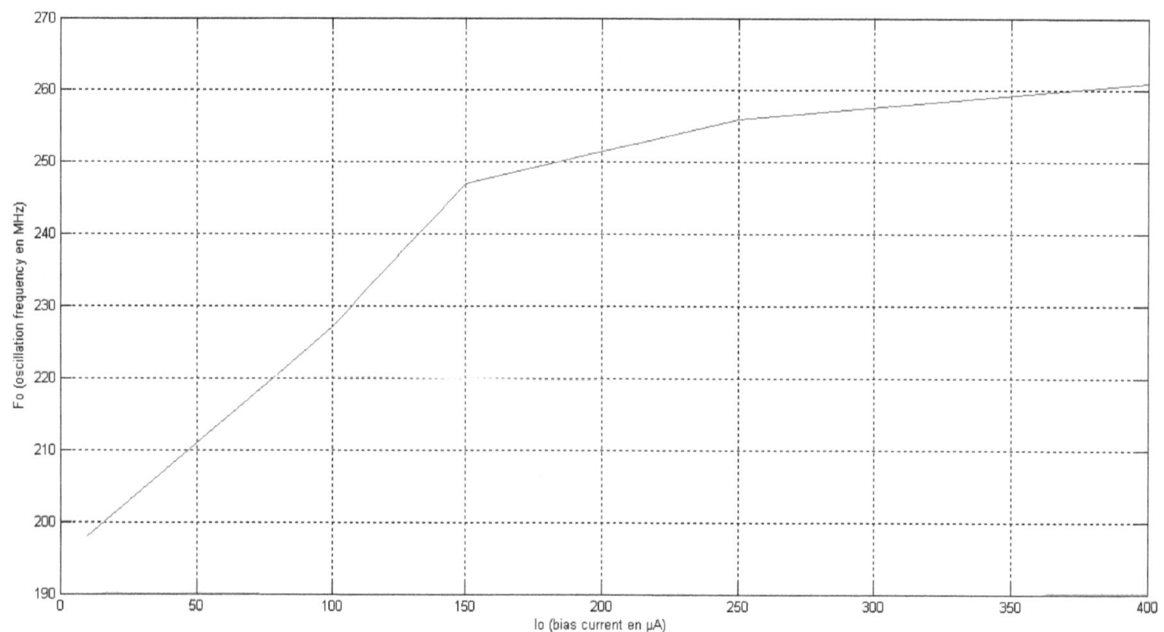

Figure 6. Oscillation frequency versus control current.

Table 1. Device scaling after optimisation process

Device Name	Aspect ratio W/L
M1, M2	12/0.35 (μm)
M3, M4	36/0.35 (μm)
Mxx (in PMOS current mirrors)	18/0.35 (μm)
Mxx (in NMOS current mirrors)	6/0.35 (μm)

The circuit was simulated using $R_1 = R_2 = R_4 = 500\ \Omega$ $R_5 = 1\ \text{K}\Omega$, $R_{X3} = 450\ \Omega$ ($I_{o3} = 100\ \mu\text{A}$), $C_1 = C_2 = 0.2$ pF and $I_{o1} = I_{o2} = 100\ \mu\text{A}$. The obtained oscillation frequency is 225 MHz and the obtained quadrature voltage waveforms are shown in **Figure 7**. Simulations were carried out using 0.35 μm CMOS process parameters.

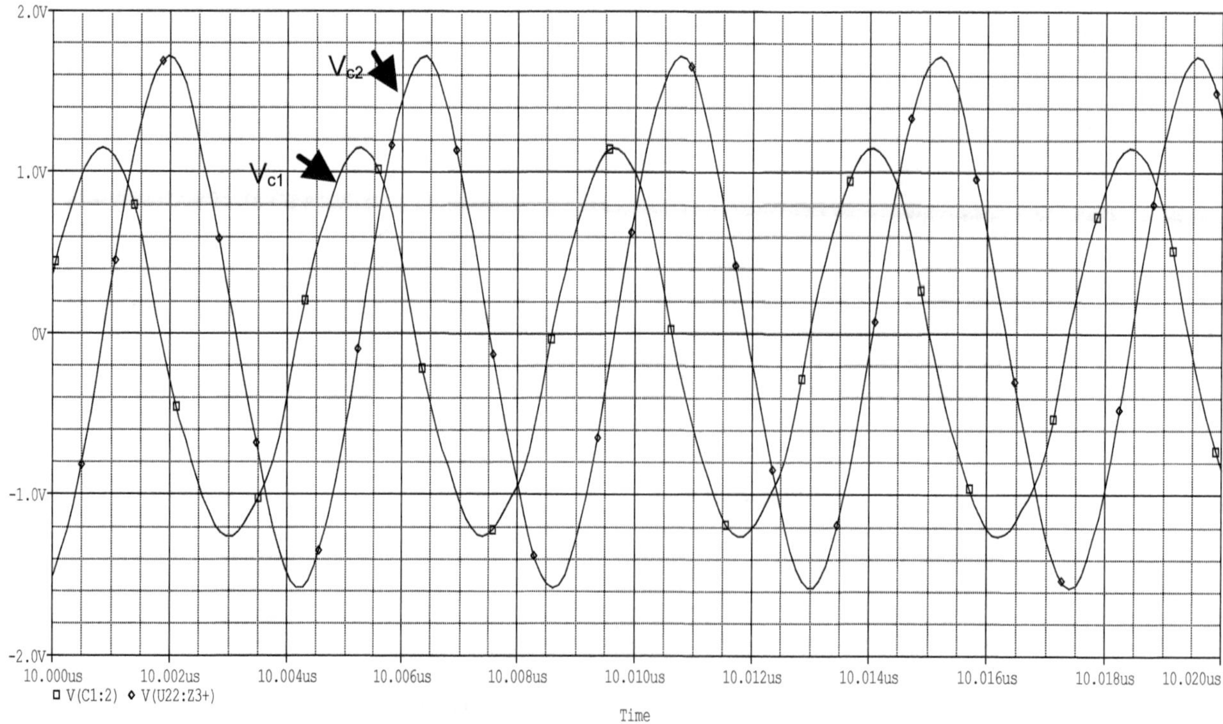

Figure 7. The simulated of Quadrature output waveforms.

4. Conclusions

In this paper, we have proposed a new design of variable frequency current controlled Quadrature oscillators. In order to get high frequency performances of the oscillator, we use an optimized translinear multi-output CCII structure in 0.35 μm CMOS process of AMS. Simulation results show that this Quadrature oscillator provides a control of the oscillation frequency which is independent from the oscillation condition in the range [198 MHz - 261 MHz] by varying the control current in the range [10 μA - 400 μA].

5. References

[1] P. Beg, I. A. Khan and M. T. Ahmed, "Tunable Four Phase Voltage Mode Quadrature Oscillator Using Two CMOS MOCCIIs," *Multimedia, Signal Processing and Communication Technologies*, Aligarh, 14-16 March 2009, pp. 155-157.

[2] S. Maheshwari, "Quadrature Oscillator Using Grounded Components with Current and Voltage Outputs," *IET Circuits, Devices & Systems*, Vol. 3, No. 4, 2009, pp. 153-160.

[3] S. Maheshwari, "Analogue Signal Processing Applications Using a New Circuit Topology," *IET Circuits, Devices & Systems*, Vol. 3, No. 3, 2008, pp. 106-115.

[4] A. Fabre, O. Saiid, F. Wiest and C. Bouchern, "High Frequency High-Q BICMOS Current-Mode Bandpass Filter and Mobile Communication Application," *IEEE Transaction on Circuits and Systems* 1: *Fundamental Theory and Applications*, Vol. 33, No. 4, 1998, pp. 614-625.

[5] H. O. Elwan and A. M. Soliman, "Low-Voltage Low-Power CMOS Current Conveyors," *IEEE Transaction on Circuits and Systems* 1: *Fundamental Theory and Applications*, Vol. 44, No. 9, 1997, pp. 828-835.

[6] D. S. Masmoudi, S. Ben Salem, M. Loulou, L. Kammoun "A Radio Frequency CMOS Current Controlled Oscillator Based on a New Low Parasitic Resistance CCII," 2004 *International Conference on Electrical, Electronic and Computer Engineering*, Egypt, 5-7 September 2004, pp. 563-566.

[7] S. B. Salem, M. Fakhfakh, D. S. Masmoudi, M. Loulou, P. Loumeau and N. Masmoudi, "A High Performances CMOS CCII and High Frequency Applications," *Journal of Analog Integrated Circuits and Signal Processing*, Vol. 49, No. 1, 2006, pp. 71-78.

[8] S. B. Salem, D. S. Masmoudi and M. Loulou "A Novel CCII-Based Tunable Inductance and High Frequency Current Mode Band Pass Filter Application," *Journal of Circuits, Systems, and Computers* (*JCSC*), Vol. 15, No. 6, 2006, pp. 849-860.

[9] S. B. Salem, D. S. Masmoudi, A. B. Saied and M. Loulou "An Optimized Low Voltage and High Frequency CCII Based Multifunction Filters," 13*th IEEE International Conference on Electronics, Circuits and Systems*, Nice, 10-13 December 2006, pp. 1268-1271.

[10] A. B. Saied, S. B. Salem, M. Fkih and D. S. Masmoudi "A New High Frequency Second Generation Current Conveyor Based Chaos Generator," 14*th IEEE International Conference on Electronics, Circuits and Systems*, Marrakech, 11-14 December 2007, pp. 387-390.

[11] C. Thoumazou, F. J. Lidgey and D. Haigh, "Integrated Circuits: The Current Mode Approach," *IEEE Circuit and Systems Series* 2, Peter Ltd., London, 1993.

23

Fully Uncoupled Electronically Controllable Sinusoidal Oscillator Employing VD-DIBAs

Data Ram Bhaskar[1*], Dinesh Prasad[1], Kanhaiya Lal Pushkar[2]
[1]Department of Electronics and Communication Engineering, Faculty of Engineering and Technology, Jamia Millia Islamia, New Delhi, India
[2]Department of Electronics and Communication Engineering, Maharaja Agrasen Institute of Technology, Rohini, New Delhi, India

ABSTRACT

Recently, voltage differencing-differential input buffered amplifiers (VD-DIBA)-based electronically controllable sinusoidal oscillator has been presented that it does not have the capability of complete independence of frequency of oscillation (FO) and condition of oscillation (CO) as well as electronic control of both CO and FO. In this article, a new fully-uncoupled electronically controllable sinusoidal oscillator using two VD-DIBAs, two grounded capacitors and two resistors has been proposed which offers important advantages such as 1) totally uncoupled and electronically controlled condition of oscillation (CO) and frequency of oscillation (FO); 2) low active and passive sensitivities; and 3) a very good frequency stability factor. The effects of non-idealities of the VD-DIBAs on the proposed oscillator are also investigated. The validity of the proposed formulation has been confirmed by SPICE simulation with TSMC 0.18 μm process parameters.

Keywords: Sinusoidal Oscillator; Voltage-Mode; VD-DIBA

1. Introduction

Sinusoidal oscillators find various applications in signal processing, instrumentation, measurement, communication and control systems. The class of single resistance controlled oscillators (SRCOs) using different active element(s)/device(s) has been of particular interest during the last four decades because of their applications in variable frequency oscillators. However, in these SRCOs, electronic control of CO and FO can be obtained by replacing the respective controlling resistor(s) with FET based or CMOS voltage controlled resistor(s). A careful inspection of the available SRCOs reveals that while many oscillators enjoy independent single element control of CO and FO, the class of fully uncoupled oscillators has not been considered adequately in the literature. In fully uncoupled oscillator circuits CO and FO are determined by two completely different sets of active and/ or passive components, that is none of the active and/or passive components appeared in CO are involved in FO and vice versa. This feature is very useful for realizing voltage controlled oscillators as FO can be controlled independently without disturbing CO, whereas the flexibility of being able to control CO independently is advantageous to incorporate amplitude stabilization. In the recent past, number of fully-uncoupled sinusoidal oscillators employing different active element(s)/devices has been introduced see [1-7] and the references cited therein. In references [1-5] the CO and FO of the proposed oscillators are adjustable through resistors (the electronic tunability can be established by replacing one of the grounded resistors by JFETs/MOSFETs [8,9]), whereas in case of oscillators presented in references [6,7], both CO and FO are electronically controllable. The VD-DIBA was introduced by Biolek, Senani, Biolkova and Kolka in [10] since then it has been found to be a useful new active building block in realizing all voltage-mode pass filters [11], inductance simulation [12], universal biquad filter [13] and an electronically controllable sinusoidal oscillator [14]. Although the paper presented by the authors in [14] employs two VD-DIBAs, two grounded capacitors and one grounded resistor but this circuit does not have the capability of complete independence of CO and FO as well as electronic control (only FO is electronically controllable). Therefore, the purpose of this

*Corresponding author.

paper is, to propose a new fully uncoupled electronically controllable sinusoidal oscillator employing two VD-DIBAs, two grounded capacitors and two resistors, which offers 1) fully uncoupled and electronically controlled CO and FO, 2) low active and passive sensitivities, and 3) a very good frequency stability factor. The feasibility of the proposed oscillator has been demonstrated by SPICE simulation with TSMC 0.18 μm process parameters.

2. The Proposed Fully Uncoupled Oscillator

The schematic symbol and behavioral model of the VD-DIBA are shown in **Figures 1(a)** and **(b)** respectively [11]. The VD-DIBAs can be described by the following set of equations:

$$\begin{pmatrix} I_+ \\ I_- \\ I_z \\ I_v \\ V_w \end{pmatrix} = \begin{pmatrix} 0 & 0 & 0 & 0 & 0 \\ 0 & 0 & 0 & 0 & 0 \\ g_m & -g_m & 0 & 0 & 0 \\ 0 & 0 & 0 & 0 & 0 \\ 0 & 0 & \pm 1 & \mp 1 & 0 \end{pmatrix} \begin{pmatrix} V_+ \\ V_- \\ V_z \\ V_v \\ I_w \end{pmatrix} \quad (1)$$

The proposed new fully-uncoupled electronically controllable sinusoidal oscillator circuit is shown in **Figure 2**.

Assuming that the VD-DIBAs are characterized by Equation (1), the characteristic equation (CE) of **Figure 2** can be given by:

$$s^2 + s\frac{1}{C_1}\left(\frac{1}{R_1} - g_{m_1}\right) + \frac{g_{m_2}}{R_2 C_1 C_2} = 0 \quad (2)$$

From this CE, the CO and FO can be found as:

CO

$$\left(\frac{1}{R_1} - g_{m_1}\right) \leq 0 \quad (3)$$

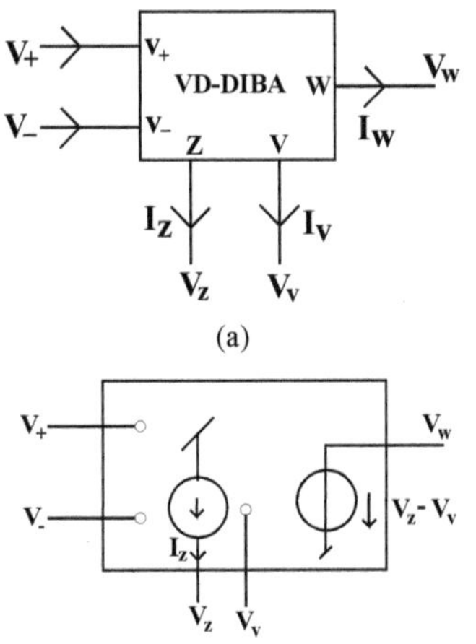

(a)

(b)

Figure 1. (a) Schematic symbol; (b) Behavioral model of VD-DIBA.

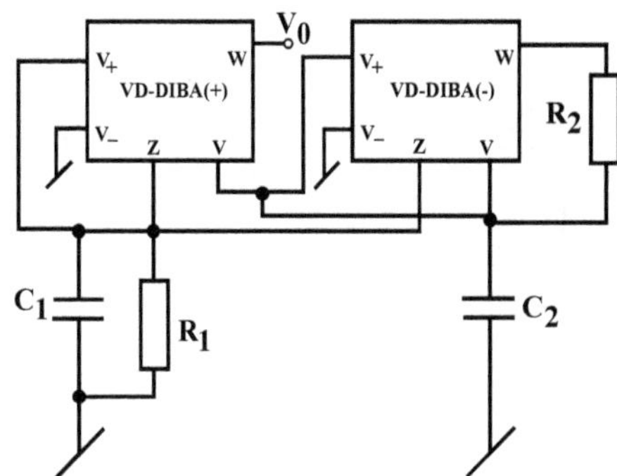

Figure 2. The proposed fully-uncoupled electronically controllable sinusoidal oscillator.

and

FO

$$\omega_0 = \sqrt{\frac{g_{m_2}}{R_2 C_1 C_2}} \quad (4)$$

Therefore, from Equations (3) and (4) it is clear that FO and CO are fully decoupled and electronically controllable *i.e.* FO is independently controllable by transconductance g_{m_2} of the VD-DIBA(−), whereas CO is also electronically controllable through the transconductance g_{m_1} of VD-DIBA(+).

3. Non-Ideal Analysis

Considering the parasitics of VD-DIBA *i.e.* R_Z and C_Z, the parasitic resistance and the parasitic capacitance of the Z-terminal respectively. Taking the non-idealities into account, namely the voltage of W-terminal $V_W = \left(\pm\beta^+ V_Z \mp \beta^- V_V\right)$ where $\beta^+ = 1-\varepsilon_p\left(\varepsilon_p \ll 1\right)$ and $\beta^- = 1-\varepsilon_n\left(\varepsilon_n \ll 1\right)$ denote the voltage tracking errors of Z-terminal and V-terminal of the VD-DIBA (+/−) respectively, then the expression for CE becomes:

$$\begin{aligned} & s^2\left(C_1+2C_z\right)C_2 \\ & +s\left\{C_2\left(\frac{1}{R_1}-g_{m_1}+\frac{2}{R_z}\right)+C_1\frac{\left(1-\beta_2^-\right)}{R_2} \right. \\ & \left. +C_z\frac{2\left(1-\beta_2^-\right)}{R_z}\right\}+\frac{\beta_2^+ g_{m_2}}{R_2} \\ & +\frac{\left(1-\beta_2^-\right)}{R_2}\left(\frac{1}{R_1}-g_{m_1}+\frac{2}{R_z}\right)=0 \end{aligned} \quad (5)$$

From Equation (5), the CO and FO can be given by:

CO:

$$\begin{aligned} & \left\{C_2\left(\frac{1}{R_1}-g_{m_1}\right)\right\}+C_1\frac{\left(1-\beta_2^-\right)}{R_2} \\ & +\frac{1}{R_z}\left\{2C_z\left(1-\beta_2^-\right)+2C_2\right\}\leq 0 \end{aligned} \quad (6)$$

FO:

$$\omega = \sqrt{\frac{\frac{\beta_2^+ g_{m_2}}{R_2} + \frac{(1-\beta_2^-)}{R_2}\left(\frac{1}{R_1} - g_{m_1} + \frac{2}{R_z}\right)}{(C_1 + 2C_z)C_2}} \tag{7}$$

The sensitivities of ω_0 with respect to active and passive elements are calculated as:

$$S_{g_{m_1}}^{\omega_0} = -\frac{(1-\beta_2^-)g_{m_1}}{2R_2\left\{\frac{\beta_2^+ g_{m_2}}{R_2} + \frac{(1-\beta_2^-)}{R_2}\left(\frac{1}{R_1} - g_{m_1} + \frac{2}{R_z}\right)\right\}}$$

$$S_{g_{m_2}}^{\omega_0} = \frac{\beta_2^+ g_{m_2}}{2R_2\left\{\frac{\beta_2^+ g_{m_2}}{R_2} + \frac{(1-\beta_2^-)}{R_2}\left(\frac{1}{R_1} - g_{m_1} + \frac{2}{R_z}\right)\right\}}$$

$$S_{\beta_2^+}^{\omega_0} = \frac{1}{2}$$

$$S_{\beta_2^-}^{\omega_0} = -\frac{\beta_2^-\left(\frac{1}{R_1} - g_{m_1} + \frac{2}{R_z}\right)}{2\left\{\frac{\beta_2^+ g_{m_2}}{R_2} + \frac{(1-\beta_2^-)}{R_2}\left(\frac{1}{R_1} - g_{m_1} + \frac{2}{R_z}\right)\right\}}$$

$$S_{R_1}^{\omega_0} = -\frac{(1-\beta_2^-)}{2R_1R_2\left\{\frac{\beta_2^+ g_{m_2}}{R_2} + \frac{(1-\beta_2^-)}{R_2}\left(\frac{1}{R_1} - g_{m_1} + \frac{2}{R_z}\right)\right\}}$$

$$S_{R_2}^{\omega_0} = -\frac{1}{2}$$

$$S_{R_z}^{\omega_0} = -\frac{(1-\beta_2^-)}{R_zR_2\left\{\frac{\beta_2^+ g_{m_2}}{R_2} + \frac{(1-\beta_2^-)}{R_2}\left(\frac{1}{R_1} - g_{m_1} + \frac{2}{R_z}\right)\right\}} \tag{8}$$

$$S_{C_1}^{\omega_0} = -\frac{1}{2} = S_{C_2}^{\omega_0}, S_{C_z}^{\omega_0} = -1$$

An inspection of Equation (8) reveals that the active and passive sensitivities of ω_0 are found to be low.

4. Frequency Stability

Frequency stability is an important figure of merit for any sinusoidal oscillator. Using the definition of the frequency stability factor S^F as given in [5,8] $S^F = \left.\left(\frac{\mathrm{d}\phi(u)}{\mathrm{d}u}\right)\right|_{u=1}$ (where $u = \frac{\omega}{\omega_0}$ is the normalized frequency and $\phi(u)$ denotes the phase of the open-loop transfer function), with $C_1 = C_2 = C, g_{m_1} = \frac{1}{R_1} = \frac{1}{R_2} = g_m$ and $g_{m_2} = ng_m$, the S^F of this oscillator is found to be $2\sqrt{n}$. Thus the new proposed oscillator circuit offers very high frequency stability factor for larger values of n.

5. Simulation Results

The proposed sinusoidal oscillator circuit has been simulated using the CMOS-based VD-DIBA [14]. The various component values used were $C_1 = C_2 = 0.05$ nF, $R_1 = 1.67$ KΩ and $R_2 = 10$ K, the CMOS VD-DIBA was biased with ±1 V D.C. power supplies with $I_{B1} = I_{B2} = I_{B3} = I_{B4} = I_{B5} = I_{B6} = 150$ μA and $I_{B7} = 30$ μA. The transconductances of VD-DIBAs were controlled through the respcctive bias currents. The SPICE generated output waveforms indicating transient and steady state responses are shown in **Figures 3(a)** and **(b)** respectively. From SPICE simulations {**Figures 3(a)** and **(b)**}, the oscillations are observed to be quite stable and the frequency of generated sine wave was found as 731.88 KHz. The THD of the output waveform was found as 1.159%. **Figure 4** shows the Monte-Carlo simulations which provide the robustness of the oscillator circuit of **Figure 2** by taking sample result for ±10% variations in R_1. Simulation results, thus, confirm the workability of the pro-

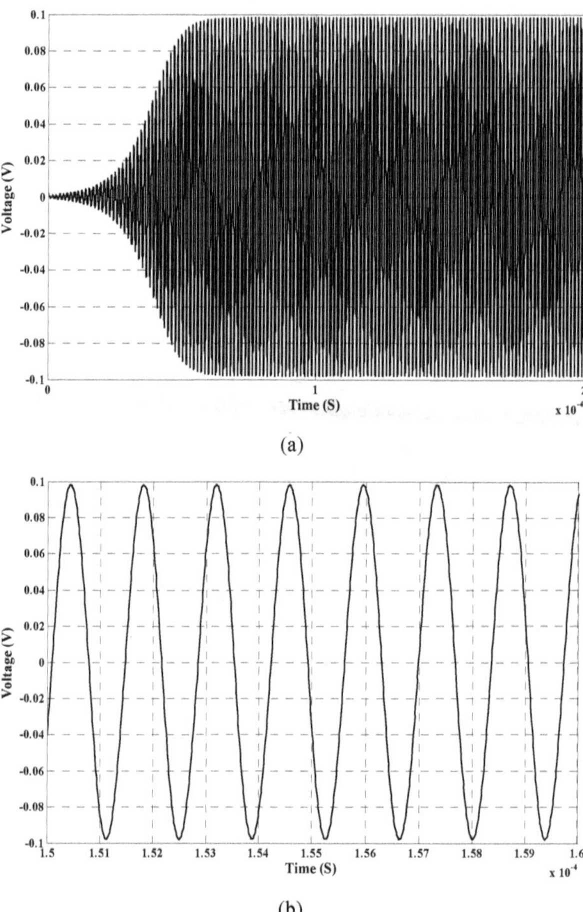

Figure 3. (a) Transient output waveform; (b) Steady state response of the output.

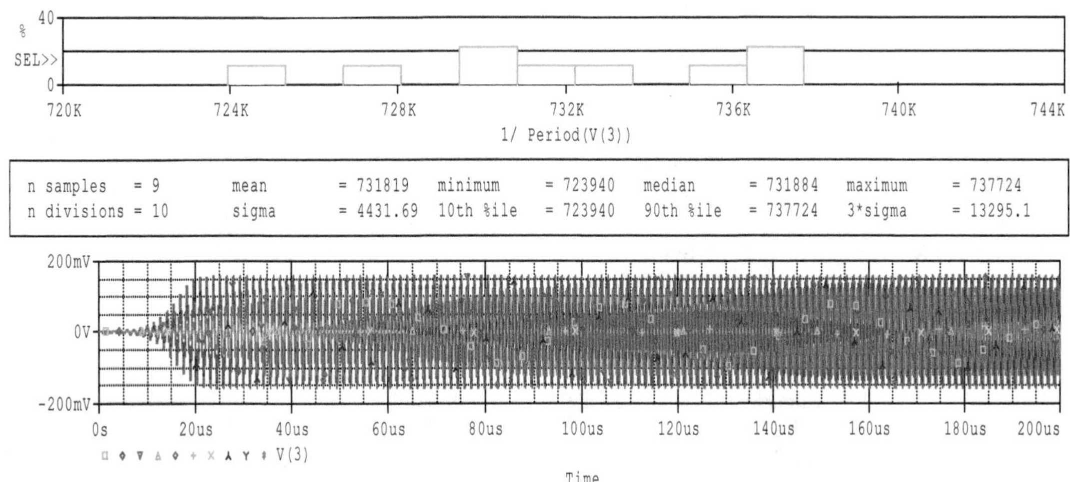

Figure 4. Result of Monte-Carlo simulation of oscillator circuit of Figure 2.

Table 1. Comparison with other previously known fully uncoupled sinusoidal oscillators.

Reference Number	No. of Active Elements	No. of Passive Elements	No. of Grounded Capacitors	Independent Electronic Tunability in Both CO and FO
[1]	2	6	2	NO
[2]	3	4 - 6	2 - 3	NO
[3]	3	5	2	NO
[4]	1 - 3	3 - 7	2 - 3	NO
[5]	3	6	2	NO
[6]	4	2	2	YES
[7]	2	2	2	YES
[14]	2	3	2	NO
Proposed	2	4	2	YES

posed oscillator. A comparison with other previously known fully uncoupled sinusoidal oscillators has been given in **Table 1**.

6. Concluding Remarks

A new sinusoidal oscillator with fully decoupled and electronically controllable both frequency of oscillation and condition of oscillation has been presented. The new oscillator configuration also enjoys 1) low active and passive sensitivities and 2) a very good frequency stability factor for larger values of *n*. The robustness of the proposed oscillator circuit has been confirmed by the Monte-Carlo analysis. The workability of the proposed configuration has been established by SPICE simulations with TSMC 0.18 μm process parameters.

REFERENCES

[1] W. Tangsrirat and S. Pisitchalermpong, "CDBA-Based Quadrature Sinusoidal Oscillator," *Journal of RF-Engineering and Telecommunication* (*Germany*), Vol. 61, No. 3-4, 2007, pp. 102-104.

[2] M. T. Abuelmatti, "New Sinusoidal Oscillators with Fully Uncoupled Control of Oscillation Frequency and Condition Using Three CCII + s," *Analog Integrated Circuits and Signal Processing*, Vol. 24, No. 3, 2000, pp. 253-261.

[3] D. R. Bhaskar, S. S. Gupta, R. Senani and A. K. Singh, "New CFOA-Based Sinusoidal Oscillators Retaining Independent Control of Oscillation Frequency Even under the Influence of Parasitic Impedances," *Analog Integrated Circuits and Signal Processing*, Vol. 73, 2012, pp. 427-437.

[4] A. M. Soliman, "Current Feedback Operational Amplifier Based Oscillators," *Analog Integrated Circuits and Signal Processing*, Vol. 23, No. 3, 2000, pp. 45-55.

[5] D. R. Bhaskar, "Realization of Second Order Sinusoidal Oscillator/Filters with Non-Interacting Controls Using CFAs," *Journal of RF-Engineering and Telecommunication* (*Germany*), Vol. 57, No. 1-2, 2003, pp. 12-14.

[6] D. R. Bhaskar and R. Senani, "New Linearly Tunable

CMOS-Compatible OTA-C Oscillators with Non-Interacting Controls," *Microelectronics Journal*, Vol. 25, No. 2, 1994, pp. 115-123.

[7] D. Prasad, M. Srivastava and D. R. Bhaskar, "Electronically Controllable Fully—Uncoupled Explicit Current-Mode Quadrature Oscillator Using VDTAs and Grounded Capacitors," *Circuits and Systems*, Vol. 4, No. 2, 2013, pp. 169-172.

[8] D. R. Bhaskar and R. Senani, "New CFOA-Based Single-Element-Controlled Sinusoidal Oscillators," *IEEE Transactions on Instrumentation and Measurement* (*USA*), Vol. 55, No. 6, 2006, pp. 2014-2021.

[9] S. S. Gupta and R. Senani, "Realisation of Current-Mode SRCOs Using All Grounded Passive Elements," *Frequenz*, Vol. 57, No. 1-2, 2003, pp. 25-36.

[10] D. Biolek, R. Senani, V. Biolkova and Z. Kolka, "Active Elements for Analog Signal Processing; Classification, Review and New Proposals," *Radioengineering*, Vol. 17, No. 4, 2008, pp. 15-32.

[11] D. Biolek and V. Biolkova, "First-Order Voltage-Mode All-Pass Filter Employing One Active Element and One Grounded Capacitor," *Analog Integrated Circuits and Signal Processing* (*USA*), Vol. 65, No. 1, 2009, pp. 123-129.

[12] D. Prasad, D. R. Bhaskar and K. L. Pushkar, "Realization of New Electronically Controllable Grounded and Floating Simulated Inductance Circuits Using Voltage Differencing Differential Input Buffered Amplifiers," *Active and Passive Electronic Components*, 2011, Article ID 101432.

[13] K. L. Pushkar, D. R. Bhaskar and D. Prasad, "Voltage-Mode Universal Biquad Filter Employing Single Voltage Differencing Differential Input Buffered Amplifier," *Circuits and Systems*, Vol. 4, No. 1, 2013, pp. 44-48.

[14] D. Prasad, D. R. Bhaskar and K. L. Pushkar, "Electronically Controllable Sinusoidal Oscillator Employing CMOS VD-DIBAs," *ISRN Electronics*, 2013, Article ID 823630.

Logic Picture-Based Dynamic Power Estimation for Unit Gate-Delay Model CMOS Circuits

Omnia S. Ahmed[1], Mohamed F. Abu-Elyazeed[1], Mohamed B. Abdelhalim[2], Hassanein H. Amer[3*], Ahmed H. Madian[4]

[1]Faculty of Engineering, Cairo University, Giza, Egypt

[2]College of Computing and Information Technology, Arab Academy for Science, Technology & Maritime Transport, Cairo, Egypt

[3]Electronics Engineering Department, American University in Cairo, Cairo, Egypt

[4]Radiation Engineering Department, Egyptian Atomic Energy Authority, Cairo, Egypt

ABSTRACT

In this research, a fast methodology to calculate the exact value of the average dynamic power consumption for CMOS combinational logic circuits is developed. The delay model used is the unit-delay model where all gates have the same propagation delay. The main advantages of this method over other techniques are its accuracy, as it is deterministic and it requires less computational effort compared to exhaustive simulation approaches. The methodology uses the Logic Pictures concept for obtaining the nodes' toggle rates. The proposed method is applied to well-known circuits and the results are compared to exhaustive simulation and Monte Carlo simulation methods.

Keywords: Dynamic Power Estimation; Logic Pictures; CMOS Digital Logic Circuits; Toggle Rate; Unit-Delay Model

1. Introduction

Power dissipation is an important parameter for digital VLSI circuits as the excessive power consumption may lead to runtime errors or permanent damages due to overheating. Hence, along with low power design techniques at different levels of the design, accurate power estimation tools are highly needed. Currently, there are many methods for estimating the power consumption; they are mainly categorized as non simulative-based [1-5] and simulative-based methods [6-9]. Non simulative-based methods can either be probabilistic or statistical. They rely on probabilistic measures for the inputs and the switching activities to estimate the power. While being efficient for large circuits with acceptable margins of errors, the power produced is not accurate but only an estimate. For simulative-based methods, the circuit is simulated with different inputs to obtain the power consumption. The main problems in simulative-based methods are the large memory requirements, time consumption and how to find the representative input vector set needed to exercise the circuit. Exhaustive simulations (where all pairs of input vectors are applied to the circuit) are very accurate but, obviously, time consuming, especially for large circuits.

In [10], an accurate method was introduced for calculating the average and the maximum dynamic power at the gate level. The paper developed the concept of Logic Pictures (LPs) in calculating the average power. As the LP is the status of gates outputs, it was found that the number of LPs was much smaller than the number of inputs patterns; hence, LPs were used instead of input patterns to obtain all the possible transitions for circuit nodes then obtaining the power consumption. The main advantage of this method is that it is deterministic and the simulations required are much less time-consuming than exhaustive simulations. The logic picture concept was modified in [11] to calculate the average power consumption for sequential circuits. In [12], the method was generalized and extended to calculate the maximum power consumption for sequential circuits including all types of Flip-Flops and their internal nodes power consumption; it was also shown how the tool could be used for design space exploration to select the appropriate Flip-Flop that consumed less power. While the method in [10-12] is accurate, it assumed that no propagation delay was associated with logic gates, *i.e.*, zero-delay model.

In this research, a method to calculate an accurate toggle rate assuming unit-delay model, is presented using

*Corresponding author.

the LP concept. The toggle rate can be directly related to the dynamic power consumption. The proposed method is backward-compatible as it can be easily modified to obtain the power consumption for the zero-delay gate model.

The rest of this paper is organized as follows. Section 2 introduces the methodology to calculate the switching activity of the circuit nodes under unit-delay model assumption for all the gates. Section 3 contains the experimental results while Section 4 has the conclusions.

2. Methodology

For CMOS logic circuits, the average dynamic power can be calculated as follows [13]:

$$P_{avg} = \frac{1}{2} V_{dd}^2 f_{clk} \sum_N \alpha_i c_i \quad (1)$$

where V_{dd} is the supply voltage, f_{clk} is the clock frequency, N is the number of gates outputs (circuit nodes), α_i is the toggle rate of the output of gate i and c_i is the output capacitance of gate i. From this equation, it can be seen that V_{dd} and f_{clk} depend on the fabrication technology while c_i is linearly proportional to the gate fan-out; the only parameter that depends on the circuit operation is α_i. Therefore, the toggle rate of the nodes is a good indicator of power dissipation [14].

Consider the circuit in **Figure 1** and assume that all inputs have equal probabilities to be 0 or 1.

The circuit has 2 gate outputs (nodes): d and e. As shown in the truth table in **Table 1**, column 3 indicates that the circuit has 3 LPs for the output nodes: 00, 01 and 11. Each LP is associated with a Logic Group (LG) composed of the input vectors that leads to this picture. For LP_1, LG_1 contains 3 input vectors that lead to LP_1: 000, 010 and 100. Hence, $\|LG_1\| = 3$. Similarly, $\|LG_2\| = 3$ and $\|LG_3\| = 2$.

Now, if the unit-delay model is assumed, a propagation delay δ is assigned for each gate and **Table 2** can be easily constructed.

Starting from an initial LP at time $t = 0$, if the input vector is from the LG that leads to the same initial LP, then it is not considered as there is no transition and hence no power consumption, while all the input vectors that belong to other LGs must be applied to get different LPs. The status of the nodes temporarily changes into other transient LPs at $t = \delta$ and finally change into a third, and final, LP at $t = 2\delta$ since there are 2 gates in the critical path. The transient LPs and the final LP are merged into one LP in the rightmost column of **Table 2**.

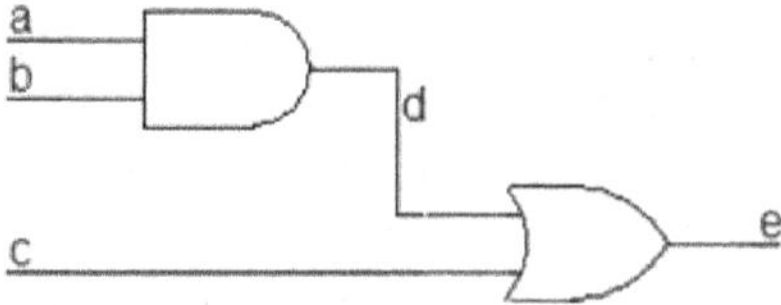

Figure 1. A simple 3-input circuit.

Table 1. Circuit logic pictures with zero-delay model.

Inputs			Outputs		Logic pictures	Logic groups
a	b	c	d	e		
0	0	0	0	0	LP_1 = "00"	LG_1
0	0	1	0	1	LP_2 = "01"	LG_2
0	1	0	0	0	LP_1	LG_1
0	1	1	0	1	LP_2	LG_2
1	0	0	0	0	LP_1	LG_1
1	0	1	0	1	LP_2	LG_2
1	1	0	1	1	LP_3 = "11"	LG_3
1	1	1	1	1	LP_3	LG_3

The number of transitions between the initial LPs and the merged LPs is calculated in **Table 3**. As an example, the transition between $LP_{1,0}$ and LP_1 can be obtained as follows: from **Table 1**, the number of inputs that leads to $LP_{1,0}$ is 3 (remember that $\|LG_1\| = 3$) while from **Table 2**, LP_1 appeared after $LP_{1,0}$ for 3 different inputs; hence, the number of different combinations of inputs that could lead from $LP_{1,0}$ to LP_1 is 3 × 3 = 9. LP_2 and LP_3 appeared only once in **Table 2** after $LP_{1,0}$; hence, the number of different input combinations that leads to LP_2 and LP_3 is 1 × 3 = 3. Finally, there is no input that leads from $LP_{1,0}$ to LP_4 or LP_5 which means zero direct transition between them.

To obtain the node transitions, if a node in the logic picture toggles from 1 to 0 or 0 to 1, then it is considered as a toggle. Then, this toggle is multiplied by the number of all possible input vectors that lead to this toggle. The same is done for all LPs through time. The possible number for transition for each node is then accumulated and divided by 2^{2n} to obtain the toggle rate. For example, $LP_{3,0}$ is "11"; the logic picture changes to $LP_{1,\delta}$ which is "01". This means that node d toggles from 1 to 0. All possible input transitions from $LP_{3,0}$ to $LP_{1,\delta}$ can be obtained from **Table 3** as $LP_{1,\delta}$ is a part of LP_1 and LP_5, then the input transitions are 6 + 6 = 12. In addition, there are toggles at node d from $LP_{1,0}$ to $LP_{2,\delta}$, $LP_{1,0}$ to $LP_{3,\delta}$, $LP_{2,0}$ to $LP_{2,\delta}$ and $LP_{2,0}$ to $LP_{3,\delta}$ with 3 possible input transitions for all 4 transitions cases. This leads to 12 other possible transitions. Hence, for node d, the number of transitions is 24. The same can be done with node e resulting into 36 transitions.

To conclude, the following equation can be used to obtain the toggle rate α_i with the unit-delay model:

$$\alpha_i = \frac{\sum_{t=1}^{s} \sum_{l=1}^{k_1(t)} \sum_{m=1}^{k_2(t+\delta)} R_{l,m} tr_t(P_l, P_m)}{2^{2n}} \quad (2)$$

where s is the number of stages in the critical path, K_1 and K_2 are the LPs in each state where the two states must be consecutive with respect to gates delay, *i.e.*, a

Table 2. All possible logic pictures for the unit-delay model.

Logic Group	Applied Inputs	Initial LP $t = 0$	Transient LP $t = \delta$	Final LP $t = 2\delta$	Merged LP
	a b c	d e	d e	d e	
LG_2	0 0 1	0 0 “$LP_{1,0}$”	0 1 “$LP_{1,\delta}$”	0 1 “$LP_{1,2\delta}$”	0 1 0 1 “LP_1”
LG_2	0 1 1	0 0 “$LP_{1,0}$”	0 1 “$LP_{1,\delta}$”	0 1 “$LP_{1,2\delta}$”	0 1 0 1 “LP_1”
LG_2	1 0 1	0 0 “$LP_{1,0}$”	0 1 “$LP_{1,\delta}$”	0 1 “$LP_{1,2\delta}$”	0 1 0 1 “LP_1”
LG_3	1 1 0	0 0 “$LP_{1,0}$”	1 0 “$LP_{2,\delta}$”	1 1 “$LP_{2,2\delta}$”	1 0 1 1 “LP_2”
LG_3	1 1 1	0 0 ’$LP_{1,0}$’	1 1 “$LP_{3,\delta}$”	1 1 “$LP_{2,2\delta}$”	1 1 1 1 “LP_3”
LG_1	0 0 0	0 1 “$LP_{2,0}$”	0 0 “$LP_{4,\delta}$”	0 0 “$LP_{3,2\delta}$”	0 0 0 0 “LP_4”
LG_1	0 1 0	0 1 “$LP_{2,0}$”	0 0 “$LP_{4,\delta}$”	0 0 “$LP_{3,2\delta}$”	0 0 0 0 “LP_4”
LG_1	1 0 0	0 1 “$LP_{2,0}$”	0 0 “$LP_{4,\delta}$”	0 0 “$LP_{3,2\delta}$”	0 0 0 0 “LP_4”
LG_3	1 1 0	0 1 “$LP_{2,0}$”	1 0 “$LP_{2,\delta}$”	1 1 “$LP_{2,2\delta}$”	1 0 1 1 “LP_2”
LG_3	1 1 1	0 1 “$LP_{2,0}$”	1 1 “$LP_{3,\delta}$”	1 1 ’$LP_{2,2\delta}$”	1 1 1 1 “LP_3”
LG_1	0 0 0	1 1 “$LP_{3,0}$”	0 1 “$LP_{1,\delta}$”	0 0 “$LP_{3,2\delta}$”	0 1 0 0 “LP_5”
LG_1	0 1 0	1 1 “$LP_{3,0}$”	0 1 “$LP_{1,\delta}$”	0 0 “$LP_{3,2\delta}$”	0 1 0 0 “LP_5”
LG_1	1 0 0	1 1 “$LP_{3,0}$”	0 1 “$LP_{1,\delta}$”	0 0 “$LP_{3,2\delta}$”	0 1 0 0 “LP_5”
LG_2	0 0 1	1 1 “$LP_{3,0}$”	0 1 “$LP_{1,\delta}$”	0 1 “$LP_{1,2\delta}$”	0 1 0 1 “LP_1”
LG_2	0 1 1	1 1 “$LP_{3,0}$”	0 1 “$LP_{1,\delta}$”	0 1 “$LP_{1,2\delta}$”	0 1 0 1 “LP_1”
LG_2	1 0 1	1 1 “$LP_{3,0}$”	0 1 “$LP_{1,\delta}$”	0 1 “$LP_{1,2\delta}$”	0 1 0 1 “LP_1”

state at δ and the other state at 2δ. $R_{l,m}$ are the repetition of the LPs p_l and p_m within a state and $tr(p_l, p_m) = 1$ if there is a node transition between p_l and p_m and equals 0 otherwise.

3. Experimental Results

The circuit used in [10] is shown in **Figure 2**. It was studied with the unit-delay model and it was noticed that the number of nodes transitions increased (compared to the zero-delay model) due to the glitches arising from the gates delays as shown in **Table 4**.

To validate the results of the proposed method, exhaustive and Monte Carlo simulations (as in [8]) are applied to the ISCAS-85 C17 benchmark circuit, the 7483 4-bit binary adder and the 74157 Quad 2-input multiplexer. The characteristics of these circuits are shown in **Table 5**. The resulting power is compared to that obtained using the proposed method. It is found that the difference between the obtained results from the proposed method and the Monte Carlo approach is negligible. Moreover, the results obtained are identical to those obtained using exhaustive simulations.

Since the simulation requires building the truth table (with size of 2^n), the tool running time is less than the time required for the exhaustive simulation approach. The memory saving ratio can be calculated as the ratio between the memory space required to store the LPs and the memory space needed for the exhaustive simulations [10]. For exhaustive simulations, $\left[2^n * \left(2^n - 1\right)\right]/2$ vectors must be stored; each vector represents a circuit input transition and consists of all the possible values for all circuit nodes; hence its size, in bits, is equal to the number of circuit nodes times the number of LPs. In the methodology proposed in this research, only $2^n * (K-1)$ vectors are required where k is the number of LGs. The size of each vector is identical to that mentioned in the exhaustive simulation method.

Finally the proposed method could be used to obtain the power consumption for the zero-delay model considering only the initial and final states; the power consumption obtained is found to be identical to the one calculated using the technique in [10].

4. Conclusion

This paper discussed a deterministic and accurate method to calculate the node toggle rate, hence dynamic power

Table 3. All transitions between initial LPs and merged LPs.

	$LP_{1,0}$	$LP_{2,0}$	$LP_{3,0}$
LP_1	9	0	6
LP_2	3	3	0
LP_3	3	3	0
LP_4	0	9	0
LP_5	0	0	6

Table 4. Node transitions with different delay models.

Node transitions	E	F	G	H
Zero-delay model	96	120	110	126
Unit-delay model	96	144	152	144

Table 5. Test circuit characteristics.

Circuit	Inputs	Nodes	LPs count	Critical path gates	Memory saving
ISCAS85-C17	5	6	10	3	1.7
7483	9	36	162	4	1.6
74157	10	15	34	4	15.5

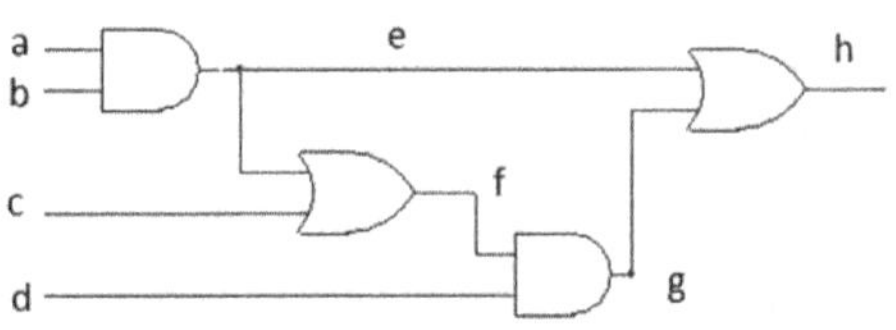

Figure 2. 4-input combinational circuit.

consumption, under the unit-delay model assumption for CMOS combinational circuits. The method is based on the logic picture concept and takes into account intermediate logic pictures that may appear due to gate delays. The proposed method was compared with both Monte Carlo and exhaustive simulations and applied to several circuits: ISCAS85-C17, 7483 4-bit binary adder and 74157 quad 2-input multiplexer. The results are identical but with much lower complexity.

REFERENCES

[1] G. Theodoridis, S. Theoharis, D. Soudris and C. Goutis, "An Efficient Probabilistic Method for Logic Circuits Using Real Gate Delay Model," *Proceedings of the International Symposium on Circuits and Systems ISCAS*, Orlando, 30 May-2 June 1999, pp. 286-289.

[2] S. Bhanja and N. Ranganathan, "Switching Activity Estimation of VLSI Circuits Using Bayesian Networks" *IEEE Transactions on VLSI Systems*, Vol. 11, No. 4, 2003, pp. 558-567.

[3] M. Xakellis and F. Najm, "Statistical Estimation of the Switching Activity in Digital Circuits," *Proceedings of the Conference on Design Automation DAC*, San Diego, 6-10 June 1994, pp. 728-733.

[4] M. Nemani and F. Najm, "Towards a High-Level Power Estimation Capability," *IEEE Transactions on Computer-Aided Design of Integrated Circuits and Systems*, Vol. 15, No. 6, 1996, pp. 588-598.

[5] A. Ghosh, S. Devadas, K. Keutzer and J. White, "Estimation of Average Switching Activity in Combinational and Sequential Circuits," *Proceedings of the Conference on Design Automation DAC*, Anaheim, 8-12 June 1992, pp. 253-259.

[6] C. S. Ding, C. Y. Tsui and M. Pedram, "Gate-Level Power Estimation Using Tagged Probabilistic Simulation," *IEEE Transactions on Computer-aided Design of Integrated Circuits and Systems*, Vol. 17, No. 11, 1998, pp. 1099-1107.

[7] S. M. Kang, "Accurate Simulation of Power Dissipation in VLSI Circuits," *IEEE Transactions on Solid-State Circuits*, Vol. 21, No. 5, 1986, pp. 889-891.

[8] R. Burch, F. N. Najm, P. Yang and T. N. Trich, "A Monte Carlo Approach for Power Estimation," *IEEE Transactions on VLSI Systems*, Vol. 1, No. 1, 1993, pp. 63-71.

[9] J. Monteiro, S. Daved, A. Chos, K. Keutzer and J. White, "Estimation of Average Switching Activity in Combinational Logic Circuits Using Symbolic Simulation," *IEEE Transactions on Computer-aided Design of Integrated Circuits and Systems*, Vol. 16, No. 1, 1997, pp. 121-127.

[10] M. F. Fouda, M. B. Abdelahlim and H. H. Amer, "Average and Maximum Power Consumption of Digital CMOS Circuits Using Logic Pictures," *Proceedings of the International Conference on Computer Engineering and Systems ICCES*, Cairo, 14-16 December 2009, pp. 14-16.

[11] M. F. Fouda, M. B. Abdelahlim and H. H. Amer, "Power Consumption of Sequential CMOS Circuits Using Logic Pictures," *Proceedings of the Biennial Baltic Electronics Conference BEC*, Tallinn, 4-6 October 2010, pp. 133-136.

[12] M. H. Amin, M. F. Fouda, A. M. Eltantawy, M. B. Abdelahlim and H. H. Amer, "Generalization of Logic Picture-Based Power Estimation Tool," *Proceedings of the First Annual International Conference on Energy Aware Computing ICEAC*, Cairo, 16-18 December 2010, pp. 133-136.

[13] F. Najm, "A Survey of Power Estimation Techniques in VLSI Circuits," *IEEE Transactions on VLSI Systems*, Vol. 2, No. 4, 1994, pp. 446-455.

[14] F. Najm, "Transition Density: A New Measure of Activity in Digital Circuits," *IEEE Transactions on Computer-Aided Design of Integrated Circuits and Systems*, Vol. 12, No. 2, 1993, pp. 310-323.

Power and Time Efficient IP Lookup Table Design Using Partitioned TCAMs

Youngjung Ahn, Yongsuk Lee, Gyungho Lee
Department of Computer Science & Engineering, Korea University, Seoul, South Korea

ABSTRACT

This paper proposes a power and time efficient scheme for designing IP lookup tables. The proposed scheme uses partitioned Ternary Content Addressable Memories (TCAMs) that store IP lookup tables. The proposed scheme enables O(1) time penalty for updating an IP lookup table. The partitioned TCAMs allow an update done by a simple insertion without the need for routing table sorting. The organization of the routing table of the proposed scheme is based on a partition with respect to the output port for routing with a smaller priority encoder. The proposed scheme still preserves a similar storage requirement and clock rate to those of existing designs. Furthermore, this scheme reduces power consumption due to using a partitioned routing table.

Keywords: IP Lookup Device; Routing Table; TCAMs; Insertion

1. Introduction

IP routers have been growing more complex with each passing year. These routers must continually support new features such as Quality of Service and Service Level Agreement monitoring, and they must perform these services at an increasing pace to match new connection speeds. The central design issue for these devices is performing IP lookup and classification at wire speed. Many routers now include a co-processor to perform the crucial task of IP lookup. The most critical issues are related to performance degradation, which occurs when a new entry is inserted into the table and due to the limitations imposed by the large encoder logic. In the worst case, the insertion will take O(N) time to be completed, where N represents the number of entries in the routing table. Table size is expected to grow in the future at an exponential rate, and the update time will linearly grow with table size [1]. On an average day, this same router may spend up to 10% of the time updating the table. No lookups are possible while an insertion is occurring. The insertion time has a dramatic effect on the performance of routers with large tables [2,3].

TCAMs allow a third matching state of "X" or "Don't Care" for one or more bits in the stored data word, thus adding flexibility to the search [4]. TCAMs have a very high cost/density ratio, and they have to search the entire table for each lookup that causes high power consumption [5]. Therefore, TCAMs are used in specialized applications such as packet classification and routing in high performance routers, where the searching speed cannot be accomplished using a less costly method. TCAMs are currently used to perform the task of the Longest Prefix Match (LPM) in high-end routers because they are able to search a table in parallel in one cycle. In such high end routers, it is crucial to have a time and power efficient scheme for updating IP lookup tables with new entry insertions. This paper proposes a novel solution that eliminates the need for routing table sorting per prefix length. As a result, the time penalty for inserting a new entry in the IP routing table is O(1). Moreover, it significantly reduces power consumption because of its partitioned TCAMs. This paper describes the proposed design and implementation details along with the simulation results and design evaluation.

2. Related Works

There have been many attempts to address the insertion problem in IP routing tables [6]. A commonly used technique involves adding empty space after each prefix group. If there is an empty slot after the required prefix group, the TCAM may keep a few empty memory locations every x non-empty memory locations ($x < N$, where N is the table size). The average case update time improves to O(x), but it degenerates to O(N) if the intermediate empty spaces are filled up [7]. A better technique is called the L-Algorithm, which can create an empty space in a TCAM in no more than L memory shifts [7]. L-Algorithm reduces the worst-case to O(L) where L is the length of the IP address. This means the algorithm would have a worst-case insertion time of O(32) for IPv4 and O(128) for IPv6. This algorithm takes advantage of the fact that sorting within each length group is unnecessary, so only one entry from each group needs to be moved. This provides a great improvement over the O(N). However, even with the L-Algorithm, problems can still occur in an actual router. A routing table update due to a new entry insertion may still need 32 or 128 cycles; this is undesirable in high-end routers. The design may also require a large overhead to manage the free space in the table. Also, when a burst of updates is received by the router, the router will not be able to route packets while the insertion is taking place. This means that the incoming packets need to be buffered. If the buffer size is not sufficient to hold all the received packets, then some will be dropped. This hurts the major selling point of routers, level of the worst-case performance and reliability. If the insertion time is reduced to O(1), then the need for additional buffering would be unnecessary since the insertions can happen at lookup speed.

TCAMs are currently used to perform the task of the Longest Prefix Match (LPM) in high-end routers because they are able to search a table in parallel in one cycle. However, TCAMs are inefficient in terms of power consumption even though the search time is fast. The size of TCAMs in IP lookup devices is increasing. There are currently many studies on reducing the power consumed by IP lookup devices by dividing routing tables [8,9].

3. Design Approach and Implementation Details

In order to keep the table sorted, the table must be updated, and the result would take O(N) moves. In the proposed design, the need for sorting is removed, and thus insertion time is improved to O(1). **Figure 1** shows the proposed design. The output port divides the table, so it is partitioned into smaller tables. The number of tables generated equals the number of output ports of the router, and each table holds a collection of all the entries that map to the output port that it corresponds with. All entries in a partitioned table map to the same output port, making it unnecessary to sort the entries in the table.

When searching, each TCAM checks the IP address in parallel. Each table outputs the matched lengths to a selection logic. The selection logic chooses the longest length, and the packet is sent to the output port based on the table that had the longest prefix match. When insertion is need, the output port matching the entry is checked by analyzing the entry. After figuring out the matching output port, the entry is inserted into an open location in the corresponding table. Note that the entry goes to "any" open location in the corresponding table.

Figure 2 shows the modified design for the partitioned table. Typical TCAM cells storing the network address prefix are shown on the left, and memory cells storing the lengths with the priority encoder removed are shown on the right. When the logic selects the table containing the LPM, the information of the output port is known, and there no longer a need for SRAM memory to store such information. Since the TCAM cells can be connected to the corresponding SRAM memory cells because they are directly related, the priority encoder and address decoders are also not needed. In addition, more than one row can be asserted at once. This is possible because there can only be one match per length. If a lookup results in more than one match of the same length, then this would mean that duplicate entries have been stored. Therefore, the maximum number of matches is 32-bits, the length of an IP address. Lengths are stored in a one-cold encoding. Since lengths are being stored instead of output ports in the SRAM cells, the number of SRAM cells needed is more than that in a typical router.

Since the TCAM cells are directly connected to the SRAMS cells, the proposed design reduces the complexity of the traditional design. For each entry, 32 TCAM cells are used to store the prefix, and 32 SRAM cells are used to store the prefix length. If more than one entry match is found, then each asserts a corresponding output line to reveal the prefix length. The selection logic checks the length output to determine the table containing the longest prefix match. This can be used to choose the longest match since there can only be a maximum of

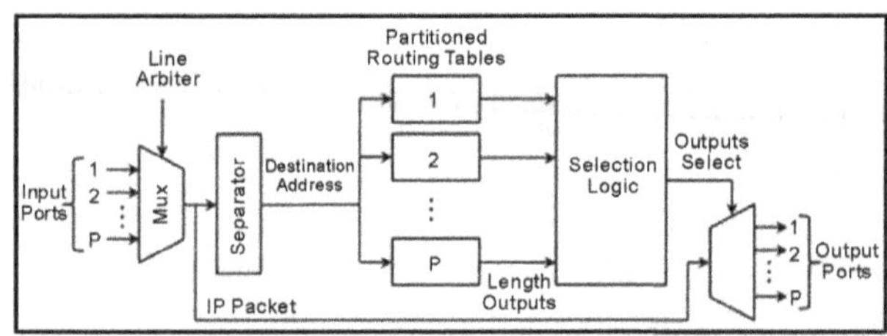

Figure 1. Proposed architecture.

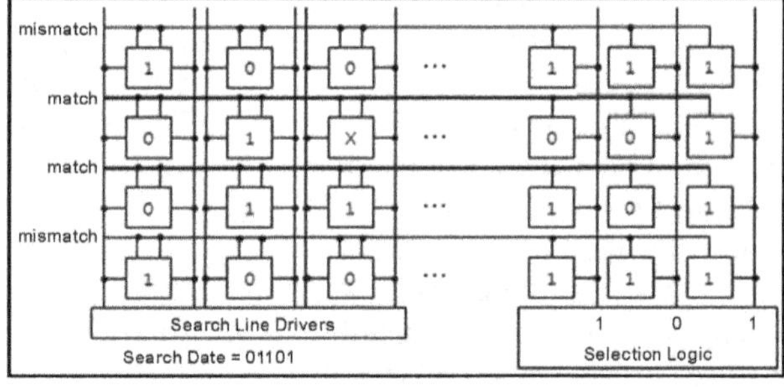

Figure 2. Modified routing table.

one matching entry for each prefix length between 1 and 32.

For the proposed design, the SRAM cell word lines are directly connected to the TCAM match lines. During normal SRAM operation, only one word line should be activated at once because if multiple word lines are activated, then the neighboring SRAM cells may become corrupt due to the shared bit line. The TCAM search may have multiple matches, and it can cause multiple SRAM word lines to be activated. Additional access transistors are added to each SRAM cell to activate the SRAM cell only if a "0" is stored in the cell. Only one SRAM cell will be activated for each column since each match can correspond to only one length, and the length is stored in a one-cold encoding. To enable access to the cell for writing, two additional transistors are needed and four transistors in total are added for each 6T SRAM cell. This is shown in **Figure 3**. The standard 6T SRAM cell is presented in the dotted line. The four extra transistors will increase the area and latency of the SRAM cell.

The size of each partition of the table should still be fairly large because the total table size is very large and the number of output ports is usually quite low. Long lines will significantly increase the latency [10]. This requires each partition to be further divided into smaller blocks, as is shown in **Figure 3**. The outputs from each block are combined in an OR scheme. Since there can only be one match for each length, there will be no conflicts.

Normally, the distribution of the prefixes will not be balanced across partitions. In some cases, more than 90% of the prefixes forward to the same port [11]. Many configurations are possible since this proposed design subdivides the partitions further to reduce the bit line length.

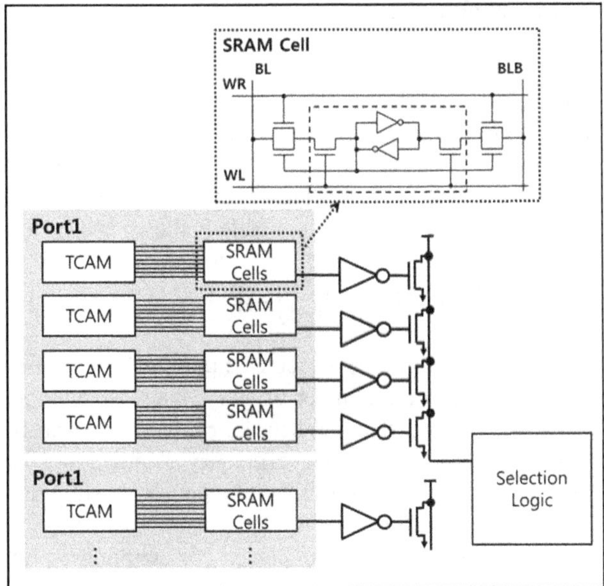

Figure 3. SRAM cell design and partitioned layout.

By combining the outputs of the blocks, *i.e.*, sub-tables, the OR scheme controls the boundaries of each partition. One end of the boundary connects to the selection logic, while the other end connects to a column pull-up. A basic switching scheme allows the partition sizes to be programmable. The number of possible configurations can be determined by the minimum grouping size. Due to hardware complexity limitations, switching connections cannot be available at all sub-table boundaries.

The selection logic takes inputs from the output lines of the partitions of the table. The logic uses 32 inputs for each output port, so if the router has four output ports, then 128 inputs are connected. The selection logic first determines the longest length that was found. Then, the output port is determined based on the table that the LPM is from. The logic finds the port with which the highest length is associated. Then, the packet can be forwarded to the correct port. This is a very simple logic and is similar in complexity to a small priority encoder.

4. Evaluation of the Design

Improving insertion time is only beneficial if the lookup latency is not slower than that of the original design. The proposed design is compared to a typical co-processor design. The typical design for this comparison contains a standard TCAM that is capable of holding up to 256 K entries. There are four and sixteen output ports in typical core routers. By analyzing this, four output ports have been used. This latency of the new and old designs could be broken down into several parts and could also be separately compared as shown in **Table 1**. As the table shows, both designs have similar latencies. Although the SRAM reading time is longer than that of the proposed design, the selection logic is much simpler than the logic of the priority encoder. The first portion of both designs begins with the TCAM search. The design of the TCAM cells remains unchanged so that the latency of the TCAM search could remain identical. In the proposed design, the next step is to access the SRAM cells that correspond to the matched prefixes from the TCAM search to determine the length of the prefix.

The overall size of the SRAM cell has increased due to the addition of access transistors. This increases the length of each bit line causing the capacitance to become larger, and this increases the necessity time to pull down

Table 1. The latency.

Original Design	TCAM Search	Priority Encoder	SRAM Read	Total
	~6.5 ns	~3.6 ns	2.7 ns	~12.8 ns
Proposed Design	TCAM Search	SRAM Read	Selection Logic	Total
	~6.5 ns	4.1 ns	~0.98 ns	~11.6 ns

the line. Since the bit lines of one large table are too long, the partition table is further broken into sub-tables. Each table outputs the bits corresponding to the lengths that were found in the sub-table. The results from each sub-table and each length are combined using an OR scheme. The optimal configuration was found by comparing the delay due to the size of each sub-table and the delay of combining the results from each sub-table. Cadence tools in a 0.25 um technology were used to simulate the access time of various SRAM configurations to compare the standard of SRAM cells. The capacitances of the bit lines were estimated based on the area increase of the additional transistors. These results show that the original SRAM performs approximately 33% faster than the new SRAM in all configurations. A full custom layout would provide more accurate results. Larger size is preferred in order to reduce the number of outputs that should be combined together. **Table 2** shows the simulation result.

In old designs, the delay of the major logic is from the priority encoder. This circuit becomes larger when it handles the input from all TCAM search lines. The proposed design directly connects the TCAM cells to the SRAM cells so that the priority encoder could be removed. The address decoder of the SRAM from the old design can be removed too. The major logic delay according to the proposed design is from the selection logic. First, the logic chooses the longest length, and it then determines the length of the partition table that was already found. The circuit is similar to a very small priority encoder.

The logic was designed by using Mentor Graphics ModelSim in Verilog. The design was synthesized using a 0.50 um technology and simulated by using Mentor Graphics LenardoSpecturm. The results show that the selection logic is much easier than the priority encoder and has a smaller delay. The results are shown in **Table 3**.

To evaluate the scalability of the proposed design, the differences between the two designs were compared. The

Table 2. SRAM simulations.

Size	Original SRAM	Proposed SRAM
128	1.4 ns	2.0 ns
256	2.0 ns	3.0 ns
512	2.7 ns	4.1 ns

Table 3. Logic simulations.

	Priority Encoder	Selection Logic
Gates	27,668	3015
Delay	14.4 ns	3.8 ns

TCAM cells have not been modified, so they will scale in the same way. When the SRAM cells were modified, they have shown about 33% difference in performance. Although the proposed design continuously has a difference, it will also scale in the same way. The largest difference between the two designs is found in the difference in logic. The selection logic scales logarithmically depend on three things. The length of the IP address, the number of output ports on the router and the size of the routing table. Since the length of the IP address is unexpected to increase after IPv6 and the number of output ports to change, the most important factor is the number of entries in the routing table. A priority encoder's delay will also scale logarithmically with respect to the number of entries in the table [12]. Its delay is not affected by the number of output ports or length of the IP address because there are no dependencies. The address decoder in SRAM will have a logN scaling factor. Based on the above analysis, both designs are expected to scale similarly as the routing table size grows. The power consumption in the partitioned routing table is shown as below. When the length of prefix is 32-bits while the number of entry of routing table is n, the power consumption of TCAMs is denoted as (1) [13]. P(n) consists of one TCAMs and describes the power consumption while the number of entry is n.

$$P(n) = \sqrt{n} \times (0.5 \times \log_2 n + 1) + 0.5 \times \log_2 n \qquad (1)$$

In IP lookup, the behavior of TCAMs can be divided by IP searching and notification of matched Prefix. According to [14], the ratio of power consumption of two functions is shown as (2). The IP search in TCAMs is advanced in all partitioned routing tables. In addition, the notification of matched Prefix is progressed in one partitioned routing tables.

$$\text{search} : \text{match} = 17 : 83 \qquad (2)$$

The proposed scheme divides the routing table corresponding to the output port. The number of entry of each partitioned table is n/x when the number of output port is x. By using this property and (2), the total power consumption of partitioned routing table is shown as (3).

$$P_{total} = (1 - 0.17) \times x \times P\left(\frac{n}{x}\right) + (1 - 0.83) \times p\left(\frac{n}{x}\right) \qquad (3)$$

Table 4 describes power consumption and efficiency corresponding to the number of entry, when the number of output port is sixteen. When the routing table can be divided into sixteen tables, efficiency is increased by approximately 28% compared to the power consumption of existing TCAMs. When the total number of entries is increased, the efficiency of power consumption is decreased because the number of x entries of each partitioned routing table is increased.

Table 4. Power consumption.

# of Entry	# of Output Port	Power Consumption		Efficiency
		TCAMs	Partitioned TCAMs	
128 K	16	3447.87	2432.89	29.44
256 K	16	5129.00	3660.05	28.64
512 K	16	7612.31	5488.88	27.89
1024 K	16	11274.00	8207.60	27.20

5. Conclusion

The purpose of IP router is to make a decision on a routing path to use and to forward a packet corresponding to the decided route. An existing router, which stores a prefix in the routing table, has a difficulty to meet QoS requirement from rapidly expanding internet environment—keep speeding up and adding new routes. The contribution of the proposed scheme is mainly to reduce routing table updating time and also the power consumption at the same time. The new design improves the routing table updating time by storing new prefix in routing table in unsorted manner: The worst case updating time in existing design O(N) reduces to O(1). In order to do this, the routing table is partitioned per output port, while the SRAM that stores a prefix length is directly connected to each partition of the routing table. This allows partitioned TCAMs to be employed in the design for shorter delay and lower power consumption. The logic of priority encoder and another logic related to existing SRAM are replaced to simple selection logic. This removes not only the needs for ordering the table by prefix length but also the lookup process for finding an output port.

6. Acknowledgements

This work was supported in part by the Basic Science Research Program through the National Research Foundation of Korea (NRF) funded by the Ministry of Education, Science and Technology (2012R1A1A2004615).

REFERENCES

[1] "Latest Version of AS65000-BGP Routing Table Statistics Analysis Report." http://bgp.potaroo.net/as2.0/bgp-active.html

[2] V. Srinivasan, B. Nataraj and S. Khanna, "Methods for Longest Prefix Matching In a Content Addressable Memory," US Patent 6237061, 1999.

[3] R. Guo and J. G. Delgado-Frias, "IP Routing Table Compaction and Sampling Schemes to Enhance TCAM Cache Performance," *Journal of Systems Architecture*, Vol. 55, No. 1, 2009, pp. 61-69.

[4] K. Pagiamtzis and A. Sheikholeslami, "Content-Addressable Memory (CAM) Circuits and Architectures: A Tutorial and Survey," *IEEE Journal of Solid-State Circuits*, Vol. 41, No. 3, 2006, pp. 712-727.

[5] S. Kaxiras and G. Keramidas, "IPStash: A Power-Efficient Memory Architecture for IP-Lookup," 36*th International Proceedings of Symposium on Microarchitecture*, San Diego, 3-5 December 2003, pp. 361-372.

[6] M. J. Akhbarizadeh and M. Nourani, "An IP Packet Forwarding Technique Based on Partitioned Lookup Table," *IEEE International Conference on Communications*, Vol. 4, 2002, pp. 2263-2267.

[7] D. Shah and P. Gupta, "Fast Updating Algorithms for TCAMs," *IEEE Micro*, Vol. 21, No. 1, 2001, pp. 36-47.

[8] T. Kocak and F. Basci, "A Power-Efficient TCAM Architecture for Network Forwarding Tables," *Journal of Systems Architecture*, Vol. 52, No. 5, 2006, pp. 307-314.

[9] V. C. Ravikumar, R. N. Mahapatra and L. N. Bhuyan, "EaseCAM: An Energy and Storage Efficient TCAM-Based Router Architecture for IP Lookup," *IEEE Transactions of Computer*, Vol. 54, No. 5, 2005, pp. 521-533.

[10] B. S. Amrutur and M. A. Horowitz, "Speed and Power Scaling of SRAMs," *IEEE Transactions on Solid-State Circuits*, Vol. 35, No. 2, 2000, pp. 175-185.

[11] The Internet Performance Measurement and Analysis Project. http://ftp.chg.ru/pub/network/routing/ipma/Manual/

[12] C. H. Huang and J. S. Wang, "High-Performance and Power-Efficient CMOS Comparators," *IEEE Journal of Solid-State Circuits*, Vol. 38, No. 2, 2003, pp. 254-262.

[13] W. Lu and S. Sahni, "Low-Power TCAMs for Very Large Forwarding Tables," *IEEE/ACM Transactions on Networking*, Vol. 18, No. 3, 2010, pp. 948-959.

[14] B. Agrawal and T. Sherwood, "Ternary CAM Power and Delay Model: Extensions and Uses," *IEEE Transactions on Very Large Scale Integration* (*VLSI*) *Systems*, Vol. 16, No. 5, 2008, pp. 554-564.

Electronically-Controllable Grounded-Capacitor-Based Grounded and Floating Inductance Simulated Circuits Using VD-DIBAs

Data Ram Bhaskar[1*], Dinesh Prasad[1], Kanhaiya Lal Pushkar[2]
[1]Department of Electronics and Communication Engineering, Faculty of Engineering and Technology, Jamia Millia Islamia, New Delhi, India
[2]Department of Electronics and Communication Engineering, Maharaja Agrasen Institute of Technology, Rohini, New Delhi, India

ABSTRACT

New Voltage Differencing Differential Input Buffered Amplifier (VD-DIBA) based lossless grounded and floating inductance simulation circuits have been proposed. The proposed grounded simulated inductance circuit employs a single VD-DIBA, one floating resistance and one grounded capacitor. The floating simulated inductance (FI) circuits employ two VD-DIBAs with two passive components (one floating resistance and one grounded capacitor). The circuit for grounded inductance does not require any realization conditions where as in case of floating inductance circuits, a single matching condition is needed. Simulation results demonstrating the applications of the new simulated inductors using CMOS VD-DIBAs have been included to confirm the workability of the new circuits.

Keywords: VD-DIBA; Inductance Simulation; Filters

1. Introduction

The importance of grounded and floating simulated inductors in the context of active network synthesis is well known [1]. Several grounded and floating inductance simulation schemes, employing different active elements such as operational amplifiers (op-amps) [2-6], current conveyors (CCs) [7-15], current controlled conveyors (CCCIIs) [16,17], current feedback operational amplifiers (CFOAs) [18,19], operational mirrored amplifiers (OMAs) [20], differential voltage current conveyors (DVCCIIs) [21], current differencing buffered amplifiers (CDBAs) [22,23], current differencing transconductance amplifiers (CDTAs) [24,25], operational transconductance amplifiers (OTAs) [26,27] have been reported in the literature. In [28], many new active building blocks have been introduced; VD-DIBA is one of them. Till now, some applications of VD-DIBAs have been reported in the open literature such as in the realization of all pass filters [29], realization of grounded and floating inductance circuits using two/three VD-DIBAs as reported in [30], electronically controllable sinusoidal oscillator in [31] and voltage-mode universal biquad in [32,33]. The purpose of this paper is to introduce new VD-DIBA-based: 1) a lossless grounded inductor using only a single VD-DIBA, one resistor and a grounded capacitor without requiring any matching condition and 2) two floating inductance simulation circuits employing two VD-DIBAs, one resistor and a grounded capacitor along with a single matching condition for floatation. The genesis of these FI circuits is inspired by [1,34,35].

2. The Proposed New Configuration

The schematic symbol and equivalent model of the VD-DIBA (−) are shown in **Figures 1(a)** and **(b)** respectively [29]. The model of VD-DIBA (−) includes two controlled sources: the current source controlled by differential voltage $(V_+ - V_-)$, with the transconductance g_m, and the voltage source controlled by differential voltage $(-V_z + V_v)$, with the unity voltage gain. The VD-DIBA (−) can be described by the following set of equations:

*Corresponding author.

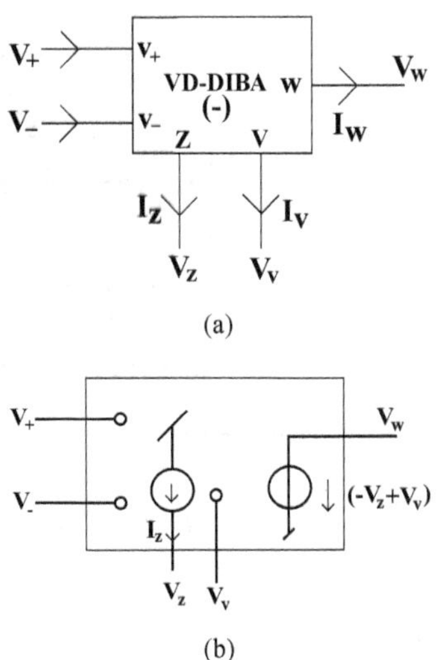

Figure 1. (a) Schematic symbol (b) equivalent model of VD-DIBA.

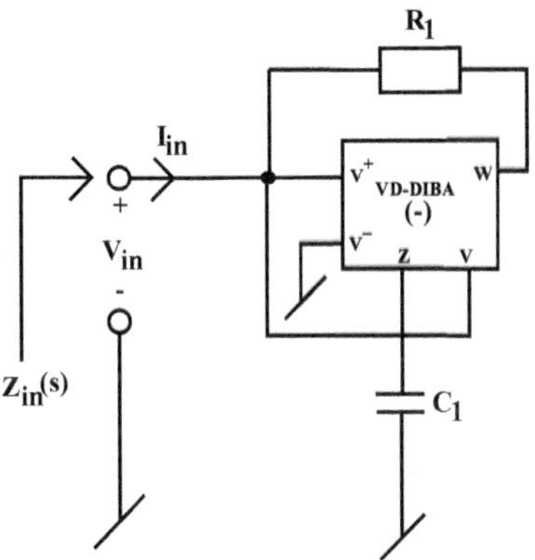

Figure 2. Proposed grounded inductance simulation configuration.

$$\begin{pmatrix} I_+ \\ I_- \\ I_z \\ I_v \\ V_w \end{pmatrix} = \begin{pmatrix} 0 & 0 & 0 & 0 & 0 \\ 0 & 0 & 0 & 0 & 0 \\ g_m & -g_m & 0 & 0 & 0 \\ 0 & 0 & 0 & 0 & 0 \\ 0 & 0 & -1 & 1 & 0 \end{pmatrix} \begin{pmatrix} V_+ \\ V_- \\ V_z \\ V_v \\ I_w \end{pmatrix} \quad (1)$$

The proposed grounded and floating inductance circuits are shown in **Figure 2** and **Figure 3** respectively.

A routine analysis of the circuit shown in **Figure 2** results in the following expression for the input impedance

$$Z_{in}(s) = \frac{V_{in}(s)}{I_{in}(s)} = s\left(\frac{C_1 R_1}{g_m}\right) \quad (2)$$

The circuit, thus, simulates a grounded inductance with the inductance value given by

$$L_{eq} = \frac{C_1 R_1}{g_m} \quad (3)$$

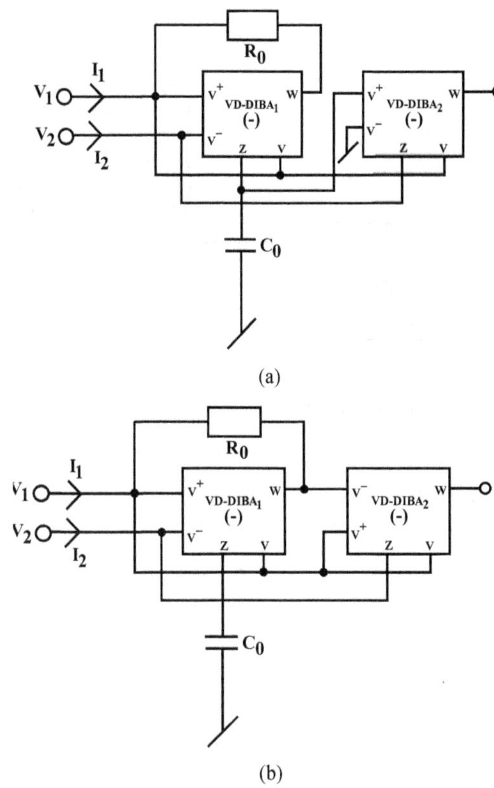

Figure 3. Proposed floating inductance simulation configurations.

On the other hand, analysis of the new FI circuits shown in **Figures 3(a)** and **(b)** yields

$$\begin{bmatrix} I_1 \\ I_2 \end{bmatrix} = \frac{g_{m_1} g_{m_2}}{sC_0} \begin{bmatrix} +1 & -1 \\ -1 & +1 \end{bmatrix} \begin{bmatrix} V_1 \\ V_2 \end{bmatrix}, \text{ with } g_{m_2} = \frac{1}{R_0} \quad (4)$$

which proves that the circuits simulate a floating lossless inductance with the inductance value given by

$$L_{eq} = \frac{C_0}{g_{m_1} g_{m_2}} \quad (5)$$

The proposed CMOS implementation of VD-DIBA (−) is shown in **Figure 4**. The CMOS VD-DIBA (−) is implemented using 0.35 μm MIETEC real transistor model which are listed in **Table 1**. Aspect ratios of transistors used are given in **Table 2**.

3. Non-Ideal Analysis and Sensitivity Performance

Let R_z and C_z denote the parasitic resistance and parasitic capacitance of the Z-terminal. Taking into account the non-idealities of the VD-DIBA (−), namely $V_w = \left(-\beta^+ V_z + \beta^- V_v\right)$, where $\beta^+ = 1 - \varepsilon_1 \left(\varepsilon_1 \ll 1\right)$ and $\beta^- = 1 - \varepsilon_2 \left(\varepsilon_2 \ll 1\right)$ are voltage tracking errors of the VD-DIBA, for the circuit shown in **Figure 2**, the non-ideal input impedance is found to be

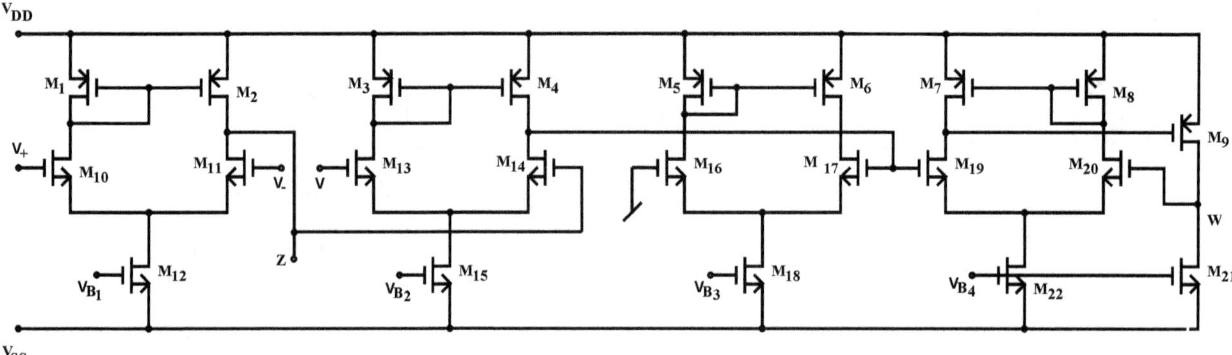

Figure 4. Proposed CMOS Implementation of VD-DIBA, $V_{DD} = -V_{SS} = 2$ V, $V_{B1} = -0.44$ V, $V_{B2} = I_{B3} = -0.22$ V and $V_{B4} = -0.9$ V.

Table 1. CMOS process parameters.

	N MOS	P MOS
LEVEL	3	3
TOX	7.9E-9	7.9E-9
NSUB	1E17	1E17
GAMMA	0.5827871	0.4083894
PHI	0.7	0.7
VTO	0.5445549	-0.7140674
DELTA	0	0
UO	436.256147	212.2319801
ETA	0	9.999762E-4
THETA	0.1749684	0.2020774
KP	2.055786E-4	6.733755E-5
VMAX	8.309444E4	1.181551E5
KAPPA	0.2574081	1.5
RSH	0.0559398	30.0712458
NFS	1E12	1E12
TPG	1	-1
XJ	3E-7	2E-7
LD	3.162278E-11	5.000001E-13
WD	7.046724E-8	1.249872E-7
CGDO	2.82E-10	3.09E-10
CGSO	2.82E-10	3.09E-10
CGBO	1E-10	1E-10
CJ	1E-3	1.419508E-3
PB	0.9758533	0.8152753
MJ	0.3448504	0.5
CJSW	3.777852E-10	4.813504E-10
MJSW	0.350872	0.5

Table 2. Dimensions of CMOS transistors.

Transistor	W/L (μm)
M1-M6	14/1
M7-M9	14/0.35
M10-M18	4/1
M19-M22	7/0.35

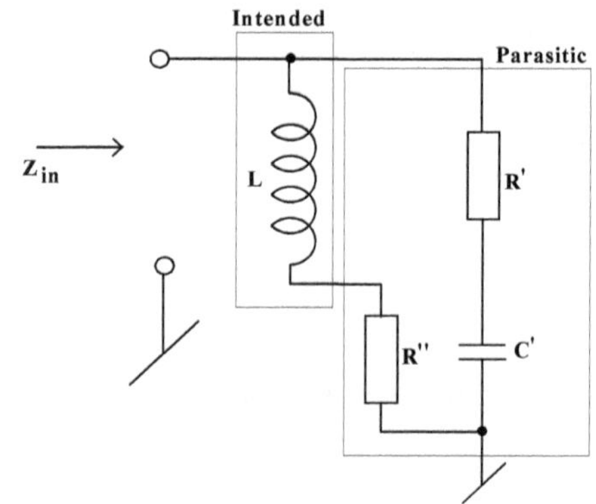

Figure 5. Non-ideal equivalent circuit of grounded inductor of Figure 2.

$$Z_{in}(s) = \frac{\left\{ s(C_1 + C_z) + \frac{1}{R_z} \right\}}{\left\{ s\frac{(C_1 + C_Z)(1-\beta^-)}{R_1} + \frac{(1-\beta^-)}{R_1 R_Z} + \frac{\beta^+ g_m}{R_1} \right\}} \tag{6}$$

From the above, a non-ideal equivalent circuit of the grounded inductor is derivable which is shown in **Figure 5**.

Where $L = \frac{(C_1 + C_z) R_1 R_Z}{\left\{(1-\beta^-) + \beta^+ g_m R_Z\right\}}$, $R' = \frac{R_1}{(1-\beta^-)}$,

$C' = \frac{(C_1 + C_Z)(1-\beta^-) R_Z}{R_1}$,

and $R'' = \dfrac{R_1}{\{(1-\beta^-)+\beta^+ g_m R_Z\}}$

From the above, the sensitivities of L with respect to various active and passive elements are found to be

$$\begin{aligned}
S^L_{C_0} &= \frac{C_1}{(C_1+C_z)}, S^L_{C_z} = \frac{C_z}{(C_1+C_z)}, S^L_{R_0} = 1,\\
S^L_{R_z} &= \frac{(1-\beta^-)}{\{(1-\beta^-)+\beta^+ g_m R_Z\}},\\
S^L_{\beta^-} &= \frac{\beta^-}{\{(1-\beta^-)+\beta^+ g_m R_Z\}},\\
S^L_{\beta^+} &= -\frac{\beta^+ g_m R_Z}{\{(1-\beta^-)+\beta^+ g_m R_Z\}},\\
S^L_{g_m} &= -\frac{\beta^+ g_m R_Z}{\{(1-\beta^-)+\beta^+ g_m R_Z\}}
\end{aligned} \tag{7}$$

similarly, for the circuit shown in **Figures 3(a)** and **(b)** for $\beta^- = \beta^+ = 1$, the input-output currents and voltages relationships are given by:

$$\begin{bmatrix} I_1 \\ I_2 \end{bmatrix} = \frac{g_{m_1} g_{m_2}}{\left\{s(C_0+C_{z_1})+\dfrac{1}{R_{Z_1}}\right\}} \times \begin{bmatrix} 1 & -1 \\ -1 & 1+\dfrac{\left\{s(C_0+C_{z_1})+\dfrac{1}{R_{Z_1}}\right\}\left(sC_{z_2}+\dfrac{1}{R_{Z_2}}\right)}{g_{m_1} g_{m_2}} \end{bmatrix} \begin{bmatrix} V_1 \\ V_2 \end{bmatrix}$$

with $g_{m_2} = \dfrac{1}{R_0}$ (8)

The non-ideal equivalent circuit of floating inductors of **Figures 3(a)** and **(b)** derivable from Equation (8) is shown in **Figure 6**.

Where $L = \dfrac{(C_0+Cz_1)}{g_{m_1} g_{m_2}}$ and $R = \dfrac{1}{R_{z_1} g_{m_1} g_{m_2}}$

The various sensitivities of L with respect to active and passive elements are:

$$\begin{aligned}
S^L_{C_0} &= \frac{C_0}{(C_0+C_{z_1})}, S^L_{C_{z_1}} = \frac{C_{z_1}}{(C_0+C_{z_1})}, S^L_{g_{m_1}} = -1,\\
S^L_{g_{m_2}} &= -1,\ S^L_{\beta^+} = 0,\ S^L_{\beta^-} = 0
\end{aligned} \tag{9}$$

Taking $g_{m_1} = g_{m_2} = 389.673\ \mu\text{A/V}$, $C_{z_1} = C_{z_2} = 0$, $R_{z_1} = R_{z_2} = \infty$, $C_0 = 0.1\ \text{nF}$ and $R_0 = 100\ \text{k}\Omega$, these sensitivities are found to be (1, 0, 1, 0, 0, −1) and (1, 0, −1, −1, 0, 0) for Equations (7) and (9) respectively. Thus, all the passive and active sensitivities of both grounded and floating inductance circuits are low.

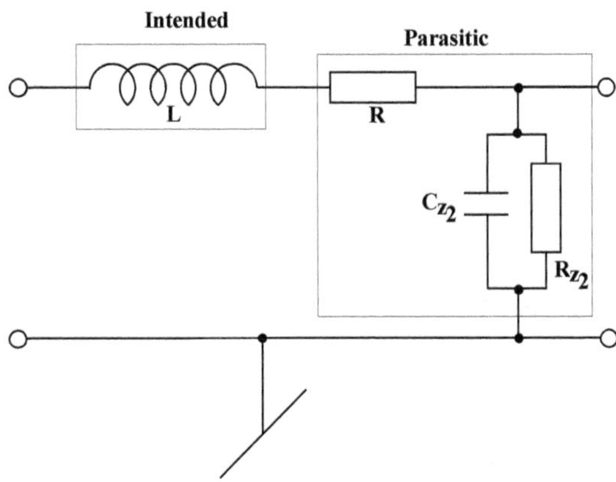

Figure 6. Non-ideal equivalent circuit of floating inductor of Figure 3.

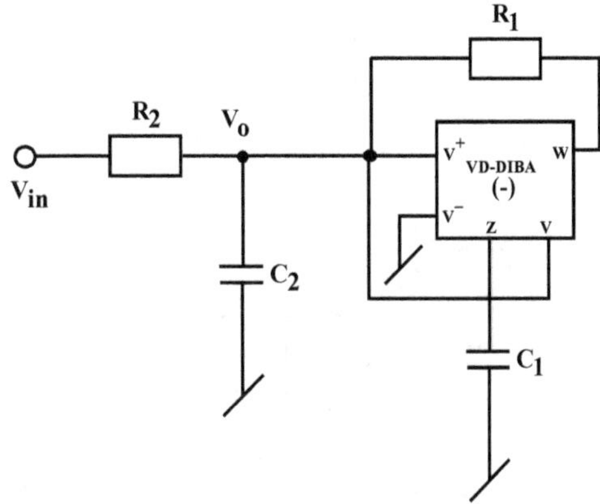

Figure 7. Band pass filter realized by the new grounded simulated inductor.

4. Simulation Results of the New Proposed Grounded/Floating Inductance Configurations

The workability of the proposed simulated inductors has been verified by realizing a band pass filter (BPF) as shown in **Figures 7** and **8**.

The transfer function realized by this configuration is given by

$$\frac{V_0}{V_{in}} = \frac{s\left(\dfrac{1}{R_2C_2}\right)}{s^2+s\left(\dfrac{1}{R_2C_2}\right)+\left(\dfrac{g_{m_1}}{C_1C_2R_1}\right)} \tag{10}$$

from where it is seen that bandwidth and centre frequency are independently tunable, the former by R_2 and the latter by any of R_1, g_{m_1} and C_1.

The transfer function realized by configuration shown in **Figure 8** is given by

$$\frac{V_0}{V_{in}} = \frac{s\left(\frac{R_1 g_{m_1} g_{m_2}}{C_0}\right)}{s^2 + s\left(\frac{R_1 g_{m_1} g_{m_2}}{C_0}\right) + \frac{g_{m_1} g_{m_2}}{C_0 C_1}} \text{ with } g_{m_2} = \frac{1}{R_0}, \quad (11)$$

In this case, bandwidth is tunable by R_1 whereas centre frequency can be tuned by C_1.

Performance of the new simulated inductors was verified by SPICE simulations. CMOS-based VD-DIBA (−) (as shown in **Figure 4**) was used to determine the frequency responses of the grounded and floating simulated inductors. The following values were used for grounded inductor: $C_1 = 0.01\text{nF}$, $R_1 = 100\ \text{k}\Omega$, $g_{m_1} = 296.468\ \mu\text{A/V}$ and for the floating inductor: $C_0 = 0.01\ \text{nF}$, $R_0 = 100\ \text{k}\Omega$, $g_{m_1} = 296.468\ \mu\text{A/V}$, $g_{m_2} = 10\ \mu\text{A/V}$. From the frequency response of the simulated grounded inductor (**Figure 9**) it has been observed that the inductance value remains constant up to 1 MHz. Similarly, from the frequency response of the simulated floating inductor (**Figure 10**) the inductance value also remains constant up to 1 MHz.

To verify the theoretical analysis of the application circuits shown in **Figures 7** and **8**, they have also been simulated using CMOS-based VD-DIBA (−) as shown in **Figure 4**. The component values used were for **Figure 7**: $C_1 = 0.1$ nF, $C_2 = 1$ pF, $R_1 = 100$ kΩ, $R_2 = 113.258$ kΩ and for **Figures 8(a)** and **(b)**: $C_0 = 0.1$ nF, $C_1 = 0.01$ nF, $R_0 = 100$ kΩ, $R_1 = 71.652$ kΩ, $g_{m_2} = 10\ \mu\text{A/V}$ (which can be maintained by taking $V_{B1} = -1.5\text{V}$). The VD-DIBA was biased with ±2 volts D.C. power supplies with $V_{B1} = -0.44\text{V}$, $V_{B2} = V_{B3} = -0.22\text{V}$ and $V_{B4} = -0.9\text{V}$. VD-DIBA (−) transconductance is controlled by V_{B1}. **Figure 11**, **Figures 12(a)** and **(b)** show the simulated filter responses of the BP filters.

The above described results, thus, confirm the validity of the application of the proposed grounded and floating simulated inductance circuits. A comparison of the various salient features of the proposed configurations as compared to other previously known grounded and FI

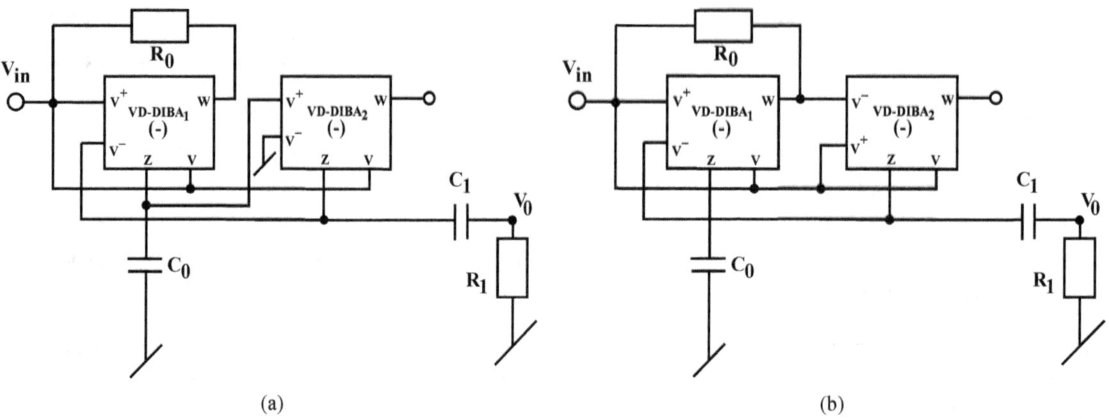

Figure 8. Band pass filters realized by the new floating simulated inductors of Figures 3(a) and (b).

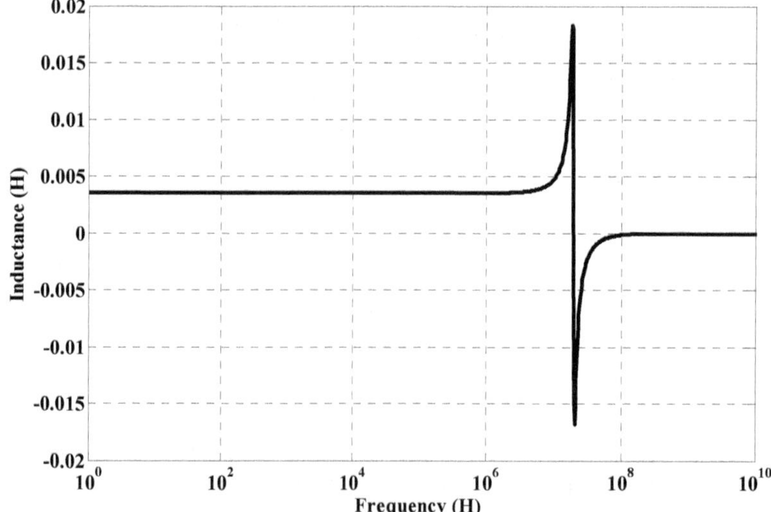

Figure 9. Frequency response of the simulated grounded inductor.

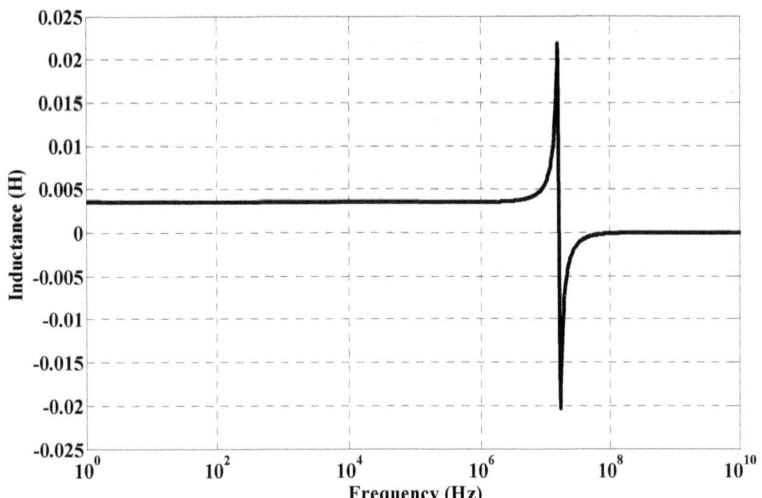

Figure 10. Frequency response of the simulated floating inductor.

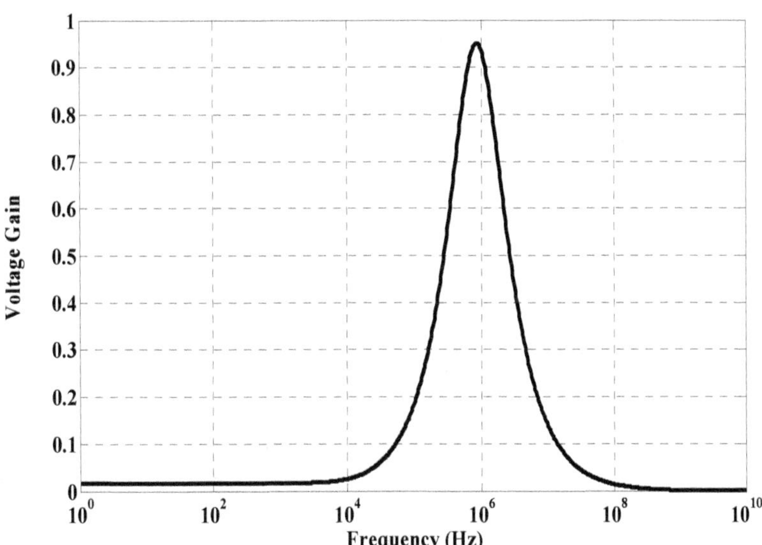

Figure 11. Frequency response of BPF using the proposed simulated grounded inductor.

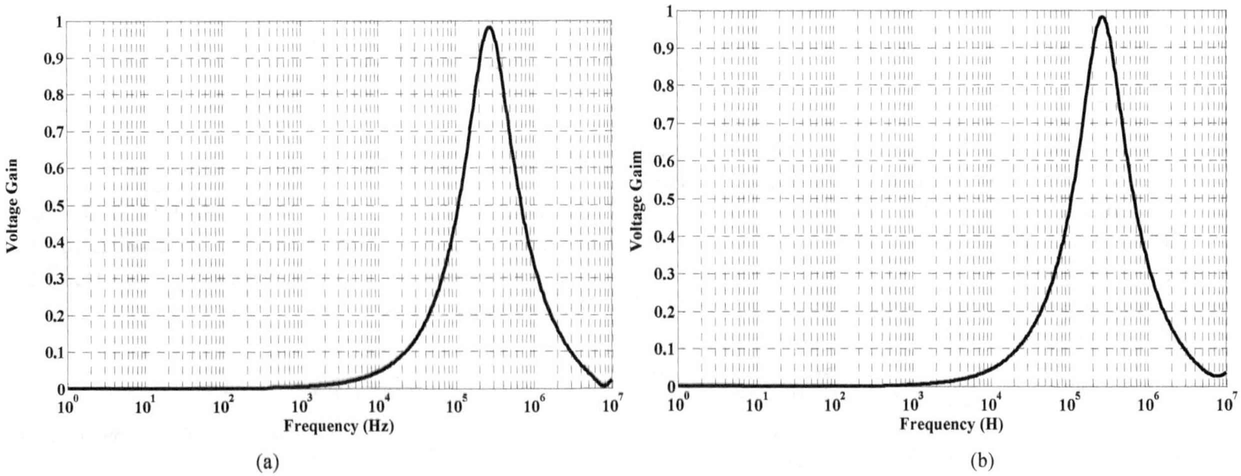

Figure 12. Frequency response of BPF using the proposed simulated floating inductor.

Table 3. Comparison with other previously published grounded and floating inductors.

Reference	Inductance type*	Number of active elements used	Number of resistors used	Number of capacitors used	Matching condition required	Availability of Electronic tunability
[4]	F	3	3	1	yes	no
[7]	F	3/2	2	1	no	no
[8]	F	4	4	1	yes	no
[9]	F	4	3	1	yes	no
[10]	F	4	2	1	no	no
[11]	F	4	2	1	no	no
[12]	F	2	2	1	no	no
[14]	G	1	2	1	yes	no
[16]	F	4/3	3	1	no	no
[17]	G	2	0	1	no	yes
[18]	G	2	2	1	no	no
[19]	F	2	3	2	yes	no
[20]	F	3	2	1	no	no
[21]	G	3	4	1	no	no
	F	3	4	1	no	no
[22]	F	3/4	4	1	yes	yes
[23]	F	3	0	1	yes	yes
[24]	F	3	0	1	yes	yes
[25]	G	2	0	1	no	yes
	F	3	0	1	yes	yes
[26]	G	2	0	1	no	yes
	F	3	0	1	yes	yes
[30]	G	2	0	1	no	yes
	F	3	0	1	yes	yes
[36]	F	3	2	1	no	no
[37]	G	3	3	1	no	no
Proposed	G	1	1	1	no	yes
	F	2	1	1	yes	yes

*F = Floating, G = Grounded.

simulators has been included in **Table 3**.

5. Conclusions

New circuits of lossless grounded and floating inductance have been proposed employing VD-DIBAs. The proposed grounded inductance circuit employs only one VD-DIBA (−), one resistor and one grounded capacitor and does not require any component matching condition. On the other hand, the two floating inductance configurations each using two VD-DIBAs (−), one resistor and one grounded capacitor, need only a single realization condition for floatation. The SPICE simulation results have confirmed the workability of the new propositions as well as the suggested application examples using them.

The problem of realizing any new single VD-DI-BA-based FI configuration using a single grounded capacitor and without requiring any matching condition appears to be an interesting problem which is open to be investigated.

6. Acknowledgements

The authors gratefully acknowledge Prof. Dr. Raj Senani, Head, Division of Electronics and Communication Engineering, and Director NSIT, New Delhi, for useful discussions/suggestions.

REFERENCES

[1] R. Senani, "New Single-Capacitor Simulations of Floating Inductors," *Electro Component Science and Technology*, Vol. 10, No. 1, 1982, pp. 7-10.

[2] A. Antoniou, "Gyrators Using Operational Amplifiers," *IEEE Electronics Letters*, Vol. 3, No. 8, 1967, pp. 350-352.

[3] A. Antoniou, "Realization of Gyrators Using Op-Amps and Their Use in RC Active Network Synthesis," *Proceedings of the IEEE*, Vol. 116, 1969, pp. 1838-1850.

[4] R. Senani, "Realization of Single Resistance-Controlled Lossless Floating Inductance," *IEEE Electronics Letters*, Vol. 14, No. 25, 1978, pp. 828-829.

[5] T. S. Rathore and B. M. Singhi, "Active RC Synthesis of Floating Immittances," *International Journal of Circuit Theory and Applications*, Vol. 8, No. 2, 1980, pp. 184-188.

[6] R. Senani, "Three Op-Amp Floating Immittance Simulators: A Retrospection," *IEEE Transactions on Circuits and Systems Part* II, Vol. 36, No. 11, 1989, pp. 1463-1465.

[7] R. Senani, "New Tunable Synthetic Floating Inductors," *IEEE Electronics Letters*, Vol. 16, No. 10, 1980, pp. 382-383.

[8] K. Pal, "Novel Floating Inductance Using Current Conveyors," *IEEE Electronics Letters*, Vol. 17, No. 18, 1981, p. 638.

[9] V. Singh, "Active RC Single-Resistance-Controlled Lossless Floating Inductance Simulation Using Single Grounded Capacitor," *IEEE Electronics Letters*, Vol. 17, No. 24, 1981, pp. 920-921.

[10] R. Senani, "Novel Lossless Synthetic Floating Inductor Employing a Grounded Capacitor," *IEEE Electronics Letters*, Vol. 18, No. 10, 1982, pp. 413-414.

[11] W. Kiranon and P. Pawarangkoon, "Floating Inductance Simulation Based on Current Conveyors," *IEEE Electronics Letters*, Vol. 33, 1997, pp. 1748-1749.

[12] P. V. Anand Mohan, "Grounded Capacitor Based Grounded and Floating Inductance Simulation Using Current Conveyors," *IEEE Electronics Letters*, Vol. 34, No. 11, 1998, pp. 1037-1038.

[13] H. Sedef and C. Acar, "A New Floating Inductor Circuit Using Differential Voltage Current Conveyors," *Journal of RF-Engineering and Telecommunications*, Vol. 54, No. 5-6, 2000, pp. 123- 125.

[14] E. Yuce, S. Minaei and O. Cicekoglu, "A Novel Grounded Inductor Realization Using a Minimum Number of Active and Passive Components," *ETRI Journal*, Vol. 27, No. 4, 2005, pp. 427-432.

[15] O. Cicekoglu, "Active Simulation of Grounded Inductors with CCII+s and Grounded Passive Elements," *International Journal of Electronics*, Vol. 85, No. 4, 1998. pp. 455-462.

[16] E. Yuce, "On the Realization of the Floating Simulators Using Only Grounded Passive Components," *Analog Integrated Circuits and Signal Processing*, Vol. 49, 2006, pp. 161-166.

[17] T. Parveen and M. T. Ahmed, "Simulation of Ideal Grounded Tunable Inductor and Its Application in High Quality Multifunctional Filter," *Microelectronics Journal*, Vol. 23, No. 3, 2006, pp. 9-13.

[18] A. Fabre, "Gyrator Implementation from Commercially Available Trans Impedance Operational Amplifiers," *IEEE Electronics Letters*, Vol. 28, No. 3, 1992, pp. 263-264.

[19] R. Senani and D. R. Bhaskar, "New Lossy/Lossless Synthetic Floating Inductance Configuration Realized with Only Two CFOAs," *Analog Integrated Circuits and Signal Processing*, Vol. 73, No. 3, 2012, pp. 981-987.

[20] R. Senani and J. Malhotra, "Minimal Realizations of a Class of Operational Mirrored Amplifier Based Floating Impedance," *IEEE Electronics Letters*, Vol. 30, No. 14, 1994, pp. 1113-1114.

[21] K. Pal and M. J. Nigam, "Novel Active Impedances Using Current Conveyors," *Journal of Active and Passive Electronic Devices*, Vol. 3, No. 1, 2008, pp. 29-34.

[22] A. U. Keskin and H. Erhan, "CDBA-Based Synthetic Floating Inductance Circuits with Electronic Tuning Properties," *ETRI Journal*, Vol. 27, No. 2, 2005, pp. 239-242.

[23] W. Tangsrirat and W. Surakampontorn, "Electronically Tunable Floating Inductance Simulation Based on Current-Controlled Current Differencing Buffered Amplifiers," *Thammasat International Journal of Science and Technology*, Vol. 11, No. 1, 2006, pp. 60-65.

[24] D. Biolek and V. Biolkova, "Tunable Ladder CDTA-Based Filters," 4*th Multi Conference* (*WSEAS*), Spain, 19-21 December 2003, pp. 1-3.

[25] D. Prasad, D. R. Bhaskar and A. K. Singh, "New Grounded and Floating Simulated Inductance Circuits Using Current Differencing Transconductance Amplifiers," *Radio Engineering Journal*, Vol. 19, No. 1, 2010, pp. 194-198.

[26] R. Nandi, "Lossless Inductor Simulation: Novel Configurations Using DVCCs," *IEEE Electronics Letters*, Vol. 16, No. 17, 1980, pp. 666-667.

[27] M. T. Abuelmaatti, M. H. Khan and H. A. Al-Zaher, "Simulation of Active-Only Floating Inductance," *Journal of RF-Engineering and Telecommunications*, Vol. 52, No. 7-8, 1998, pp. 161- 164.

[28] D. Biolek, R. Senani, V. Biolkova and Z. Kolka, "Active Elements for Analog Signal Processing; Classification, Review and New Proposals," *Radioengineering*, Vol. 17, No. 4, 2008, pp. 15-32.

[29] D. Biolek and V. Biolkova, "First-Order Voltage-Mode All-Pass Filter Employing One Active Element and One Grounded Capacitor," *Analog Integrated Circuits and Signal Processing*, Vol. 65, No. 1, 2010, pp. 123-129.

[30] D. Prasad, D. R. Bhaskar and K. L. Pushkar, "Realization of New Electronically Controllable Grounded and Floating Simulated Inductance Circuits using Voltage Differencing Differential Input Buffered Amplifiers," *Active and Passive Electronic Components*, 2011, Article ID 101432.

[31] D. Prasad, D. R. Bhaskar and K. L. Pushkar, "Electronically Controllable Sinusoidal Oscillator Employing CMOS VD-DIBAs," *ISRN Electronics*, Vol. 2013, Article ID 823 630, 6 Pages.

[32] K. L. Pushkar, D. R. Bhaskar and D. Prasad, "Voltage-

Mode Universal Biquad Filter Employing Single Voltage Differencing Differential Input Buffered Amplifier," *Circuits and Systems*, Vol. 4, No. 1, 2013, pp. 44-48.

[33] K. L. Pushkar, D. R. Bhaskar and D. Prasad, "A New MISO-Type Voltage-Mode Universal Biquad Using Single VD-DIBA," *ISRN Electronics*, Vol. 2013, Article ID: 478213, 5 Pages.

[34] R. Senani, "Some New Synthetic Floating Inductance Circuits," *AEU: International Journal of Electronics and Communications*, Vol. 35, 1981, pp. 307-310.

[35] R. Senani, "Canonic Synthetic Floating-Inductance Circuits Employing Only a Single Component-Matching Condition," *Journal of IETE*, Vol. 27, No. 6, 1981, pp. 201-204.

[36] S. A. Al-Walaie and M. A. Alturaigi, "Current Mode Simulation of Lossless Floating Inductance," *International Journal of Electronics*, Vol. 83, No. 6, 1997, pp. 825-830.

[37] E. Yuce, "Grounded Inductor Simulators with Improved Low Frequency Performances," *IEEE Transactions on Instrumentation and Measurement*, Vol. 57, No. 5, 2008, pp. 1079-1084.

27

An Improved SOI CMOS Technology Based Circuit Technique for Effective Reduction of Standby Subthreshold Leakage

Manish Kumar[1], Md. Anwar Hussain[1], Sajal K. Paul[2]
[1]Department of Electronics and Communication Engineering, North Eastern Regional Institute of Science and Technology, Arunachal Pradesh, India
[2]Department of Electronics Engineering, Indian School of Mines, Jharkhand, India

ABSTRACT

Silicon-on-insulator (SOI) CMOS technology is a very attractive option for implementing digital integrated circuits for low power applications. This paper presents migration of standby subthreshold leakage control technique from a bulk CMOS to SOI CMOS technology. An improved SOI CMOS technology based circuit technique for effective reduction of standby subthreshold leakage power dissipation is proposed in this paper. The proposed technique is validated through design and simulation of a one-bit full adder circuit at a temperature of 27°C, supply voltage, V_{DD} of 0.90 V in 120 nm SOI CMOS technology. Existing standby subthreshold leakage control techniques in CMOS bulk technology are compared with the proposed technique in SOI CMOS technology. Both the proposed and existing techniques are also implemented in SOI CMOS technology and compared. Reduction in standby subthreshold leakage power dissipation by reduction factors of 54x and 45x foraone-bit full adder circuit was achieved using our proposed SOI CMOS technology based circuit technique in comparison with existing techniques such as MTCMOS technique and SCCMOS technique respectively in CMOS bulk technology. Dynamic power dissipation was also reduced significantly by using this proposed SOI CMOS technology based circuit technique. Standby subthreshold leakage power dissipation and dynamic power dissipation were also reduced significantly using the proposed circuit technique in comparison with other existing techniques, when all circuit techniques were implemented in SOI CMOS technology. All simulations were performed using Microwindver 3.1 EDA tool.

Keywords: Standby Subthreshold Leakage; SOI Technology; Low Power; Multi-Threshold Voltage; Stack Effect; Reverse Gate Voltage

1. Introduction

In recent years, the demand for reducing the standby subthreshold leakage power has grown significantly. This tremendous demand is mainly due to the fast growth of battery-operated portable applications such as notebook and laptop computers, personal digital assistants, cellular phones, and other portable communication devices, which remain in the standby state for a significant time interval. This leakage power dissipation is mainly noticeable in electronic portable battery operated systems having burst-mode type integrated circuits, where computation occurs for only short intervals and the system spends the majority of time in standby state [1]. Reduction of this subthreshold leakage power is highly desirable for battery operated portable systems, which remain in the standby state for the majority of their operating time.

Scaling of MOS transistors allow higher density of logic integration on a single chip. With the scaling down of MOS transistors, supply voltage has to be reduced to lower the dynamic power dissipation. The threshold voltage of the transistor has also to be scaled down to maintain the desired performance. However, reducing the threshold voltage in small geometry MOSFETs results in an exponential increase in the standby subthreshold leakage current [2]. With the scaling down in technology, recent research has shown that the subthreshold leakage current will become even greater than the dynamic current in the overall power dissipation [3]. Leakage power dissipation arises from the leakage currents flowing through the transistor when there are no input transitions and the transistor has reached the steady state. Excessive standby subthreshold leakage power dissipation is a primary hindrance for the advancement of CMOS integrated circuits with further scaling down in technology. Suppressing subthreshold leakage current in integrated circuits is essential for achieving green computing and facilitating the proliferation of portable electronic devices. This leakage power is expected to increase 32 times per device by the year 2020 [4]. CMOS logic circuit having submicron MOSFETS involves a number of complex tradeoffs in device dimensions, which supply voltage, and the threshold voltage for minimizing this subthreshold leakage power dissipation.

Today most electronic circuits are realized using a bulk CMOS technology, which is a very mature technology. Both die size and power dissipation of electronic circuits using this bulk CMOS technology will become difficult to reduce in the future [5]. So, new advanced technologies have to be developed for reducing these emerging problems. The most promising one for ultra-low power circuit implementation is silicon-on-insulator (SOI) CMOS technology [5-7]. The ability to use a low supply voltage and to simultaneously reduce parasitic capacitances is of high importance in designing low power digital circuits [8]. Instead of a bulk silicon substrate, SOI CMOS technology employs an insulator below a thin layer of silicon which eliminates most of the parasitic capacitances found in bulk CMOS technology. This allows SOI CMOS circuits to operate with a reduced supply voltage, thus further reducing the system power consumption.

Short channel effects (SCE) such as short channel threshold voltage roll off and drain induced barrier lowering (DIBL) are becoming major challenges in deep submicron MOS transistors and circuits in CMOS technology. In order to minimize SCE, advanced MOSFET technologies have to be used. Short channel effects of MOSFETs are much less in silicon-on-insulation (SOI) technology in comparison with conventional CMOS bulk technology [9]. The main advantage of SOI technology is its reduced junction capacitance due to oxide isolation of individual circuit elements, resulting in the overall lower power dissipation. Silicon-on-insulator (SOI) technology has attracted considerable attention as a potential alternative substrate for low power application. The use of silicon-on-insulator (SOI) technology is bringing new possibilities for effective reduction of the standby subthreshold leakage power dissipation. However, the main drawback with SOI CMOS technology is its high manufacturing cost which can be prohibitive for products where low system cost is of primary concern.

Techniques such as multi-threshold CMOS (MTCMOS) technique [10,11], and super cutoff CMOS (SCCMOS) technique [12] are available in the literature for the reduction of standby subthreshold leakage power in CMOS bulk technology. In MTCMOS technique, the high V_{TH} MOS transistor can limit the down scaling of the supply voltage, V_{DD} for ultra-low power applications due to the increase in the circuit delay. The delay is influenced by the reduced effective supply voltage and use of high V_{TH} MOS transistors. The main advantage of SCCMOS technique over MTCMOS technique is the reduction in the circuit delay due to the use of low V_{TH} sleep MOS transistors. However, in SCCMOS technique, a complex controller circuit is used for providing both negative and positive gate voltages, V_{GS} to completely turn off nMOS and pMOS transistors respectively.

In this paper, an improved SOI CMOS technology based circuit technique is proposed for effective reduction of the subthreshold leakage power dissipation in standby mode. To compare the proposed technique in SOI CMOS technology with existing (MTCMOS and SCCMOS) standby subthreshold leakage control techniques in CMOS bulk technology, a one-bit full adder circuit is designed and simulated using the proposed technique. The proposed and existing techniques are also implemented in SOI CMOS technology and compared. The proposed circuit technique in SOI CMOS technology is found to dissipate the least standby subthreshold leakage power and also dynamic power dissipation is reduced significantly in comparison with other existing circuit techniques in CMOS bulk technology. Standby subthreshold leakage power dissipation and dynamic power dissipation are also reduced significantly using the proposed circuit technique in comparison with other existing techniques, when all circuit techniques are implemented in SOI CMOS technology.

The rest of the paper is organized as follows: Section 2 describes about the fundamentals and advantages of silicon-on-insulator technology for low power applications over bulk CMOS technology. Section 3 describes the subthreshold leakage power dissipation model in more details. In Section 4, a methodology for reducing the subthreshold leakage power dissipation in standby mode is discussed. Section 5 describes the proposed SOI CMOS technology based circuit technique for effective reduction of the standby subthreshold leakage power dissipation. In Section 6, simulation results are provided for a one-bit full adder circuit and the obtained results are compared using the existing circuit techniques in CMOS bulk technology and the proposed SOI CMOS technology based circuit technique. Finally, conclusion is provided in Section 7.

2. Silicon-on-Insulator CMOS Technology

Silicon-on-insulator CMOS technology refers to the use of a layered silicon-insulator-silicon substrate in place of conventional silicon substrates in semiconductor device-manufacturing. Instead of using silicon as the substrate, as in bulk CMOS transistors, an insulating substrate can be used to improve device characteristics [13]. SOI CMOS circuits consist of single-device islands which are dielectrically isolated from each other and also from the underlying substrate. Since there are virtually no isolation constraints for individual devices, transistor and interconnect densities can be very high. In bulk CMOS devices every junction produces undesirable parasitic capacitances as well. These junction capacitances do exist in SOI CMOS devices also, but they are reduced by a factor ranging from 4 to 7 [14,15]. The main advantage of SOI technology is its reduced junction capacitance, resulting in the overall lower power dissipation.

3. Subthreshold Leakage Power Dissipation Model

Subthreshold leakage current occurs in a MOS transistor when the gate voltage, V_{GS} is below the threshold voltage of the MOS transistor. BSIM 4 subthreshold leakage current model [16] can be expressed as:

$$I_{SUB} = I_O e^{\frac{V_{GS}-V_{THO}-\eta V_{DS}+\gamma V_{BS}}{nV_T}} \left(1 - e^{\frac{-V_{DS}}{V_T}}\right) \quad (1)$$

$$I_0 = \mu C_{OX} \frac{W}{L} V_T^2 e^{1.8} \text{ and } V_T = \frac{KT}{q} \quad (2)$$

where V_{GS}, V_{DS} and V_{BS} are the gate to source, drain to source, and bulk to source voltages respectively, μ denotes the carrier mobility, C_{ox} is the gate oxide capacitance per unit area, W and L denote the channel width and channel length of the leaking MOS transistor respectively, K is the Boltzmann constant, T is the absolute temperature, q is the electrical charge of an electron, V_T is the thermal voltage, V_{THO} is the zero biased threshold voltage, γ is body effect coefficient, η denotes the drain induced barrier lowering coefficient, and n is the subthreshold swing coefficient.

In a logic circuit, the subthreshold leakage power dissipation can be calculated as the product of the number of nMOS and pMOS transistors (N_{nMOS} & N_{pMOS}), the average subthreshold leakage current per MOS transistor ($I_{SUBAVG.}$), and the supply voltage, V_{DD}. Hence it may be expressed as:

$$P_{SUB} = \left(N_{nMOS} + N_{pMOS}\right) \times I_{SUBAVG} \times V_{DD} \quad (3)$$

where $I_{SUBAVG.}$ is calculated by computing the average leakage current per MOS transistor for the given logic circuit using gate-level subthreshold leakage power estimation.

4. Methodology Adopted

Methodology for designing the proposed technique for effective reduction of the standby subthreshold leakage power is adopted after careful investigation of the subthreshold leakage current equations described in section 3.

Gate voltage, V_{GS} can be lowered by utilizing the principle of reverse gate voltage, V_{GS} to MOS transistors. There is an exponential decrease in the standby subthreshold leakage current due to the application of positive and negative gate voltages to pMOS and nMOS transistors respectively [16,17]. So, subthreshold leakage power dissipation can be reduced effectively by applying reverse gate voltages to MOS transistors.

Figure 1 [18] shows the reduction of the subthreshold leakage current due to the increase in the barrier height and the reduction in V_{DS} (= $V_{DD} - V_m$) after stacking of two cutoff nMOS transistors in comparison with a single cutoff nMOS transistor. When both nMOS transistors, Q_1 and Q_2 are turned off due to the application of $V_{GS} < V_{TH}$, then the intermediate node voltage, V_m has a positive value due to the existence of a small drain current. Thus, the gate to source voltage of Q_1 is negative, due to which the subthreshold leakage current reduces exponentially. The body effect of Q_1 (due to $V_m > 0$), further increases V_{TH} of Q_1, thereby, reduces the subthreshold leakage current. Drain induced barrier lowering (DIBL) is also reduced due to the positive value of node voltage, V_m. This increases V_{TH} of Q_2, which also contributes to the reduction of the subthreshold leakage current. Thus, the subthreshold leakage current is reduced considerably, due to stacking effect of MOS transistors.

Threshold voltage of a MOS transistor plays a vital role in low power VLSI circuit design. In the active mode of circuit operation, low V_{TH} MOS transistors are preferred for higher performance. However, for the standby mode of circuit operation, high V_{TH} MOS transistors are used for reducing the subthreshold leakage power dissipation. Hence, MTCMOS circuit technique-can be utilized for effectively reducing the standby subthreshold leakage power dissipation.

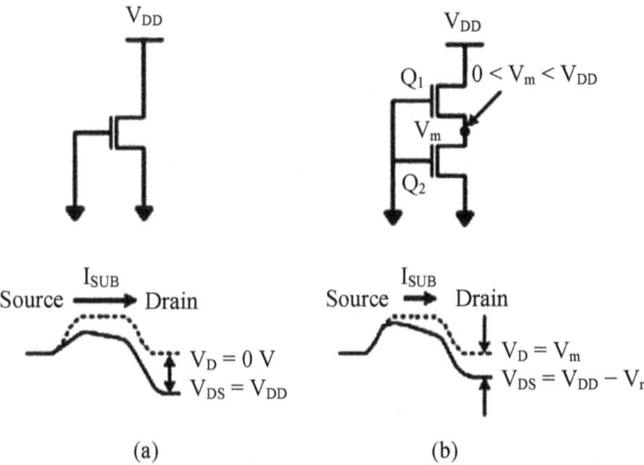

Figure 1. Standby subthreshold leakage current differences between (a) a single cutoff nMOS transistor and (b) a stack of two cutoff nMOS transistors.

Silicon-on-insulator (SOI) is a non-bulk CMOS technology. The reduction in the effective parasitic capacitance in SOI technology due to isolation from the bulk silicon makes it attractive for ultra-low power applications. The dynamic power dissipation is proportional to the total circuit capacitance and the square of the supply voltage. This means that SOI technology is very much suitable for low power operations as the parasitic capacitance is reduced and the supply voltage can be lowered. A steeper subthreshold swing helps to achieve low subthreshold leakage power dissipation.

The subthreshold swing S of a MOS transistor can be expressed as [19]:

$$S = \frac{KT\ln 10}{q}\left(1+\frac{C_{\mathrm{d}}}{C_{\mathrm{ox}}}\right) \quad (4)$$

where K is the Boltzmann constant, T is the absolute temperature, q is the elementary charge, and C_{d} and C_{ox} are the capacitance of the depletion layer and gate oxide.

In SOI technology, $C_{\mathrm{d}}/C_{\mathrm{ox}}$ is close to zero as the depletion capacitance is negligible. An important feature in SOI technology is the steeper sub threshold slope due to a reduction in the substrate body effect. For a given $I_{\text{off-current}}$, the SOI technology has a much smaller threshold voltage, which means that the circuit can operate at a lower supply voltage. SOI technology has lower DIBL, lesser short channel effects, very good subthreshold swing, and lesser junction and parasitic capacitances in comparison with the bulk CMOS technology. Thus, the subthreshold leakage current in SOI technology is much lower than the bulk CMOS technology for the same threshold voltage.

5. Proposed Circuit Technique

The proposed circuit technique is designed after analyzing the dependence of MOS transistor parameters on the subthreshold leakage current. Methodology adopted for designing this SOI based circuit technique is discussed in detail in Section 4.

Figure 2 show salogic circuit designed using MTCMOS technique in SOI CMOS technology. This logic circuit is designed using low V_{TH} MOS transistors, and a high V_{TH}pMOS transistor is inserted between the supply voltage, V_{DD} and the logic circuit while a high V_{TH}nMOS transistor is inserted between the logic circuit and the ground. During standby mode of operation, V_{GS1} is connected to a positive gate voltage, while V_{GS2} is connected to the ground as per MTCMOS technique. **Figure 3** shows a logic circuit using the proposed SOI CMOS technology based circuit technique, which is designed from **Figure 2** after stacking high V_{TH} MOS transistors and applying reverse gate voltages, V_{GS1} and V_{GS2} (*i.e.* positive gate voltage, V_{GS1} to the stacked high V_{TH}pMOS transistors and negative gate voltage, V_{GS2} to the stacked high V_{TH}nMOS transistors) to the stacked high V_{TH}pMOS and nMOS transistors respectively in SOI CMOS technology.

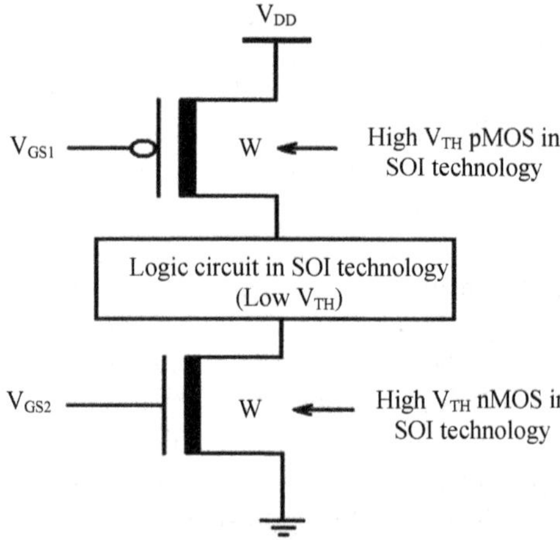

Figure 2. A logic circuit using MTCMOS techniquein SOI CMOS technology.

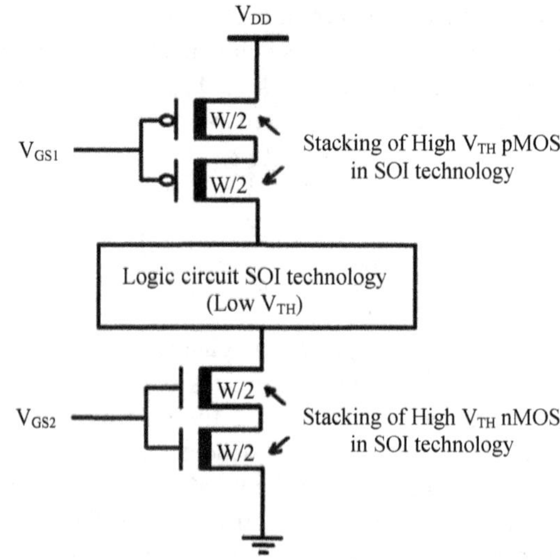

Figure 3. A logic circuit using the proposed circuit technique in SOI technology.

In this proposed technique, standby subthreshold leakage current is reduced effectively by utilizing multi-threshold MOS transistors, stacking of MOS transistors, applying reverse gate voltages, V_{GS1} and V_{GS2} (positive gate voltage, V_{GS1} to the stacked high V_{TH}pMOS transistors and negative gate voltage, V_{GS2} to the stacked high V_{TH}-nMOS transistors) to MOS transistors, and using silicon-on-insulator (SOI) CMOS technology.

6. Simulation Results and Observations

Figure 4 shows the circuit diagram of a one-bit full adder using the proposed technique in SOI CMOS technology. The proposed technique in SOI CMOS technol-

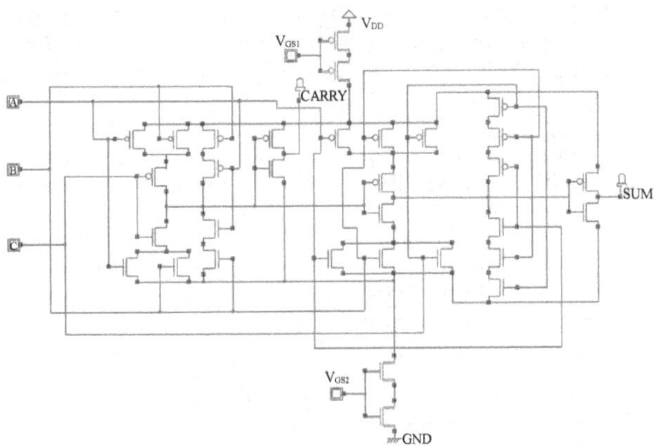

Figure 4. Circuit diagram of a one-bit full adder using the proposed technique in SOI CMOS technology.

ogy is compared with the existing techniques in CMOS bulk technology in terms of standby subthreshold leakage power dissipation, and also dynamic power dissipation. Layout of a one-bit full adder circuit was designed and simulated using Microwind ver. 3.1 EDA tool. All simulations were performed at a temperature of 27°C and supply voltage, V_{DD} of 0.9 V in 120 nm SOI CMOS and bulk CMOS technologies. W/L of low V_{TH}nMOS and pMOS transistors were taken as 0.72 µm/0.12 µm and 1.20 µm/0.12 µm respectively. Similarly, W/L of high V_{TH}nMOS and pMOS transistors were taken as 0.72 µm/ 0.24 µm and 1.20 µm/0.24 µm respectively.

Standby subthreshold leakage power dissipation was measured by combining all possible input vector combinations. For calculation of standby subthreshold leakage power dissipation in a logic circuit, the voltage magnitude of all input vectors should always be less than the magnitude of the threshold voltage of the MOS transistor of the logic circuit. In this proposed technique, subthreshold leakage power dissipation in standby mode for a one bit full adder was calculated by connecting reverse gate voltages, V_{GS1} and V_{GS2} (positive gate voltage, V_{GS1} to stacked high V_{TH}pMOS transistors and negative gate voltage, V_{GS2} to stacked high V_{TH}nMOS transistors) to high V_{TH} stacked MOS transistors and applying all combinations of static input voltages, $V_{in} < V_{TH}$ to the logic circuit. Dynamic power dissipation using this proposed technique was calculated by applying input clock signals at a frequency of 5 GHz.

Standby subthreshold leakage power dissipation and standby subthreshold leakage reduction factor for a one-bit full adder circuit using the proposed technique in SOI CMOS technology in comparison with existing techniques in CMOS bulk technology are shown in **Tables 1** and **2** respectively. **Figures 5** and **6** are the graphical representations of **Tables 1** and **2** for standby subthreshold leakage power and standby subthreshold leakage reduction factor respectively. Similarly **Figures 7** and **8** are

Table 1. Standby subthreshold leakage power dissipation and dynamic power dissipation for a one-bit full adder circuit using the proposed technique in SOI CMOS technology and existing techniques in CMOS bulk technology.

References	Techniques	Standby subthreshold leakage power dissipation	Dynamic power dissipation
[10,11]	MTCMOS	0.054 nW	0.050 µW
[12]	SCCMOS	0.045 nW	0.041 µW
Proposed	Proposed	0.001 nW	0.012 µW

Table 2. Standby subthreshold leakage reduction factor and dynamic power dissipation reduction factor using the proposed technique in SOI CMOS technology in comparison with other existing techniques in CMOS bulk technology.

Techniques	Standby subthreshold leakage power dissipation	Standby subthreshold leakage reduction factor for the proposed technique in comparison to the existing techniques
Multi-threshold	0.012 nW	12x
Super cutoff	0.009 nW	9x
Proposed	0.001 nW	-

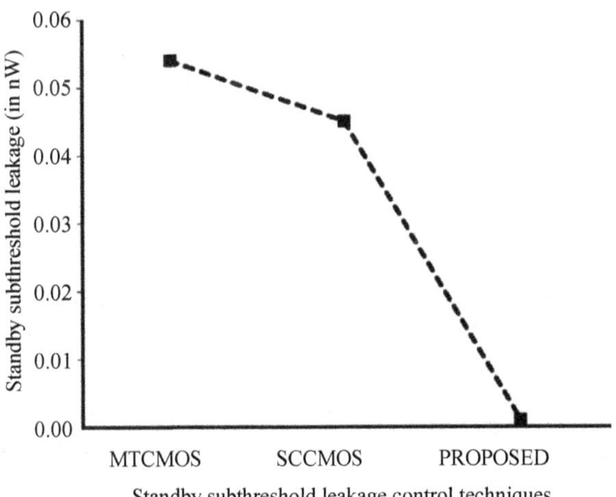

Figure 5. Standby subthreshold leakage power dissipation for a one-bit full adder circuit in MTCMOS, SCCMOS and proposed techniques.

the graphical representations of **Tables 1** and **2** for dynamic power dissipation and dynamic power reduction factor respectively. **Table 3** shows standby subthreshold leakage power dissipation and standby subthreshold leakage reduction factor for a one-bit full adder circuit, when both the proposed and existing circuit techniques are implemented in SOI CMOS technology. **Table 4** shows dynamic power dissipation and dynamic power dissipation reduction factor for a one-bit full adder circuit when both the proposed technique and existing circuit techniques are implemented in SOI CMOS technology.

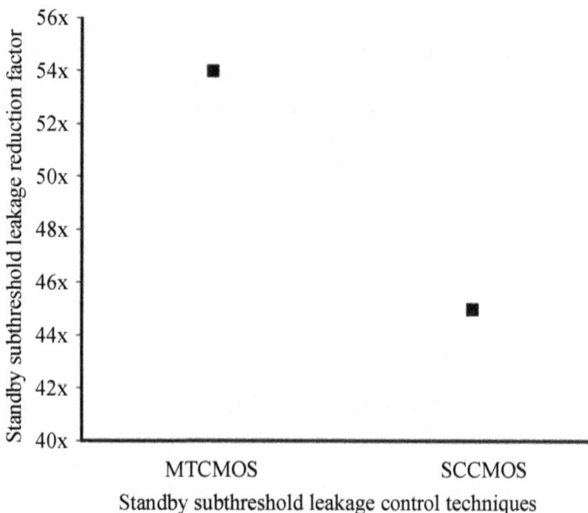

Figure 6. Standby subthreshold leakage reduction factor of the proposed technique in comparison to MTCMOS and SCCMOS techniques for a one-bit full adder circuit.

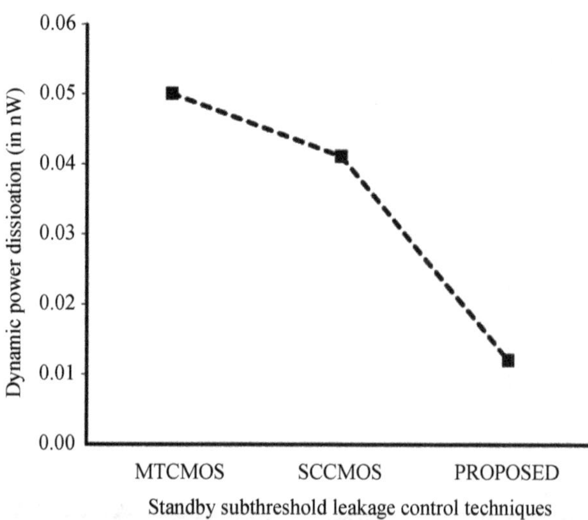

Figure 7. Dynamic power dissipation for a one-bit full adder circuit in MTCMOS, SCCMOS and proposed techniques.

Table 3. Standby subthreshold leakage power dissipation and standby subthreshold leakage reduction factor for a one-bit full adder circuit when both the existing techniques and the proposed technique are implemented in SOI CMOS technology.

Techniques	Dynamic power dissipation	Dynamic power dissipation reduction factor for the proposed technique in comparison with existing techniques
Multi-Threshold	0.037 μW	3.083x
Super Cutoff	0.031 μW	2.583x
Proposed	0.012 μW	-

Reduction in the standby subthreshold leakage power

Table 4. Dynamic power dissipation and dynamic power reduction factor for a one-bit full adder circuit using both the existing techniques and the proposed technique in SOI CMOS technology.

Standby subthreshold leakage reduction factor using the proposed technique in SOI CMOS technology in comparison with existing techniques in CMOS bulk technology		Dynamic power dissipation reduction factor using the proposed technique in SOI CMOS technology in comparison with existing techniques in CMOS bulk technology	
MTCMOS technique	SCCMOS technique	MTCMOS technique	SCCMOS technique
54x	45x	4.167x	3.417x

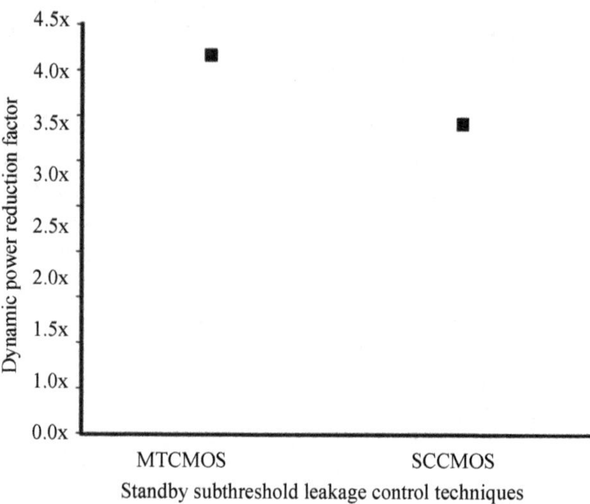

Figure 8. Dynamic power reduction factor of the proposed technique in comparison to MTCMOS and SCCMOS techniques for a one-bit full adder circuit.

dissipation by reduction factors of 54x and 45x foraone-bit full adder circuit is achieved using the proposed SOI CMOS based circuit technique in comparison to the existing MTCMOS and SCCMOS techniques respectively in CMOS bulk technology. Dynamic power dissipation is also reduced significantly by reduction factors of 4.167x and 3.417x using the proposed SOI CMOS technology based circuit technique in comparison with MTCMOS and SCCMOS techniques respectively in CMOS bulk technology. It is also observed from **Tables 3** and **4** that the standby subthreshold leakage power dissipation and dynamic power dissipation are also reduced significantly using the proposed circuit technique in comparison with other existing techniques, when all circuit techniques are implemented in SOI CMOS technology.

7. Conclusion

This paper has presented migration of standby subthreshold leakage control technique from a bulk CMOS to SOI CMOS technology. An improved SOI CMOS technology based circuit technique for efficient reduction of standby subthreshold leakage power dissipation is presented in this paper. The proposed technique is validated through layout design and simulation of a one-bit full adder circuit using the proposed and other existing standby subthreshold leakage control techniques. The proposed SOI CMOS technology based circuit technique dissipated the least standby subthreshold leakage power in comparison to other existing techniques in CMOS bulk technology. Dynamic power dissipation is also reduced using this proposed technique in SOI technology in comparison with other presented techniques in CMOS bulk technology. It also reveals that when both the proposed and existing techniques are implemented in SOI CMOS technology, the proposed technique maintains the trend of reduced power dissipation in both standby and dynamic modes. Hence it may be concluded that the proposed SOI CMOS technology based circuit technique showed a significant improvement in the standby subthreshold leakage power dissipation, which makes it attractive for ultra low-power applications.

8. Acknowledgements

This research work was partially supported by the Indian National Science Academy, New Delhi through INSA-visiting fellowship programme for the year 2012-13 vide number SP/VF-21/2012-13/306.

REFERENCES

[1] M. Anis and M. Elmasry, "Multi-Threshold CMOS Digital Circuits: Managing Leakage Power," Kluwer Academic Publishers, Norwell, 2010.

[2] R. X. Gu and M. I. Elmasry, "Power Dissipation Analysis and Optimization of Deep Submicron CMOS Digital Circuits," *IEEE Journal of Solid-State Circuits*, Vol. 31, No. 5, 1996, pp. 707-713.

[3] N. S. Kim, *et al*., "Leakage Current: Moore's Law Meets Static Power," *IEEE Computer*, Vol. 36, No. 12, 2003, pp. 68-75.

[4] S. Borkar, "Design Challenges of Technology Scaling," *IEEE Micro*, Vol. 19, No. 4, 1999, pp. 23-29.

[5] Y. Kado, "The Potential of Ultrathin-Film SOI Devices for Low-Power and High-Speed Applications," *IEICE Transactions on Electronics*, Vol. E80-C, No. 3, 1997, pp. 443-454.

[6] S. Cristoloveanu and G. Reichert, "Recent Advances in SOI Materials and Device Technologies for High Temperature," *Proceedings of High-Temperature Electronic Materials, Devices and Sensors*, San Diego, 22-27 February 1998, pp. 86-93.

[7] R. Reedy, *et al*., "Single Chip Wireless Systems Using SOI," *Proceedings of the International SOI Conference*, San Diego, 4-7 October 1999, pp. 8-11.

[8] T. Iwamatsu, *et al*., "Analysis of the Delay Distributions of 0.5 μm SOI LSIs," *IEICE Transactions on Electronics*, Vol. E80-C, No. 3, 1997, pp. 464-471.

[9] R. Yan, A. Ourmazd and K. F. Lee, "Scaling the Si MOSFET: From Bulk to SOI to Bulk," *IEEE Transactions on Electron Devices*, Vol. 39, No. 7, 1992, pp. 1704-1710.

[10] S. Mutoh, *et al*., "1-V Power Supply High—Speed Digital Circuit Technology with Multi-Threshold Voltage CMOS," *IEEE Journal of Solid-State Circuits*, Vol. 30, No. 8, 1995, pp. 847-854.

[11] M. Anis, S. Areibi and M. Elmasry, "Design and Optimization of Multi-Threshold CMOS (MTCMOS) Circuits," *IEEE Transactions on Computer-Aided Design of Integrated Circuits and Systems*, Vol. 22, No. 10, 2003, pp. 1324-1342.

[12] H. Kawaguchi, K. Nose and T. Sakurai, "A Super Cutoff CMOS (SCCMOS) Scheme for 0.5 V Supply Voltage with Picoampere Standby Current," *IEEE Journal of Solid-State Circuits*, Vol. 35, No. 10, 2000, pp. 1498-1501.

[13] S. J. Abou-Samra and A. Guyot, "Performance/Complexity Space Exploration: Bulk vs. SOI," *Proceedings of the International Workshop on Power and Timing Modelling*, Optimization and Simulation, Lyngby, 7-9 October 1998.

[14] J. P. Colinge, "Silicon-on-Insulator Technology: Materials to VLSI," Kluwer Academic Publishers, Boston, 1997.

[15] J. B. Kuo and J.-H. Lou, "Low-Voltage CMOS VLSI Circuits," John Wiley & Sons, Inc., New York, 1999.

[16] A. Chandrakasan, W. J. Bowhill and F. Fox, "Design of High-Performance Microprocessor Circuits," IEEE Press, New York, 2001.

[17] B. S. Deepaksubramanyan and A. Nunez, "Analysis of Subthreshold Leakage Reduction in CMOS Digital Circuits," *Proceedings of the 13th NASA VLSI Symposium*, Post Falls, 5-6 June 2007, pp. 1-8.

[18] H. Jeon, Y. B. Kim and M. Choi, "Standby Leakage Power Reduction Technique for Nanoscale CMOS VLSI Systems," *IEEE Transactions on Instrumentation and Measurement*, Vol. 59, No. 5, 2010, pp. 1127-1133.

[19] S. M. Sze, "Physics of Semiconductor Devices," Wiley-Interscience, New York, 1981.

28

Switched Capacitor Biquad Filter Using CDTA

Meeti Dehran[1], Indu Prabha Singh[1], Kalyan Singh[2], Rabindra Kumar Singh[3]
[1]Department of Electronics and Communications Engineering, Shri Ramswaroop Memorial Group of Professional Colleges (SRMGPC), Lucknow, India
[2]Department of Physics and Electronics, R.M.L. University, Faizabad, India
[3]Department of Electrical and Electronic Engineering, Kamla Nehru Institute of Technology (KNIT), Sultanpur, India

ABSTRACT

A switched capacitor biquad filter using current differencing transconductance amplifier (CDTA) is presented in this paper. The proposed circuit employs only one CDTA, two virtually grounded capacitors and one switched capacitor. It is a resistorless circuit, so it is beneficial to IC implementation in terms of space consideration. The proposed circuit is a second order single input multiple output (SIMO) current-mode filter. This filter can simultaneously realize all basic filter functions high pass, low pass and band pass responses without any component-matching conditions. All the active and passive sensitivities are low. The natural angular frequency (ω_0) and quality factor (Q) of proposed filter can be electronically controlled. Owing to current mode operation it consumes less power. PSPICE simulation results are used to verify the theoretical analysis.

Keywords: Current Differencing Transconductance Amplifier (CDTA); Biquad Filter; Current-Mode Circuit

1. Introduction

Since the introduction of the current differencing transconductance amplifier (CDTA) in 2003, it has been acknowledged to be a versatile current-mode active building block in designing analog circuits [1]. This device with two current inputs and two kinds of current output provides an easy implementation of current-mode active filters [2]. It also exhibits the ability of electronic tuning by the help of its transconductance gain (g_m). All these advantages together with its current-mode operation nature make the CDTA a promising choice for realizing the current-mode filters. As a result, a variety of CDTA applications has also been considered by various researchers.

The work in [2] introduces universal biquad filters which can simultaneously realize lowpass (LP), highpass (HP) and bandpass (BP) current responses. However, they suffer from the use of a large number of passive components. On the other hand, a lowpass filter circuit using CDTAs is proposed in [3]. However, this configuration is restricted for only lowpass transfer function design and it also requires an additional passive resistor. In [4], the CDTA-based current-mode single-input three-output filter is reported. It permits the realization of only three basic filter functions LP, BP, and HP responses simultaneously at high impedance output. While the circuit proposed in [5] requires four CDTAs, and an external passive resistor for its realization. In [6], a universal current-mode biquad, providing four basic transfer functions (low-pass, band-pass, high-pass, and band-reject) simultaneously is described. However, this circuit labors with the following drawbacks: 1) only the output current of the low-pass section flows to an independent load. All the remaining output currents flow through the working impedances and thus they cannot be directly utilized without negative influence on the filter behavior. 2) The additional resistor R_3 does not represent any increase of the filter versatility and thus it can be removed from the filter structure without decreasing its functionality. The paper published in [7] employed two CDTA to perform all three basic filter functions. Second order filter using single CDTA is published in [8,9]. The paper proposed in [8] provides only BP and HP outputs or LP and BP responses after interchanging RC network to CR. The filter introduced in [9] uses single CDTA and provides several transfer functions depending on the position of applied input current, but at low frequency.

In this paper, a current-mode filter, consisting of a single CDTA, two grounded capacitors and one switched capacitor is used to realize the filter. It provides the advantage of using switched capacitor instead of a resistor that is beneficial to IC implementation in terms of space consideration. The proposed circuit can be used as high pass, low pass, and band pass filter. PSPICE simulation results are used to verify the performance of the proposed circuit.

2. CDTA

Digital signal processing is becoming increasingly more powerful while advances in IC technology provide compact efficient implementation of its algorithms on silicon chips. Although many types of signal processing have indeed moved to digital domain, analog circuits are fundamentally necessary in many of today's complex, high performance systems. This is caused by the reality that naturally occurring signals are analog. Therefore analog circuits act as a bridge between the real world and digital systems. In the beginning, operational amplifiers were the main building blocks for analog circuit design. Unfortunately, their limited performance such as bandwidth, slew-rate etc. led the analog designer to search for other possibilities and other building blocks. As a result, new current-mode active building blocks such as Operational Transconductance Amplifiers (OTA), second generation Current Conveyors (CCII), Current-Feedback Op-Amps (CFOA), Differential Voltage Current Conveyor (DVCC), Differential Difference Current Conveyor (DDCC), third-generation Current Conveyor (CCIII), Dual X Current Conveyors (DXCCII), Current Controlled Current Conveyors (CCCII), Current Differencing Buffered Amplifier (CDBA) And Current Differencing Transconductance Amplifier (CDTA) receive considerable attention due to their larger dynamic range and wider bandwidth. Employing these new active elements for analog design and using CMOS technology for implementation, the circuit designers obtained new possibilities to solve their problems. CDTA device is a synthesis of the well-known advantages of the CDBA and an output transconductance amplifier to facilitate the implementation of current-mode analog signal processing.

The electrical symbol of the CDTA is shown in **Figure 1**.

The terminal relation of the CDTA can be characterized by the following set of Equation (1).

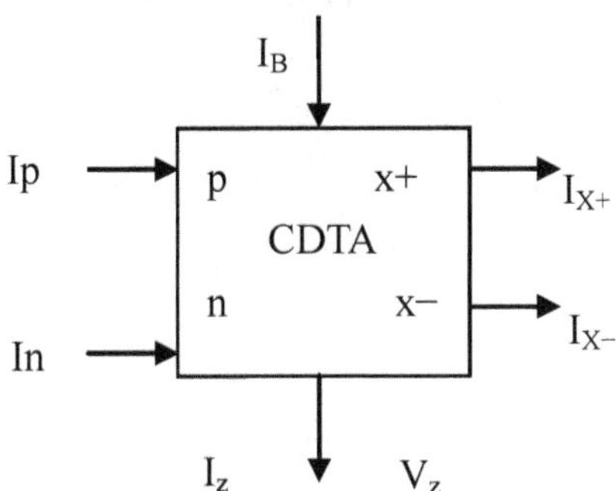

Figure 1. Electrical symbol of CDTA.

$$\begin{bmatrix} V_p \\ V_n \\ I_z \\ I_x \end{bmatrix} = \begin{bmatrix} 0 & 0 & 0 & 0 \\ 0 & 0 & 0 & 0 \\ 1 & -1 & 0 & 0 \\ 0 & 0 & \pm g_m & 0 \end{bmatrix} \begin{bmatrix} I_p \\ I_n \\ V_z \\ 0 \end{bmatrix}$$

$$\begin{aligned} V_p &= V_n = 0 \\ I_z &= I_p - I_n \\ I_{x+} &= g_m V_z \\ I_{x-} &= -g_m V_z \end{aligned} \tag{1}$$

Where

P and n are input terminals;

z and $\pm x$ are output terminals;

g_m is the transconductance gain;

And Z_z is external impedance connected at the terminal z.

According to above equation, the current flowing out of the terminal z (I_z) is a difference between the currents through the terminals p and n (I_p - I_n). The voltage drop at the terminal z is transferred to a current at the terminal x (I_x) by a transconductance gain (g_m), which is electronically controllable by an external bias current (I_B). These currents, which are copied to a general number of output current terminals x, are equal in magnitude but flow in opposite directions.

The (CDTA) is composed of a unity-gain current source controlled by the difference of two input currents and a multi-output transconductance amplifier providing electronic tuning ability through its transconductance gain (g_m). Therefore, this device is quite suitable for the synthesis of current-mode filters with electronically tunability properties. Moreover, the use of the CDTA as an active element provides the circuit implementations with a reduced number of passive elements, thereby leading to compact structures in some applications. All these advantages together with its current-mode operation nature make the CDTA a promising choice for implementing the current-mode continuous-time signal processing circuits consecutively.

Figure 2 shows a CMOS realization of the CDTA element [10]. The transistors M1 to M17 form the input DCCCS stage and M21 to M28 form the dual-output transconductor stage Aspect ratios of the transistors in **Figure 2** are given in **Table 1**.

3. Proposed Circuit

The proposed current-mode multifunction filter employing CDTA, two grounded capacitors and a switched capacitor is shown in **Figure 3**.

Since all the grounded capacitors are employed, the circuit is suitable for IC implementation [11,12]. The switched capacitor (SC) functions as a resistor and re-

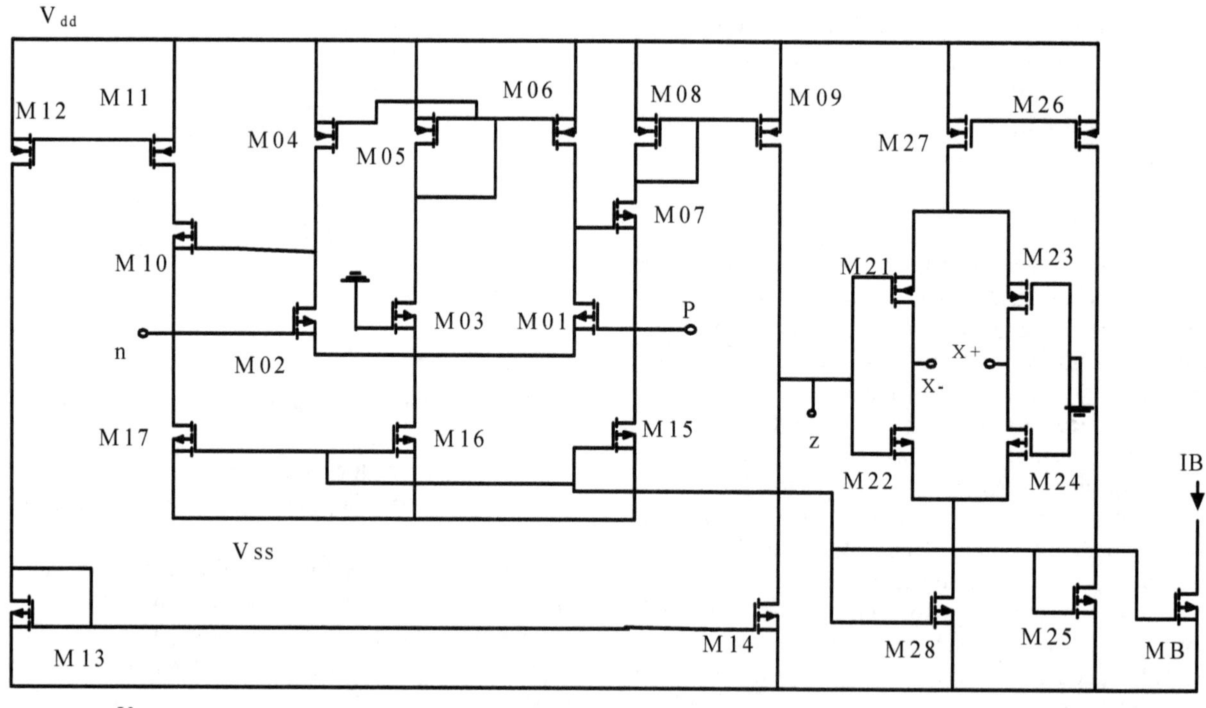

Figure 2. CDTA CMOS implementation from [10].

Table 1. Aspect ratios of the transistors.

M1 = 70 µm/0.7 µm	M15 = 35 µm/0.7 µm
M2 = 70 µm/0.7 µm	M16 = 35 µm/0.7 µm
M3 = 70 µm/0.7 µm	M17 = 35 µm/0.7 µm
M4 = 28 µm/0.7 µm	M21 = 28 µm/0.7 µm
M5 = 28 µm/0.7 µm	M22 = 16 µm/0.7 µm
M6 = 28 µm/0.7 µm	M23 = 28 µm/0.7 µm
M7 = 42 µm/0.7 µm	M24 = 16 µm/0.7 µm
M8 = 10.5 µm/0.7 µm	M25 = 56 µm/0.7 µm
M9 = 10.5 µm/0.7 µm	M26 = 59 µm/0.7 µm
M10 = 42 µm/0.7 µm	M27 = 56 µm/0.7 µm
M11 = 10.5 µm/0.7 µm	M28 = 56 µm/0.7 µm
M12 = 98 µm/0.7 µm	MB = 7 µm/0.7 µm
M13 = 10.5 µm/0.7 µm	M30 = 50 µm/0.7 µm
M14 = 10.5 µm/0.7 µm	M31 = 50 µm/0.7 µm

duces the required space for the fabrication. The SC is compatible with CMOS technology. The proposed circuit is able to perform the basic filter functions *i.e.* low pass, high pass, band pass. The low pass, high pass and band pass current outputs have been shown in **Figure 3**. From routine calculations for the proposed filter, the current responses can be given by:

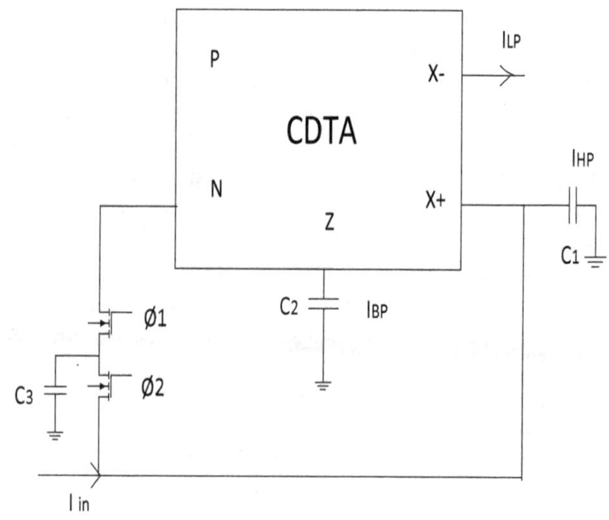

Figure 3. Biquad filter using CDTA element.

$$I_{LP} = \frac{\frac{g_m}{RC_1C_2}}{S^2 + \frac{1}{RC_1}S + \frac{g_m}{RC_1C_2}} I_{in} \tag{2}$$

$$I_{BP} = -\frac{\frac{1}{RC_1}S}{S^2 + \frac{1}{RC_1}S + \frac{g_m}{RC_1C_2}} I_{in} \tag{3}$$

$$I_{HP} = \frac{S^2}{S^2 + \frac{1}{RC_1}S + \frac{g_m}{RC_1C_2}} I_{in} \quad (4)$$

Bandwidth (BW), natural frequency (ω_0) and quality factor (Q) are given by

$$BW = \frac{1}{RC_1}, \omega_0 = \sqrt{\frac{g_m}{C_1C_2R}}, Q = \sqrt{g_m R \frac{C_1}{C_2}} \quad (5)$$

From Equation (5), the parameter ω_0 can be controlled by transconductance g_m independently of bandwidth. The transconductance values can be changed through adjusting the biasing current of the CDTA.

From the expression of Equation (5), the sensitivities of ω_0 and Q to variations in various parameters is given as

$$S_{g_m}^{\omega_0} = \frac{1}{2}, S_{C_1,C_2,R}^{\omega_0} = -\frac{1}{2}, S_{g_m}^{Q} = \frac{1}{2}, \quad (6)$$
$$S_{C_1,R}^{Q} = \frac{1}{2}, S_{C_2}^{Q} = -\frac{1}{2}$$

Hence all the sensitivities are low as calculated in Equation (6).

The value of the capacitor C_3 used in switched capacitor is calculated using the formula given as

$$C_3 = \frac{1}{Rf} \quad (7)$$

Where, R is the equivalent resistance value of the switched capacitor and f is the frequency of clock signal (Φ_1) and (Φ_2), applied at two mosfets (M30, M31) of switched capacitor.

4. Simulation Results

The performance of the proposed filter is verified using the simulation in PSpice. According to the analysis from Sections 2 and 3, the single input excitation is given. The CDTA model employing the n-well CMOS process TSMC 0.35 mm is used. The transconductanceis set to 888 µS via a bias current of 40 µA.

As an example design, the capacitors $C1 = C2 = 10$ pF, $C_3 = 2.96$ pF and the biasing current $I_{bias} = 40$ µA are given. This setting has been designed to obtain the LP, BP and HP, filter responses. The simulated responses of the BP, LP and HP of the proposed filter are shown in **Figure 4**. Both the natural frequency and the quality factor are in accordance with the proposed values.

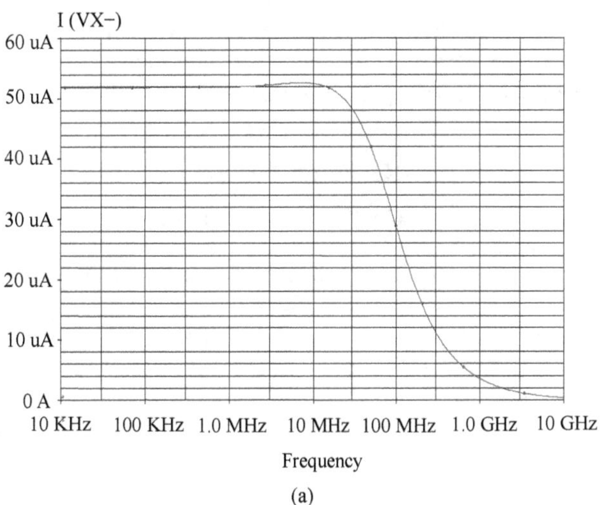

(a)

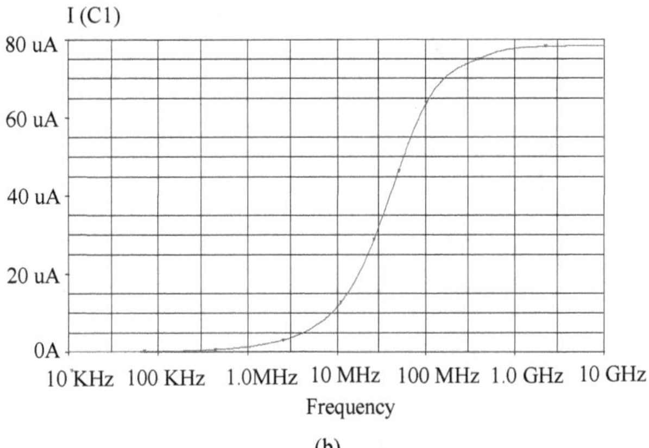

(b)

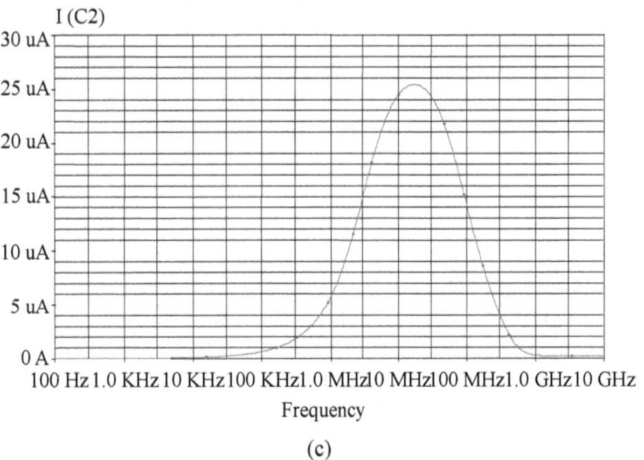

(c)

Figure 4. Response of biquad filter using CDTA element. (a) Low pass response; (b) High pass response; (c) Band pass response.

5. Conclusion

A 2nd-order single input multiple output (SIMO) current-mode filter employing a single CDTA is described in the paper. The natural angular frequency ω_0 and the bandwidth ω_0/Q can electronically be controlled by adjusting the transconductance gain g_m of the CDTA. The simulated responses with PSPICE have been used to prove the theory. It possesses the properties as the following: 1) employment of only grounded capacitors which is suitable for IC implementation; 2) ability of realizing the LP, BP, and HP filter responses without any component-matching condition; and 3) Electronic control of the parameter ω_0. The switched capacitor has good linearity. The PSPICE simulation results demonstrate the close agreement with the presented theory.

REFERENCES

[1] D. Biolek, "CDTA-Building Block for Current-Mode Analog Signal Processing," *Proceedings of European Conference on Circuit Theory and Design* (*ECCTD*), Poland, 1-4 September 2003, pp. 397-400.

[2] D. Biolek and V. Biolkova, "Universal Biquad Using CDTA Elements for Cascade Filter Design," *Proceeding of 7th International Multiconference on Circuits, Systems Communications and Computers* (*CSCC*), Athens,7-9 July 2003, pp. 8-12.

[3] A. T. Bekri and F. Anday, "Nth-Order Low-Pass Filter Employing Current Differencing Transconductance Amplifiers," *Proceeding of the* 2005 *European Conference on Circuit Theory and Design*, Cork, 28 August-2 September 2005, pp. 193-196.

[4] D. Biolek and V. Biolkova, "CDTA-C Current-Mode Universal 2nd Order Filter," *Proceeding of the* 5*th WSEAS International Conference on Applied Informatics and Communications*, Malta, 15-17 September 2005, pp. 411-414.

[5] W. Tanjaroen, T. Dumawipata, S. Unhavanich, W. Tangsrirat and W. Surakampontorn, "Design of Current Differencing Transconductance Amplifier and Its Application to Current-Mode KHN Iquad Filter," *Proceeding of ECTI-CON*, Ubon Ratchathani, 10-13 May 2006, pp. 497-500.

[6] D. Prasad, D. R. Bhaskar and A. K. Singh, "Universal Current-Mode Biquad Filter Using Dual Output Current Differencing Transconductance Amplifier," *International Journal of Electronics and Communications*, Vol. 63, No. 6, 2008, pp. 497-501.

[7] A. Uygur and H. Kuntman, "Design of a Current Differencing Transconductance Amplifier (CDTA) and Its Application on Active Filters," *SIU*'2005: *IEEE* 13*th Signal Processing and Communication Applications Conference*, Kayseri, 16-18 May 2005, pp. 340-343.

[8] N. A. Shah, M. Quadri and S. Z. Iqbal, "Current Mode Multifunction Filter Using Current Differencing Transconductance Amplifier," *Indian Journal of Pure & Applied Physics*, Vol. 45, No. 9, 2007, pp. 767-769.

[9] D. Biolek, V. Biolkova and Z. Kolka, "Single-CDTA (Current Differencing Transconductance Amplifier) Current-Mode Biquad Revisited," *WSEAS Transactions on Electronics*, Vol. 5, No. 6, 2008, pp. 250-257.

[10] D. Biolek, E. Hancioglu and A. U. Keskin, "High-Perfor-Mance Current Differencing Transconductance Amplifier and Its Application in Precision Current-Mode Rectification," *International Journal of Electronics and Communications*, Vol. 62, No. 2, 2008, pp. 92-96.

[11] M. Bhusan and R. W. Newcomb, "Grounding of Capaci-Tors in Integrated Circuits," *Electronics Letters*, Vol. 3, No. 4, 1967, pp. 148-149.

[12] K. Pal and R. Singh, "Inductor Less Current Conveyor All Pass Filter Using Grounded Capacitors," *Electronics Letters*, Vol. 18, No. 1, 1982, p. 47.

Current Processing Current Tunable Universal Biquad Filter Employing Two CCTAs and Two Grounded Capacitors

Ravindra Singh Tomar[1], Sajai Vir Singh[2], Durg Singh Chauhan[3]
[1]Department of Electronics Engineering, Anand Engineering College, Agra, India
[2]Department of Electronics and Communications, Jaypee Institute of Information Technology, Noida, India
[3]Department of Electrical Engineering, Indian Institute of Technology, Banaras Hindu University, Varanasi, India

ABSTRACT

This paper presents a current processing current-tunable universal biquad filter employing two current conveyor transconductance amplifiers (CCTAs) as active element and two grounded capacitors as passive element. It realizes all the five standard filtering responses such as low pass (LP), band pass (BP), high pass (HP), band reject (BR) and all pass (AP) through appropriate selection of applied current inputs. Proposed circuit does not require minus input current signal and double input current signal to realize different filtering responses. It also does not require component matching condition to realize any filtering responses. Moreover, the circuit offers the advantage of orthogonal electronic tunability of pole-frequency and quality factor. The circuit exhibits low active and passive sensitivities. The circuit performance is verified through P-SPICE simulation software.

Keywords: Biquad; Current-Mode; Universal Filter; CCTA

1. Introduction

The applications, advantages and realizations of high performance continuous-time (CT) current-mode (also called current processing) active filters have been receiving considerable attention, since the last few decades [1,2]. Thus, a number of papers deal with the design of biquad current-mode (CM) filter in the literature [3-27] using different current-mode active elements. However, all of them are realized either in the form of the single-input multiple-output (SIMO) or multiple-input single output (MISO) category. SIMO filters [3-13] simultaneously realize different filtering functions (in general three or more) at different outputs, without changing the connection of the input signal. On the other hand MISO filters [15-27] can realize multifunction filtering responses at single output terminal by altering the way in which multi-input signals are connected. Moreover, the MISO configuration in comparison with SIMO configuration may lead to a reduction in number of active elements for circuit realization and hence, seems to be more suitable than that of SIMO configuration to realize all the standard biquad filter functions. However, one critical issue with CT filters is the RC time constant variation problem due to process tolerance, the environmental effects of temperature drift, humidity and aging of the components [14]. As a consequence, the performance of the filter circuit differs from the nominal design. The continuous-time filter approach typically compensates for this problem with the tunable filter, by electronically varying the time constant. So there is a growing interest towards designing of electronically tunable filters to compensate for deviation in the circuit due to process tolerance, parasitic, temperature drift and component aging. During the last one decade and recent past, several electronically tunable MISO type current-mode active filters have been proposed in the literature [15-27], using different current-mode active elements such as second generation current controlled current conveyor (CCCII) [15-21], current differencing transconductance amplifier (CDTA) [22], current follower transconductance amplifier (CFTA) [23], voltage differencing transconductance amplifier (VDTA) [24], current controlled transconductance amplifier (CCTA) [25] and current controlled current conveyor transconductance amplifier (CCCCTA) [26,27] etc.

Each MISO current-mode filter based on CCCII reported in [15-21] uses two [15-17] or more [18-20] CCCIIs and two grounded capacitors but all of them [15-20] require minus input current signal(s) [15-20] and/or component matching conditions [18,20] to realize at least one filter function. Thus, they need one or more active component to obtain minus input current signal/matching condition. The single CCCII-based current-mode filter [21] with three input single output uses two grounded capacitors and one resistor. However, it still needs minus input current signal(s) to realize BP, BR and AP filter functions. Few more three input single output current-mode filters based on two active elements in the form of CDTA [22], CFTA [23], VDTA [24] and CCTA [25] are also proposed in the literature. Each circuit [22-25] consists of two grounded capacitors and realizes all the standard filtering functions but they also require minus input current signal(s) [22-24] or/and double input current signal(s) [22-25] to realize at least one filter function. Other novel circuits based on two CCCCTAs [26,27] each having two grounded capacitors can also be used as three input single output tunable current-mode filter but they still require minus input current signal [26] or matching conditions [27] to realize AP response.

In this paper, a current processing current-tunable universal biquad filter is proposed which consists of two current conveyor trans-conductance amplifiers (CCTAs) and two grounded capacitors. It can realize LP, BP, HP, BR and AP in the current form at high impedance output through appropriate selection of the input signals, without any matching conditions. Moreover, the proposed circuit realizes all the filtering responses without requiring any minus input current signal and double input current signal. Also, the circuit offers the advantage of electronic tunability of pole-frequency independent of quality factor. The circuit exhibits low active and passive sensitivities. The circuit is simulated through P-SPICE simulation.

2. CCTA and Proposed Biquad Filter

The CCTA [13,25] is a combination of second generation current conveyor (CCII) and operation transconductance amplifier (OTA). The block diagram of the CCTA is shown in **Figure 1**. It consists of two input terminals (X, Y). Port X is low input impedance terminal while port Y is the high input impedance terminal. Port $\pm Z$ and port $\pm O$ are the high output impedance terminals. The input-output current-voltage relationship between different terminals of the CCTA can be described by the following equations.

$$I_Y = 0, V_X = V_Y, I_{\pm Z} = \pm I_X, I_{\pm O} = \pm g_m V_Z \qquad (1)$$

where g_m is the trans-conductance of CCTA and depends upon the biasing current I_s of the CCTA. The MOS implementation of CCTA is proposed in **Figure 2**. For a

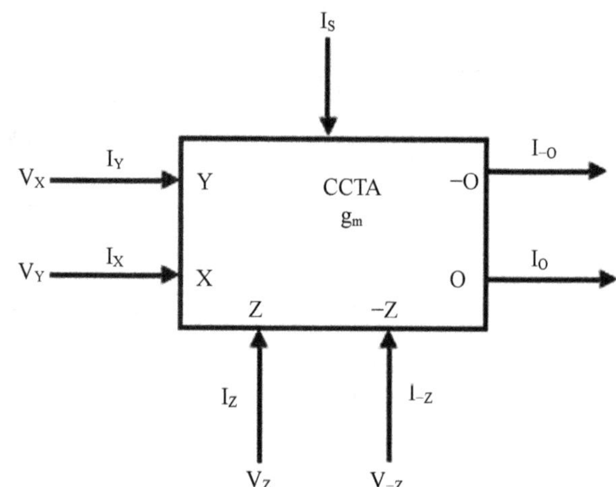

Figure 1. CCTA symbol.

MOS CCTA, the g_m can be expressed as

$$g_m = \sqrt{\beta_n I_s} \qquad (2)$$

Where β_n is given by

$$\beta_n = \mu_n C_{OX} \frac{W}{L} \qquad (3)$$

where μ_n, C_{OX} and W/L are the electron mobility, gate oxide capacitance per unit area and transistor aspect ratio of M13 and M14 NMOS, respectively.

The proposed current-processing universal filter with three inputs (I_1, I_2 and I_3) and single output (I_{out}) is shown in **Figure 3**. The circuit employs only two CCTAs and two grounded capacitors. A routine analysis of the circuit in **Figure 3** yields the following current output expression.

$$I_{out} = \frac{-\left(s^2 C_1 C_2 I_1 - s C_2 g_{m2} I_2 + g_{m1} g_{m2} I_3\right)}{D(s)} \qquad (4)$$

Where

$$D(s) = s^2 C_1 C_2 + s C_2 g_{m2} + g_{m1} g_{m2} \qquad (5)$$

It is evident from (4) that various biquad filtering responses in current form can be obtained at current output (I_{out}) through appropriate selection of input currents.

1) Inverted HP response at I_{out}, with $I_1 = I_{in}$, *and* $I_2 = I_3 = 0$.

2) Inverted LP response at I_{out}, with $I_3 = I_{in}$, $I_1 = I_2 = 0$.

3) Non-inverted BP response at I_{out}, with $I_2 = I_{in}$, *and* $I_1 = I_3 = 0$.

4) Inverted BR response at I_{out}, with $I_1 = I_3 = I_{in}$, *and* $I_2 = 0$.

5) Inverted AP response at I_{out}, with $I_1 = I_2 = I_3 = I_{in}$, thus, the circuit is capable of realizing all the standard filtering responses in current form from the same configuration. Moreover, there is no requirement of minus-

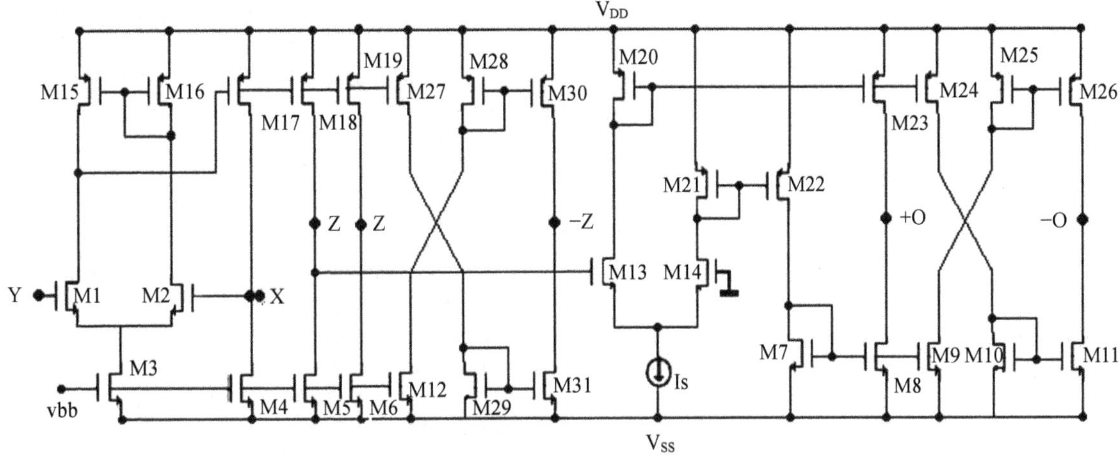

Figure 2. CMOS implementation of CCTA.

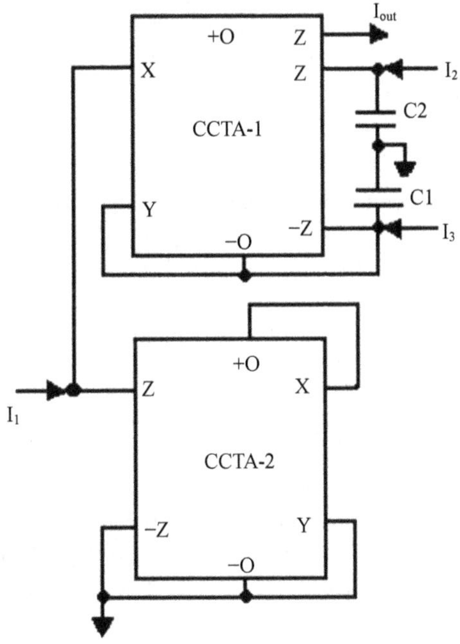

Figure 3. Proposed universal current-processing biquad filter.

type input current signal(s) and double input current signal(s) to realize all the responses in the design. Moreover, the proposed circuit also realizes all filtering responses without any component matching condition. The filter parameters such as pole frequency (ω_0) and quality factor (Q_0) can be formulated as

$$\omega_0 = \sqrt{\frac{g_{m1}g_{m2}}{C_1C_2}} = \sqrt{\frac{\beta_n\sqrt{I_{S1}I_{S2}}}{C_1C_2}} \tag{6}$$

$$Q_0 = \sqrt{\frac{g_{m1}C_1}{g_{m2}C_2}} = \sqrt{\frac{C_1}{C_2}\sqrt{\frac{I_{S1}}{I_{S2}}}} \tag{7}$$

From (6) and (7), it can be noted that the pole frequency can be adjusted by I_{S1} and I_{S2} without affecting the quality factor by keeping the ratio of I_{S1} and I_{S2} as constant. Similarly, Q_0 can also be adjusted by I_{S1} and I_{S2} without affecting the pole frequency by keeping the product of I_{S1} and I_{S2} as constant. In addition, bandwidth (BW) of the system can be expressed by

$$BW = \frac{\omega_0}{Q_0} = \frac{g_{m2}}{C_1} = \frac{\sqrt{\beta_n I_{S2}}}{C_1} \tag{8}$$

It can also be noted that ω_0 and Q_0 of the filter can be simultaneously controlled independent of the BW through I_{S1}.

3. Non-Ideal Aspects

A non-ideal CCTA, implemented with the transistors is characterized by finite voltage, current and trans-conductance tracking errors occurred due to the mismatching in the transistors. Therefore, taking the non-idealities of the CCTA into account, the relationship of the terminals voltage and current of the ith CCTA described by (1) can be modified by (9) which is as follows

$$\begin{gathered} I_{Yi} = 0, V_{Xi} = \beta_i V_{Yi}, I_{Zi} = \alpha_{pi} I_{Xi}, \\ I_{-Zi} = -\alpha_{ni} I_{Xi}, I_{\pm Oi} = \pm\gamma_i g_{mi} V_{Zi} \end{gathered} \tag{9}$$

Where α_{pi}, α_{ni}, β_i and γ_i are the tracking errors of ith CCTA (i^{th} = 1, 2) and practically deviated from unity. Taking the non-idealities of CCTA given in (9) into consideration and re-analyzing the circuit of **Figure 3**, the current response of the proposed circuit of **Figure 3** are changed to

$$I_{out} = \frac{-\left(s^2C_1C_2I_1 - \beta_1 sC_2 g_{m2} I_2 + \gamma_1\beta_1 g_{m1} g_{m2} I_3\right)}{D(s)} \tag{10}$$

Where

$$D(s) = s^2C_1C_2 + \beta_1\alpha_{n1} sC_2 g_{m2} + \beta_1\alpha_{p1}\gamma_1 g_{m1} g_{m2} \tag{11}$$

With involved non-idealities, ω_0, Q_0 and BW are modified to

$$\omega_0 = \sqrt{\frac{\beta_1 \alpha_{p1} \gamma_1 g_{m1} g_{m2}}{C_1 C_2}} \quad (12)$$

$$BW = \frac{\beta_1 \alpha_{n1} g_{m2}}{C_1} \quad (13)$$

$$Q_0 = \frac{1}{\alpha_{n1}} \sqrt{\frac{\alpha_{p1} \gamma_1 g_{m1} C_1}{\beta_1 g_{m2} C_2}} \quad (14)$$

This shows that ω_0 and Q for the ideal current-mode filter are slightly affected by non-ideal tracking errors. Sensitivity analysis of the proposed filter with respect to active and passive elements yields

$$S^{\omega_0}_{C_1,C_2} = -\frac{1}{2}, S^{\omega_0}_{\beta_1,\alpha_{p1},\gamma_1,g_{m1},g_{m2}} = \frac{1}{2} \quad (15)$$

$$S^{\omega_0}_{\alpha_{n1},\alpha_{p2},\alpha_{n2},\gamma_2,\beta_2} = 0 \quad (16)$$

$$S^{Q_0}_{C_2,g_{m2},\beta_1} = -\frac{1}{2}, S^{Q_0}_{\gamma_1,\alpha_{p1},C_1,g_{m1}} = \frac{1}{2} \quad (17)$$

$$S^{Q_0}_{\alpha_{n1}} = -1, S^{Q_0}_{\alpha_{p2},\alpha_{n2},\gamma_2,\beta_2} = 0 \quad (18)$$

From above results, it can be found that all the active and passive sensitivity are within "unity" in magnitude and hence, proposed circuit ensures a good sensitivity performance.

4. Simulation Results

To verify the theoretical analysis of the proposed current-processing filter circuit of **Figure 3**, PSPICE simulation has been used. In simulation, the CCTA was realized using CMOS implementation as shown in **Figure 2**. The MOS transistors were simulated using 0.35 um MOS process parameters from TSMC (the model parameters are given in **Table 1**). The supply voltages were $V_{DD} = -V_{SS} = 1.75$ V and $V_{bb} = -0.55$ V. The dimensions of M13 and M14 NMOS were determined as W = 14 µm and L = 2 µm while the dimensions of all remaining NMOS were determined as W = 10 µm and L = 2 µm. In PMOS transistors, the dimensions were W = 10 µm and L = 1 µm. The circuit was designed with $I_{S1} = I_{S2} = 100$ µA, and $C_1 = C_2 = 26$ pF. **Figure 4** shows the simulated current gain and phase responses of BP, LP, HP, BR and AP for the proposed current-mode filter. The simulation results show the simulated pole frequency as 2.04 MHz that agree quite well with the theoretical analysis. **Figures 5** and **6** shows the responses of BP and BR functions, respectively, where I_{S1} and I_{S2} were equally set and changed for several values, by keeping its ratio to be constant for constant Q_0 (= 1). From **Figures 5** and **6**, it can be seen that pole frequency can be electronically tuned by the bias currents (I_{S1} and I_{S2}) without affecting quality factor. Similarly, Q_0 tunability independent of pole frequency is shown in **Figures 7** and **8** which display the BP and BR responses, respectively, for different sets of value of I_{S1} and I_{S2} with their product to be maintained as constant. The time domain response of current-mode HP output is shown in **Figure 9**. It was observed that 120 µA peak to peak input current sinusoidal signal levels having frequency 40 MHz are possible without significant distortions.

5. Conclusion

In this paper, a new current processing current tunable universal biquad filter employing two CCTAs and two grounded capacitors is proposed. The proposed filter offers the following advantages: 1) employment of only two active elements; 2) ability of realizing all current-mode standard filtering functions; 3) employment of minimum number of grounded capacitors (only two) to realize any biquad filtering function; 4) low sensitivity figures; 5) electronically orthogonal tunability of ω_0 and Q; 6) availability of explicit current output (*i.e.* high impedance output node) without requiring any additional active elements; 7) no requirement of components matching conditions to get all filtering responses; 8) no requirements of inverting-type input current signal(s) and double input current signal(s) to realize the filtering response(s) in the design, all of which are not available simultaneously in any of the previously reported current-controlled current-mode biquad filter of [15-27]. With above mentioned features, it is very suitable to realize the proposed circuit in monolithic chip to use in battery powered, portable

Table 1. The SPICE model parameters of MOSFET for level 3, 0.35 µm CMOS process from TSMC.

NMOS	LEVEL = 3 TOX = 7.9E - 9 NSUB = 1E17 GAMMA = 0.5827871 PHI = 0.7 VTO = 0.5445549 DELTA = 0 UO = 436.256147 ETA = 0 THETA = 0.1749684 KP = 2.055786E - 4 VMAX = 8.309444E4 KAPPA = 0.2574081 RSH = 0.0559398 NFS = 1E12 TPG = 1 XJ = 3E - 7 LD = 3.162278E - 11 WD = 7.046724E - 8 CGDO = 2.82E - 10 CGSO = 2.82E - 10 CGBO = 1E - 10 CJ = 1E-3 PB = 0.9758533 MJ = 0.3448504 CJSW = 3.777852E-10 MJSW = 0.3508721
PMOS	LEVEL = 3 TOX = 7.9E - 9 NSUB = 1E17 GAMMA = 0.4083894 PHI = 0.7 VTO = −0.7140674 DELTA = 0 UO = 212.2319801 ETA = 9.999762E - 4 THETA = 0.2020774 KP = 6.733755E - 5 VMAX = 1.181551E5 KAPPA = 1.5 RSH = 30.0712458 NFS = 1E12 TPG = −1 XJ = 2E - 7 LD = 5.000001E-13 WD = 1.249872E - 7 CGDO = 3.09E - 10 CGSO = 3.09E - 10 CGBO = 1E - 10 CJ = 1.419508E - 3 PB = 0.8152753 MJ = 0.5 CJSW = 4.813504E - 10 MJSW = 0.5

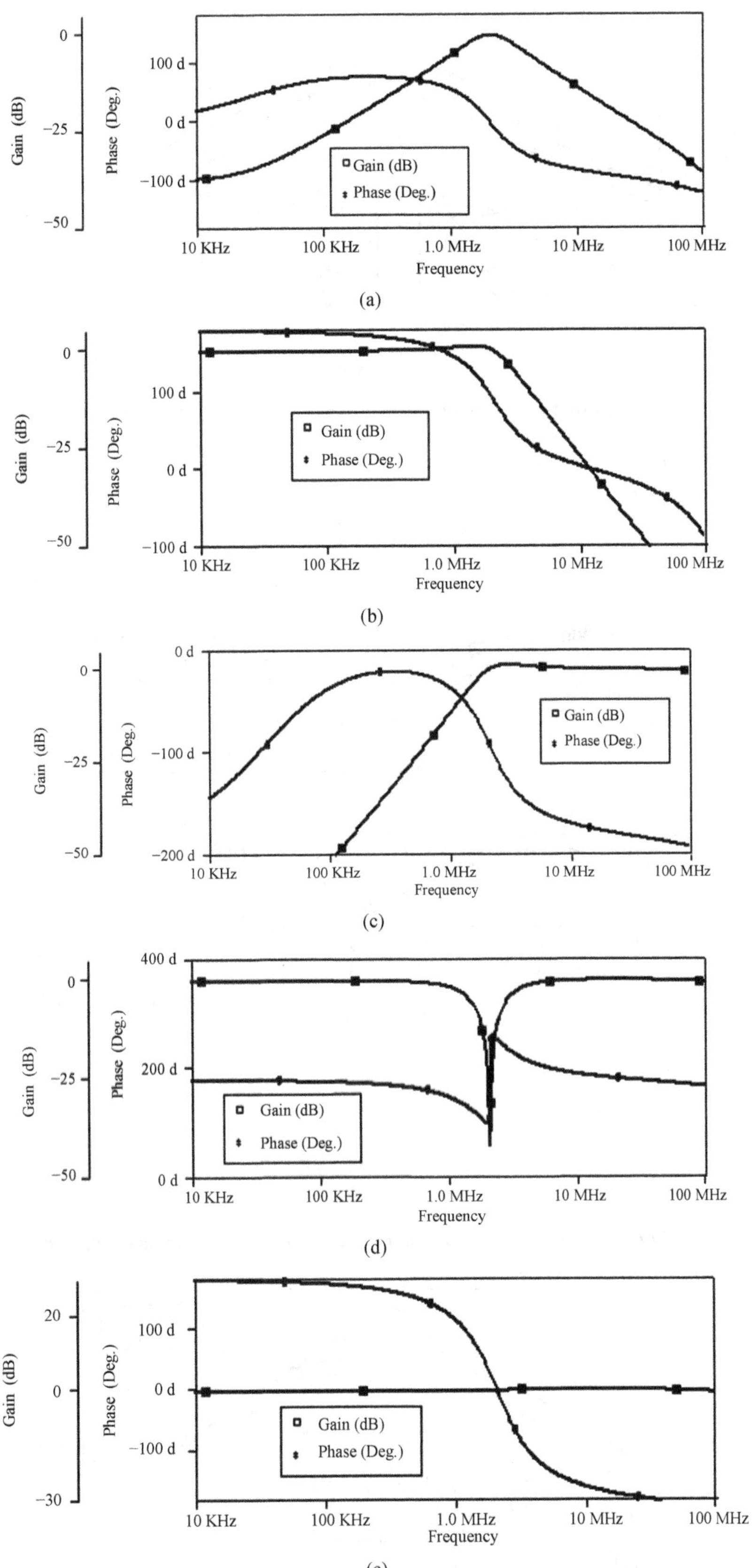

Figure 4. Current gain and phase responses of the (a) BP, (b) LP (c) HP (d) BR (e) AP for the proposed biquad filter in Figure 3.

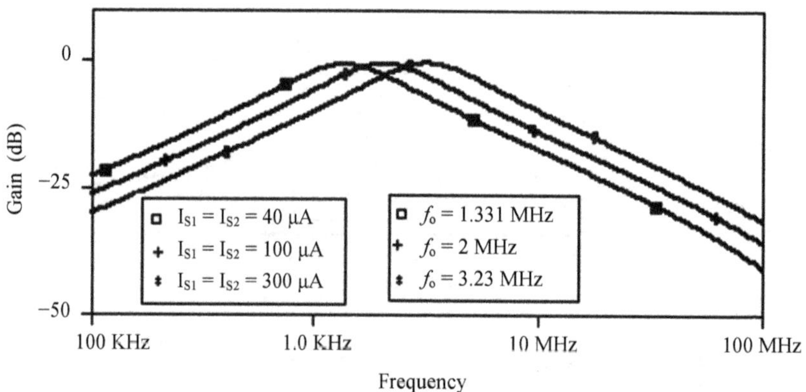

Figure 5. BP responses for different value of $I_{S1} = I_{S2}$ to show the electronic tunability of pole frequency.

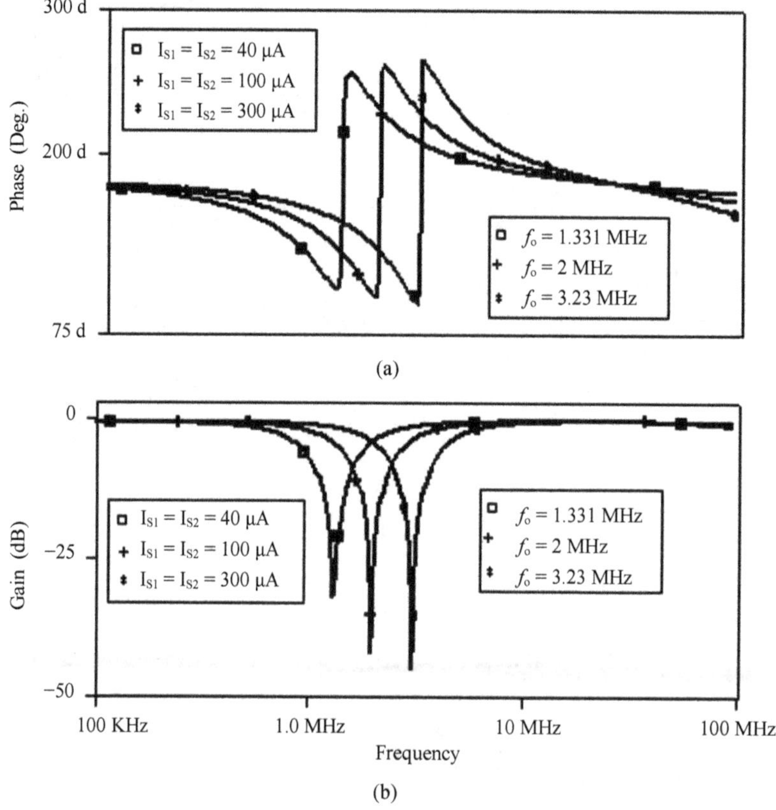

Figure 6. BR responses (a) Gain (b) Phase, for different value of $I_{S1} = I_{S2}$ to show the electronic tunability of pole frequency.

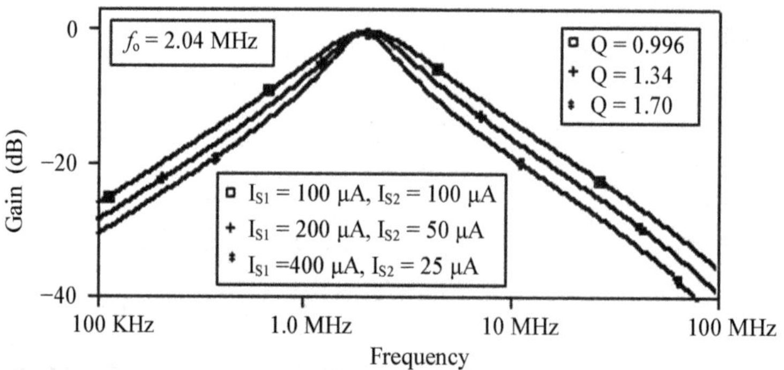

Figure 7. BP responses for different value of I_{S1} and I_{S2} to show the electronic tunability of quality factor.

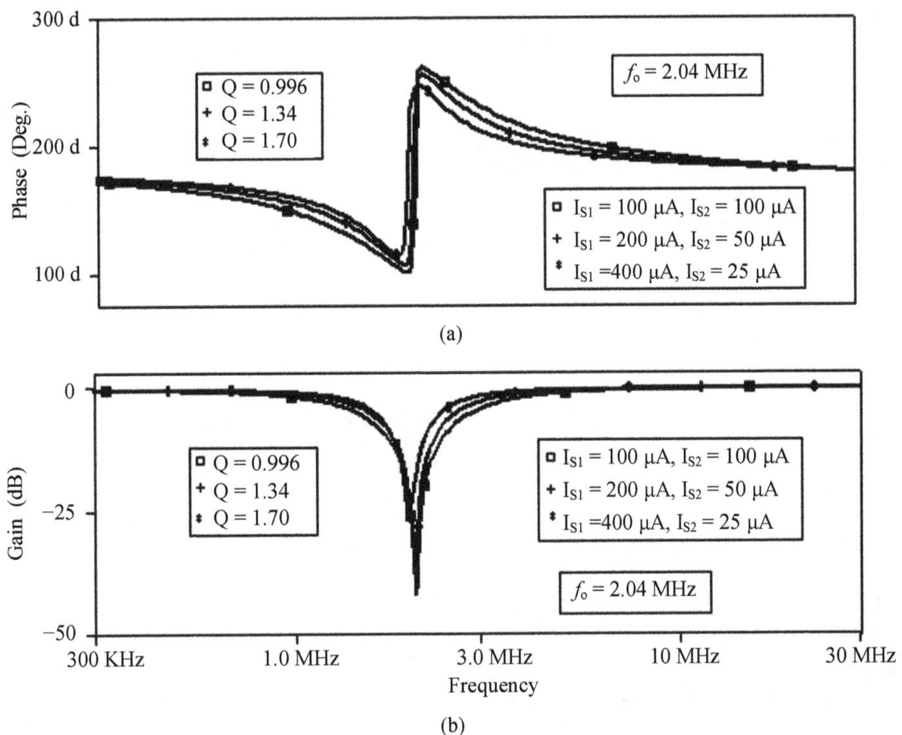

Figure 8. BR responses (a) gain (b) phase, for different value of I_{S1} and I_{S2} to show the electronic tunability of quality factor.

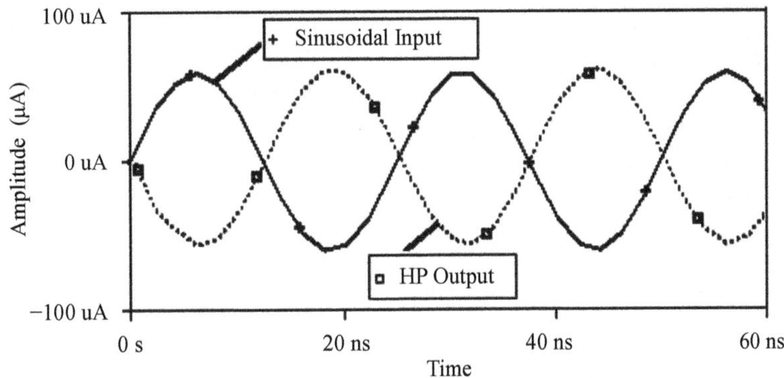

Figure 9. The time domain input waveform and corresponding response at HP current output.

electronic equipments such as wireless communication system devices.

REFERENCES

[1] B. Wilson, "Recent Developments in Current Conveyors and Current Mode Circuits," *IEE Proceeding-G*, Vol. 137, No. 2, 1990, pp. 63-77.

[2] M. A. Ibrahim, S. Minaei and H. A. Kuntman, "A 22.5 MHz Current-Mode KHN-Biquad Using Differential Voltage Current Conveyor and Grounded Passive Elements," *Int'l J. Electronics and Communication* (*AEÜ*), Vol. 59, No. 5, 2005, pp. 311-318.

[3] A. M. Soliman, "Current Mode Universal Filter," *Electronics Letters*, Vol. 31, No. 17, 1995, pp. 1420-1421.

[4] R. Senani, V. K. Singh, A. K. Singh and D. R. Bhaskar, "Novel Electronically Controllable Current Mode Universal Biquad Filter," *IEICE Electronics Express*, Vol. 1, No. 14, 2004, pp. 410-415.

[5] S. Maheshwari, S. V. Singh and D. S. Chauhan, "Electronically Tunable Low Voltage Mixed-Mode Universal Biquad Filter," *IET Circuits, Devices and Systems*, Vol. 5, No. 3, 2011, pp. 149-158.

[6] M. T. Abuelma'atti and A. M. Shabra, "A Novel Current Conveyor-Based Universal Current-Mode Filter," *Microelectronics Journal*, Vol. 27, No. 6, 1996, pp. 471-475.

[7] S. Minaei and S. Türköz, "New Current-Mode Current-

Controlled Universal Filter with Single Input and Three Outputs," *Int'l J. Electronics*, Vol. 88, No. 3, 2001, pp. 333-337.

[8] A. U. Keskin, D. Biolek, E. Hancioglu and V. Biolkova, "Current-Mode KHN Filter Employing Current Differencing Transconductance Amplifiers," *Int'l J. Electronics and Communications*, Vol. 60, No. 6, 2006, pp. 443-446.

[9] S. V. Singh, S. Maheshwari and D. S. Chauhan, "Universal Current-Controlled Current-Mode Biquad Filter Employing MO-CCCCTAs and Grounded Capacitors," *Journal of Circuits, Systems, and Computers*, Vol. 1, 2010, pp. 35-40.

[10] T. Tsukutani, Y. Sumi, S. Iwanari and Y. Fukui, "Novel Current-Mode Biquad Using MO-CCCIIs and Grounded Capacitors," *Proceeding of* 2005 *Symposium on Intelligent Signal Processing and Communication* (*ISPACS*), Hong Kong, 13-16 December 2005, pp. 433-436.

[11] B. Singh, A. K. Singh and R. Senani, "New Universal Current-Mode Biquad Using Only Three ZC-CFTA," *Radioengineering*, Vol. 21, No. 1, 2012, pp. 273-280.

[12] D. Biolek and V. Biolkova, "CDTA-C Current-Mode Universal 2nd Order Filter," *Proceeding of the 5th WSEAS Int'l Conference on Applied Informatics and Communications*, Malta, 15-17 September 2005, pp. 411-414.

[13] N. Herencsar, J. Koton and K. Vrva, "Single CCTA-Based Universal Biquad Filters Employing Minimum Components," *International Journal of Computer and Electrical Engineering*, Vol. 1, No. 3, 2009, pp. 307-310.

[14] B. Metin, "Electronic Tunability in Analog Filters," Ph.D. Thesis, Bogazici University, Istanbul, 2007.

[15] W. Tangsriart and W. Surakampontorm, "Low Component Current-Mode Universal Filter Using Current Controlled Conveyors and Grounded Capacitors," *Journal of Active and Passive Electronic Devices*, Vol. 8, 2009, pp. 259-264.

[16] M. Kumngem, J. Chanwutitumt and K. Dejhan, "Current-Tunable Current-Mode Universal Filter Using Minimum Elements," *Proceeding of the 6th IEEE Int'l Conference on Electrical Engineering/Electronics and Information Technology* (*ECRI-CON*), Pattaya, 6-9 May 2009, pp. 582-585.

[17] E. Yuce, A. Kircay and S. Tokat, "Universal Resistorless Current-Mode Filters Employing CCCIIs," *Int'l Journal of Circuit Theory and Applications*, Vol. 36, No. 5-6, 2008, pp. 739-755.

[18] W. Tangsriart and W. Surakampontorm, "Electronically Tunable Current-Mode Universal Filter Employing Only Plus-Type Current-Controlled Conveyors and Grounded Capacitors," *Circuits Systems and Signal Processing*, Vol. 25, No. 6, 2006, pp. 701-713.

[19] N. Jangsamsi, T. Pukkalanun and W. Tangsrirat, "CCCII-Based High-Output Impedance Current-Mode Universal Filter Employing Only Grounded Capacitors," *SICE-ICASE International Joint IEEE Conference*, Busan, 18-21 October 2006, pp. 5695-5698.

[20] M. T. Abuelma'atti and M. L. Al-qahtani, "Universal Current-Contolled Current-Mode Filter with Three Inputs and One Output Using Current Controlled Conveyor," *Active Passive Electronic Components*, Vol. 21, No. 1, 1998, pp. 33-41.

[21] C. M. Chang, T. H. Huang, S. H. Tu, C. L. Hou and J. W. Horng, "Universal Active Current Filter Using Single Second-Generation Current Controlled Conveyor," *Circuits, Systems and Signal Processing*, Vol. 1, No. 2, 2007, pp. 194-198.

[22] W. Tangsrirat, T. Dumawipata and W. Surakampontorn, "Multiple-Input Single-Output Current-Mode Multifunction Filter Using Current Differencing Transconductance Amplifiers," *Int'l Journal of Electronic and Communication* (*AEÜ*), Vol. 61, No. 4, 2007, pp. 209-214.

[23] S. Lawnwisut and M. Siripruchyanun, "A Current-Mode Multifunction Biquadratic Filter Using CFTAs," *Journal of King Mongkut's University of Technology, North Bangkok*, Vol. 22, No. 3, 2012, pp. 479-484.

[24] J. Satansup, T. Pukkalanum and W. Tangsrirat, "Electronically Tunable Current-Mode Universal Filter Using VDTAs and Grounded Capacitors," *Proceeding of the International Multiconference of Engineers and Computer Scientists*, Hongkong, 13-15 March 2013, pp. 6-9.

[25] T. Thosdeekoraphat, S. Summart, C. Saetiaw, S. Santalunai and C. Thongsopa, "Resistor-Less Current-Mode Universal Biquad Filter Using CCTAs and Grounded Capacitors," *World Academy of Science, Engineering and Technology*, Vol. 69, 2012, pp. 559-563.

[26] W. Jaikla, S. Siripongdee and P. Suwanjan, "MISO Current-Mode Biquad Filter with Independent Control of Pole Frequency and Quality Factor," *Radioengineering Journal*, Vol. 21, No. 3, 2012, pp. 886-891.

[27] S. V. Singh and S. Maheshwari, "Current-Processing Current Controlled Universal Biquad Filter," *Radioengineering Journal*, Vol. 21, No. 1, 2012, pp. 317-323.

Permissions

The contributors of this book come from diverse backgrounds, making this book a truly international effort. This book will bring forth new frontiers with its revolutionizing research information and detailed analysis of the nascent developments around the world.

We would like to thank all the contributing authors for lending their expertise to make the book truly unique. They have played a crucial role in the development of this book. Without their invaluable contributions this book wouldn't have been possible. They have made vital efforts to compile up to date information on the varied aspects of this subject to make this book a valuable addition to the collection of many professionals and students.

This book was conceptualized with the vision of imparting up-to-date information and advanced data in this field. To ensure the same, a matchless editorial board was set up. Every individual on the board went through rigorous rounds of assessment to prove their worth. After which they invested a large part of their time researching and compiling the most relevant data for our readers. Conferences and sessions were held from time to time between the editorial board and the contributing authors to present the data in the most comprehensible form. The editorial team has worked tirelessly to provide valuable and valid information to help people across the globe.

Every chapter published in this book has been scrutinized by our experts. Their significance has been extensively debated. The topics covered herein carry significant findings which will fuel the growth of the discipline. They may even be implemented as practical applications or may be referred to as a beginning point for another development. Chapters in this book were first published by Scientific Research Publishing Inc.; hereby published with permission under the Creative Commons Attribution License or equivalent.

The editorial board has been involved in producing this book since its inception. They have spent rigorous hours researching and exploring the diverse topics which have resulted in the successful publishing of this book. They have passed on their knowledge of decades through this book. To expedite this challenging task, the publisher supported the team at every step. A small team of assistant editors was also appointed to further simplify the editing procedure and attain best results for the readers.

Our editorial team has been hand-picked from every corner of the world. Their multi-ethnicity adds dynamic inputs to the discussions which result in innovative outcomes. These outcomes are then further discussed with the researchers and contributors who give their valuable feedback and opinion regarding the same. The feedback is then collaborated with the researches and they are edited in a comprehensive manner to aid the understanding of the subject.

Apart from the editorial board, the designing team has also invested a significant amount of their time in understanding the subject and creating the most relevant covers. They scrutinized every image to scout for the most suitable representation of the subject and create an appropriate cover for the book.

The publishing team has been involved in this book since its early stages. They were actively engaged in every process, be it collecting the data, connecting with the contributors or procuring relevant information. The team has been an ardent support to the editorial, designing and production team. Their endless efforts to recruit the best for this project, has resulted in the accomplishment of this book. They are a veteran in the field of academics and their pool of knowledge is as vast as their experience in printing. Their expertise and guidance has proved useful at every step. Their uncompromising quality standards have made this book an exceptional effort. Their encouragement from time to time has been an inspiration for everyone.

The publisher and the editorial board hope that this book will prove to be a valuable piece of knowledge for researchers, students, practitioners and scholars across the globe.

List of Contributors

Jeff Rebacz, Erdal Oruklu and Jafar Saniie
Department of Electrical and Computer Engineering, Illinois Institute of Technology, Chicago, USA

Renbo Xu
School of Physics Science and Technology, Central South University, Changsha, China
School of Materials Science and Engineering, Central South University, Changsha, China
Hunan Information Science Vocational College, Changsha, China

Hongjian Li
School of Physics Science and Technology, Central South University, Changsha, China
School of Materials Science and Engineering, Central South University, Changsha, China

Yongzhi Li
College of Physics and Information Science, Hunan Normal University, Changsha, China

Changqian Zhang
School of Physics Science and Technology, Central South University, Changsha, China

Mehmet Sağbaş
Department of Electronics Engineering, Maltepe University, Istanbul, Turkey

Nihal Kularatna and Chandani Jindasa
The University of Waikato, Hamilton, New Zealand

Montree Kumngern
Department of Telecommunications Engineering, Faculty of Engineering, King Mongkut's Institute of Technology, Ladkrabang, Bangkok, Thailand

Sudhanshu Maheshwari and Ankita Gangwar
Department of Electronics Engineering, Z. H. College of Engineering and Technology, Aligarh Muslim University, Aligarh, India

Saurabh Chaudhury
Department of Electrical Engineering, National Institute of Technology, Silchar, India

Anirban Dutta
Department of Electronics & Communication Engineering, National Institute of Technology, Silchar, India

Seyed Reza Hadianamrei, Masoud Sabaghi, Maziyar Niyakan Lahiji and Mehdi Rahnama
Research School of National Science & Technology Research Institute (N.S.T.R.I), Tehran, Iran

Raj Senani
Division of Electronics and Communication Engineering, Netaji Subhas Institute of Technology, Delhi, India

Kasim Karam Abdalla and Data Ram Bhaskar
Department of Electronics and Communication Engineering, Faculty of Engineering and Technology, Jamia Millia Islamia, New Delhi, India

Mohamed Mabrouk and Leila Bousbia
CIRTACOM and ISETCOM of Tunis, University of Carthage, Tunis, Tunisia

David Hentrich, Erdal Oruklu and Jafar Saniie
Department of Electrical and Computer Engineering, Illinois Institute of Technology Chicago, Illinois, USA

Tadeusz Kaczorek
Faculty of Electrical Engineering, Bialystok University of Technology, Bialystok, Poland

Shilpi Birla
Department of Electronics and Communication (ECE), Sir Padampat Singhania University (SPSU), Udaipur, India

Rakesh Kumar Singh
Department of Electronics and Communication (ECE), Bipin Tripathi Kumaon Institute of Technology (BTKIT), Dwarahat Almora, India

Manisha Pattanaik
VLSI Group, Atal Bihari Vajpayee Indian Institute of Information Technology & Management (ABV-IIITM), Gwalior, India

Vasil G. Angelov
Department of Mathematics, University of Mining and Geology, Sofia, Bulgaria

Marin Hristov
Department of Microelectronics, Technical University of Sofia, Sofia, Bulgaria

Stefano Perticaroli, Nikend Luli and Fabrizio Palma
Department of Information Engineering, Electronics and Telecommunications, Sapienza Università di Roma, Rome, Italy

Mahmood Ashoori-Lalimi and Sedigheh Ghofrani
Electrical Engineering Department, Islamic Azad University, South Tehran Branch, Tehran, Iran

Neeraj Kumar Shukla
Department of ECE, ITM University, Gurgaon, India

Kapil Rathi
Texas Instruments, Bangalore, India

Vandana Vikas Thakare
Department of Electronics and Instrumentation Engineering, Anand Engineering College, Keetham, Agra, India

Pramod Singhal
Department of Electronics Engineering, Madhav Institute of Technology & Science, Gwalior, India

Jorge Garcia, Antonio J. Calleja, Emilio L. Corominas, David Gacio, Lidia Campa and Ramón E. Díaz
Department of Electrical Engineering, EEC-IEL Research Group, University of Oviedo, Asturias, Spain

Xiaomao Hou
Hunan Information Science Vocational College, Changsha, China

Chin-Hsin Lin and Marek Syrzycki
School of Engineering Science, Simon Fraser University, Burnaby, Canada

Ashwek Ben Saied
Computer Imaging and Electronic Systems Group (CIEL), Research Unit on Intelligent Design and Control of complex Systems (ICOS), Sfax, Tunisia
University of Sfax, National Engineering School of Sfax (ENIS), Sfax, Tunisia

Samir Ben Salem
University of Sfax, National Engineering School of Sfax (ENIS), Sfax, Tunisia
Development Group in Electronics and Communications (EleCom), Laboratory of Electronics and Information Technology (LETI), Sfax, Tunisia

Dorra Sellami Masmoudi
Computer Imaging and Electronic Systems Group (CIEL), Research Unit on Intelligent Design and Control of complex Systems (ICOS), Sfax, Tunisia
University of Sfax, National Engineering School of Sfax (ENIS), Sfax, Tunisia

Dinesh Prasad
Department of Electronics and Communication Engineering, Faculty of Engineering and Technology, Jamia Millia Islamia, New Delhi, India

Kanhaiya Lal Pushkar
Department of Electronics and Communication Engineering, Maharaja Agrasen Institute of Technology, Rohini, New Delhi, India

Omnia S. Ahmed and Mohamed F. Abu-Elyazeed
Faculty of Engineering, Cairo University, Giza, Egypt

Mohamed B. Abdelhalim
College of Computing and Information Technology, Arab Academy for Science, Technology & Maritime Transport, Cairo, Egypt

Hassanein H. Amer
Electronics Engineering Department, American University in Cairo, Cairo, Egypt

Ahmed H. Madian
Radiation Engineering Department, Egyptian Atomic Energy Authority, Cairo, Egypt

Youngjung Ahn, Yongsuk Lee and Gyungho Lee
Department of Computer Science & Engineering, Korea University, Seoul, South Korea

Manish Kumar and Md. Anwar Hussain
Department of Electronics and Communication Engineering, North Eastern Regional Institute of Science and Technology, Arunachal Pradesh, India

Sajal K. Paul
Department of Electronics Engineering, Indian School of Mines, Jharkhand, India

Meeti Dehran and Indu Prabha Singh
Department of Electronics and Communications Engineering, Shri Ramswaroop Memorial Group of Professional Colleges (SRMGPC), Lucknow, India

Kalyan Singh
Department of Physics and Electronics, R.M.L. University, Faizabad, India

Rabindra Kumar Singh
Department of Electrical and Electronic Engineering, Kamla Nehru Institute of Technology (KNIT), Sultanpur, India

Ravindra Singh Tomar
Department of Electronics Engineering, Anand Engineering College, Agra, India

Sajai Vir Singh
Department of Electronics and Communications, Jaypee Institute of Information Technology, Noida, India

Durg Singh Chauhan
Department of Electrical Engineering, Indian Institute of Technology, Banaras Hindu University, Varanasi, India